The Art of SEWING

Basics and Beyond

4-21-87
Dear Gerry - I hope this helps with the sewing projects
Shirley Smith

by
Shirley Smith

MP
Morton Publishing Company
925 W. Kenyon Ave., Unit 4
Englewood, Colorado 80110

Printed in the United States of America.

ISBN: 0-89582-168-0

This book is dedicated
to my husband, Don
for guidance, patience, and a willing ear

and

to my wonderful students
who requested that I write this book.

A Special Thank You to Nancy Dwight
for editing the manuscript.

Photography
by
Lynette Swanson-O'Kane

Soft Sculpture
Kathleen Williams

Hand printed fabric
Douglas Ram Samuj

SHIRLEY SMITH

Shirley Smith is a designer, fashion coordinator, and teacher who teaches custom workshop sewing classes at her Sewing Arts studio. She formed the Sewing Arts in 1975. Her goal was to assist those who had a creative desire to design and construct wardrobes for themselves. Shirley developed her sewing expertise at an early age. Constructing garments out of necessity led to her interest and expertise in sewing and design. She has studied under European as well as domestic designers, recently with Charles Kleibacker. Shirley is a member of the Denver Fashion Group and The American Sewing Guild, Denver Chapter.

Contents

Introduction ■

- Introduction
- Choices! Choices!

INTRODUCTION

This book is written at the request of many of my students. In my classroom I use step samples of all the procedures that I find are fast and effective methods of sewing. For years my students have asked me to illustrate in book form the step samples and handouts I use in my classes. These step samples have been wonderful teaching aids, and I hope you find them useful illustrations for the text of this collection of my class handouts. I have tried my best to bring you into my studio in Denver. I hope you will use this book along with your pattern guide and find it to be a helpful tool in your sewing. I hope you will share with me a love and enjoyment of sewing.

I began sewing at a very early age, first hand stitching doll clothes, then machine quilting on my mother's treadle sewing machine. Quilting is a great way for a beginner to learn to cut and sew straight. I was raised on a farm in Central Washington State. Along with other crops, my father raised chickens and, consequently, we had a lot of chicken feed sacks. At that time the sacks came in prints. Since the fabric was free with the purchase of the feed, my mother didn't care what I made of it. I polished my early sewing skills on yards and yards of feed sacks. By the time I reached high school I was constructing most of my wardrobe, although not of feed sacks!

I've always loved to sew, because I feel as if I'm accomplishing something. A seam stitched is something done. Even if my sewing time is very limited, sooner or later I have a finished garment I can wear and enjoy. AN ACCOMPLISHMENT! It doesn't have to be done over; it isn't boring like cleaning the floors, or making beds, or cooking every day. Sewing lets me be **powerful — creative — individual!**

I can have my clothing exactly the way I want it to be. I can sew exactly the way I want. I can throw it together and wear it once, or spend hours on a couture garment to treasure and wear for years. The only restriction on my creativity is my imagination, the availability of fabric, and of course, my time. Occasionally, I create my own pattern. Most often I combine and change patterns to create my own styles. Sometimes I use a pattern exactly as it is and let my choice of fabric make the garment mine alone.

I sew the common sense way. I don't follow the pattern directions exactly. I always read them and change what needs to be changed to make the garment better or save time. Some rules I sew by:

- I always pre-shrink all fabrics, zippers, interfacings, linings, etc.
- I always check the fit, the wearing ease, and design ease of any new pattern.
- I always do a sample seam to test the stitch length, the needle size and condition, the thread weight, and how my fabric presses.
- I always test for the best seam finish.
- I am always careful of my workmanship and finishing.

Sewing is an **ART** form. Like other art forms, to become proficient, you must practice. But unlike some other art forms, you get an immediate reward — A new garment to wear!

If you are a beginner, your first garments won't be perfect, but as your skill improves each garment will be better. When beginning students insist on **absolute perfection** I remind them that perfection requires practice. Proficient seamstresses are generally very critical of their handiwork. Do strive for great looking clothes, but don't deprive yourself of the joy of sewing by demanding absolute perfection. Few garments you purchase, even the most expensive ones, are perfect. Each time you sew you will improve and soon you will be creating clothing worth many hundreds of dollars.

In this book I'm sharing with you the knowledge I have gained from many wonderful teachers: Hendy Cameron and the late Elizabeth Nash of Portland, Oregon; Julia Tobias of Denver, Colorado; Charles Kleibacker of New York; and, of course, my wonderful, creative and challenging students who have made sewing for me relaxing, fun and very rewarding. I hope this book helps sewing be relaxing, fun, and very rewarding for you, too.
Every woman who sews can have beautiful clothing — Challenge yourself to make your garments special.

CHOICES! CHOICES!

Think first of your needs and your skill level. Then of fashion. To help you make a choice, take a day each season to shop at the better stores. Shopping the best ready-to-wear helps keep you current and does inspire and give you ideas. Try on new styles, see what works for you. Notice the fabric in good clothing. Then go fabric shopping and buy the best fabric you can afford! The work and time you put into a garment are the same for good or poor fabric. Only good fabric makes a good garment.

Decide what garment you will make: skirt, trousers, dress, blouse, jacket, or coat. Look for appropriate fabrics. Many inexperienced seamstresses make the mistake of selecting a pattern first, and then match the fabric to the pattern. **Wrong!** Let the fabric be the driver in creating your garment. A pattern should be the last choice.

If you need to buy fabric and you do not have a pattern, you can judge the amount of fabric you will require by knowing what garment you would make from that fabric. For slacks you need two lengths. If the fabric is 60″ wide, and you wear no larger than a size 14, one length plus waistband will be enough. For a blouse, dress, or coat you need two lengths plus a sleeve length plus hems. A skirt usually requires two skirt lengths. A pleated or many-gored skirt, three lengths plus a waistband. Purchase an extra 1/8 yard for shrinkage. If buying a plaid, buy a plaid repeat for every major pattern piece. These are just basic requirements. If your garment is to be very full, add another length.

Always begin a garment or a design with the fabric. In the store, unwind it from the bolt and drape it on you in front of the mirror. Drape it lengthwise, crosswise and on the diagonal. Hold it fitted to your body, gather it, pleat it. Listen to your fabric! For instance, will it gather beautifully? If it won't gather, will it pleat flat? Keep trying new bolts of fabric until you find something you like for the garment you need. Now choose a pattern as close to your idea as possible. Always use a reliable old pattern if you can. A collection of basic patterns is a wonderful help and they can be combined to create new styles. If using a new pattern, always measure your new tissue and compare it either with some clothing of similar style that fits you or an old pattern of similar style. Pin the tissue together and try it on. If you are still unsure of the fit, make a muslin. This may seem like a lot of work, but actually this takes less time than redoing a garment. You can check the fit, hang, and style and correct anything you do not like before cutting your fashion fabric.

Learn by progressing from one garment to another more difficult garment. The easiest projects have the fewest pattern pieces. If you are a beginner, start with a simple project. The easiest garment to make is a simple skirt, especially one having a wrap or elastic waistline. A top with no sleeves or a dolman or a raglan sleeve is very easy. Watch neck openings. Often a pattern will look very easy and have a placket opening. Placket openings are too difficult for a beginner. Pants with an elastic or drawstring are also an easy project for a beginner.

Garments listed in order of increasing skill level:

1. Wrap skirt or elastic waistline skirt. Drawstring or elastic waistline pant. Top with no set-in sleeve and no button opening.

2. Skirt with a zipper and waistband. It could have patch pockets or pockets in a seam. Slacks with a fly front, waistband, and pockets.

3. Blouse or dress with sleeves and a tie or a collar. Make several with different details. Garments with gathers, pleats or tucks. Garments with different openings listed in the degree of difficulty: zipper, buttons and buttonholes, placket openings. Garments with dolman sleeves, raglan sleeves, dropped shoulder sleeves, shirt sleeves, gathered sleeves, and the most difficult, a smooth set-in sleeve. Garments with a rolled collar on a sporty garment, then a full roll collar in heavier fabric, and finally a collar with a collar band.

4. Simple jacket, no collar, with a lining. Jacket with a collar and a lining.

5. Tailored jacket or coat with a lining.

Different fabrics present new problems and give you new skills as you sew. While you are perfecting your skills in cutting and sewing, stay away from the difficult fabrics. Prints or fabrics with texture or design hide sewing mistakes, while a plain color or little texture really shows off your sewing skills.

Fabrics listed in order of increasing skill level:

1. Cotton and polyester blend knit, wool knit, especially if it is a print. Stay away from plaids or stripes for a first project.
2. Cotton or a cotton blend woven print. Most challis would be easy for a beginner, no plaids or stripes.
3. Denims, linen or linen blends, wools, corduroys, silks, but not slippery silk. Any of the above fabrics in a stripe or a plaid. Be careful when you buy stripes or plaids. They often are not printed on grain. Try to buy woven stripes or plaids. Refer to Layouts For Special Fabrics.
4. Polyester or silk fabrics in a slippery weave.
5. Novelty fabrics, such as velvet, ribbon silk, lace, and chiffons.

I find that there is always a new challenge in sewing and always something new to learn. That's what keeps me sewing and loving every minute of it.

Preparation For Cutting · 1

FITTING YOUR GARMENTS – PATTERN ADJUSTMENT

In sewing classes at my studio, if there is any question of correct pattern size, I try the basic dress or pants muslin on my student to determine the size pattern she should be using. Even though I have done this for students, we still check each new tissue, do any necessary changes, and try on the bodice tissue before we cut. Since many of you reading this book will not be in my sewing classes, the following are some general rules to help you buy the correct size pattern and to adjust it before you cut.

When you purchase a pattern for a dress, blouse, or any garment that must fit through the shoulder and bustline, **always choose the pattern size closest to your high bust measurement.** If you buy the pattern to fit your bust measurement over the bust tip it usually will not fit in the shoulders and neckline. Garments hang from the shoulders, so the fit in the shoulder area is most important. The waist and hipline are easy to adjust. Buy skirt and slack patterns using the 9″ hip measurement. If you are making all the garments in a pattern, buy the pattern using your high bust measurement and plan on adjusting the skirt or slack pattern. Patterns are designed for a "B" cup bra. If you wear a "C" cup bra or larger you will probably have to increase in the bust line. If you are an "A" cup you may have to take in the bust area.

The most accurate way to choose the correct size pattern is to try on a basic fitting muslin. I know that will not be possible for all of you, but if you get the opportunity to try on a basic dress or slacks, take advantage of the chance to check and make sure you are using the correct size patterns. If you have trouble getting your garments to fit, I would recommend having a basic dress or slack pattern adjusted for your figure. You cannot do this for yourself. You cannot take accurate measurements on your own body. You should have someone who is an expert in fit do this for you. I offer this as a service by private appointment. I take the measurements, do all the pattern adjusting, and have my customer do the sewing.

Some rules to keep in mind when you are fitting:

Fabric will not travel. You must add more where you need it and take away where you have excess. If you are larger in the front and flat in the back, add only to the front.

Don't over-fit. You only want to accommodate figure faults for comfort and good looks. If you fit too closely you can accentuate the problem.

Safety first. If you are in doubt, and haven't used the pattern before or haven't had experience with your fabric, allow extra large seam allowance along the side seams. You can always take in, but if you have cut too small, you have lost your garment.

I don't recommend taking a class to make a basic pattern unless the teacher is doing all the measurements and most of the pattern work. If you make mistakes and then get them into fabric, it is very hard to tell what is wrong. Basic patterns are a wonderful tool. They have all the facts you need to adjust all your patterns to fit. You still have to check the **design ease** and make sure it is what you want, but you know that it will fit the differences in your body and the **average size.** All patterns are designed for an average size and not many of us fit that ideal.

When you buy a new pattern always check the fit and the amount of wearing ease and design ease before you cut the garment out of fashion fabric. **Wearing ease** is a fairly snug fit. **Design ease** is any amount the designer wants to achieve the **look** she desires.

Always take bust and waist measurements with a finger under the tape, and breathe. A good test for a nice wearable ease in a straight skirt is to hold the tape between the finger and thumb and loosen it until it will drop off the hip line without any help from the other hand.

Basic Amounts Of Wearing Ease

Bust 2″-3″, Waist 1″-1½″, Hip 2½″-3″.

Design Ease

Design ease depends on the silhouette of the garment. Design ease also depends on your taste, your build and height. Taller people can handle the big loose styles. If you like to have a little less ease, and the design is very loose fitting, buy one size smaller pattern than you would normally wear. That is the only time to ever buy a pattern that is not the correct size. You are borrowing problems if you try and use a pattern one size too large or too small. Vogue patterns always describe the amount of design ease in their patterns on the back of the pattern envelope by naming the different silhouettes. The amount of ease in each silhouette is listed below.

Silhouette	dresses, blouses skirts, tops, vests	jackets lined or not	coats lined or not
close fitting	0 - 2⅞″	not applicable	not applicable
fitted	3 - 4″	3¾ - 4¼″	5¼ - 6¾″
semi-fitted	4⅛ - 5″	4⅜ - 5¾″	6⅞ - 8″
loose fitting	5⅛ - 8″	5⅞ - 10″	8⅛ - 12″
very loose fitting	over 8″	over 10″	over 12″

On Vogue patterns you can expect those amounts of design ease. As you can see on the chart, they do vary in the design ease. Some other patterns also give you clues as to how much ease is in their styles.

Sometimes I am surprised by a pattern. The description is not always accurate and sometimes the drawings on the envelope are misleading. That is why I never take a chance. I always measure and compare to make sure before I cut.

If you have a basic pattern, adjust your new tissue the same amount as your basic was adjusted. This will give you the wearing ease you must have plus the design ease the new pattern intended for that style.

Is that the amount of ease you want? There are several good ways to judge design ease. A fast way to check the walking room in a skirt pattern is to make a circle with the tape measure and hold it around your legs. Can you move? For a simple design, pin the fashion fabric width the pattern calls for together and hold it around you. Is that the look you want?

For a more complete check, flat measure a garment or a pattern that you have used before as similar as possible in general style to your new pattern. Subtract your measurements from the flat measure of the garment or the pattern you have already used. To determine the amount of ease the new pattern has, compare these findings to the eases of your new tissue.

To determine the design ease built into a new pattern, write down the bust, waist and hip measurements of your size from the pattern envelope. Flat measure the tissue. DO NOT INCLUDE THE SEAM ALLOWANCE in the measurements. The difference in the pattern envelope and the tissue is the amount of ease the design has built into it. On the example below, ignore for a moment the personal measurements and notice the pattern envelope, flat tissue measurements, and design ease.

Example:

Pattern Size 12

Personal measurements		pattern envelope	flat tissue	design ease
High bust	34.5			
Bust over tips	37	34	40	6
Waist	27.5	26.5	27.5	1
Hip - 9″ from waist	39	36	44	8
Back waist length	16.25	16.25	16.5	0.25

The waist and center back length are only showing us amounts of **wearing ease.** The bust and hip measurements reflect **design ease. For the garment to fit the way the pattern intends, you must add the amount of design ease the pattern calls for to your measurements.**

Sometimes you may want all the ease the pattern calls for and sometimes you may want to adjust that ease to suit your personal preference. The chart below shows adding all the design ease the pattern calls for. If you want less just make sure that you have at least the wearing ease called for. Also remember the garment will not look like the picture on the pattern envelope if you remove all the design ease that has been allowed.

Example:

Personal Measurements		pattern envelope	flat tissue	design ease
Bust	37	34	40	6

Your bust measure (37) + design ease (6) = 43″. Flat tissue is 40″. Add 3″ to the pattern. Divide 3″ by 4 (the number of seams) = 3/4″ added to the front and back at the side seams. I divide with my tape measure. It is easy and accurate. Fold 3″ in half = 1½″, fold again = 3/4″.

Waist	27	26.5	27.5	1

Your waist measure (27) + wearing ease (1) = 28″. Flat tissue is 27.5″. Add 1/2″ length to the waistband pattern.

Hip - 9″ from waist	39	36	44	8

Your hip measure (39) + design ease (8) = 47″. Flat tissue is 44″. Add 3″ to the front and back of the pattern, again dividing the 3″ by the number of seams = 3/4″ added to the front and back at the side seams.

Back waist length	16.25	16.25	16.5	0.25

No change is needed for the back waist length.

If the tissue is too large, pin the tissue in and take the pattern in that amount. **Be careful!** It is much safer to leave a little room in a tissue. You can always take in and it is impossible to let out if you have cut too small. Divide the amount to be removed in half and add or subtract equally to the front and back at the side seams.

Adjusting The Tissue

There are several ways to adjust the tissue. You can slash and spread or you can trace and pivot. I use a combination of these methods.

The pivot method, using tracing paper and a tracing wheel, works great for most adjustments, especially if you are reluctant to cut the tissue. I prefer tracing paper from an art supply store to wax paper or sheets of tissue. Wax paper is hard to mark and to press and many times the sheets of tissue available must be pieced. If I am shortening, I usually tuck the pattern. I slash and add tissue if I am lengthening.

To add using the pivot method, trace the seam and the cutting line.

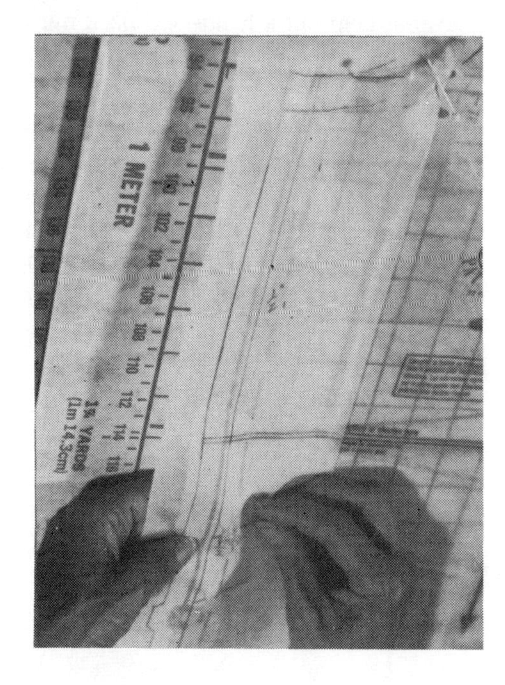

Pivot it out to increase. Pivot in to decrease. Do this along an entire side seam or only the part of a seam that needs adjusted.

After one side seam is done you can lay the corresponding pieces together matching the seam lines, and pin along the seam line. Cut the excess tissue from both pieces.

Cutting the seams you are adjusting together saves tracing and adjusting the second piece.

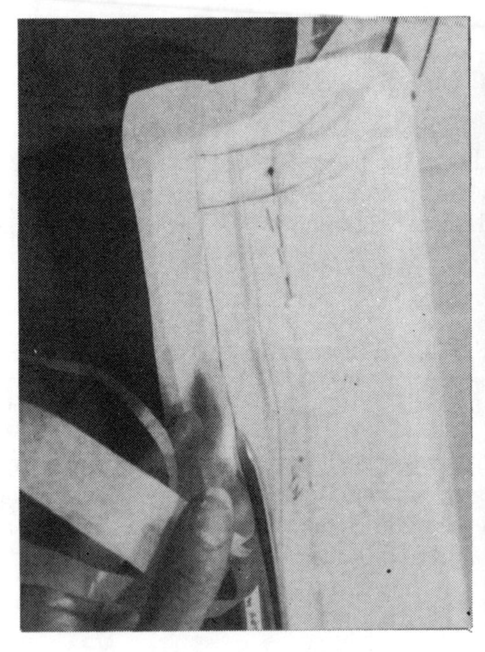

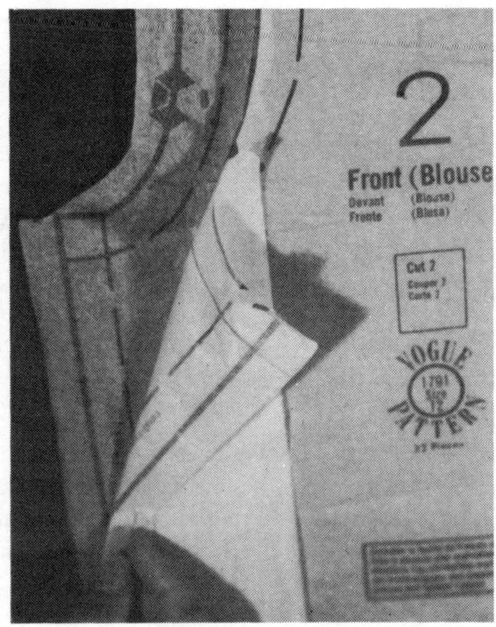

The Dritz French Curve and the Dritz See-thru Ruler are valuable aids in pattern adjustments. Also utilize the 5/8″ width of your tape measure for adding seam allowance markings, especially helpful when working with multiple size patterns. It is very helpful to do this type of work on a cutting board so you can fasten the pattern down to it with pins while you are working. Tissue and scotch tape are difficult to manage unless you hold the tissue in place while you are taping.

Try The Tissue On To Check The Fit And Style

Always press your tissue with a dry iron. A wrinkled tissue can certainly affect the fit of your garment. Pin the tissue together and try the tissue on. Check the fit in front of a full length mirror. A three-way mirror is a great help but a hand-held back mirror will work.

Pin the tissue bodice front and back together at the sides and shoulders. If there is a skirt, pin it onto the bodice. Pin the sleeve together, but don't try to pin the sleeve into the armhole. If the sleeve has a cuff,. pin it on the sleeve. Pin up any hem lines. **Be sure you pin with seamline on seamline,** not cutting line on cutting line. Pin a seamtape or a ribbon, long enough to go around your waist, to the pattern at the waistline. On a close fitting garment, put the tape or ribbon on the outside.

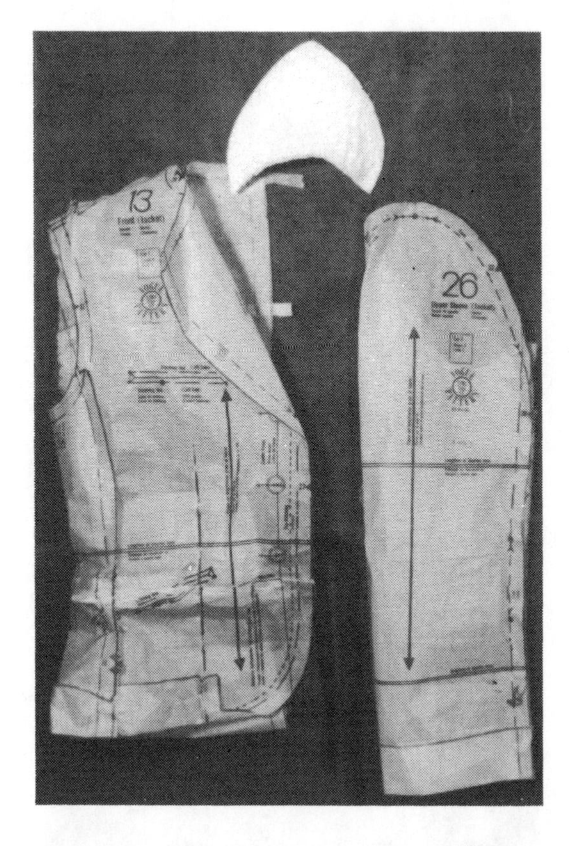

On a loose fitting garment, pin the tape on the inside of the pattern. If the garment calls for a shoulder pad, you will need it to fit the pattern.

Check The Lengths And Widths Of Bodice, Skirt, Jacket, And Sleeves

Slip the tissue on your body. The seam tape at the waistline of the pattern will secure the pattern at the waist and help you judge the waist length of the pattern. (Some help here is great but it is possible to do this on your own.)

Try the pattern on over the garments you will wear with it. Pin the tissue to your garments at center front and center back at the waist. Pin the bustline at center front to hold it in place. Pin the tissue to you at center back, at your bra, and tape the tissue to you at the neckline. Slip the sleeve on and pin it at the notches in the front and the dot at the shoulder. If you have a helper, she can pin the back. Bend your arm to check sleeve length. Check the front neckline. Too high? Too low? Check the amount of blousing in the bodice. Check the skirt length of your garment. Patterns vary a lot in the length. It is safer to cut a little long if you have the fabric. For more detailed information on skirts, refer to pages 9-11. For more detailed information on slacks, refer to pages 12-14.

Use a shoulder pad in the shoulder if the pattern calls for a pad. This trying-on will give you a good idea of how the pattern will look on you. You can see how the pattern and the resulting garment will hang on you. The center front should come to your center front, the back to your center back without tearing the tissue.

If, after adjustments, the pattern will not reach center front and back, take the pins out of the side seams and let the pattern spread till the center back and front are at your center back and front. Measure the amount the pattern has spread. That is the amount you will need to add to the side seam for the garment to fit you with wearing ease. This will not give you design ease.

Often a pattern is too narrow in the reach room in the back. We women seem to have broad backs and narrow fronts. You need enough room to hug a man! The seam line should be where your arm attaches to your body.

If you don't need a lot of room, this can be done by straightening the line of the armhole which is usually quite curved. Often I will also add to the back of the sleeve cap and taper to nothing at the top of the sleeve. If that is not enough room, add more to the back pattern to enlarge it. Split the pattern as it is marked. Add the necessary width and a shoulder dart to take in the added amount at the shoulder seam.

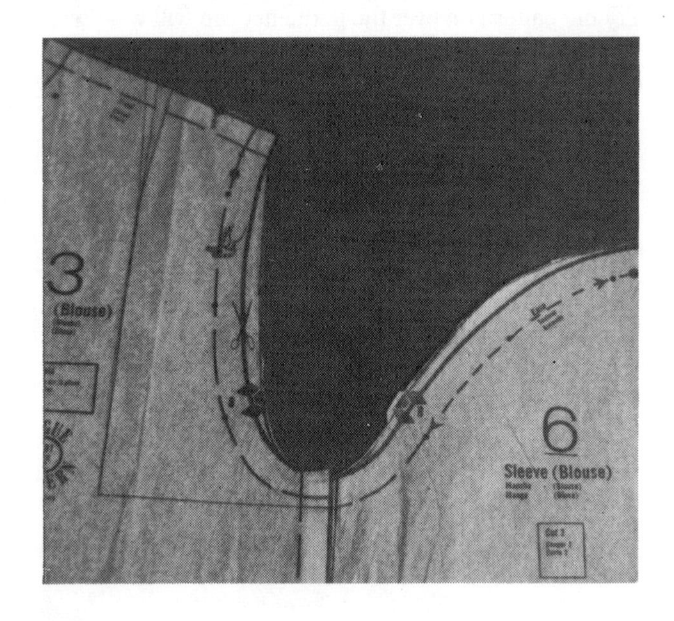

A fitted garment must fit you in the armhole. Many patterns are too low in the armhole. If your pattern is fitted, always raise the armhole of both the sleeve and the front and back bodice. If the seam is too low, you will not be able to move your arm freely. You can always lower the seam if you don't need the extra fabric you have added.

The time you spend getting the pattern to fit is so important to good results in sewing. Many people just assume that the garment will fit and are very disappointed when it doesn't turn out the way they thought it would. Even if you have used a size 10 Vogue for years, check each new pattern you use. Often you will change something that you could not correct after you cut.

If you do extensive changes or are using expensive fabric, it is a very good idea to make the pattern up in muslin before you cut your fashion fabric. I do this often, especially for coats and jackets, and for very fitted garments.

When the tissue is adjusted and the fabric preshrunk, you are ready to cut. Refer to Cutting and the pattern directions for the layout.

As you sew, try your garment on as soon as possible, and often, to see how it is fitting. Your fabric influences the fit, and minor adjustments may be necessary. Also, pin-fitting a garment really customizes the fit and makes your clothing very comfortable.

SKIRTS

Check For Figure Faults

These are fitting problems you would learn how to adjust by having a Basic Dress Pattern. Put a narrow belt around your waist snugly and settle it comfortably at your waistline. Have someone measure the distance from the bottom of the belt to the floor at **right and left sides,** and **center front and back.** If you have to measure yourself, stand close to a table and put a pin in your garment where the table comes. Then measure the distance from the waistband to the pin.

If the side measurement is not the same, you have a high hip. Example: Left side 43″; Right side 43.5″. If one side is higher, it is also usually larger. Increase the side seams to a 1″ seam. That will allow room for you to pin-fit the larger hip. If the back is lower than the center front, you probably have a sway back and/or a prominent tummy. Often you will see a wrinkle across the back of the skirt when you have the band pinned or basted on for a fitting. This is commonly called a sway back. Sometimes a prominent tummy will cause the wrinkles in the back. If you have a prominent tummy, often you will need to add (raise) the waist seam at the center front.

Example: Center front 42.5"; Center back 42". Since the right hip is 1/2" higher than the left hip, trace the waist seam of the pattern, both back and front, and pivot it 1/2" higher at the side seams. Since you also have 2.5" higher center front, raise the center front 1". This will give you room to adjust the hang of your skirt.

Check the hang of your skirt by using a belt with two plumb lines (a measuring tape with a drapery weight makes a great plumb line) around your waist and adjust at the waist seam until the skirt is hanging correctly. The seams of the skirt must hang straight. Put a row of pins at the bottom of the belt. That is your corrected waist seamline. Note the changes you have made and in the future do those adjustments to all garments with waist seams.

Check Your Measurements Against The Pattern

Measure your waist with wearing ease

Measure your waist with interfacing the same width as the waistband pattern. Sit and relax. It should be comfortable.

Measure the length of the waistband pattern

Measure from the center front to the center back and double the measurement. Adjust the waist measurement to fit your waist measure. Standard ease over a snug measure is usually 1" - 1½". **Exception:** A skirt that is very full and heavy needs a rather snug waistband. A little less ease than normal should be used.

Measure the waist seam of the pattern

It should be 1/2" to 1" larger than your waistband pattern measures. The amount of ease depends on your size, your shape, and your fabric. Many patterns do not allow any ease here and often skirts will ride up and have a wrinkle just below the waistband. 1" ease is pretty standard unless you are flat or have fabric that will not ease. In that case, allow less than 1". Divide the amount you are short or long by 4, and add or take in that amount at the side seams or in the darts.

Measure your hip with wearing ease

Put a tape around your hips. Hold it with your fingers and loosen the tape till it will drop over the largest part of the hipline without any help from your other hand. Standard ease over a snug hip line is 2"-3". Style dictates the ease. Check the design ease, as explained earlier, if your skirt if full or gored, page 4. For a straight skirt, proceed as follows:

Measure how far from the waist you are the largest

The pattern should measure the same as your largest hip measure, plus the ease. If the pattern is not the same as your hip measurement plus ease, divide the difference by 4, and add or take in that amount at the side seams. If you have pockets in the side seams, it is easier to split the pattern and add tissue instead of redrawing the seam lines.

Adjusting The Tissue To Your Measurements

Waistband

Example:

personal measurement	tissue	amount to add
28.5	27	1.5

You can add to one end of the waistband pattern or split the pattern at the side seam marking and add equally at each side seam. The notches won't match if you have to make pattern adjustments. Check to see if the waistband is the same length in the front as the back.

Measure the distance from center front to side seam and the distance from center back to side seam on the waistband pattern. If it is even, you can divide the waistband in fourths and match center front, center back, and side seams.

Example:

14¼″ skirt front	14¼″ skirt back
7⅛″ from side to center front	7⅛″ from side to center back

Often the waistband is larger in the front. If that is the case, divide the waistband as the pattern shows.

Example:

28½″	14½″ skirt front	14″ skirt back
	7¼″ from side to center front	7″ from side seam to center back

Waist seam of pattern

Example:

personal measurement	tissue	amount to add
29.5	27	2.5

Divide 2.5 by 4 (the number of seams) = 5/8″ added to each side seam at the waist seam and taper to 1/2″ at the hipline.

Hip at the largest (10″ from the waist)

Example:

personal measurement	tissue	amount to add
42	40	2

Divide 2 by 4 (the number of seams) = 1/2″ added to each side seam. Continue the addition through the hem.

If you are curvy, you need darts. If you are more flat, you could get the extra 1/2″ in the waist by letting out the darts and just increase 1/2″ along the entire side seam. Be sure you do both the skirt front and back.

Check the length of the skirt pattern and adjust if needed. Always allow a little extra, if you can, in case you decide the garment should be longer than you planned.

When the tissue is adjusted and the fabric preshrunk, you are ready to cut. Refer to Cutting and the pattern directions for the layout.

Try your garment as soon as possible, and often, to see how it is fitting. Your fabric influences the fit, and minor adjustments may be necessary. Also, pin-fitting a garment really customizes the fit and makes your clothing very comfortable.

SLACKS

Check And Adjust The Pattern

If you have a basic slack pattern, use that pattern to make the slacks, if you can. Or, if you want a different style, use the basic slack pattern as a guide for adjusting a new pattern. Slacks are the most difficult garment to fit and sometimes a new pattern adjusted from a pattern that fits you is not as good a fit as the old pattern would be. If you don't have a basic, check the following points.

Check the crotch depth and adjust if needed

Take your measurements. Put a narrow belt snugly around your waist. Sit on a flat surface and measure from the bottom of the belt over the hip curve to the flat surface. Add ease, 3/4″-1½″, depending on your size. Allow a minimum of 3/4″ for size 6-10, 1″ for size 12-14, and 1½″ for 16-20. A fuller slack needs more depth in the crotch. So if your pattern has gathers or pleats, allow ⅜″ extra ease in the crotch depth.

Measure the front pattern. Draw a line at a right angle to the straight of grain that intersects the crotch seam. Measure from that line to the waist seam at the side seam of the pattern. That measurement should equal your crotch depth measurement. If it does not, adjust the crotch.

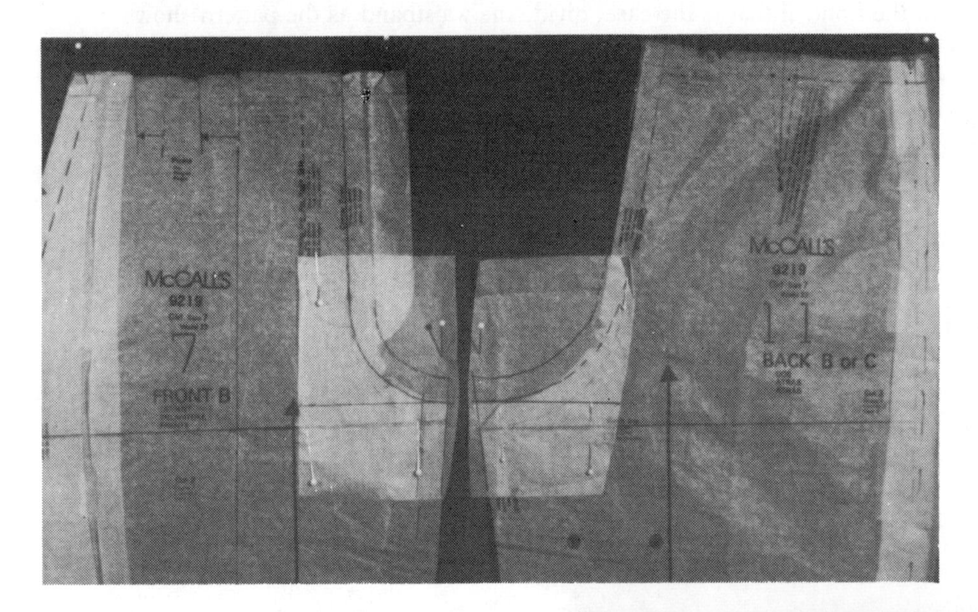

Trace the crotch on tracing paper. Pivot it up to shorten the crotch depth. Do both the front and back patterns the same amount.

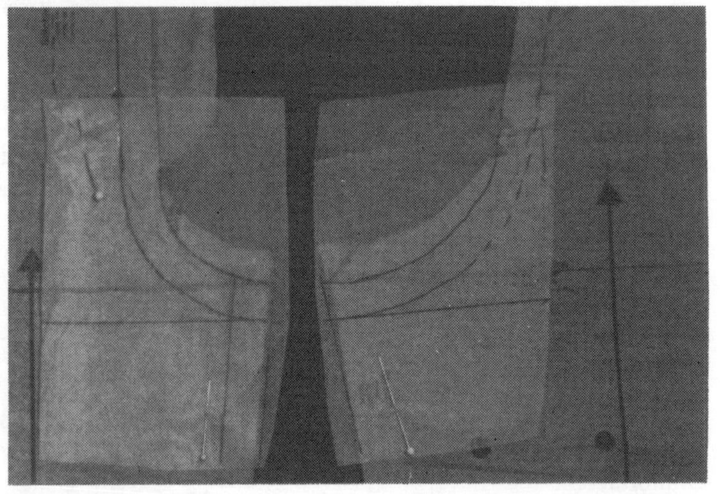

Pivot the crotch down to lengthen. Do both the front and the back pattern pieces.

Check the crotch total length

Measure your total crotch length, both sitting and standing. Measure the crotch between the legs from center back to center front, from the bottom of the narrow belt at both center front and back. This measurement is a guide to help you judge the amount you should have in the pattern when you measure the total crotch. Usually you need a minimum of the measurement of the total crotch length sitting.

Measure the pattern from the waistline at center back to the waist line at center front around the crotch curve. Since you are measuring a curve, stand the tape on edge. You must have at least the sitting measurement in the pattern. To help know what crotch length you are comfortable in, measure a pair of slacks from the waistband to waistband along the crotch seam. If your measurements are not the same as the pattern, after the crotch depth is adjusted, adjust the pattern by adding to the inner leg seam.

Crotch Depth and Length are Very Individual

Always check the crotch depth and length after you have the band stitched on. Lower it by stitching the crotch seam deeper if you need more room. If the crotch is too long, you must set the band down to shorten the crotch length and depth. If you have other figure problems, such as a prominent tummy, high hip, or sway back, refer to the Skirt on page 9-10 . Those same adjustments should be made when you put the waistband on slacks.

Check the length of the slack pattern

Measure the pattern from the waistline at the side seam to the hem line at the bottom of the slacks.

Adjust the length at lengthen/shorten line on the pattern. If you must adjust over 4″, remove 2″ at the lengthen/shorten line and 2″ between the crotch and the knee.

Check the waist measure

Measure your waist with interfacing the same width as the waistband pattern.

Measure the length of the waistband pattern and adjust it to fit your waist measure.

Ease over a snug measurement of your waist is usually 1-1½″. I feel that a waistband on slacks should be a bit longer than on other garments because of the pull at the waist when you sit. So I usually allow 1½″ ease in slacks.

I like a waistband with a center back seam if the slack has a front opening to allow for adjustment in the waistline.

Waistband

Example:

personal measurements	pattern envelope	flat tissue	design ease
27	26.5	27.5	1

Your waist measure (27) + wearing ease (1½″) = 28½″. Flat tissue is 27.5″. Add 1″ length to the waistband pattern. Refer to waistband of skirts, page 11, for information on where to add.

Measure your hip with wearing ease

Put a tape around your hips, hold it with your fingers and loosen the tape till it will drop over the largest part of the hipline without any help from your other hand. Measure how far from the waist you are the largest.

The pattern should measure the same as your hip measures with wearing ease. If the pattern has extra fullness, darts or gathers, check to see how much ease the pattern has allowed in the hipline. Add that amount to your snug hip measurement. If the pattern does not correspond with your measurement plus wearing and/or design ease, divide the difference by 4 and add or take in that amount at the side seams. Taper to the regular seam at the knee for a slim leg or add the full length of the pattern piece.

Wearing ease over a snug hip measurement is usually 2-2½″. Design ease can be any amount the designers added to get the look they desire.

Hip - 9″ from waist

Example:

personal measurements	pattern envelope	flat tissue	design ease
39	36	44	8

Your hip measure (39) + design ease (8) = 47″. Flat tissue is 44″. Add 3″ to the front and back of the pattern, again dividing the 3″ by the number of seams = 3/4″ added to the front and back at the side seams. I divide with my tape measure. It is easy and accurate. Fold 3″ in half = 1½″, fold again =3/4″.

A Summary Of The Changes That Were Needed On This Tissue

The **crotch** measure is 10″ + 1″ ease = 11″. The pattern is 11¼″. Shorten the crotch 1/4″ both on the front and back pattern. The **length** of the pattern. The length is 37″ from the waistline to the hem line. The pattern tissue measures 39″. Fold out 2″ at the lengthen/shorten line.

The **waist** measure is 28½″. The waistband pattern tissue measures 27″. Add 1½″ to the waistband pattern.

The **waist seam** needs to be 29½″ (1″ ease should be added over the waistband length). The pattern tissue is 27″. Add 2½″ to the waist seam of the pattern.

The **hip** measurement is 42″, 10″ from the waist. The pattern tissue measures 40″, 10″ from the waist. Add 2″ to the pattern, 1/2″ on each side seam 10″ from the waist. Add 5/8″ at the waist line or let out the darts a bit to get the 2½″ you need at the waist seam.

If you have pockets in the side seams, it is easier to split the pattern and add instead of redrawing the seam line.

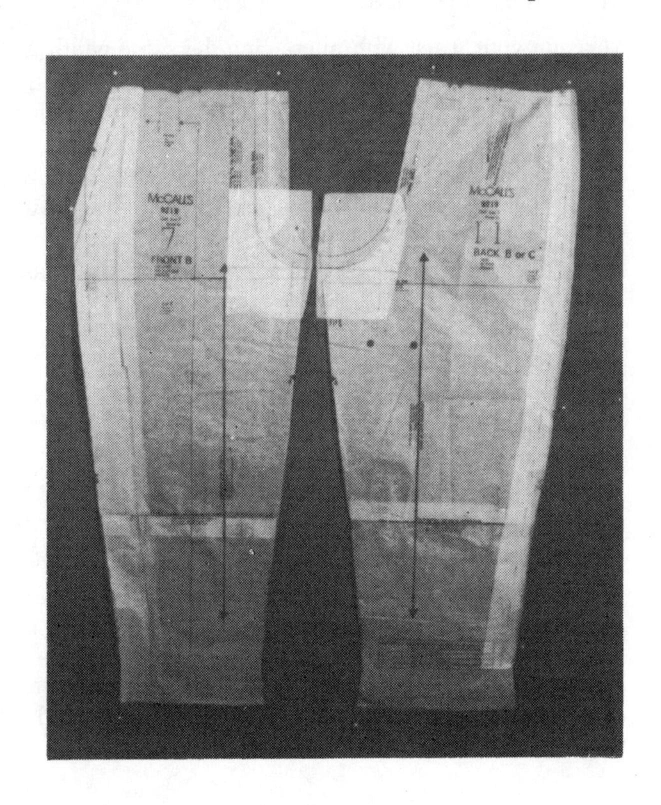

The pattern tissue with the crotch, the slack length, and width adjusted at the side seams. The front pattern was split because of the pocket. The back width was adjusted by tracing the side seam and pivoting out the needed amount.

GRAIN IN FABRICS

Grain is of prime importance in the fit and hang of a garment. Just as plumb or straight is important in building houses so is it important in making garments. For garments to hang and fit correctly they must be cut straight on the grain of the fabric. All woven and knit fabrics have grainlines.

Woven Fabric

Woven fabric has a lengthwise grain, a crosswise grain, and a bias.

Lengthwise—the direction of the warp thread, is the strongest, straightest hang, and has the least give. The selvage is the lengthwise grain.

Crosswise—the direction of the woof or filling thread, has more give, drapes differently giving a fuller look to a garment.

Bias — runs diagonally across the weave, is a direction not a grain. It cuts through the grain.

The **lengthwise** and the **crosswise** are always at right angles to each other, no matter what the surface texture of the fabric may be. **Bias** stretches the most, drapes softly and tends to be unstable at the hemline.

Knit Fabric

Knit fabric has a lengthwise grain and a crosswise grain and no selvage edge. **Lengthwise** grain is indicated by the ribs running with the yardage. Usually this direction does not have much give. **Crosswise** grain is at right angles to the rib-line and can have considerable give. Crosswise grain is used where the bias would be used in a woven fabric.

A pinned rib-line is the only straight of grain on a knit!

For further instructions on pinning a rib-line and cutting a knit refer to Cutting on pages 31-32.

Grain lines and the human figure

The relationship of fabric to figure is simple and direct. The lengthwise grain is established down the center front, center back, and sleeve center. In all work done to shape the garment, seams, darts, gathers, steaming and pressing, this grain direction must be maintained. **The grain must hang plumb on the figure.** This basic rule of sewing cannot be disregarded without sad results in the fit and hang of a garment. In **almost** all garments the lengthwise grain corresponds to the up and down of the figure. Fabric design may make it necessary to reverse this and use the crosswise grain. Some garments are cut on the true bias. **Drape your fabric in front of a mirror** to see how it hangs on all grainlines and to see which you like the best for your fabric and garment.

Grain and fabric finishes

Fabric, as it comes from the loom, is grain perfect. The lengthwise and crosswise threads are exactly at right angles. Rolling the fabric from bolt to bolt, and the various finishes with which fabrics are treated, very often cause the crosswise grain to be pulled out of line making the weave off-grain. If the finish is temporary, this can be corrected. If the finish is permanent it cannot be corrected. Permanent finishes lock the grain in position and cannot be straightened. Always **read the bolt end** when you are buying fabric. If the grain is crooked it will remain that way without impairing the hang of the garment. There is no need to straighten the fabric. You could pull and pull on it but when it hangs it will go back to its crooked state. Permanent finishes are usually mentioned on the bolt end. **Read the bolt end.** Permanent-press, crease-resistant, durable-press, stain-resistant, water-repellant, and bonded fabrics are permanent finishes. Temporary finishes are not mentioned on the bolt ends. Pre-shrunk, shrink-resistant, sanforized, and flame-retardant are not permanent finishes and do not affect the grain.

Straightening the fabric

Woven fabric is lengthwise straight with the selvage. Sometimes the crossgrain has been pulled out of line causing the weave to be off grain. Straighten the fabric if it is **woven** of untreated cotton, wool, silk, linen, or rayon. Straighten the end (crossgrain) by tearing, pulling a thread, or cutting on a prominent design line. Cutting on a prominent design line is possible with a woven-in stripe, plaid, or other woven design. It will not work if the design is printed on the fabric.

Tearing is the fastest method but it works only on firmly woven fabrics.

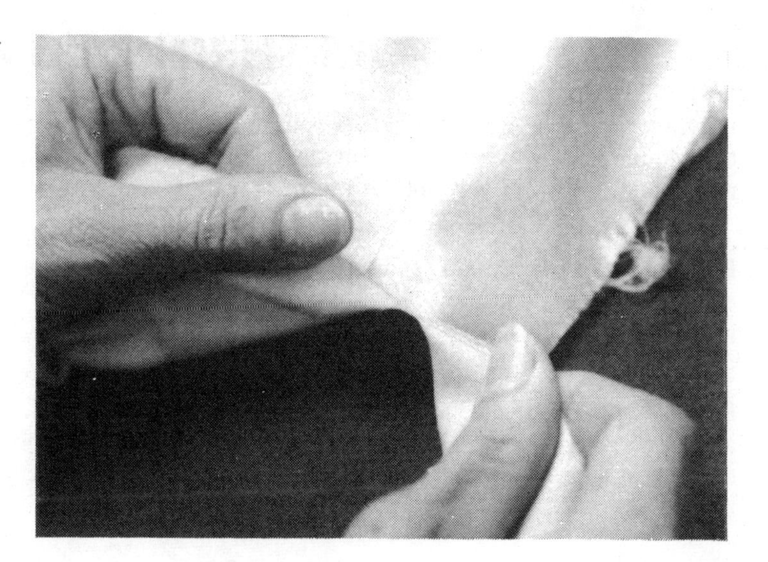

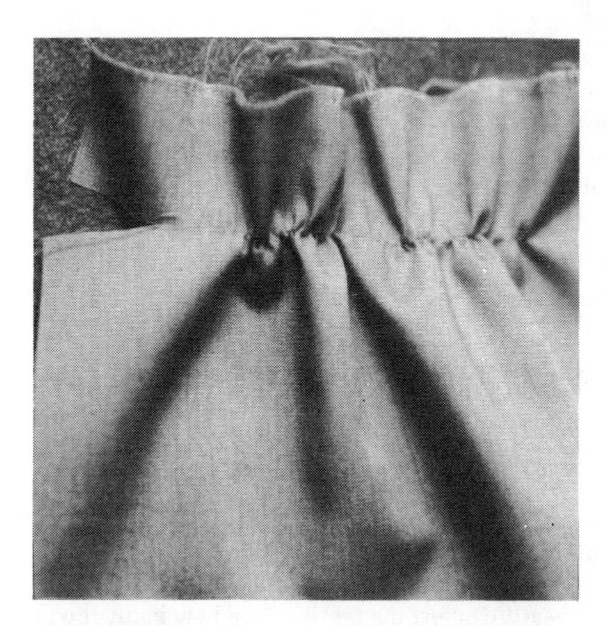

Pulling a thread and cutting the puckered fabric along the pulled line works for most woven fabrics. Don't expect to pull one thread across the entire width of your fabric. Pull a thread. If it breaks, cut as far as you can see that thread. Gently tug on the cut edge till you can find another thread, pull that thread, and continue across the entire width of the fabric.

I feel it is necessary to straighten only one end of the fabric unless the fabric is very crooked. Lay the selvages together and lay the crosswise grain together. If the fabric will lie flat (no ripples) that is sufficient. If you must pull the fabric on the bias for it to lie flat and straight of grain it is necessary to straighten both ends. If after straightening and preshrinking the fabric it will not lie flat with the crossgrains even and the selvages even, it has been treated with a permanent finish that was not noted on the bolt end. Cut it with the selvages together. The lengthwise grain will be straight. Only the crosswise grain will be off.

I have had the sad experience of having a garment hang crooked after working very hard to get the fabric straight. Usually this does not happen but if your fabric won't behave listen to it. Cut it as if you were sure it had a permanent finish. Lay the selvages together and let the straightened ends be uneven.

Hair canvas

I have been unsuccessful in attempts to straighten hair canvas. Use hair canvas as it is.

PRE-SHRINKING FABRIC

Always preshrink the fabric before you cut it. I never cut a garment without pre-shrinking my fabric. Even though many of today's fabrics do not shrink they will handle more easily after pre-shrinking. If the fabric does not launder well, you may not wish to work with it.

Pre-shrink your fabric after it has been straightened. Baste the straightened edges together before washing, especially if you plan to dry the fabric in the drier. If it will be hung or laid flat to dry you can pull it straight while it is wet.

Fabrics should be treated as the finished garment will be treated. Washable fabrics should be washed with soap and dried as you will dry the garment. Dry-cleanable fabrics should be taken to the cleaners for pre-shrinking or they can be pre-shrunk at home using the London Shrink method.

London Shrink Method

Straighten one end of the fabric. Fold in half lengthwise, baste ends, clip the selvages if they pucker. Spread the fabric on a damp sheet. Then fold the fabric and the sheet together. Place them, all folded, in a plastic bag for a few hours till the fabric is damp. Dry the fabric flat making sure it is lying straight. Press with a steam iron. I usually preshrink my fabric in the morning, then lay it out flat to dry in the evening, and by morning it is ready to be pressed.

If you have decided not to pre-shrink your fabric, (**I don't recommend this**) then at least press it with a steam iron.

Sample Seam

When you are working with a fabric that is unfamiliar to you, test a scrap of it to see how it stitches on the lengthwise, crosswise, and bias grainline. Do a sample seam and press the seam open. Test a scrap of your fabric to see how it reacts to pressing. Use a large enough piece to compare a pressed section with a unpressed part. Check to see how the fabric reacts to moisture as well as heat. Also test the fabric to see how badly it will ravel and what seam finish will be the most desirable for the fabric. Often testing will steer you away from a design which would cause you extra work or an undesirable finished garment.

Preparation For Sewing · 2

INNER CONSTRUCTION

Inner Construction Consists Of Interfacing, Underlinings, Linings, And Paddings

Interfacings are used to support the fashion fabric, to add body and crispness without bulk, to provide strength and stability, and to prevent stretching. Interfacing should not be heavier or show through the fashion fabric.

To choose the correct weight of interfacing for your garment feel two layers of your fabric with one layer of the interfacing between them. Determine the effect by draping. Will it roll back nicely if you have a lapel, will it stand up for a mandarin collar, will it be soft and let the front of a blouse drape without sticking out? The interfacing, plus your fabric, should have the feel you want one area of garment to have. Mix interfacing weights if you want one area of the garment to be crisp and one to be soft. Example: Crisp for a mandarin collar and soft for the button opening on a blouse.

Choosing an interfacing is difficult at first, especially if you just take what is recommended and don't consider what you want it to do for you. You know what you want you garment to do. Choose your interfacings to suit your needs. Interfacing must have the same care and should wear as well as the fashion fabric.

There are many interfacings on the market. They are not all my favorites so they will not be listed here. I don't use fusible interfacings as a general rule, but there are times I like them. I don't believe they are any easier or faster to apply in most garments than the regular sew-in interfacing. I use glue-stick to hold my interfacings in place until they are secured in the seam. Dot the glue-stick along the edge of the interfacing in the seam allowance and lay the fashion fabric on it. I use this method to secure interfacings and underlinings for all types of fabric. Be careful, use the glue sparingly. Dot the glue along the edge of the seam allowance. If you are underlining, lay the fashion fabric and the underlining together, matching all the edges. Smooth the layers with your hands or press them together on a large flat surface. If the pieces are large, they must be folded once on the lengthwise with the underlining on the inside to accommodate the body curve. Loosen one long edge by running a finger between the two layers of fabric while the glue is still wet. Let the underlining scoot out past the edge of the fashion fabric. This makes the underlining slightly smaller than the fashion fabric which prevents wrinkles in the underlining when the garment is on the body. Hand baste through the center front and back if they are on a fold. Also baste through the center of any dart or tuck to hold the layers together during construction. Treat the two layers as one during construction. After the seam is stitched and trimmed most of the glued area has been trimmed off. I do like fusible interfacings on knits and on some woven cottons and cotton blends. I do not like them on silks or silky polyesters. I wear my garments for years and it has been my experience that nonfusibles hold up best in the laundry and cleaning.

Always preshrink any washable interfacing by washing it in warm water with soap. Preshrink hair canvas by soaking it in warm water, then let the water drip out. Or spin the water out in the washing machine. Either dry flat or line dry. Always preshrinking your fusible by soaking it in a basin of fairly warm water, drip the water out or spin in the washing machine, and lay out flat to dry. Do not put fusible interfacings in the drier. Always test your fusible interfacing before you apply it. The fusing agent when cool can make for a stiffer interfacing than you anticipated.

Many times the pattern tells you to put the interfacing on the garment itself. As a general rule, I prefer to put the interfacing on the facings and the under-side of the collar and cuffs.

There are exceptions. If your fab ric is sheer and the seam shows through to the right side, then, of course, you would interface the top layer.

Lightweight Interfacings

Organdy:

A very fine, thin, transparent cotton cloth with a crisp finish, woven of tightly twisted yarns. Prewash and iron it while wet. It is nice and crisp and does not ravel.

There are two weights of organdy available and both are nice for interfacing. The crispest and therefore the most expensive per yard is the best for bound buttonholes, welt pockets, and square corners. Some stores do not carry this type of organdy. The less expensive organdy works well for any area that could not curl, such as a plain neckline or under buttons on a blouse. It works great for voile blouses where you need a thin, sheer interfacing. Organdy would not be suitable for any area that could roll or curl such as French cuffs or a collar.

Organza:

A fine transparent fabric similar to organdy using highly twisted yarns. Made in silk and synthetics. I prefer the polyester organza. It is less expensive and can be washed. The silk organza needs to be dry cleaned and it frays more easily than the polyester organza. Organza can be used anywhere you would use organdy, but it does ravel more than organdy.

Sheath Lining:

100% cotton sheath lining has the same hand after it is washed as imported 100% bastiste and is much less expensive. Use it anywhere you need a soft interfacing. It is softer than a cotton polyester blend batiste but it does wrinkle.

Batiste:

A soft sheer cotton, linen, or synthetic fabric of plain weave. I prefer the cotton/polyester blend because it doesn't wrinkle. Prewash it and it can be dried in the dryer.

Use batiste for interfacing any light weight fabric. It is especially nice for interfacing in the collars, cuffs, and under the buttonhole closing in blouses and dresses.

Broadcloth:

I like the cotton/polyester blend broadcloth for just a little heavier interfacing than batiste. Preshrink it by washing and drying it in the drier.

Easy-knit:

A nylon tricot with a fusible back. Preshrink by soaking in a basin of medium hot water for about ten minutes. Let the water drip out and lay flat to dry, Do not put fusible interfacing in the dryer.

Use easy-knit for interfacing any knit where you want just a little body and stability. I also like easy-knit in cotton and cotton blend wovens and for Ultrasuede and Facille where I want just a light interfacing.

Whisper Weft:

A woven fusible 60% polyester and 40% rayon by Armo. Preshrink by soaking in a basin of medium hot water for about ten minutes. Let the water drip out and lay flat to dry. Do not put fusible interfacing in the dryer.

Whisper Weft combines the best properties of knit and woven fabrics, stability and resiliency. Use it in any fabric where you want just a light interfacing and wish to use a fusible.

Medium Weight Interfacings

Super Siri:

A blend of polyester/rayon that comes in both soft and firm and in black and white. Preshrink it by machine washing. It can be dried in the dryer.

Use Super Siri for interfacing medium weight fabric. Drape the interfacing with your fabric to determine the finish to use. It comes in soft and crisp. Siri is getting hard to find.

Armo-press:

A blend of cotton/polyester that comes in both a soft and crisp finish. Preshrink by washing. It can be dried in the dryer.

Use Armo-press for interfacing any medium weight fabric when you want a little more body that batiste or organza would give. The soft Armo-press is similar to batiste or broadcloth, but personally, I prefer the hang of batiste or broadcloth. Since the fiber content of Armo-press was changed from polyester/rayon to polyester/cotton it has not been one of my favorite interfacings.

Taffeta:

A basic group of fine plain-weave fabrics, smooth, crisp, usually lustrous. Taffeta can be rayon, polyester, or silk. Use taffeta for interfacing ties or belts that you want to hold a bow. Taffeta especially heavy taffeta also works great in some fabrics for a crisp cuff or collar interfacing.

Muslin:

A wide variety of plain-woven cotton fabrics ranging from sheer to coarse.

Use muslin for interfacing the back of a jacket or coat. Muslin is the choice in tailoring for a channel on hair canvas when working with heavy fabric. Also use muslin for a light weight interfacing for hems.

Stay-shape:

A perma-prest interfacing by Stacy with a little more body and crispness than armo-press. If your garment will ever be washed, wash the stay-shape. It loses a bit of its body when it is washed.

Use Stay-shape for interfacing for light weight jackets and coats where other interfacing would be too light and hair canvas would be too heavy.

Armo Weft:

A woven fusible 60% polyester and 40% rayon by Armo. Preshrink by soaking in a basin of medium hot water for about ten minutes. Let the water drip out or spin the water out in the washing machine. Lay it flat to dry or line dry it. Do not put fusible interfacing in the dryer.

This is my favorite fusible interfacing for Fusible Tailoring for medium weight fabrics, both woven and knits. I would use this if I were making a jacket out of less expensive fabric that I did not plan to have in my closet for 10 years. I also use it for tailoring Ultrasuede when I want a little heavier interfacing than whisper weft or easy-knit.

Heavy Weight Interfacings

These interfacings would be used mostly for tailoring.

Sta-shape #50:

A very crisp perma-prest washable hair canvas. Use sta-shape #50 to interface jackets or coats of crisp fabrics. Be sure and handle both interfacing and fabric together to test the hand. Sta-shape #50 does not lose any of its crispness.

Hair canvas:

Most hair canvases are made by Armo/Crown Textile Co. or Stacy Fabric Corp. and are available in light, medium, and heavy weights. Check the bolt end for fiber content. Commonly they are some combination of wool, polyester, cotton, rayon, and goat hair and must be dry cleaned. I do preshrink by soaking in warm water and laying out flat to dry. I also like a 100% wool hair canvas usually available at better stores that carry tailoring supplies. Use hair canvas for shaping and underlining the appropriate weight fabric. Hair canvas is used mostly in tailoring. Always drape with your fabric as discussed earlier and choose the weight you like. I don't pay much attention to brand names when choosing a hair canvas. I use what I like the feel or hand of. What is available in one area may not be available in another area, so take a piece of your fashion fabric and go shopping.

Fusible Acro:

A fusible, washable hair canvas by Armo which is fairly stiff in the garment. It also comes in nonfusible. Be sure and test a piece on your particular fabric. I like the nonfusible but the fusible Acro is too stiff.

Collar Linen:

This is hard to find but it makes the best collar interfacing for tailoring. I usually can find it at a tailoring supply house. Collar Linen comes in two weights and is only drycleanable.

Pre-padded Felt and Collar Linen:

This usually must be purchased at a tailor supply outlet. Use Pre-padded Felt and Collar Linen to tailor a sporty jacket.

Paddings

Use paddings for shoulder pads, sleeve heads, and for quilting.

Lamb's wool:

The soft and elastic fleece obtained from a seven or eight month-old lamb's first shearing. Can be woven into a superior fabric.

Use for padding and for underlinings. I often use lamb's wool for a light weight sleeve head in tailoring.

Lamb's wool is a wonderful backing for the lining of a coat where you want to add warmth. Underlining the lining, instead of the garment, helps to eliminate the bulk in the coat itself and still gives the extra warmth needed.

Pellon fleece:

Use Pellon fleece for making shoulder pads, and for a lofty sleeve head in tailoring. Good for padding in a quilted belt.

Thermolan:

Is similar to Pellon fleece. Thermolan is made by Stacy and is heavier in weight than Pellon fleece. I use them both and often combine the different weights in shoulder pads.

Polyester batting or fleece:

Use for quilting jackets and vests. Try to purchase a batting that can be split in two layers. Often you want a thinner batting for a garment than you would use for a quilt. This works great for anything you want to have a soft puff.

Underlinings

For several years underlining has been out of favor except on the very expensive couture garments done by top designers. It costs money and more important, takes time and labor to put underlining in a garment. I believe that is why so much of even the better ready-to-wear garments no longer have underlinings.

Use an underlining when your fabric needs more body to hang well. Underlining reduces wrinkling and adds strength to a garment. Underline when you can see through a fabric and you don't want to. Underlining hides hems and facings and gives you a place to tack hems and facing to.

The underlining fabric must have the same care and should wear as well as the fashion fabric. It usually is lighter in weight than the fashion fabric. If you don't want to add weight and bulk to your garment use a very light weight underlining.

Be sure you preshrink both your fashion fabric and your underlining. Drape both fabrics over your hand to make sure they relate well to each other. A tightly woven fabric is best for preventing stretching and to preserve the shape of the garment.

Lightweight Underlinings

China Silk:

A plain weave silk in various weights. Use for lining skirts, dresses, or loose fitting jackets where you need a very lightweight lining. China silk can be handwashed or washed in the delicate cycle of the washing machine.

Sheath Lining:

100% cotton sheath lining has the same hand after it is washed as imported 100% batiste and is much less expensive. It works well for underlining silks and anywhere else you need a soft underlining. It does wrinkle more than a cotton/polyester blend batiste. Sheath lining is getting hard to find.

Batiste:

A soft sheer cotton, linen, or synthetic fabric of plain weave. I prefer the cotton/polyester blend because it doesn't wrinkle. Prewash it and it can be dried in the dryer.

Use batiste for underlining any time you want something a little heavier than China silk or the cotton sheath lining. I use it mostly for underlining trousers.

Siri:

A woven fabric blend of polyester/rayon with either a soft or crisp finish.

Use siri for underlining all weight garments for a soft or crisp hand depending on which finish you use. Siri is getting hard to find.

Medium Weight Underlinings

Muslin:

A wide variety of plain-woven cotton fabrics ranging from sheer to coarse. Always buy a good grade of muslin. Underline any garment of medium to heavy weight fabric where the hand is right. Muslin will not add any crispness. I have used muslin when I was unable to get out and get anything else. Works fine.

Armo-press:

A blend of cotton/polyester that comes in both soft and crisp finish. Preshrink by washing and drying in the dryer.

Use for underlining any medium weight fabric. Drape your fabric to determine which weight to use.

Outing flannel:

A soft, lightweight, plain, or twill woven fabric with a nap on one or both sides. Made from cotton or rayon, it is used mostly for infants' wear, sleepwear, diapers, etc.

Use outing flannel to underline satin for a luxurious look and for warmth and comfort. Outing flannel has been used to underline an entire wedding dress when inexpensive satin was used. The weight and the drape of the flannel makes polyester satin look like expensive silk satin. For a most luxurious feel, and to hide the flannel, line the garment with china silk. Also use flannel for underlining a satin bodice or camisole.

Linings

Linings give your garment a smooth luxurious feel and a finished custom look. Lining also lengthens the life of the garment by covering the inner construction and by protecting the fashion fabric from abrasion. It prevents stretching, reduces wrinkling, and adds body to limp fabrics, although not as much as underlining. Lining must have the same care and should wear as well as the fashion fabric. Generally, lining should be softer and lighter in weight than the fashion fabric, but not so lightweight as to reveal inner construction. **Lining should be opaque and slippery** when used for jackets and coats. It is desirable for linings to be static-free and absorb moisture. I often mix the lining in a suit. I put a more expensive lining or one that is opaque in the jacket and a less expensive one in the skirt. The majority of trade-name linings are color-fast, perspiration-proof, wrinkle-resistant, and have non-cling finishes. Common trade names are Skinner, Logantex, Earl-glo, Balsom, Pogo, and Robert Kaufman. Linings are often hard to find, especially if you have an unusual color. Silky blouse fabrics make a good lining but are usually more expensive than a lining fabric.

Lightweight Linings

I have not listed any fabric that would not be slippery. However, if that is not a factor for your garment, you could consider other fabrics than those listed.

Chinа silk:

A plain weave silk in various weights. Use for lining skirts, dresses, or loose fitting jackets where you need a very lightweight lining. China silk can be handwashed or washed in the delicate cycle of the washing machine.

Silk crepe-de-chine:

Use only if the garment will always be dry cleaned. Silk crepe-de-chine would be the most expensive and luxurious lining.

I would consider it for a very fine wool jacket, especially if I were making a blouse to match.

Use silk crepe-de-chine for lining a coat or suit jacket and for making a blouse to match.

Polyester crepe-de-chine:

This would be a nicer lining than just a polyester lining. Polyester crepe-de-chine would also make a nice blouse. Skinner makes one that is dyed to match Ultrasuede.

Polyester lining:

Use when washability and long wear are important. Make sure your lining fabric is opaque and preferably non-static. Fashionaire or polyester pongee by Pago is a nice lining.

Rayon lining:

Rayon is a very comfortable lining and absorbs moisture but it does not launder or wear as well as polyester. A good choice if polyester is too hot for you and if you will not wear the garment hard. Rayon has been much improved in recent years. Satellite by Balson is a nice light weight rayon lining. Duet by Robert Kaufman is an acetate lining suitable for a skirt.

Medium Weight Linings

Rayon lining:

Rayon is a more comfortable lining and absorbs moisture but it does not launder or wear as well as polyester. A good choice if polyester is too hot for you and if you will not wear the garment hard. Rayon has been much improved in recent years. Earl-glo makes a twill rayon lining. Ambiance, Chesterfield, and Hangloose by Logantex of 100% bemberg rayon are good medium to heavy weight rayon linings. Drape the linings with your fabric to choose which is best for your purpose.

Satin Royale:

This is not an easy lining to find, but it is one of my favorites for a medium weight coat. It is 59% rayon and 41% silk. It is fairly expensive but feels wonderful. It can be purchased through Maxine's Fabrics in New York City.

Silk broadcloth:

Use only if the garment will always be dry cleaned. I would consider it for a very fine wool jacket or coat especially if I were making a blouse to match.

Broadcloth has more body than the other silks listed for lining.

Polyester linings:

Ala Creme by Skinner and Coupe de Ville by Burlington are both good choices if you need a medium weight polyester lining.

Crepeback satin:

Acetate and rayon or 100% polyester. These would be found in the bridal section of most fabric stores.

Heavy Weight Linings

You could underline a medium or light-weight lining with outing flannel or lambswool if you can't find a suitable heavy weight lining.

Lutesong:

100% polyester satin, quite heavy in weight. A very long wearing lining. Use lutesong for a coat that would be worn a lot.

Milium lining:

Earl-glo and Skinner both make a rayon lining that is insulated with milium for warmth. Use for a warm coat which won't be worn a lot.

Sunback satin:

Balson and Skinner both make a satin rayon lining backed with wool fleece. Dry clean. Use for a very warm coat or jacket.

Quilted lining:

Rayon or polyester satin quilted with a fill. Use for lining a very warm jacket, I use this especially for lining sleeves when I am lining the remainder of the garment with fleece.

CUTTING

Be sure your **fabric** has been **straightened** and **preshrunk** (refer to Grain in Fabric and Preshrinking), and your **pattern adjusted** to fit you before you cut. Don't hurry into a sewing project without first doing those two jobs. Never cut expensive fabric without preparing the fabric and pattern. I can't resist lovely fabric so I have quite a collection. If you too collect fabric, try to straighten, preshrink, and measure your fabric when you buy it. If there is anything wrong with it, the fabric can be returned to the store. That is a little hard to do a couple of years later. Label the fabric after pre-shrinking so you know it is needle-ready. **Press** any wrinkles out of your **fabric** before cutting. **Press** your adjusted **pattern** with a dry iron. A wrinkled pattern or fabric can certainly affect the fit of a garment.

Many of you may be cutting on your floor or the dining room table. A cutting board, with straight lines and a non-slippery surface you can pin to, is a great help in cutting. Another option is a long counter in the kitchen and an adjustable ironing board. Put the ironing board along the counter and put the cutting board on top. Saves your back! In my classroom, I have 4′ x 8′ padded tables with cutting boards on top of them. Four sawhorse brackets, "two-by-fours" for legs and cross-bars, and the 4′ by 8′ piece of plywood makes a great table for cutting. You can make it any height that is comfortable for you. Pad it and you have a great table for all your sewing needs.

Before Cutting

Always check to make sure you have enough fabric to cut all the pieces before you cut the first piece. You needn't pin them all but lay them all in place. I don't always use the pattern layout but I do always refer to it. Often it is the best way to cut, and it has important information for cutting the garment. If you are a beginning seamstress, **cut the notches out. Never cut notches in.** If you are an experienced seamstress, it's fine to use little snips for the notches unless the fabric ravels badly. Then cut the notches out because the snips would soon be lost. **Cut carefully.** If you make a mistake cutting, it can be costly. Often if I am cutting expensive fabric, I will lay it out one day and cut it the next morning after I have checked my layout. If you can save fabric by changing the layout, do it. Always remember, the minute you buy a pattern, it is yours! Don't do anything just because the pattern says to, especially if you know you have a better way.

Tips For Fabric And Pattern Layouts

When cutting either knit or woven fabric, I usually cut with the right side of the fabric inside. There are exceptions. If you are matching a design that doesn't show through, or cutting a knit and the rib-line is easier to see on the right side, then, of course, cut with the right side out. I find it easier to mark with the right side inside, but that is a personal preference.

Difficult fabrics

If the fabric is slippery (crepe de chine, linings, silky polyesters), fastening it to a cutting board with pins is a big help. Fastening it along the straight lines of the cutting board keeps the grain lying straight. If you have trouble cutting slippery fabrics straight, pin on both sides of the cutting line. A pair of scissors with one serrated blade is very helpful in cutting the slippery, silky fabrics. If your fabric is really difficult (moves when you breathe, example: ribbon silk chiffon, polyester chiffon), pin it to tissue paper before cutting. After it is cut, stay-stitch around all the edges through the tissue. You may want to cut double tissue paper or cut the garment singly so you have the extra piece of tissue you need for the stay-stitching. Then carefully remove the tissue. The stay-stitching will preserve the grain-line while you are handling the delicate fabric.

Nap layout

Always use a nap layout if you can. A nap layout is laying all the pattern pieces in the same direction.

Patterns always give the fabric requirements for with and without nap. Be sure you have enough to cut the nap layout if your fabric has nap. Notice on the pattern layouts below one illustration says without nap when it is in fact with nap.

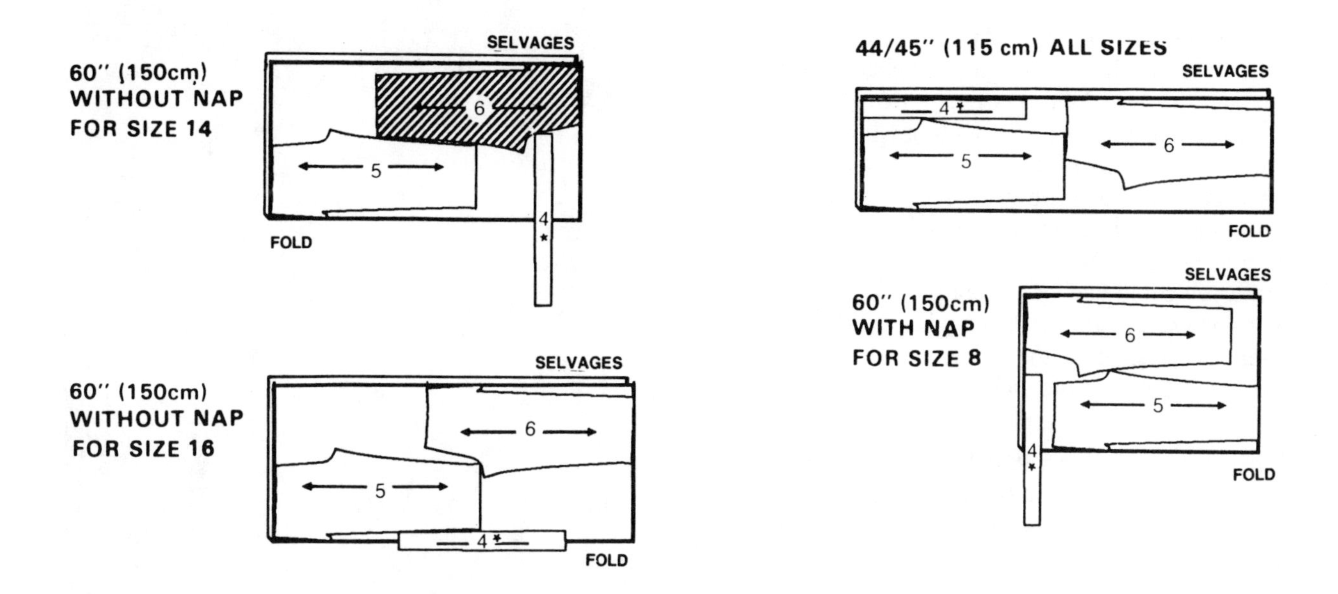

If you must turn the pieces, very carefully check to make sure there is no nap to the fabric. Put the fabric around your neck and look at it in the mirror. Can you see any difference in the two pieces of fabric? If there is no difference, it is safe to turn the pieces and have some lying one direction and some lying the opposite direction.

Some fabrics that always require a nap layout are velvets, corduroys, brushed denims, and Ultrasuede. Usually, nap fabrics are cut with the nap running up so the fabric looks darker and richer. Some coating fabrics also have a nap and they are usually cut with the nap going down so it is smooth against your hand.

Other fabrics that don't appear to require a nap layout often do. Check plaids, uneven stripes, and all-over prints. Some will have a subtle one-way design. Over the years, I have just made it a practice always to use a nap layout. That saves me the worry that I might miss a subtle difference that would show up after I had cut the garment. Refer to Layouts For Special Fabrics for information on the Wiggle Method of cutting plaids and stripes, page 35.

Cutting Woven Fabrics

If you need to fold your woven fabric to fit the width of a pattern piece, as in the illustration, it's quick and accurate to measure the pattern to determine the width needed. Then do a row of pins that distance from the selvage through just one layer of the fabric. Fold the fabric along the row of pins. This preserves the straight of grain.

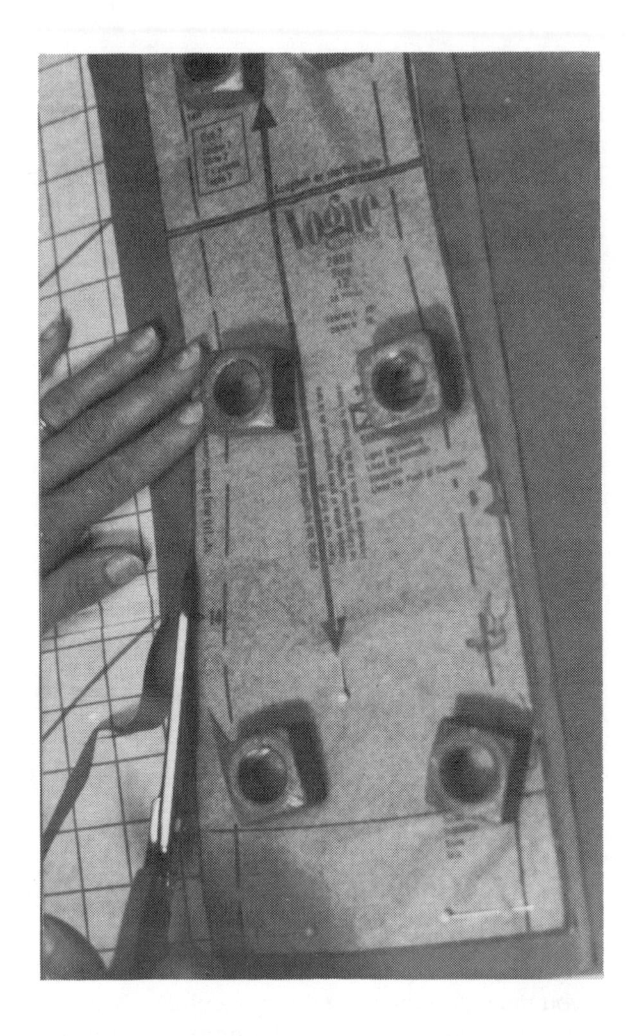

I use weights a lot, but I also pin the straight of grain, the corners of the pattern, and weight the remainder of the pattern edges. **When you cut, don't pick the fabric up.** Hold the fabric flat with one hand and cut with the other hand. **Don't cut beyond the corner of your pattern.** Put the end of your scissor to the edge of the pattern as you take the final snip. If you are short fabric, cutting beyond the corners of your pattern can ruin a scrap you could use for a small pattern piece. If a weight is in the way, just move it. Weights are much faster and often more accurate than lots of pins. They allow the fabric to lie flat on the table.

When measuring your straight of grain, fit your pattern pieces onto the fabric at the widest point of each piece. Pin to hold. Measure the distance from straight of grainline to the fold or selvage.

Move up to the other end of the pattern piece and move the pattern till it is the same distance from the fold or selvage.

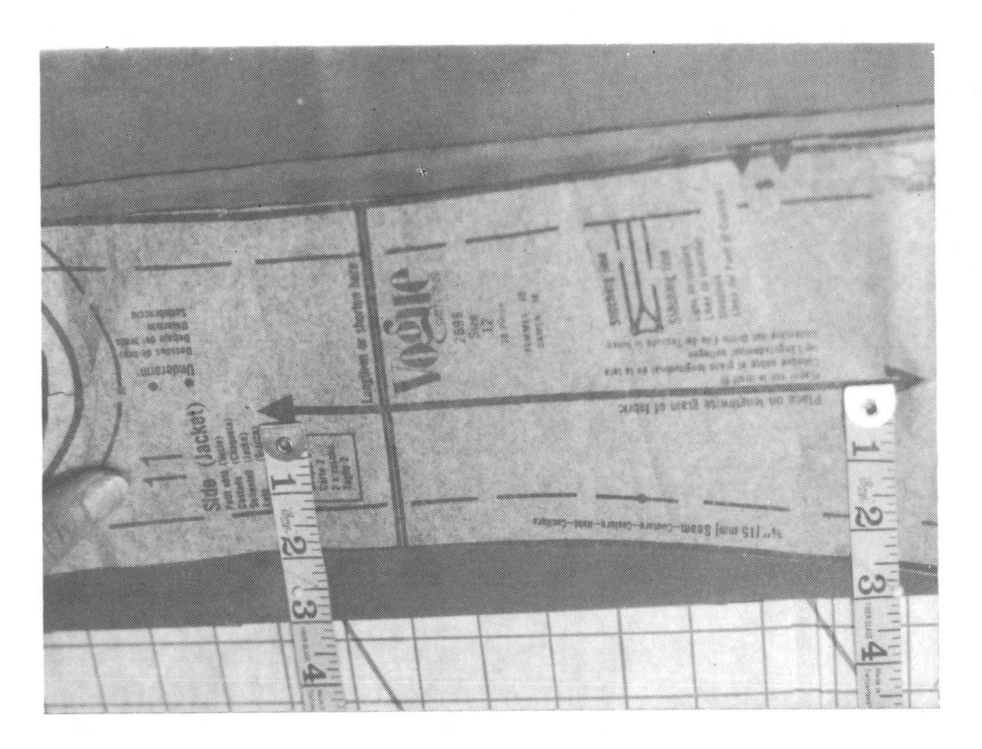

Pin to hold. Check the first end pinned — sometimes it may shift — and check the middle. If both ends are the same and the middle is off, gently pull your fabric on the crossgrain till it is the correct distance.

Cutting Knits

If your fabric is a **knit** you must **pin a rib-line** for the straight of grain. Check your pattern layout. Determine the width needed for each piece. Establish a fold the needed width. Usually the rib-line, which runs lengthwise with less give, will be easier to see on one side of the fabric.

Pinch the fabric between your forefinger and thumb and slide your fingers along a rib-line. Pin at right angles to the fold. Knit fabric is often crooked. If you begin on an end, often you will not have the needed width at the opposite end when you are finished pinning. Begin in the middle of each length needed and pin along **one** rib-line the length needed for your pattern piece.

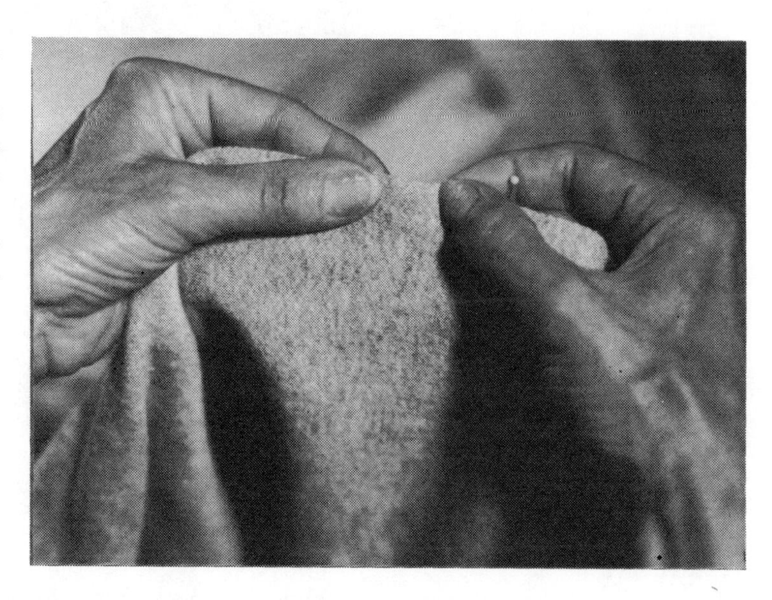

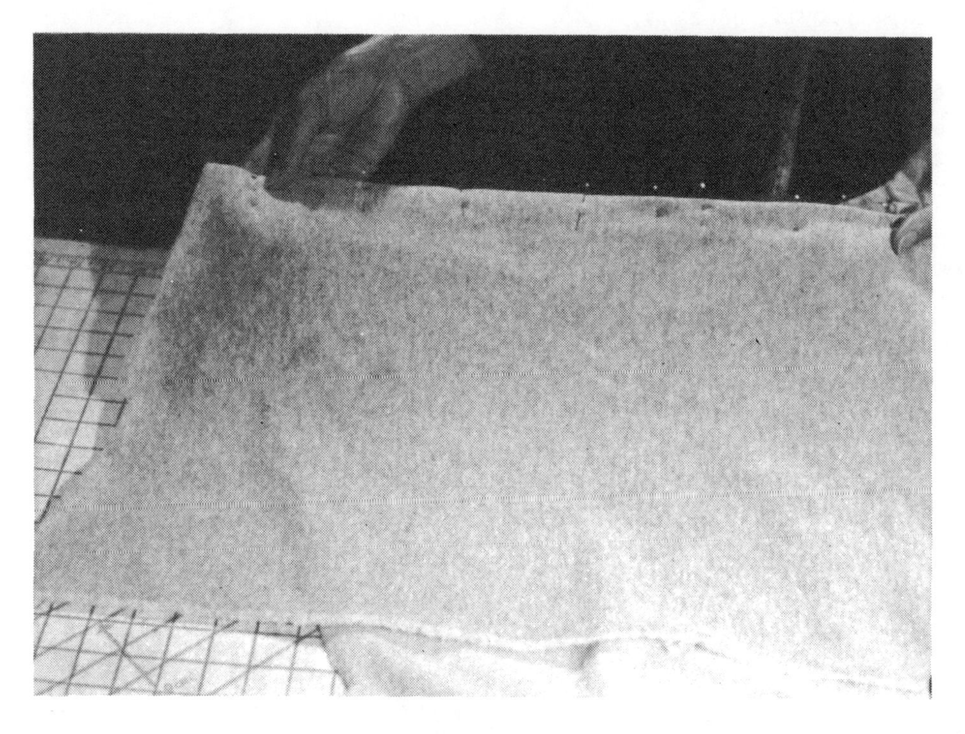

After pinning the rib-line, give the fabric a gentle shake and lay it out on the table.

Do not let knit fabric hang over the edge of the table because it stretches. If your knit fabric has a design or is striped and the design is not straight with the grain, you cannot cut the garment on the grain and have the design match. It usually looks best to use the design as the straight of grain. The garment seams will not hang properly but you can't have your cake and eat it too. I check knit fabric with a design before buying to make sure it is printed straight. If it is crooked, leave it in the store.

Cut as many pieces as possible using that pinned rib-line as the straight of grain.

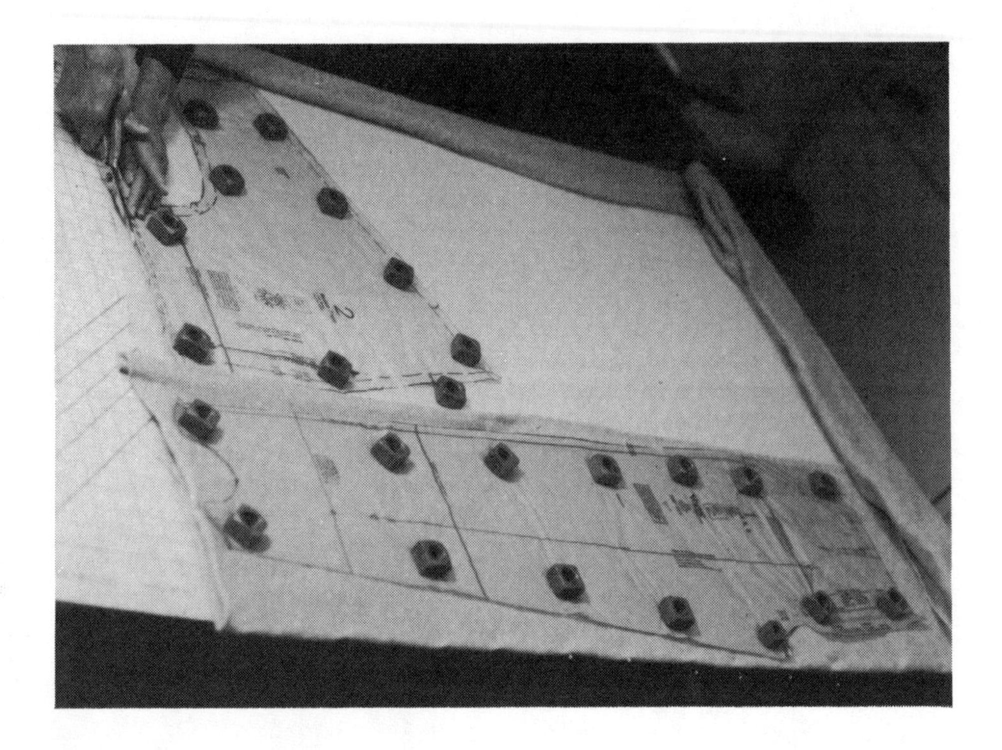

When cutting either a knit or woven fabric, any piece that does not require a fold can be cut singly next to a piece on the fold.

Be sure to cut a right and left of each piece cut singly. Cut one piece with the pattern printed side up and the remaining piece with the printed side down.

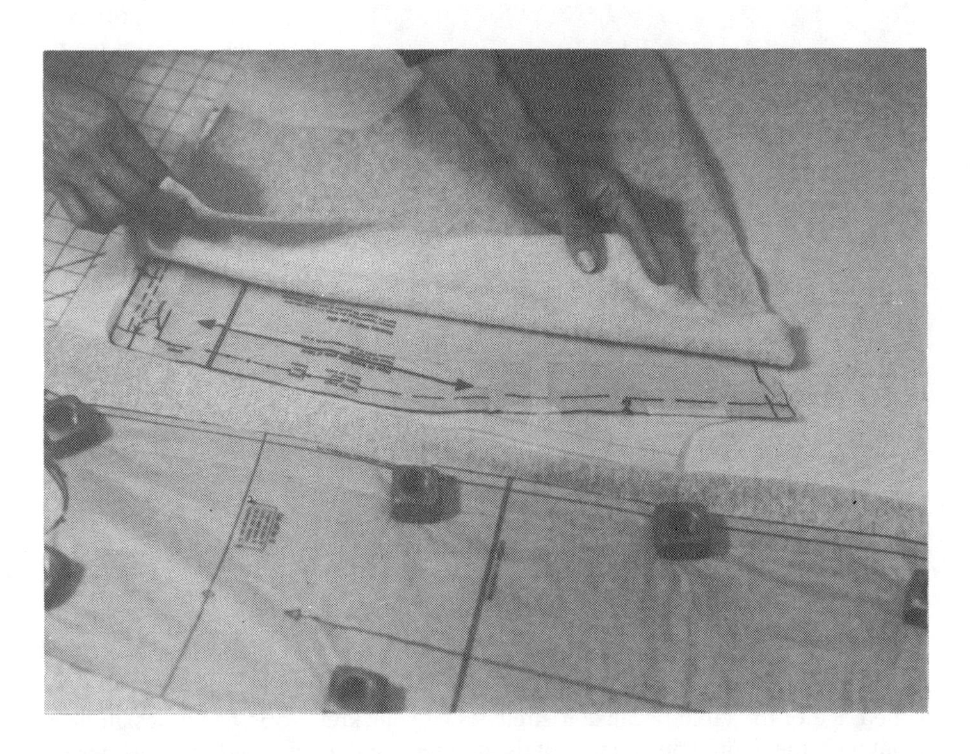

Always check your cutting of the second piece by laying the first piece on top of the second piece, right or wrong sides together, to make sure you have it right before cutting the second piece. This prevents your making the mistake of cutting two rights or two lefts.

Cutting correctly is the most important part of making a garment. Take the time to cut carefully. Cutting carefully will save you sewing time and the expense of buying extra fabric. Try to have a segment of time without interruption to cut fabric, especially expensive fabric.

LAYOUTS FOR SPECIAL FABRICS

Special fabrics include plaids, stripes, diagonals, napped fabrics, and any print that has a strong horizontal or vertical design that resembles a stripe. Check the back of the pattern envelope to assure that pattern and fabric are suited to each other. More fabric is often required for matching special fabrics. When buying fabric, especially if it is a plaid, consider the size of the pattern repeat and number of lengths needed for the major pattern pieces. Buy a pattern repeat for each large pattern piece. Is the fabric printed or woven? If it is printed, check to see that it is on grain. If the print is crooked on the crossgrain, leave it in the store. Napped fabrics require that all the pattern pieces be laid in one direction. If no nap layout is given, check the layout to see how many pieces must be turned. Buy enough extra fabric to do this.

Plaids and Stripes

Plaids and stripes can be either even or uneven. Even plaids and stripes are easier to match. To test the plaid, first fold the fabric diagonally through the center of any repeat. (Plaid must be perfectly on grain.) If the spaces and colors match, test further by folding the plaid vertically and horizontally through the center of any repeat.

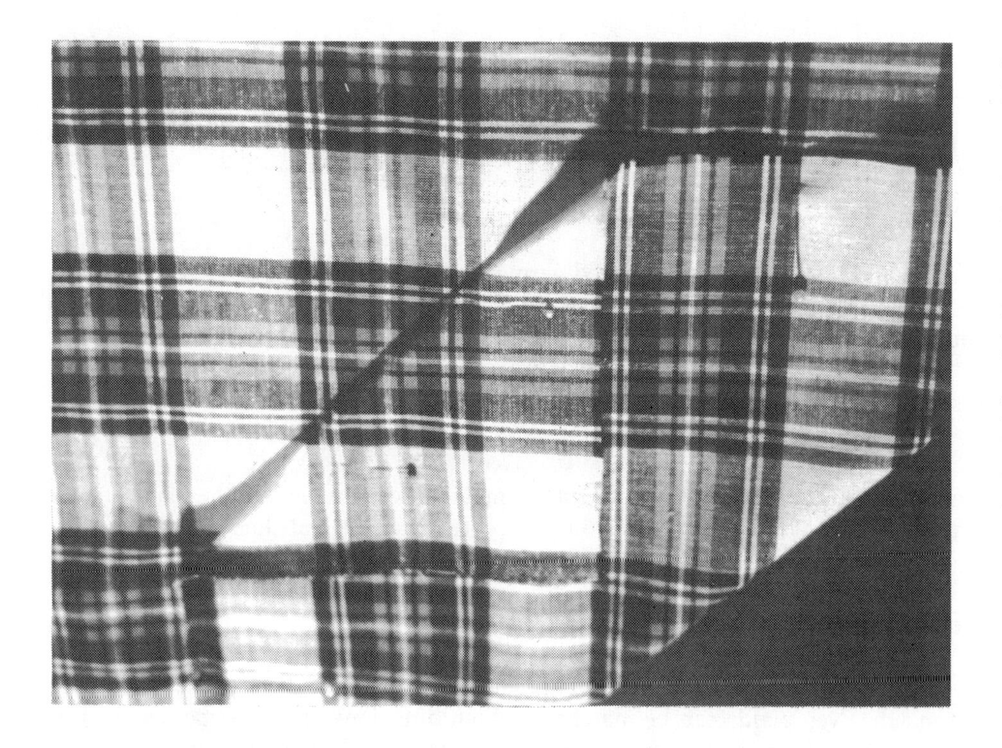

An even plaid forms a perfect square when folded diagonally, horizontally, or vertically through the center of any repeat and all the spaces and colors match in both directions. I have never found a perfectly even plaid but some are very close. This is a balanced plaid. The colors all are coming from the center in a balanced pattern. It is almost even.

In the picture, the plaid forms a perfect square on the diagonal and the vertical or the lengthwise grain. It is slightly off on the horizontal or crossgrain of the fabric.

In an uneven plaid, the spaces and colors do not match in both directions when folded on the diagonal, and/or the spaces and colors do not match in both directions when it is folded vertically or horizontally.

This plaid is also unbalanced. The colors are not balanced from the center of a design on the horizontal or crossgrain of the fabric.

Dominant plaid lines

Plan carefully where the dominant lines will be on your finished garment. Use the following guidelines:

- Dominant vertical lines should be at center front and center back and should be continuous from front to back.
- Dominant horizontal lines should be placed at the hemline (exception: curved hemline). Determine the finished length before cutting.
- Don't place a dominant line at the bustline or waistline. If you are making two garments of the plaid, match the plaids of one garment to the plaids of the other garment at the centers and the waistline.

Layout For Even Plaids and Stripes

Cutting plaids is the moist challenging part of making a plaid garment. If you don't cut them properly (so they match), your garment will not match. Even plaids can be matched in both directions and must be matched in both directions if you want your seams to form a chevron. If you do not have enough fabric to match the plaid in both directions, match the horizontal lines.

Drape the plaid on you in front of a mirror and pick out the proiminent plaid line. Where do you want that to come on your body? Decide what part of the plaid you want down your center front, where the plaid looks the best at bustline, hipline, and hem.

Fold the plaid so the center of the dominant plaid (the plaid you want down the center) is at the fold. Plaid lines should be somewhat matched on the upper and under pieces of the fabric.

Areas that must be on the center of the dominant plaid

- Center front
- Center back
- Center of the upper collar
- Center (big dot) of the sleeve cap
- Front facing must be a mirror image of the center front piece

Areas that must match as you cut

Match the horizontal and vertical lines across all the pattern pieces at the bottom of the fabric and at the notches on the seamline. (If you do not have enough fabric to match both the horizontal and vertical lines, match the horizontal lines).

Match the sleeve (upper sleeve if it is a two-piece sleeve) to the garment by matching the middle dot in the armhole of the garment to the corresponding dot on the sleeve cap.

The Wiggle Method of Cutting Plaids

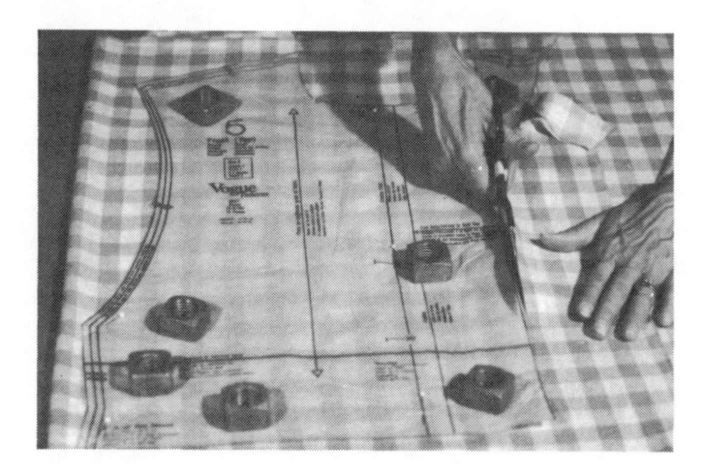

Lay all the pattern pieces out on the double of the fabric and pin. Use the plaid lines as straight of grain. Cut a single layer of fabric. Slip the scissors between the layers of fabric to cut. When cutting on a fold, make a big snip through both layers, then slip the scissors between the layers and cut singly.

When the top layer is cut, un-pin and remove the pattern. Remove all the extra fabric from around the cut piece.

Match the piece you just cut exactly to the plaid fabric underneath. Pin in place and use the piece you have just cut as the pattern to cut the second piece.

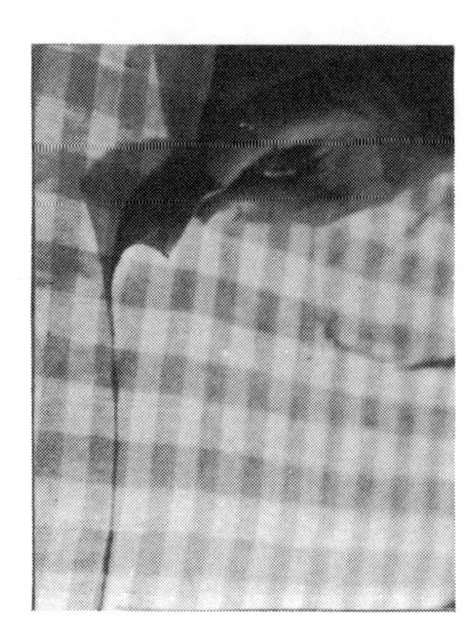

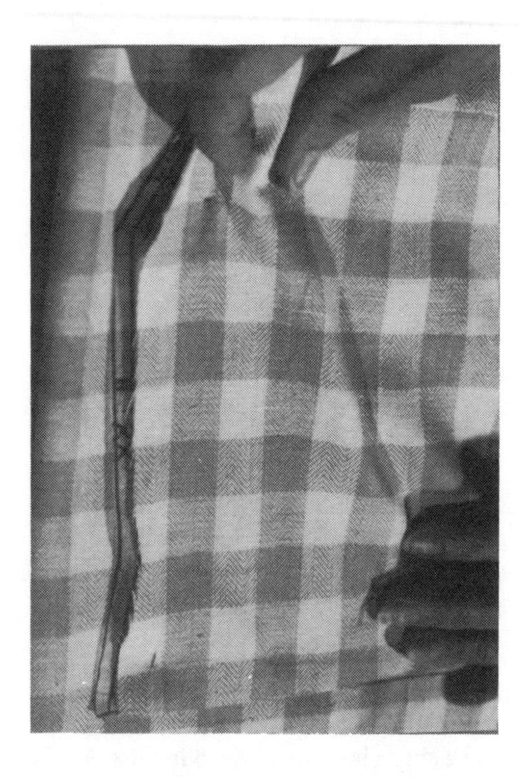

Match each piece you have cut to the corresponding piece before you cut. In that way you are again checking your plaid layout. The illustration shows matching the horizontal lines. The vertical lines should match also if you have enough fabric.

A good sequence for cutting plaids

1. Cut the center front piece.
2. Cut the front facing. It must be a mirror image of the center front piece.
3. Cut the side front matching the corresponding seam of the side front to the center front piece.
4. Cut the side back matching the corresponding seam of the side front to the side back.
5. Cut the center back matching the corresponding seam of the side back.
6. Cut the upper sleeve, matching the mid-point dot or the notches in the front armhole to the corresponding dot or notches in the sleeve.
7. Cut the under sleeve, matching the corresponding seams of the upper sleeve.

If you don't want to match the small pieces, such as pockets, pocket flaps, undercollars, yokes, and cuffs, they can be cut on the bias.

Uneven Plaids and Stripes

When working with uneven plaids and stripes, choose a pattern with as few construction lines as possible. The matching and layout are the same as for even fabrics except that uneven plaids cannot be matched in both directions. Pick the vertical stripe you want for the center front. Fold fabric, matching two stripes for the front sections. The horizontal lines are matched, then the vertical lines as the fabric allows. Cut uneven plaids and stripes using the Wiggle Method, or lay out the pattern on a single layer of fabric. The Wiggle Method is safer; there is no danger of cutting two pieces for the same side.

Stripes are treated basically the same when laying out as plaids except that stripes are easier to match — you need only match one set of designs.

Consider your figure before choosing a stripe. Horizontal stripes tend to shorten and also emphasize the bust and hips. Vertical stripes tend to lengthen the figure. Thin stripes are more slenderizing than bolder, thicker stripes. Drape the fabric before you buy it.

Bias-cut plaids

Choose an **even** plaid or one as close to even as you can find without a pronounced diagonal weave. Drape the fabric in front of a mirror. You don't want any strong lines going in only one direction. Unless your pattern is recommended for a bias-cut, you will need to draw a new straight of grainline at a 45 degree angle to the lengthwise grain. Use the bias lines on your cutting board for easy marking. To perfectly match a bias cut skirt, the front and back pieces must be the same size. If they are not the same size, use the skirt front pattern piece to cut the back as well as the front. If the skirt has no center front seam, make a whole front pattern piece. Cut the front, then match the seamlines before cutting the back. It is a good idea to allow for 1" side seams as the hang of the bias differs with each weight of fabric.

Diagonal Fabrics

Diagonal fabrics include twill weaves, such as flannel, serge and gabardine. On some fabrics, the diagonal is hardly noticeable and unless the fabric has a nap, special attention is not needed (example: denim and some gabardines). Other twills will have a very distinct diagonal pattern that must be carefully matched. Diagonally striped fabric is usually printed, not woven, but they are treated in the same manner as obvious diagonal weaves.

Choose designs carefully. Check the pattern envelope for the warning: "Obvious diagonal fabrics are not suitable." Check your fabric to see how obvious the diagonal is, drape it on yourself and study it in a mirror. Avoid design features such as:

- Collars cut on the fold and roll-back lapels.
- V-neck lines in which the diagonals run in different directions on the V.
- Bias cut side seams, A-line and gored skirts pieces will not match.
- Long bias darts will look different on the left and the right side of the garments.
- Any sleeve that is cut-in-one with the bodice is a poor choice.

Study your pattern and check for those features which will give a pleasing effect when using diagonal fabrics. Look for designs with slim skirts, few seams, set-in sleeves, stand-up collars, no darts or straight underarm darts. If you are planning a garment that has a design feature that is not recommended, drape your fabric and make sure you like the effect before you proceed.

Layout for Diagonal Fabrics

Use the Wiggle Method using a nap layout, or lay out the pattern on a single layer of fabric. Match the seamlines as you did with plaids. If your collar has a fold, be sure to cut it on the bias instead of straight of grain. A design with a center front fold is nice. It saves matching a center front seam.

Reversible Diagonal Fabrics (exactly the same on one side as the other) enable you to lay out your pattern so the diagonal forms a chevron. A design with a center front and center back seam is necessary. Open the fabric to its full width and cut it in half. (Never cut the fabric in half till you have checked to make sure you have enough fabric to cut all the pattern pieces. Many times a garment can be cut singly that you cannot get if you cut the fabric).

Place one length of fabric on top of the other length of fabric with the right side of one piece to the wrong side of the other piece. Match the diagonal stripes. This can be done whether the stripe is even or uneven. Lay your pattern pieces on the fabric and cut, using the Wiggle Method.

If your fabric is not reversible but is an even stripe and does not have a nap, you can achieve the same results by cutting the pattern out one thickness at a time in opposite directions.

Create special effects by cutting the diagonal on the bias for pockets, cuffs, and trims.

Bias printed fabrics are harder to match than diagonal fabrics since they run in two directions and must be matched in both directions. They are suitable for more styles than a one-way diagonal and if they cannot be matched it isn't as noticeable as with a diagonal. Bias-cut seams can be matched if the print is on the true bias. Sleeves cut-in-one with the bias can be used. In general, a bias-printed fabric will match more often than a true diagonal.

MARKING

Being thorough and accurate when you are marking your fabric really speeds up your sewing. While my pattern piece is still on the fabric, I snip — just a mini clip — about 1/8", each center fold or anything that marks center of a piece. Don't put the tip of your scissors any deeper than you want to snip. It's so easy to do a deep snip. Do a mini snip at the shoulder marking of the collar and at the underarm seam marking on the cuff and the dots along the cuff and the bottom of the sleeve if the sleeve is gathered. Refer to Sleeves, pages 193 and 194. Those markings help you to distribute the gathering evenly. Also snip the top of each leg of all darts, pleats, and tucks.

I mark the wrong side of each piece of fabric if it is hard to distinguish the right side from the wrong side. A little piece of paper or Scotch tape with a "wrong" on it can save you lots of frustration.

I was taught in high school to do tailor tacks, but now I use pins. I don't do tailor tacks! I'm not too lazy to put them in, but I resent having to put them in and then having an awful time getting some of them out after stitching across them. Pins or marking pencils are more accurate than tailor tacks or tracing paper and wheel. I still use the tracing paper and wheel when I am doing a basic dress which requires a great deal of marking. Some of my students prefer to use the marking pencils. The new marking pencils work very well, but do test them on a scrap of your fabric to make sure they will come off. I have used pins for years and like them. Whether you use pins or marking pencil, the procedure is the same.

Marking With Pins

Put the pin in the middle of each dot or important marking on the pattern. Do it first on the pattern side then on the other side. I also mark seam junction lines if the top edges are on an angle. Example: the angle seam of a two-piece sleeve, princess lines on a jacket or dress, the angle seams of a jacket with no side seam.

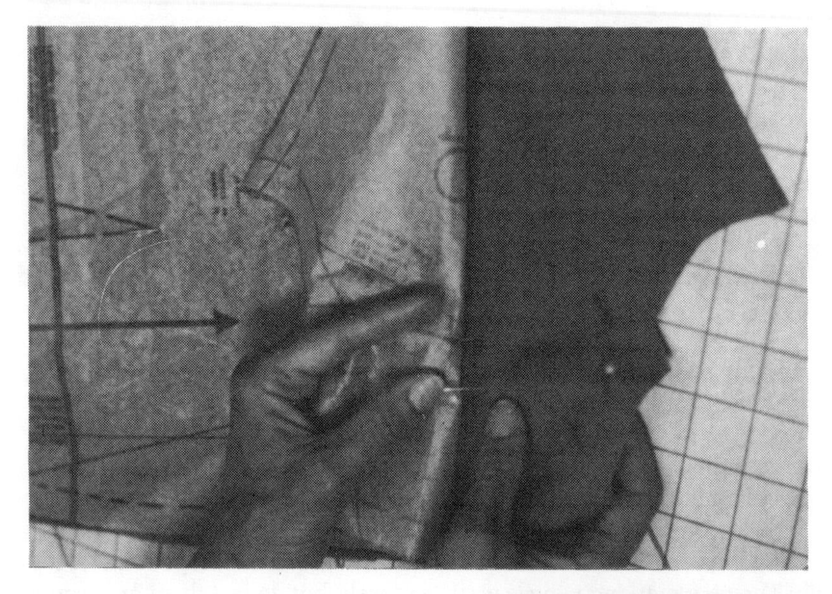

When you have put pins at every mark on both sides of the fabric, gently pull the pattern off the fabric.

Then gently pull the pieces apart.

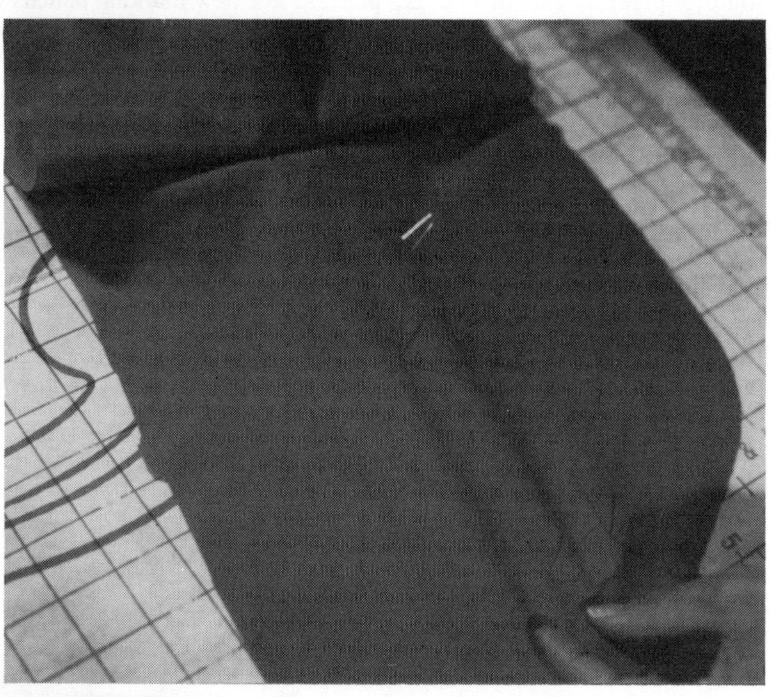

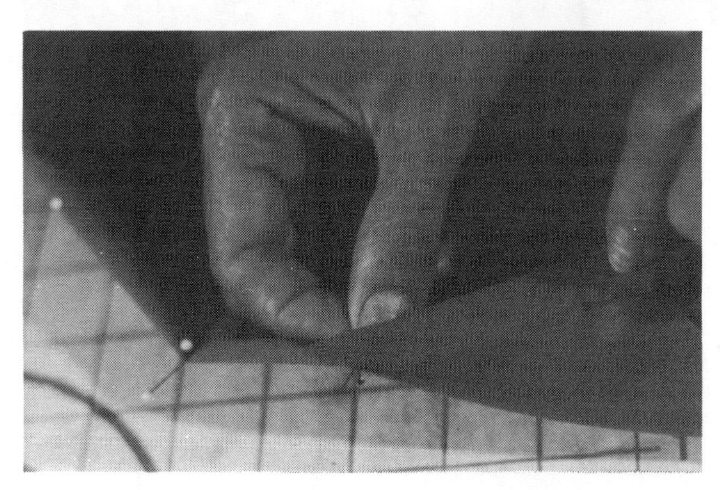

Where you have darts, tucks, or pleats, pin them in now.

On your other symbols, weave your pins through the fabric as if you are taking several stitches with a hand needle. The point where the pin enters the fabric is the center of the symbol. If you lose a pin (that doesn't happen very often), get the pattern piece out and re-establish the mark.

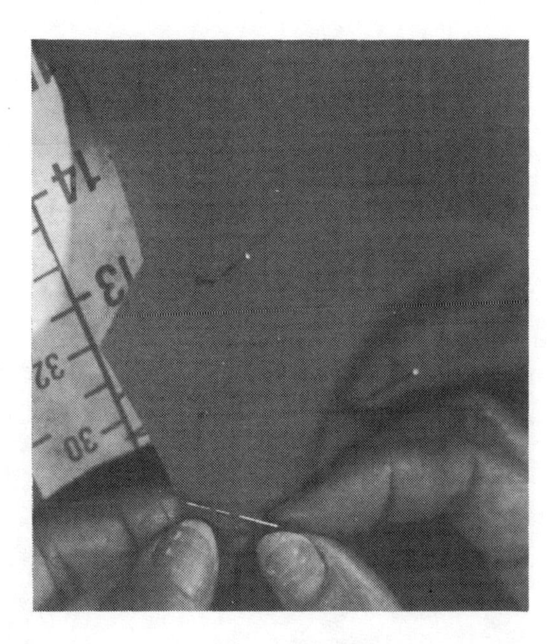

Taping and Stitching Darts

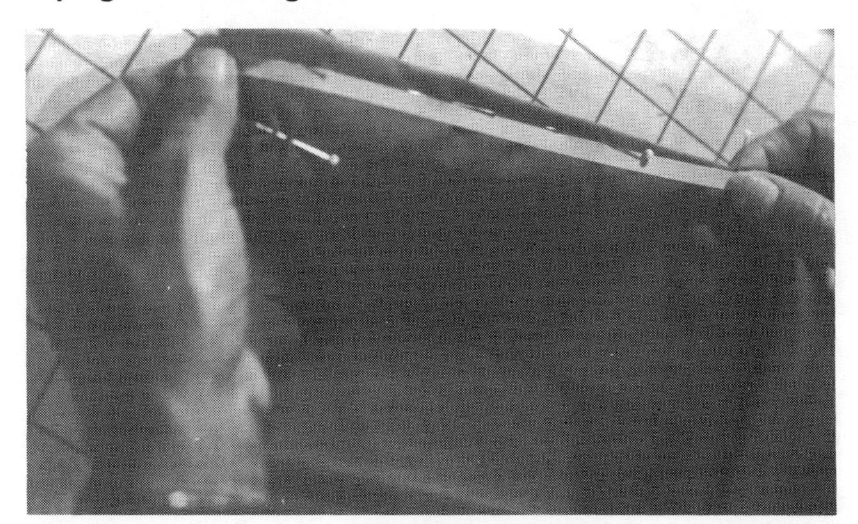

Before stitching the dart, lay a narrow (1/4" wide) piece of masking tape along the pin line and move the pins away from the stitching line. Leave the pin marking the end of the dart. The tape gives you a straight or curved tapered stitching line.

Stitch just next to the tape, never through it, and remove it immediately. **Don't ever leave tape on your fabric.** It can be very difficult to remove. If you have a pile fabric (velvet or corduroy), check on a scrap before using tape.

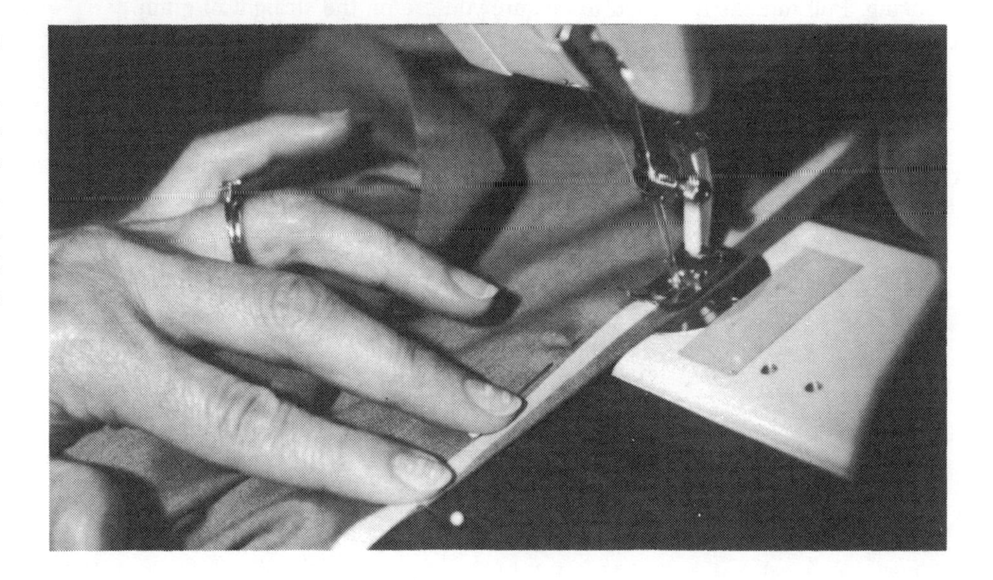

Sometimes just the weight of the presser foot can make the tape adhere, thus pulling the pile off the fabric. On such difficult fabrics, mark the darts with a thread trace or with a marking pencil.

Always stitch two stitches on the fold of the fabric when you come off the end of a dart. Stitching on the fold prevents that little bubble on the right side of the garment at the end of the dart. On Ultrasuede and Facile, stitch four stitches just on the fold of the fabric, then come off the fold.

Tying a tailor's knot

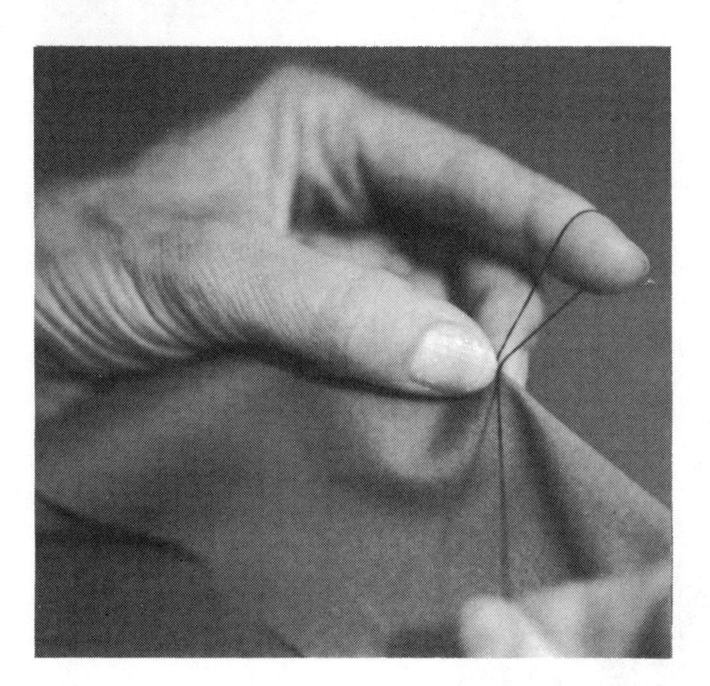

Never backstitch at the end of the dart. Tie the threads. A **tailor's knot** is easy to do and holds threads tightly. Make a circle of the thread, pull the end through the circle, and keep the thread at the end of the fabric with your thumbnail or a pin while you pull the thread down to the knot. Leave a little tail on the thread when you cut it.

Marking and Stitching Tucks and Pleats Before Cutting

If the garment requires small tucks in a large area, I prefer to tuck the fabric before cutting. Cut a square of fabric the length and width needed for the pattern piece. Allow a few inches extra in the direction you will be tucking. Pull threads if needed to be sure you are on the straight of grain.

If you are tucking the entire width of the front, mark the center of that piece of fabric with a close handbaste in a contrasting thread. Then work from the center marked with the baste line to the edges. If you are tucking half the front, work from the edge of the center front to the side seam. Measure the distance between the tucks and the depth of the tucks as you pin and stitch them. It is so easy to be off a sixteenth of an inch, and when that is multiplied by several tucks it can affect the fit of the garment.

After all the tucks are stitched and pressed as they will lie in the garment, fold the tucks in the pattern and then cut that piece out of the tucked fabric.

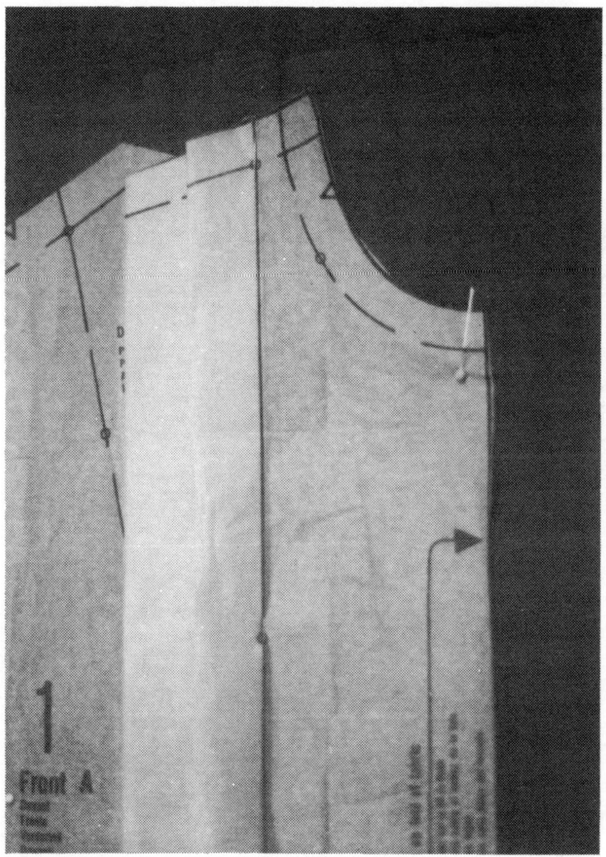

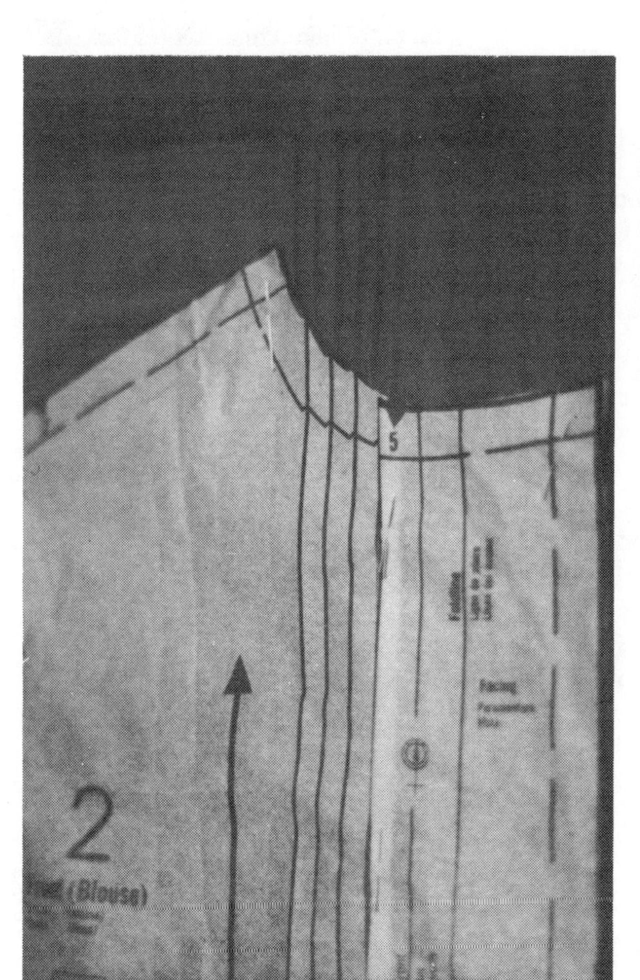

If you have many small pleats, measure the amount of width you will lose and fold that amount out of the width of the pattern.

If you have a favorite pattern that you wish were tucked, you can tuck the fabric and then cut the garment.

Marking and Stitching Tucks and Pleats After Cutting

When marking pleats or wide tucks, use a mini clip at the top and bottom of the fabric. Then either use pins or a marking pencil or, if the fabric is hard to mark, use a thread trace. I often will do pins at several intervals down my fabric and pin the pleat or wide tuck.

Put a piece of tape on the bed of your sewing machine to mark the depth of the tuck or pleat and stitch it.

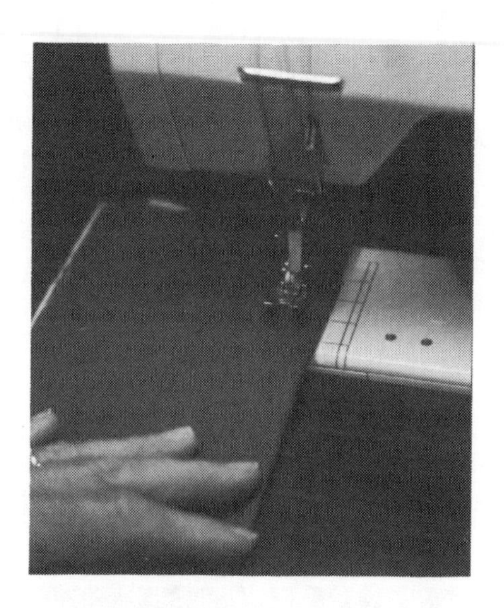

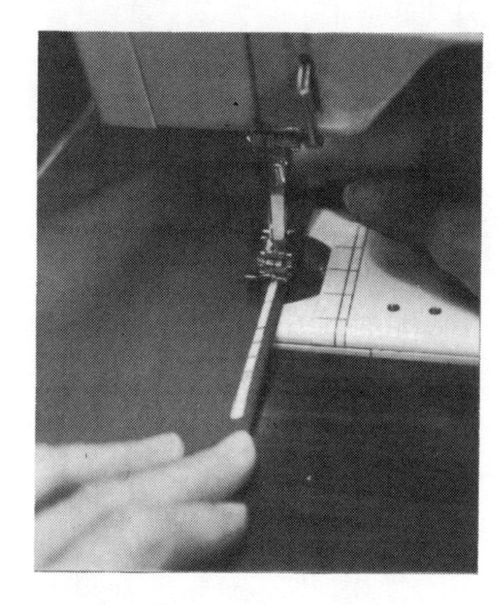

If you have trouble sewing a straight line, use a piece of masking tape along the line to be stitched as a guide.

Thread Trace

A thread trace is a line of basting through one layer of fabric. I often will use the same procedure to baste a pleat, stitching through two layers of fabric.

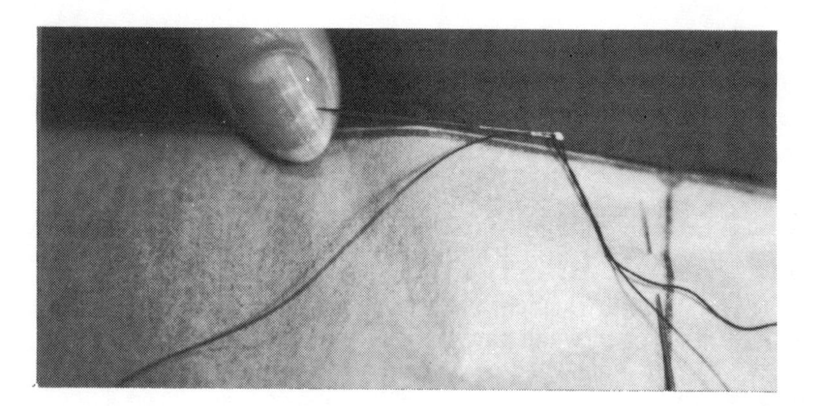

To thread trace, fold your pattern along the line to be marked and baste next to the pattern edge.

The thread trace must be a straight line. If you have difficulty basting straight, put a piece of masking tape along the pattern as a guide.

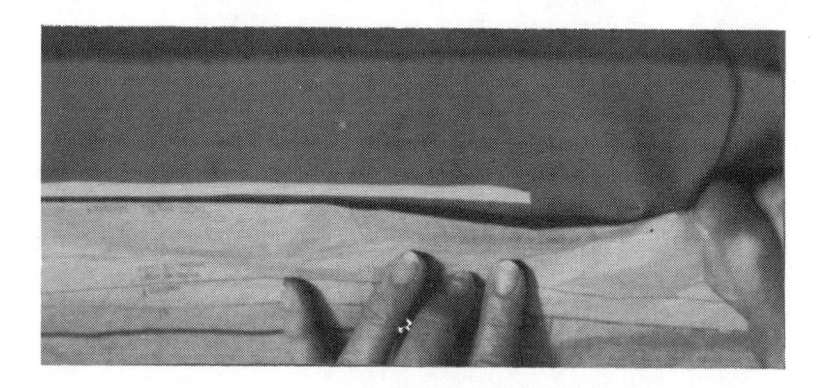

Identifying Pieces

Leave the pattern pieces attached to the fabric until you are ready to sew the pieces together. Often you need to refer to the pattern piece. Much information, such as depth of hem, is on the pattern piece and not in the pattern directions. When this information on the pattern piece is handy, it speeds your sewing. Leaving the pattern pieces pinned to the fabric keeps them handy and easily identifies each piece of the garment.

Storing Patterns

As the garment grows and you are finished with the pattern pieces, lay them together, out flat, and pin them together to prevent losing pieces. When the garment is done, fold them all together to form a nice flat package which will fit in the pattern envelope. Folding each piece separately is so time consuming and makes finding a pattern piece a real chore.

Pattern Referral

Note any changes you would make if you were to use the pattern again. Also note the date, your weight, and the garment you have made on the pattern envelope before putting it away. This is a big help when you are comparing a new pattern to an old one or using the pattern for a second garment. I use my patterns many times and when hunting through patterns I can refer to my notes and know without question how I liked that particular pattern, how it fits, and if I still like the garment.

For a 1" waist band

1" = 2" + 1 1/4 seam allowance 3 1/4

w/ selvage 2 7/8 (neatest)

For a 1 1/4" w.b. - 2 1/2 + 1 1/4 = 3 3/4

w/ selvage 2 1/2 + 5/8 + 3/8 = 3 1/2

Line up stiff stuff along edge

Then fold along edge & press using ss. as guide

Mark the sewing line using edge of armoflex & then stitch one notch over so that sewing line isn't against S.S.

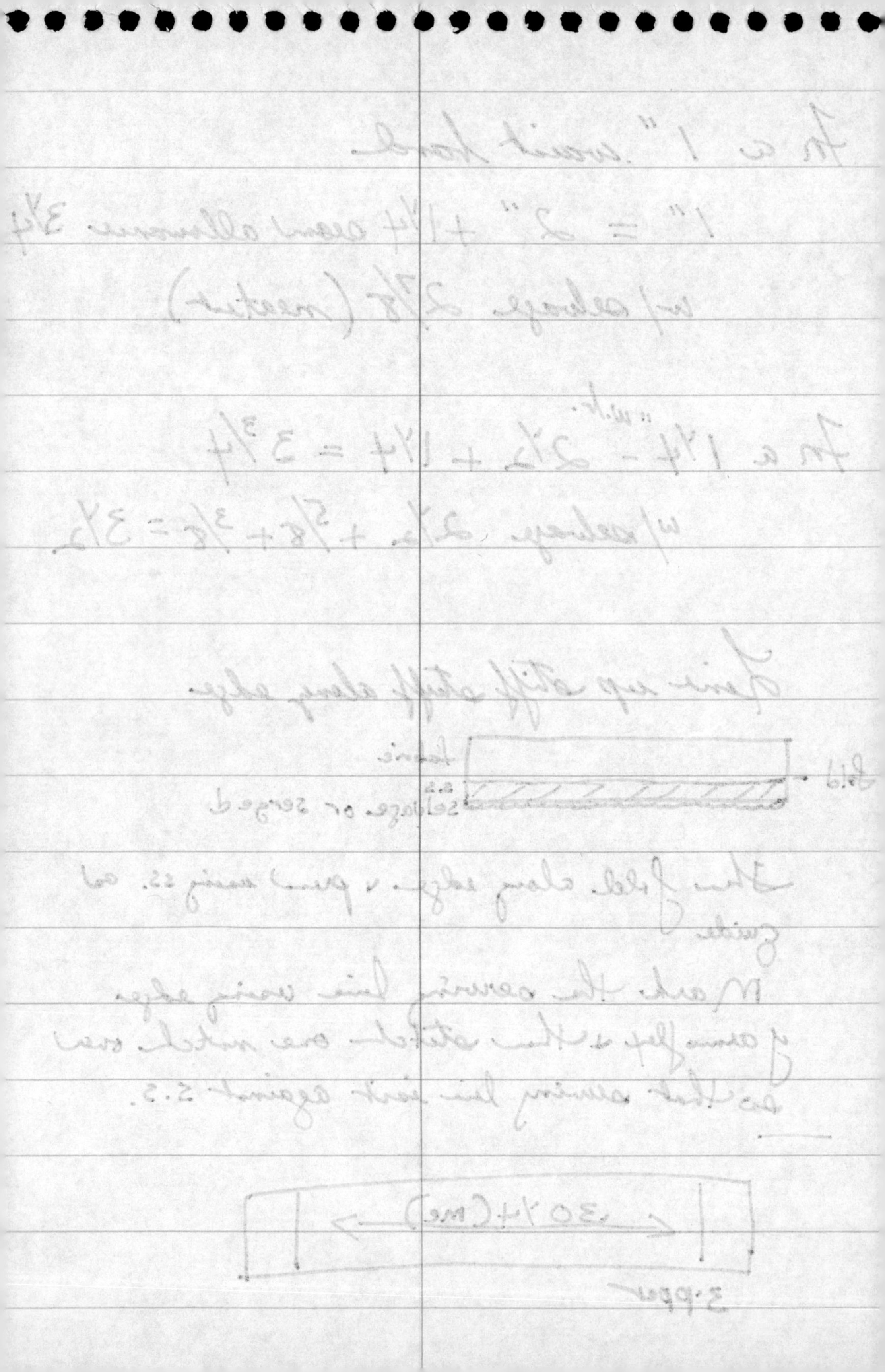

Sewing Techniques For Skirts and Slacks · 3

SKIRTS

If you are using a new pattern that has not been checked and adjusted refer to Fitting your Garments-Pattern Adjustment page 9-11.

Cut And Mark The Skirt

Refer to Preparation For Sewing page 28-32 and 39-45.

Also follow your pattern directions.

Exception: Cut the waistband with the unnotched edge on the selvage if possible. The band can be a bit narrower (a scant 1/4″) as you will not be turning it under. Cut the waistband interfacing the same length as the waistband. My favorite interfacing is Armo-flex or Ban-roll.

Skirt Construction

Do a sample seam refer to Sample Seams and Pressing Techniques. Read your pattern instruction sheet. Your particular skirt style may influence the construction. I usually follow this sequence. Stitch the darts if there are darts. Refer to page 41-42. If there are pockets put the pockets on skirt fronts and backs. If there is a zipper put it in before stitching the side seams. To apply a lapped zipper refer to Zippers page 77. Stitch the side seams (refer to Slacks, page 58), then try the skirt on and check the fit in the waist and hipline. Adjust if needed. Finish the seams. Refer to Seam Finishes. Press the seams open. Refer to Pressing Techniques, page 66.

Apply the waistband

If your skirt has a gathered waistline refer to the Gathering pages 92-95. Pin-baste or baste the waistband in place, then try it on and check to see how the skirt is hanging. Are the side seams hanging straight? Is it skimming the body through the hip line? Are pleats, if any, hanging properly? To adjust, if needed, put a belt with two plumb lines (a measuring tape with a drapery weight makes a great plumb line) around your waist and adjust at the waist seam till the skirt is hanging correctly. When everything looks fine put a row of pins along the bottom of the belt and use that line for your waist seam.

If you need to make changes to the waist seam note them on your pattern so you can adjust your skirts in the future without all that work.

Pin the right side of the band to the right side of the skirt. Ease the skirt onto the band matching center front and back, side seams, and notches. Pin or baste the band in place.

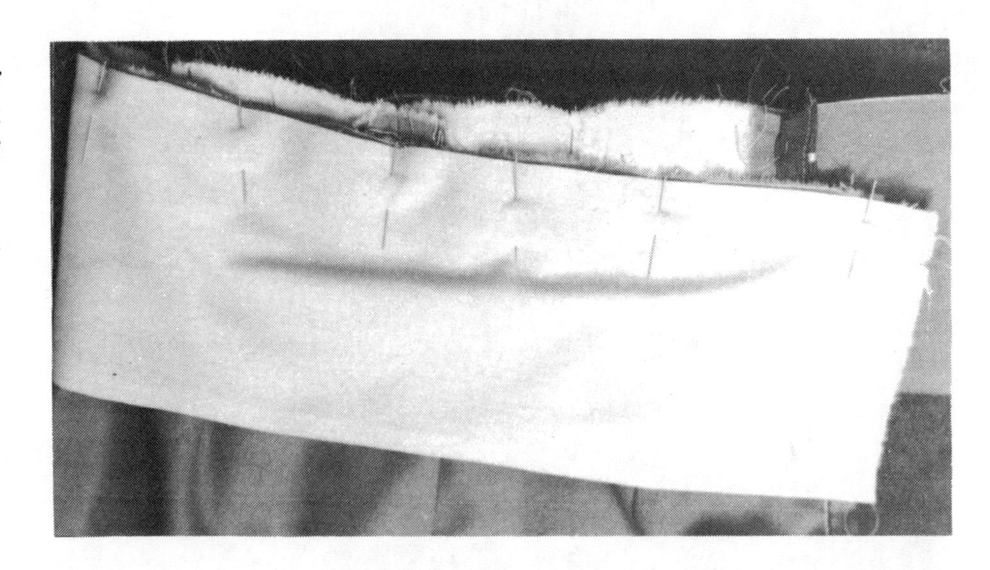

Your notches and side seams may not match because of pattern alterations. If they don't match, check your waistband pattern to see if the skirt is evenly divided between the front and the back. Sometimes the pattern has allowed a bit more in the front than the back. Refer to Fitting Your Garments - Pattern Adjustment, page 11. Apply the band as your pattern dictates. If your fabric is difficult to ease, do a machine-baste stitch around the waist seam. Refer to Gathering instructions, page 96. If you are unable to get the waistband eased onto the waist seam without puckers, take in the side seams or darts a bit and taper to the normal seam about 3″ from the waist.

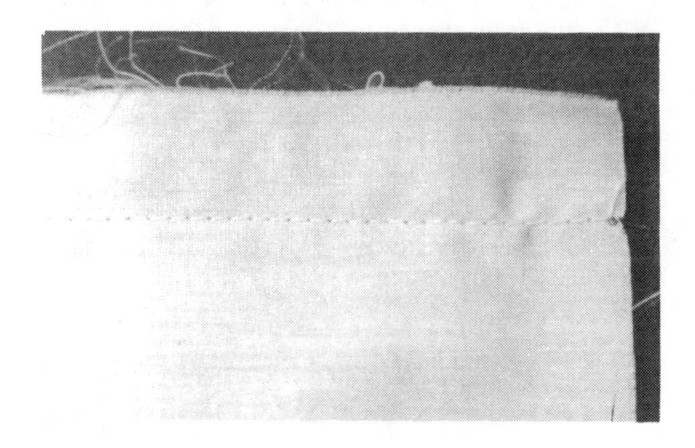

Stitch the band onto the skirt, stitching to the ends of the waistband. Press the seam toward the band.

Lined Skirts

High Hip: Be sure and reverse your lining when you stitch the seams as it must go wrong side of lining to wrong side of skirt. Stitch the lining together and attach to the skirt.

Lay the lining into the skirt with the wrong side of the lining to the wrong side of the skirt. Match up the seams, center front and back and baste the waist seam of the lining to the waist seam of the skirt.

Hand whip the lining to the skirt along the edge of the zipper tape. This gives enough room so the lining is not caught in zipper teeth.

Interface The Waistband

My favorite waistband interfacing is Ban-roll or Armo-flex. It should be purchased in the desired width as it cannot be cut without resealing the edge.

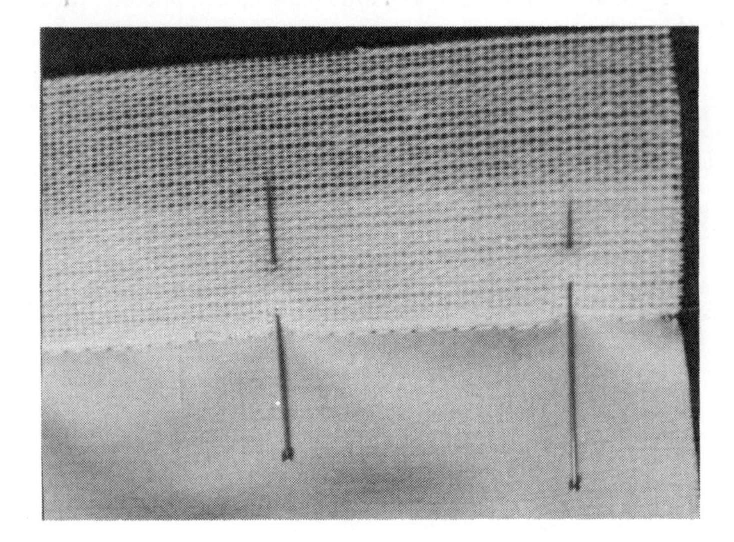

Lay the interfacing on the wrong side of the band with one edge of it lying on and covering the seam allowance. The edge of the interfacing should just clear the seamline. Pin in place to hold.

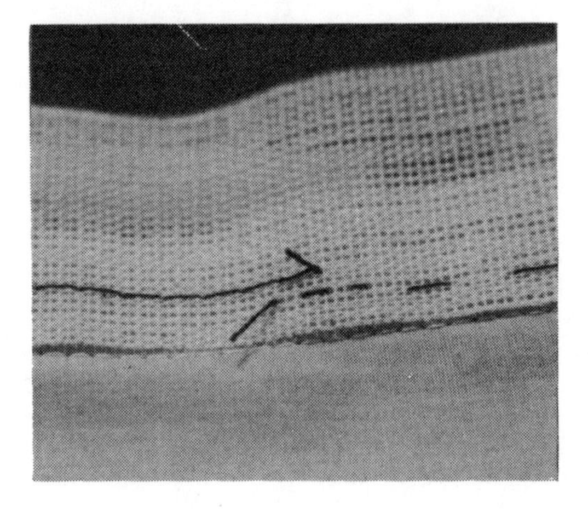

Machine- or hand-baste about 1/4″ from the lower edge of the interfacing.

Finish The Ends Of The Waistband

Extension End Of The Waistband

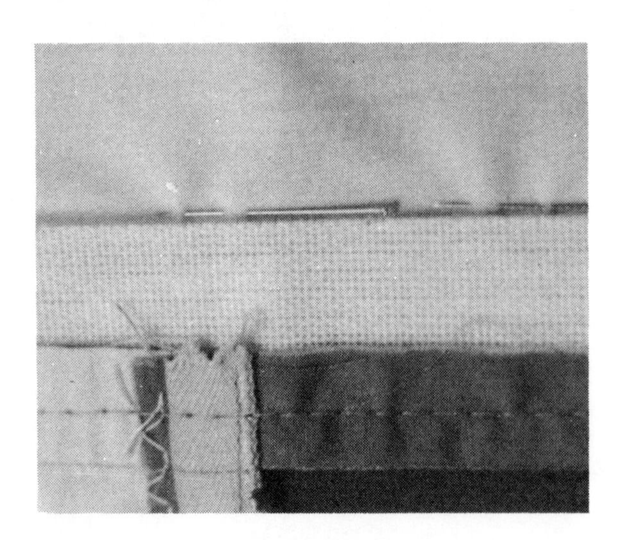

On the extension end of the waistband mark the foldline of the band just at the top of the interfacing.

Fold the band in half, right sides together, along the foldline. Pin the two layers of the band together. Lay the interfacing down toward the body of the skirt so it's out of the way. Stitch along the edge of the interfacing from the end of the band to the skirt.

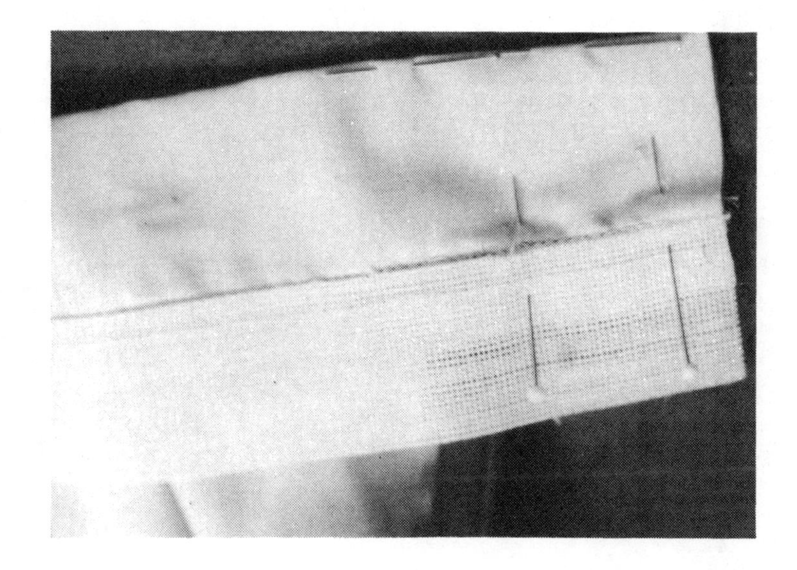

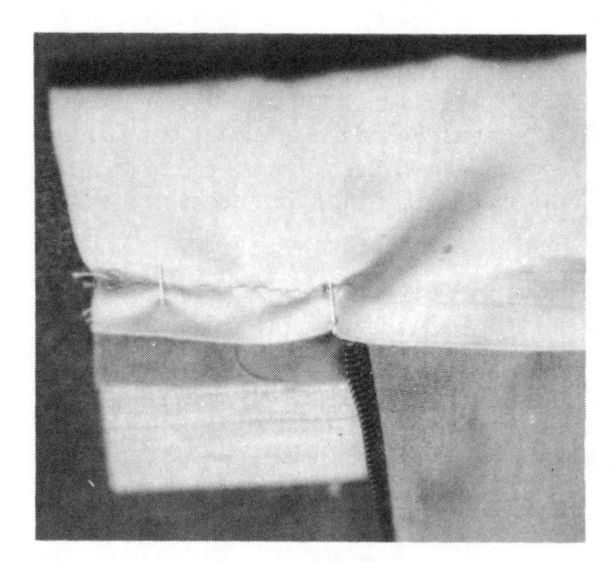

(You are stitching through two thicknesses of the band.)

Fold the interfacing back up against the waistband and stitch across the end of the band. (You are stitching through two thickness of the waistband the interfacing). Trim the seam to 1/4″.

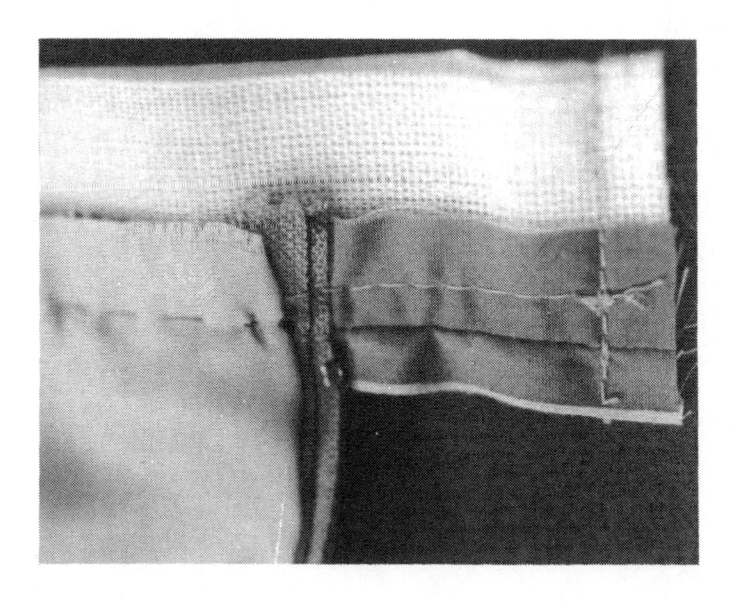

Turn rightside out. It's a little hard to turn. A point pusher or a small screwdriver helps.

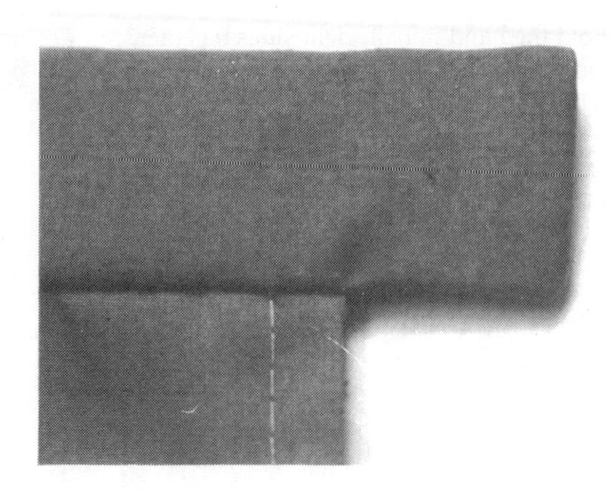

Flush End Of The Waistband

On the flush end of the band, mark the fold line. Fold the band in half, right sides together. Fold the seam allowance up and pin to hold. Stitch across the end of the band, going straight up from the edge of the skirt.

Trim the seam and turn right side out.

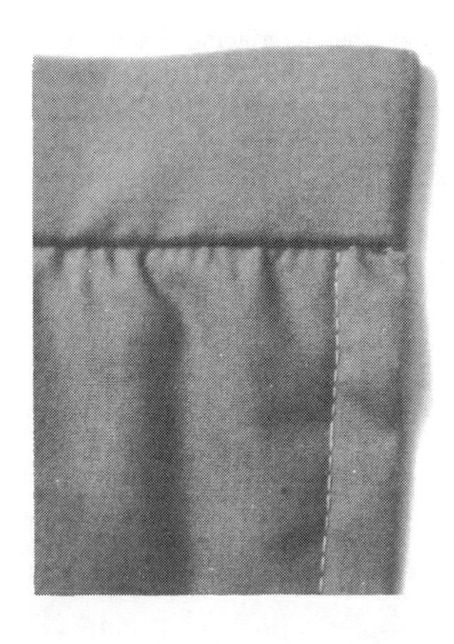

Bring the loose edge of the waistband up and over the interfacing to the wrong side of the skirt and pin in place.

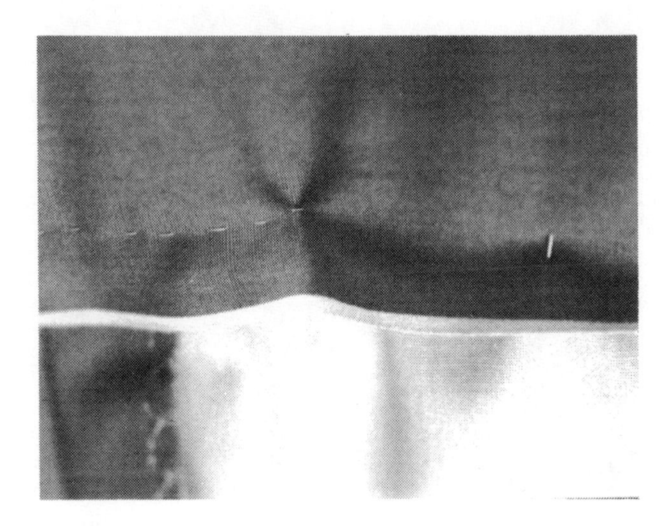

I let the selvage edge hang down into the skirt. It's less bulky than turning the seam under. If you were unable to cut the band with one edge on the selvage you can turn the edge under if your fabric is lightweight. If it is too heavy finish the edge of the band with machine overcasting, Seams Great, or a Hong Kong finish using a piece of the lining cut on the bias. Refer to Seam Finishes on pages 68, 69, and 71.

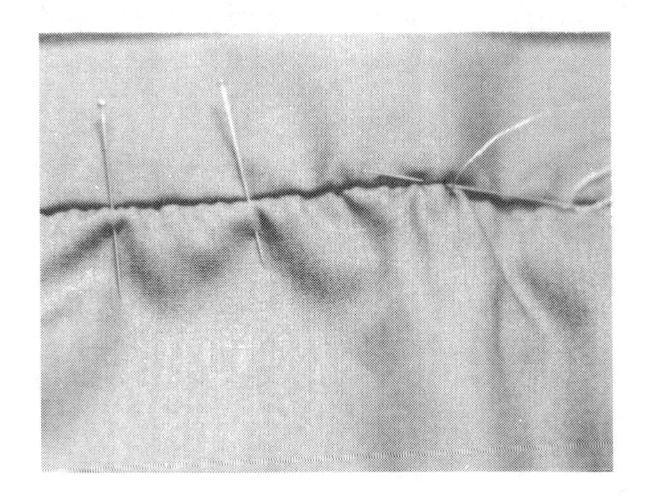

Stitch in the well of the seam on the **right** side of the skirt, either by hand or machine, catching the band on the wrong side.

Hem The Skirt

Refer to the Hems on page 97. I usually hem a skirt by hand. I never use hem tape on a knit fabric, and rarely use hem tape at all.

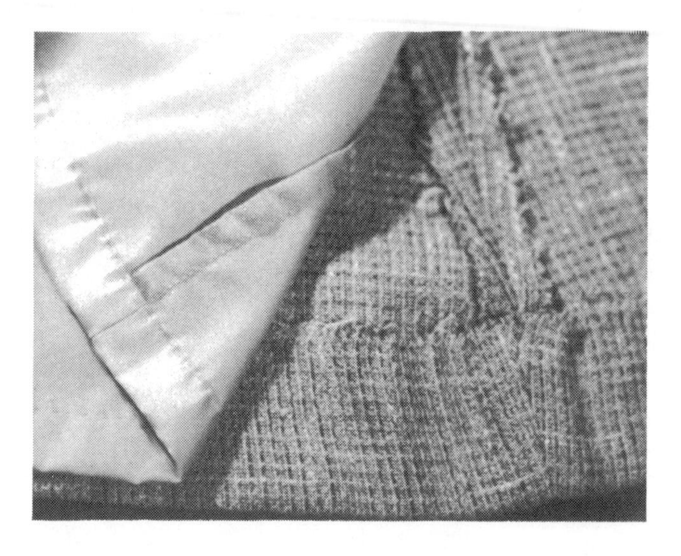

If your skirt is lined, hem the lining separately. Turn under the raw edge of the lining and either hand stitch or machine stitch it in place. The lining hem need not be very deep.

Closures

Attach a fastener to the end of the band. I use a flat metal hook and eye. Attach the eye first. Slip the hook snugly in the eye. Stitch the hook to the waistband enough to hold it. Unhook and finishing stitching the hook to the waistband.

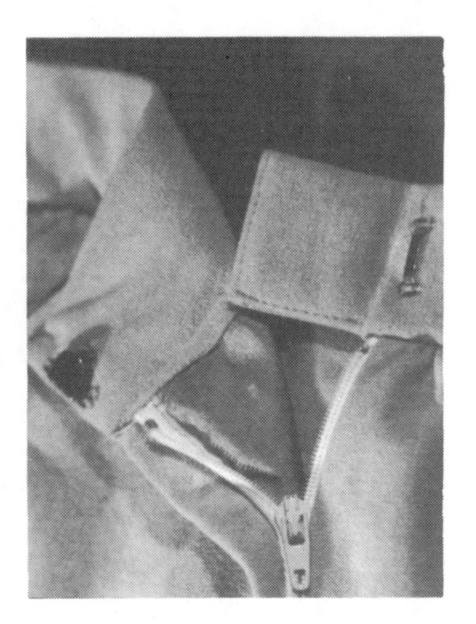

If the under extension is long as in a skirt with a pocket closing and no zipper, put one hook on the end of the under extension and another on the flush end of the band. The hook on the extension should take the pull so the top hook lies flat.

SLACKS

If you are using a new pattern that has not been checked and adjusted refer to Fitting your Garments-Pattern Adjustment page 12-14.

Cutting The Slacks

Follow the pattern directions except cut the waistband with the unnotched edge on the selvage if possible. If you can cut the waistband with one edge on the selvage it can be a bit narrower than the pattern, a scant 1/4" if your fabric is bulky and a fat 1/4" if your fabric is lightweight.

I like a center back seam in the waistband if I am using a center front opening. It is great for adjusting for weight loss or gain. Cut the waistband apart at the center back and add a 5/8" seam allowance to both pieces.

Many patterns have pockets and pocket stays cut entirely of the fashion fabric. If your fabric is medium to heavy weight, or if you are short of fabric make a new pattern to cut just pocket facings of the fashion fabric instead of cutting the whole pocket of your fashion fabric. This can be done on a slash pocket or a pocket in the side seam.

Drafting new pocket pattern pieces

On the side front pocket piece draw a line between the pocket location markings. Measure in 1 and 1/2" from that pocket location line and draw another line parallel to it. This will be the side front pocket facing. Lay a piece of tissue or tracing paper on top of the side front pocket piece and trace the new pocket facing. Transfer the straight of grain from the original pattern to the new pattern. Use this for your side front pocket facing and cut two of your fashion fabric.

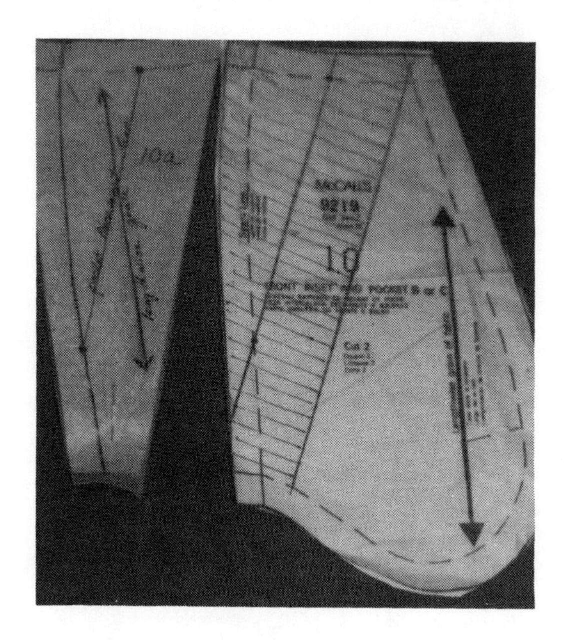

Optional: Make a facing for the inside pocket piece of fashion fabric. If your lining is a good match and your garment will not get excessive wear you can use lining for this entire place.

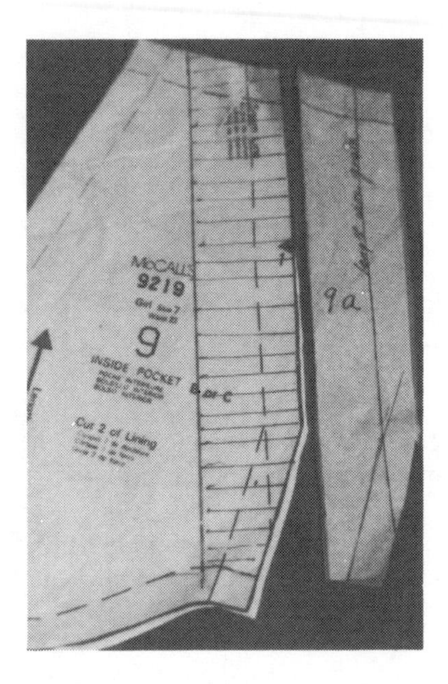

On the pocket opening of the inside pocket pattern piece measure over 1″ - 1 & 1/2″ from the stitching line and draw a line parallel to the stitching line. This will be the inside pocket facing. Lay a piece of tissue or tracing paper on top of the inside pocket piece and trace the new pocket facing. Use the seam line as the straight of grain line. This will strengthen and stabilize the pocket opening. You don't need to tape the pocket opening if your facing is straight of grain.

Cut the side pocket, pocket stay (if there is one), and inside pocket of lining. Cut the new pattern pieces you have traced of fashion fabric.

Stitching the pocket facings and lining

Lay the wrong side of the facing to the right side of the lining and stitch along the inside edge. Zig-zag the raw edge. Glue stitch or baste the outer edges. Follow the pattern directions for the pocket.

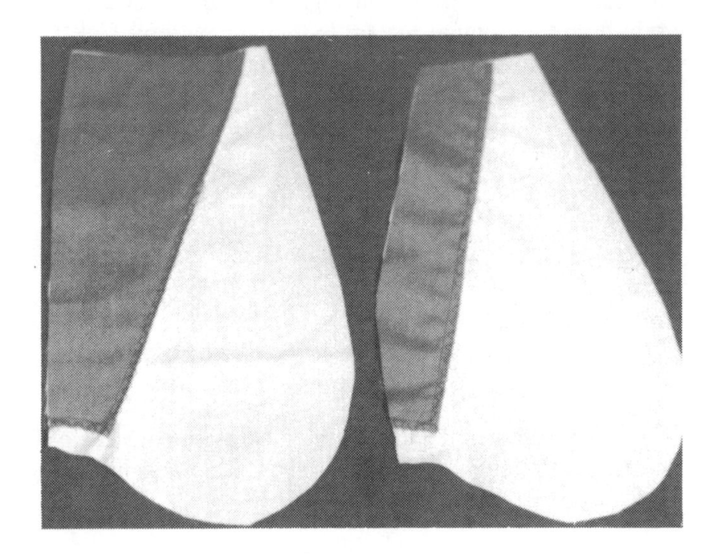

Cutting The Lining For Slacks

If the pattern does not have separate pieces for lining and you wish to line your slacks, use the front pattern and side front pocket (if there is a pocket) and the back pattern pieces. Cut the lining as long as the finished slack. Cut the back pattern as it is, except for the length. Pin the hem up. Pin the front pattern and the side front pocket together as shown in picture on page 57.

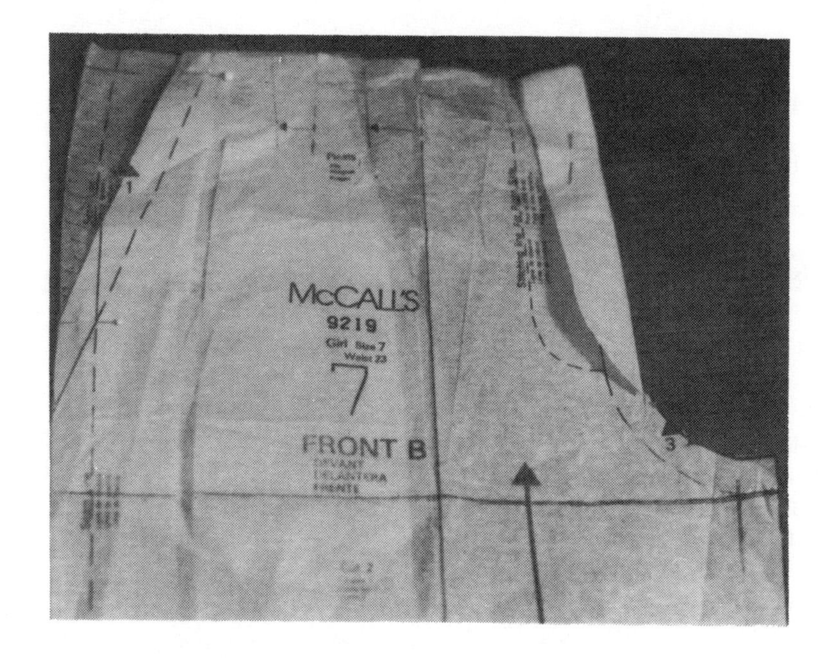

On the front pattern piece fold the cut-on fly facing back, leaving a 5/8" seam from the center front.

If the pattern has a pocket that involves the side seam, pin the side front pocket to the front pattern, matching the markings for the pocket opening. Pin the hem up.

Slack Construction

Read your pattern instruction sheet. Your particular style may influence the construction. If possible, I follow this sequence.

1. Mark the darts, center front, and the front crease line. Refer to Marking. If the front crease is not marked on your pattern, lay the edges of the front leg together at the bottom of the leg and up the leg to the knee. Crease the pattern to the waist seam. Draw a line along the crease. Label it **front crease line.**

2. Press the front crease line. Press the crease either to the waist seam or to the darts, whichever you prefer. If there are pleats, the crease should go into one of the pleats. Press the crease in firmly with a damp cloth and pounding block. Refer to Pressing, pages 66 and 67.

3. Stitch the darts and press toward the center. Refer to Marking, page 41.

4. If there are pockets, put them in now. Follow the pattern directions. If the pattern calls for welt pockets and you have heavy fabric, or if the welt pocket has a flap or an outside or inside welt, refer to Welt Pockets, page 232. If your fabric is medium to light weight and the welt pocket is a bound buttonhole welt, follow the pattern directions for the welt pockets and refer to page 249.

Apply the zipper

5. Refer to the Fly Front Zipper instructions, page 86. For other zippers, refer to the Zippers, pages 74-75, and 83. When stitching the front or the back crotch below the zipper, be sure to leave 1" unstitched at the crotch.

Pin baste before stitching seams

I rarely baste a seam unless I am unsure of the fit. I do pin baste all seams before basting or stitching. I often pin baste to try on the garment by placing the pins on the seam line vertically.

Lay both layers of fabric together on a flat surface, preferably one to which you can fasten the fabric. Example: Padded table, cutting board or an ironing board. Match the top and bottom edges of the seam with the two seam allowances lying open. If the seams are angled, match the seam junctions instead of the edges. Pin the layers to your working surface so they are taut. Pin from one end to the middle of the piece. Pin the opposite end to the middle. Insert the pins into the seam allowance with the head of the pin toward the seam. Having the pin head toward the seam facilitates removing the pins quickly as you sew. On straight seams pin about every 6″. On curved seams pin more closely.

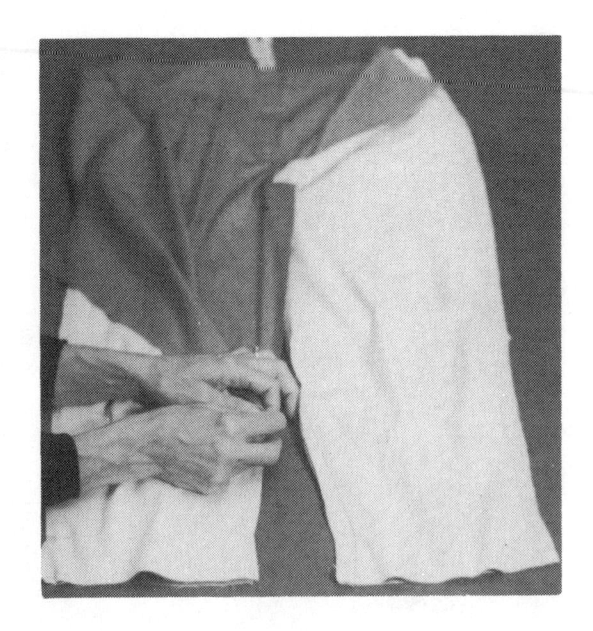

6. Stitch a front leg to a back leg at the side seam and the inseam. Match the notches and fabric edges and ease the leg if needed. It is easier to ease if you have the smaller area on top and **taut stitch** the area to be eased.

   Taut stitch: Hold your fabric firmly in front of and behind the needle. Hold it taut and let the machine feed the fabric through. The feed dogs will help ease the larger area. If you have quite a lot of ease on the inseam on the front of the slacks, steam and stretch the back inseam of the slack to facilitate easing.

7. Press the seams open and finish the edges if they will ravel. Refer to Seam Finishes and Pressing Techniques. Lightweight fabrics can be pressed to one side and finished together. Turn the legs right side out.

8. Hold the slacks with the side seams together, both legs in one hand at the waistline, and put your hand down in one leg. Grab the other leg and turn them wrong side out. One leg will be inside the other leg.

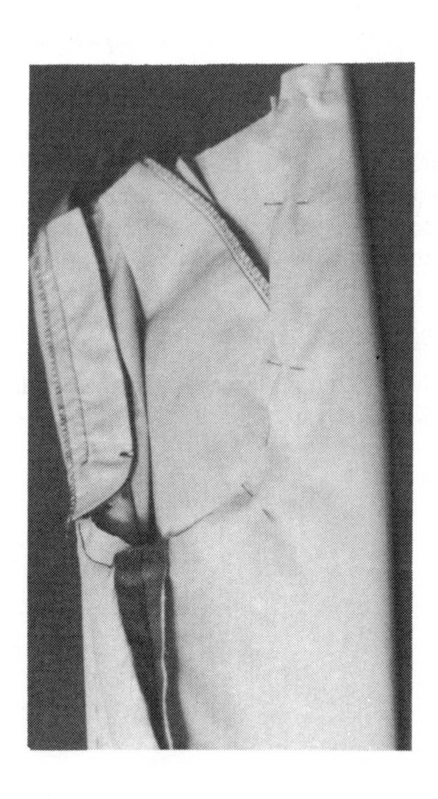

9. Match the inner leg seams and the edges at the waistline. Machine baste the crotch seam and try the slacks on to check the fit. Do any adjusting needed in the hipline. Wait until the waistband is stitched on to fit the crotch seam.

Waistband

10. If you are using a two-piece waistband, stitch the band onto slacks. Apply the interfacing before the final stitching of the crotch seam.

If you are using a one-piece waistband, permanently stitch the crotch seam before you apply the waistband.

Ultrasuede slacks

Put the lining in the slacks before permanently stitching the crotch seam. Refer to Lined Slacks, page 62. The lining in Ultrasuede slacks should be stitched with the suede at the crotch seam and the waistline to support and to prevent splitting of the Ultrasuede.

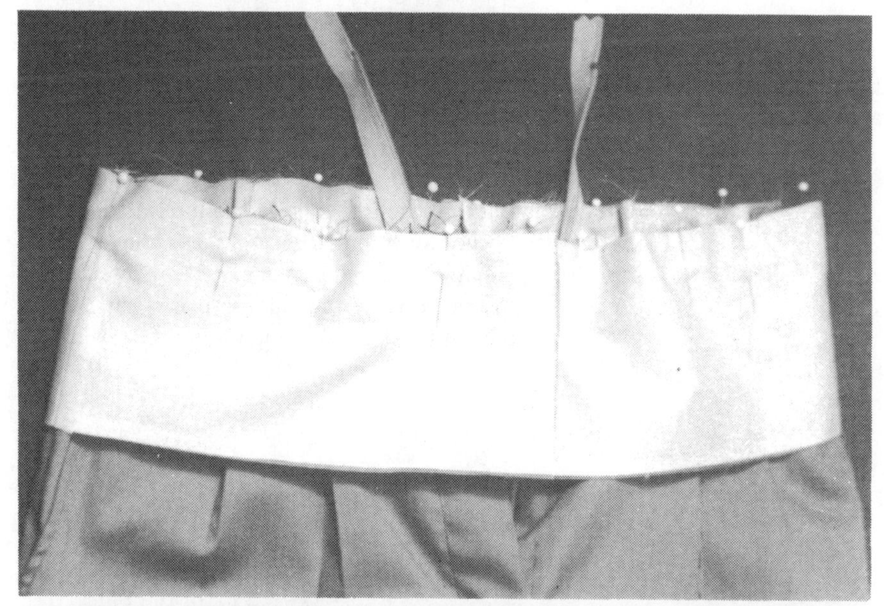

Pin the right side of the bands to the right side of the slacks. **Ease** the slacks onto the band, matching the center fronts and the center backs. Refer to Easing, page 96. Most fabrics will ease. A few very firm fabrics will not. If you can't get the waist eased onto the waistband, take the seams or darts in a little. Stitch the band onto the slacks. Stitch the entire length of the waistband.

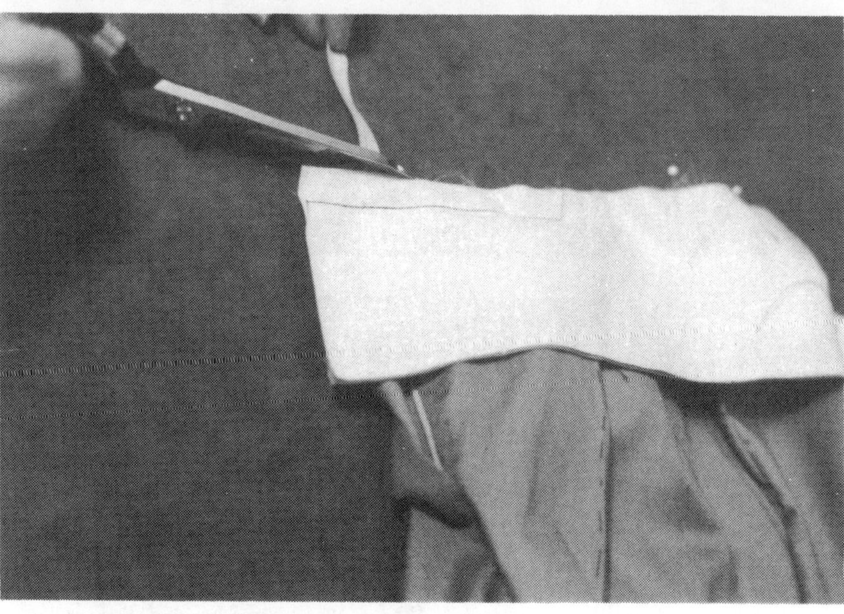

After the band is stitched on, cut off the excess length of the zipper. **Never cut the zipper off until you have stitched across it.**

11. Interface the waistband. My favorite waistband interfacing is Armo-flex or Ban-roll. (They are the same thing, just different brand names.)

Lay the interfacing on the **wrong side of the waistbands** with one edge of it lying on and covering the seam allowance. The lower edge of the interfacing must not cover the waist seam. Pin the interfacing in place, and machine or hand baste it about 1/4″ from the lower edge of the interfacing. You are stitching through the interfacing and both layers of the seam allowance. Be sure to carry the interfacing to the ends of the band.

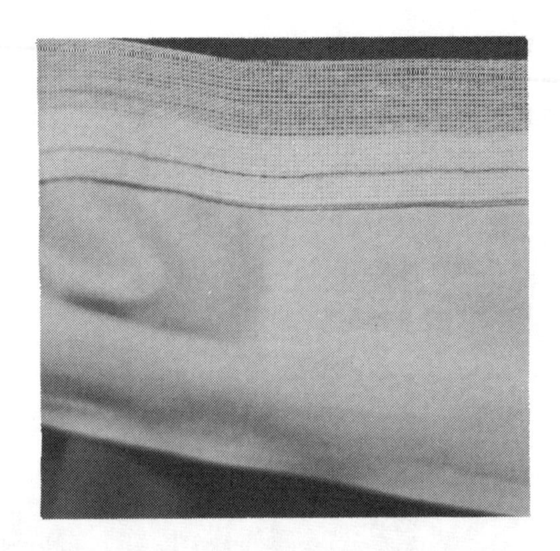

12. Finish the ends of the waistband. On some patterns the extension end will be under and some patterns have it on the upper side. It is a matter of style and preference. Do it as you prefer.

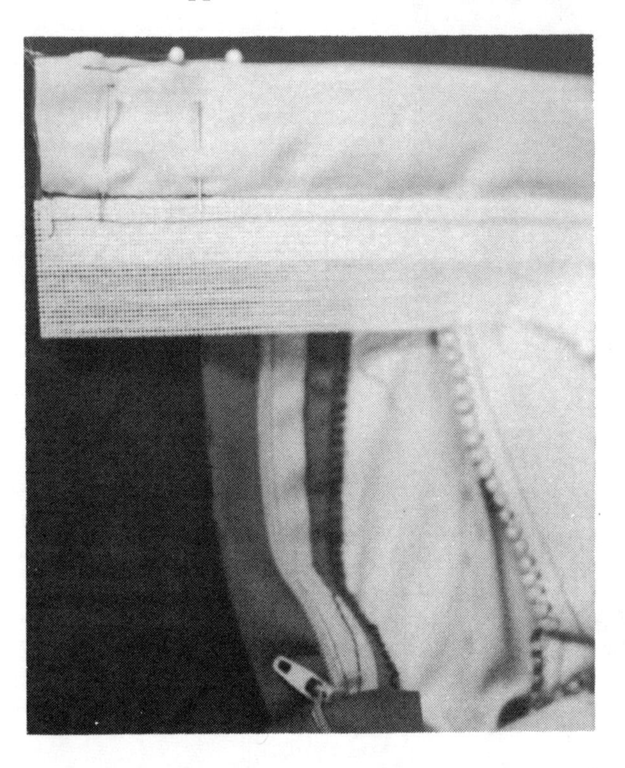

On the **extension end** of the band mark the fold line of the waistband at the top edge of the interfacing. Fold the waistband in half, right sides together along the fold line, and pin to hold the fold in place. Lay the interfacing down toward the body of the slacks so it is out of the way. Stitch along the edge of the interfacing from the end of the waistband to the center front of the slacks.

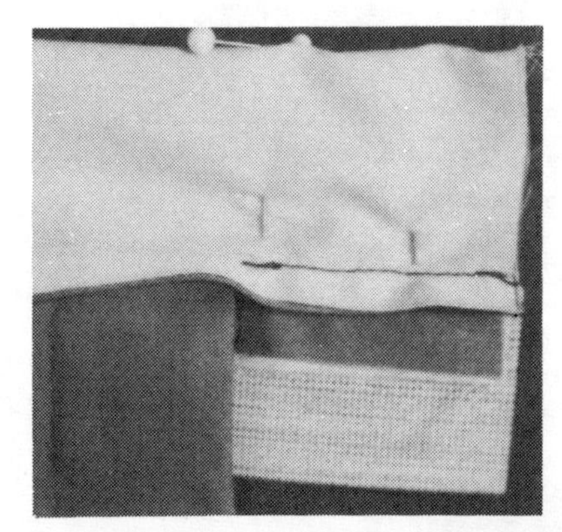

You are only stitching through two thicknesses of the band.

Fold the interfacing back up against the waistband and stitch across the end of the band, stitching through the interfacing and two layers of the waistband. Trim the seam to 1/4″, trim the corner, and turn right side out.

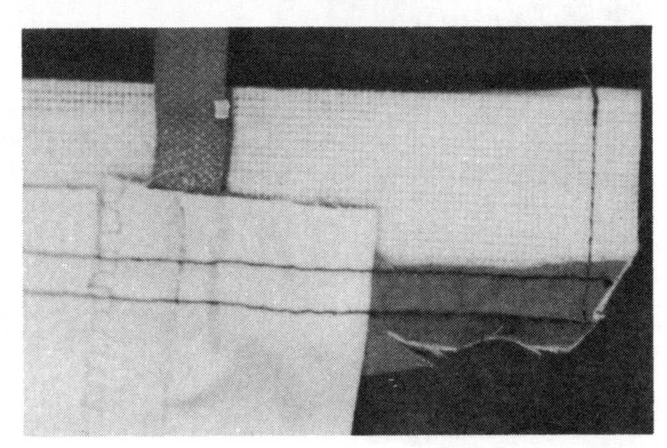

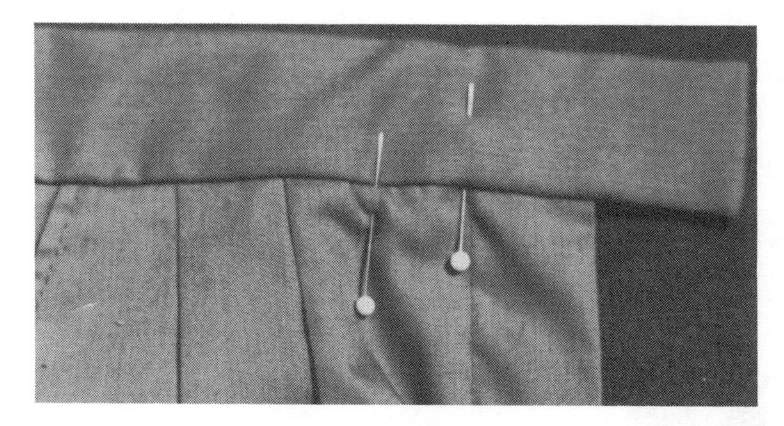

It's a little hard to turn. A screwdriver or point pusher helps get the corners turned neatly.

On the **flush end** of the band, mark the fold line.

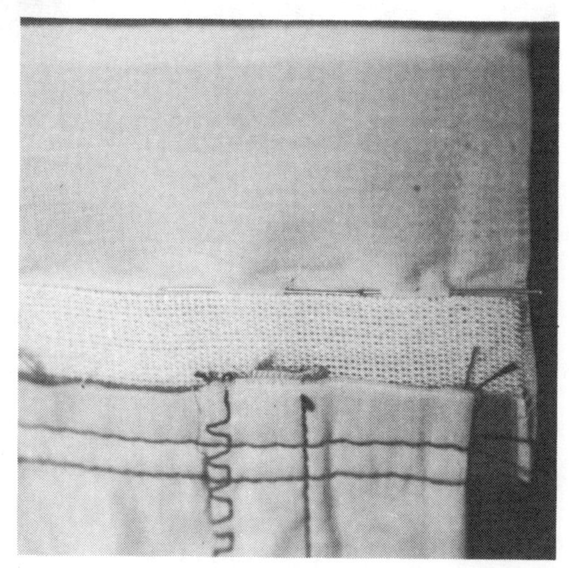

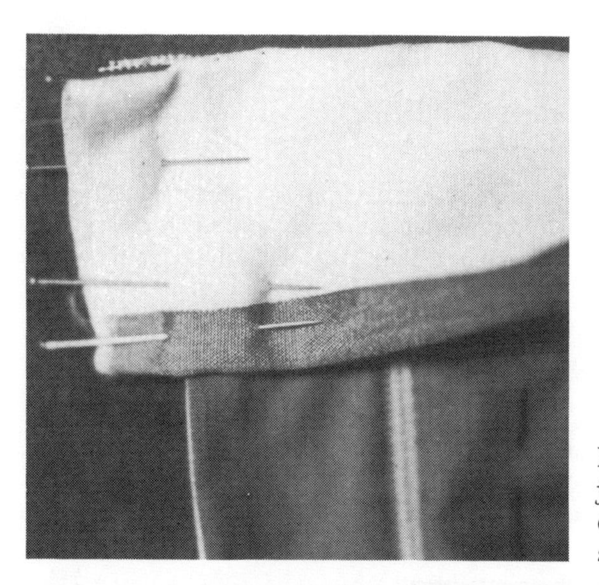

Fold the band in half. Fold the seam allowance up till it just covers the seam and pin to hold it. Stitch across the end of the band, going straight up from the edge of the slacks.

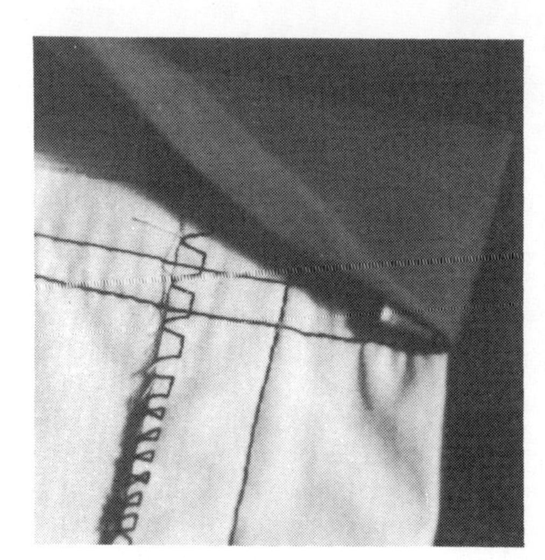

Trim the seam to 1/4″ and turn the waistband right side out.

The picture on the right shows the flush end under (on the left front). It can be on the upper (the right front) as well. It is a matter of style and personal preference.

Permanently stitch the crotch seam and press the seam open to the top of the crotch curve. Stitch the crotch seam together 1/4″ in to the seam allowance from the top of the crotch curve on the back to the zipper opening on the front. Trim close to the last row of stitching. If you have a zig-zag stitch, trim the seam first to 1/4″ then stitch.

Press the back crease line

Press the back crease line, ending just below the crotch line. The front crease determines where the back crease will be up to the knee. Then put the inseam and the side seam together at the crotch and finish pressing the back crease. Use a press cloth and plenty of steam and a pounding block. Press, then hold the pounding block firmly on the crease.

Lined Slacks

Stitch the lining together and attach to the slacks after you have stitched the waistband onto the slacks.

High Hip: If you adjust your patterns for a higher hip on one side be sure and reverse your lining when you stitch it together. It must be exactly opposite of your slacks.

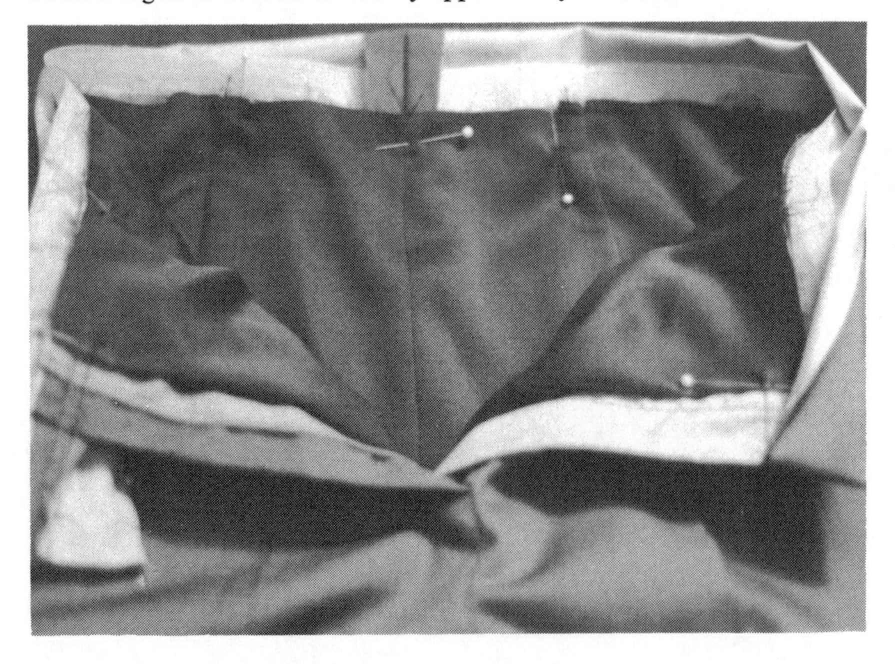

Pin the lining to the slacks at the waist seam — wrong side of lining to the wrong side of the slacks. Baste the lining to the slacks at the waistline. Whipstitch the lining to the slacks along the edge of the zipper tape on the left front. On the right front the lining must be left free to allow the zipper to be closed. Press or stitch the edge to establish a fold.

13. Bring the loose edge of the waistband up and over the interfacing to the wrong side of the slacks and pin in place. I let the selvage edge hang down into the slacks. It's less bulky than turning the seam under. If you were not able to cut the band with one edge of it on the selvage, finish the edge (refer to Seam Finishes, pages 68 and 71) or turn it under, before stitching. Stitch in the well of the seam on the right side of the slacks, either by hand or by machine, catching the band on the wrong side.

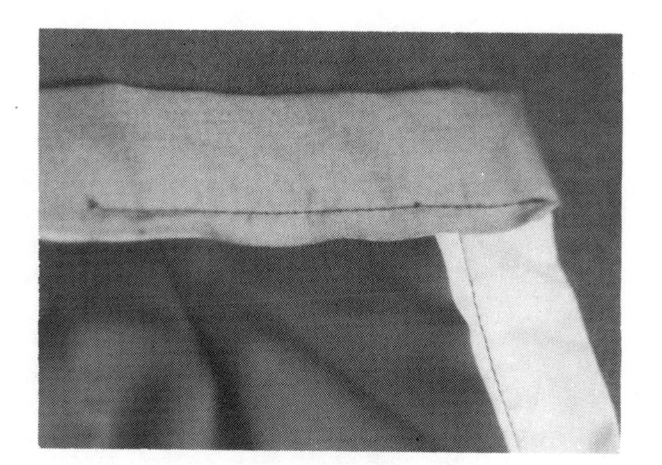

Hem The Slacks

14. A 2″ hem is ample. I hem a good pair of slacks by hand, and casual slacks by machine. Refer to Hems, pages 97-98 and 101.

Hemming lined slacks

Either hem the slacks and the lining separately or do a jump hem in the lining. I prefer the jump hem in the lining.

Slacks and lining hemmed separately.

To do a jump hem, first hem the slacks. Fold the lining up so it is from 3/4″ to 1″ shorter than the slacks. Pin along the top of the slack hem.

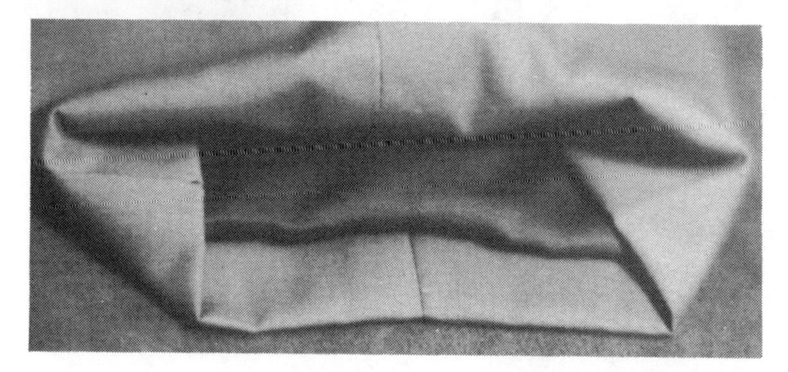

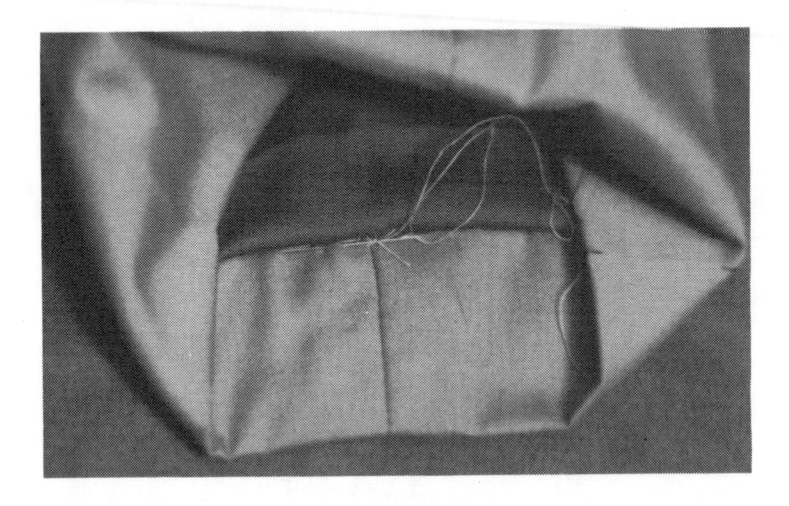

Lift the hem of the lining and pin again through one layer of the lining. Hand stitch the lining to the hem just below the top edge of the hem of the slacks.

Attach A Fastener To The Waistband

15. If the extension end of the band is on the outside, hand stitch a metal hook and eye directly above the zipper. Either put a second hook and eye or a button and buttonhole at the end of the band. Refer to Skirts, page 54.

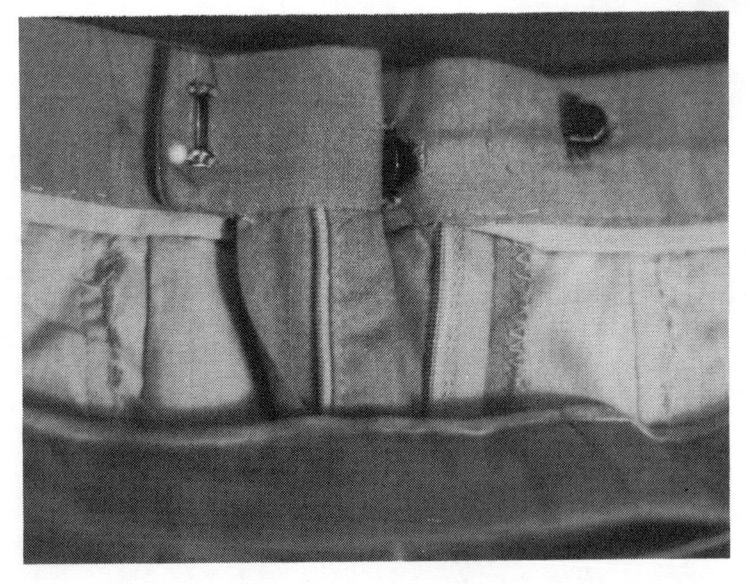

If the extension end of the band is underneath and the flush end is on top, hand stitch a metal hook and eye to both ends of the band. Make sure the pull is on the hook on the underneath.

SAMPLE SEAMS AND PRESSING TECHNIQUES

Sample Seam

When you are working with a fabric that is unfamiliar to you, test a scrap of it to see how it stitches on the lengthwise, crosswise, and bias grainline. Do a sample seam and press the seam open. Test a scrap of your fabric to see how it reacts to pressing. Use a large enough piece to compare a pressed section with an unpressed part. Check to see how the fabric reacts to moisture as well as heat. Also test the fabric to see how badly it will ravel and what seam finish will be the most desirable for the fabric. Often testing will steer you away from a design which would cause you extra work or an undesirable finished garment.

Turn Of Cloth

If you are using heavier fabric than is called for on the pattern envelope, you should check for the turn of cloth on the collar and lapel pieces. If the fabric is heavier than the pattern expected it to be, you could be short of fabric for the collar and lapel roll. Also be aware of it when you check your pattern. If there is any other area that has a roll plus seams where the fabric has to turn on the seam as well as on a roll, allow more along the seam line.

To help you know how much larger you need to cut, check the turn of cloth by doing a sample.

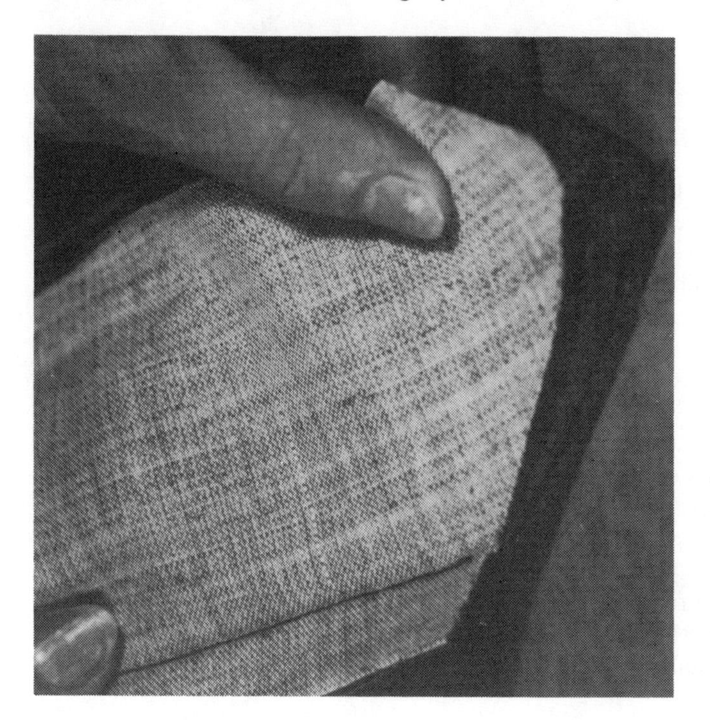

Cut two pieces of fabric about 5″ by 7″ exactly the same size (this can be scraps) and one piece of the interfacing. Stitch a seam with the interfacing included. Press the seam open and trim the seam.

Turn to the right side. Fold the sample as a collar or lapel will fold. Press the seam allowances separately to the wrong side on the opposite edge from the seam that you stitched. Measure the difference in the two seam lines. The upper collar and front facing should be that much larger than the undercollar and the front facing in the lapel area and any other area that rolls to accommodate the turn of cloth.

Pressing Techniques

A beautiful garment depends as much on the pressing as it does on the sewing.

Pressing is not ironing!

It is the lifting of the iron and setting it down again, putting heat and steam plus pressure in the right place to shape and mold the garment.

You need the proper equipment — a good steam iron and a press cloth are most important. A firm cotton cloth, like an old cotton sheet, will work for most things. A wool cloth is best to preserve the spongy texture of wool. Several layers of cheesecloth or cotton organdy will work if you need to see through the pressing cloth. Other pressing aids I use are a sleeve roll, a ham, a ham holder, a mitt, a tailor's clapper, a sleeve board, and a point presser. Another helpful tool is a large artist paint brush. Painting the opened seam with water before pressing puts the moisture exactly where you need it.

Often a point presser is combined with a clapper. I have a nice sleeve board that is combined with a point presser. A sleeve board with a mitt slipped over the end of the board gives a nice small curved area for shrinking in the fullness of small areas you have eased.

Some General Rules For Pressing

Always test a scrap of your fabric to see how it reacts to pressing. Use a large enough piece to compare a pressed section with an unpressed part. Check to see how the fabric reacts to moisture as well as heat.

Press with the grain of your fabric as much as possible. This is especially important when working with a bias cut. Be careful not to stretch edges and curves.

Press on the wrong side of the fabric as much as possible. If you must press on the right side, use a press cloth faithfully.

To prevent the impression of seams, hems, or pleats on the right side of the garment, cut strips of brown paper 2″ wider than the seam or pleat and tuck them under the area before pressing. Pressing seams open on a sleeve-roll also prevents seams from showing because of the curve of the roll.

Often just the steam from the iron is enough moisture but sometimes you need more. Use a paint brush to get the seam wet, then press. That gets the moisture just where you need it. If you need to get a larger area damp, wet half your press cloth, wring it out, fold it in half with the dry part and wring it again. Use that slightly dampened cloth for pressing.

Always press seams and darts before they are crossed with other seams.

When you press the dart, press it flat first to set the stitches but just press to the end of the dart, not past the end. Then press the dart to one side usually toward the center on the wrong side of the fabric. Check the dart on the right side of the fabric to make sure you have pressed a nice tapered point.

Don't press any seams or sharp creases in until after your garment is fitted. A pounding block is helpful in setting a crease, however you needn't pound with it. Shoot the steam to the fabric and press down with the pounding block. Just that pressure is adequate.

Try to use the tip of the iron and work in the same direction you stitched. Don't press over basting threads or pins.

Above all, don't over-press. Be careful of the heat setting on your iron. When pressing pleats or shaping an area, let it dry before handling it. I use a Teflon guard on my irons. It helps to prevent scorching.

SEAM FINISHES

All seams on woven fabrics should be finished unless they will be covered by a lining. A finished seam helps to support the garment shape, insures long life, prevents raveling, and makes a garment look better. If a garment is intended for limited wear, it may be a waste of your time to finish the seams. I have listed only the seam finishes I have used and like. Do a test seam to see how your fabric stitches and presses, and to check for the best seam finish for your particular fabric and garment. Sometimes you will need to use a different seam finish on curved seams than you are using on straight seams.

Hand Overcast

The finest seam finish is one you don't often find on purchased garments because of the cost. Some very-well-done and expensive couture garments still have hand overcast seams. I hand overcast my expensive silks or silky polyesters if other seam finishes show when pressed. Hand overcast with a cotton thread on silk, a polyester thread on polyesters.

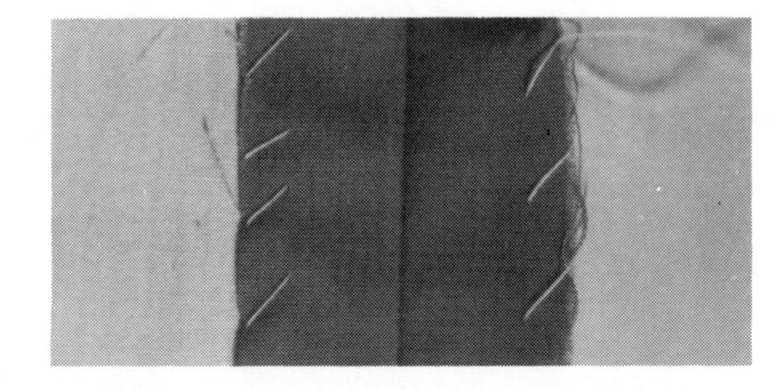

Beeswax the thread, then press it. The beeswax helps eliminate knotting. Use a fine long needle. Take a stitch about 1/4″ deep in the fabric, pull the thread to the fabric edge. Slant the needle so the stitches lie at an angle and take the next stitch.

A hand overcast can be done quite fast by wrapping your needle around the edge of the fabric and taking several stitches. Then pull the stitches through and adjust a bit so the edge is lying flat.

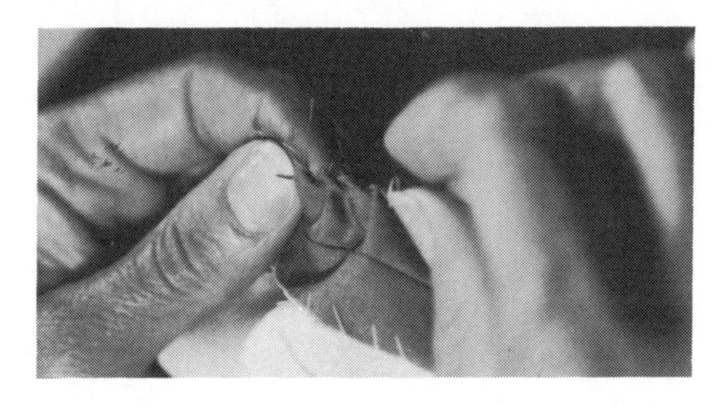

Serged, Overlock, Or Overedge

This finish is done with a special machine. It sews up to 1500 stitches per minute and trims the edge of the material as it sews. I do not recommend sewing the seams of your fine garments with the serger, but it is wonderful for finishing seams on even the finest fabrics. The edge lies flatter than with a regular sewing machine.

I use my serger for sewing sporty garments when I am sure of the fit. The serger sews, cuts seams to 1/4″, and finishes the edge of the seam at the same time.

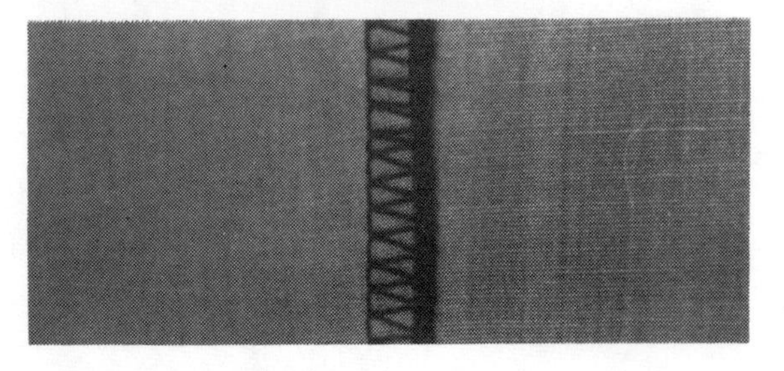

Machine Overcast

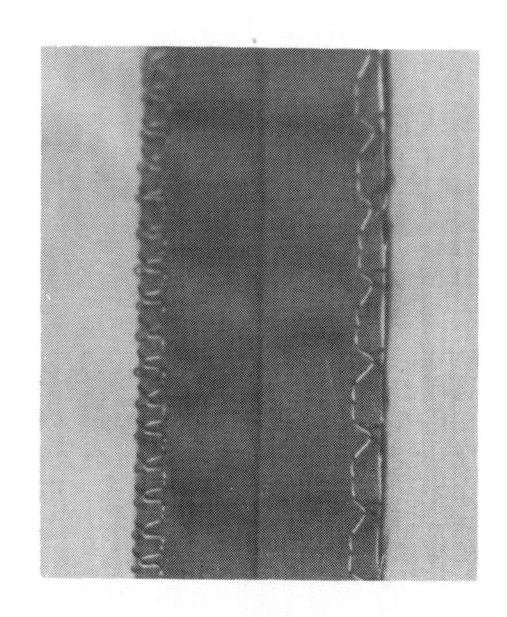

Suitable for many fabrics, usually done after the seams are stitched and pressed open. However, if your fabric frays badly, overcast the edges before you stitch the seams. If your machine does not have an overcast stitch, use your zig-zag stitch in place of the overcast. The blind hem stitch works as well as the overcast if you put your fabric on the right side of the needle. (Normally your fabric would be on the left side of the needle.)

French Seams

Use only for lightweight and sheer fabrics. French seams work only on straight seams. Use the self-bound seam finish for the curved seams on your garment.

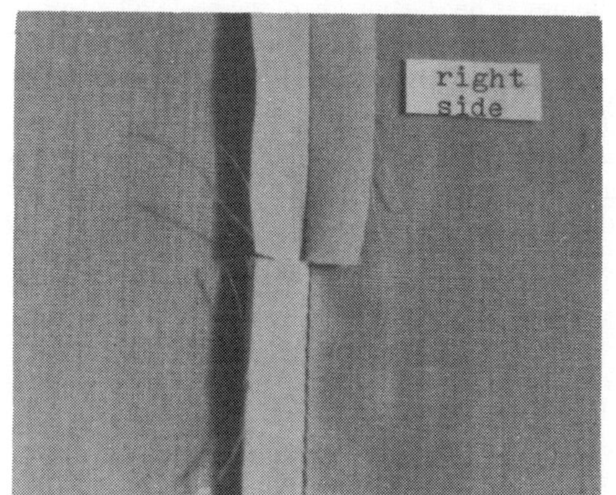

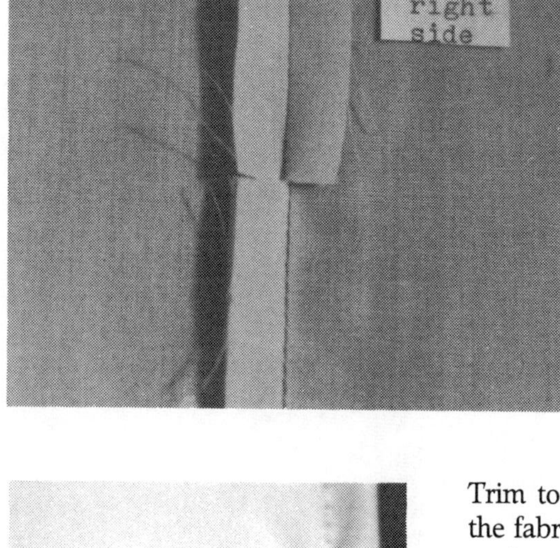

Stitch your seams with the wrong sides together, using a 3/8″ seam. Press the seam open, then press to one side.

Trim to 1/8″. Put the right sides of the fabric together and pin the seam again with the seamline on the fold.

Stitch, this time using a 1/4″ seam. Press to one side. In fine garments, a narrow French seam looks wonderful. I often do French seams in linings for my skirts. To make them faster and stronger I stitch the first time with the wrong sides together using a 1/4″ seam. Press, then stitch with the right sides together using a 3/8″ seam.

Self-Bound French Seam

Stitch the seam using the 5/8″ seam allowance. Trim the seam allowance to 1/2″ and fold both seams under 1/4″. It is easier to fold one seam under 1/4″ and pin it, then as you are hand stitching fold the other seam under.

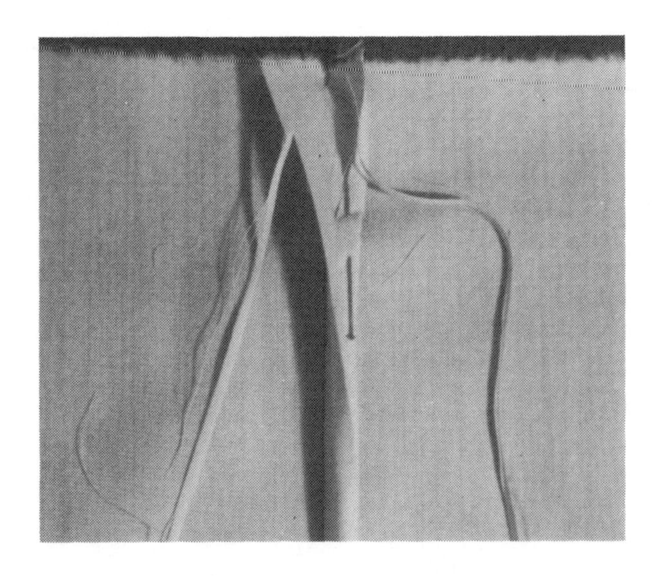

Stitch, preferably by hand, through all layers of the seam. This looks very much like a French seam, only the final row of stitching is on the outside of the seam allowance. I use this finish on curved seams in garments in which the other seams have been finished with a French seam. It is an especially nice finish for the armhole of sheer blouses. Also use it if you are matching horizontal stripes in a sheer fabric where a conventional French seam would be very difficult.

Turned Under

Suitable for only lightweight and medium weight fabrics. Turn under the edge of the seam allowance and stitch on the edge of the fold.

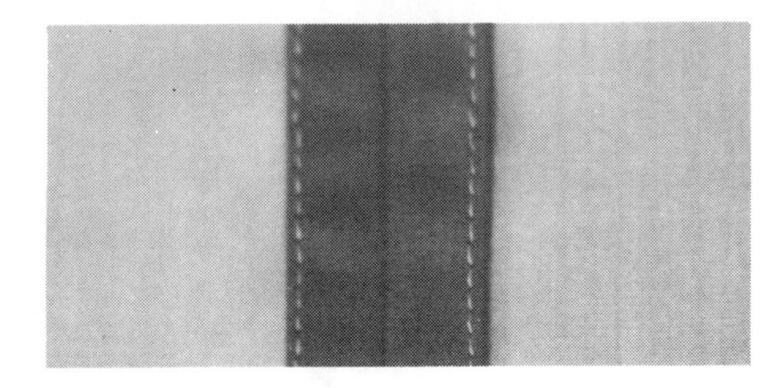

Pinked Seams

Suitable for firmly woven fabric which doesn't ravel. A stronger finish is to stitch 1/4″ from the edge and then pink. Sometimes, if the only finish for a slippery, silky polyester is a hand overcast, I will do a pinked seam instead. My seam finish depends on the garment, the cost of the fabric, and my time.

Hong-Kong

Use for underlined garments and for unlined jackets and coats. Cut bias strips 1″ wide of a lightweight fabric such as batiste, broadcloth, or linings. Refer to Blouses and Dresses, page 127. Seams Great, which is 15-denier tricot cut on the bias, also works to bind seams. Buy the wider Seams Great. The 5/8″ wide is difficult to work with. I used 15-denier tricot on the straight of grain or the cross grain to bind seams long before Seams Great was available packaged. It is much less expensive than the packaged bias tricot.

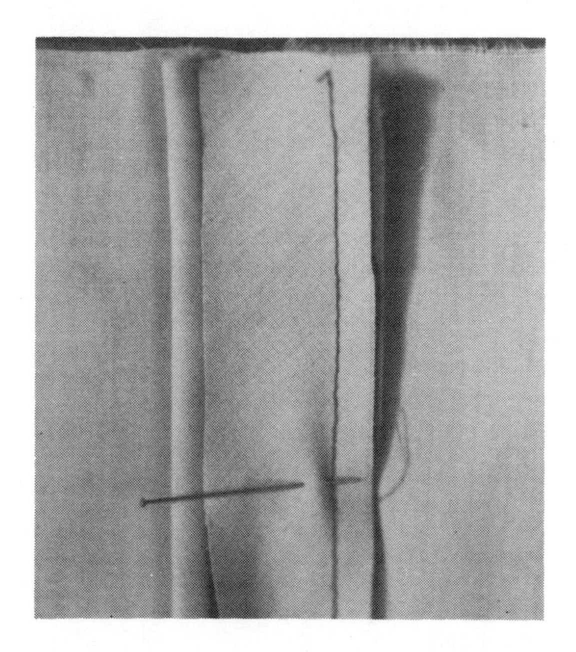

Stitch the bias or the tricot to the seam edge using a 1/4″ seam.

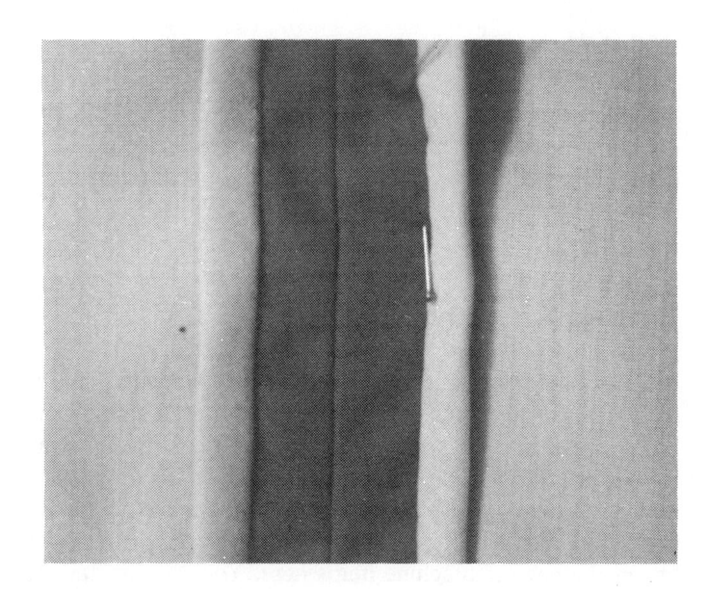

Turn the seam finish to the inside over the seam and stitch again in the well of the seam with the right side up, either by hand or machine.

Seams Great could also be applied using the package directions. For this application the 5/8″ size would be all right.

TOPSTITCHING AND EDGESTITCHING

Topstitching

Topstitching is used to accent seams and style lines, to give garments a structured finished look, and to hold seams flat. It is usually done 1/4″-3/8″ from the seam line.

Edgestitching

Edgestitching which is done to hold seams flat is always done very close to the edge, usually 1/16″.

Both topstitching and edgestitching are done on the right side of the garment. It is always your choice to topstitch, edgestitch, or not to stitch. The particular garment and fabric and your taste determine which you will choose to do. Throughout the remainder of this chapter I am referring to both topstitching and edgestitching.

When To Topstitch

Some topstitching is done during construction. When topstitching, make sure of the fit before doing the topstitching on any seams that will affect the fit. Small areas such as pocket flaps, belts, and other trims are topstitched before being attached. Patch pockets are usually topstitched onto the garment. Always do topstitching before lining the garment.

Accurate Topstitching

When topstitching, accuracy is necessary. Hand basting the areas to be topstitched holds the layers of fabric together and saves lots of ripping. Straight, even stitches are important. Topstitching or masking tape, or a hand baste thread line are good guides to keep the stitching straight. The blind hem presser foot is a wonderful guide for edgestitching. Hold the bar close to the edge of the fabric and move the needle to achieve the desired width for edgestitching. Refer to Couture Patch Pockets, page 231. Use care on curves. If the curve is tight with the needle down, pick up the presser foot every few stitches to stitch the curve and achieve a smooth line. A knee lift on the sewing machine helps here. You can lift the presser foot slightly and still keep both hands on your fabric. Mark the distance from the corners so you know when to pivot. A long thread through the corner is a help in keeping the machine from stalling on the corner. With a hand needle and long thread, take one stitch through the point of the corner. Gently tug the thread after you pivot to keep the sewing smooth as you go away from the corner. Refer to Collars, page 164.

Topstitching Sample

Always do a sample topstitching through all the thickness of the fabric to check the tension of your machine, the thread, the needle, and the stitch length. Since it is always your choice to topstitch, this gives you the opportunity to judge topstitching on your particular fabric and garment.

Different effects can be realized when topstitching by changing the length of the stitch, the type of thread you use, and the manner in which you finish the seam. Regular thread, silk buttonhole twist, polyester topstitching thread, or two strands of regular or silk thread are all options. Two strands of thread through the needle are much easier than heavy thread and give similar results. The two threads should be threaded separately through the machine tension. Refer to Couture Tailoring, page 314.

A fine even outline is achieved with regular thread and small stitches. A more defined outline is achieved by using a heavier thread and larger stitches. If you choose to use heavier thread, it is necessary to use a larger needle. The needle must fall easily along the thread for it to sew smoothly at the machine.

The seam finish also affects the look of topstitching. Often the seam is pressed one direction and then topstitched. For a more defined look pad the seam. Trim the under layer of the seam just slightly narrower than the topstitching for a slightly padded look.

ZIPPERS

There are four different ways to put a zipper in a garment. They are the lapped zipper, the center zipper, the unique zipper, and the fly front zipper.

If the garment has a facing either at the neckline or the waistline, the facing must be put on before the zipper is put in. A couture zipper application can be done at the waistline. In this application, the zipper goes up into the waistband. Refer to page 83.

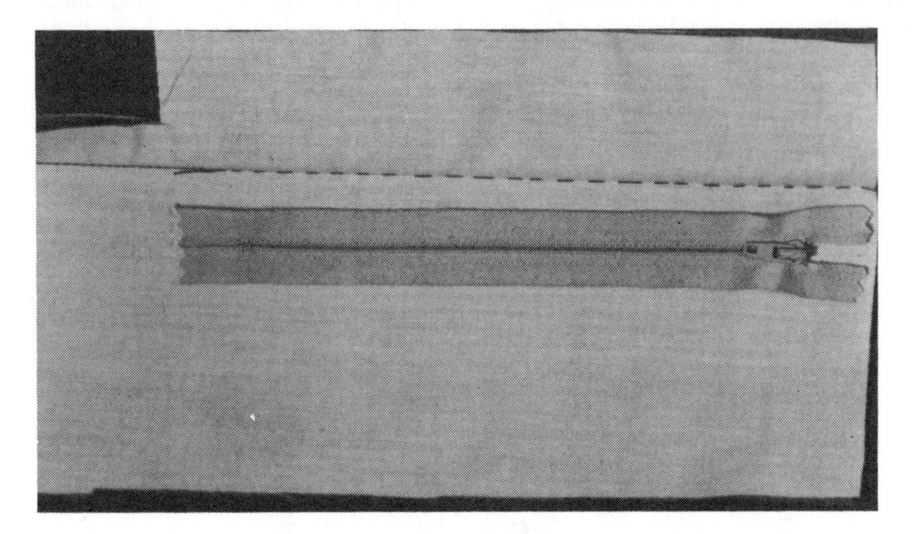

Any zipper is easier to put in and lies flatter if, when cutting, you allow an extra wide seam allowance in the zipper area. Marking the seam line with a thread trace is also a big help. Marking the seam keeps the seam line in the correct place and since you can be accurate the first time you never need to do the zipper twice.

Any time a garment has a facing you must prepare the neckline of a bodice or the waistline of a skirt for the zipper. **Exception:** If you are using a Unique zipper, the neckline or waistline seam must be finished after the zipper is put in. If the garment is finished with a collar or a neck trim, no facing, it is not necessary to prepare the neckline before you put the zipper in the garment. The same is true for a skirt with a waistband. Refer to page 75.

Lapped Zipper

The lapped zipper is set under a seam line 1/8" and the seam laps over the zipper. The seam lines must still meet on the seam line. The lapped zipper is the easiest zipper to put in and the most commonly used. Refer to page 77.

Center Zipper

The center zipper is centered under a seam. Both edges of the seam line must lap over the zipper slightly or the zipper will show. This zipper is difficult to put in so it does not show. Use it only when the fabric is too bulky for a lapped zipper or the style dictates that you must use a center zipper. This zipper is best done entirely by hand. Refer to page 81.

Unique Zipper

The zipper itself is made differently from other zippers. It takes a special foot on the sewing machine to sew the unique zipper into a garment. This zipper looks like a seam because there is no stitching on the right side of the fabric. Only the little pull tab of the zipper shows. Use this zipper **only** in heavier fabrics or it does show and looks terrible. The unique zipper is a fairly stiff, heavy zipper so the fabric must be heavy, stiff, or bulky to support the zipper. Example: Velvets, double knits, heavy wools, and Ultrasuede. Use it in place of the lapped or center zipper in those heavy fabrics. Refer to page 84.

Fly Front Zipper

A fly front refers to the zipper opening on a pair of slacks or skirt. Refer to page 86.

Facing Application For Zippers

Mark the length needed for the zipper opening

Mark the length of the zipper opening using the zipper itself as a guide. Do not go by the marking on the pattern. Zippers vary in length. A 7″ zipper is around 7″. The opening must be the exact length of the zipper plus whatever you need for the seam or for a snap or hook at a neckline.

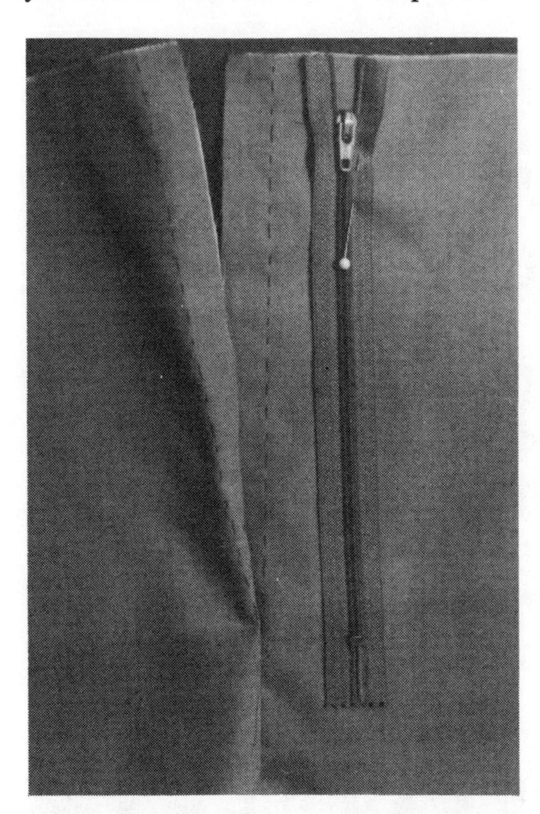

Stitch the seam of the garment, usually a center back seam, below the zipper opening. Mark the seam line with a hand baste stitch before putting the zipper in. With the seam marked it is easy to be accurate. When the zipper is in, the seam lines must be lying exactly together.

Neck opening: Hold the zipper pull tab about 1/2″ below the seamline to give space for a hanging snap or a hook & eye.

Skirt opening: Hold the zipper just slightly below the seam allowance.

Stitch the side seams of a skirt or the shoulder seams of a bodice. Stitch the facing in the same manner. Interface the facing of the garment. A French finish is nice on a facing. Refer to Blouses and Dresses, pages 119-120. If you have a serger, you can serge the edge of the facing and the interfacing together to finish the edge. If you are using fusible interfacing, do not use a French finish.

Press the garment seams open and pin the facing to the garment with the center back edges even.

Before stitching the neckline seam, fold the facing back in the following manner:

Lapped zipper

On the lapped (left) side, fold the facing back on itself 1″ and pin to hold it. It should be 3/8″ short of the seam line. The wrong sides will be together. Fold the garment seam allowance over the facing on the 5/8″ seam line and pin to hold it.

On the unlapped (right) side of the garment, fold the facing back 1/2″ and pin to hold it. The picture shows the facing finished with a French finish.

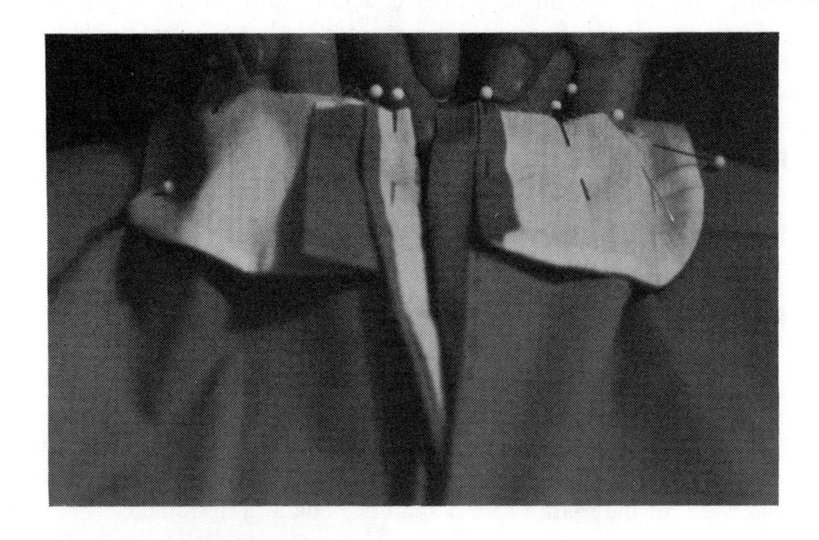

Center zipper

Treat both sides of the center zipper the same as the left or lapped side of the lapped zipper. The facing can be folded back 7/8″ instead of 1″, otherwise it is the same. The picture shows the waistline of a skirt with part of the waistline seam stitched and trimmed.

Stitch around the neckline or waistline opening. On the lapped (left) side, clip to the seam line at the edge of the center back seam allowance as in the picture above. Also trim the seam to the corner.

Clip any curves and understitch. (Stitch the seam to the facing about 1/8″ from the seam with the right side up. You are stitching on the facing and catching the seam.)

Trim the seam allowance to the understitching and press the facing into place. The picture shows facing finished with a serged edge.

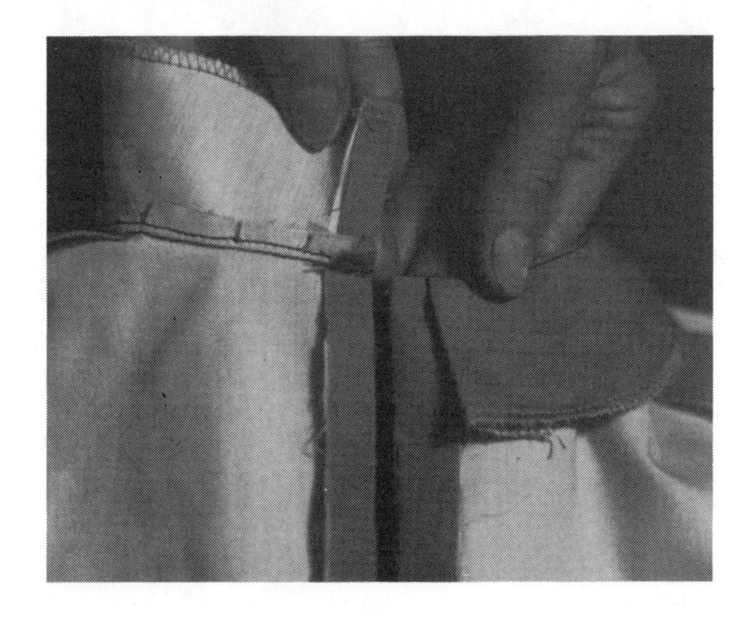

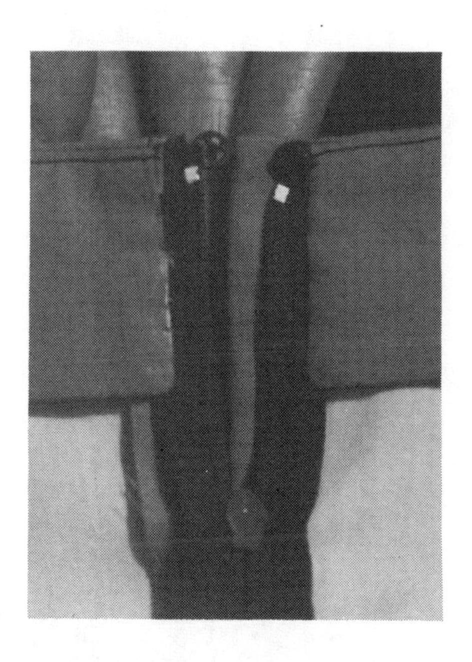

Neck opening

After the zipper is in, hand stitch the facings into place and sew a hanging snap fastener to the top of the garment. A hanging snap above the zipper is nicer than a hook and eye. It is easy to fasten and will not hook into your garment and make a hole.

The pictures show the lapped zipper on the right and wrong side.

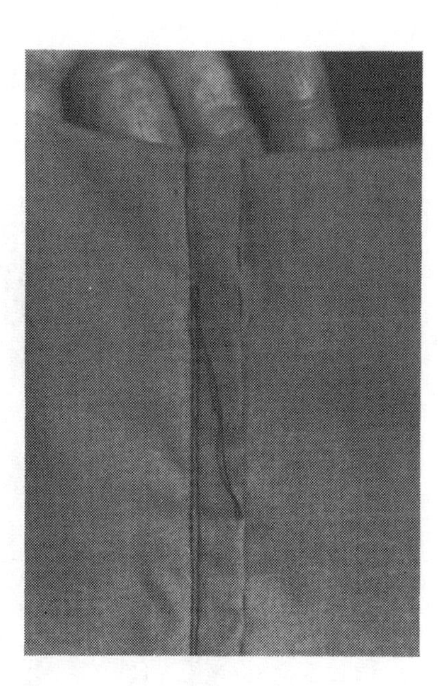

LAPPED ZIPPER

I prefer a lapped zipper on most garments. Use a center zipper only if you must because of the design of a garment or the weight of the fabric. A lapped zipper always hides the zipper and is the easiest to apply.

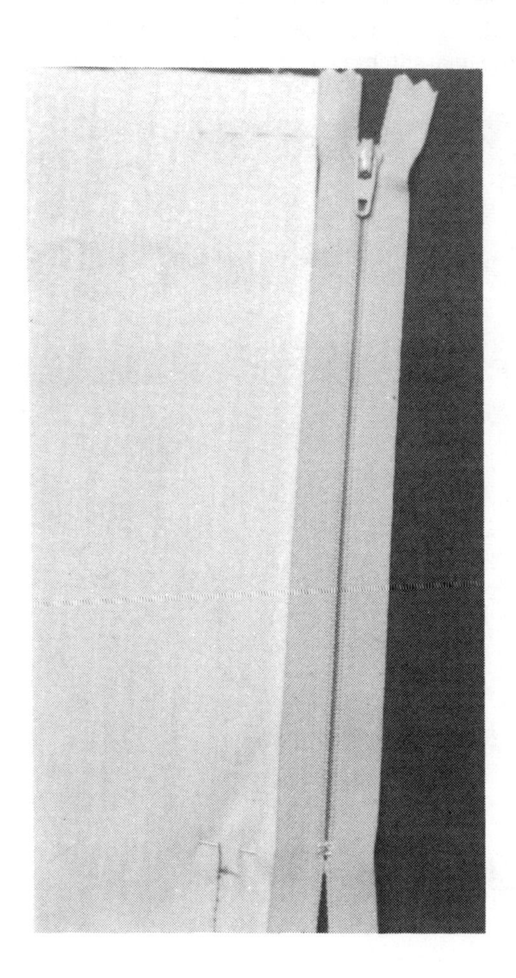

Preparation For Lapped Zipper

Mark the length needed for the zipper. Always use the zipper to mark the length as a 7″ zipper isn't always exactly 7″.

Neck opening: Hold the zipper pull tab about 1/2″ below the seamline to give space for a hanging snap or a hook and eye.

Skirt opening: Hold the pull tab just slightly below the seam line. Mark the bottom of the opening with a pin just above the metal stop of the zipper.

Stitch the remaining seam from the hem to your pin. Back-stitch or tie the threads. The zipper is easier to install and lies flatter if, when you are cutting, you allow for a larger seam allowance in the zipper area. At least be sure the seam is a generous 5/8″.

Marking the seam keeps the seam line in the correct place and since you can be accurate the first time, you do not need to do the zipper twice. If your fabric is stretchy, machine baste the zipper opening before pressing the seam open.

Press the seam open as follows: 5/8″ on the lapped (left) side, 1/2″ on the unlapped (right) side. This leaves a 1/8″ pleat at the bottom of the zipper opening. Be sure you have this pleat. Don't destroy it with the iron.

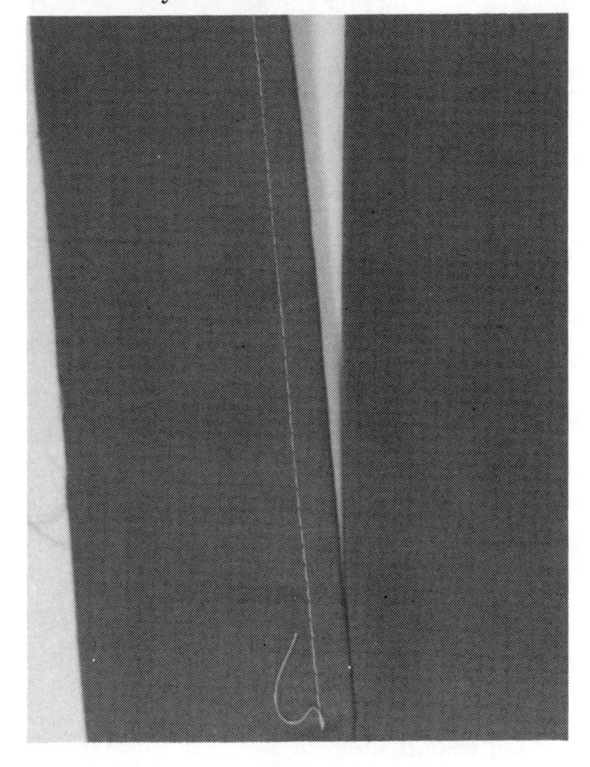

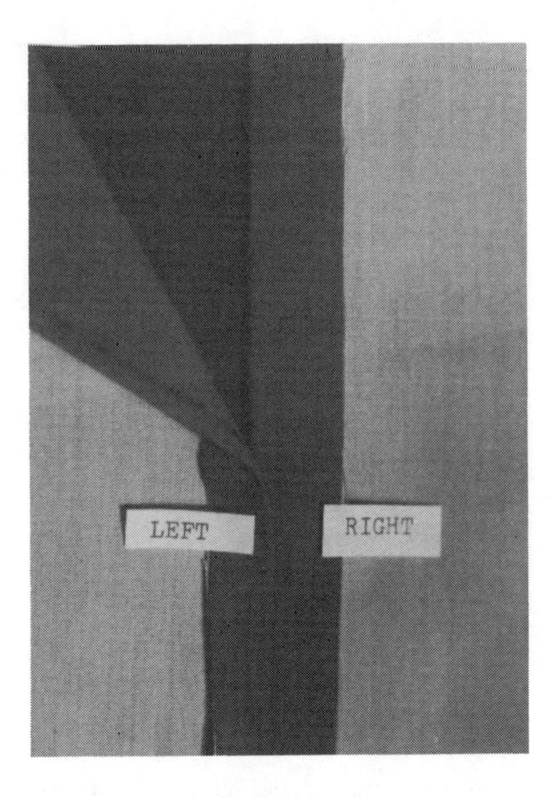

On the right side of the fabric, machine or hand baste 3/8″ from the folded edge on the lapped (left) side. This is a guide line for the final stitching. Use a contrasting thread.

Stitch The Lapped Zipper

Scotch tape the wrong side of the zipper. Lay the garment and the zipper on a flat surface with the ends of both lying in the same direction. Turn the zipper over so that the wrong side is up. Scotch tape the left side of the zipper. Turn the zipper over so the sticky side of the tape is up.

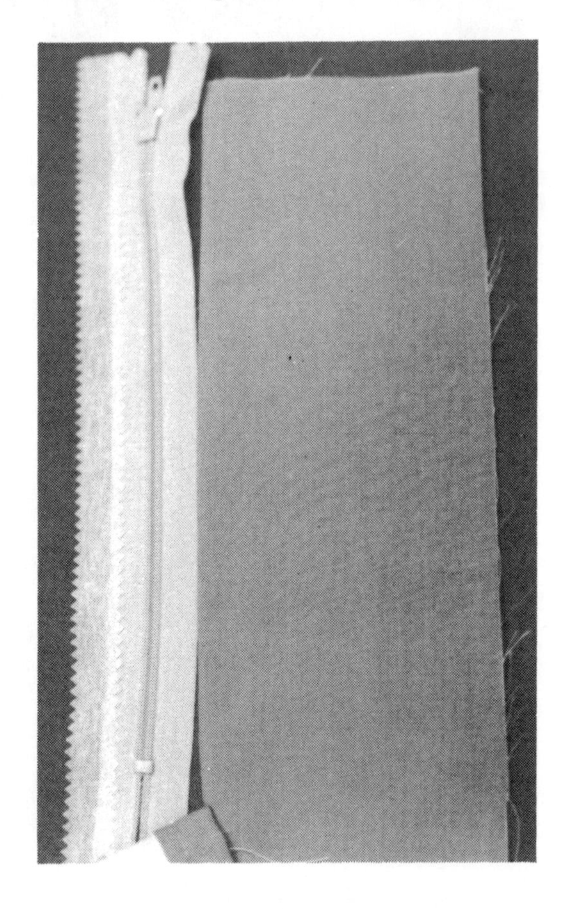

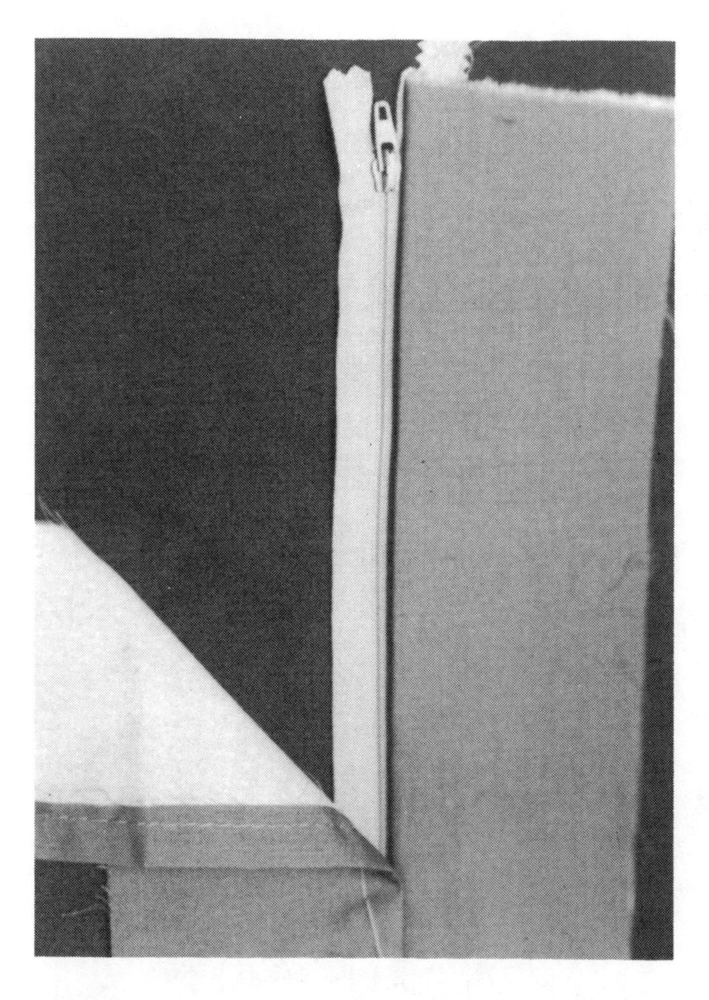

Fasten the zipper, with the sticky side of the tape up, to the cutting board or any padded surface to hold it. Lay the garment unlapped side (the one with the 1/2″ seam) in place along the zipper teeth. The tape acts as a quick baste. Some fabrics don't adhere very well to the tape. If that is the case, pin the zipper in a couple of places until you get to the sewing machine with it.

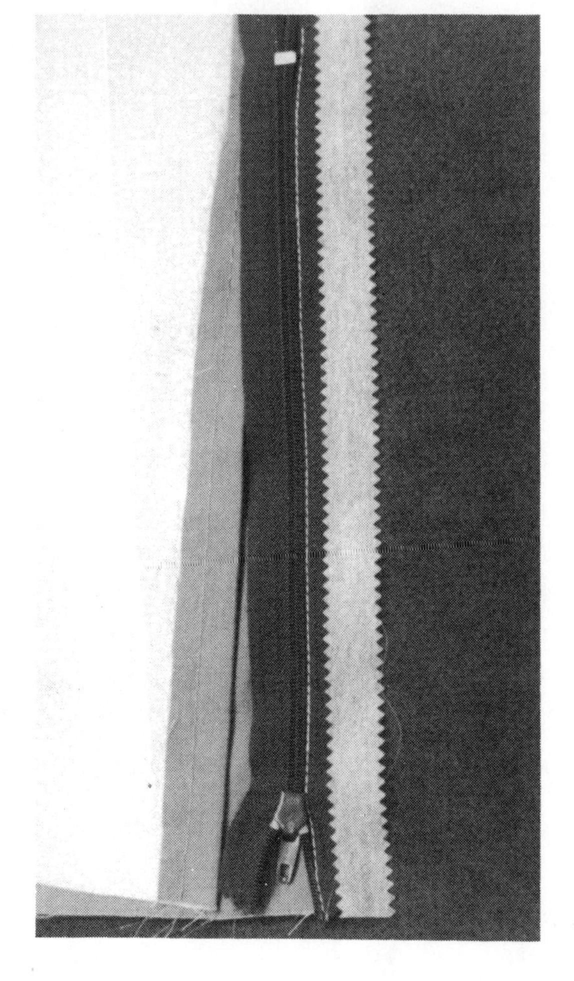

Extend the seam out flat and stitch the zipper tape to the seam allowance. The zipper is up and you are stitching through the zipper and the seam only. Stitch from the bottom to the top, breaking the stitching to move the pull tab. When the pull tab is in the way, stop and cut the thread. Pull the tab down out of the way and begin stitching a bit below the stopping point. This way you stay uniformly close to the zipper teeth. There is no stitching line showing on the right side of the garment. The picture is shown as the fabric should lie at the sewing machine. When the zipper is stitched, check to make sure you still have the 1/8″ pleat at the bottom of the zipper. Then press so the zipper is lying flat. The zipper should be 1/8″ from the marked seam line.

Lay the lapped side in place and baste or tape to hold. The left side laps 1/8" over the right side.

The seam lines are not marked with a thread trace in the picture. You can see how helpful it is to have them marked. The left side must lap over and just meet the seam line on the right side.

You can scotch tape the wrong side of the unstitched side of the zipper if you wish to have it held for you. In delicate fabric it is better to hand baste.

Putting a small piece of tape at the upper edge of the zipper helps to hold the zipper in place when you have lowered the pull tab.

Be sure the top edges of the garment are even.

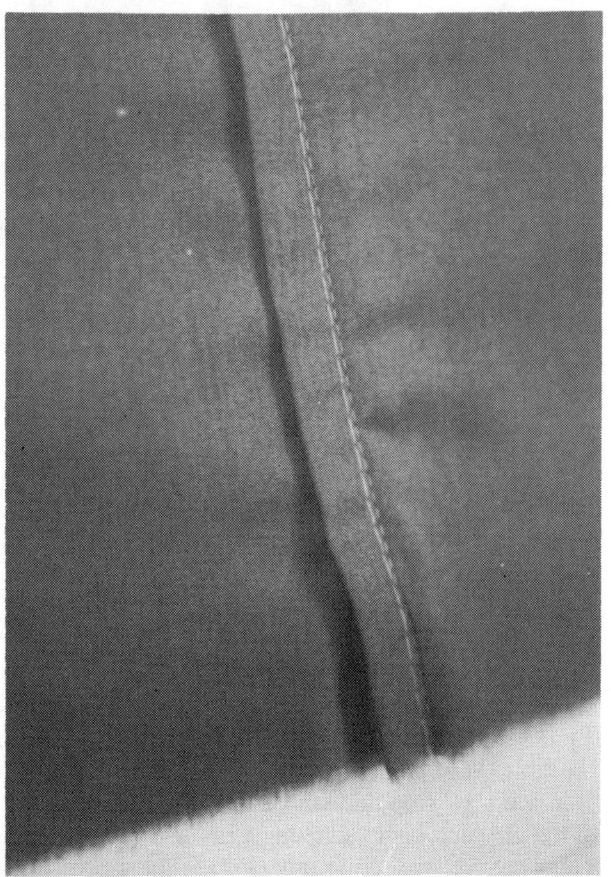

If the fabric is delicate, baste the folded edge to hold the zipper in place. Always tape the top to hold the zipper in place when you lower the pull tab.

On the right side, stitch from the bottom up with matching thread using the contrasting basting line as a guide. The picture shows the fabric lying as it would be at the sewing machine. Refer to page 81 for a couture finish.

Do not stitch across the bottom of the zipper. Often that will cause a bubble at the bottom. This is especially true in knit fabrics. Pull the thread through to the wrong side and tie.

Remove all bastings. Proceed with the garment. Refer to the pattern directions and the pertinent chapters of this book.

Couture finish

I always do a couture finish on a good garment. It shows less and though not quite as fast, is easier to get perfect than at the sewing machine.

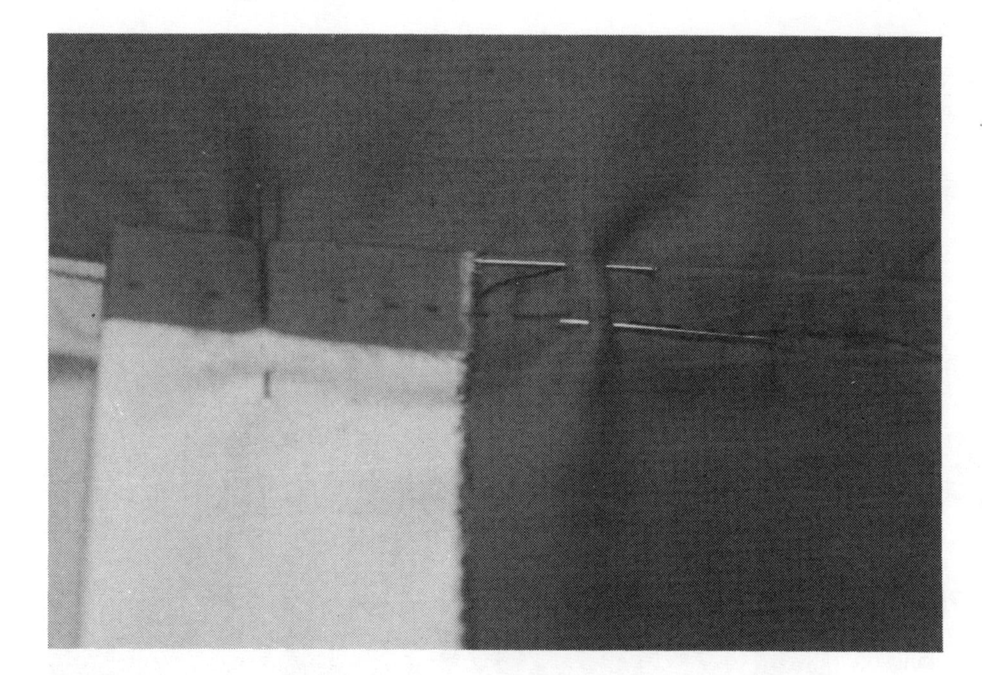

Handstitch the lapped side of the zipper using a small backstitch or a hand pick if you prefer. Use a narrow piece of tape 3/8″ from the folded edge if you need a solid guide line to keep your stitches straight.

Hand stitching is easier if you beeswax and iron your thread. The wax prevents the thread from knotting. Remove the basting and press.

Proceed with the garment. Refer to the pattern directions and the pertinent chapters of this book.

CENTER ZIPPER

Only use this zipper if the fabric is too bulky for a lapped zipper or the style dictates the use of a center zipper. This zipper is more difficult to apply and harder to hide the zipper. It is done the most adequately by hand.

Preparation For Center Zipper

Mark the length needed for the zipper opening. Mark the length of the zipper opening using the zipper itself as a guide. Do not go by the marking on the pattern. Zippers vary in length. A 7″ zipper is around 7″. The opening must be the exact length of the zipper plus whatever you need for the seam or for snap or hook at a neckline.

Neck opening: Hold the zipper pull tab about 1/2″ below the seamline to give space for a hanging snap or a hook and eye.

Skirt opening: Hold the zipper just slightly below the seam allowance.

Stitch the remaining seam. Be sure you have a minimum 5/8″ seam allowance. If you can cut a wider seam allowance in the zipper area, so much the better. Mark the seam line with a hand baste stitch before putting the zipper in. With the seam marked, it is easy to be accurate. When the zipper is in, the seam lines must be lying exactly together.

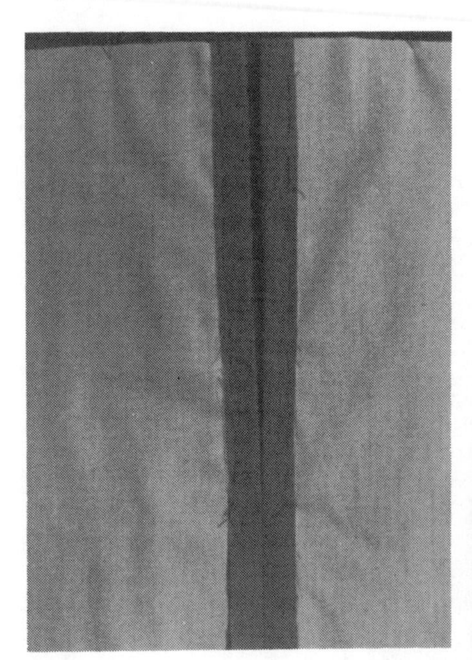

Do not press the seam allowance. Hand baste the seam line to hold it and leave it unpressed. If your fabric is stretchy, insert a seam tape in the seam allowance and hold it in place with the hand basting.

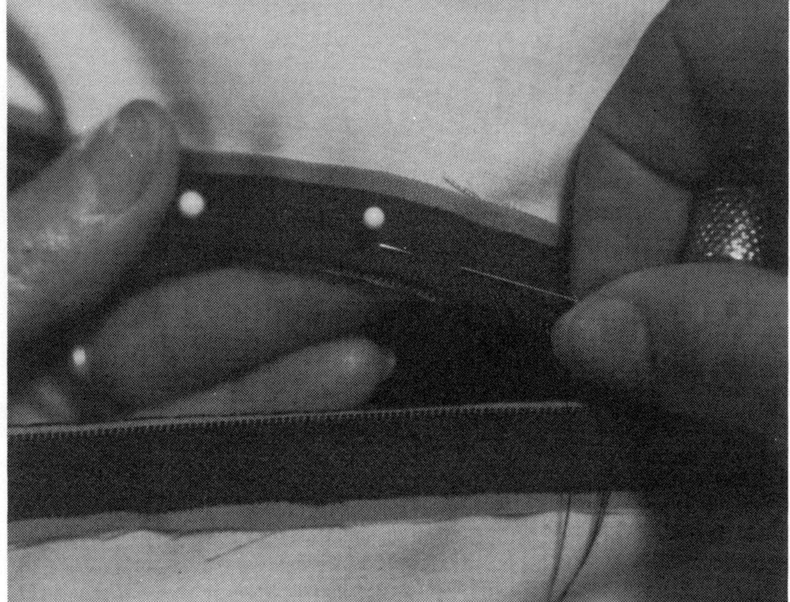

Stitch The Center Zipper

With the zipper open and working on the wrong side of the fabric, put the zipper teeth 1/16″ from the edge of the fabric and pin to hold. Baste firmly in place, removing pins as you go. Baste close to the zipper teeth.

Thread a short needle (size 10 betweens for quilting is good) with beeswaxed thread or 3 ply silk thread. Start with a knot on the wrong side.

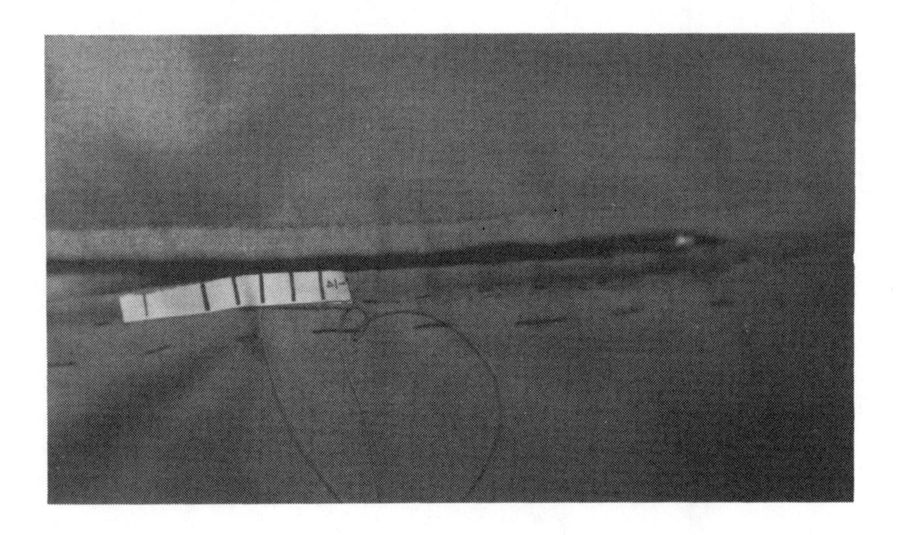

Place a 1/4″ wide piece of tape along the edge of the fold to give a straight line for the stitching. Bring the needle to the right side and stitch close to your basting. Do a backstitch or a small running stitch the length of the zipper.

For added strength, stitch the zipper tape to the seam allowance using cotton thread. Then press with the zipper open with a damp cloth. Be sure to keep the narrow fold of fabric along the zipper teeth.

Bar-tack at the bottom of the zipper with several small stitches. If the zipper tape is bulky where it folds back on the top of the zipper, cut it off at the zipper stop and hand overcast very closely to prevent raveling.

Remove all bastings. Proceed with the garment. Refer to the pattern directions and the pertinent chapters of this book.

COUTURE ZIPPER APPLICATION

The zipper goes up into the waistband. The pull never shows and there isn't that funny little bulge at the top of the zipper. Put the waistband on the skirt before the zipper is put in the skirt. The extension end is always on the top of the waistband with this application.

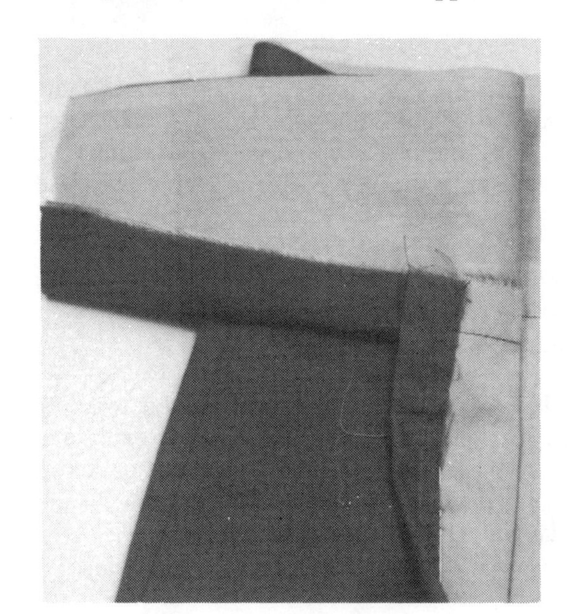

On the **lapped (left) side** of the skirt, fold the seam allowance under 5/8″ and stitch across it when you put the waistband on the skirt. Put the waistband on the skirt, matching the center front, side seams, and center back. The extension end of the band must be on the left side of the skirt.

The **unlapped (right) side** of the cut edge of the waistband must be even with the cut edge of the skirt seam allowance.

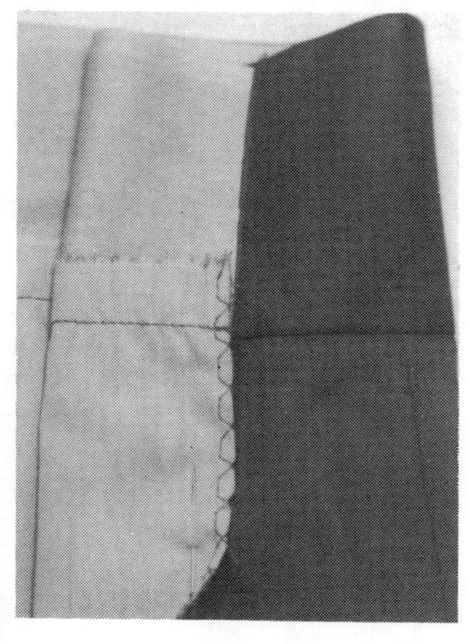

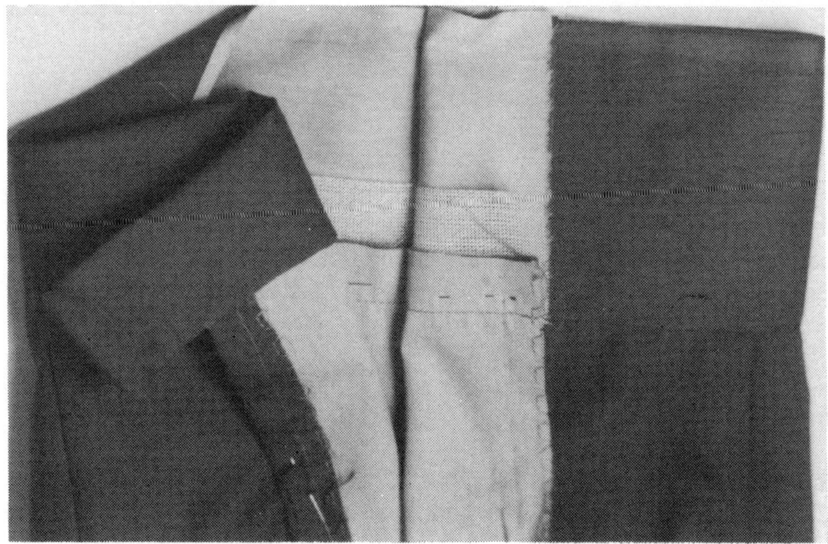

Put the waistband on the skirt. Interface the waistband. Stitch and turn the extension end of the waistband.

Put the zipper in following the **lapped** (page 77) or **center zipper** (page 81) instructions. Keep the tab of the zipper slightly below the top of the waistband. I usually do the unlapped side of the zipper by machine and hand stitch the lapped side. After the zipper is in, put the lining in if the skirt is to be lined. You must hold the lining to the edge of the zipper tape.

Continue with the skirt construction. Refer to Skirts, page 49. A skirt hook, snap fastener, or small hook and eye will hold the extension end in place.

UNIQUE ZIPPER

The zipper itself is made differently from other zippers. Use this zipper **only** in heavier fabrics or it does show and looks terrible. The fabric in the picture below is not quite heavy enough to support the zipper. It shows just a little instead of looking like a seam line. The unique zipper is a fairly stiff, heavy zipper so the fabric must be heavy, stiff, or bulky to support the zipper. Example: Velvets, double knits, heavy wools, and Ultrasuede. Use it in place of the lapped or center zipper in those heavy fabrics.

This zipper looks like a seam. There is no stitching on the right side of the fabric. Only the little pull tab shows on the right side of the garment.

You must have a special foot for your machine to apply this zipper. The foot is a short shank so anyone with long shank feet on his or her machine will need an adapter to help that foot fit the machine. Most sewing machines come with an adapter.

Instructions for the zipper foot.

Be sure the needle is exactly in the center of the foot. Use the groove on the right side of the foot to stitch the right side of the zipper and the groove on the left side of the foot to stitch the left side of the zipper. The groove fits over the zipper teeth and the needle goes into the zipper tape very close to the zipper teeth. Do not try to stitch any seams other than the zipper itself with this foot. Change back to the regular sewing foot to close the seam after the zipper is in.

Preparation For The Unique Zipper

Leave the seam open. If it is an opening with a facing, hold the pull tab 1/2″ below the seam line to allow room for a hanging snap or hook and eye. If it is an opening with a waistband, hold the pull tab just below the seam line. Mark the seam line with a machine baste.

Stitch The Unique Zipper

Lay the zipper right side down on the right side of the fabric. Place the zipper teeth on the 5/8″ seam line with the edge of the zipper tape next to the cut edge of the fabric. Pin the zipper to the fabric at the top and bottom. Then tape the zipper along the seam. The tape keeps the zipper from scooting on the fabric and if your fabric is a knit, the tape stabilizes the knit.

Using the special zipper foot for the Unique zipper, stitch from the top down until you are stopped by the pull tab. Make sure the needle is on the zipper tape side of the zipper. Hold the zipper taut while you are stitching.

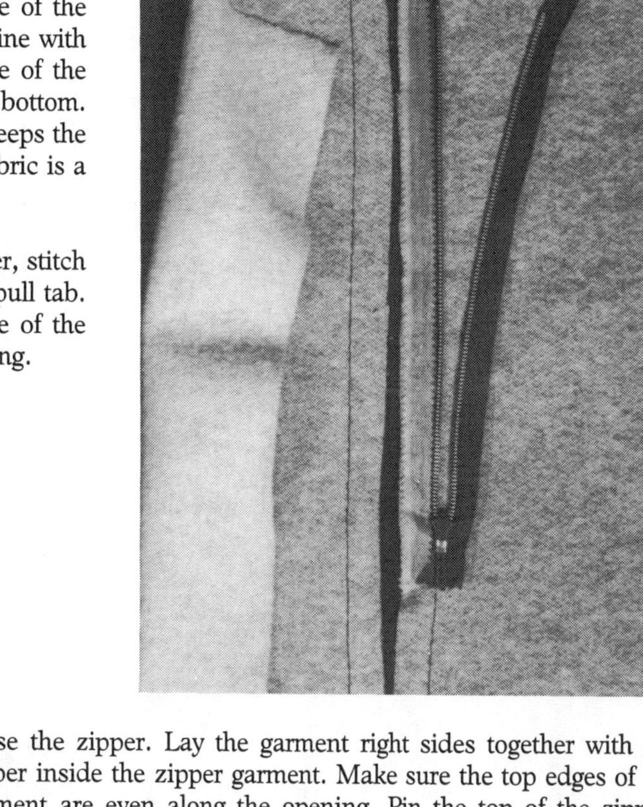

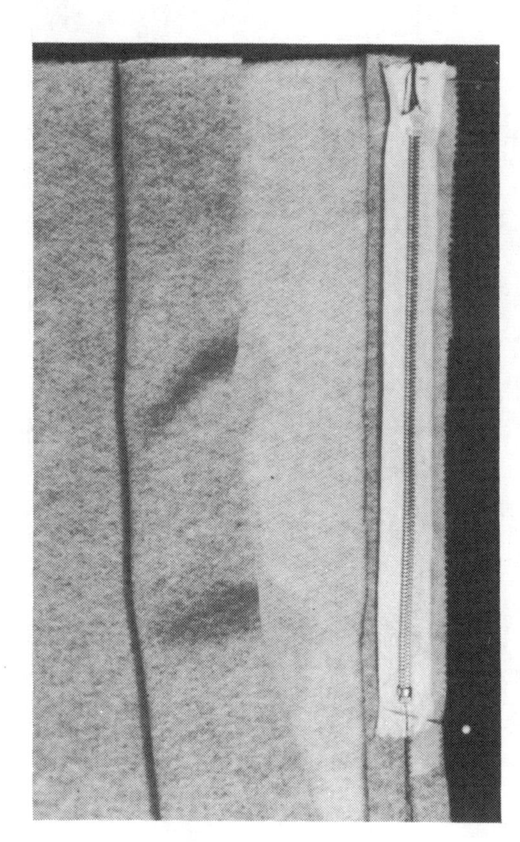

Close the zipper. Lay the garment right sides together with the zipper inside the zipper garment. Make sure the top edges of the garment are even along the opening. Pin the top of the zipper. Open the zipper. Put the zipper teeth on the 5/8″ line. Pin the bottom of the zipper. Then tape the zipper to the seam.

Stitch from the top to the bottom as before. This time you will use the opposite groove in the foot. Make sure the needle is on the zipper tape side of the zipper.

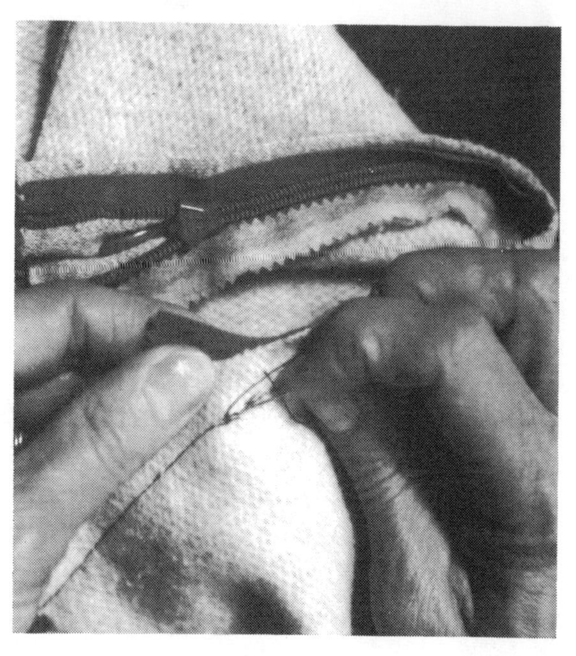

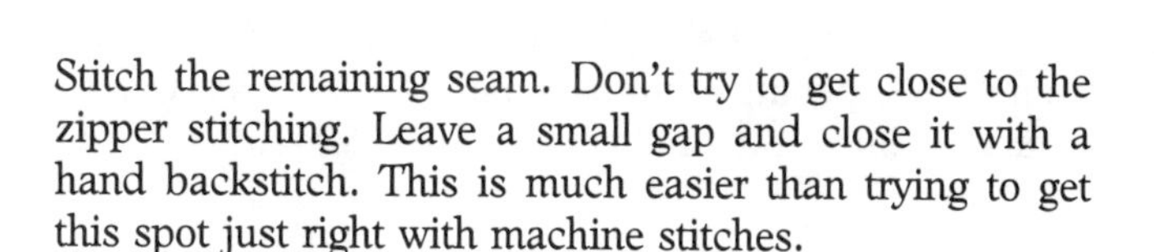

Stitch the remaining seam. Don't try to get close to the zipper stitching. Leave a small gap and close it with a hand backstitch. This is much easier than trying to get this spot just right with machine stitches.

Proceed with the garment. If you have neck facings, follow the instructions for the center zipper. Refer to page 76.

FLY FRONT ZIPPER

A fly front refers to the zipper opening on a pair of slacks or skirt. It is much easier to use a 9″ zipper for fly front openings. The pull tab is up out of the way when you are stitching the zipper. After the waistband has been stitched, cut off the excess length of the zipper.

Zipper guard pattern and fly front template

Most patterns do not have a zipper guard. A zipper guard is optional; however, most expensive slacks have one. A zipper guard does exactly that, it guards the zipper from excessive strain. If your pattern does not have one, make a trace of the cut-on facing and the curved stitching line on the slack front in the zipper area.

Trace from the fold line for the right side (center front) to the front edge of the pattern, and from the bottom of the curve to the waistline of the pattern. Label this piece "zipper guard". Cut one zipper guard of your fabric with the straight part of the curved edge on the selvage if possible.

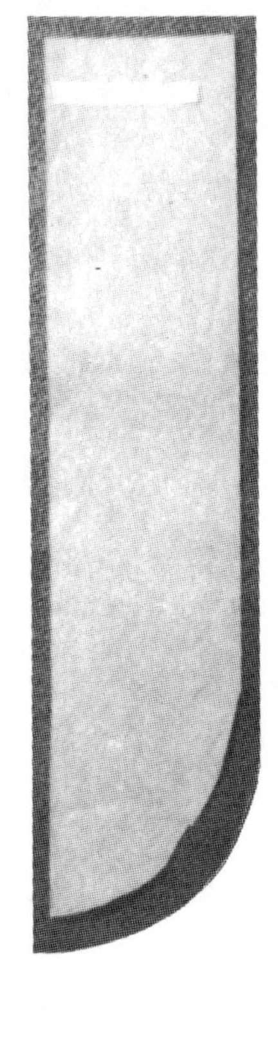

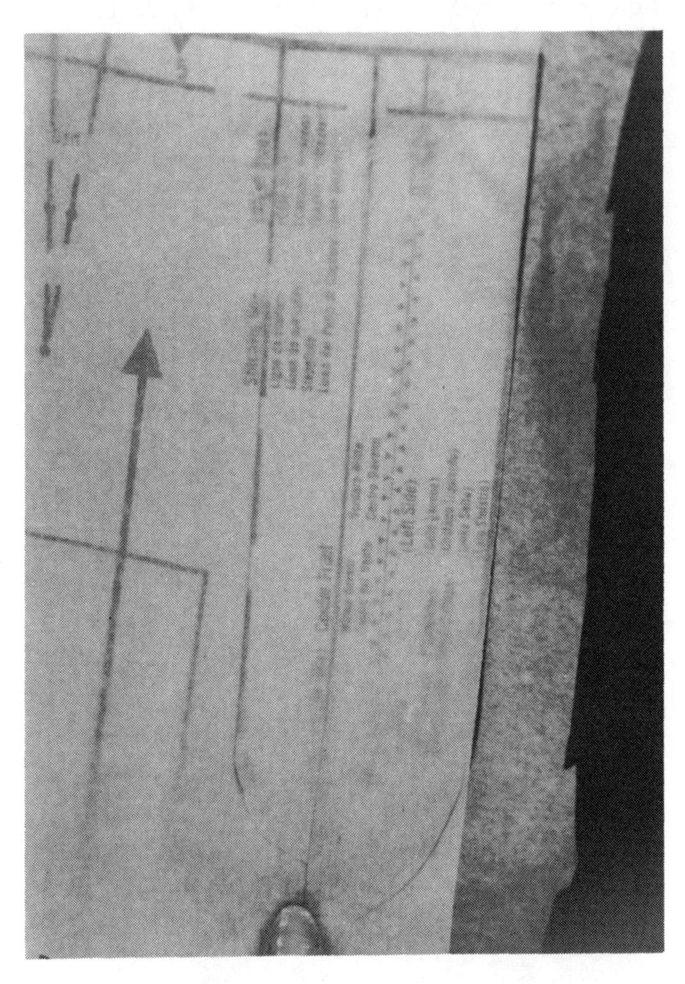

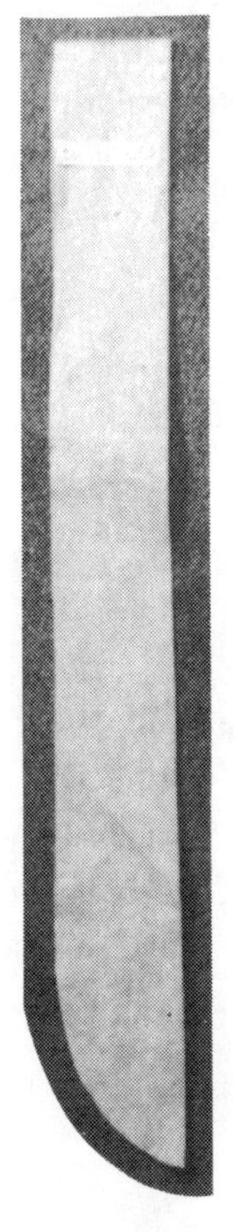

Also make a pattern for the curved stitching line on your slack front. Trace the center front and the curved stitching line from the bottom of the opening to the waistline of the slacks. Use this as a template for marking the curved stitching line on the right front of the slacks.

Preparation For Fly Front Zipper

Mark the center front on the right side of the **left** front of the slacks. Use pins, marking pencil, or a thread trace. I often use a tape measure when I am marking a seam. The tape is 5/8″ wide and is easy to mark along.

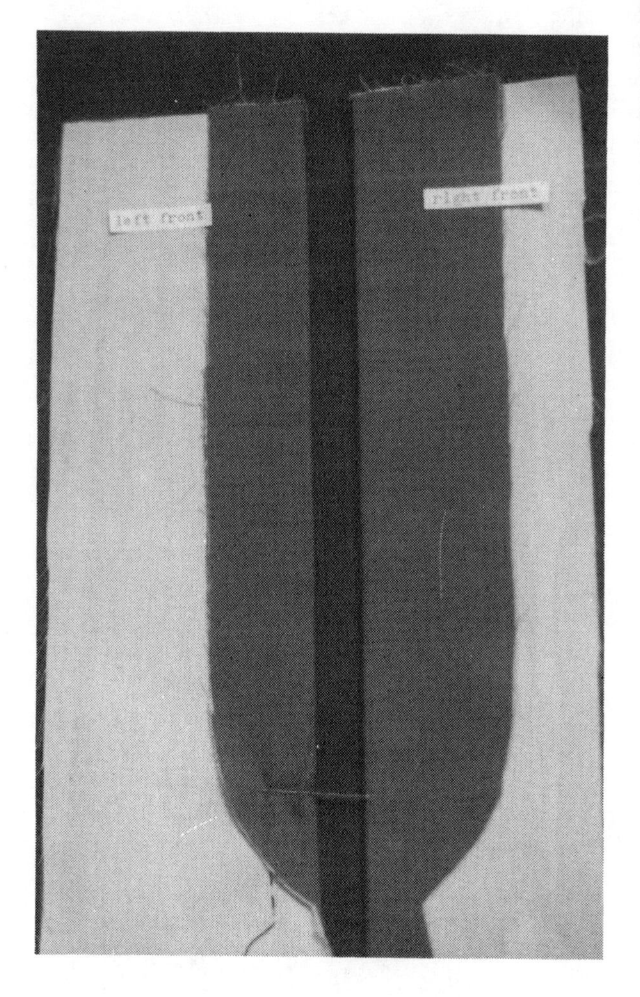

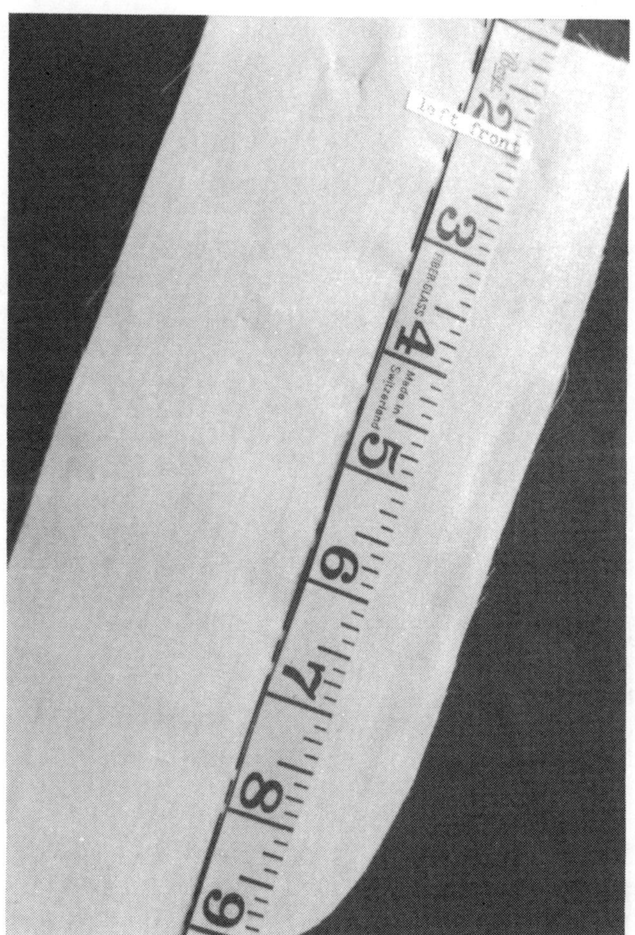

Press the cut-on facings to the wrong side of the slacks. Follow the lines marked on your pattern. On the **right front** press the facing back exactly on the center front. (On the Vogue basic this is 1⅝″ from cut edge of the facing and 5/8″ at the crotch just below the facing). On the **left front** press the facing back on the fold line marked for the left side. (On the Vogue basic this is 1⅛″ from the cut edge of the facing.)

On the **left front** mark the length of the zipper opening with a pin. Usually the zipper opening is 7⅝" to 8" from the top edge of the slack.

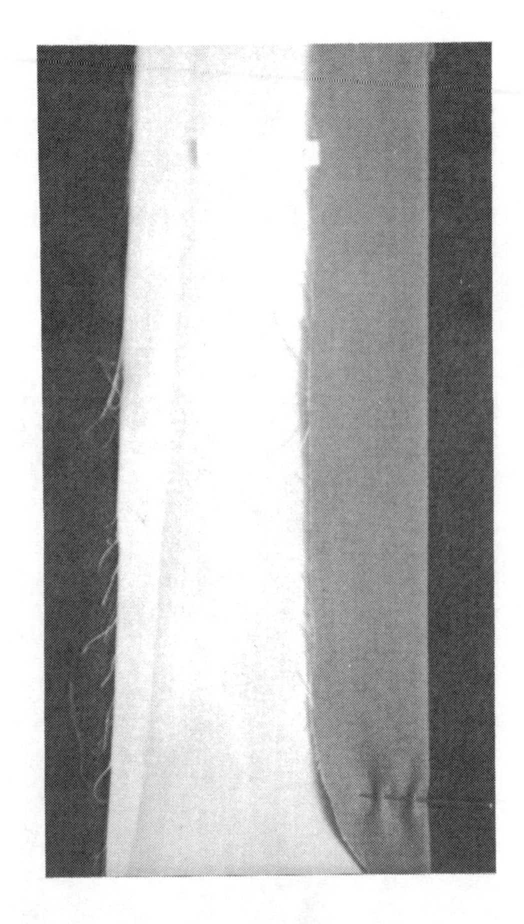

Stitch The Fly Front Zipper

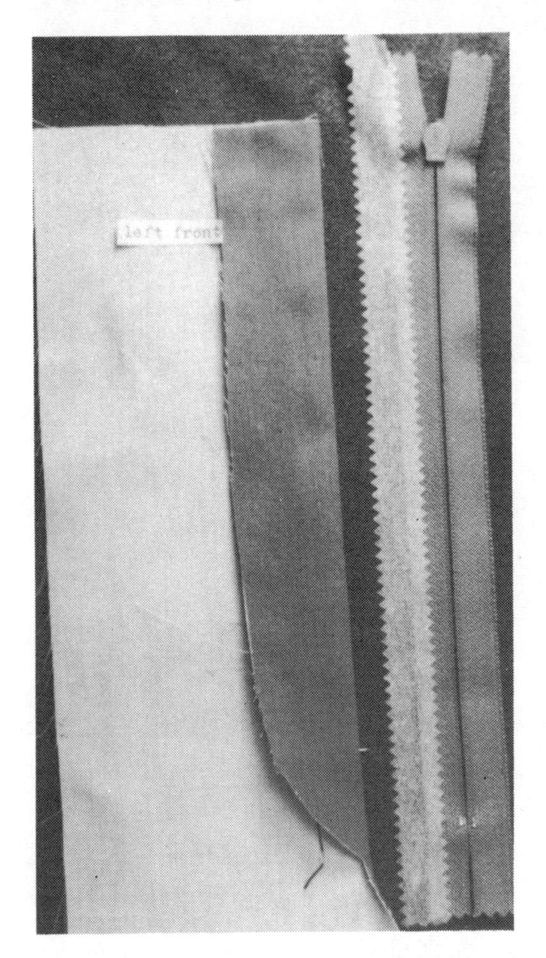

With the zipper top away from you, scotch tape the **left** edge of the **wrong** side of the zipper. Turn the zipper over so the sticky side of the tape is up.

Place the **left front** with the facing folded back along the zipper teeth. The pin marking the zipper length should be just above the metal stop at the bottom of the zipper. Press your fingers along the zipper. The tape will act as a quick baste.

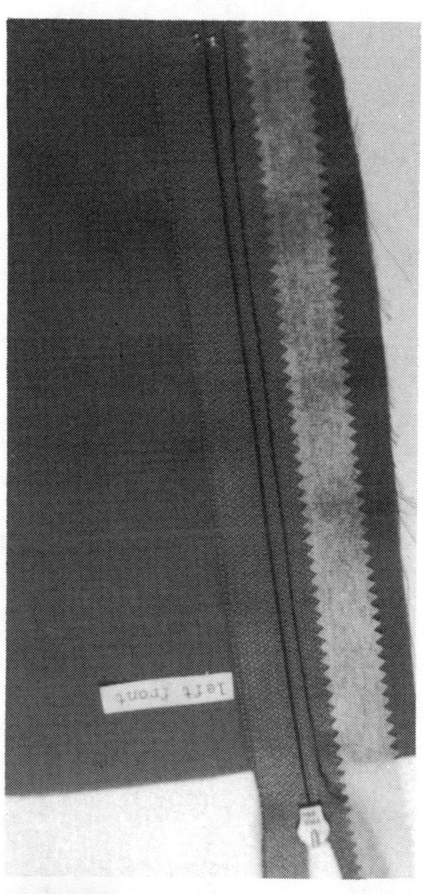

Extend the facing out. With the zipper foot on your machine, stitch the zipper to the facing close to the zipper teeth. Start stitching at the metal stop at the bottom of the zipper on the same side of the zipper as the scotch tape. Sew up to the top of the slacks. The picture shows the fabric lying as it would at the sewing machine.

Press the zipper as it will lie in the completed garment.

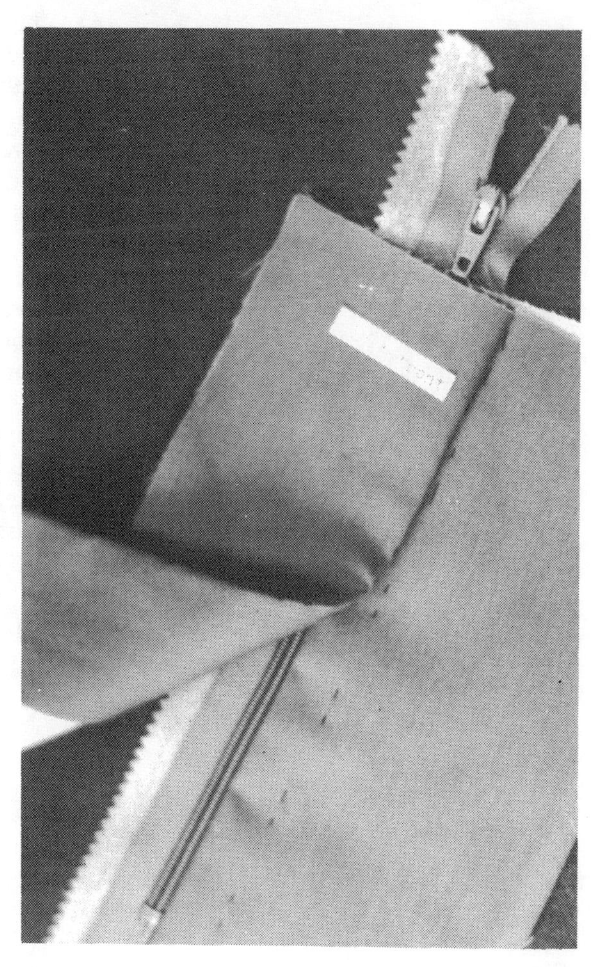

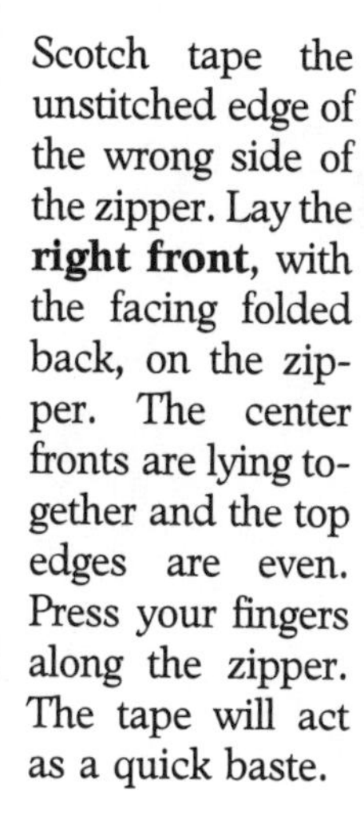

Scotch tape the unstitched edge of the wrong side of the zipper. Lay the **right front**, with the facing folded back, on the zipper. The center fronts are lying together and the top edges are even. Press your fingers along the zipper. The tape will act as a quick baste.

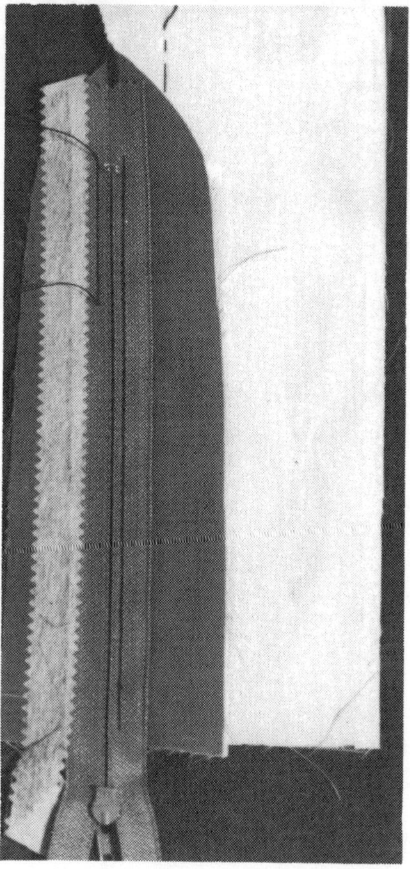

Lay the slacks, right sides together, with the zipper up. With the zipper foot on your machine, stitch the zipper to the facing. Start stitching at the metal stop at the bottom of the zipper on the same side as the tape. Stitch up to the top of the slacks.

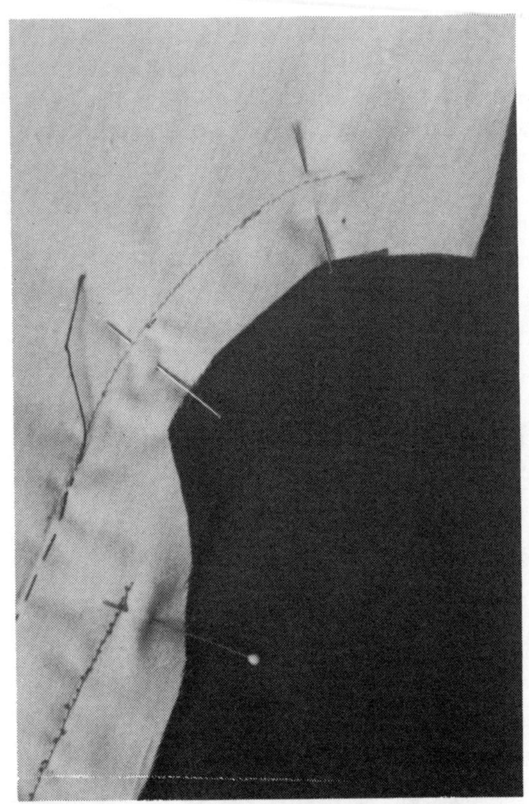

Pin the crotch seam of the slacks, lining up the edges of the crotch and the cut-on facing. Stitch the front crotch seam of the slacks, leaving about an inch open at the inseam so you can later attach the back leg. Backstitch at the square marking the end of the zipper opening. Use the regular foot on your machine. I often double stitch this seam.

Lay the template of the curved stitching line on the slacks with the straight edge on center front. Be careful to extend the end of the curve just below the metal stop at the bottom of the zipper. Hand baste then machine stitch along the curved line through all thicknesses. It is a temptation to skip the hand basting. The layers slip, so do hand baste.

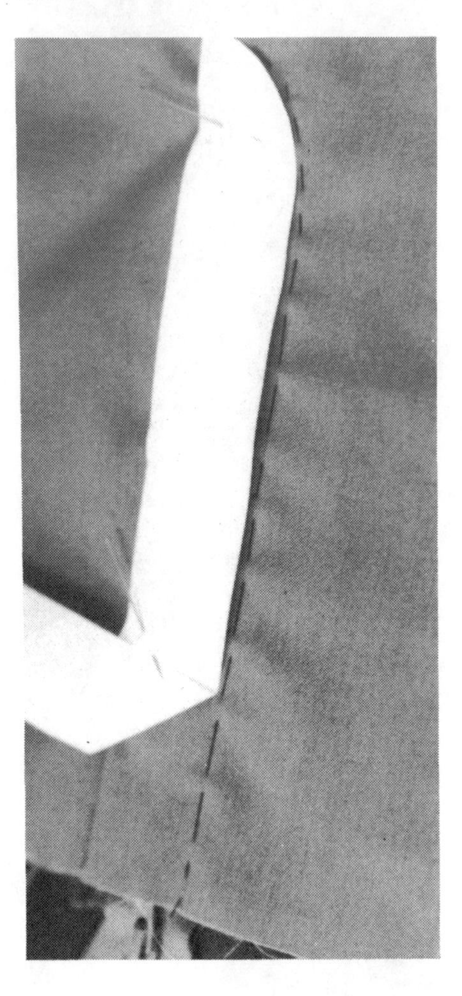

Optional zipper guard

Trim the excess facing of the **left front** to a 5/8″ seam. Lay the zipper guard on top of the wrong side of the zipper and stitch the zipper guard to the seam allowance. Use a zig-zag or an overcast stitch to finish the raw edge.

Lay the slacks right side up and stitch along the zipper on the **left** front. You are stitching through the slack front, the zipper, and the facing. This holds the zipper and the zipper guard flat.

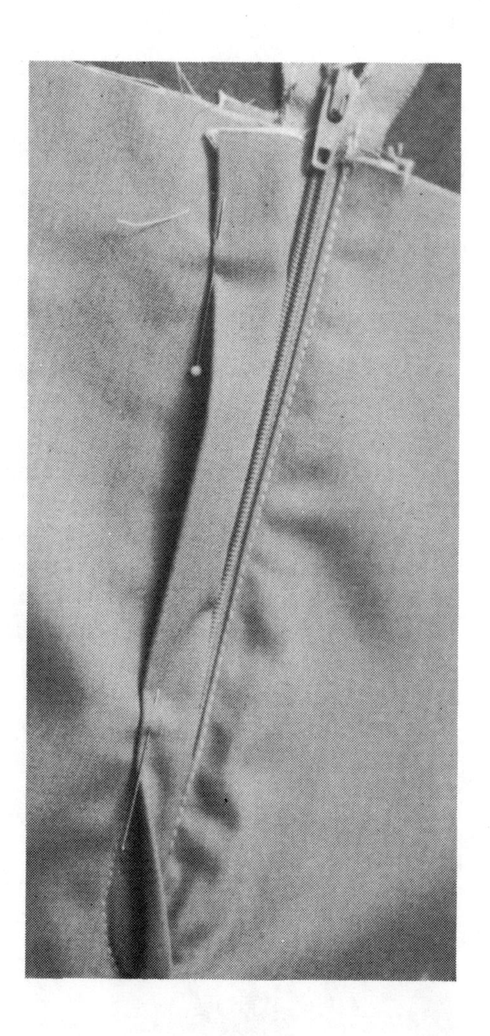

Open the zipper and hold the zipper guard and the facing together. Pin and stitch them together at the spot near the bottom of the zipper where the strain will be taken from the zipper when you put on and take off the slacks.

Continue with the construction of the slacks. Refer to Slacks, page 58.

GATHERING

Gathering is the process of drawing a given amount of fabric into a smaller area to create soft, even folds. This would seem like a simple enough procedure but many of my students find gathering difficult. Check your pattern instructions for areas to be gathered. Do all the gathering the pattern calls for at the same time. If your fabric is lightweight, gathering can be done over the seams after they have been stitched, finished, and pressed. If your fabric is medium to heavy weight, follow the pattern instructions for gathering before seams are stitched.

Stitch Length, Tension and Thread

The stitch length for gathering is longer and the upper thread tension is looser than usual. I don't find it necessary to change the tension on the Bernina machines, only the stitch length. It helps to test both tension and stitch length on a fabric scrap. Stitch length varies from 6-12 stitches per inch. Shorter stitches for sheer or lightweight fabrics and longer stitches for thick, heavy, or firm fabrics. The shorter the stitch length, the more control you have in gathering. The bobbin thread is the thread that should be pulled, and a looser upper tension makes it easier to slide the fabric along the thread. If you pull both the bobbin and the top thread, your stitch will lock and you will not be able to pull either the top or the bottom thread to gather the fabric. Be careful and pull only the bobbin thread.

Using a different color thread in the bobbin helps to identify the correct thread to pull and helps to use up old thread. Gathering all the areas of a garment at the same time speeds up your sewing.

On the right side of the fabric, stitch two parallel rows. The first row is stitched one thread width below the seam line and the second row is stitched 1/4″ higher (into the seam allowance). Leave thread ends long for pulling and DO NOT backstitch.

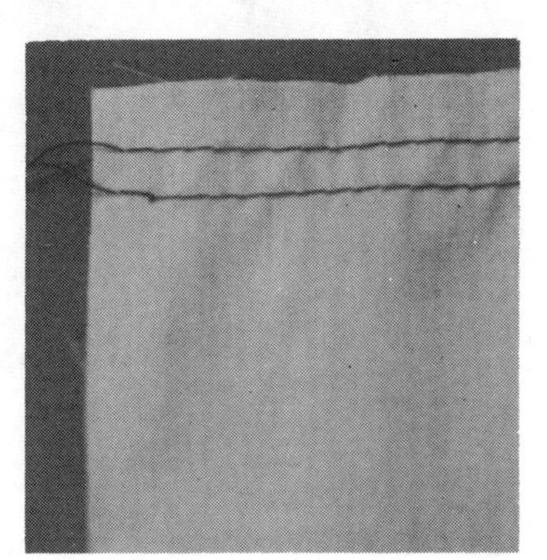

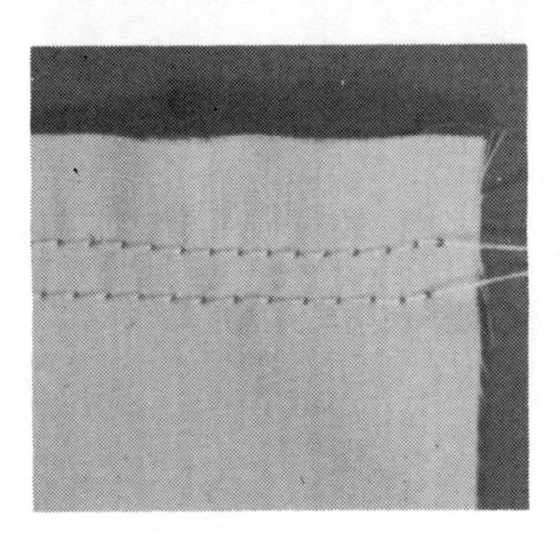

For heavy fabric or extensive gathering, use an extra strong thread in the bobbin. You usually must loosen the bobbin tension to use a heavier thread.

You can also use a small zig-zag stitch over a strong cord to gather. However, this method does not give as much control over the gathers as regular stitching. The gathering is not as fine as with regular stitching.

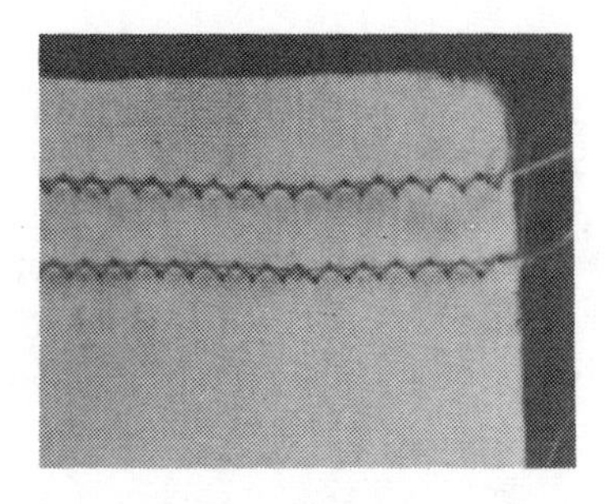

If your fabric is heavy, break the stitching at the seams leaving them free. If the fabric is lightweight, stitch over the seams. Usually, pockets and pleats are held free and are not gathered.

Gathering The Fabric

Pin the gathered area to the corresponding flat area, right sides together, matching seams, notches, and centers.

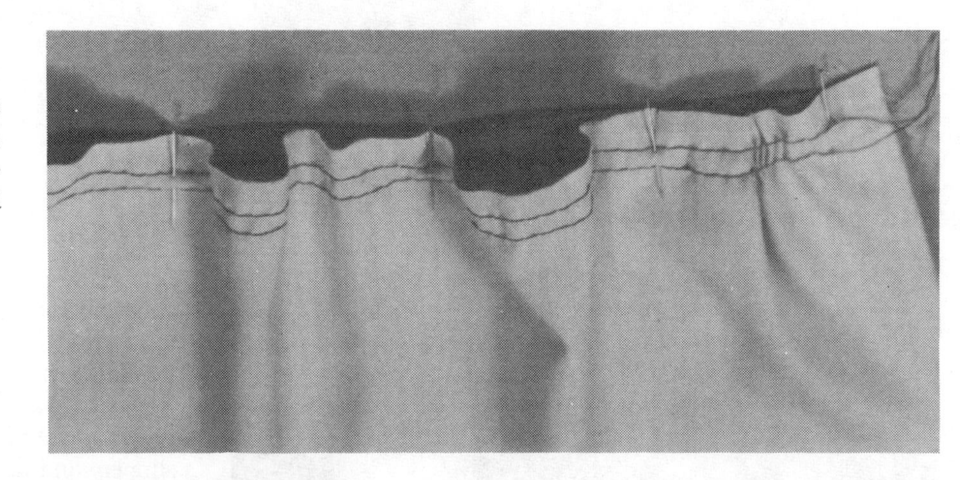

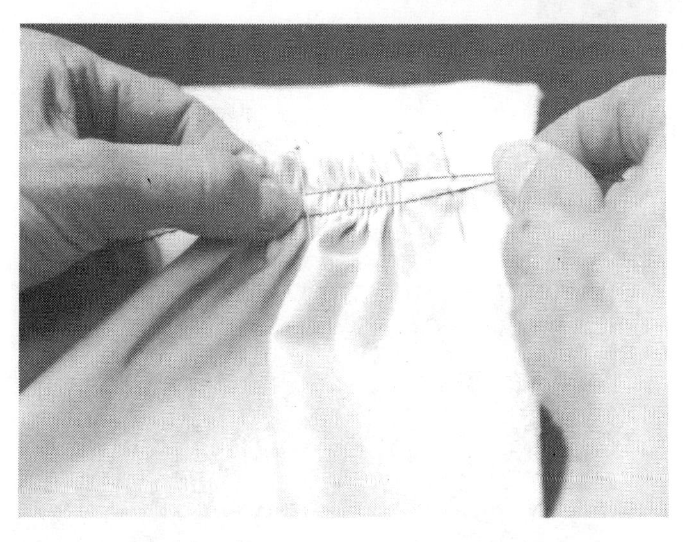

Pull the bobbin threads of both rows of gathering together, slipping the fabric gently along the bobbin threads. Be careful not to pull the upper thread, which locks the stitch, and makes it impossible to gather the fabric.

If you are unlucky enough to break your thread or lock it, it is best to remove the whole piece and re-stitch it. If you try to start and stop, it makes gathering a very difficult, time-consuming task with poor results.

Pull the bobbin threads from one end to the center until the gathered area is a bit smaller than the flat corresponding area. Secure the thread ends by wrapping around a pin in a tight figure 8. Use the same procedure from the other end to the center.

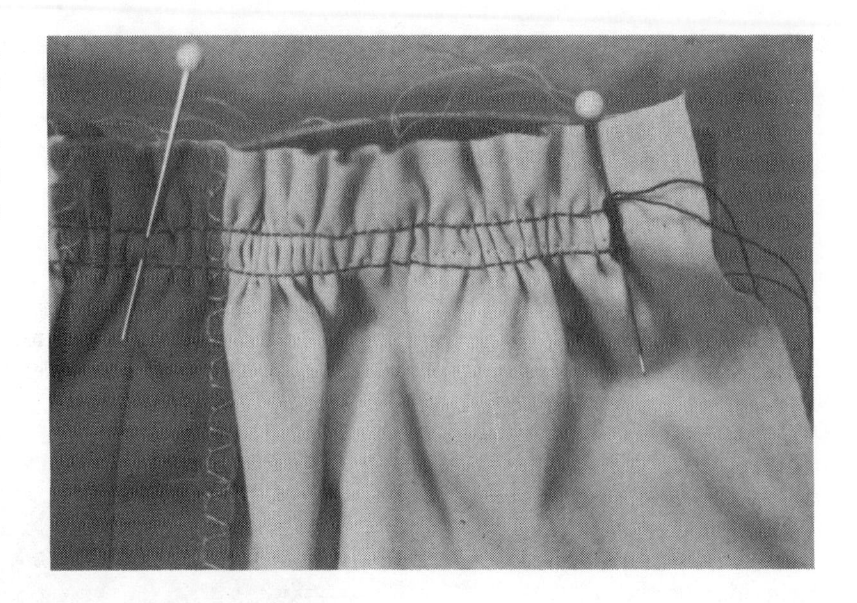

Stitching The Gathered Seam

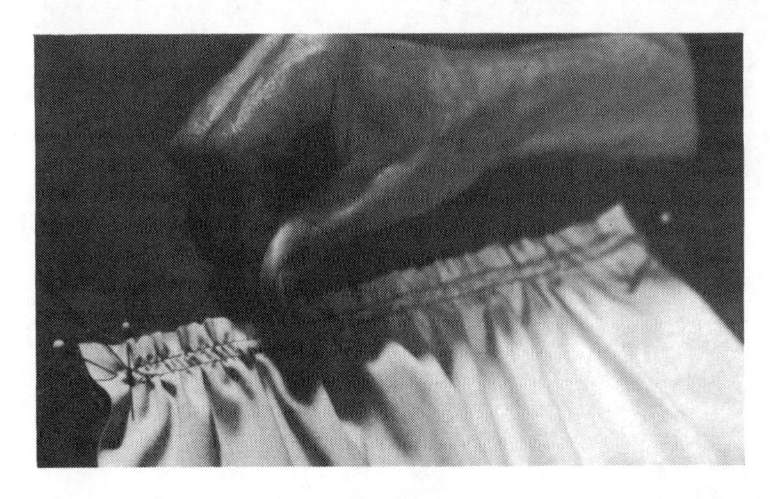

Adjust the gathers uniformly with a pin or your fingernail. It helps to fasten your work to a cutting board or ironing board. Pin at frequent intervals to hold the folds in place. You can hand baste before stitching if you prefer. I only hand baste if my fabric is slippery and difficult to handle.

Set the machine stitch back to normal stitch length, change the bobbin thread back to the matching color, and stitch with the gathered area up. Hold the fabric on either side of the needle so the gathers will not be stitched in uneven pleats. Stitch on the seam line, between the rows of gathering, one thread width away from the first (deeper) row of gathering.

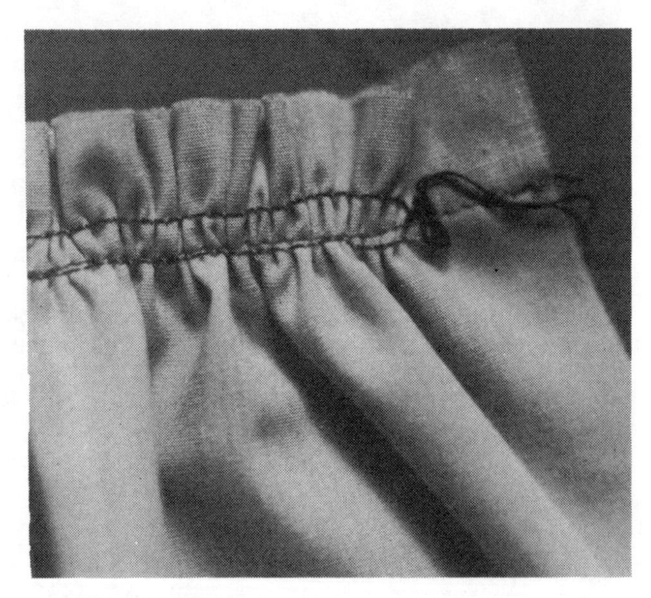

Press the seam allowance using the tip of the iron. Don't press the gathers below the seam allowance. Finish the edge of the seam. Sometimes you must use a different seam finish on a gathered seam. Do a sample seam to test for the best seam finish. Press the seam as it will lie in the garment.

Remove the gathering stitch that shows on the right side of the garment. The remaining row of gathering can be left in or taken out.

Staying A Gathered Seam

A lightweight stay can be of woven seam tape (rayon seam tape with no woven lines is the best lightweight stay) or unpuckered selvage of the fabric. Twill tape or grosgrain ribbon works fine for medium to heavy weight stays. Use a lightweight stay in lightweight fabric, and a heavier stay in medium and heavy weight fabrics. If the gathered area is attached to a bias area (example: a shoulder seam), stay the bias area before attaching the gathered fabric to it. Use your pattern tissue as a guide for the length of the stay.

Lay the edge of the stay just below the seam line. Baste it in place. Woven seam tape or selvage of your fabric works best for this application.

After the stay is basted in place, stitch the gathered piece to the stayed section with the gathered part up, catching the stay in the permanent stitching line.

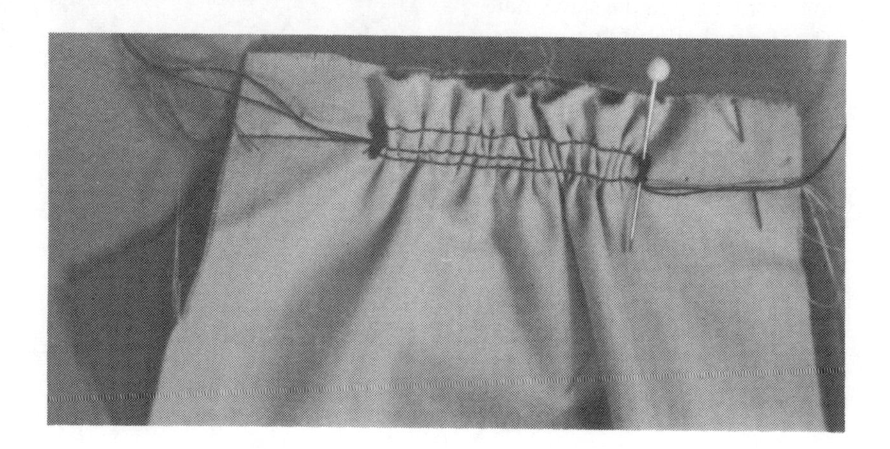

Often a gathered area (example: the waistline of a dress) is stayed after the pieces are stitched together.

Lay the edge of the stay next to the permanent stitching line, over the gathers, straight stitch close to the lower edge of the stay, through all thickness. Trim the seam allowance even with the top edge of the stay tape. If the fabric ravels, overcast or zigzag the top edge of the fabric to the stay. If the stay is used at the waistline of a buttoned or zippered garment, leave one end long enough so it can be fastened inside the garment to hold the waistline at the opening.

Easing

Often the pattern will call for you to ease an area. This is accomplished in much the same manner as gathering except you do not have any folds in the fabric (example: elbow area, sleeve cap, waistline). Some areas such as waistlines call for easing, but it is usually not necessary to do any easing stitch. Hold the fabric rolled over your fingers with the area to be eased on top. Refer to Tailoring, page 294. Just the difference in the turn of cloth with the smaller area under on a small curve eases a surprising amount. If that doesn't work, it is necessary to put in an easing stitch.

Do the stitching in the same manner as for gathering. Often one row on the 5/8" seam line is sufficient instead of two rows of stitching. Pull on the bobbin thread till the fabric is gathered up, then ease all the fullness back out again.

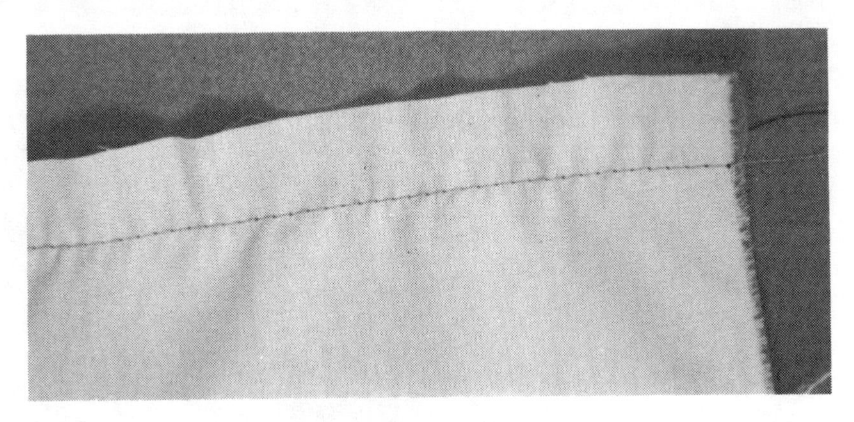

Pin it to the corresponding piece. Stitch them together and remove the easing stitch.

HEMS

The hem is the last detail on a garment. A beautifully done hem is never seen. A badly-done hem looks terrible and on a handmade garment says, "Loving hands at home."

To achieve a good hem

- Reduce extra fullness.
- Eliminate the bulk.
- Press carefully to prevent ridges.
- **Never** pull the stitches tight.

Hem Depth

The normal hem is 2½" deep, 3" is maximum in a straight skirt. The fuller (flared) the skirt the narrower the hem. If the hem is in a very full skirt or a sheer fabric, the depth will vary from 1/4" to 1" for a circular skirt and as narrow as 1/8" or as wide as 6" for a straight full chiffon overskirt. If the skirt has any bias areas, it should hang at least overnight to let the bias set and to prevent the hem from sagging after it is hemmed.

Marking A Hem

When marking a hem, wear the garment with a belt if it is called for. Wear the proper undergarments and a heel the height you will wear with the garment. Stand straight with arms down and with your weight on both feet. Try to stand still.

The most accurate marking is done by a helper using a hem marker or a yardstick. Put pins at regular intervals around the hem, 3"-4" apart for a full flared skirt and 5"-6" apart for a straight skirt.

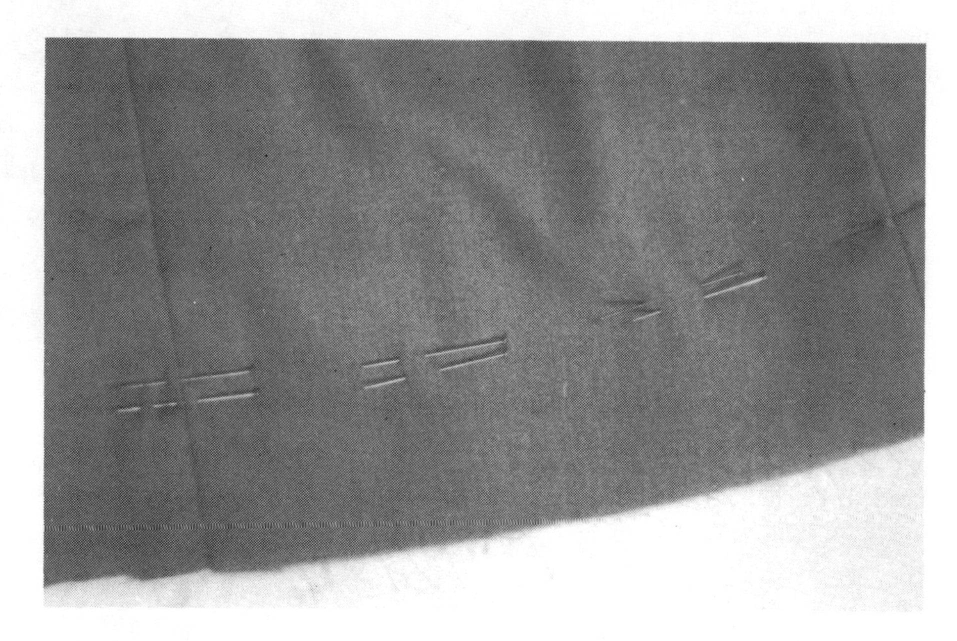

Take the garment off and lower the pins 1/4" at center back. Taper to the marked hem line at the side seams. For coats or long skirts, lower 1/2" at center back and taper to 1/8" at the side seams and to the hem turn at center front.

Your hems will always look better if you do this lowering. Often when someone sees you from across a room you are leaning slightly forward and your garments will appear to be shorter in the back. Slightly longer in the back is a very flattering look anytime.

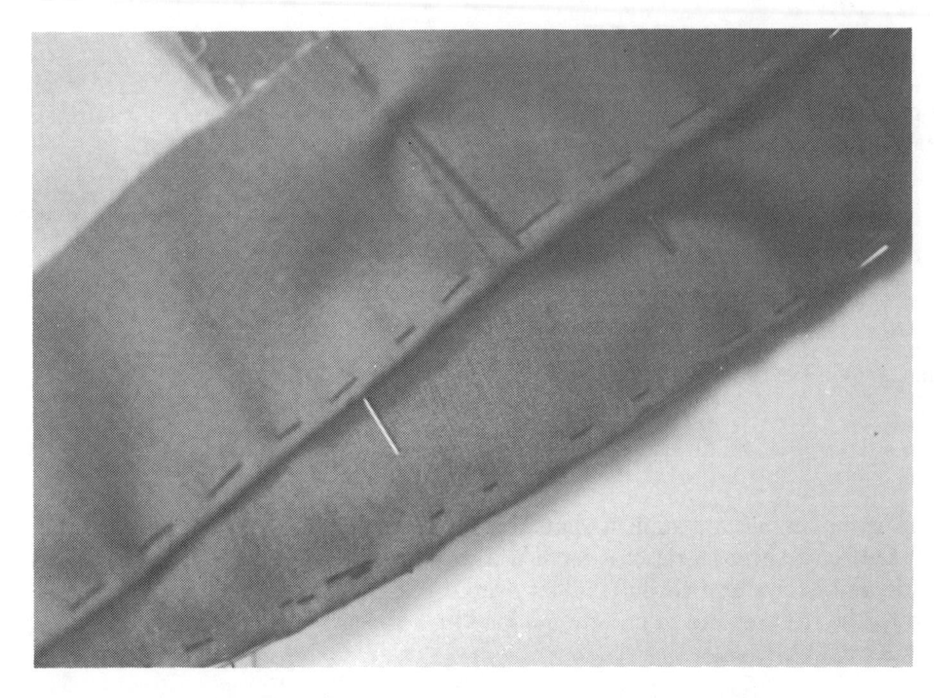

Fold the hem to the wrong side along the pin line. Make sure the curve is an even-flowing line with no abrupt ups or downs. If a pin causes an abrupt up or down, ignore that pin. Hand baste close to the edge of the hem fold. Pin up the excess hem and try the garment on to make sure the hem is hanging straight and you are happy with the length.

Mark the desired width of the hem as discussed earlier and trim the excess fabric away. The hem should be the same width around the entire skirt. Let the narrowest area determine the width if you have a narrow amount for the hem. If that is too narrow, you can add Seams Great (bias sheer tricot) or some of your fabric as a facing. It is always better to allow enough for an adequate hem when you cut the garment.

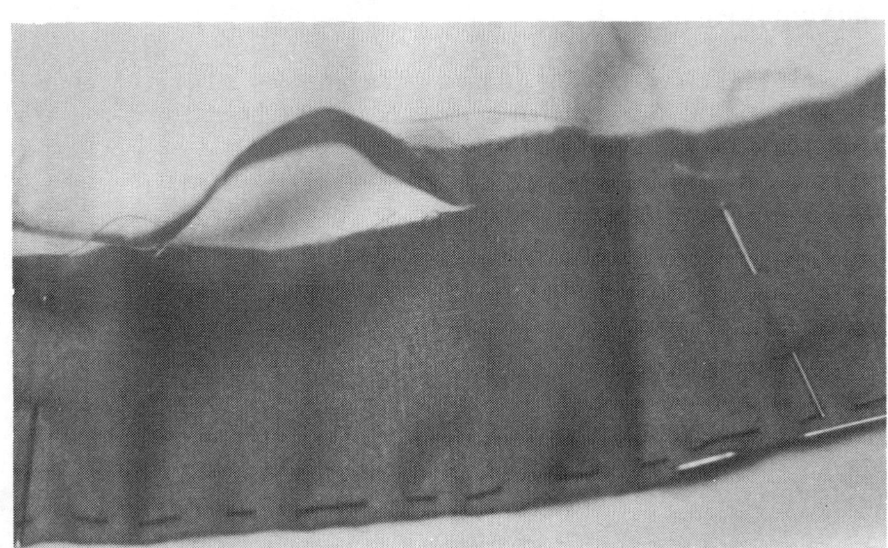

Ease in the fullness on flared skirts

My favorite method is ease-plussing. Ease-plus without any thread in the machine. Several rows can be done if needed. The more flared the skirt, the more rows you should do. Begin about 3/4" from the hem turn and work out to the edge.

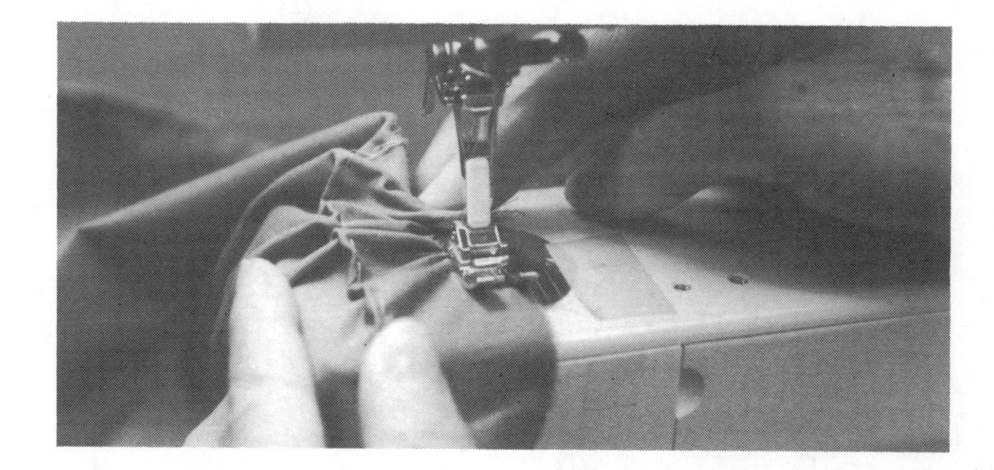

To ease-plus, hold your finger firmly behind the pressure foot and sew through the hem only, letting the fabric pile up between the foot and your finger. This eases in the hem fullness.

If your fabric is stubborn, do the last row of ease-plus at the hem edge with thread in the machine. For very stubborn fabrics, it may be necessary to use a gathering thread to ease the excess, but usually ease-plussing works great.

Eliminate the bulk

Grade the seam allowances in the hem line if the fabric is bulky. One disadvantage to grading the side seam seam allowance in the hem turn is that you can no longer let the garment out. You must decide if it would be best to have a little extra bulk in the hem so that you could let the garment out in the future.

If the hem is curved and full, you may need to take a deeper seam in any seam lines in the hem area to reduce extra fullness. Take the seam in the deepest on the hem edge and taper to nothing 1/4" from the hem line. This is a last resort measure to reduce fullness in the hem turn and only works if the garment has several seams and is quite shaped.

Press carefully to prevent ridges

Press lightly with steam to shrink in the excess. I prefer a soft hem in most garments. A hand baste line close to the hem fold will hold the hem turn until the hem is in. Then I press lightly. I never make a hard crease on a hem unless I have pleats and they must be pressed with a crisp edge. Use a paper between the hem and the garment to buffer the hem edge. Pin the hem in place. Let any excess fullness go where it wants to. If you try to move it, it will show. When you are hemming, let the little pleats hang loose. If you fasten them down, they show.

Finish The Edge Of The Hem

Test for the easiest and best finish on a scrap of your fabric and press as you will press the hem. I try the fastest finish first and, if that shows, then I try others until I find the best finish for the fabric. If a ridge shows on the right side of the sample hem when it is lightly pressed, try another of the methods discussed here. I never use seam tape or lace on the edge of a hem. They do show through when the garment is pressed at the cleaners. The finest finish is a hand overcast. The next finish to try is the serged edge. Then the machine overcast. I rarely turn under the raw edge because it usually shows. However, sometimes a double thickness on a very lightweight or sheer fabric will look the best. A Hong Kong finish (refer to Seam Finishes, page 71) is lovely but it is often too heavy, even using Seams Great.

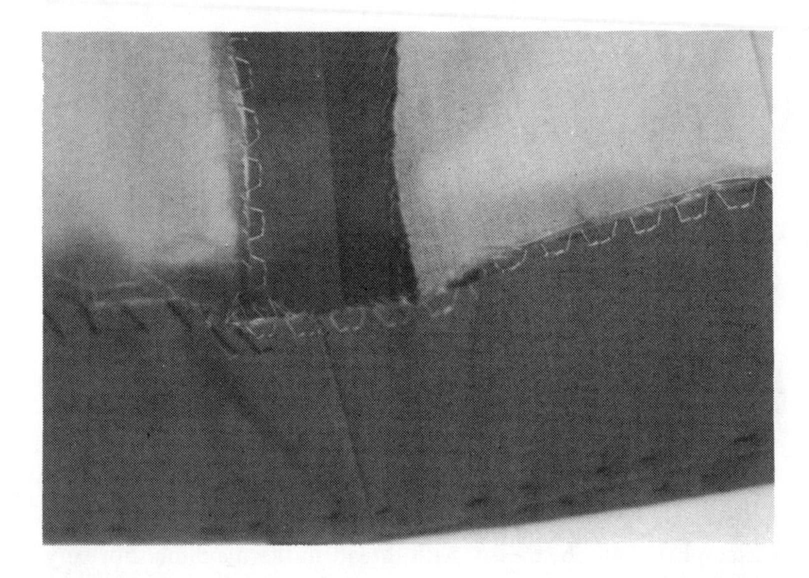

A machine overcast will work nicely on many fabrics. The finest finish is a hand overcast. Do this anytime the machine overcast shows through when you press. Refer to Seam Finishes, page 69.

A hand overcast can be done quite fast by wrapping your needle around the edge of the fabric and taking several stitches, then pulling the stitches through and adjusting a bit so the edge is lying flat. Refer to Seam Finishes, page 68.

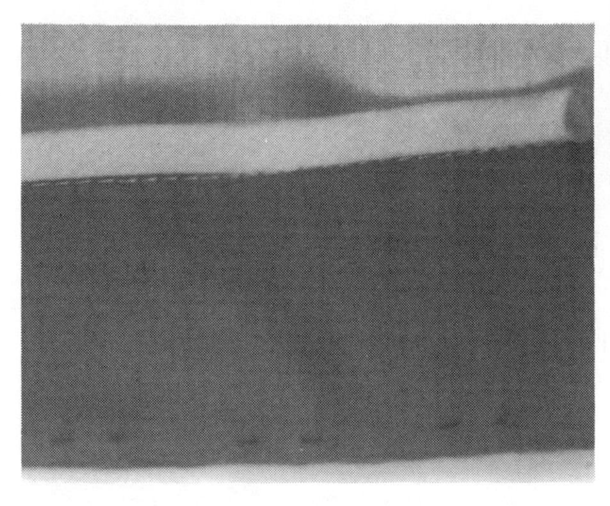

A Hong Kong finish can be used if you finished the other seams in that manner and if it is not too heavy to cause a ridge when it is pressed. Refer to Seam Finishes, page 71.

Hand Stitching The Hem

Most hems are best done by hand, but on some knits and everyday garments a machine hem is fine. The blind hemming stitch on your sewing machine will work here. For dressy garments of good fabric, the hem should be done by hand. Use a small needle (a quilting needle size, 9 or 10, or an embroidery needle, size 5-8), beeswax the thread, then press it for hand stitching. The beeswax helps eliminate knotting. Refer to page 220. Beeswax and press enough thread to do the hem. Don't make your pieces too long. Sit in a comfortable chair. Handstitching a hem takes time and is easier to do if you are comfortable.

The stitches are taken inside, between the hem and the garment. In the finished hem, no stitches are visible and the edge of the hem does not press into the garment. It helps to fasten the garment to a table or your knee. This acts as a third hand to hold the garment so you are pulling against it. Hold the hem in your left hand at right angles to your body. Work toward yourself. Fold the edge of the hem back 1/8″-1/4″ and fasten the thread inside on the hem. Take a very small stitch 1/4″ toward you in the hem. Take the next stitch 1/4″ toward you in the garment. Continue to alternate stitches from hem to garment, spacing them 1/4″-1/2″ apart. **Don't pull the stitches tight.** Only catch a thread or two in the garment. Your stitches in the hem can be larger. To make the hem stronger you can take a securing stitch every few inches in the hem. Be sure to leave any fullness (little pleats) loose.

Press the hem gently from the wrong side. I prefer a soft hem, so on most garments I never press the crease in. Just steam it and hand pat the hem fold.

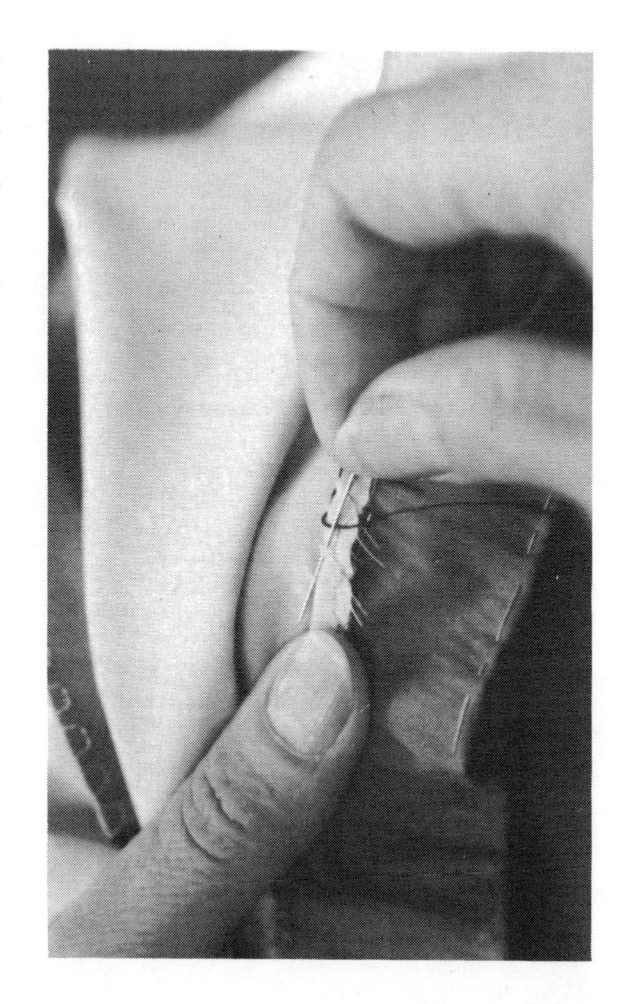

Narrow Machine Hems

A narrow machine hem is fine for some garments. It is especially good for circle skirts and for blouse hems. Many purchased garments, even silk dresses, have this hem.

Mark the hem as usual if it is a skirt. Trim to 5/8″. Work on a flat surface, preferably one you can fasten your work to.

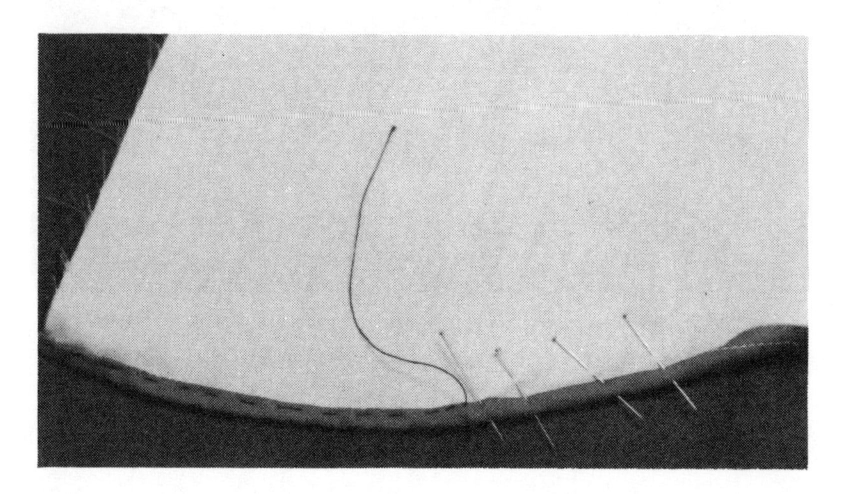

Roll about 1/4″ of fabric to the wrong side. Roll again, keeping the raw edge tight against the fold. If you have difficulty rolling evenly, machine stitch a scant 1/4″ from the edge. Roll the edge till the stitching doesn't show, then roll again. Pin and, for best results, hand baste before you machine stitch. Basting is especially important on a curved hem or if you are working with slippery fabric.

Designer's Fine Thin Hem

A designer's fine thin hem is especially nice for sheer fabric and for circle skirts or very full skirts.

Mark the length of the garment and trim to 5/8". Slip tissue paper under the fabric each time you stitch. Using matching thread, 15-20 stitches per inch, machine stitch around the lower edge of the skirt on the line marking the length. After stitching, carefully tear the paper away.

Turn up the lower edge to the stitching line. Stitch again just above the edge, always using tissue. Remove the paper.

Repeat, again stitching over paper. Stitch just above the last row of stitching. Remove the paper, then trim away the excess fabric as close as possible to the stitching line. Two rows of stitching do show on the right side of the garment.

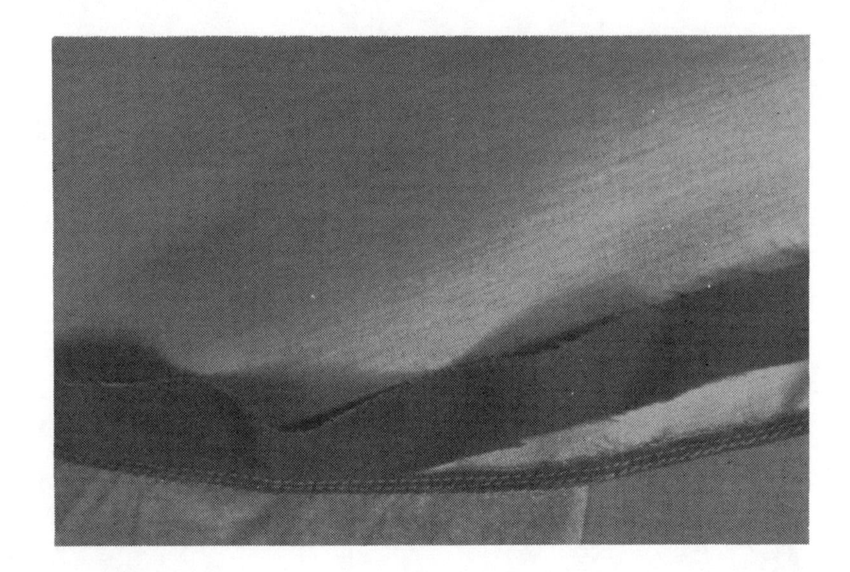

Sleeveless Garments ■ 4

SLEEVELESS GARMENTS WITH AN OPENING

Garments with a front or back opening

Vests, jumpers, and shell tops are easy and quick to line. The same technique can be used to finish the neckline and armholes if they are faced instead of lined and if they have a one-piece facing.

With the side seams unstitched, the neckline and armholes are stitched and pulled through the shoulder area. Then the hem is stitched and pulled through an opening in the side seam. This is possible because the garment is not a circle.

Pattern Adjustment For Facings

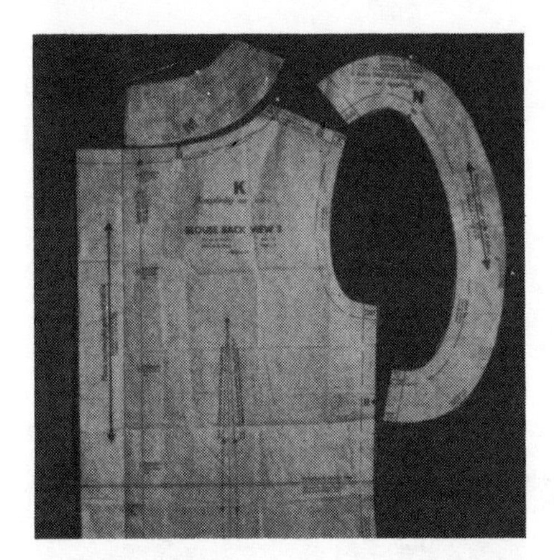

If the pattern gives a facing for the neckline and another facing for the armhole as in the picture, combine those facings and make one facing for the front of the pattern and one facing for the back of the pattern.

Changing the facing in this manner does require more fabric. Check to make sure you have adequate fabric before making the changes.

Lay the armhole facing on the pattern matching the armhole seam. Mark the shoulder line on the armhole piece and cut the armhole facing at the shoulder so that you have a back armhole facing and a front armhole facing. Lay them on the corresponding pattern pieces. Lay the neck facing on the pattern matching the neckline seam. Pin or tape them together where they lap.

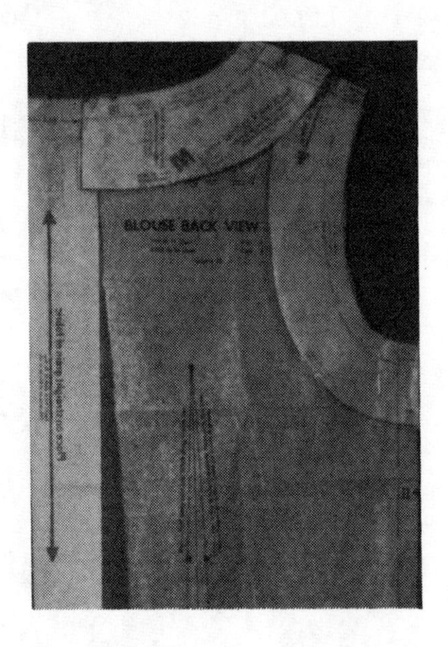

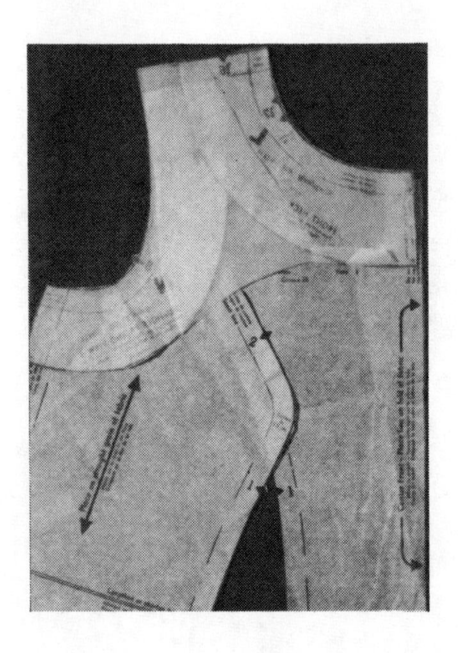

Put some tracing paper underneath and add a gentle curve on the outer edge of the facing. Add a seam allowance to the area on the shoulder that is missing a seam allowance.

Cut the garment and the new facing pieces of fashion fabric.

A few patterns are cut this way, but the directions are much different from those given here, especially the directions for garments with no openings.

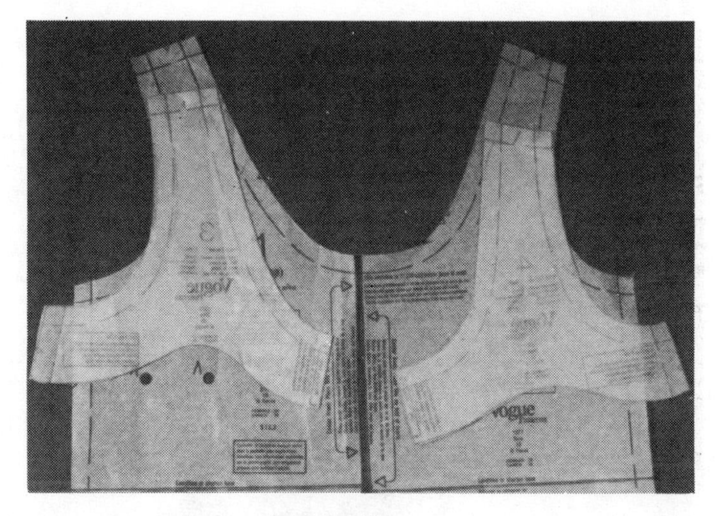

Pattern Adjustment For Lining Sleeveless Garments With An Opening

Lining to the Edge

If the pattern does not call for lining, but you would rather line the garment to the edge than use the facings, just eliminate the facings and cut the pattern again out of lining. This would line the garment to the edge all the way around.

Cut the garment once out of fashion fabric and once out of lining.

Pattern Adjustment For Lining With Facings

If the pattern does not call for lining, but you would rather line the garment and you want a facing under a button opening and around the neckline, make the following changes to both the front and back pattern pieces.

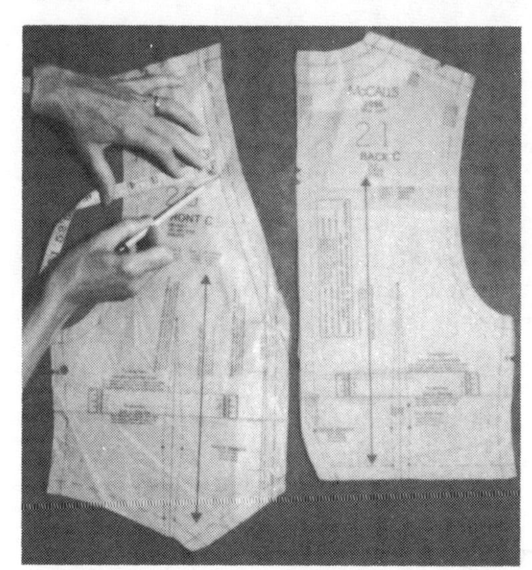

Lay the facing under the front pattern piece, matching the front edge, the neckline, and the shoulder line. Lay the back neck facing under the back pattern piece, matching the center back, the neckline, and the shoulder line.

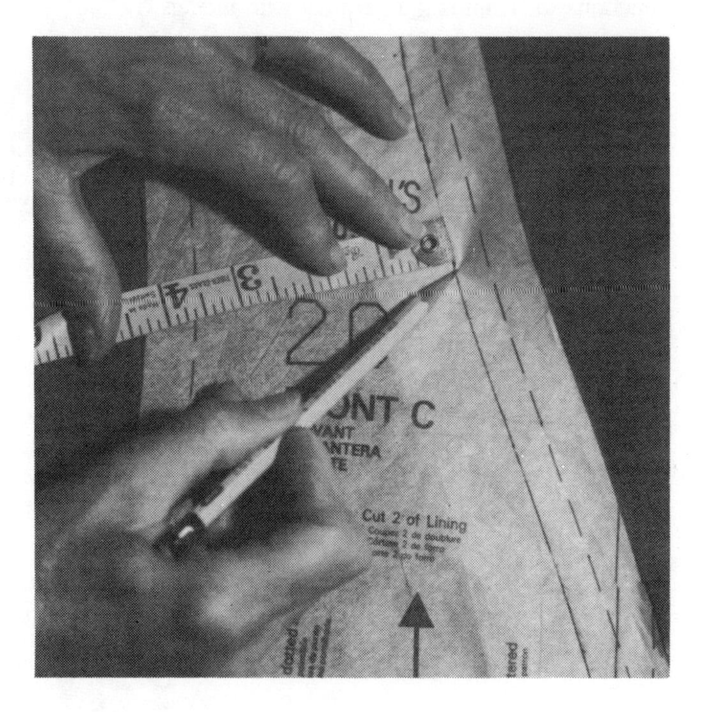

With a pencil and a measuring tape or a French curve, draw a line 1¼ inches from the inside edge of the facing (toward the neckline). Label this line the cutting line for lining. The 1¼ inches allows two 5/8″ seam allowances so you can stitch the facing to the lining. If the facing is narrow, use a smaller seam allowance. Mark 1/2″ from the facing edge. This would allow two 1/4″ seam allowances.

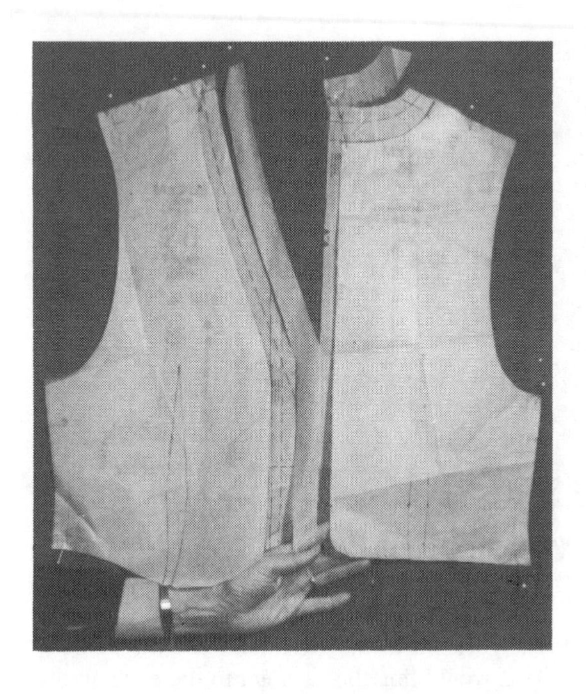

Make new pattern pieces for the lining by laying the front and back pattern pieces on tracing paper and cutting around all the edges. Mark the cutting line for the lining on the tracing paper copy and cut on that line. This is your lining pattern piece. The picture shows the lining pattern pieces with the areas to be cut already cut off.

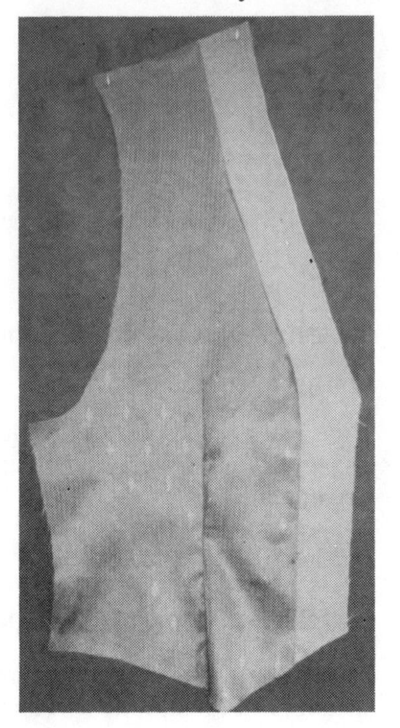

Cut the garment and facing of fashion fabric as the pattern layout shows. Cut the lining using the pattern pieces you made.

Stitch the facing to the lining on the new seam line you have created and proceed with lining the garment as follows.

Constructing Garments With A Front Or Back Opening

The stitching procedure using facings or a lining is the same for the neckline and armholes. Follow the pattern directions for hemming a garment with facings.

Stitch the garment as the shoulder seam. Stitch the lining or facings together at the shoulder line. Press the seams open.

Lay the garment and the lining or facings right sides together, and **stitch** the garment and the lining or facings together around the neckline and down the front or back opening. If there is a pointed hem line, stitch around the point so that it is easy to turn.

Trim the neckline and center front seam to 1/4″. If you have a facing instead of just a lining, grade the seam if your fabric is medium to heavy weight. Grading is cutting the layer of fabric that lies closest to the garment to 3/8″ and cutting the under layer to 1/4″.

Clip the neckline seam and stagger the clips on the facing and the garment.

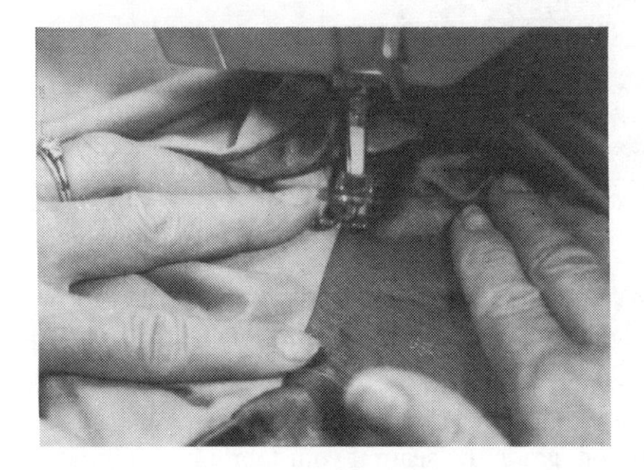

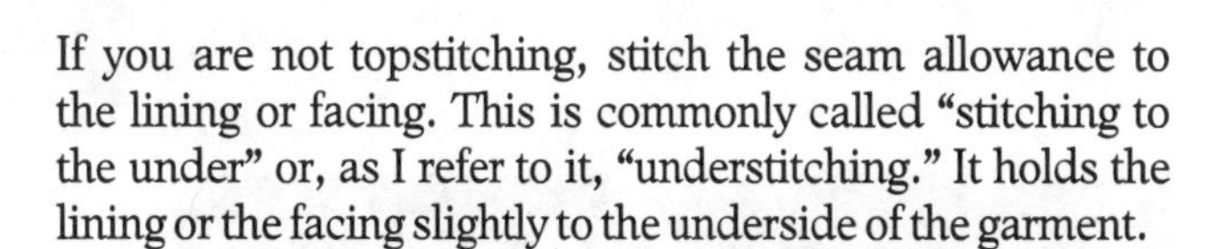

If you are not topstitching, stitch the seam allowance to the lining or facing. This is commonly called "stitching to the under" or, as I refer to it, "understitching." It holds the lining or the facing slightly to the underside of the garment.

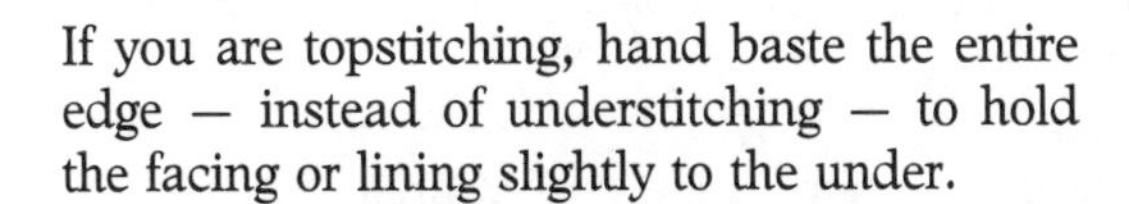

If you are topstitching, hand baste the entire edge — instead of understitching — to hold the facing or lining slightly to the under.

Press the neckline and front opening seams flat as they should be on the finished garment.

(The vest in the picture is understitched.)

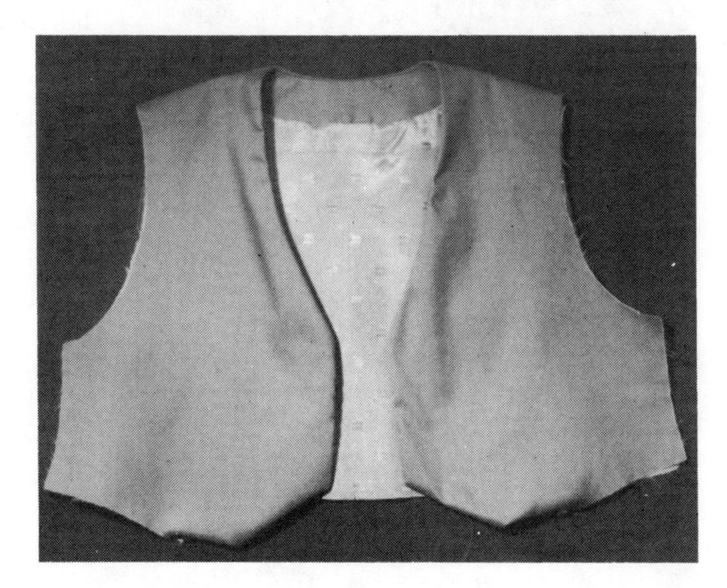

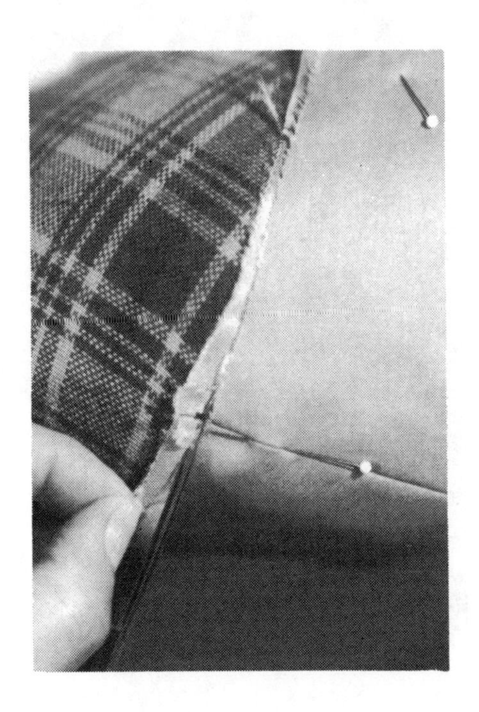

Pin around the upper part of the armhole. Do you have excess lining or facing extending past the garment armhole? If so, trim just the area that has the excess. Trim another 1/16″ off the shoulder and down into the curve of the armhole. Do not trim around the entire armhole. This trimming will accommodate the turn of cloth and keeps the lining or facing slightly to the under on both the neckline and the armhole. If you do not trim that small amount as well as trimming to make the edges even, the lining will end up too large at the shoulder area to remain underneath.

Lay the right side of the garment on the right side of facing or lining, matching the shoulder seams and side seams. Pin from the shoulder seam to the side seams on both the front and back of the garment, matching the fabric edges. Stitch around the armhole.

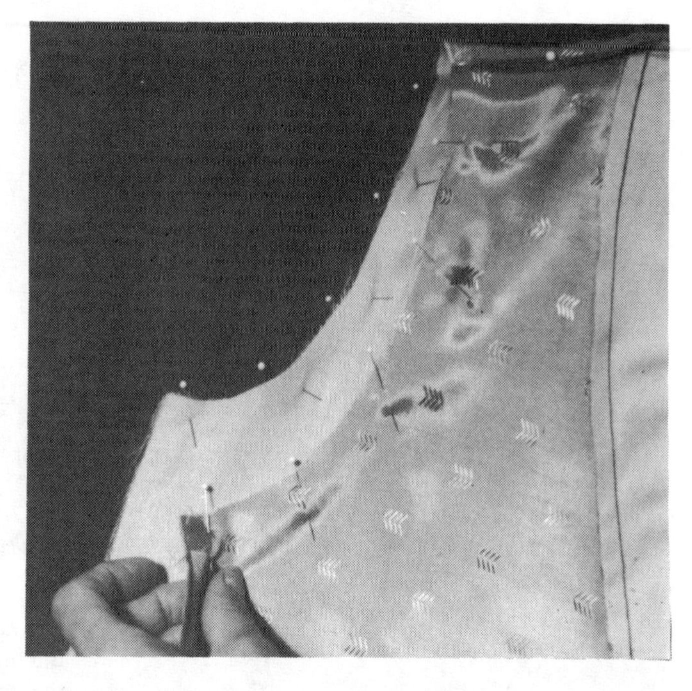

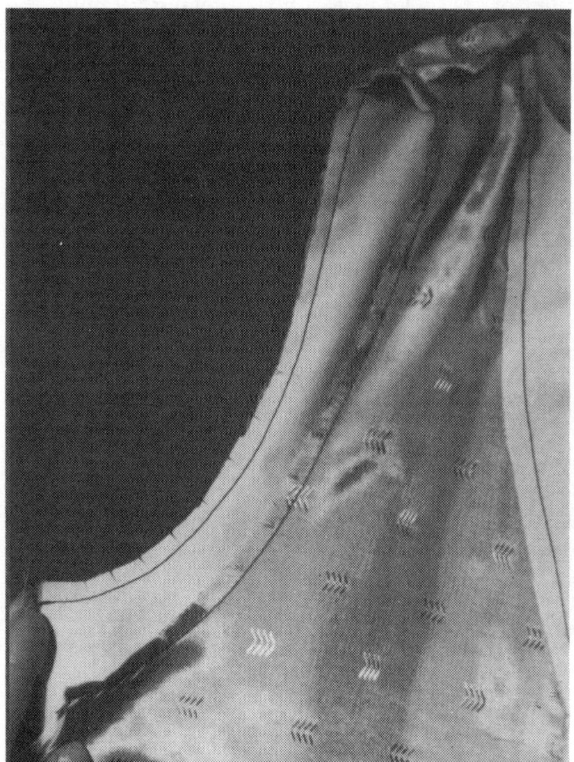

Trim the seam to 1/4″. If you have a facing instead of just a lining, grade the seam if your fabric is medium to heavy weight. Grading is cutting the layer of fabric that lies closest to the garment to 3/8″ and cutting the under layer to 1/4″.

Clip the armhole seam in the curved area. Stagger the clips if there is a facing. If the garment is lined to the edge, you need not stagger the clips.

Pull the garment to the right side by pulling the opening, one side at a time, through a shoulder. If the shoulder seam is narrow, it is a little difficult to get it started. Take a corner, feed it through the shoulder and gently pull the garment through.

Finish the armhole edge in the same manner as you did the neckline, with either understitching or handbasting before topstitching.

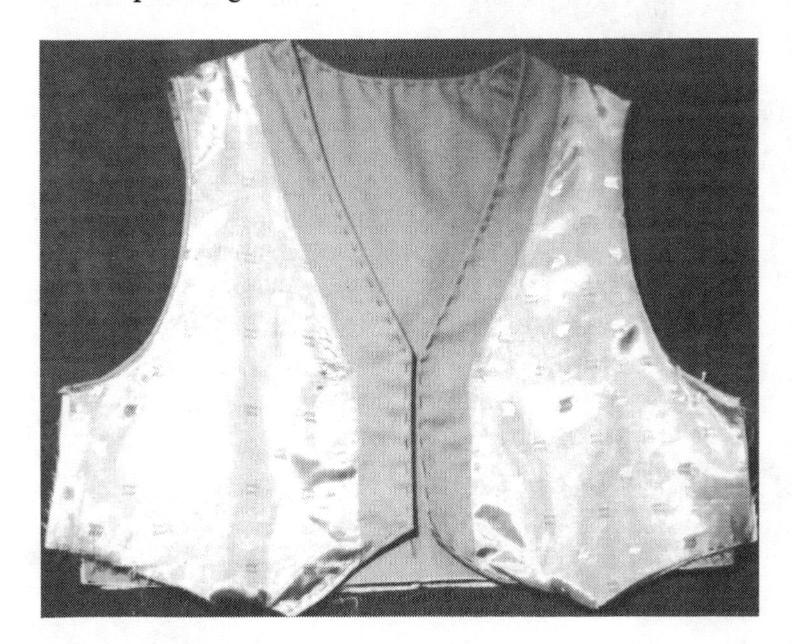

If you choose to understitch, you cannot stitch completely around the armhole. Stitch from the side seams to the shoulder seam or as far as you can stitch into the shoulder area. If you choose to handbaste before topstitching in place of understitching, wait until the side seams are stitched to handbaste and topstitch.

The step-sample vest pictured is understitched on one armhole. The other armhole will be basted after the side seams are stitched. Press the armhole seams flat, as they will be on the finished garment.

Finishing The Garment

Before you stitch the side seams of the garment and the facing or lining, determine how the hem will be handled. If your garment has a hem, follow the pattern directions for hemming and refer to Hems, pages 97 and 101. If you added a lining and the garment has a hem, refer to Tailoring, pages 323 and 324.

If the garment is lined to the edge, leave a 2″ or 3″ opening in one side seam of the lining so that you can stitch around the bottom of the garment and pull the garment through the opening in the lining to turn it. Match the side seams at the underarm and stitch the side seams. Press the seams open.

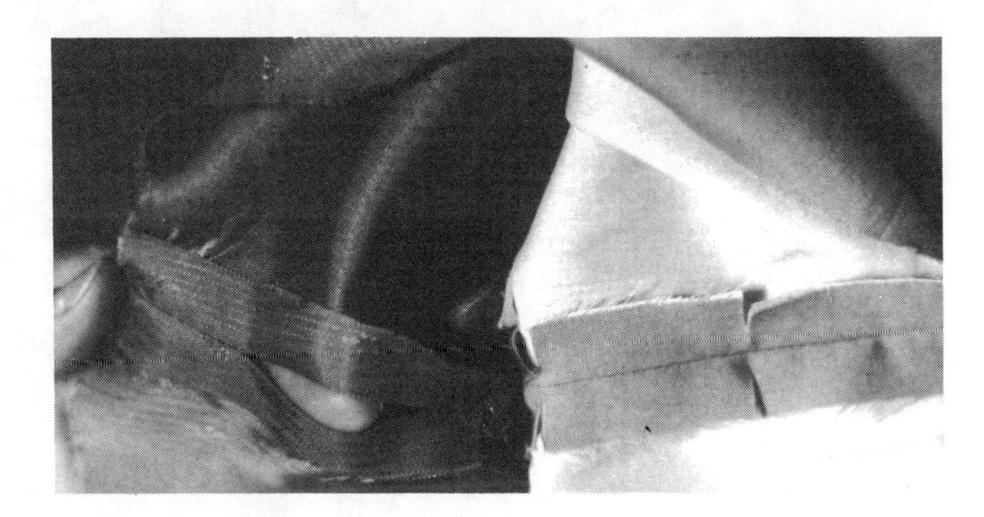

If the garment will be hemmed, you need not leave an opening in the side seam as there will be no need to turn the vest.

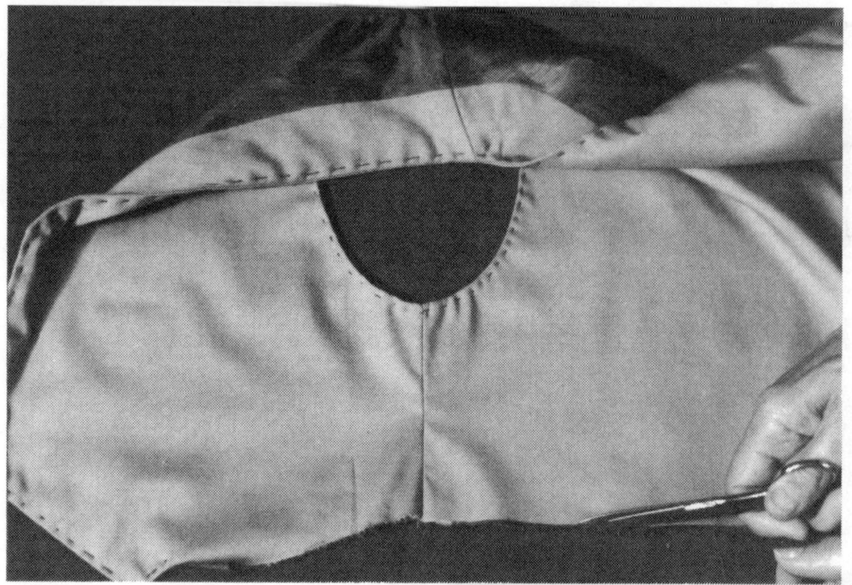

Hand baste the armhole seam if you did not understitch.

Press the armhole seams. Lay the garment out flat and check to make sure the garment and the lining are the same length. If the lining is shorter, mark the difference so you can allow for the difference when you stitch the bottom. If the lining is longer, trim the excess.

Turn the garment wrong side out (only from the armhole down) and pin the bottom edge, matching the side seams and center back. Line up the fabric edges if they were even, or make the allowances you noted. Stitch the bottom of the garment.

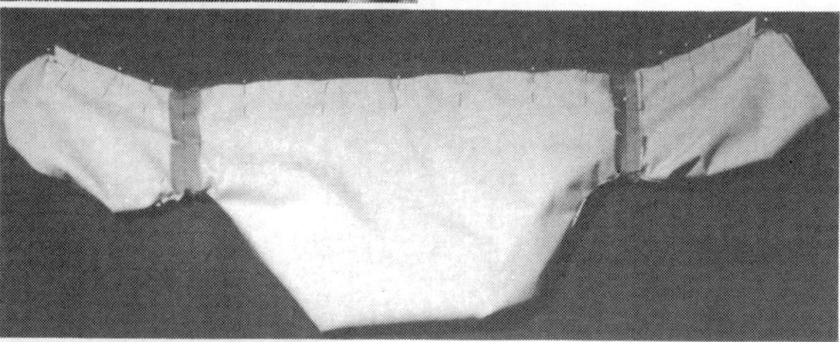

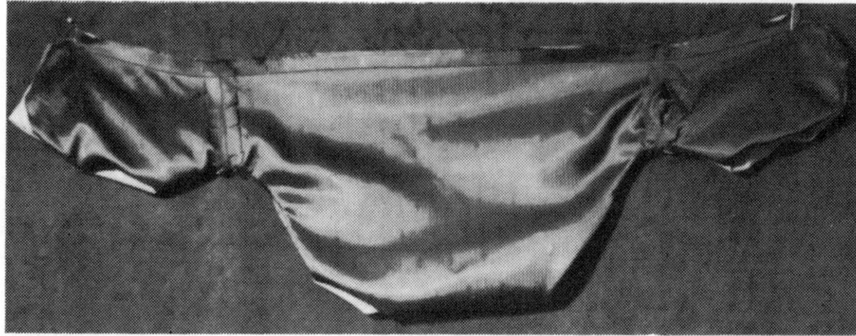

Turn the garment to the right side through the opening in the side seam. Hand baste the lower edge. The garment should hang without any pulls. Then close the opening in the lining side seam with hand stitching. Hand baste the bottom edge.

Topstitch all the edges if you did not understitch. Remove all the bastings. Press the garment and do any finishing that the pattern calls for, such as buttons and buttonholes. Refer to Machine Buttonholes, pages 206-211.

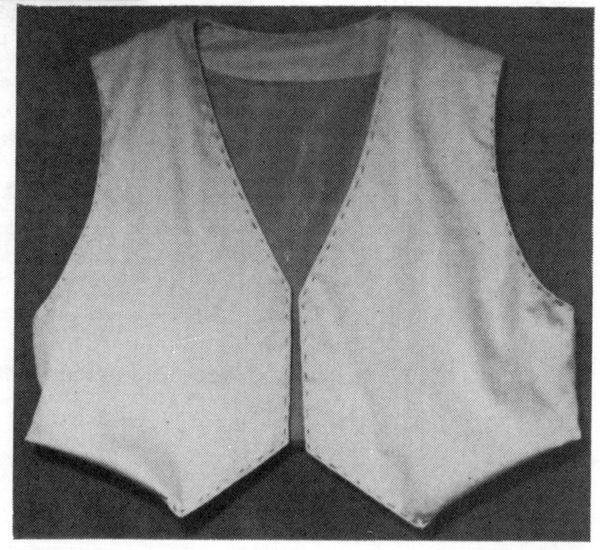

SLEEVELESS GARMENTS WITH NO OPENING

Sleeveless, collarless shell tops are easy and quick to line. The same technique can be used to finish the neckline and armholes if they are faced instead of lined and if they have a one-piece facing. For pattern adjustment for lining or facings, refer to Sleeveless Garments With An Opening, page 104-106.

Tops with no opening must be stitched in halves, because you are working with a circle. You must stitch half the armhole first, then the other half. Stitch a large part of the hem then pull the remaining hem through an opening in the lining side seam. Stitch the remaining area then turn right side out.

Lining Or Facing Sleeveless Garments With No Opening

Before you stitch the lining, determine how the hem will be handled. If the garment is lined to the edge, leave a 2-3″ opening in one side seam of the lining so that you can stitch the bottom of the garment and turn the garment through the opening in the lining. Make the opening at least 2″ below the armhole and backstitch on either end of the opening. Stitch the garment together at the shoulder line and side seams. Stitch the lining or facings together at the shoulder line and side seams. Press all the seams open.

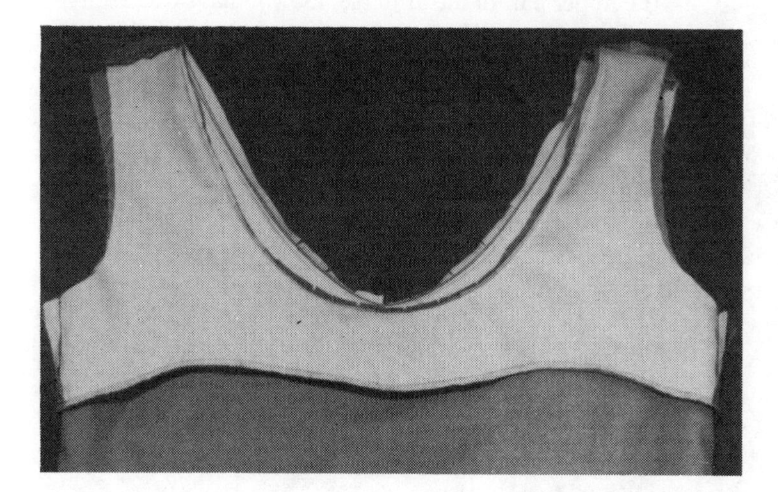

Stitch the garment and the lining or facings together around the neckline. Trim the seam to 1/4″. If you have a facing instead of just a lining, grade the seam if your fabric is medium to heavy weight. Grading is cutting the layer of fabric that lies closest to the garment 3/8″ and cutting the under layer to 1/4″.

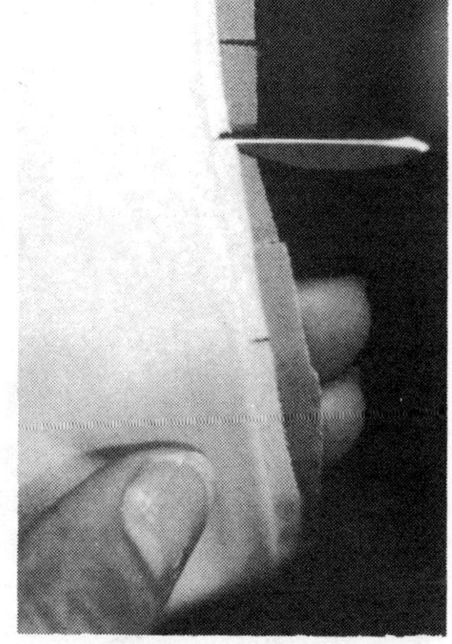

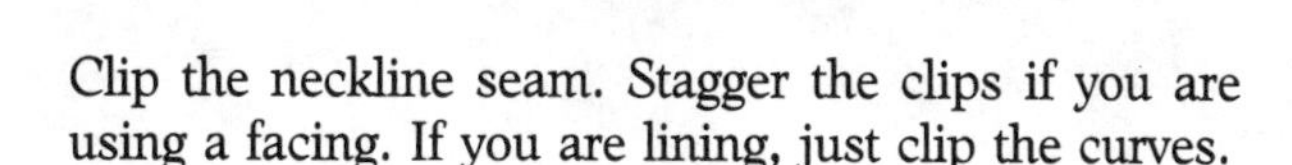

Clip the neckline seam. Stagger the clips if you are using a facing. If you are lining, just clip the curves.

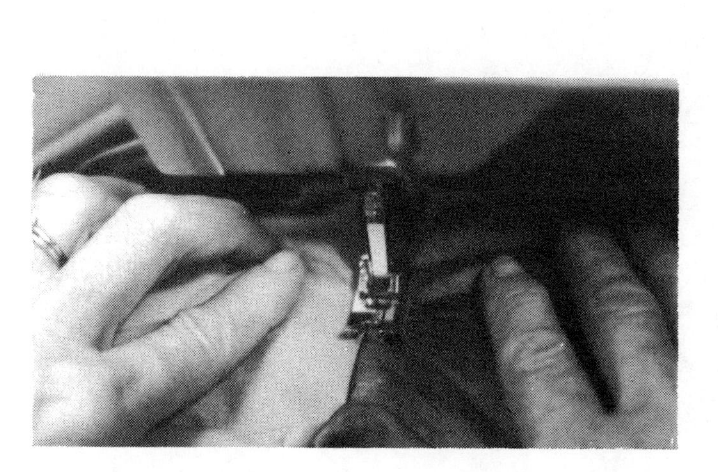

If you are not topstitching, stitch the seam allowance to the lining or facing. This is commonly called stitching to the under or, as I refer to it, understitching.

If you are topstitching, hand baste the entire edge to hold the facing or the lining slightly to the under. (The shell in the picture was understitched.) Press the neckline seam flat as it will be on the finished garment.

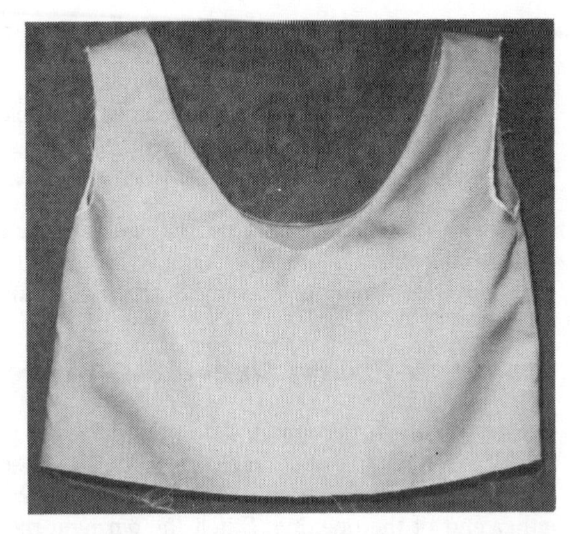

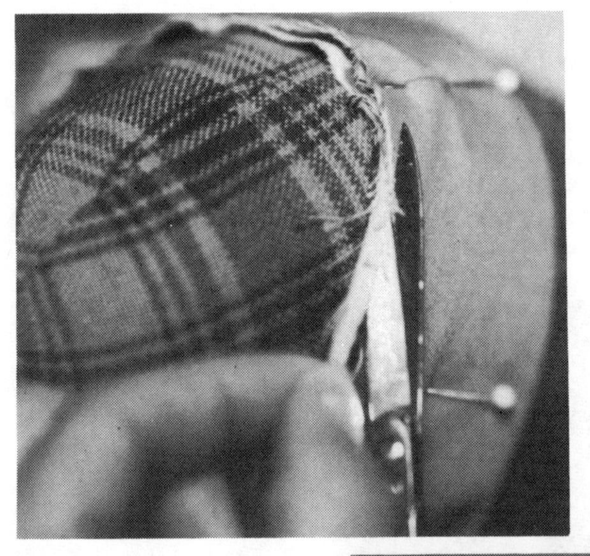

With the wrong sides of the fabric together, pin around the upper part of the armhole. Do you have excess lining or facing extending past the garment armhole? If so, trim that amount off the lining or facing. Also trim a small amount (a scant 1/8″) off the lining or facing in the shoulder area. Trim just the area that had the excess. Do not trim around the entire armhole. This trimming will accommodate the turn of cloth and will keep the lining or facing slightly to the under on both the neckline and the armhole.

Turn in the seam allowance of a small area on the **front armhole** of both the garment and the facing or lining. Hold the turned seam allowance with the fingers of one hand.

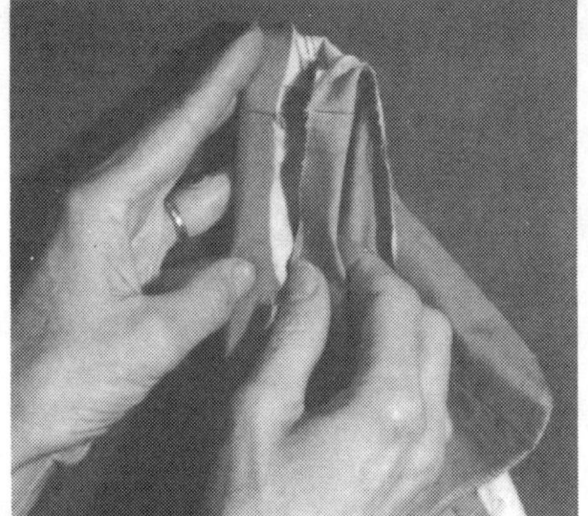

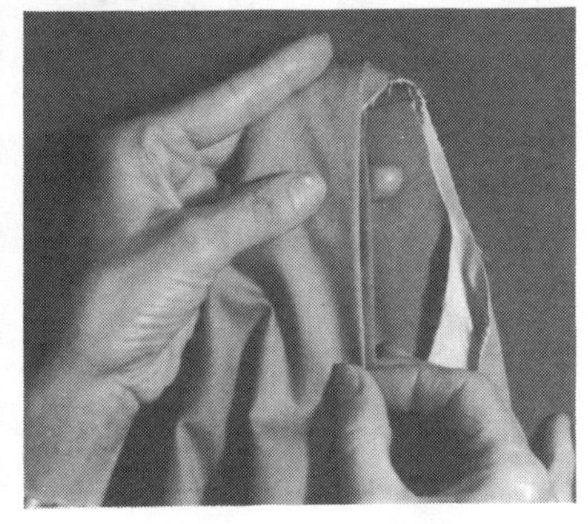

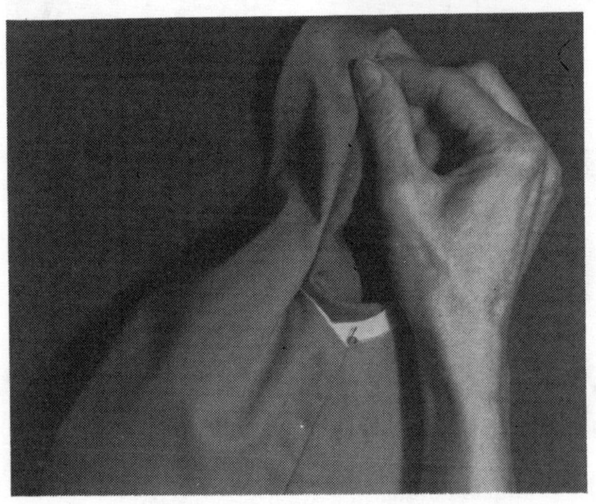

With the other hand, reach inside and hold the turned seam. While you are holding the seam, turn the garment to the wrong side and pin the front armhole from the shoulder seam to the underarm seam. Match the shoulder seam and the underarm seam of the lining or facing to the corresponding seams of the garment.

Line up the edges of both layers when pinning. Carefully push the other layers down inside the circle, out of the stitching line, and pin deeper than the seam allowance to hold the layers out of the way.

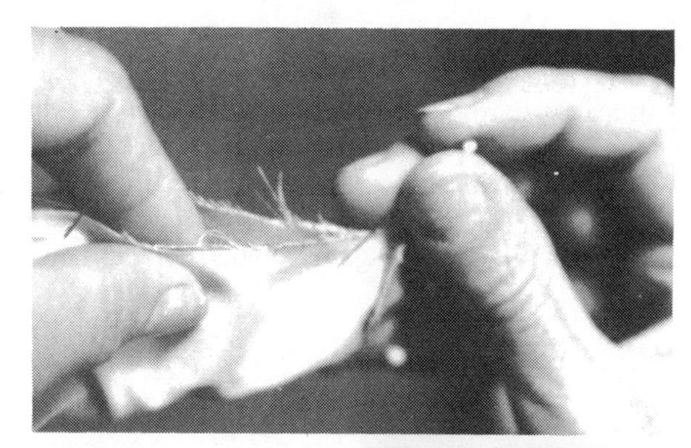

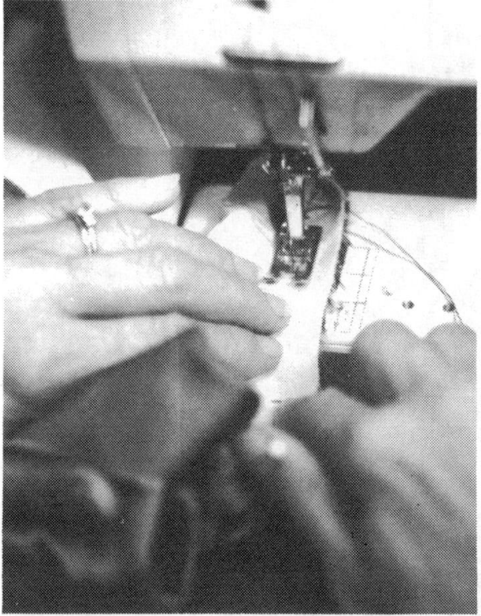

Stitch the front armhole from the shoulder to the underarm crossing the sideseam. If the shoulder area is quite narrow, use the zipper foot to stitch this seam. You must stitch a small area then pull the fabric in front of the needle and stitch again until you have reached the underarm seam. (Picture on the right is of the front armhole stitched.)

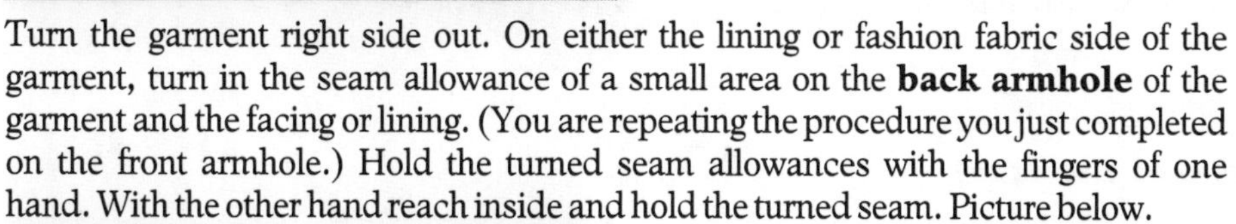

Turn the garment right side out. On either the lining or fashion fabric side of the garment, turn in the seam allowance of a small area on the **back armhole** of the garment and the facing or lining. (You are repeating the procedure you just completed on the front armhole.) Hold the turned seam allowances with the fingers of one hand. With the other hand reach inside and hold the turned seam. Picture below.

While you are holding the seam, turn the garment to the wrong side and pin the back armhole from the shoulder seam to the underarm seam, matching the shoulder seam and the

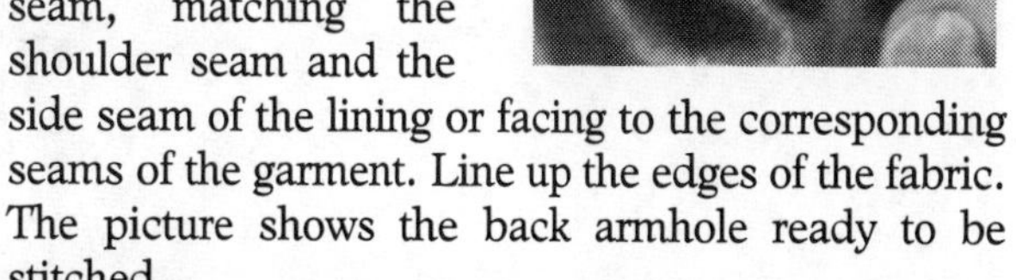

side seam of the lining or facing to the corresponding seams of the garment. Line up the edges of the fabric. The picture shows the back armhole ready to be stitched.

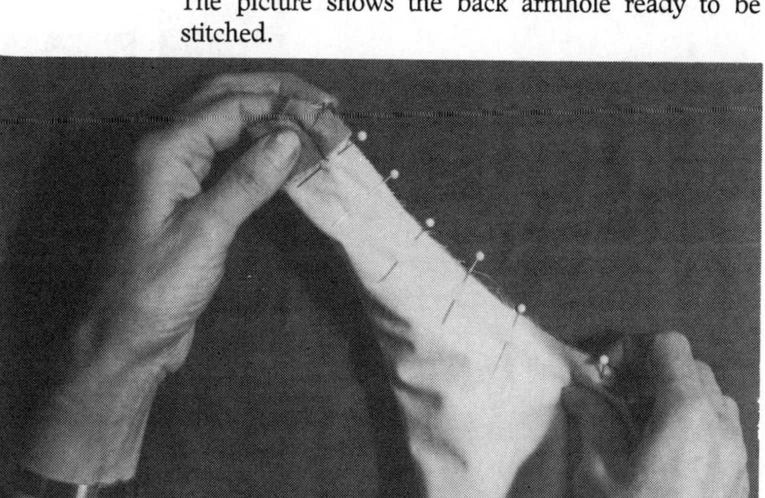

Stitch the back armhole from the shoulder to the underarm seam. Trim, clip, and understitch. If the shoulder area of the garment is narrow, you cannot understitch the entire area. Stitch up into the shoulder as far as you can. If you are topstitching, hand baste to hold the facing or lining slightly to the under. (Picture is of the armhole front and back stitched before trimming, clipping, and understitching.)

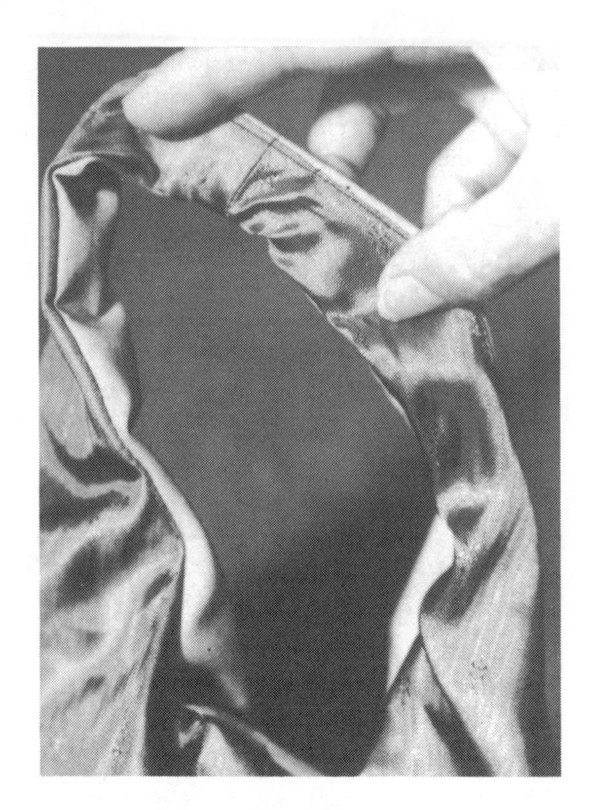

Finishing The Garment

If your garment has a hem, refer to Hems, pages 97 and 101, or follow the pattern directions for hemming. If you added a lining and the garment has a hem, also refer to Couture Tailoring, pages 323-324.

Hemming a Garment Lined to the Edge

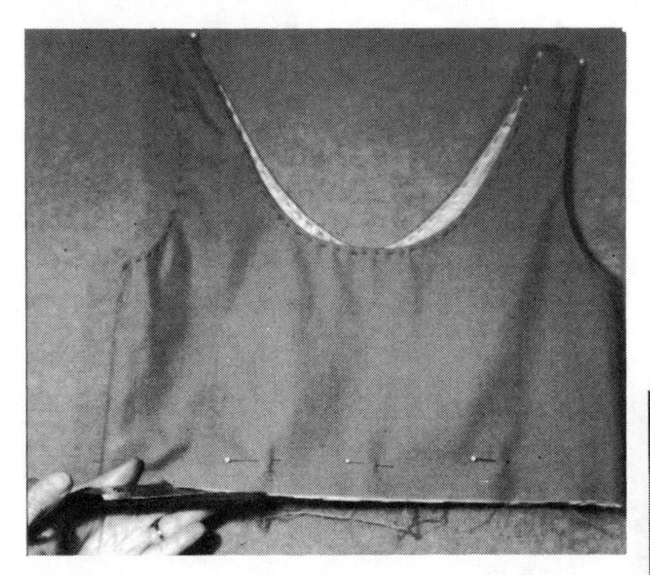

Press the armhole seams. Lay the garment out flat and check to make sure the garment and the lining are the same length. If the lining is shorter, mark the difference so you can allow for the difference when you stitch the bottom. If the lining is longer, trim the excess.

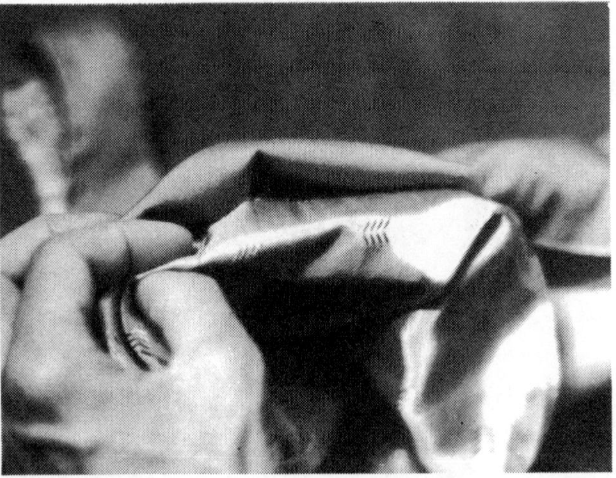

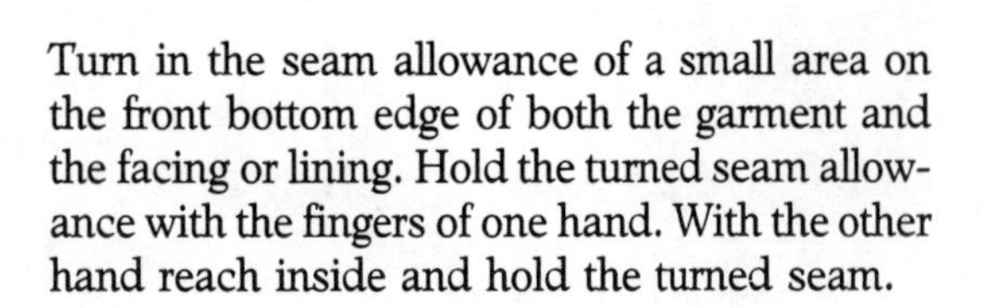

Turn in the seam allowance of a small area on the front bottom edge of both the garment and the facing or lining. Hold the turned seam allowance with the fingers of one hand. With the other hand reach inside and hold the turned seam.

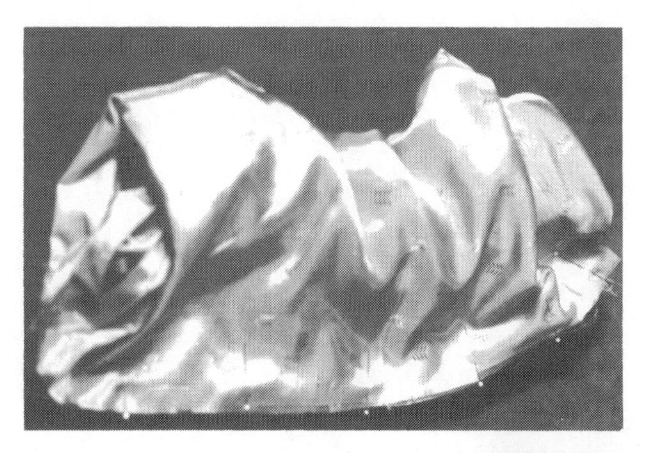

While you are holding the seam, turn the garment to the wrong side and pin the front bottom edge, matching the side seams. Begin pinning on the side seam that has the opening and pin around the front to the other side seam. Pin as far as you can into the back bottom edge. You cannot go all the way around the bottom as it is a circle. Line up the edges of both layers when pinning or if there was a difference in length allow for the difference. Stitch the pinned area.

Turn the garment right side out.

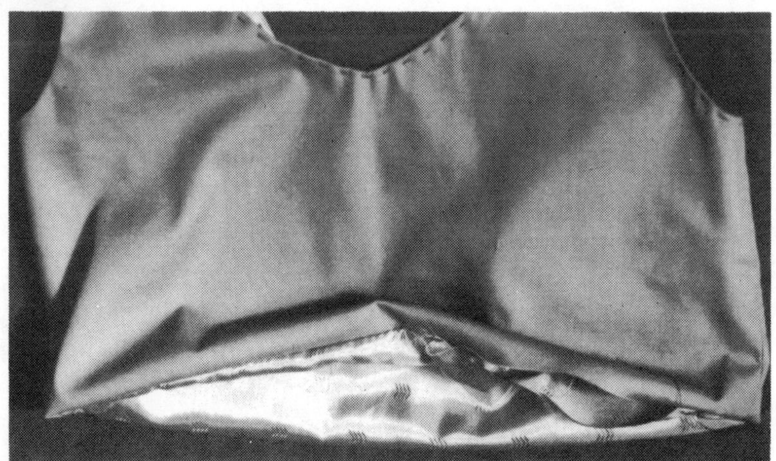

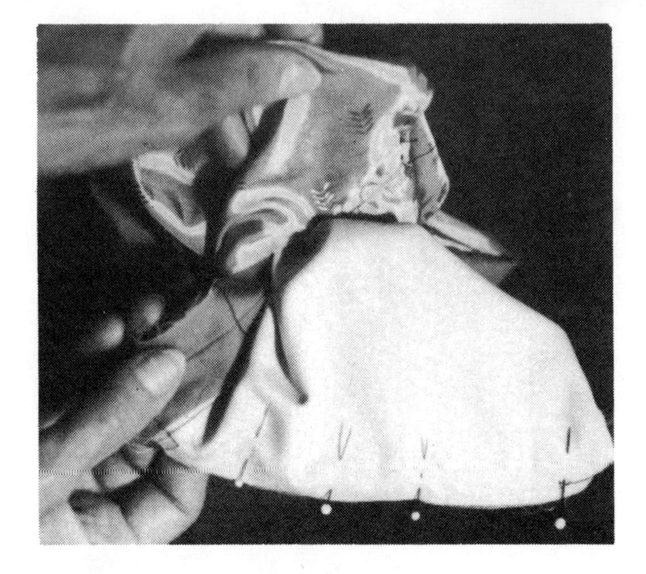

Pull the unstitched area through the opening in the side seam and pin. Finish stitching the bottom edge.

Turn the garment to the right side through the opening in the side seam. Hand baste the lower edge. The garment should hang without any pulls. Then close the opening in the lining side seam with hand stitching.

Topstitch all the edges if you did not understitch. Press the garment.

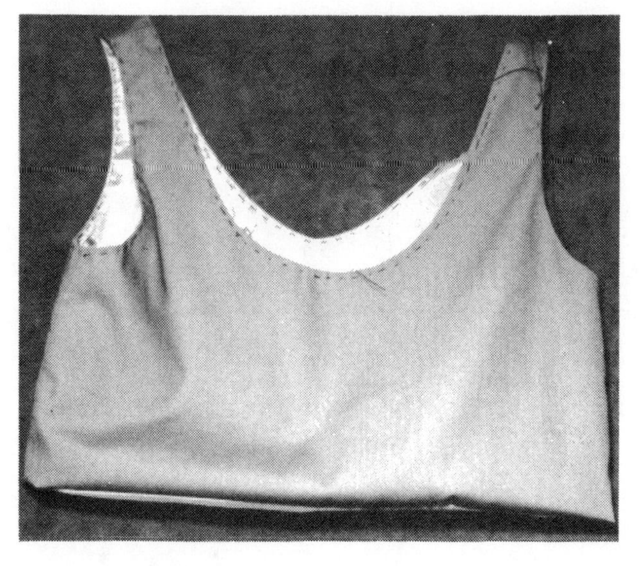

Sewing Techniques For Blouses And Dresses

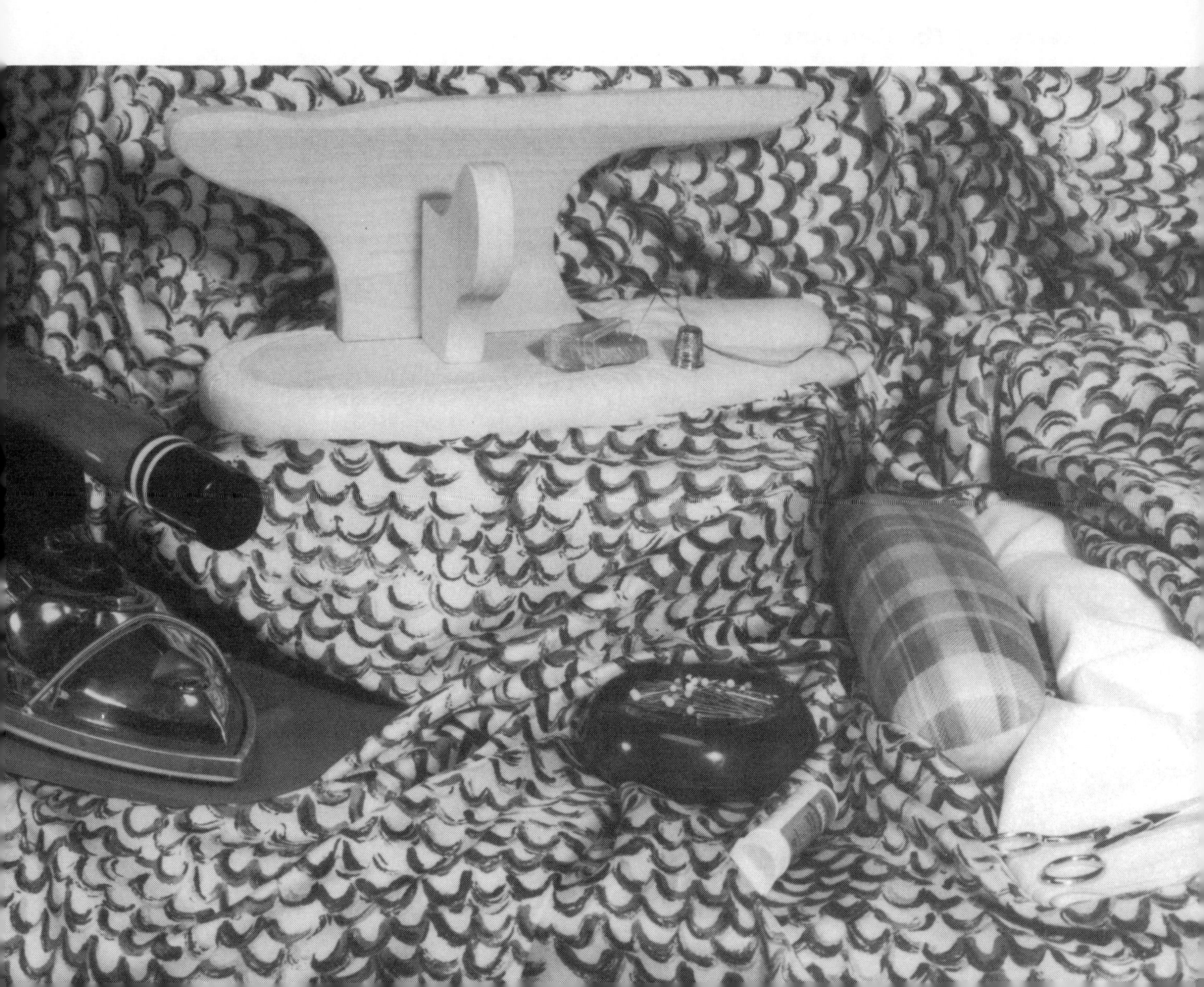

BLOUSES AND DRESSES

Blouses and the top of a dress require the same sewing techniques. Use these basic directions along with your pattern instruction sheet for either blouses or dresses.

Check your pattern by flat measuring the bust, hip, sleeve length, and dress or blouse length. Compare those measurements with a trusted pattern or a favorite garment. Do any adjustments to the pattern you normally change so it will be custom fit to you. Refer to Pattern Adjustments, pages 1-6.

After the changes are made on the tissue, pin it together and try on over the underclothes you normally wear. Refer to pages 6-8. Make any further changes you can see need to be done to the tissue after trying it on. Refer to pages 8-9.

Prepare your fabric. Refer to and follow the chapters on Grain In Fabric and Preshrinking.

Follow the pattern directions for the layout. Cut the blouse or dress and cut all the interfacing pieces shown on the pattern layout. Refer to the chapter on Cutting. If you are working with difficult fabric, refer to page 28. If your fabric is a plaid, stripe, or a diagonal, refer to page 35. Refer to the chapter on Inner Construction, page 20, for guidelines in helping you choose the correct interfacing for your fabric.

Interfacing The Garment

I almost always interface the underside of the collar, the collarband, and the cuffs. I interface the facing on the garment opening, instead of the garment. This usually looks better because the seams naturally lie a little to the side that is interfaced. The only exception would be a sheer fabric which would look better with the interfacing on the right side to hide the seam. I like a soft interfacing for the garment opening and a more crisp interfacing for the collar and cuffs.

Mark any details on your fabric or interfacing as indicated on your pattern. Do the marking for the collar and cuffs on the interfacing seam allowance. Refer to Marking. If your garment has lots of tucks or pleats, refer to pages 42-43.

If you prefer to use fusible interfacing, do not trim the seam allowance off the fusible interfacings before fusing. Fuse it very lightly in the seam allowances. After the seams are stitched, pull the fusible free and trim the interfacing out of the seam allowance. Fusible interfacing should be held in the seam by stitching to insure its staying in place through many launderings.

Save time by interfacing the collar, the cuffs, and the front facing at the same time. Then stitch everything you can. Refer to Sample Seams and Pressing Techniques, pages 69-71 and page 58. Trim all the areas that get trimmed, then press all the seams open. Doing everything you can at the same time saves time and trips to the ironing board. Feeding one seam after another into the sewing machine, backstitching each edge, then cutting the threads instead of leaving threads to tie, also saves time and thread.

Interface The Garment Opening

A great way to interface the garment opening is with the **French finish** method of attaching the interfacing. A **French finish** gives a very smooth and fast finish to the edge of the facing. Do not use the French finish if you are using fusible interfacing. Simply fuse the interfacing on the facing and finish any edges not enclosed in a seam with a finishing stitch or the serger.

If you have a back neck facing, stitch the shoulder seams of the garment. Stitch the front facing to the back facing. Finish the shoulder seams. Refer to Sample Seams and Pressing Techniques, pages 65-67 and Seam Finishes, pages 68-71. Stitch the front interfacing to the back interfacing before attaching the interfacing to the garment.

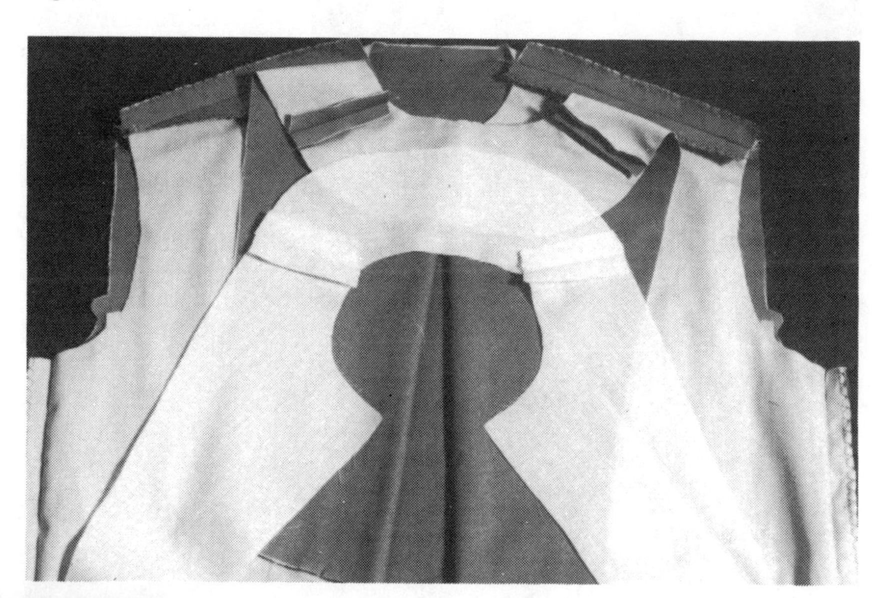

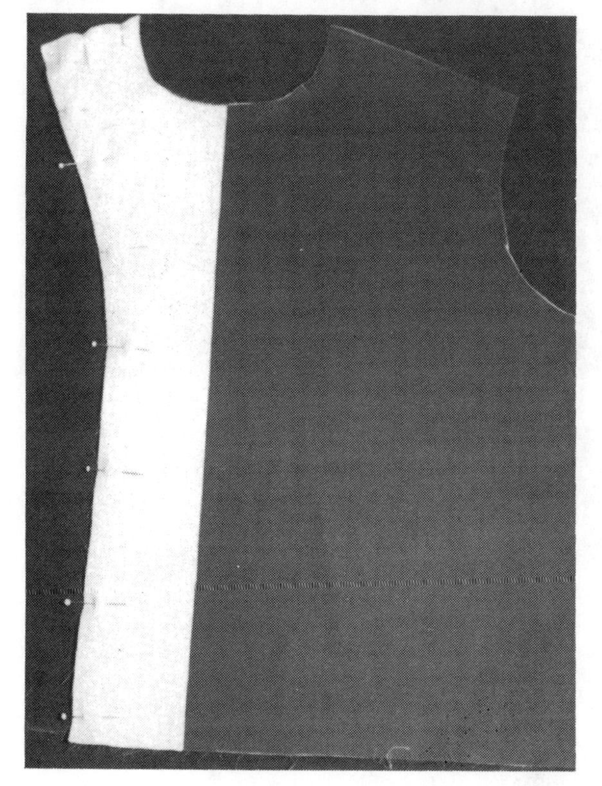

Pin the interfacing to the right side of the garment.

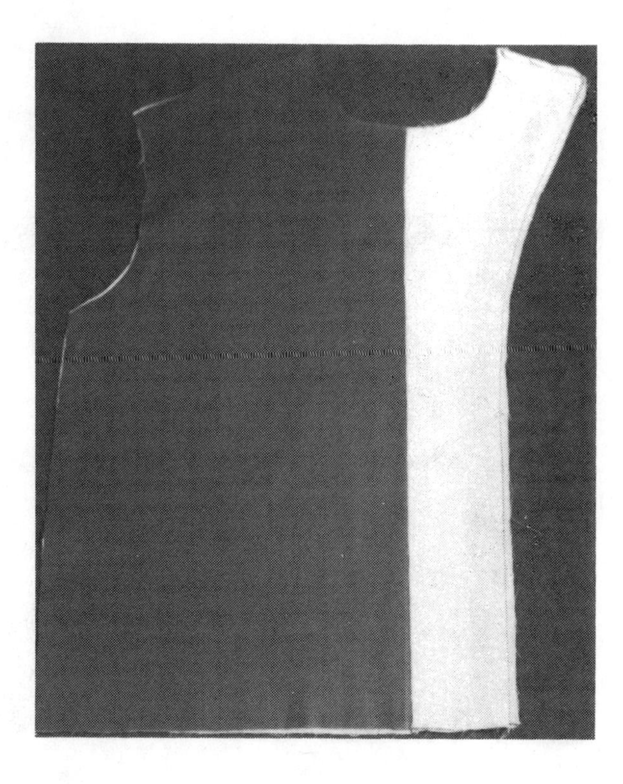

Stitch the outer edge of the facing to the interfacing with a narrow seam, 1/4″-1/8″. Some pattern directions say to understitch this seam. It is easier to press but two rows of stitching makes a stiffer edge along the facing.

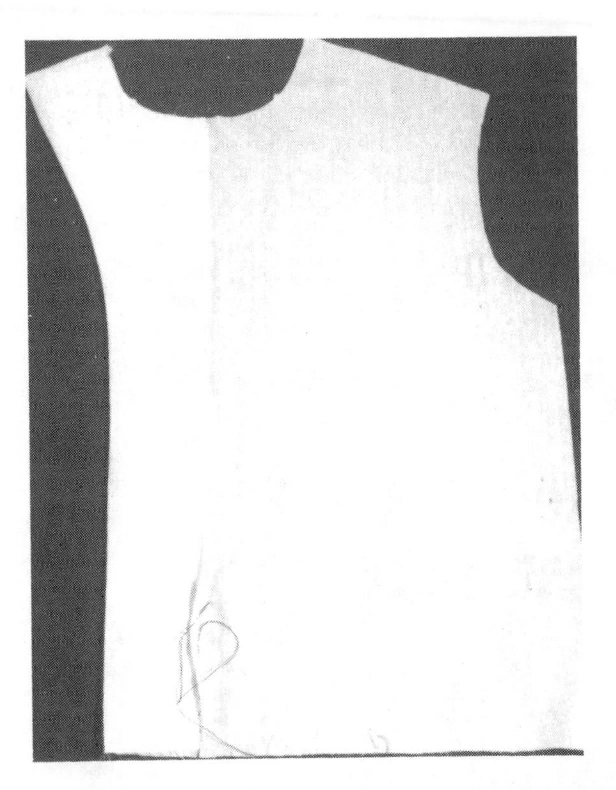

Turn the interfacing to the wrong side of the garment. Press the seam so no interfacing shows on the right side of the garment. If you are interfacing to a fold line, catch the edge of the interfacing to the fold line with tiny hand stitches.

Exception: If you are topstitching the front edge so the interfacing would be caught, either hand baste or glue stick the edge to hold the interfacing in place until the topstitching will secure it.

Interface the collar, the collar band if you have one, the cuffs, and any other pieces the pattern indicates. If I am using nonfusible interfacing, I use a glue stick to hold the interfacings in place until they are secured in the seam.

Using the glue sparingly, dot the glue stick along the edge of the interfacing in the seam allowance and lay the fashion fabric on it. Smooth with your hands or press the pieces together. After the seam is stitched and trimmed most of the glued area is trimmed off.

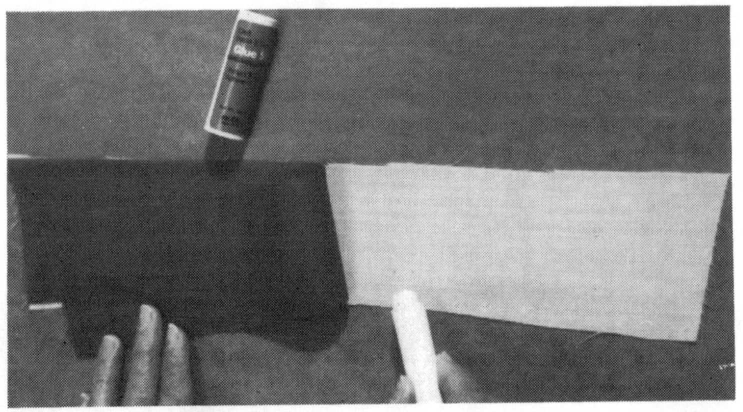

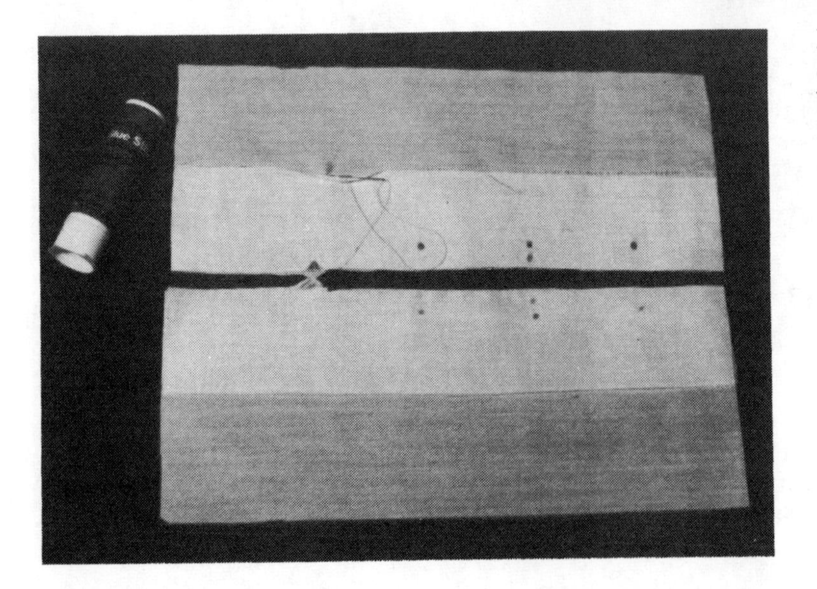

Be sure to identify the wrong side of the cuffs so you have a right and left cuff before you interface and stitch. It is very easy to do both cuffs for the same sleeve.

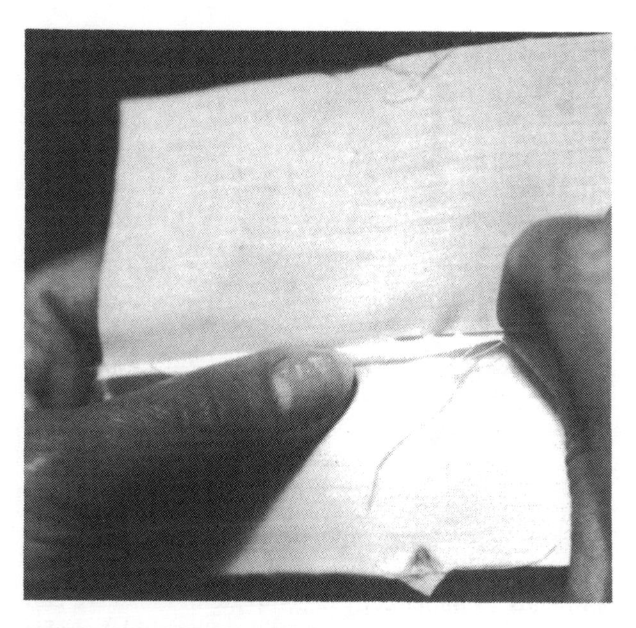

If the cuffs call for interfacing to a fold line and you are using nonfusible interfacing, you must fasten the edge of the interfacing to the fold line with tiny hand stitches.

Exception: If the cuff is topstitched so the interfacing would be held in the fold, either hand baste or glue stick the edge to hold the interfacing in place until the topstitching will secure it.

Garment Construction

Check your pattern instructions and do anything the pattern calls for to the blouse before stitching the shoulder seams. This would normally include the blouse opening, pockets, tucks, or darts. Refer to Sample Seams and Pressing Techniques, pages 65-67 and Seam Finishes, pages 58 and 68-71, before stitching the garment seams.

Stitch the shoulder seams

Always ease the back shoulder seam onto the front shoulder seam. The back shoulder is often cut from 1/16″ to 1/4″ longer than the front shoulder to accommodate the curve of the back. If the blouse has gathering on a lowered front shoulder seam, be sure and put a stay on the seam. Refer to Gathering, page 95. If the blouse has a yoke, refer to Yokes, page 139.

Cuffs and collars

I never follow the pattern directions for clipping or turning under the seam allowance of the under collar or the cuffs. Often the turn of cloth causes a problem. I find it best to eliminate that step in the pattern directions and stitch with the seam extended. Then I can turn the seam allowance under the amount the turn of cloth dictates.

Cuffs and collar construction

For detailed instructions for the collar, refer to Collars, pages 161-164.

Lay the cuffs right side together and pin. If you have a big dot on the cuff pattern, your cuff has an extension. Stitch that extension as illustrated.

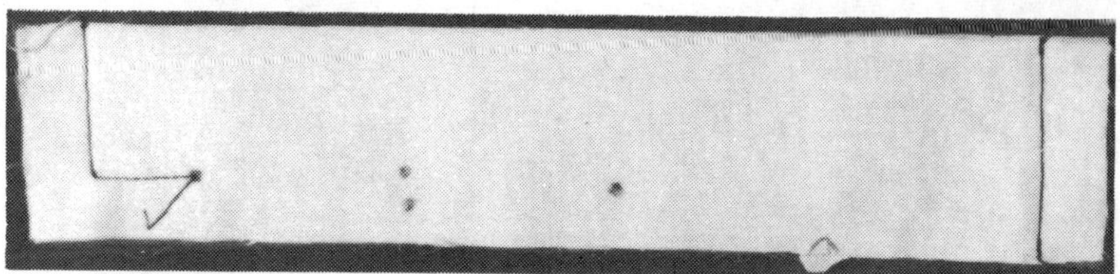

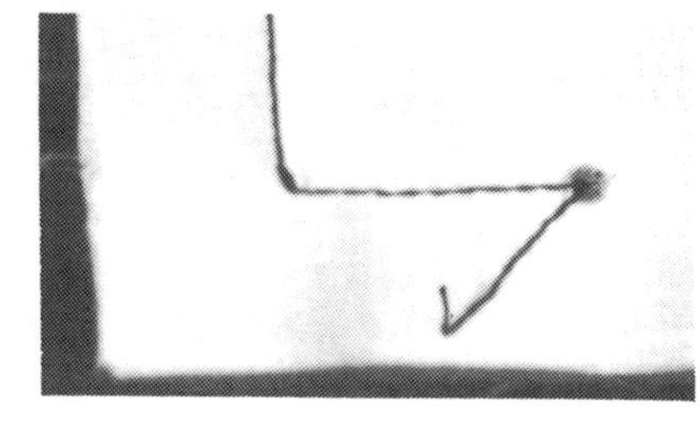

If you have bulky or heavy weight fabric, be sure to stitch one stitch on the diagonal at each outside corner. (I like to backstitch that stitch to strengthen the corner.) This slightly rounds the corner stitching and makes for a better corner in heavier fabrics than if you just pivot on your needle. Pivot on your needle if your fabric is light to medium weight.

If you have curved ends, put the pattern piece back in place over the interfacing. Stick pins along the seam line and pencil dot at each pin to mark the curved stitching line on the interfacing.

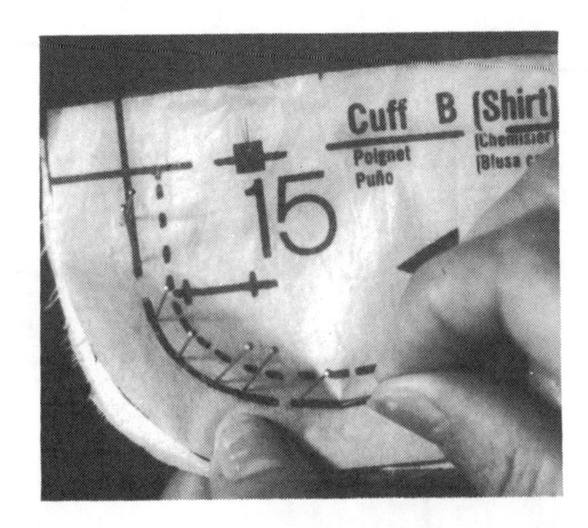

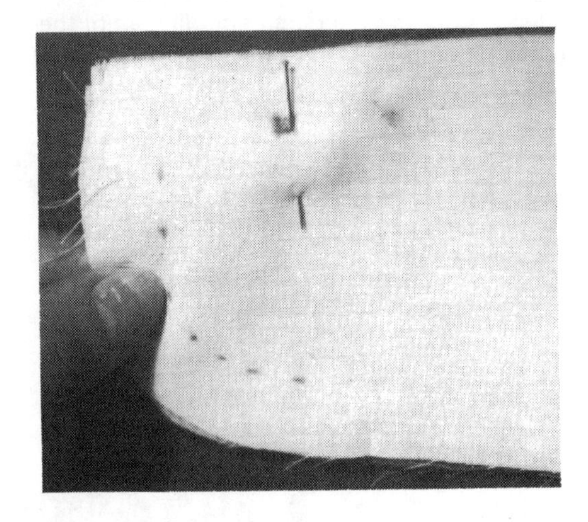

This will insure the same curve on both ends of the cuff and on both cuffs. Without a guide it is very difficult to stitch the same curve on both ends. A paper copy or template of the curve can be cut and stitched around. For an example of a template, refer to Pockets, pages 224-225.

Trim the interfacing to 1/8″. If the fabric is lightweight, trim the seam to 1/4″. If your fabric is medium or heavy weight, grade the seams. To grade, cut the layer that will lie closest to the garment to 3/8″ and the inner layer to 1/4″. Trim the corners to 1/4″. Refer to pages 162-164.

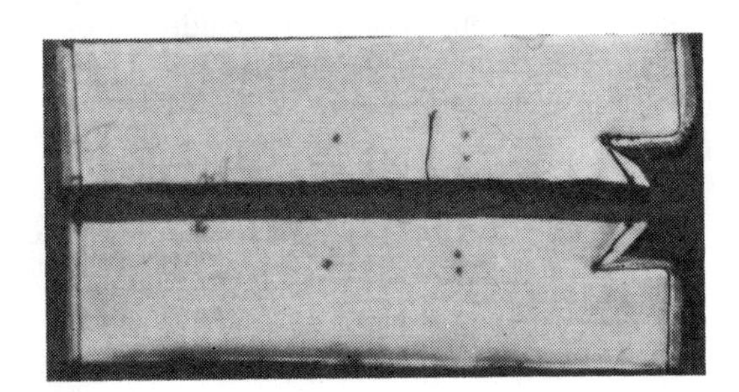

Press the seams of the collar and cuffs so the seam is favoring the interfaced side slightly. The seam should not show on the right side.

Exception: If the fabric is sheer and the interfaced side looks better, press the seam so it shows on the uninterfaced side. In that case, use the interfaced side as the right side.

Set the cuffs aside until they are needed.

Stitch the collar onto the garment

Refer to Collars and use the method listed below best suited to your garment.

Four Methods Of Stitching Collars

Method One

Refer to page 165.

I would use this method on sport garments of lightweight fabric or children's clothing. The collar never lies quite as nicely as the Four Point Collar (Method Three) and unless the fabric is lightweight, the neckline seam is very bulky.

You must use both a back and front facing for this method.

Method Two

Refer to page 168.

Much the same as Method One but there is no back neck facing. I prefer this to Method One because I like to eliminate the back neck facing when I can.

I would use this method on sport garments of lightweight fabric or children's clothing. The collar never lies quite as nicely as the Four Point Collar, and unless the fabric is lightweight the neckline seam is very bulky.

Method Three

Refer to page 171.

Method three must be used on medium and heavy weight fabric to reduce the bulk of the neckline seam. It is always used in tailoring. I often use it when constructing good blouses of lightweight fabric because it lies beautifully.

Use for garments with a front and sometimes a back neck facing. If there is no back neck facing and the garment is lined, the lining is used in place of the back neck facing. If the garment is not lined and there is no back neck facing, the upper collar is used to finish the back neck seam as in Method Two.

Method Four

Refer to page 180.

Use for garments with no facings, usually a shirt blouse with a collar and a collarband. The collar can have a stitched-on band or a cut-on band. The cut-on band is easiest to construct. The stitched-on band fits more closely and usually is seen on more expensive clothing.

After the neckline of a garment is completed, the next step is the sleeve. Always complete the neckline of a garment before setting in a set-in sleeve because the neckline influences the fit of the sleeve a great deal.

Three Methods Of Setting In Sleeves

Open Method

Directions begin on page 194.

Use the Open Method for the dropped shoulder sleeve and the shirt sleeve. Some designs must have this type construction because of the cut. Check your pattern instruction sheet. If it is directing you to use the Open Method, follow the instructions. The Open Method also works well for casual knit garments.

The Open Method of setting in a regular set-in sleeve never fits as well as the Modified Open Method or a regular Set-In Sleeve because the seam under the arm is not a continuous seam. It is broken by the side seam. The side seam is a continuous seam from the bottom of the blouse to the end of the sleeve.

Set-In Sleeve

Directions begin on page 196.

This method of setting in sleeves must be used on a two-piece sleeve and is the best way of setting in the sleeve if you have not used the pattern before. It gives you the opportunity of pin-fitting the sleeve before it is permanently stitched.

A set-in sleeve fits better and is more comfortable when the sleeve seam is a circle.

Modified Open Method

Directions begin on page 203.

The Modified Open Method finished is the same as the Set-In Sleeve but it has the ease of putting the sleeve in flat.

The Modified Open Method works well when the pattern has been fitted and you previously checked and adjusted the hang and fit of the sleeve and the fit of the garment.

Three Sleeve Openings

Your fabric and design will determine which is suitable for your garment.

I do not like some pattern directions for sleeve openings. Some patterns have you stitch a dart and then do a rolled hem on the edges of the opening. Some tell you to clip to the seam allowance and do a small rolled hem. Either of these methods leaves a clip with raveling edges at the sleeve opening. The opening in a dart is a little better than just clipping, but neither is very satisfactory. Other patterns have a small facing that is difficult to hold in place.

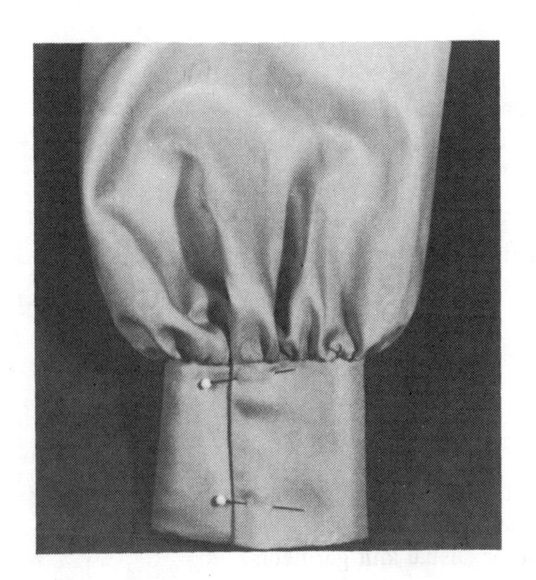

No-Slash Opening

Pictured right side out. This opening is especially nice for lightweight fabrics such as silks, silky polyesters, lightweight cottons, and cotton blends. Stitch the sleeve seam and gather or tuck the bottom of the sleeve before doing the No-Slash Opening.

If you are using the Open or Modified Open Method of putting the sleeve in the garment, the sleeve would have to be in the garment before the No Slash Opening is done. Directions begin on page 125.

No-Slash Opening pictured wrong side out with a Hong Kong seam finish and with a serger finish.

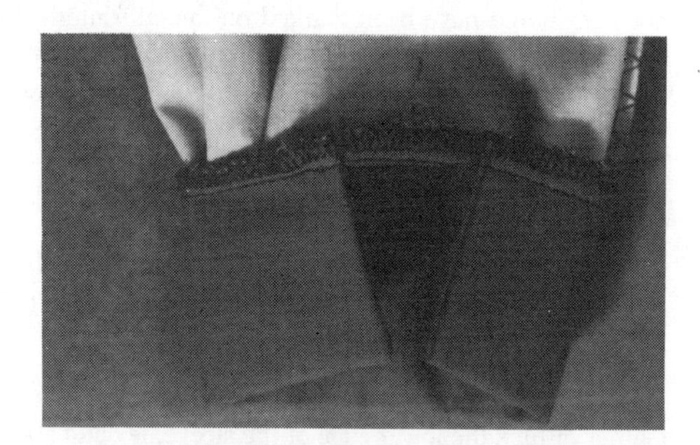

Slash Opening

Use this for any weight fabric but I prefer to use it for medium weight or heavy weight fabrics when I don't want to go to the work of the Tailored Placket Opening. Stitch the sleeve seam and gather or tuck the bottom of the sleeve after the Slash Opening is done. Directions begin on page 130.

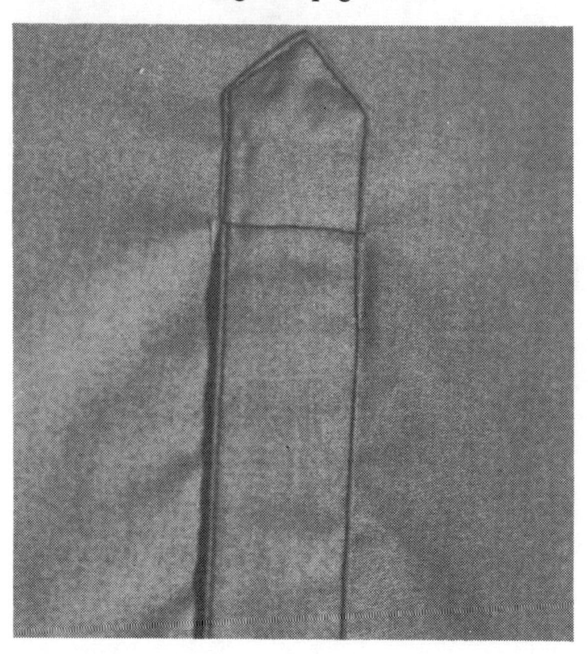

Tailored Placket Opening

Use for any weight fabric if the style dictates a tailored opening. This is the most difficult sleeve opening I recommend. Stitch the sleeve seam and gather or tuck the bottom of the sleeve after the placket opening is done. Directions begin on page 134.

Directions For Sleeve Openings

No-Slash Opening

Use for lightweight fabric. I particularly like this finish. I make my opening just large enough to fit over my elbow. (The length of the cuff plus the amount of the opening should equal your above-the-elbow measurement.) I can then push up my sleeves and keep them up if I need to be in the kitchen in my good clothes. If you are using the open or the modified open method of sewing the sleeve and the no-slash opening, you must sew the sleeve to the garment before doing the no-slash opening.

Preparation for No-Slash Opening

Be sure all the necessary marking was done on the cuff and the sleeve. All the dots, the sleeve seam, and the notches should have been marked on the cuff interfacing. The dots and notches and the sleeve opening should be marked on the sleeve. Refer to Marking, pages 39 and 43.

Stitch the sleeve seam. Refer to Sample Seams and Pressing Techniques, pages 58 and 65. I often use a French seam on lightweight fabrics. If no French seam is used, press the seam open and finish the seam. Refer to Seam Finishes, pages 68-70.

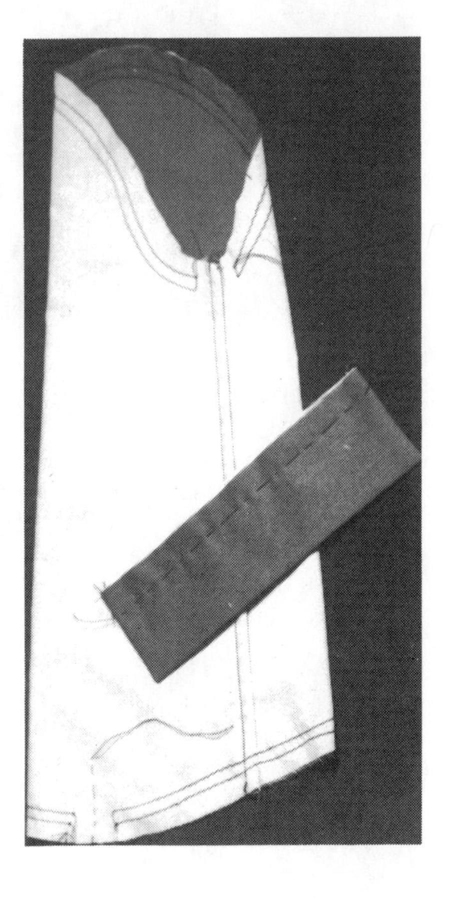

The cuffs were interfaced, stitched, and turned earlier. If this wasn't done earlier, refer to pages 121 and 122. Baste the unfinished edges together.

Gather or tuck the lower edge of the sleeve, leaving about 1" ungathered where the slash would have been. Gather the cap of the sleeve as shown. Refer to Gathering, pages 92-94.

Stitch the cuff to the sleeve

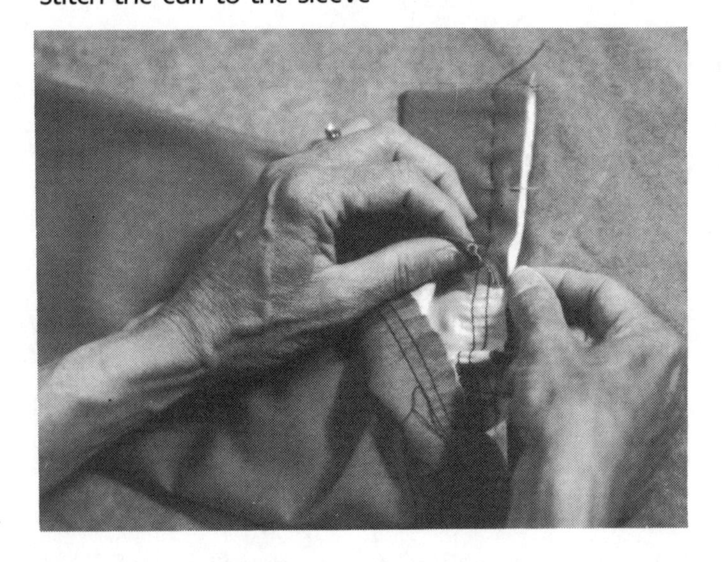

With the right (uninterfaced) side of the cuff to the right side of the sleeve, pin the cuff to the sleeve, matching all the marking of the cuff to the corresponding marks of the sleeve. The buttonhole end of the cuff lies on the back of the sleeve which is always marked with double notches on the armhole.

Turn the sleeve to the wrong side. If the sleeve is gathered, pull the threads together and adjust the fullness evenly around the cuff. Pin in place. On most garments I prefer to bind the seam with a piece of the fabric cut on the bias. This is called a Hong Kong seam finish. Refer to Seam Finishes, page 71.

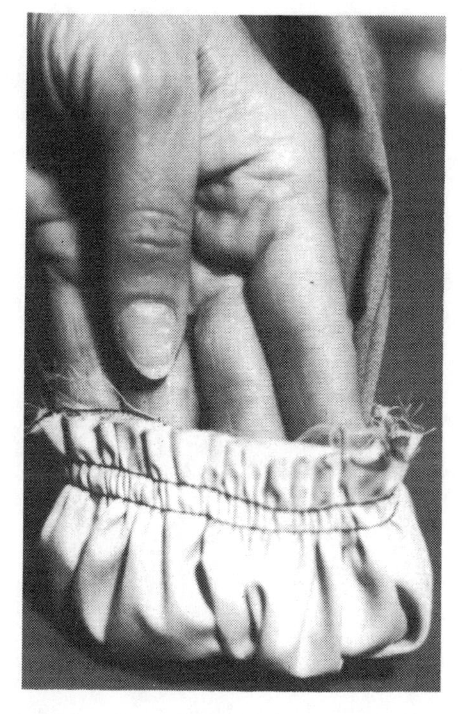

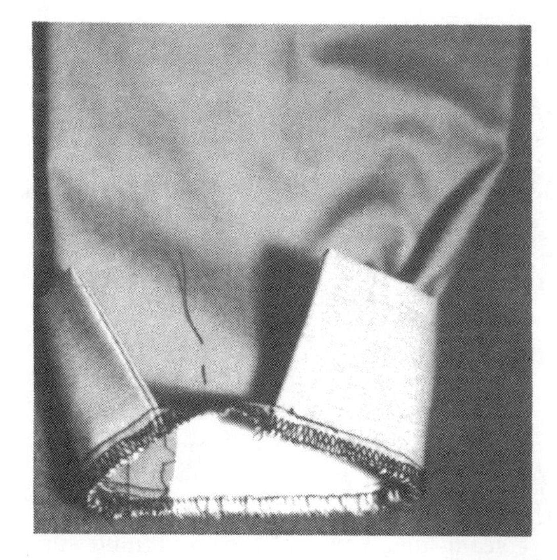

If you are not going to bind the seam with a bias finish, stitch the cuff onto the sleeve. Stitch with the sleeve up. Sew completely around the sleeve through all thicknesses. Finish the seam with a close overcast or zig-zag stitch, or stitch it on the serger. Refer to Seam Finishes, pages 68-69. Some purchased garments are finished in this manner. I would do inexpensive sport or children's garments in this way.

To bind with a Hong Kong finish, cut two pieces of bias of the fashion fabric 1½″ wide and long enough to go around the cuff and the opening plus two 1/4″ seam allowances.

To find the true bias, measure an equal distance along the straight of grain and the crossgrain. Draw a line between the two marks. Measure the width needed and cut the strips. Cut the ends of the strips on the straight of grain and have both angles the same.

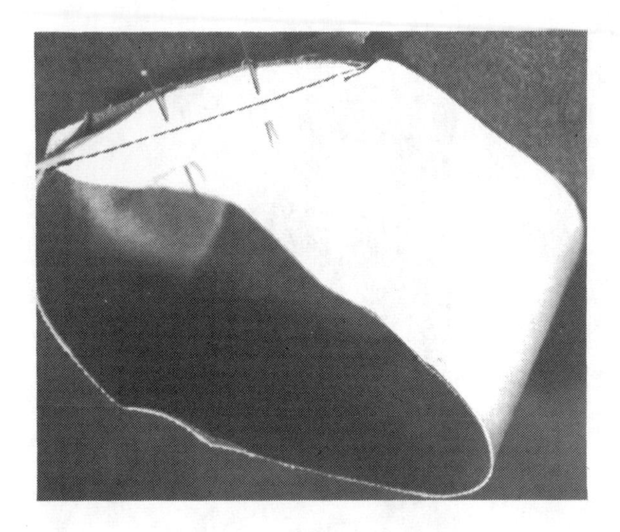

Stitch the bias strips in circles — one circle for each sleeve. Press the seam open.

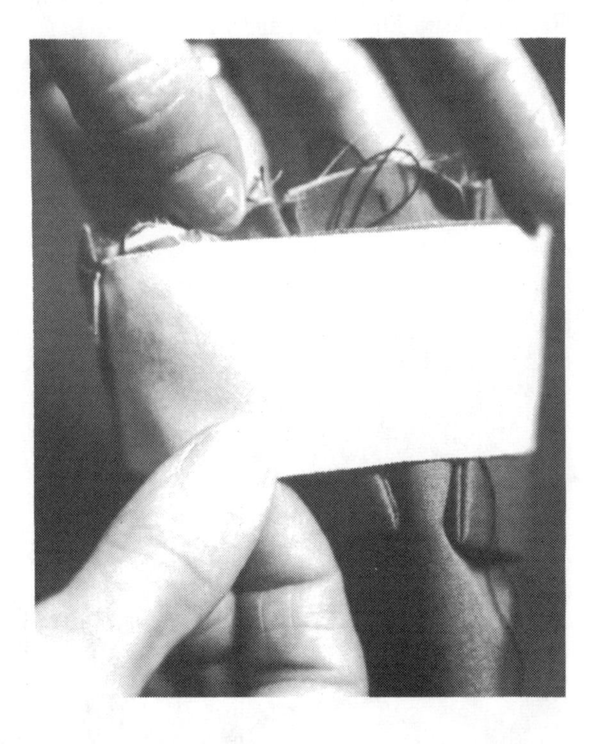

Slip the bias circle over the cuff and pin in place. (Don't put the seam of the bias strip on the opening of the cuff.)

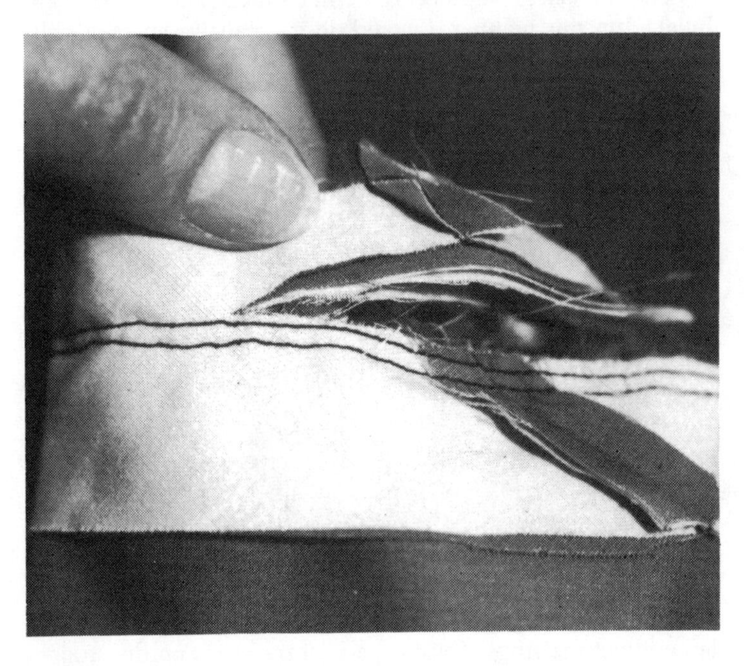

With the sleeve up, stitch along the 5/8″ seam line. You are stitching through the sleeve, the cuff, and the bias strip. Check and make sure both ends of the cuff are the same width. Then stitch again 1/8″ from the 5/8″ seam line into the seam allowance. Trim the seam close to the last stitching. Pull out any basting threads that would show.

Extend the bias strip out from the seam and trim, if needed, so the bias is no more than 5/8″ wide from the seam line.

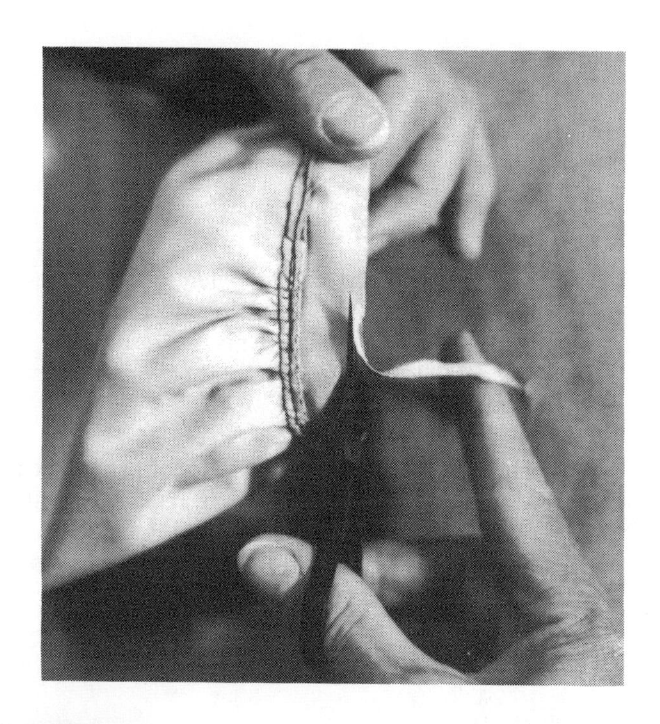

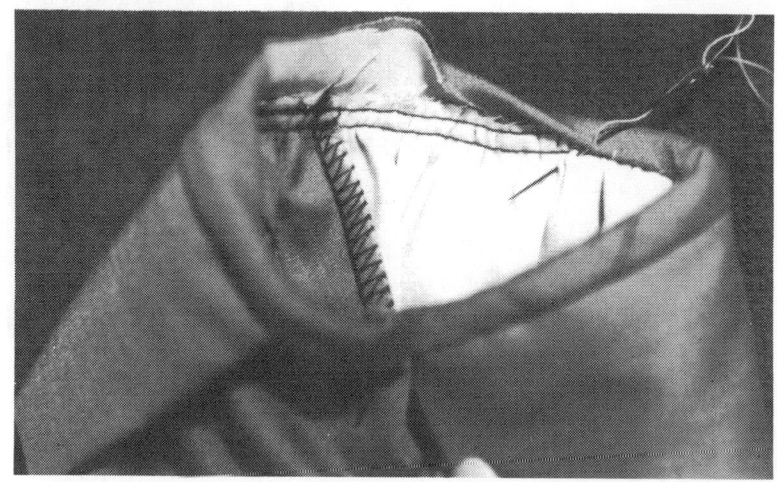

Fold the bias in half, turn under the raw edge and pin in place. Hand whip the bias fold to the seam on the wrong side of the garment.

Hand tack a tiny pleat at the buttonhole end of the cuff. This causes a nice pleat when the cuff is buttoned.

This is my favorite finish for lightweight fabric. It is the easiest sleeve opening.

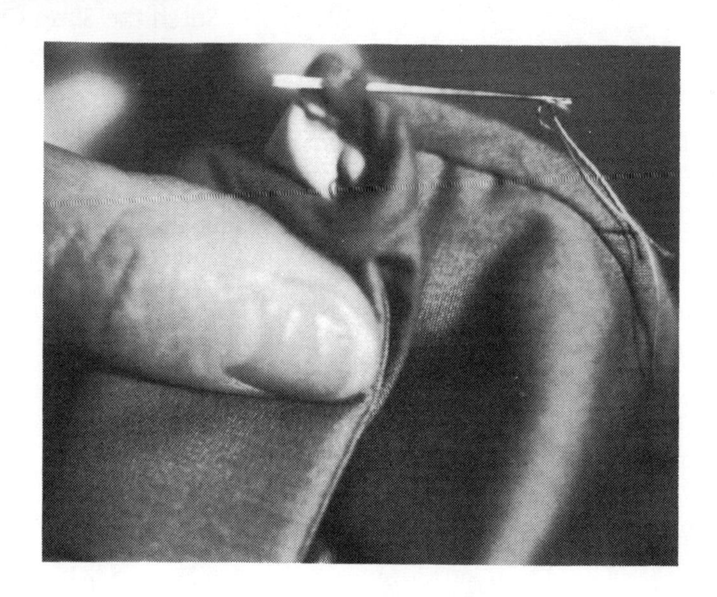

Slash Opening

Use for medium to heavy weight fabric. Mark the sleeve opening with a pencil line. You will cut on the line so it won't show.

Preparation for a Slash Opening

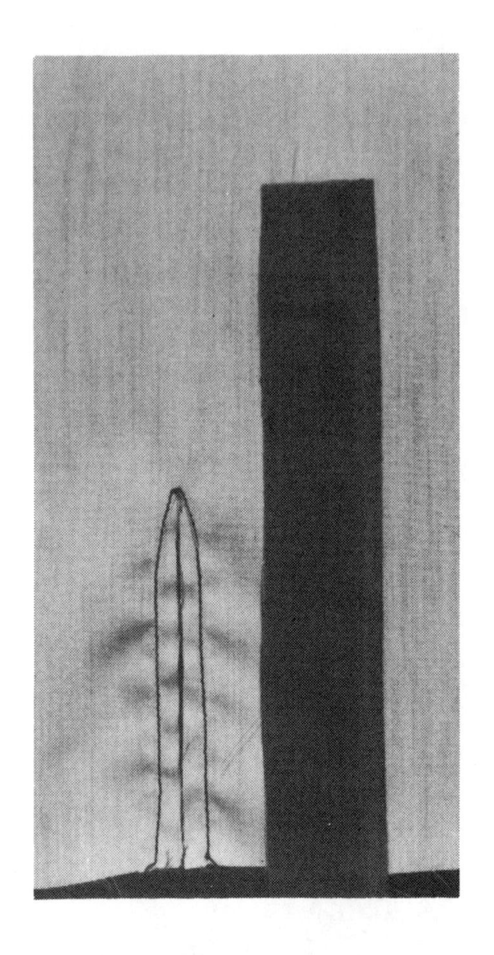

Cut a piece of fashion fabric 1⅛" wide and twice the length of the opening plus a little extra. If possible, one edge should be on the selvage. If no selvage is available, make the strip 1⅜" wide and turn under one edge. Use this piece in place of any pattern piece as they are usually too wide.

With small stitches (15-20 stitches per inch) stitch a curved V where the sleeve opening is marked. Take one stitch across at the point and backstitch at the same place. Then stitch down the remaining leg of the V. The legs of the V should be no more than a scant 1/2" apart.

Slash to the point. You **must** slash clear to the backstitch. Put a pin on the backstitch so you can't cut through the stitching.

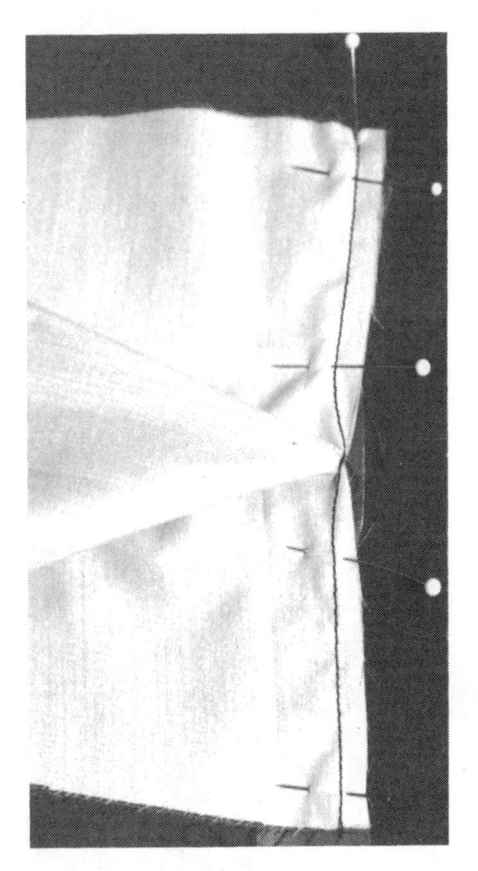

Stitch the Slash Opening

Lay the cut edge of the strip along the slash with the right sides together, keeping the selvage or the turned under edge free. The seam allowance on the strip is a scant 1/4". The seam allowance on the sleeve will be very narrow at the point of the V and a scant 1/4" wide only at the ends. With the sleeve up, pin the sleeve to the strip by pinning one end of the strip to the sleeve with right sides together. Then fasten both ends of the strip to a padded table or the ironing board with pins. Stretch the sleeve slightly as you near the point of the V so the slash fits the straight strip. Pin to hold.

It helps to fold and pin the excess fabric of the sleeve into a triangle to keep it out of the way as you are stitching across the point. With the sleeve up, stitch just inside the reinforced stitching line. Overcast the point with a small zigzag or hand overcast.

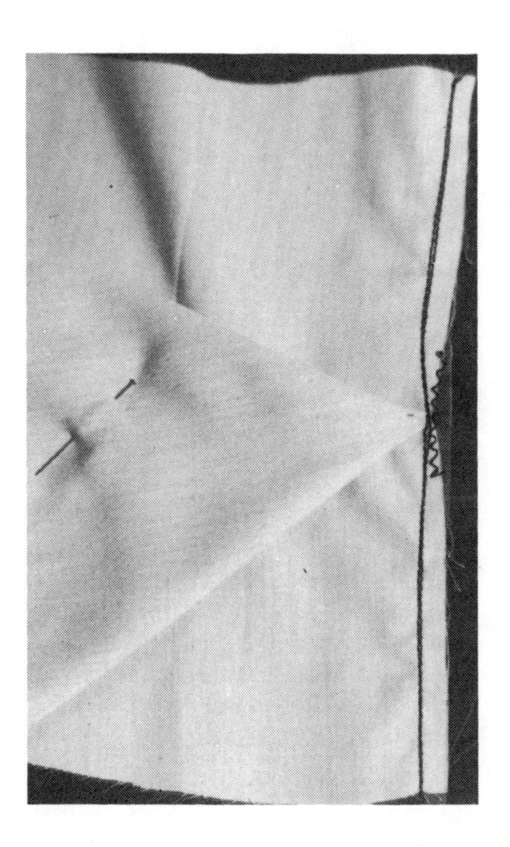

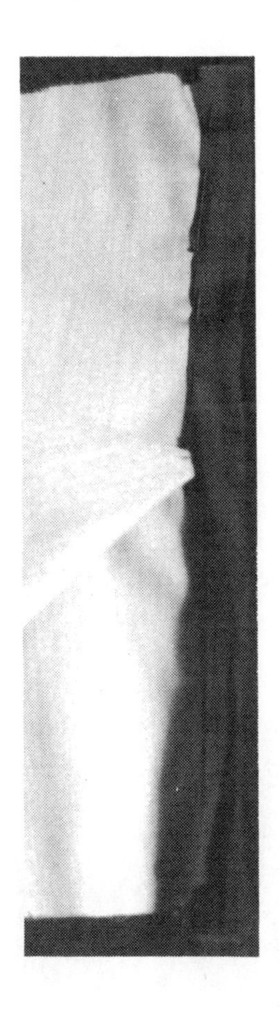

Press the seam toward the strip. Press the strip in half so the selvage barely covers the seam. Pin or baste in place.

Stitch on the right side of the sleeve in the well of the seam either by machine or hand. Handstitching is softer and finer. Machine stitching is faster and stronger.

Fold the strip in half as it will lie and tack the fold to hold it flat. Press the strip so it will extend on the area closest to the sleeve seam and turn under on the remaining side. The turned under edge corresponds with the buttonhole end of the cuff.

Now stitch the sleeve seam and finish the seam edges. Refer to Sample Seams and Pressing Techniques, pages 65-67 and Seam Finishes, pages 58 and 68-71. If you are using the Open or the Modified Open Method of setting in the sleeve, wait to stitch the sleeve seam and wait to attach the cuff until the sleeve is stitched on the garment. Refer to Sleeves, pages 194 and 203.

Stitch The Cuff On The Sleeve

Put the cuff on the sleeve by pinning the right (uninterfaced) side of the cuff to the sleeve. (If your fabric is sheer and the interfaced side of the cuff looks better, pin the interfaced side of the cuff to the sleeve.) Keep the under side of the cuff free. If the sleeve is full and gathered, it is especially important to match all the dots and notches. This distributes the gathering correctly. The buttonhole end of the cuff lies on the back of the sleeve which is always marked with double notches at the armhole. Be sure the edge of the sleeve opening is exactly on the end of the cuff.

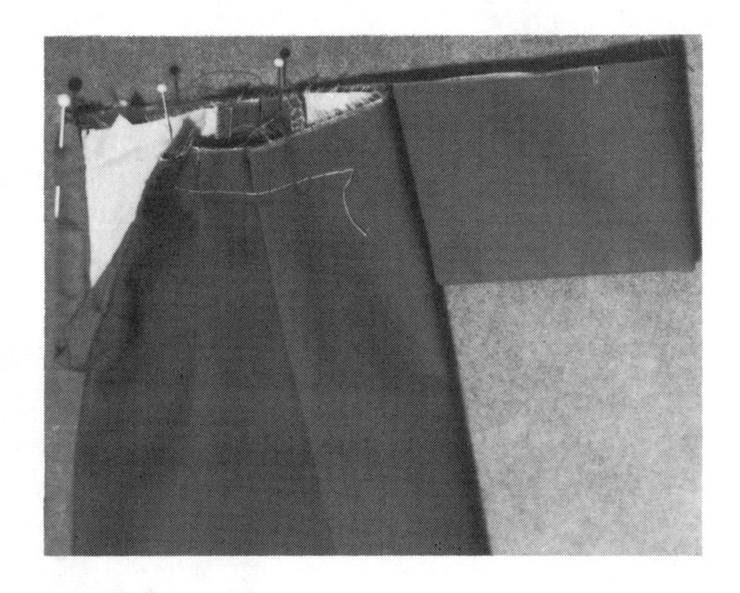

Stitch the cuff to the sleeve, keeping the seam at the cuff ends free. Stitch with the cuff up unless the sleeve is gathered. In that case, always stitch with the gathered area up.

The inside edge of the cuff can be finished by machine or by hand. I like to finish it by machine instead of hand stitching as the pattern directs. Self-finish by machine is fast, strong, and allows the seams to be trimmed after they are stitched. This method also works beautifully on some collars (refer to pages 182 and 183), yokes (refer to pages 140-141), and blouse ties.

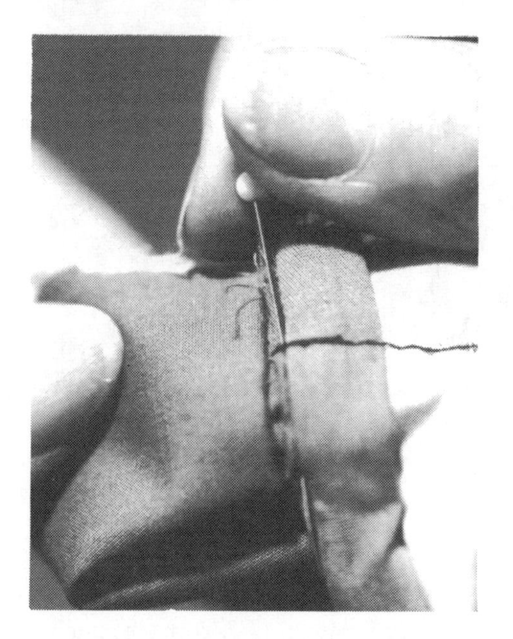

Pin the stitched sleeve to the cuff very close to the cuff seam to hold the sleeve in place while you are stitching the end. Pin with the head of the pin up toward the seam.

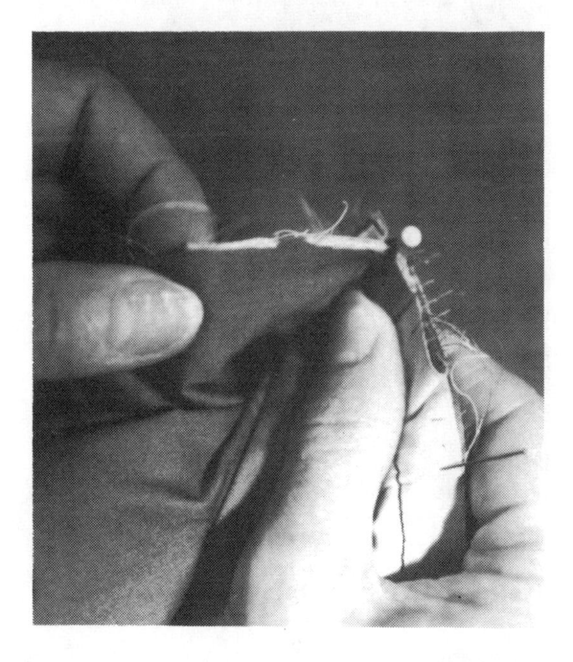

Turn the cuff back on itself and pin in place for a few inches. The cuffs will be right sides together with the sleeve in between.

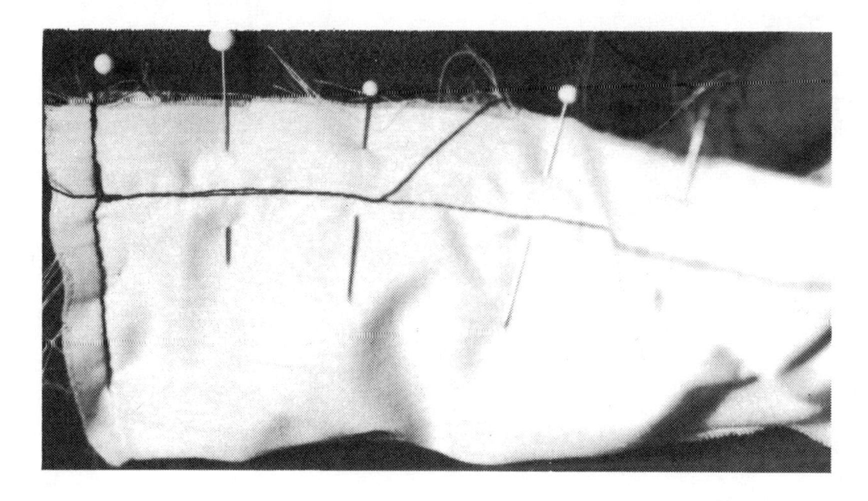

Stitch, using the first stitching line as a guide.

Pull the cuff right side out and check the stitching. If everything looks okay, turn it back to the wrong side and trim the seam to 1/4". Trim the corner to eliminate bulk. Do the other end of the cuff in the same manner.

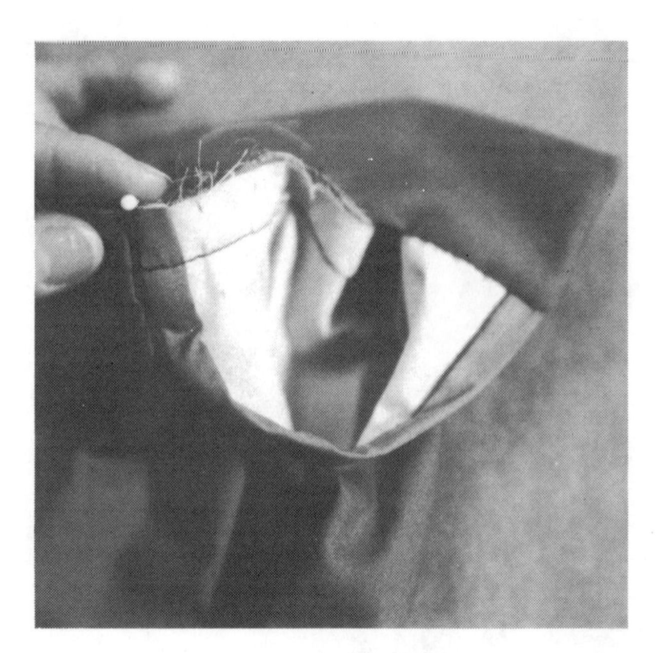

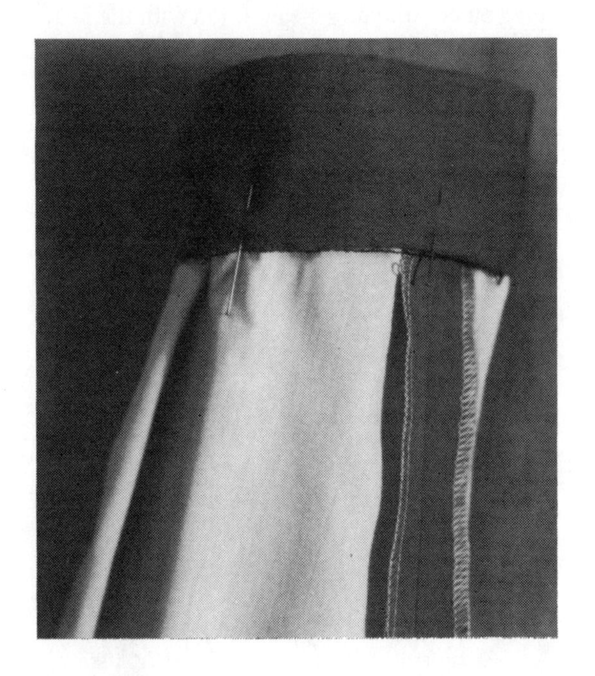

Trim the remaining sleeve/cuff seam to 1/4". Turn the remaining area of the cuff in along the seam line and whip stitch along the fold line.

Tailored Placket Opening

Your pattern will have a pattern piece for the Tailored Placket Opening. Cut two of them per pattern directions.

Preparation for a Tailored Placket Opening

Mark the slash line on the placket and the sleeve with pins, marking pencil, or thread baste line. On the placket, mark the center of the point with a dot or a pin. Mark the stitching lines on the placket with tape or a marking pencil. Refer to Placket Openings, page 149. Make the opening 1/8" narrower than the pattern is marked. A smaller opening is much easier to cover. Lay the placket on the sleeve. The right side of the placket should lie on the wrong side of the sleeve. **Be sure the pointed end of the placket is on the front of the sleeve.** Match the slash line of the placket to the slash line of the sleeve. Pin the placket in place.

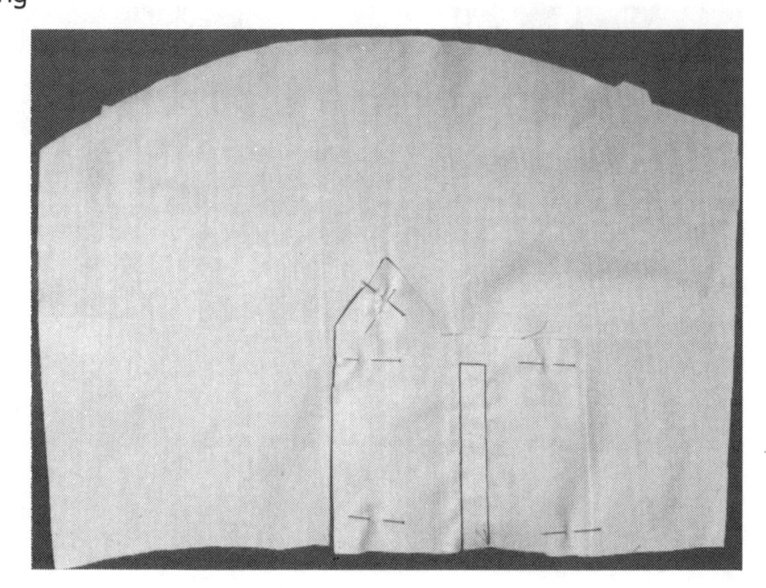

Stitch the Tailored Placket Opening

Stitch around the opening using small stitches and pivot at the corners. If your fabric frays easily, reinforce the corners with double stitching.

Slash between the stitching lines, clipping diagonally into the corners. You must clip to but not through the stitching line. Put a straight pin on the stitching line to guard against clipping through it.

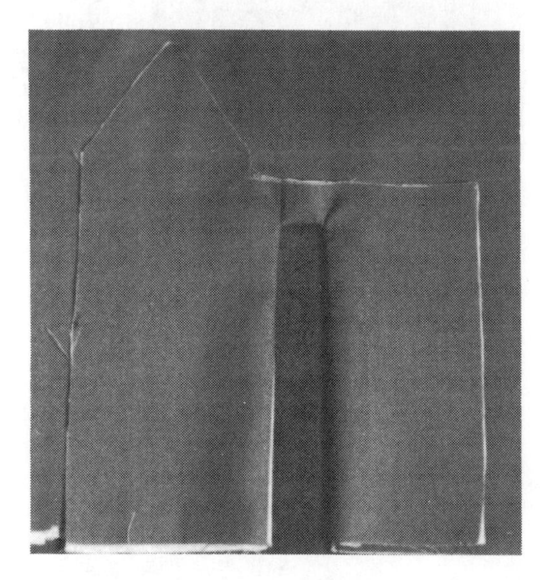

Turn the placket to the right side of the garment and press. First press the seams open. Then press so the square opening lies flat.

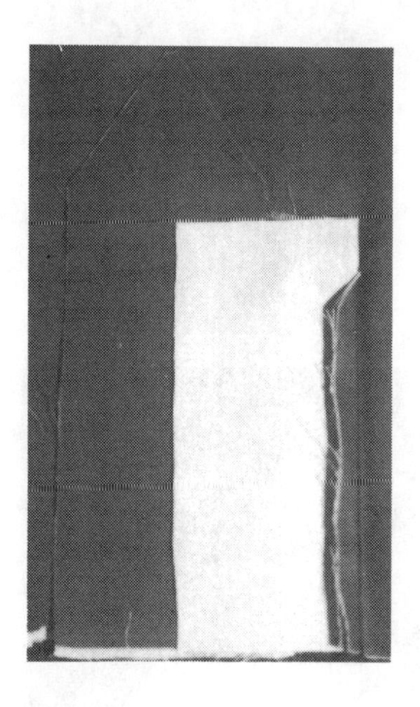

Still working on the right side, press so the seams lie toward the placket.

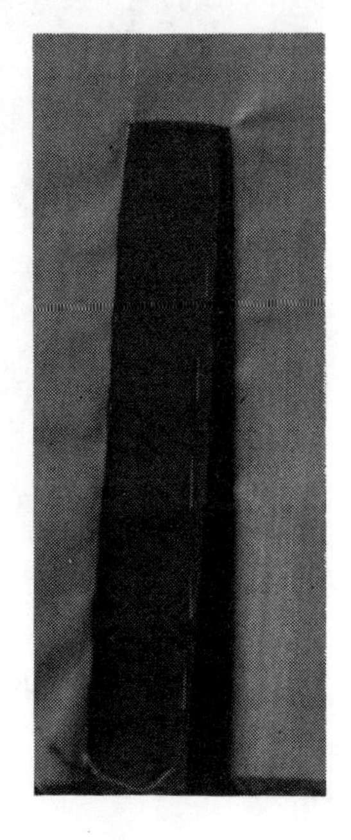

The **under** (unpointed) side of the placket must be only wide enough to fill the opening. Work from the top of the placket on the wrong side of the sleeve. Measure the distances carefully from the seam line and pin. Now baste along the fold line.

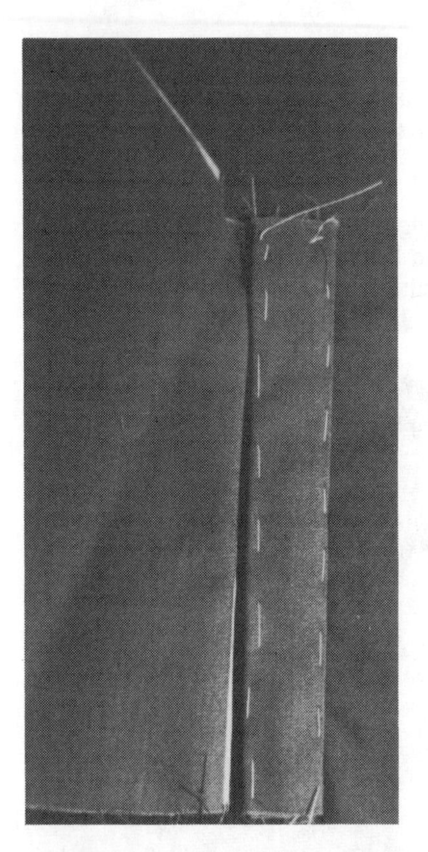

On the right side of the sleeve, turn the seam allowance under so it just covers the seam. Trim the seam allowance, if needed, and baste in place. Edgestitch both basted edges. If you have a Bernina machine, use the blind hem foot, and move the needle one or two spaces to the left. This keeps the edgestitching perfectly straight. Refer to Couture Patch Pockets, page 231.

Fold the **upper** placket along the fold line, making sure the fold covers the under placket completely, and baste to hold.

Edgestitch from the bottom of the placket to the top of the opening.

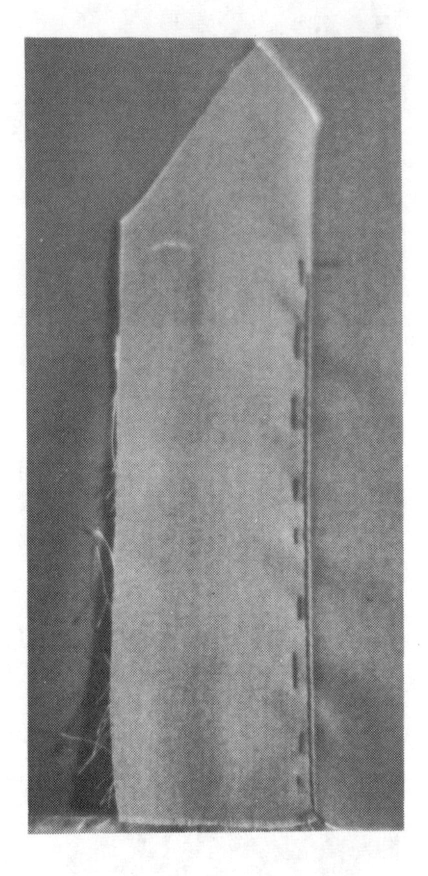

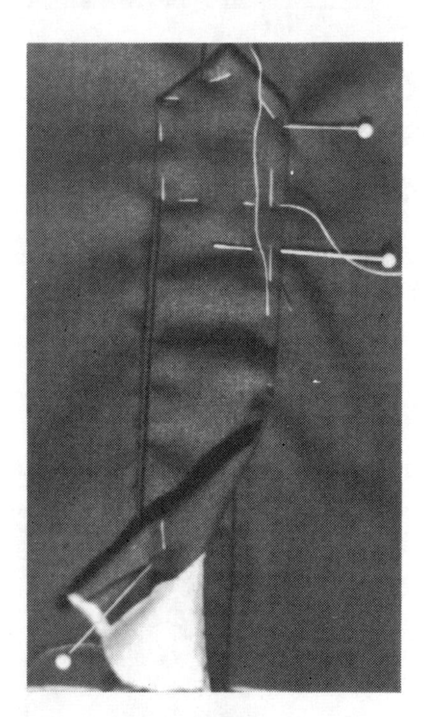

Turn the remaining seam allowance of the upper band under so it covers the seam. Pin to hold. Measure to find the center of the band at the point. This was marked earlier but sometimes the marking can be off enough to make the point uneven.

For easy turning of the point, fold the band in half, right sides together, and stitch across the point at the seam line.

Trim and turn right side out. Turn the point evenly along the band edges.

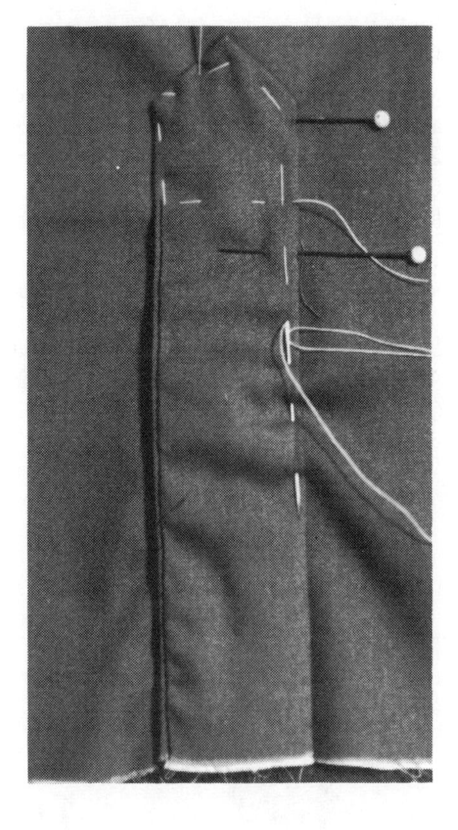

Pin and baste the point and the band. Also baste across the placket, catching the opening underneath.

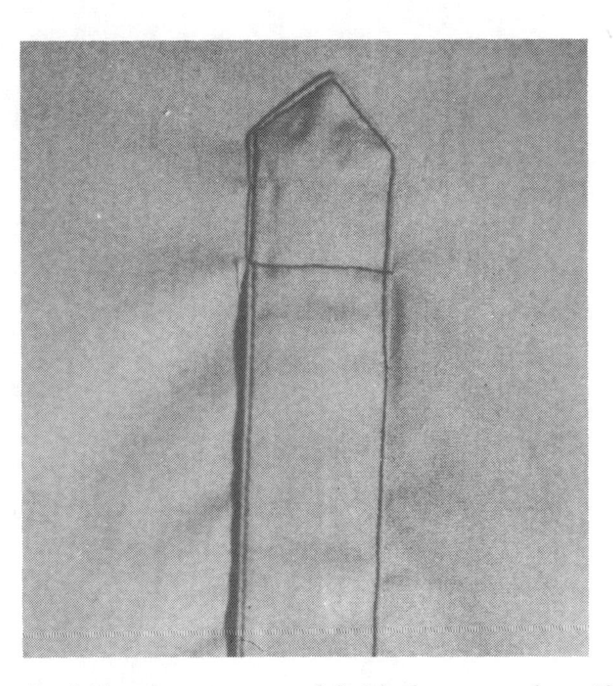

Edgestitch across the placket, around the point, and down to the bottom of the placket.

Stitch the sleeve seam and finish the seam edges. If you are using the Open or the Modified Open Method of setting in the sleeve, wait to stitch the seam until the sleeve is stitched on the garment. Refer to Sleeves, pages 194 and 203.

Stitch the cuff on the sleeve

Refer to cuff instructions on page 132 of this chapter. If there is no cuff, treat the bottom of the sleeve as your pattern directs.

Finish the blouse or dress

Hem a blouse using a machine stitched small rolled hem. Refer to Hems, page 101.

To hem a dress, refer to Hems, pages 97-102.

Make any buttonholes on the right side of the garment. Follow the pattern directions for the size of buttons, the amount of lap, and the direction (horizontal or vertical) of the buttonholes. Refer to Machine Buttonholes, page 206, for the placement of the buttonholes. Refer to 207-209 for marking the buttonhole location and length. Cord the buttonholes if your fabric is a knit. Otherwise they will stretch and become too large for the button. Refer to page 210 and your machine buttonhole directions.

On fine fabrics I prefer a narrow buttonhole. Refer to page 212.

Sew on the buttons. Make sure you have enough shank on the buttons to allow the garment to hang properly. All buttons need some shank. The amount of shank depends on the thickness of the garment. Refer to Sewing On Buttons, page 220.

YOKES

There are two ways yokes are used in garments. In one application they are simply a part of the neckline. In the other application they are used as part of the neck facing. Read your pattern directions and see how the yoke is being used in your garment. If the yoke is being used as a part of the neck facing continue to use it in that manner. Refer to Collars, pages 165 and 171.

If both thicknesses of the yoke are simply being stitched onto the back of the blouse with the under yoke being attached by hand, use the following method. It eliminates any hand stitching on the yoke and allows you to reinforce the yoke seams, trim the seam, and topstitch without the chance of puckers in the yoke.

Pin one yoke to the back of the blouse with the right side of the yoke to the right side of the blouse.

Pin the right side of the other yoke to the wrong side of the blouse. The yokes are right sides together with the back of the blouse between them.

Pin or hand baste the yoke seam and stitch. Stitch again 1/4″ into the seam allowance. Trim the seam to that second row of stitching.

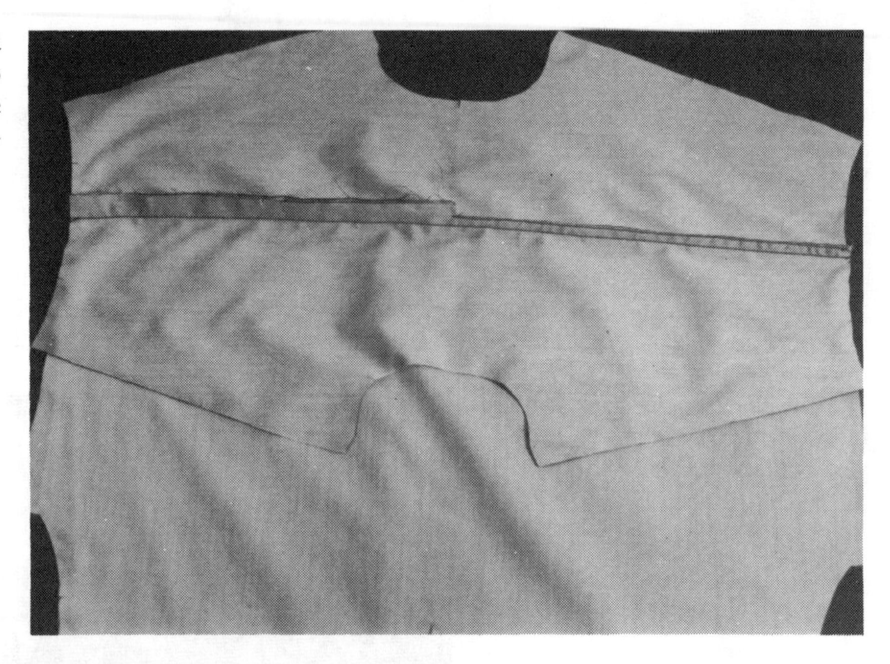

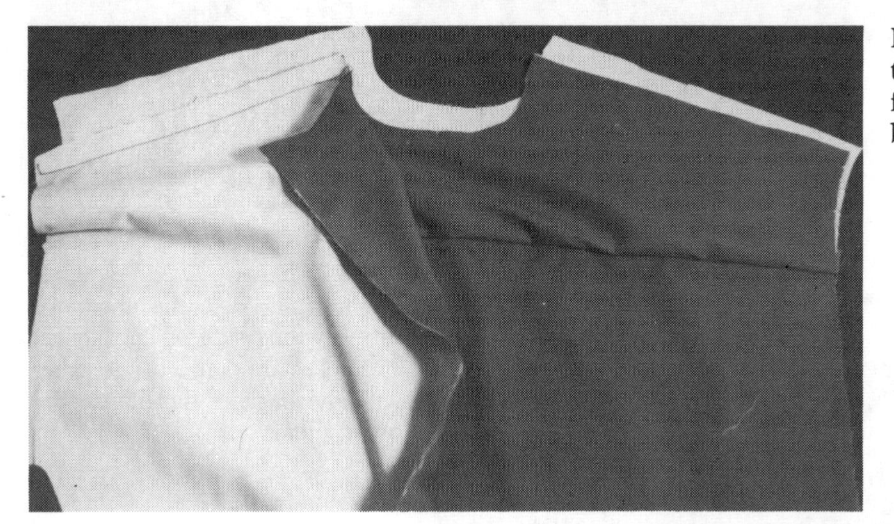

Pin the right side of the front of the blouse to the right side of the front of the yoke. Machine or hand baste the seam.

Bring the shoulder seam of the under yoke around the front of the blouse.

Pin it along the seam you just basted. The yokes are right sides together with the blouse front between the yokes.

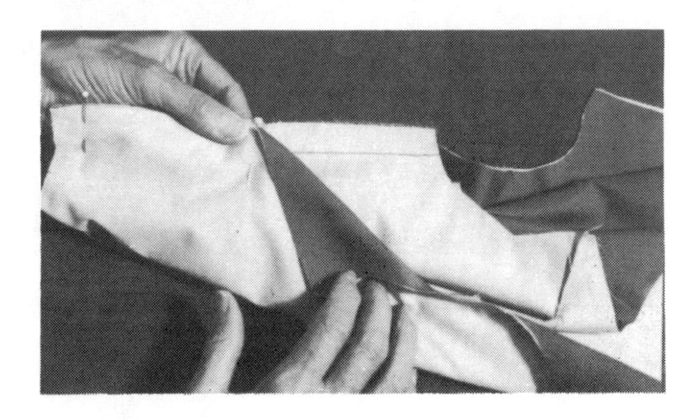

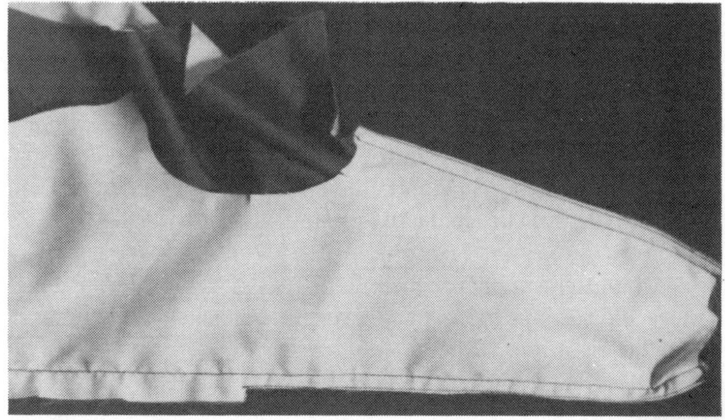

Stitch the seam. Stitch again 1/4″ into the seam allowance. Trim the seam to the second row of stitching.

Pull the blouse so it is right side out.

Do the other side in the same way.

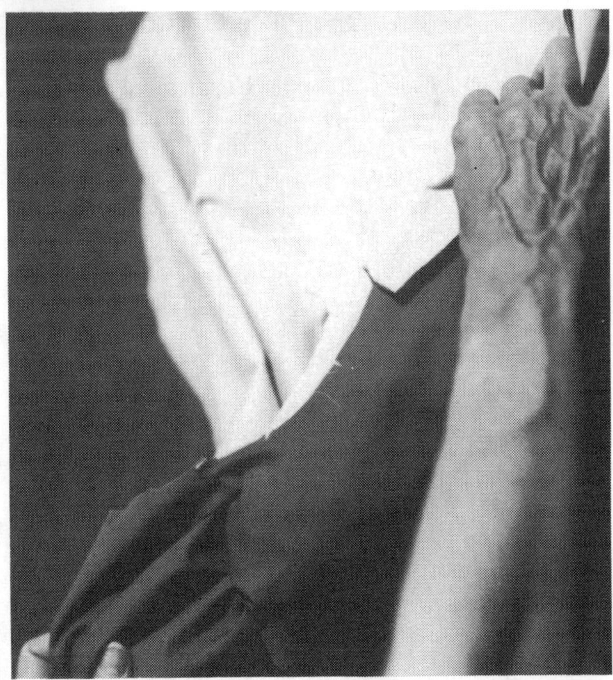

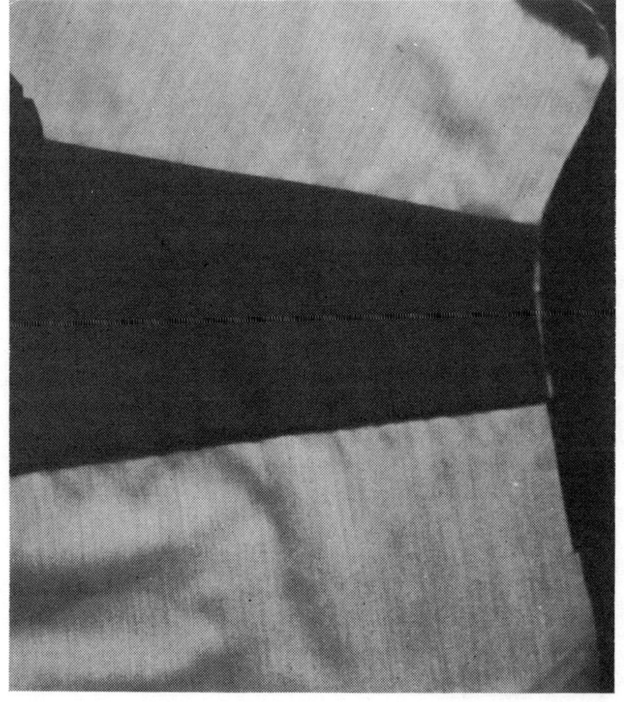

Press the yoke seams. Continue with the pattern directions for the garment. If the pattern calls for topstitching or edge-stitching, refer to pages 72-73, 231, and 314.

PLACKET OPENINGS

A placket opening looks easy but can be difficult because you must be exact. If the placket is to look professionally done, the angled seams must be stabilized with organdy. If the band is finished on the right side of the garment, the left side width must be adjusted. The left side width must be slightly narrower than the right side. The right side laps over and covers the left side. Usually a garment with a placket opening will not have a center front seam. If it does have a center front seam, the seam must be exactly in the center of the band when it is finished.

The patterns having a placket opening or a buttoned band closing can have one or two pieces for the placket. The construction method is different for a one-piece placket than it is for a two-piece placket. Sometimes a two-piece placket will use the same pattern piece for the right and left side.

This Is A One-Piece Placket

The front pattern piece is pictured on the following page.

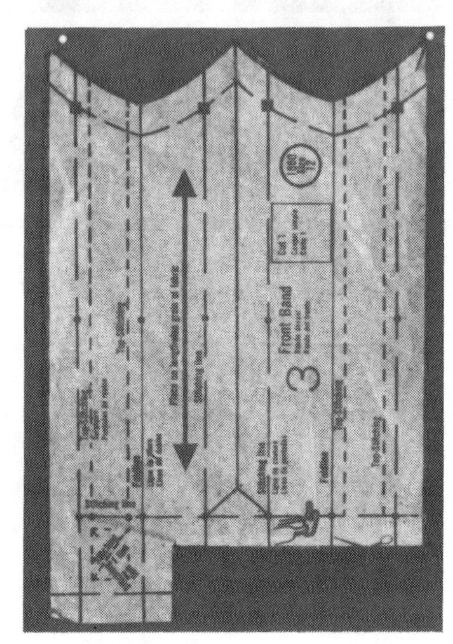

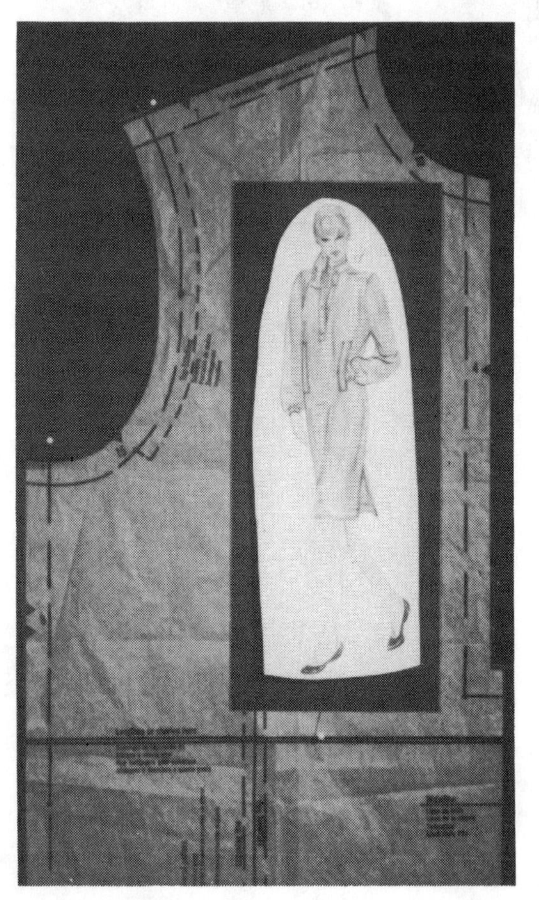

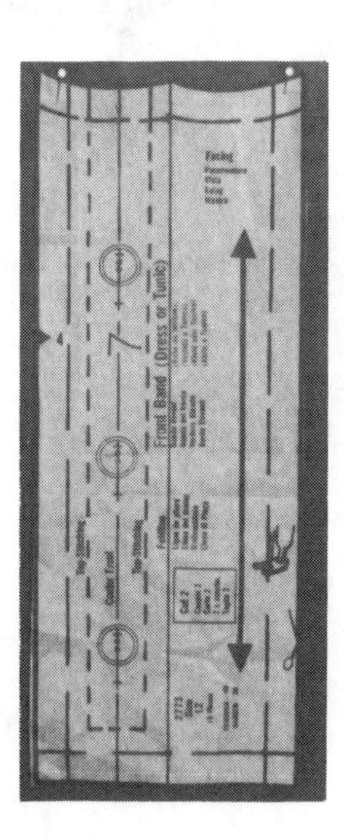

This Is A Two-Piece Placket

The same placket pattern piece is used for both the right and left side of the garment.

This Is A Two-Piece Placket

It has two placket patterns. A pattern for the right side and one for the left side. Notice all the angled seams on this blouse pattern. The sleeves are sewn with angled seams as is the front of the collar.

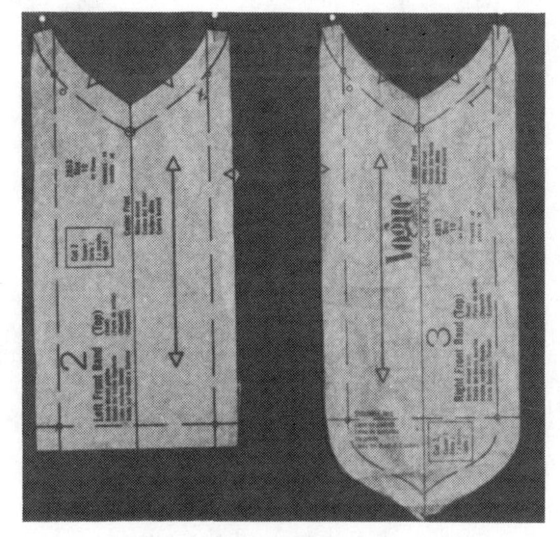

Cut The Garment

When cutting a two-piece placket, cut as the pattern directs with a rectangular hole cut in the center front of the garment.

If the pattern has a one-piece pattern for the placket (as in the picture), do not cut the fold at the center front of the placket opening of the garment. If the pattern has cutting lines there, ignore them and leave the front of the garment uncut. This pattern has a center front seam. Stitch the seam to the neckline and use that seam as the center front marking.

TWO-PIECE PLACKET

Preparation For A Two-Piece Placket Opening

Mark the center front on both the garment and the right placket piece with a thread trace. Placing a piece of masking tape with an edge along the center front is a help in basting a straight line.

Cut a piece of pre-shrunk organdy 2½″ deep and two inches wider than the width of the opening.

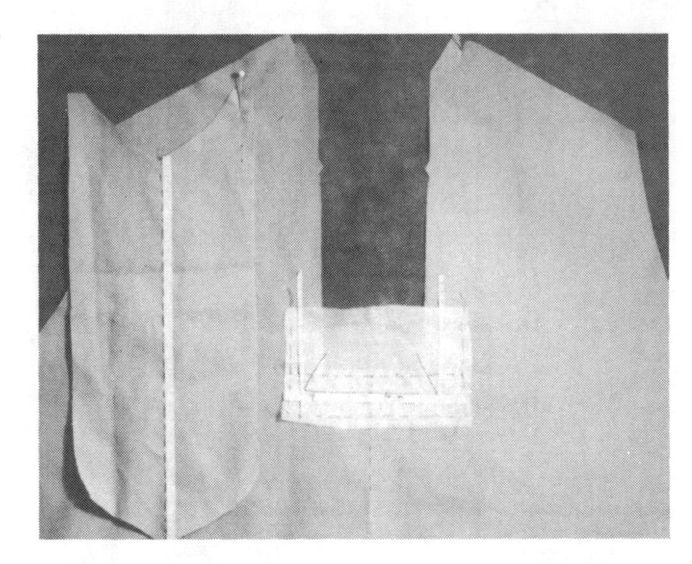

Place the organdy on the right side of the garment. Center the organdy on the placket opening with 1½″ of organdy below the opening. Baste around the outside edges of the organdy. Mark the stitching lines on the organdy with masking tape or topstitching tape.

On the right front of the placket mark the pattern stitching line usually 5/8″. On the left front of the placket mark the stitching line 1/16″ narrower. (The left front is on the right side of the picture.)

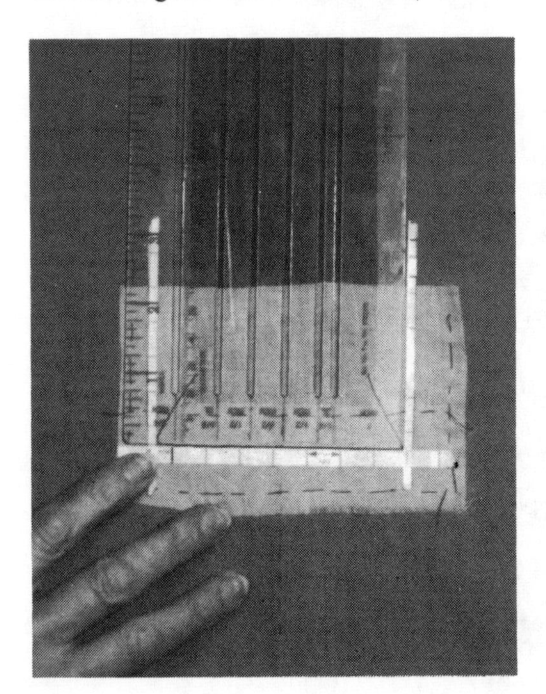

This slight difference in the width enables the right side to cover the left side completely as it must. If the fabric is bulky, allow 1/8″ difference.

Measure with a right angle (the Dritz see-through ruler is being used) to make sure the bottom edges are exactly even. Be especially careful if the bottom of the placket is stitched on the inside of the garment. if the bottom of the placket is finished on the outside of the garment, the right side of the placket will cover the opening.

Stitch the organdy in two V's, one at each corner. Clip to the point. Be careful. Don't clip through the stitching at the point of the V. Press the organdy to the wrong side. Then press the organdy toward the seam allowance. It is pictured clipped and turned in lower right photograph.

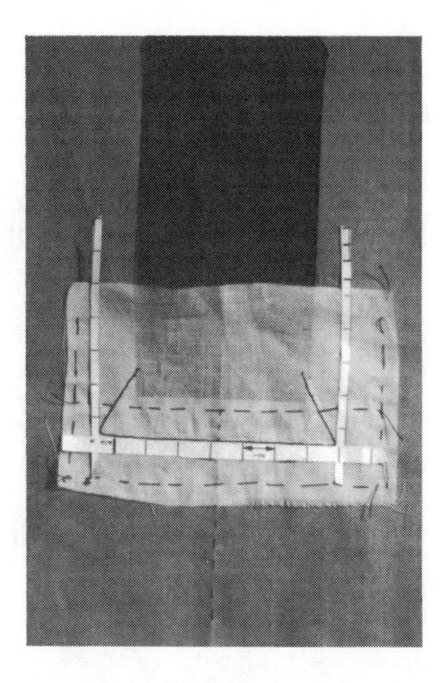

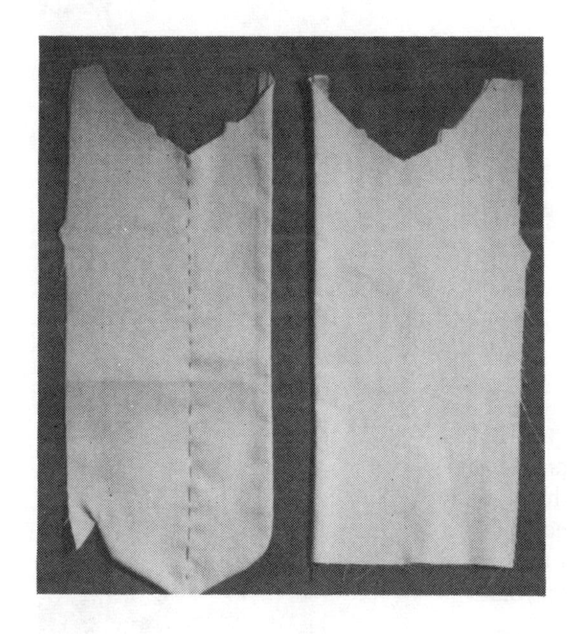

Interface the placket sides as the pattern directs. Do not establish any fold lines or trim any seam allowances on the placket. The turn of cloth can cause them to change. Refer to turn of cloth, page 65. Stitch the plackets and finish the end of the right placket as the pattern directs.

Stitching The Two-Piece Placket

On the left side of the placket opening pin a single thickness of the left placket to the garment with the right side of the placket to the right side of the garment. Extend all the organdy into the seam allowance. Baste, marking the seam line slightly narrower than 5/8″.

Stitch the left front, with the garment up, from the corner to the neckline. Be sure you are at or beyond the corner. It is easier to remove a few stitches than it is to restitch. The stitching must start exactly at the corner. Do not backstitch in the corner. Leave long threads for tying. The stitch must be just to the garment side at the corner. This prevents the organdy reinforcement from showing. The picture shows the seam stitched and the fabric is lying as it should at the sewing machine.

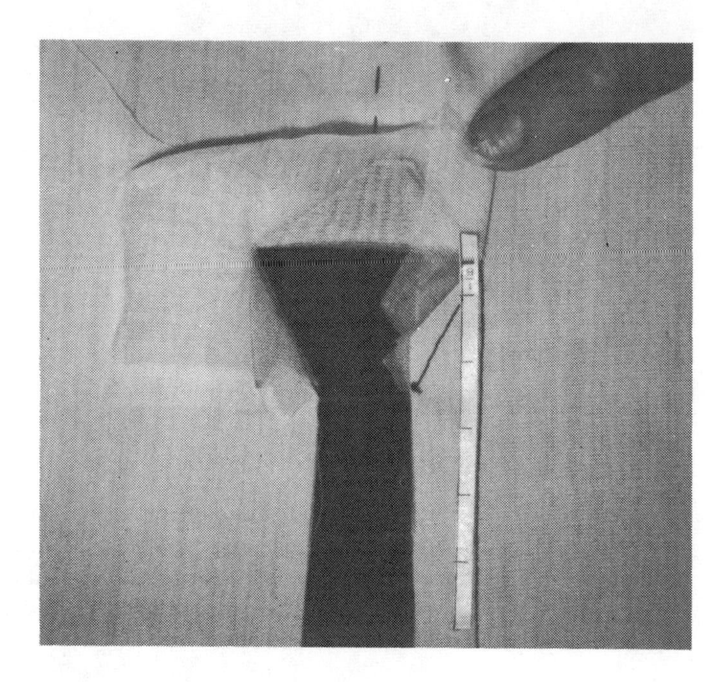

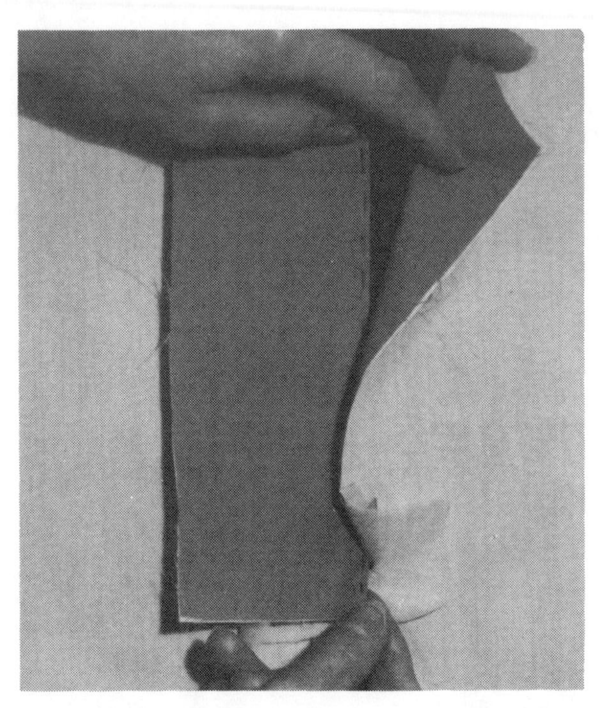

Press the seam toward the band. Fold the band so that it exactly fills the opening. Measure the width at the bottom of the opening and baste a fold to hold that width the entire length of the band.

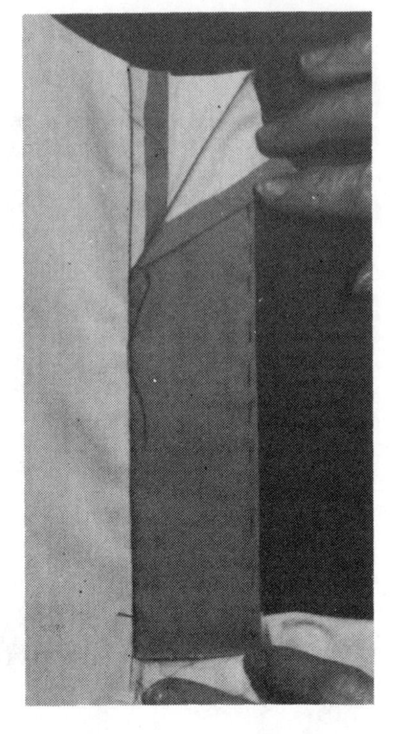

On the wrong side turn the seam allowance in so that it just covers the seam. Press or baste the fold. Trim the seam allowances to 1/4″. Trim the organdy and fold a narrow edge over the band. Slipstitch the folded edge to the stitching line. The band must just cover the seam. Do not stitch the end of the left band to the garment as the pattern directs until the right band is attached.

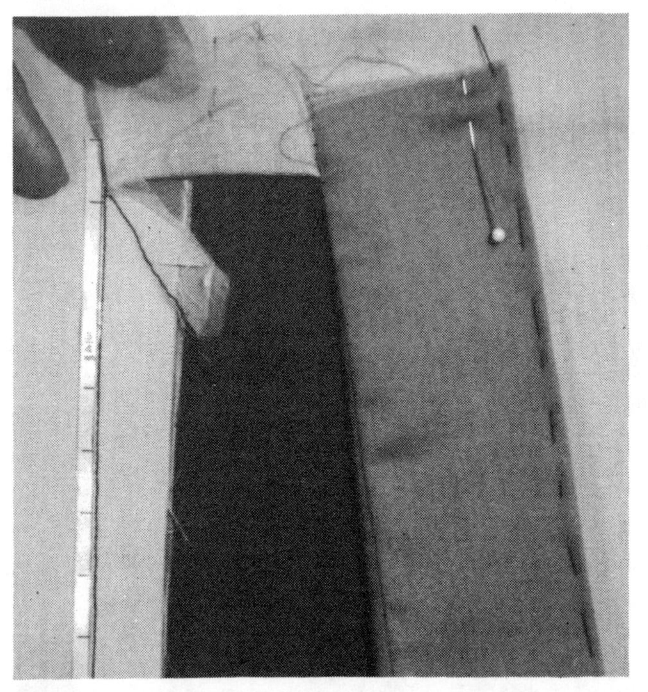

On the right side of the placket opening baste the right band to the right garment using a 5/8″ seam line.

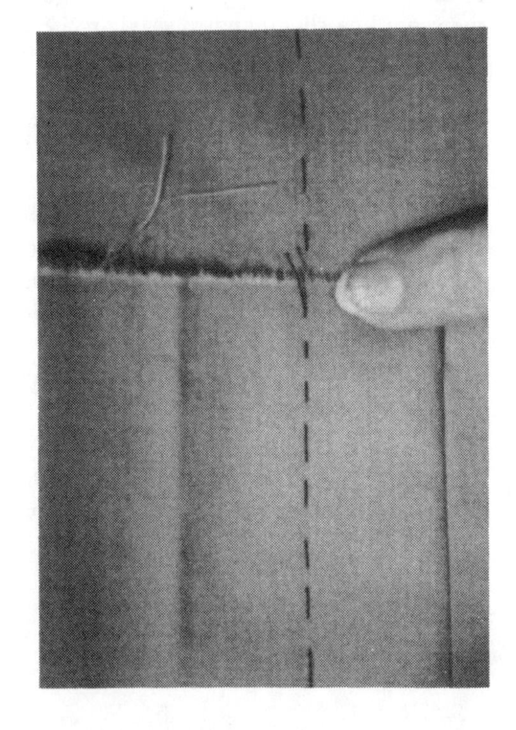

Check to see that the center front of the band lines up with the center front of the garment. If you have a pointed band, the center fronts must match. If the band is not shaped, they can be off a bit and it won't matter. Stitch the band from the corner to the neckline in the same way the left band was stitched.

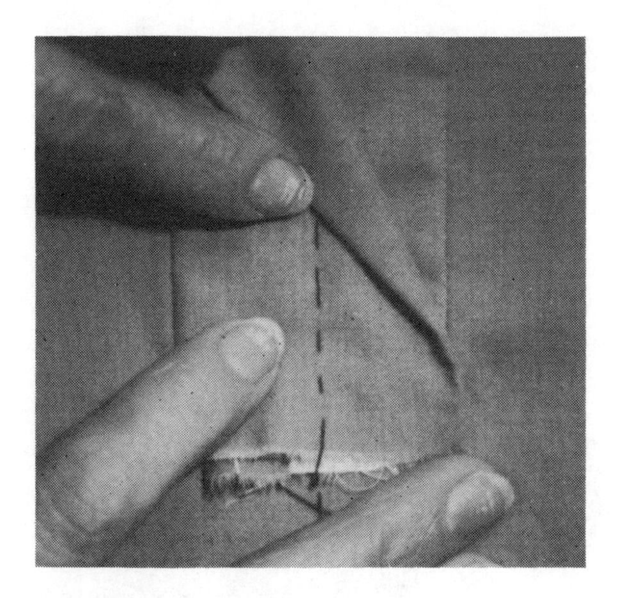

Press the seam toward the band. On the right side establish the band width. The band must be just wide enough to cover the opening. Measure the width at the bottom of the opening and baste a fold to hold that width the entire length of the band.

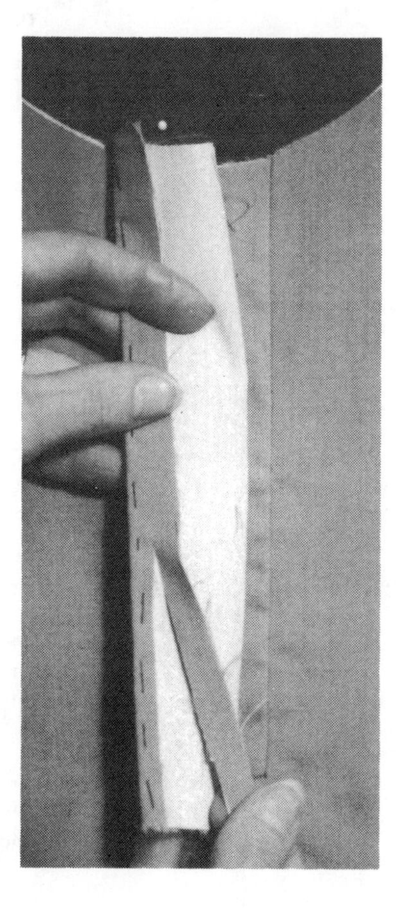

Follow the pattern directions for finishing the ends of the bands. Often the left band is stitched to the bottom of the placket opening on the inside of the garment. The right band end is finished and it covers the bottom of the placket opening. Sometimes both ends are stitched on the inside. If both ends are stitched on the inside, the fold line of the right band must just meet, not cover, the opening.

On the wrong side of the right band turn the seam allowance in so it just covers the seam. Press or baste the fold. Trim the seam allowance to 1/4″.

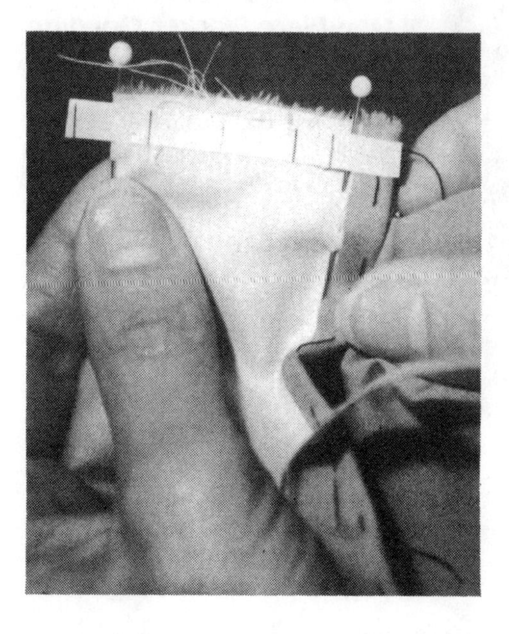

Finish the end of the right band if it was not done earlier. Mark the fold of the band. Fold the band right sides together and stitch the end. Mark the seam with tape to get it straight. Turn it right side out and check the stitching before trimming. When everything is straight, trim the seam.

Slipstitch the loose folded edge of the right band to the stitching line. The band must just cover the seam. Fasten the end as the pattern directs.

Proceed with the garment.

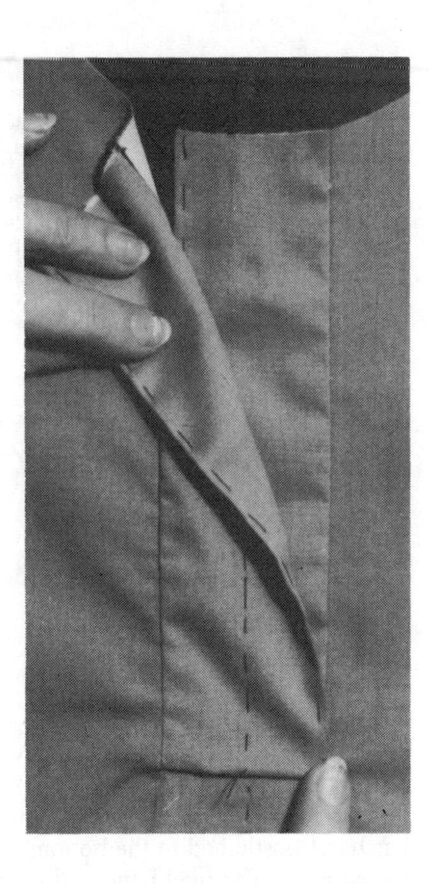

ONE-PIECE PLACKET OPENING

One-piece placket openings are very similar to the tailored placket on the sleeve of a blouse. Only the marking and the placement of the placket is different. Only the beginning and the end of the one-piece placket are covered here. For the stitching and turning instructions, refer to Dresses and Blouses, pages 135-137.

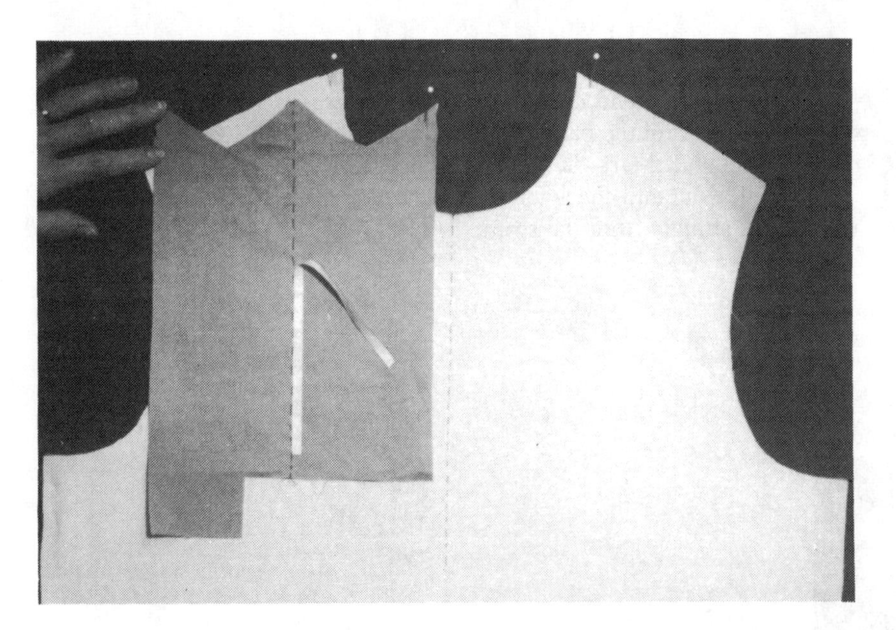

Preparation For A One-Piece Placket Opening

Mark the center front of the garment and the cutting line of the placket with a thread trace.

Mark the stitching lines on the wrong side of the placket with the masking tape or topstitching tape. On the right front (buttonhole side) of the placket, mark the pattern stitching line (5/8″). On the left front of the placket, mark the stitching line 1/16″ narrower.

This slight difference in the width enables the right side to cover the left side completely as it must. If the fabric is bulky, allow 1/8″ difference in the width.

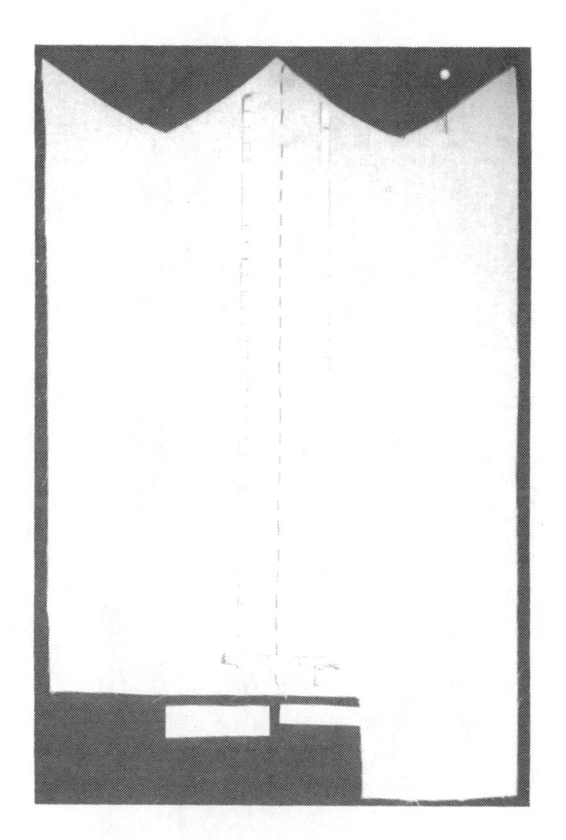

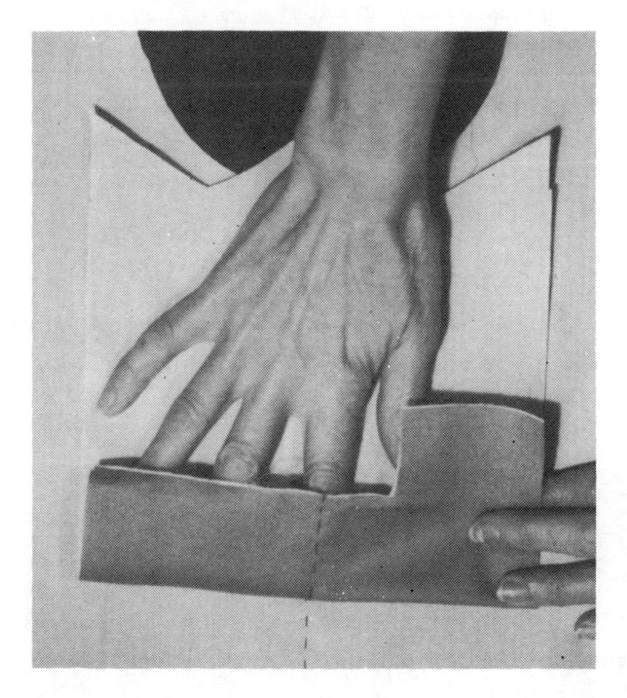

Lay the placket on the garment with the right side of the placket on the wrong side of the garment. For women's clothing the long end (buttonhole side) of the placket must be on the right front of the garment when you hold it up with the right side out. Match the center front of the plakcet to the center front of the garment. Pin or baste the placket to hold it securely.

Stitching The One-Piece Placket

Refer to Dresses and Blouses, pages 135-137, for detailed stitching instructions. Refer to your pattern instructions and the remainder of this chapter for finishing the bottom end of the placket.

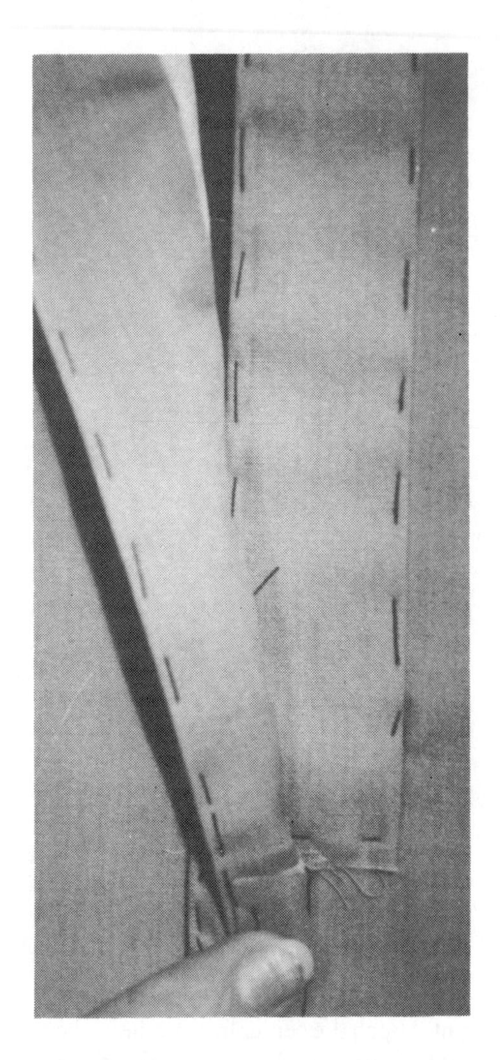

The left end is held on the right side of the fabric.

Trim any bulk out that you can and baste the edges down to hold them flat. The picture on the left shows the left side with the right side coming over to cover it. The picture on the right shows the placket on the wrong side of the garment.

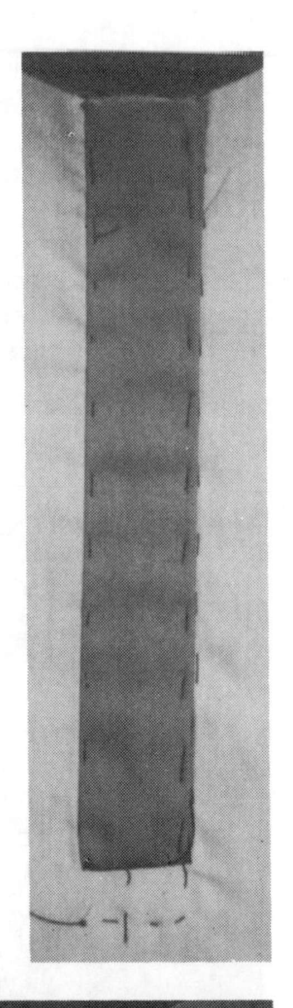

Topstitch or edgestitch as the pattern directs or the fabric dictates. Always baste before you topstitch. Topstitching must be done in steps on a placket as the pattern instructions direct. Refer to Topstitching and Edgestitching, pages 72, 231, and 314.

The bottom of the right side must just cover both sides of the bottom of the placket opening.

Proceed with the garment. Refer to the pattern instructions and any pertinent chapter in this book.

PARTIAL BUTTON OPENING

A buttoned area above a seam on a blouse can be a trouble spot. Such a blouse usually buttons partly up the back.

The shape of the opening is shown in the picture. It seems like a simple procedure. Do not reinforce the seam with a stitching line and clip to the stitching as many pattern directions suggest. For good results the seam must be clipped after the stitching is all completed.

Interface the facing to the fold line and stop the interfacing at the large dot. A French finish is a good choice for finishing the facing edge. Fasten the interfacing to the fold line with a small stitch. Mark the seam line in the facing area to be sure you have a 5/8″ seam. Stitch the seam leaving the back open above the large dot. (If French seams, page 69, are used on the blouse seams use the self-bound French seam, page 70, on the back seam.) Backstitch or tie the threads. Press the seam open.

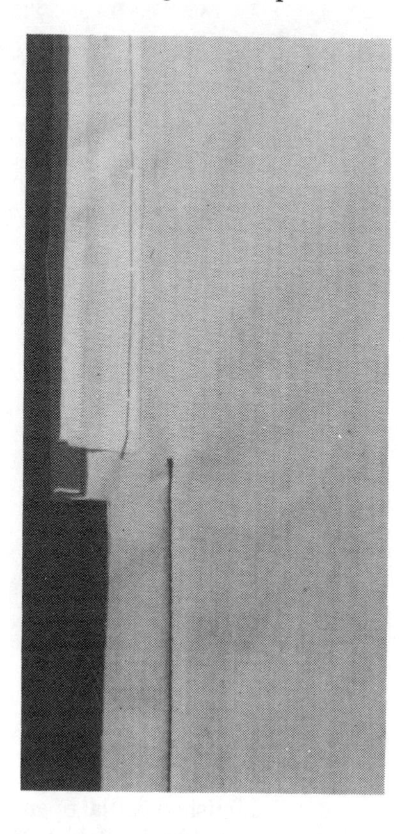

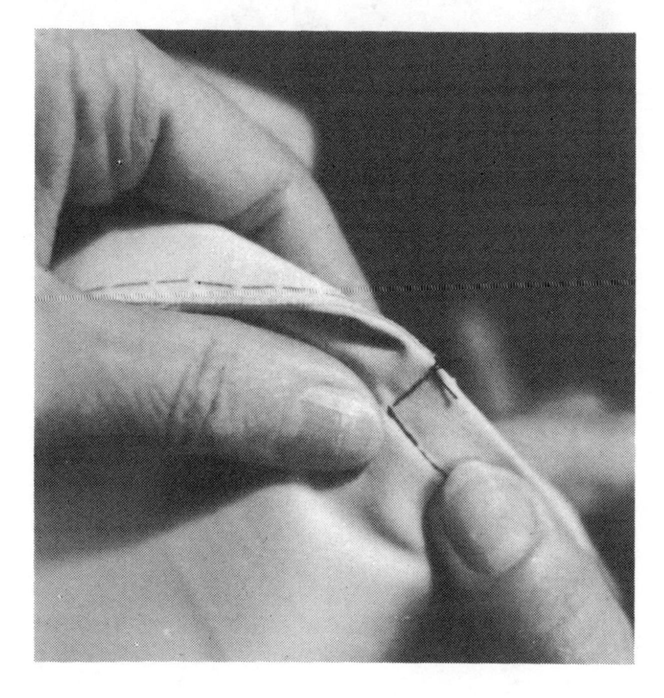

At the bottom of the facing fold the facing back on itself right sides together along the fold line. Stitch from the fold to the seam which ended at the large dot. Stitch with the facing down so you can see the seam. Just meet the seam line. Do not backstitch. Tie the threads. Stitch both the left and the right side of the opening.

Clip from the end of the extension to the fold. Then clip through the seam allowance only to the corner stitching. Trim the end of the band. Turn the band gently pushing the corner with a point pusher.

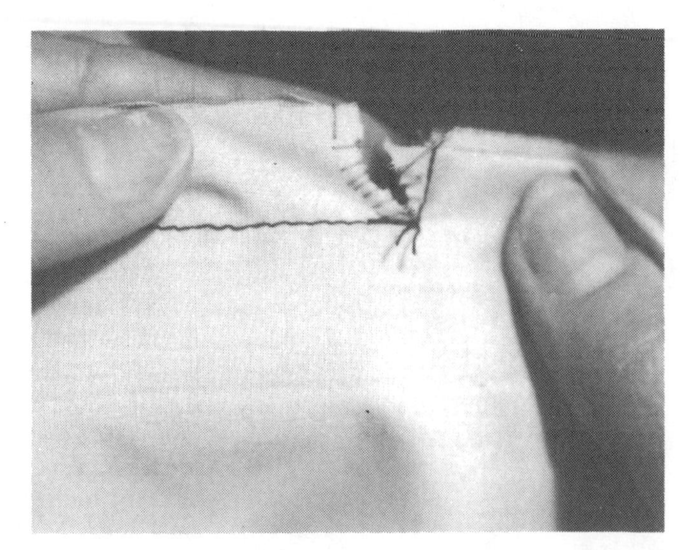

If your fabric ravels hand overcast the narrow area at the junction of the seams. Lap the bands as they should lie and invisibly stitch the band ends together on the inside. Finish the back seam. Refer to Seam Finishes, page 68-70.

The finished partial opening with the left back lapped over the right back.

Proceed with the garment.

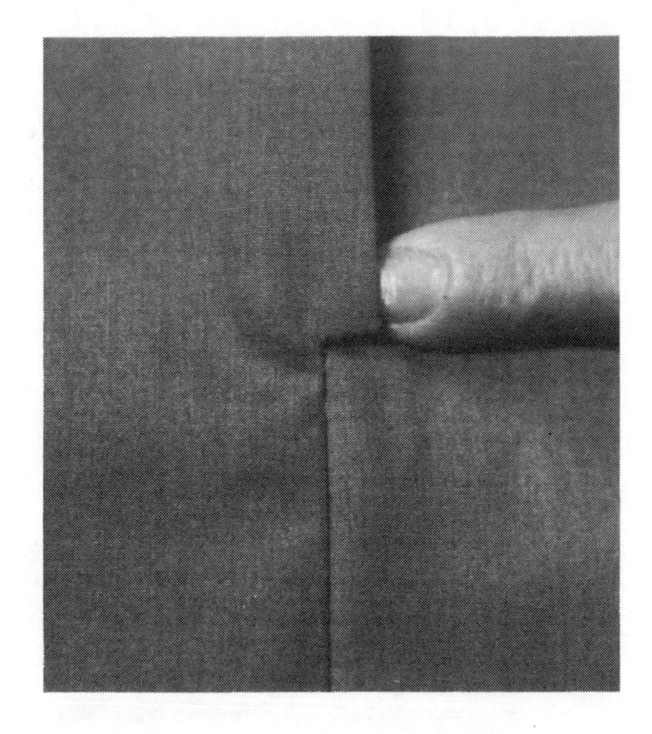

ANGLED SEAMS

Many places in a garment give us the challenge of getting a nice point or right angle. Patterns which will have angled seams are those with square or V necklines, shaped yokes, shawl collars, square armholes, and some tailored blazers. Some blazers have an angled seam in the neckline seam.

Many times the pattern instruction sheet tells you to stitch the angle and clip to the stitching. If you have a V neckline with a facing it is not necessary to reinforce it as the facing will turn back to the wrong side of the garment and reinforce the point. However, if the point were in a yoke and were to be stitched to the bodice you would need to reinforce the corner. It is very difficult to get a nice square corner and to keep it from fraying unless you reinforce the area. When you reinforce the angled seam stitch a small piece of fabric on the right side of the garment to preserve the corner when you sew the corresponding pieces together.

It is not necessary to reinforce artificial suedes. There are some styles of square armholes, in which the square is in a tuck, that do not need to be reinforced.

The best fabric for reinforcing corners is cotton organdy. I prefer the organdy that is thin and crisp. It is quite expensive but it works better for angled seams than ordinary cotton organdy. Organza could also be used but it does ravel more than organdy. Be sure and preshrink the organdy and iron it while it is wet. I buy a yard or two of organdy and keep it on hand to use for doing angled seams among other things. Refer to Inner Construction, page 21.

V NECKLINES

Pin the tissue together and try it on. Refer to Fitting Your Garments - Pattern Adjustment, pages 6-9. Make sure the V is not cut too low for you. It can easily be raised before cutting.

Adjust The Pattern Tissue

To raise the neckline extend the line from the center front fold. Raise the neckline as much as you need. Redraw the neckline and taper it into the neckline seam. You may need to curve the neckline. Follow the curve of the original neckline seam. Do the same changes to the neckline facing pattern piece.

Preparation for a V Neckline

Mark the exact center of the V on both the garment and the facing with a small hand baste. Fold the pieces in half to establish the center.

If the pattern calls for a neck stay of rayon seam binding follow the pattern instructions.

Stitching the V Neckline

Stitch the shoulder seams of both the garment and the facing.

Interface the neckline. A French finish is fine for a V neckline. That finishes the entire outer edge of the facing. Refer to Blouses and Dresses, page 118-120. If you have a serger it is very flat to serge the edges together instead of a French finish.

Lay the facing on the garment right sides together. Match the shoulder seams, the center back, and the center front. Match the baste lines on the center front and facing. Pin or baste to hold it exactly in place.

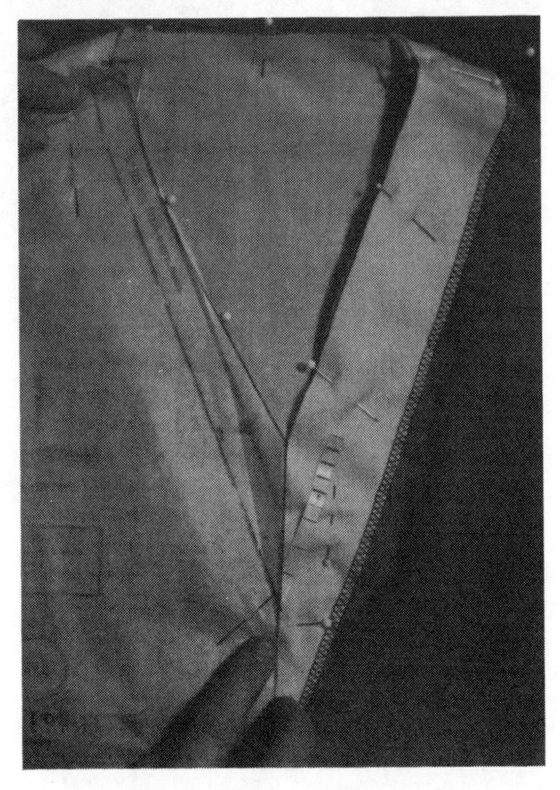

Mark the stitching line of the V with narrow tape. Lay the pattern back on the fabric and check the tape to make certain the angle is correct.

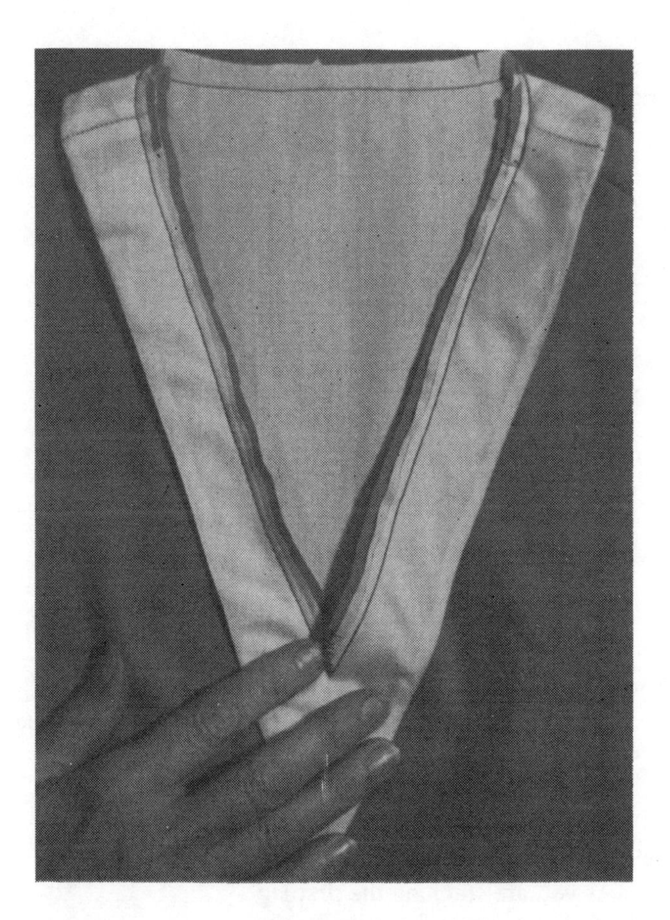

Stitch the neckline seam beginning at the back neckline. At the point shorten the stitches and pivot on the needle. Check the stitching to make sure the point is exactly on the center front baste line.

When the V point stitching is perfect reinforce it with small stitches just on the point. Clip to the stitching. Only clip at the point of the V and the curve around the back neckline. Grade the neckline seam if your fabric is medium to heavy weight. Hand overcast the point or use Fray Check. Refer to Seam Finishes, page 68. Be careful with the Fray Check. It must stay on the seam allowance.

Finish the neckline as the pattern directs. It is usually done with understitching or topstitching. Refer to Sleeveless Garments, pages 107 and 111, and to Topstitching and Edgestitching, pages 72, 231, and 314.

Proceed with the garment. Refer to the pattern directions and the pertinent chapters of this book.

ANGLED SEAMS

Preparation for stitching an Angled Seam

Cut a small square of organdy on grain. A 2″ square of organdy is adequate.

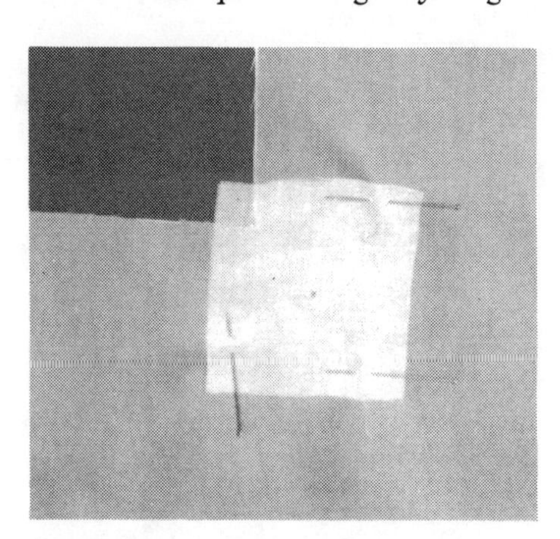

Place the organdy on the **right side** of the fabric. Pin the organdy to the fabric so that the largest part of it is on the fabric and just enough to stitch a wide V (about a 3/8″ square) extends beyond the edge. Pin the edges of the organdy to hold it in place.

Lay the pattern back on the fabric and mark just slightly inside the point of the right angle on the 5/8″ seam line. Mark with a tiny pencil dot on the organdy.

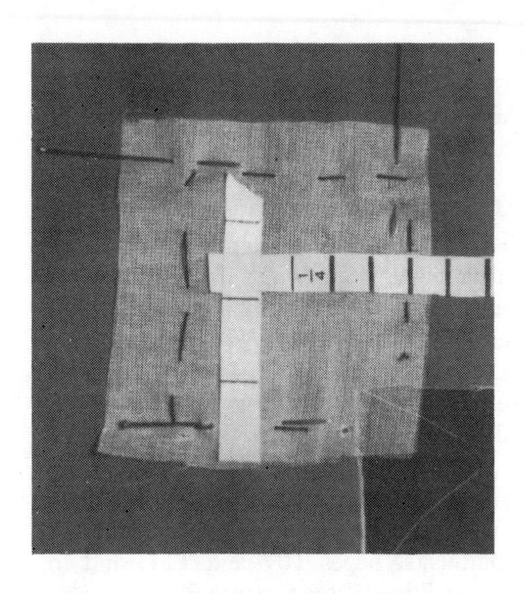

Hand baste the organdy square in place so it cannot slip. Mark the seam line with tape forming the corner.

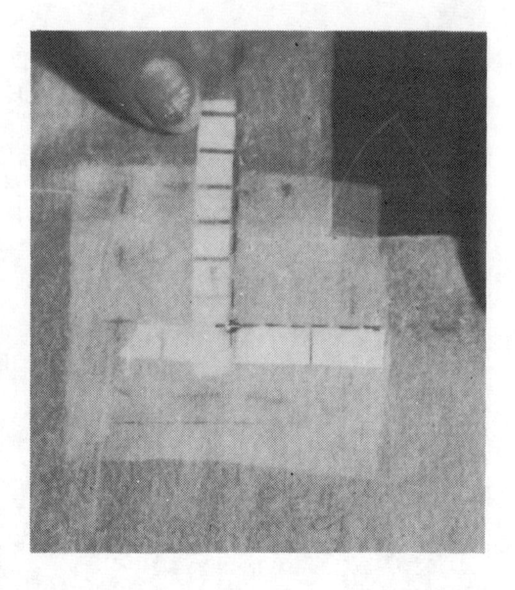

Lay the pattern back on the fabric to check the corner marking. It must be exact.

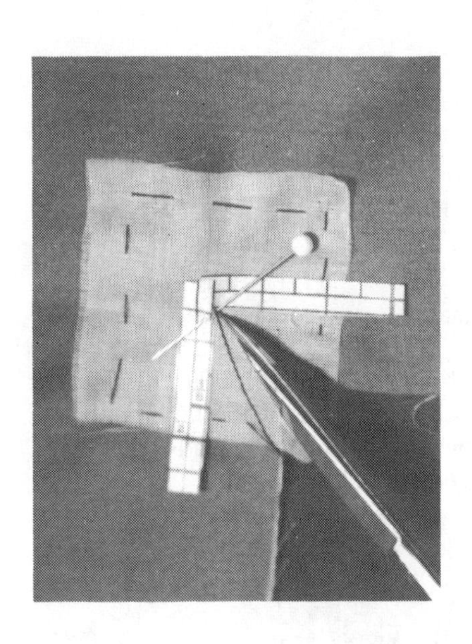

Stitch a wide V. The top legs of the V should be about 1/2″ apart. As you are stitching the first leg on the V aim for the entry of the marking pin. Leave the needle down, lift the presser foot, and pivot on the needle and stitch the remaining leg of the V. Use small stitches (20 per inch). Remove the tape and the basting.

Clip to the stitching. Put a pin across the point to keep you from clipping through the stitches.

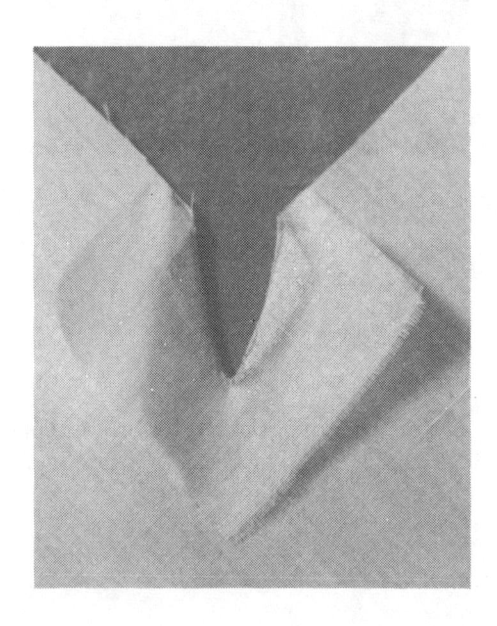

Press the organdy to the wrong side of the garment. The organdy must not show on the right side of the fabric.

Stitching an Angled Seam

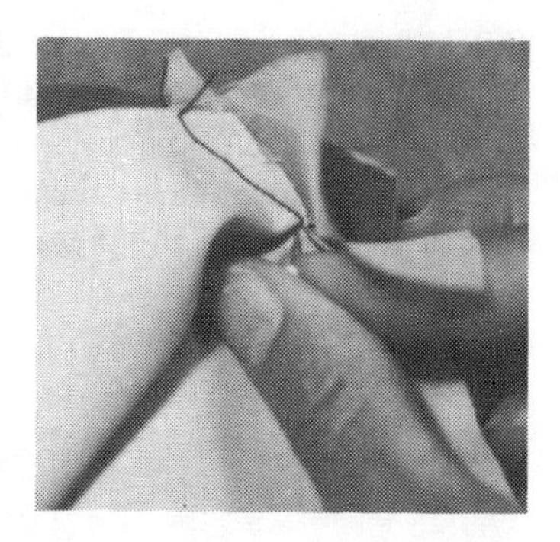

Lay the reinforced point on the corresponding piece of the garment. Extend the organdy away from the point and insert a pin in the point of the V exactly on the 5/8″ line. Insert the pin in the corresponding mark and pin to hold. Pin the organdy to the corner to hold the point.

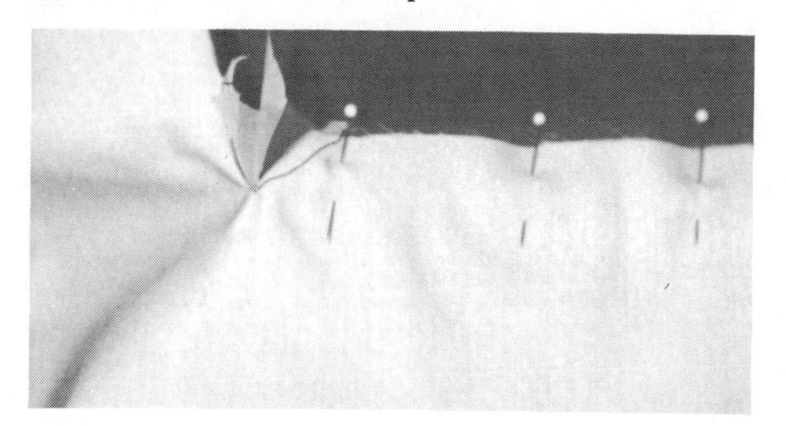

Line up the remaining seam allowance and pin to hold. Extend all the organdy into the seam.

Stitch from the point on both sides of the angle. Stitching from the point prevents a pucker on the corner. Do not backstitch and leave a long thread. Use small stitches at the point and change to a normal stitch length (10 to 12 stitches to the inch) for the remainder of the seam. You must stitch just inside the first stitching which holds the organdy and reinforces the corner.

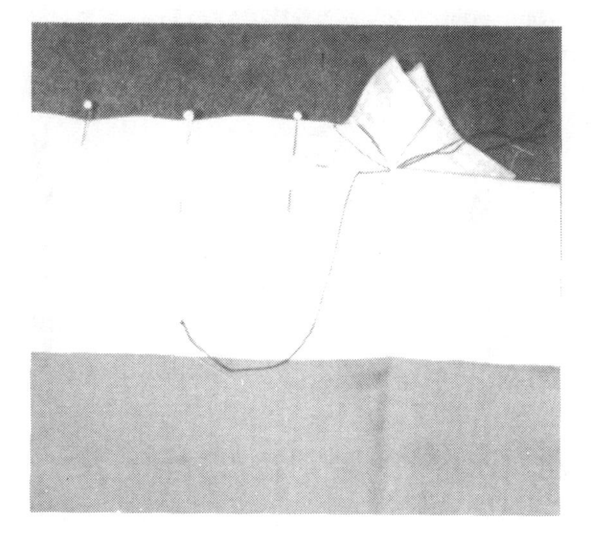

Mark the seam line for stitching the second (left) side of the point. Most machines do not have a seam gauge on the left side of the needle. If your machine has the seam allowances marked, there is no need to mark the seam.

Stitch from the point as you did the first side and follow the marked seam line. It is fine to start stitching a bit beyond the point in the organdy. It is easier to remove a stitch than it is to have to stitch again because you started short of the point.

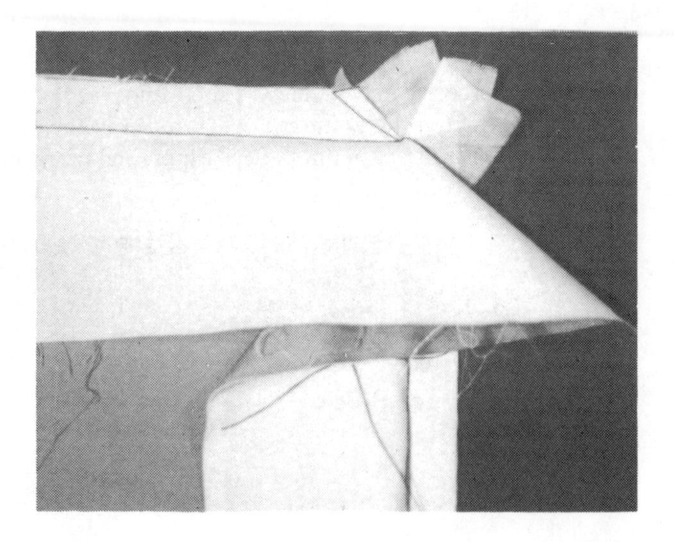

Check the corner on the right side of the garment. It should be smooth with no puckers. None of the organdy should show on the right side of the garment. If you have organdy showing, you must stitch a bit deeper.

Tie the threads securely and cut the threads, leaving a small amount beyond the knot.

Press the seam open unless the pattern directions tell you to press another way. Trim the organdy to a scant 1/4″. Trim the corner so that the seam allowance lies in a miter.

Hand overcast the point if your fabric frays. Refer to seam finishes, page 68.

Proceed with your garment.

COLLARS

The collar must be skillfully done if the garment is to be a success. Many sewers have some difficulty with collars. Therefore this chapter is very detailed in the construction of collars and attaching the collar to the garment.

Basic collar styles include a mandarin, a full roll, a partial roll, and a flat roll collar.

The shape of the neckline of the collar determines the amount of roll the collar will have. Judge the amount of roll at the back of the neck as collars tend to flatten out at an opening. The shorter the outside edge the more the collar stands up. The longer the ouside edge the more a collar lies down.

The illustration below is a full roll collar.

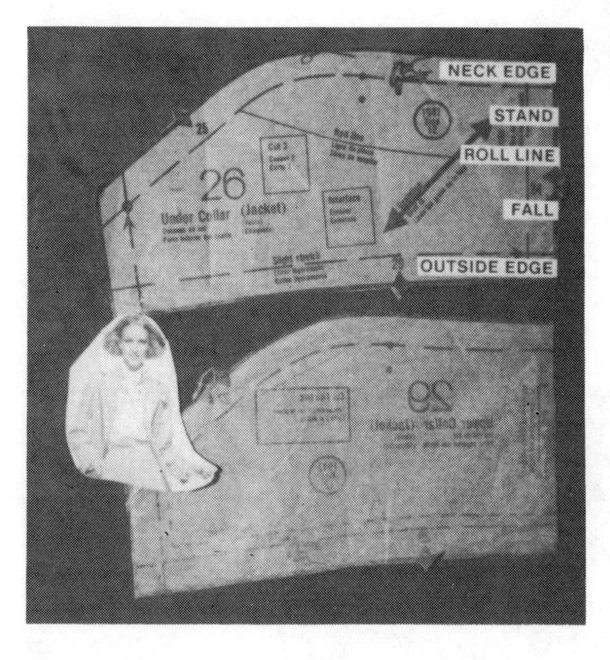

Basic parts of the collar are the outside edge, the neck edge, the roll line, the stand, and the fall. The fall of the collar should always be larger than the stand. This allows the collar to cover the neck seam at the back of the garment. The roll line is usually labeled on patterns that require tailoring. It is not important that it be labeled on patterns that do not require pad stitching, as in tailoring. Some patterns requiring tailoring do not mark the roll line. If it is not marked, establish the roll line when you are fitting the tissue. Fold the back collar so the fall is longer than the stand.

The roll line of the collar extends to the roll line of the lapel and ends at the first button. Crease the pattern as it folds and use that as the roll line for the collar and the lapel.

If you have altered the neckline of your pattern, check the collar pattern. The collar should be the exact length of the neckline or a bit shorter (1/16″) than the neckline of the garment. It should never be longer than the neckline. Check the lengths by standing a tape measure on edge on the seamlines to measure the length of the neckline and the collar.

Stretch the neckline in the shoulder area when you are pinning, basting and stitching the collar to the garment. I rarely staystitch a neckline. I find it makes it much harder to fit the collar on because the neckline will not give. If you feel you must staystitch, break the stitching line every few stitches to allow the neckline to accommodate the collar.

Interchanging Collars of Different Patterns

The necklines should be similar. Example: if a collar style needs facings the garment should have facings.

1. Measure the neckline of the front and back of the garment. Measure the collar. They should be equal, or the collar can be 1/16″ shorter than the neckline of the garment.
2. If they are not equal compare the necklines of the different patterns to determine what is different. If you like the neckline of the pattern, adjust the collar to fit that neckline. If you like the neckline of the pattern the collar came from, change the neckline of the new pattern to match the neckline of the pattern the collar came from. Also change the facing to match the neckline.
3. Adjust the collar to fit the neckline by checking the length and shape. If it is a straight collar, adjust the length at the center back. If it is a curved collar, adjust the length at the shoulder area of the collar. The shoulder seam is marked on the collar with two small dots.

Check Before Cutting Collars

Each collar has an under and upper collar. The upper collar should be a bit larger than the under collar to allow for the turn of cloth and for the roll of the collar. Refer to page 65. The heavier your fabric the larger the upper collar should be cut. In lightweight fabrics the upper and under collars are usually the same pattern piece. They are cut the same size and an adjustment is made, if necessary, when they are stitched together. If an adjustment is necessary, use a slightly smaller seam for the upper collar when you stitch the collars together.

Some patterns using a full roll collar in medium to heavy weight fabric will have a bias undercollar. If the under collar is on the bias, it should always have a seam at center back. Otherwise the collar ends have different grain lines and often do not lie the same. The upper collar pattern (here lying underneath) should always be larger than the under collar pattern to allow for turn of cloth.

Be careful of using an upper collar on the bias. They have a tendency to ripple especially if the fabric is soft.

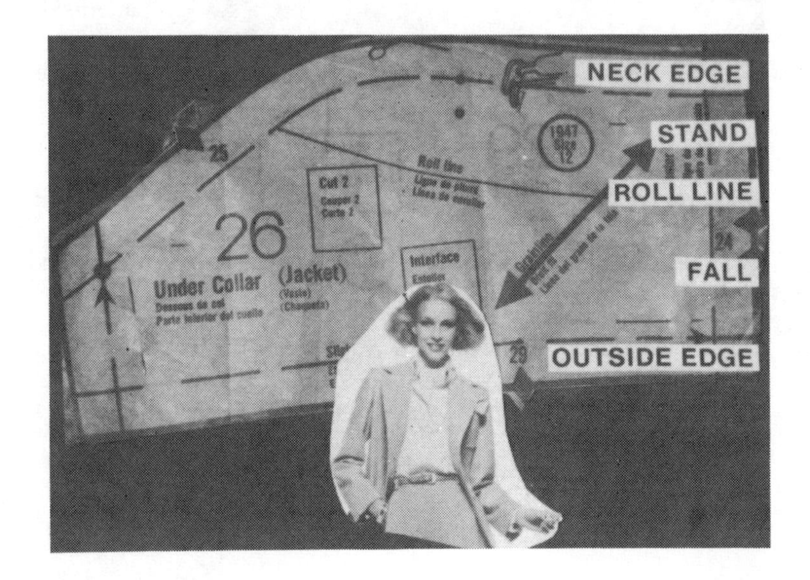

Collar Construction

Interfacing the collar

I usually interface the under collar. If the fabric is lightweight or sheer and the seam would show through on the right side, then interface the upper collar. Or, if you want a crisp collar, interface both the under and upper collars with a lightweight interfacing. Refer to Interfacing, page 21. If I am using nonfusible interfacing, I use a glue stick to hold the interfacings in place until they are secured in the seam.

Use the glue stick sparingly. Dot the glue stick along the edge of the interfacing in the seam allowance. This acts as hand baste, but it is much easier to get layers of fabric lying together without bubbles than a hand baste as you can work with them on a flat surface.

If you prefer to use fusible interfacing, do not trim the seam allowance off the fusible interfacings before fusing. Fuse it very lightly on the seam allowances. After the seams are stitched, pull the fusible free and trim the interfacing out of the seam allowance. I believe that fusible interfacing should be held in the seam by the stitching. I don't trust fusibles to hold through many washings.

Stitch the collar

Pin the upper and under collar right sides together.

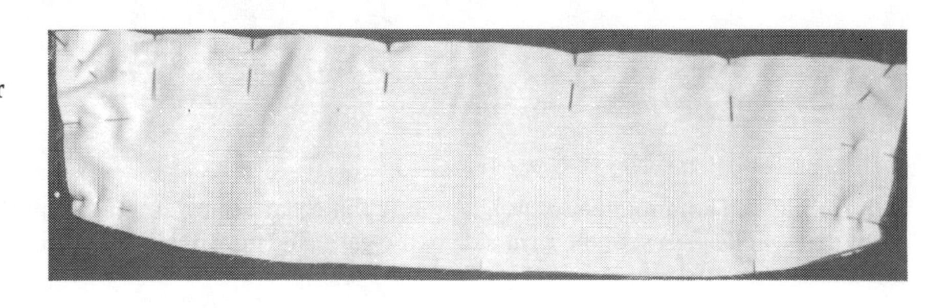

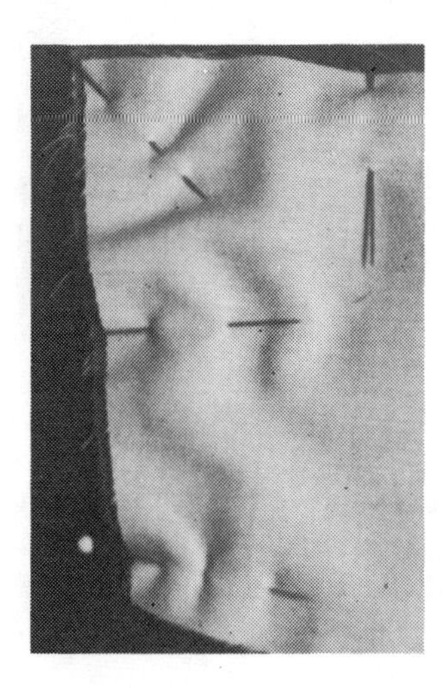

If the fabric is medium to heavy weight, allow a little extra on the upper collar for turn of cloth. Do this by scooting the upper collar cut edge in a small amount if you are using the same pattern piece for both upper and under collar.

Stitch with the interfacing up using small stitches on the corners. If your fabric is light to medium in weight, pivot on the needle at the corners. If the fabric is bulky or heavy in weight take one stitch or two small stitches on the diagonal at the corners.

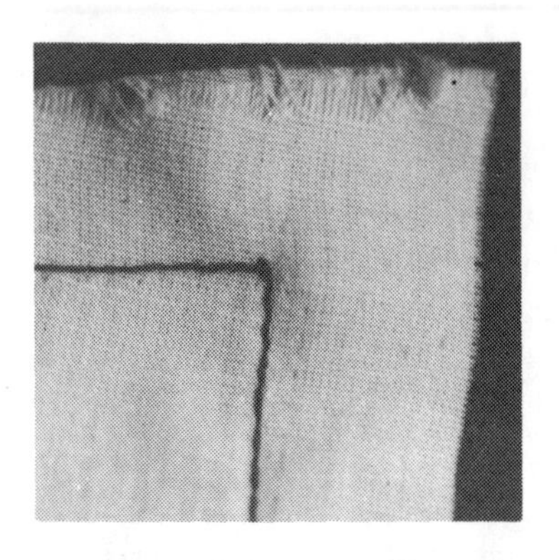

To do this easily mark your 5/8″ line and stop just short of it. Leave the needle in the fabric, raise the presser foot, turn the fabric to the diagonal. Lower the presser foot. Take one stitch then, with the needle down, raise the foot and complete the turn of the corner. This slightly rounded corner will always turn with a more square appearance in bulky fabric than a corner you simply pivot on the needle. I like to backstitch those stitches on the diagonal to give a bit more strength to the corner. You can accomplish the same thing by stitching the corners twice.

If you have curved ends, put the pattern piece back in place over the interfacing. Stick pins along the seam line and pencil dot the curved stitching line on the interfacing. This will insure the same curve on both ends of the collar. Without a guide it is very difficult to stitch the same curve on both ends of the collar. A paper template of the curve can be stitched around. For an example of a paper template, refer to Pockets, pages 224 and 225.

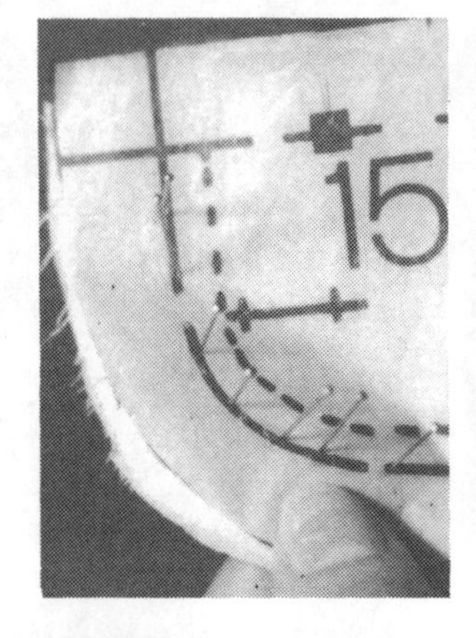

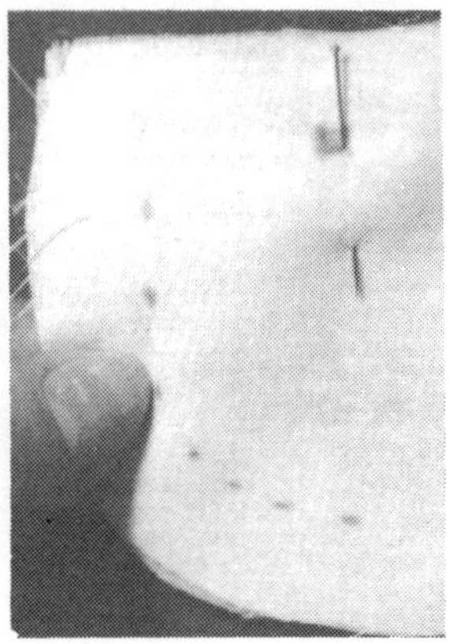

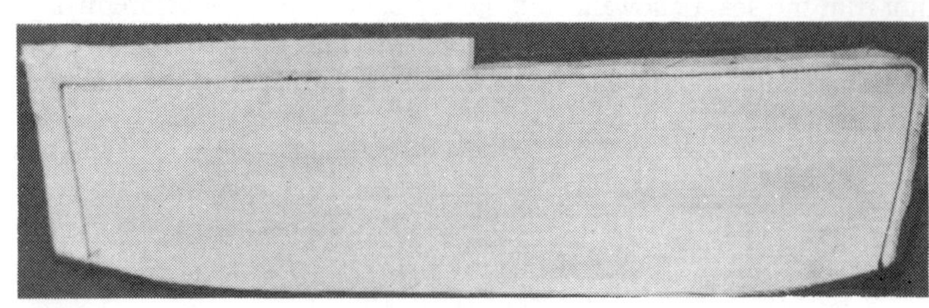

Trimming

Trim the interfacing to 1/8″. If the fabric is light weight, trim the seam to 1/4″.

If the fabric is medium to heavy weight, grade the collar seam. To grade, cut the seam that will lie closest to the right side of the garment (upper collar) to 3/8″ and the under collar to 1/4″.

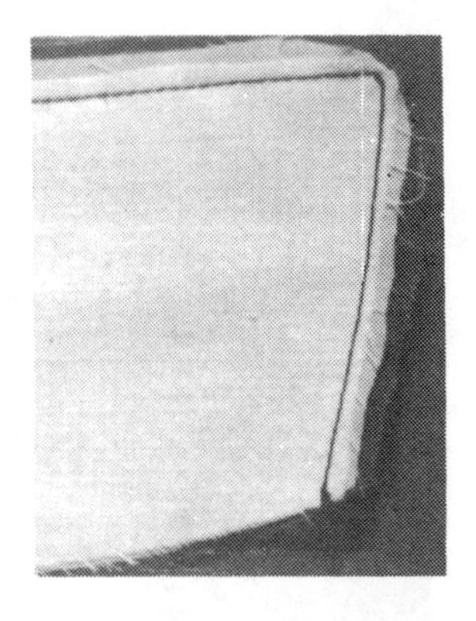

Clip the corners on the diagonal to 1/4. Fold the corner so the seam is in the middle of the point and trim the seam until just a tiny bit is extending past the fold of the collar point. Be careful. Don't clip the fold of the corner.

Trimming in this manner miters the corner and removes all bulk from the collar point but does not trim it too close. If your fabric ravels badly, put a little Fray Check on the corner. Be careful to get it only on the seam allowance. It can discolor the fabric permanently.

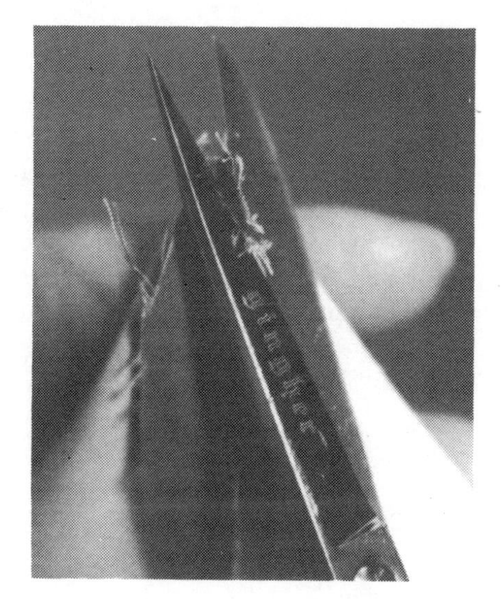

Pressing

Press the seam open on a point presser. A point presser is a necessary tool for turning a good collar. Slip the collar on the point presser.

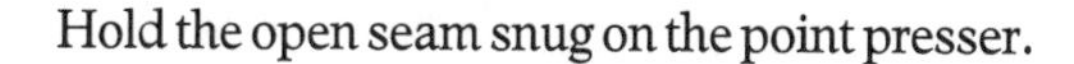

Hold the open seam snug on the point presser.

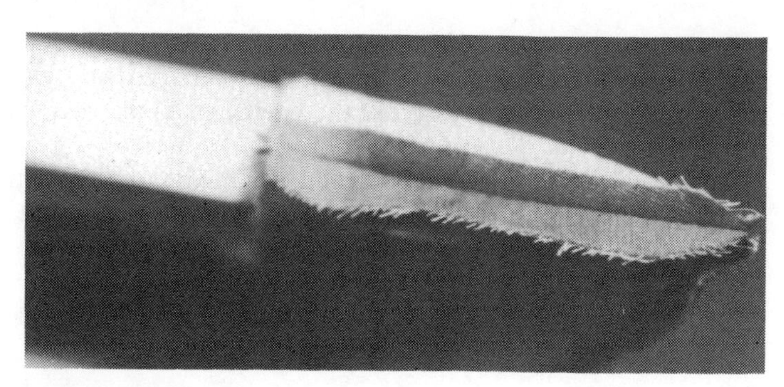

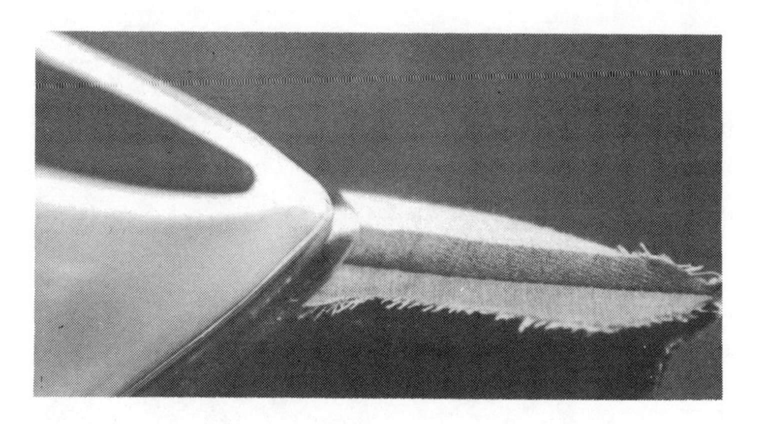

Press all the seams open with steam. I often wet the seam with a paint brush and then press. That keeps the moisture exactly where it is needed. Turn the collar on the point presser until all the seams are pressed open.

Hold the collar as shown and turn the collar right side out making sure the corners are completely turned. Use a point pusher or a small screwdriver and gently work the fabric against it. Don't ever use scissors or a pin to turn the corner. It is so easy to poke scissors through the fabric or snag a thread pulling the corner with a pin. It is much safer to thread a needle and take a stitch in the corner and gently pull. Massage the corner with your fingers while it is still damp from the steam to achieve a nice point.

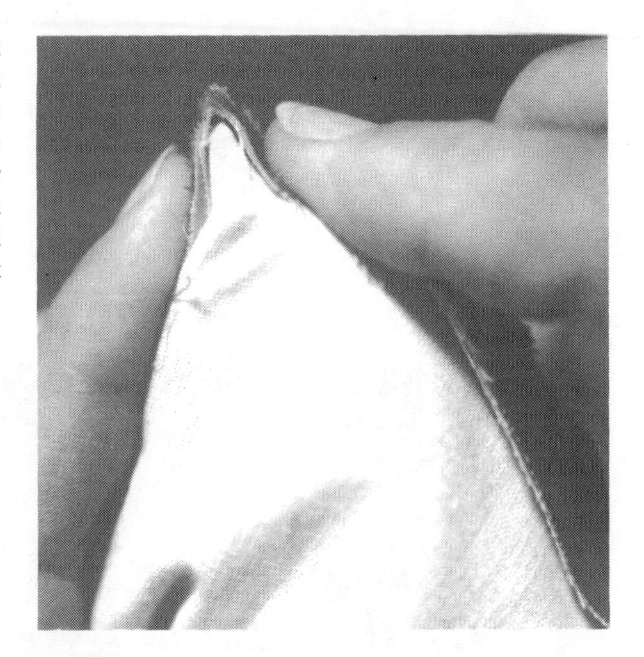

Press the seams of the collar so the seam is favoring the interfaced side. The seam should not show on the right side of the collar.

Exception: If the fabric is sheer and the interfaced side looks the best, press the seam so it shows on the uninterfaced side. In that case use the interfaced as the right side.

All collars should be interfaced, stitched, trimmed, turned, and pressed before they are stitched onto the garment. Garment construction determines whether they are topstitched before they are stitched on the garment. Check your pattern instruction sheet.

If the pattern has a collar band, topstitch the collar before stitching the band to the collar. If the collar is all in one piece, follow the pattern directions for topstitching.

When topstitching a collar, thread a needle and take a stitch right on the corner. Pull until you have both ends of the thread. Then as you are pivoting the corner you can pull on the thread to keep the topstitching smooth on the corner.

Four Methods Of Stitching Collars

Method One

I would use this method on sport garments of lightweight fabric or children's clothing. The collar never lies quite as nicely as the Four Point Collar (Method Three). Unless the fabric is lightweight the neckline seam is very bulky.

You must use both a back and front facing for this method.

Method Two

Directions begin on page 168.

Much the same as Method One but there is no back neck facing. I prefer this to Method One because I like to eliminate the back neck facing when I can.

I would use this method on sport garments of lighweight weight fabric or children's clothing. The collar never lies quite as nicely as the Four Point Collar (Method Three). Unless the fabric is light weight the neckline seam is very bulky.

Method Three

Directions begin on page 171.

Method Three must be used on medium and heavy weight fabric to reduce the bulk of the neckline seam. I often use it when constructing good blouses of lightweight fabric because it lies beautifully.

Use for garments with front and sometimes a back neck facing. If there is no back neck facing and the garment is lined, the lining is used in place of the back neck facing. If the garment is not lined and there is no back neck facing, the upper collar is used to finish the back neck seam as in Method Two.

Method Four

Directions begin on page 180.

Use for garments with no facings, usually a shirt blouse with a collar and a collarband. The collar can have a stitched-on band or a cut-on band. The cut-on band is easiest to construct. The stitched-on band fits more closely and usually is seen on more expensive clothing.

Method One

Steps 1-5.

1. Interface, stitch, trim, turn and press the collar.

Topstitch if the garment has topstitching. Refer to page 164. Also refer to Topstitching and Edgestitching, page 72-73.

2. Interface the blouse opening.

Stitch the shoulder seams of the garment. Stitch the back neck facing to the front neck facing. Finish the shoulder seams.

Refer to Blouses, pages 118-120.

I rarely staystitch a neckline. I find it makes it much harder to fit the collar on because the neckline will not give. If you feel you must staystitch, break the staystitching every few stitches to allow the neckline to accommodate the collar.

3. Pin the collar to the neckline.

Pin both layers of the collar to the garment with the under collar next to the garment. Pin with the collar up matching the center backs, notches, and the big dot marking the collar junction. Work from the center back to either end of the collar. Stretch the neckline to fit the collar. If necessary, clip the neckline. Be careful. Don't clip deeper than 3/8". Hand baste.

4. Pin the neck facing over the collar.

Match the shoulder seams and collar junctions. Make sure the front extensions are the same length and the ends of the collars are the same width on both sides of the garment. As you are pinning hold the seam in your fingers and run them along the seam to check for puckers. When everything looks and feels smooth, machine or hand baste if you wish.

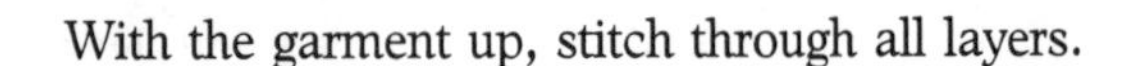

With the garment up, stitch through all layers.

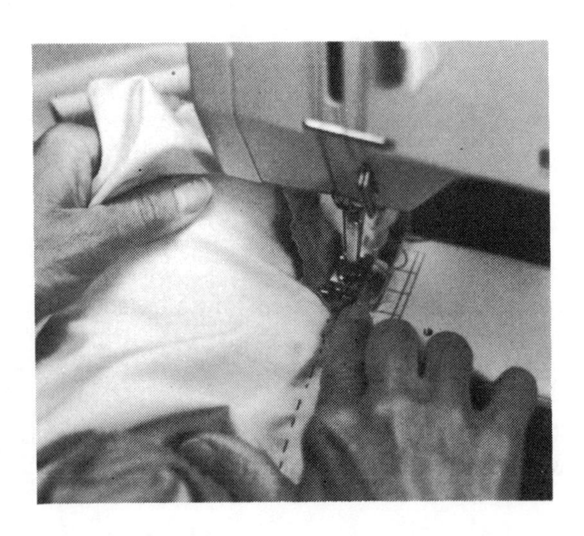

Gently tug the garment at right angles to the needle as you stitch to help prevent puckers.

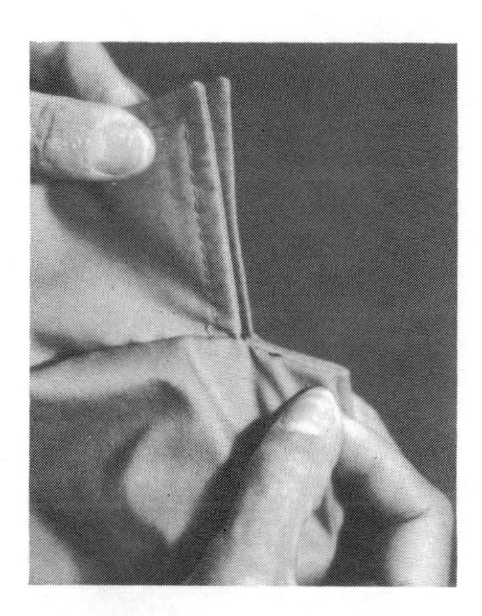

Check the length of the front extensions and the width of the collars. Check to see if you have a smooth seam without any tucks or unevenness.

5. Clip, grade, and press the collar seam.

Trim the interfacing to 1/8″. Grade the seam. Grading is cutting the piece that will lie closest to the right side of the garment 3/8″ and the under section to 1/4″. Clip the seam. Any inward curve must be clipped to allow it to lie properly.

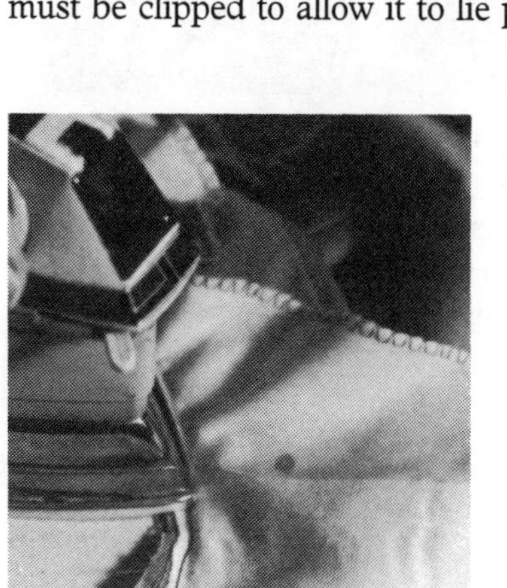

Press the neckline seam as it was stitched.

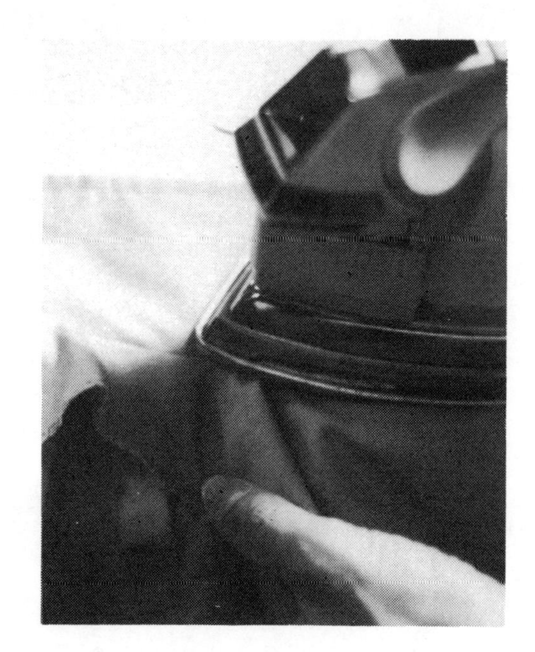

Then press the facing down with the collar extended as it will lie in the finished garment.

Continue with garment.

Method Two

Steps 1-5

1. Interface, stitch, trim, turn, and press the collar.

Refer to Collars, pages 161-164. Topstitch if the garment has topstitching. Refer to pages 72, 231, and 314.

2. Interface the garment opening.

Refer to Blouses or Dresses, pages 118-120. Stitch the shoulder seams of the garment. Refer to Sample Seams and Pressing Techniques, page 65. Finish the shoulder seams. Refer to Seam Finishes, page 68-70.

3. Pin the under collar to the neckline.

With the right sides together, pin from the center back to either end of the collar. Pin with the collar up matching the center backs, notches, and the big dot marking the collar junction. Stretch the neckline to fit the collar. If necessary, clip the neckline. Be careful. Don't clip deeper than 3/8″.

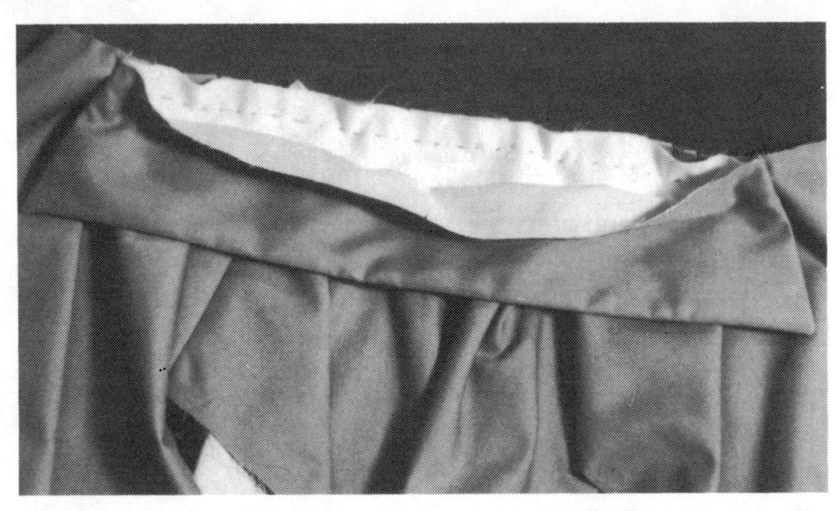

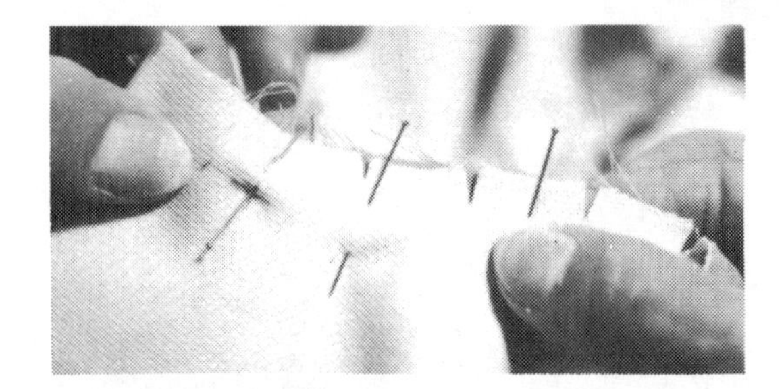

As you pin hold the seam in your fingers and run them along the seam to check for puckers. When everything looks and feels good you are ready to stitch unless you wish to hand baste the collar to the neckline first.

Stitch the under collar to the back neckline from 1″ beyond the shoulder seam on one side of the garment to 1″ beyond the shoulder seam on the other side of the garment.

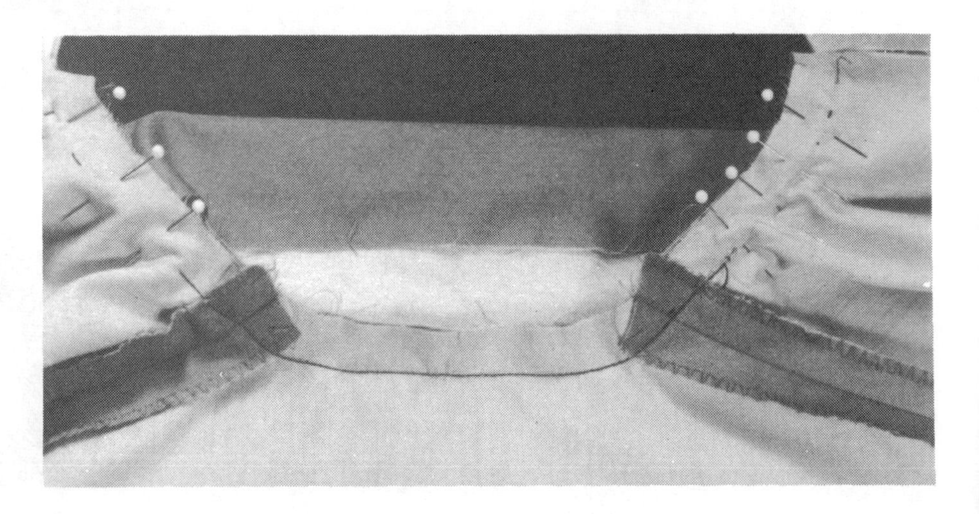

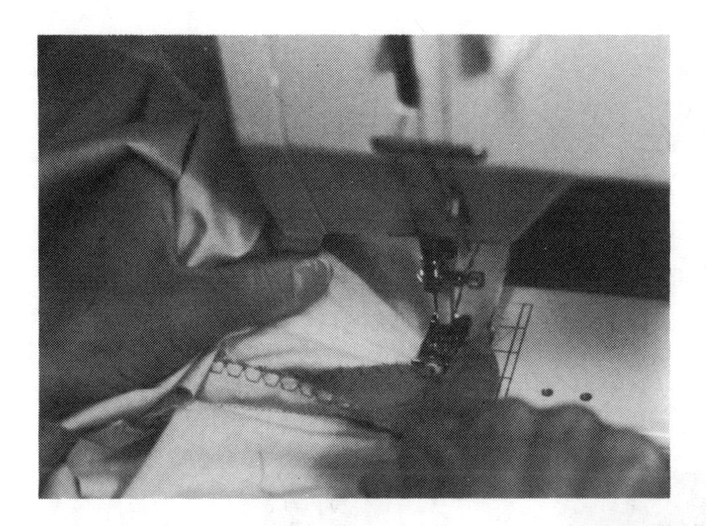

Stitch with the garment up, keeping the upper collar free underneath and slightly stretching the garment at right angles to the needle to prevent puckers.

4. Pin the collar (both upper and under collar) to the neckline

Then pin the facing to the neckline seam, matching notches and the big dot marking the collar junction. Be sure the facing ends at the shoulder seam on both sides of the garment. Be sure the extensions at center front are the same length and the collars are the same width on both sides of the garment. Hand baste if you wish.

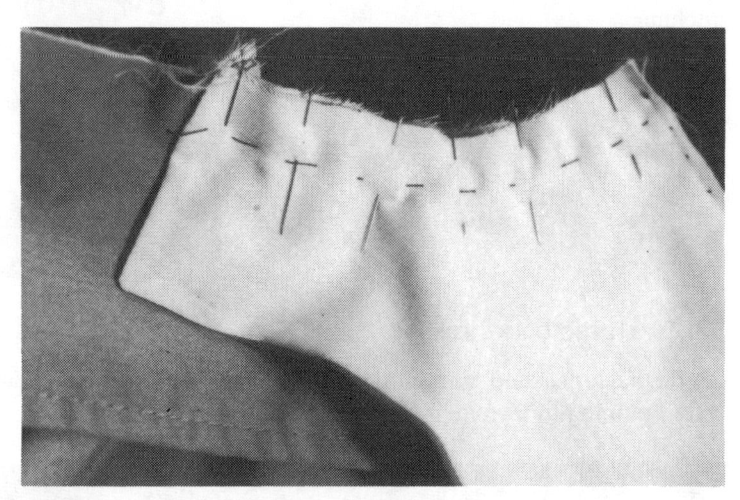

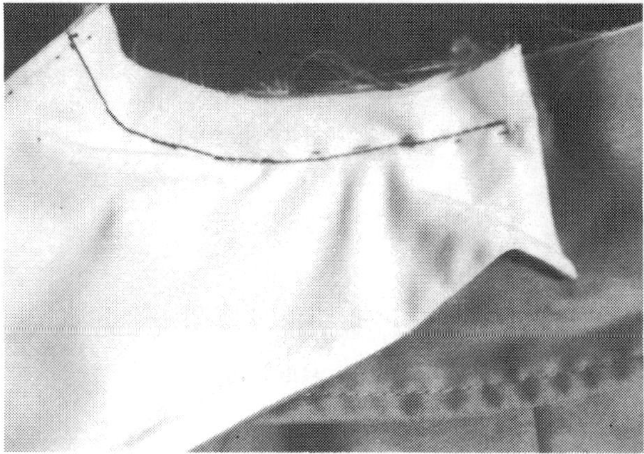

Stitch, with the facing up, from the front fold of the garment to within 1/4″ of the end of the facing. Back-stitch or leave long threads for tying.

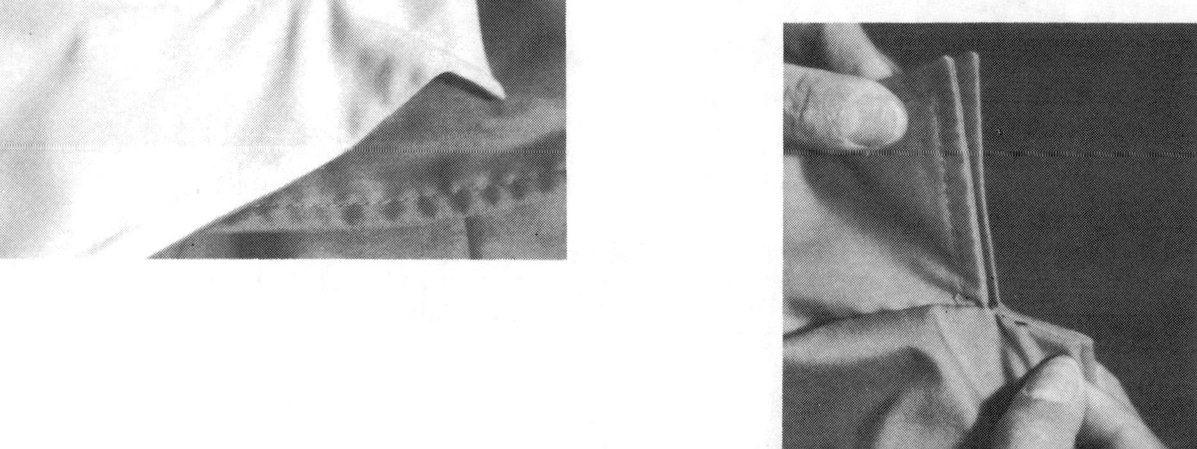

Check the length of the front extensions and the width of the collars. Check to see if you have a smooth seam without any tucks or unevenness. Pull out the bastings. Tie the threads if needed.

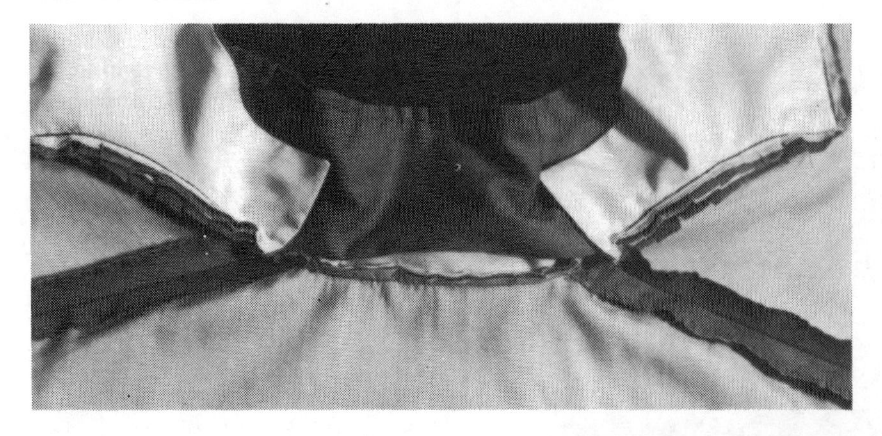

5. Trim, grade, clip, and press the neckline seam.

Do this from the end of the facing to the center front of the neckline. Don't trim the upper collar on the back neckline. Trim the back neckline seam to 1/4″.

Press the collar first as it was stitched and then as it will lie. Press the back neckline up into the collar.

Clip the neck seam on the diagonal where the front facing ends. You must clip to the stitching.

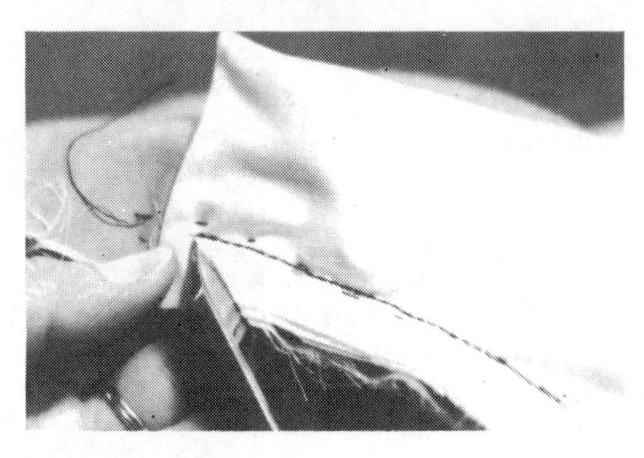

6. Finish the back neckline.

On the back neckline, turn all the seams in toward the collar. Always have the collar rolled as it will lie on you before pinning this seam.

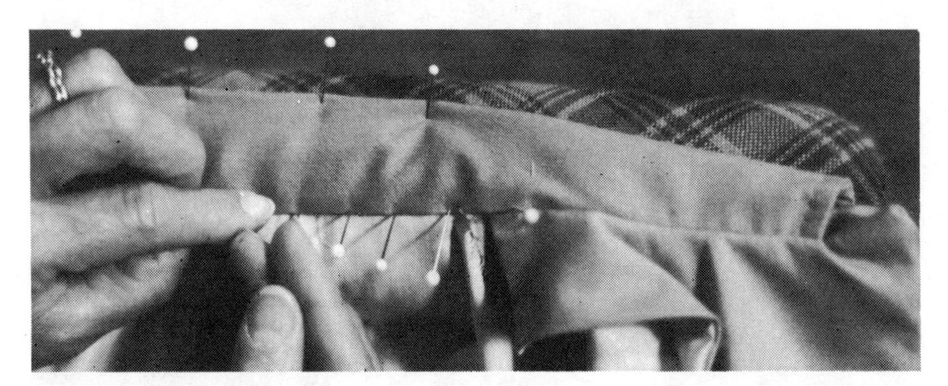

It's easiest to do this on a sleeve roll. Fasten the collar to the sleeve roll with the collar rolled as it will be on you. This allows enough fabric to let the collar roll as it should.

Fold the upper collar seam allowance in so it just covers the neck seam. Stick pins into the sleeve roll all along the seam. Pull the collar off the roll and finish pinning. Hand baste before machine stitching.

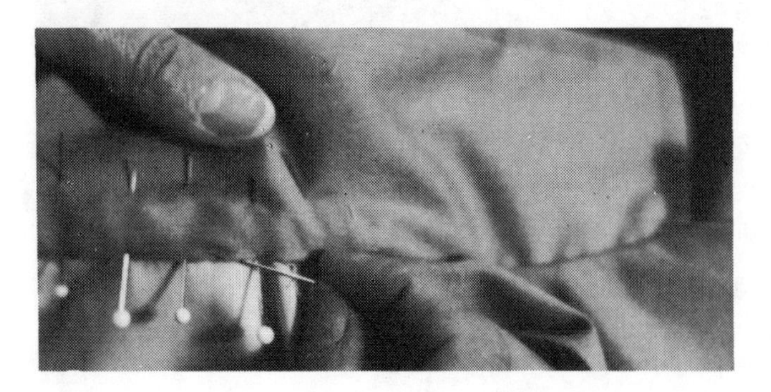

I usually machine stitch close to the fold on a sport garment and hand stitch a finer garment using a hidden whip stitch. Tack the facing to the shoulder seam. Continue with the garment.

Method Three

If the front facing is a separate piece, it should be cut a little larger in medium to heavy weight fabrics than the garment front to allow for the turn of cloth and the turn of the lapel. (Just as the upper collar is cut larger than the under collar.) Most patterns are adjusted for this, but if your fabric is heavy or bulky, check to make sure the pattern is large enough to allow for turn of cloth. Refer to Sample Seams and Pressing Techniques, page 65.

If there is any doubt, allow extra fabric when cutting.

If there is no back neck facing and the garment is lined, the lining is used in place of the back neck facing. Refer to Tailoring, pages 299 and 315-316.

If the garment is not lined and there is no back neck facing, the upper collar is used to finish the back neck seam as in Method Two, page 170.

Method Three is often referred to as the **Four Point Collar** as four seams are stopping at the same junction. Don't let this intimidate you. Just take care that all four seams are meeting at the **same level** (5/8" line) and that you are stopping **exactly** at the collar junction marked by a large dot on the front neck line. Never backstitch at the large dot. Leave a long thread and when all the seams are stitched make any corrections needed. Even the expert seamstress finds it difficult to stitch exactly to the junction of four seams accurately. If you have stitched too far, take out the stitches until you are at the large dot. If you have stopped short of the large dot, put a hand needle on the long thread you left when stitching and close the hole with small hand stitches. When all the seams are correct and the collar looks right on the outside, tie all the threads securely and clip the thread, leaving about 1/4" beyond the knot.

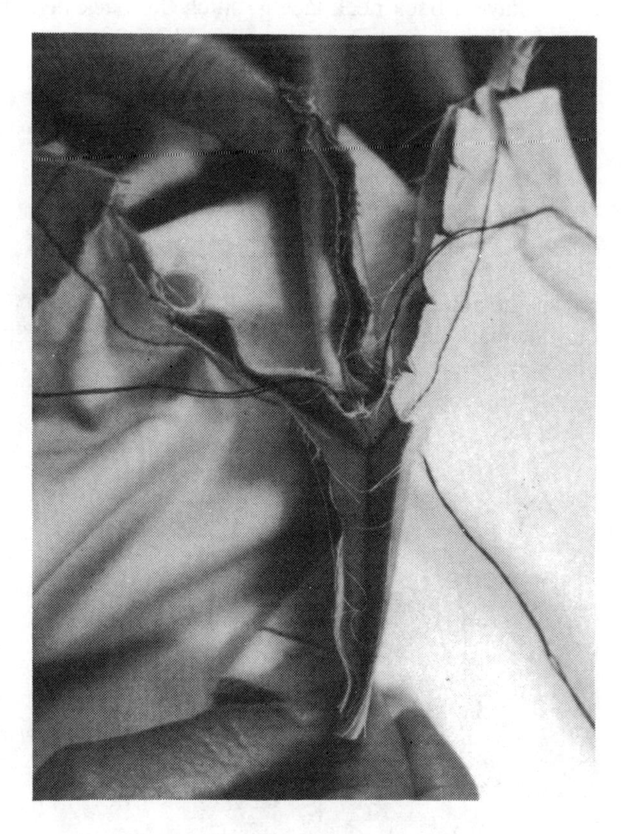

Variation:

Sometimes the collar will be even with the front fold of the garment. If that is the case, it works very well to stitch around the front fold over the opened collar seam. This would not be a four-point collar construction as four seams would not be stopping at the same junction.

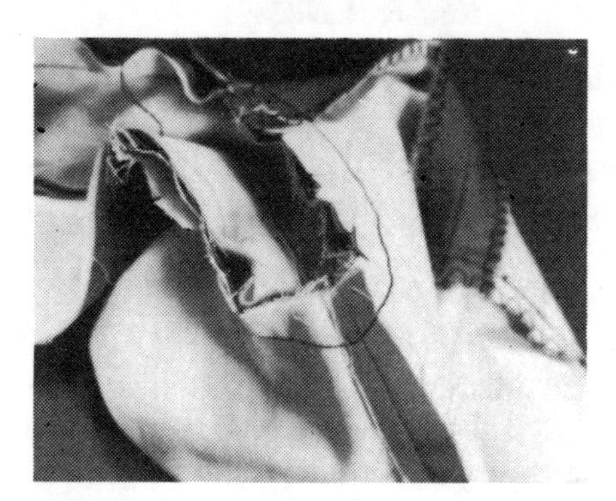

But, if the collar is even with the front of the garment, it is much easier to do a continuous stitch at the center front fold or seam than to start and stop at that point. The neckline seam would then be finished in the normal manner.

Method Three

Steps 1-7. It is important to do this in the sequence given.

1. Interface, stitch, trim, and press the collar.

It is much easier to achieve a well-turned collar if you construct it before attaching the collar to the garment as many pattern instructions tell you to do. Refer to Collars, pages 161-164. This collar cannot be topstitched before attaching it to the garment.

2. Interface the garment opening.

Stitch the shoulder seams of the garment. Refer to Sample Seams and Pressing Techniques, pages 58 and 65-67. Finish the shoulder seams. Refer to Seam Finishes, pages 68-71.

If you have a back neck facing, stitch the back neck facing to the front neck facing. For interfacing directions, refer to Blouses and Dresses, pages 119-120.

3. Attach the under collar to the garment.

With right sides together and the collar up, pin the under collar to the neckline. Match the center backs, the notches, and the big dot marking the collar junction. Work from the center back to either end of the collar.

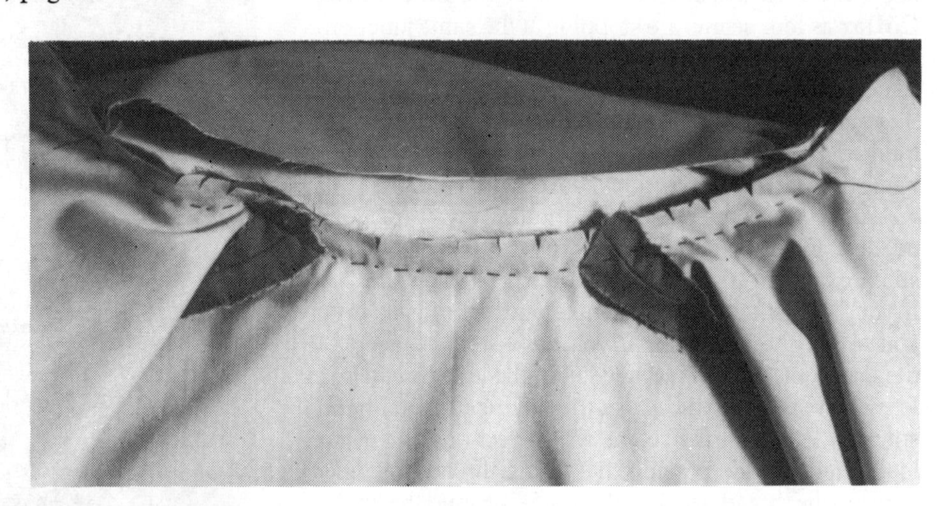

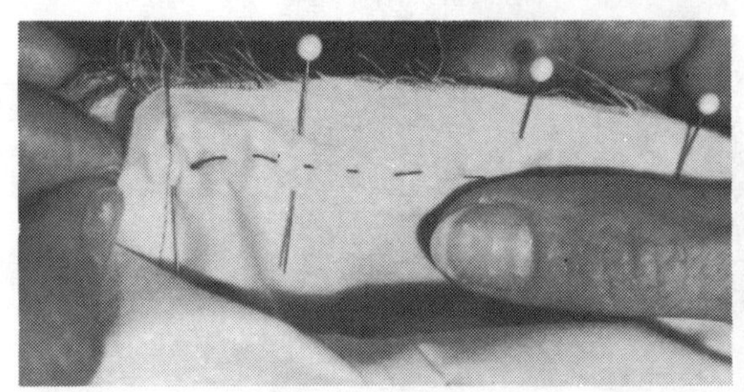

Keep the end seam of the collar free. The picture is with the collar up. Stretch the neckline in the shoulder area to fit the collar. If necessary, clip the neckline. Be careful. Don't clip deeper than 3/8″.

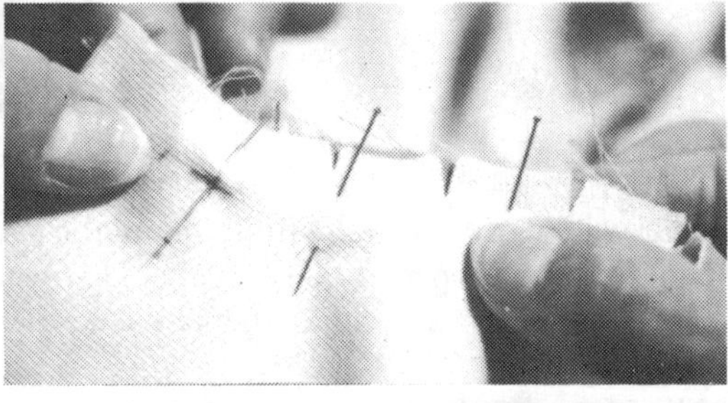

Pin or hand baste on the 5/8″ seam line and, as you do, hold the seam in your fingers and run them along the seam to check for possible puckers when you stitch the seam. If the seam feels smooth, you can usually stitch it without any puckers.

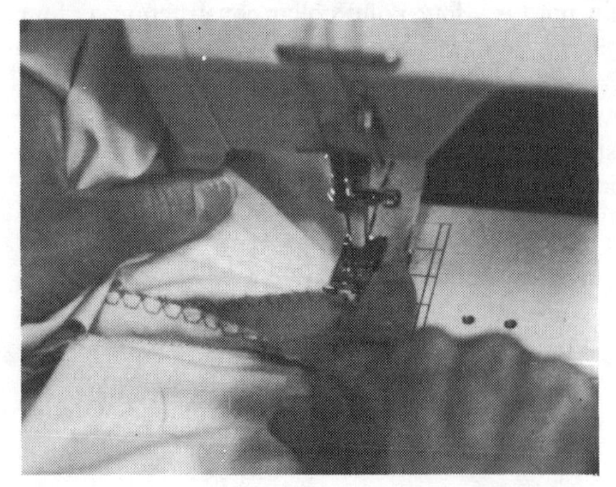

When everything looks and feels good, stitch the under collar to the garment. Stitch with the garment up. Gently tug the garment as you stitch to help prevent puckers in the seam.

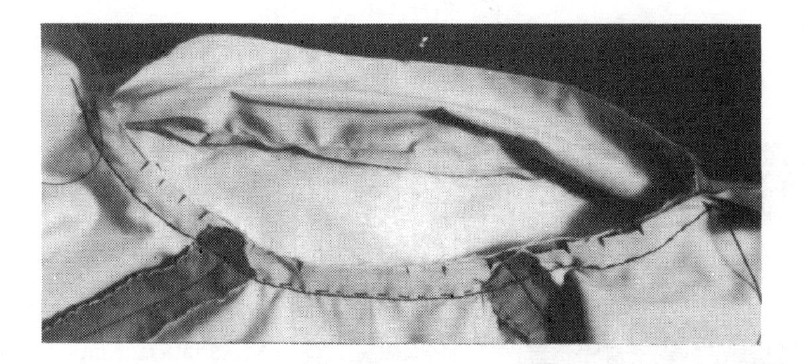

When stitching the under collar to the neckline, keep the end seam of the collar free and the upper collar pullled out of the way. Don't backstitch. Leave a long thread. (You will be tying this thread later.)

4. Attach the upper collar to the facings.

Pin the upper collar to the facing. Pin with the collar up, matching the center backs, notches, and the big dot marking the collar junction. As you are pinning, hold the seam in your fingers and run them along the seam to check for possible puckers when you stitch. Work from the center back to either end of the collar. Stretch the facing neckline in the shoulder area to fit the collar. If necessary, clip the neckline. Be careful. Don't clip deeper than 3/8″.

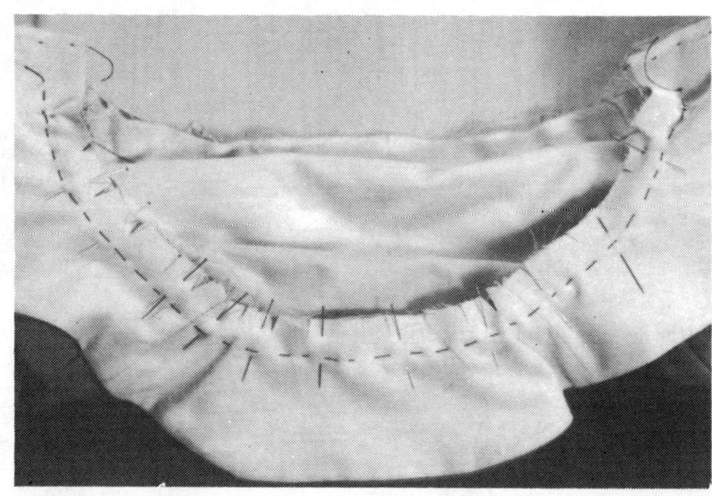

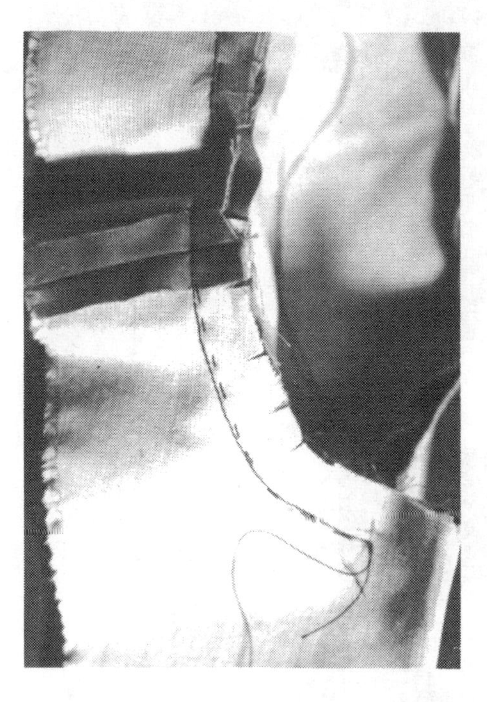

When no back neck facing is used, be sure the front facing ends at the correct place on the collar. This is usually the shoulder seam which is marked by two small dots on the collar pattern.

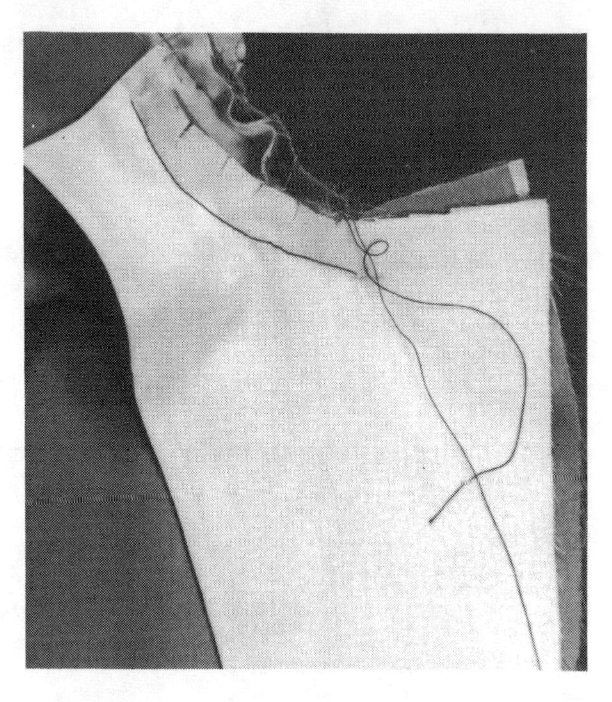

If the garment has no lining and no back neck facing, stop the stitching 1/4″ from the end of the facings. Backstitch or tie the threads. **Stitch** the upper collar to the facing, or facings if you are using a back neck facing. Stitch with the facing up. As you stitch gently tug the garment on both sides of the needle to prevent puckers in the seam. Pictured on page 172. Keep the end seam of the collar free. Refer to picture on the upper left, page 172.

5. Attach the lapel.

Check the placement before stitching the lapel.

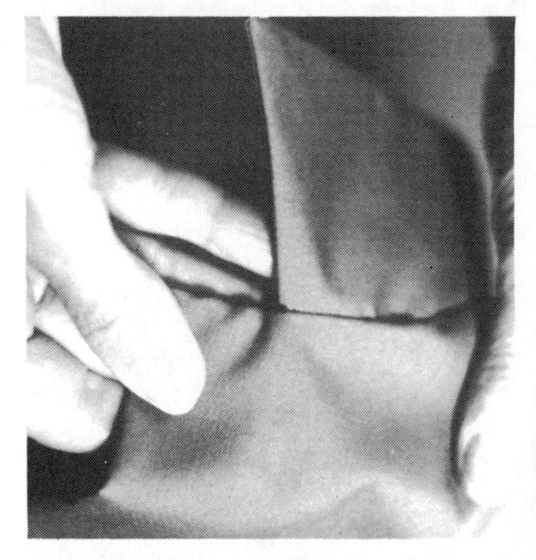

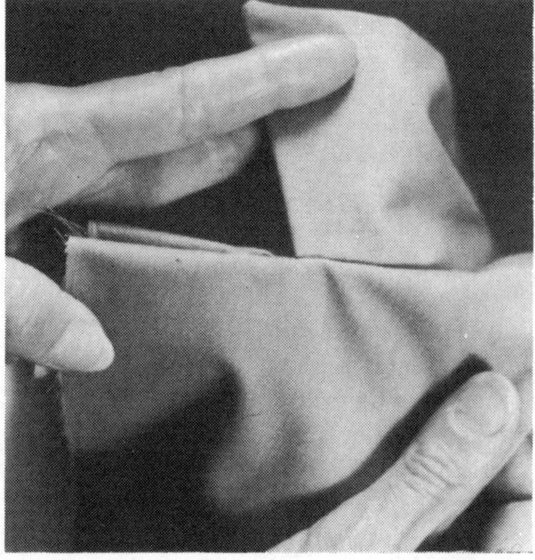

Some patterns will have a front fold with an extension. Some will have a seam with a shaped lapel. To assure that the extension or lapel are lying correctly, turn the garment right side out.

With the seam lying as it will be stitched, make sure the collar seam cannot be seen as it will lie on the garment.

Reach inside and hold the seam with your fingers.

Picture on the left is the facing side which will lie on the right side when the lapel is rolled. The picture on the right is the garment side of the lapel. It will lie under when the lapel is rolled.

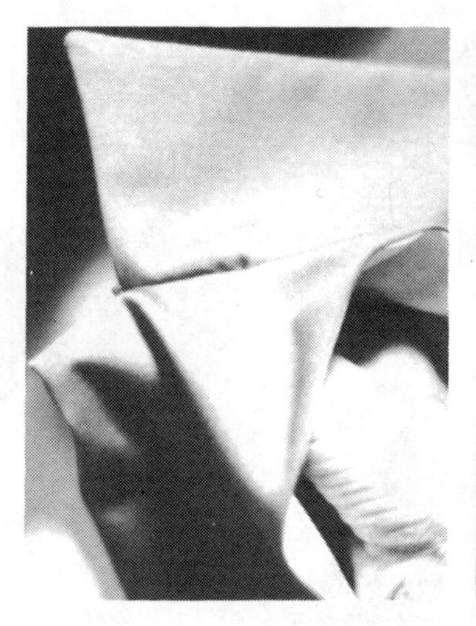

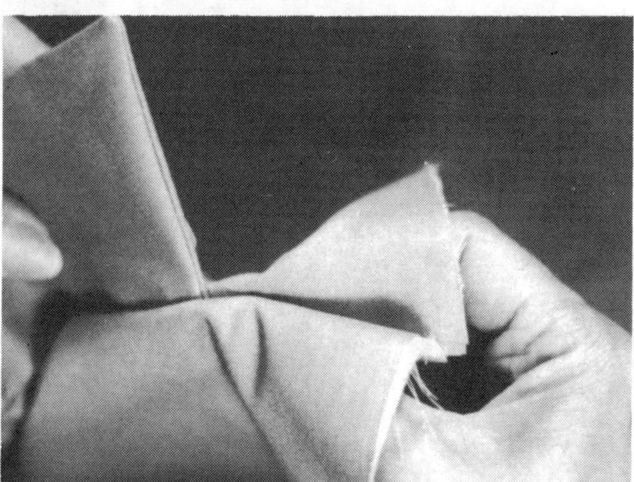

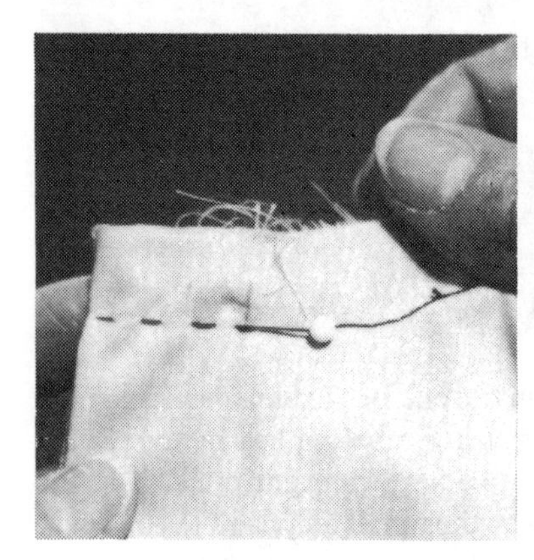

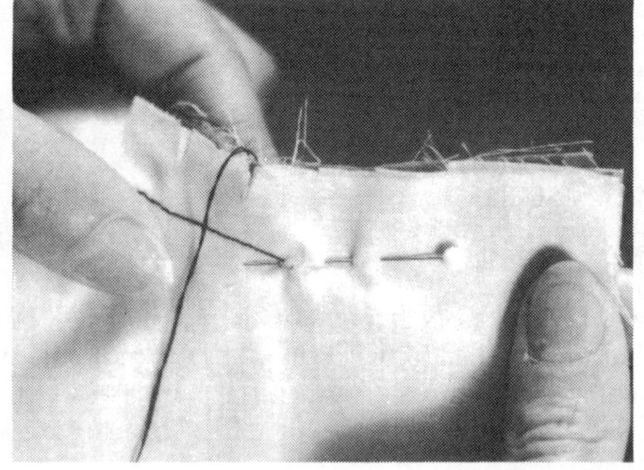

Turn the garment to the wrong side and pin the seam as you are holding it. Pin lengthwise along the seam line.

Turn to the right side. Check the collar and the lapel. Are they lying so that no seam shows on the right side of the garment as it will lie on you? If so, pin or hand baste to hold the seam in place. Photograph on the right is the under side.

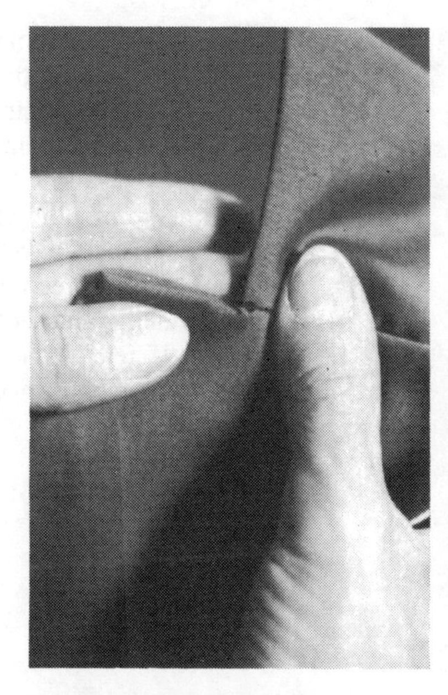

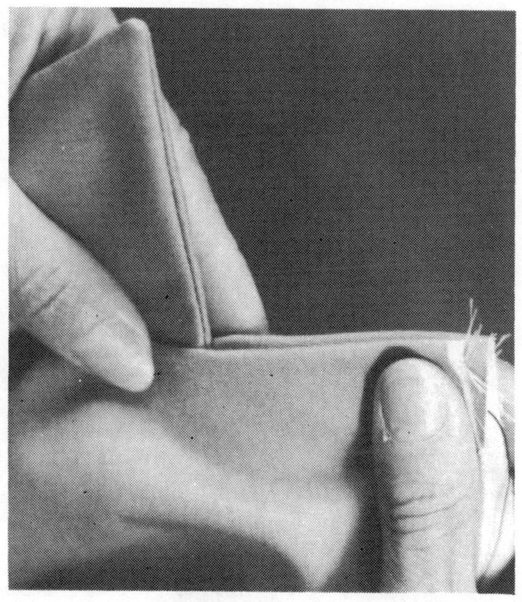

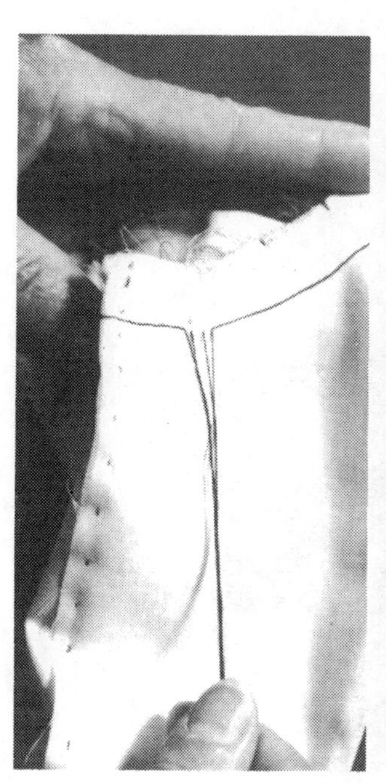

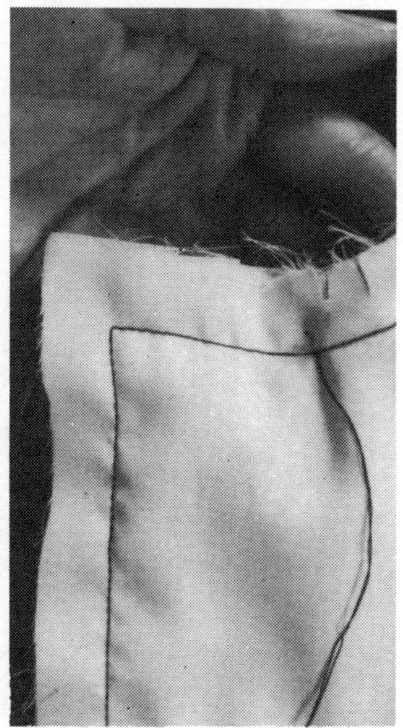

Stitch from the big dot to the fold or, if it is a lapel, stitch the entire lapel seam to the bottom edge of the garment. The lapel seam must be on the same level (5/8″) as the collar seam. Do not backstitch. Leave long threads for tying later.

Check These Points

- Be sure the front extensions at the end of the collar are of equal length on both sides of the garment.
- Be sure the collar points are of equal size and shape at the center front.
- The seams on the end of the collar should lie to the underside as it was pressed.
- The lapel seam should lie to the underside so it does not show when the lapel is folded back against the garment.
- The lapel ends should lie flat. If they curl out, you have not allowed enough fabric for the turn of cloth on the corner of the lapel. Refer to page 65.

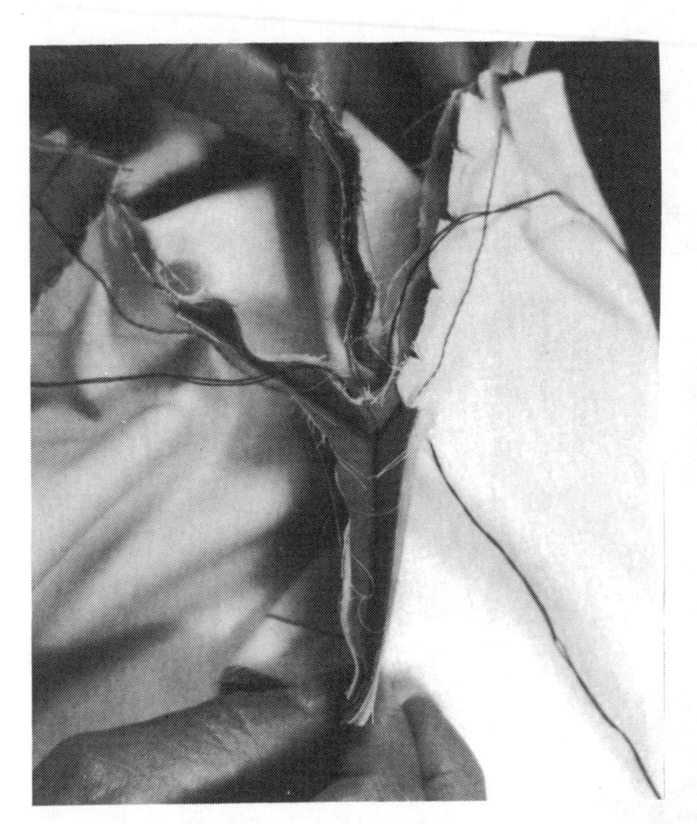

When everything looks satisfactory, pull all the threads to one side of the fabric and tie them. If you have trouble pulling the threads to one side of the fabric, thread them on a needle to get them on one side of the fabric for tying. If you have stitched too far, take out the stitches until you are at the large dot. If you have stopped short of the large dot, put a hand needle on the long thread you left when stitching and close the hole with small hand stitches. When all the seams are correct and the collar looks good turned to the right side, tie all the threads securely and clip them, leaving about 1/4″ beyond the knot.

6. Clipping, trimming, and pressing seams.

Trim all interfacing to a scant 1/8″ from the seam line.

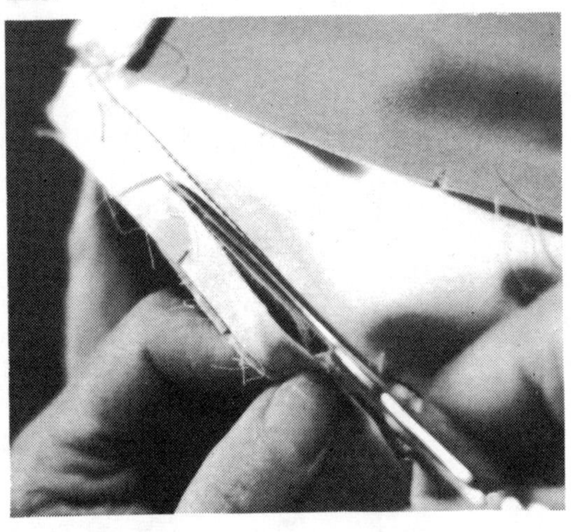

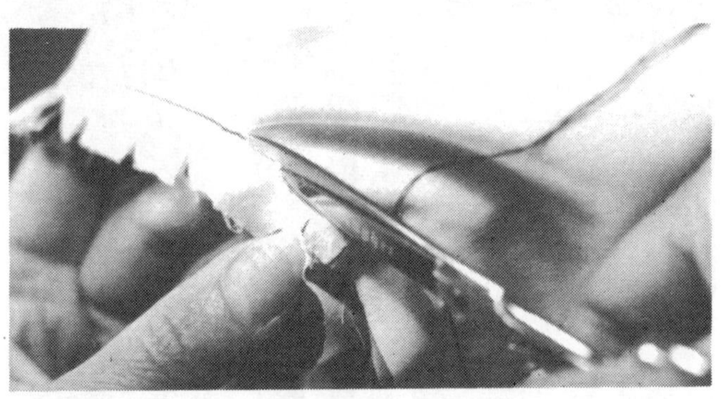

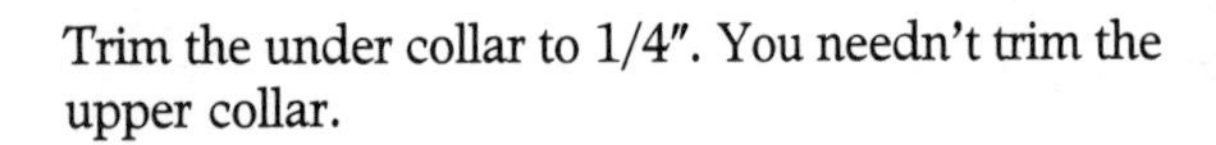

Trim the under collar to 1/4″. You needn't trim the upper collar.

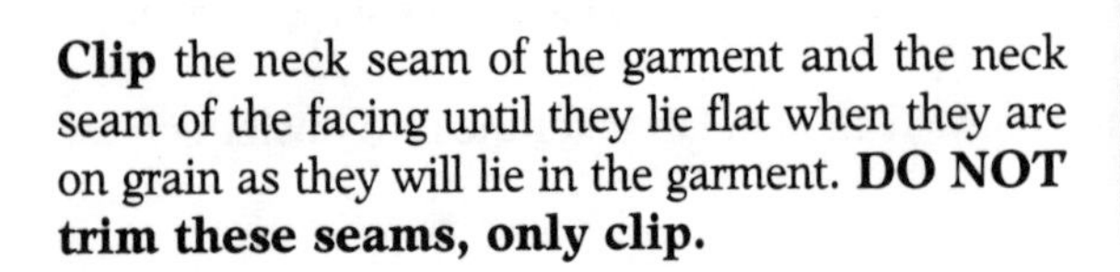

Clip the neck seam of the garment and the neck seam of the facing until they lie flat when they are on grain as they will lie in the garment. **DO NOT trim these seams, only clip.**

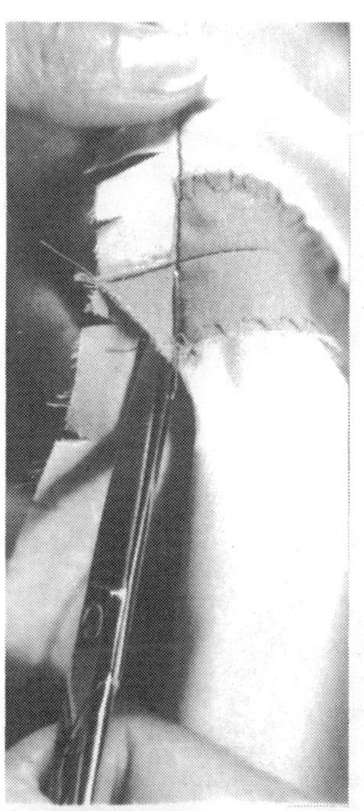

At all seam junctions trim the seam allowance out of the seam allowance to eliminate bulk.

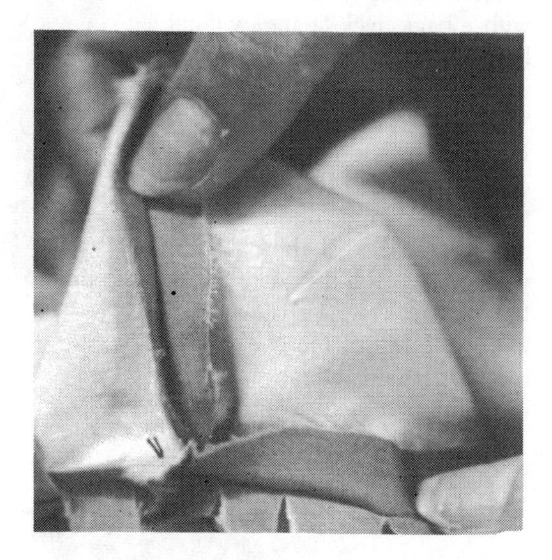

Trim the junction of garment and collar to eliminate unnecessary bulk.

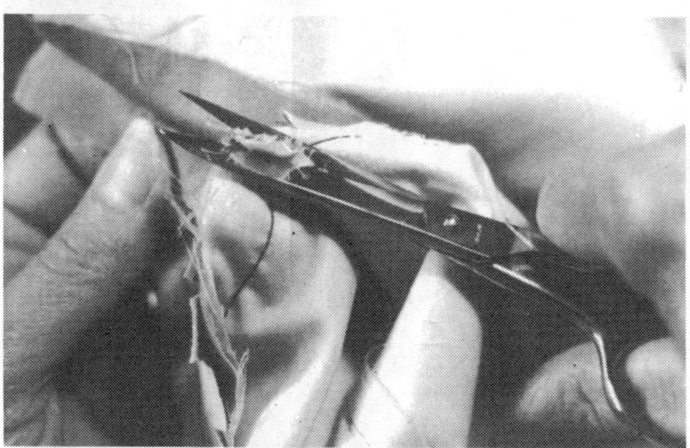

Trim the collar and neckline seam allowance to lie in a miter when it lies up into the collar. Trim the lapel seam to eliminate all unnecessary bulk. Refer to Collars, pages 162-163 and to Couture Tailoring, page 296.

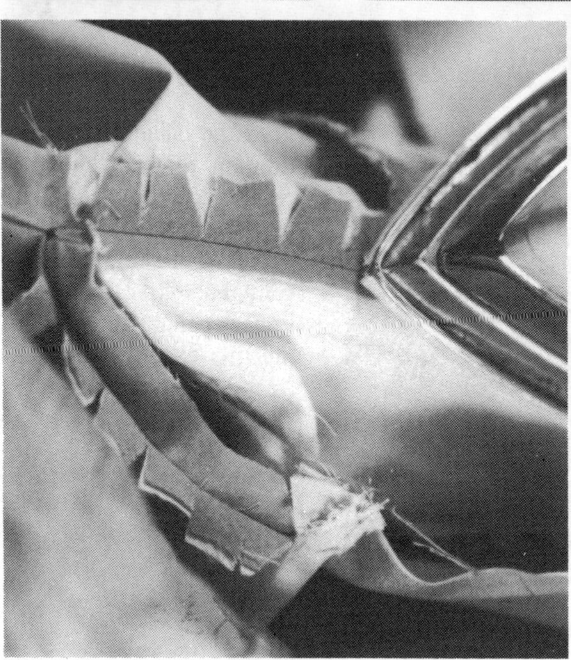

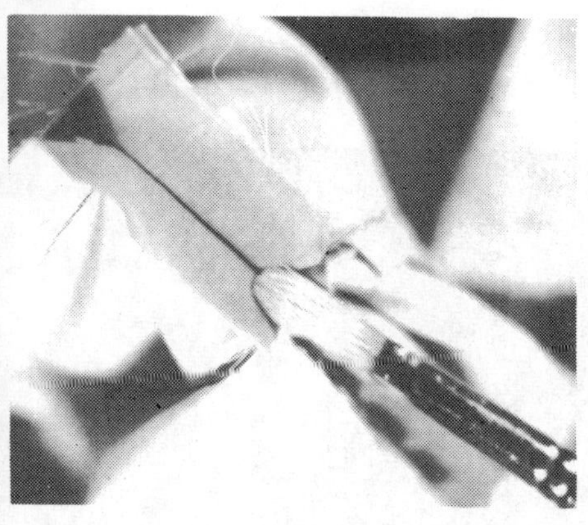

Paint the seams with a wet paint brush. Press. This keeps the moisture just where you need it.

Press the seams open on a point presser. Press the under collar seam, the upper collar seam, and the lapel seam. As you press, make sure you have clipped the neckline seams so that they can lie flat when they are lying on grain.

7. Finishing the collar.

Directions are given for garments with a back neck facing, without a back neck facing, and with a lining in place of a back neck facing.

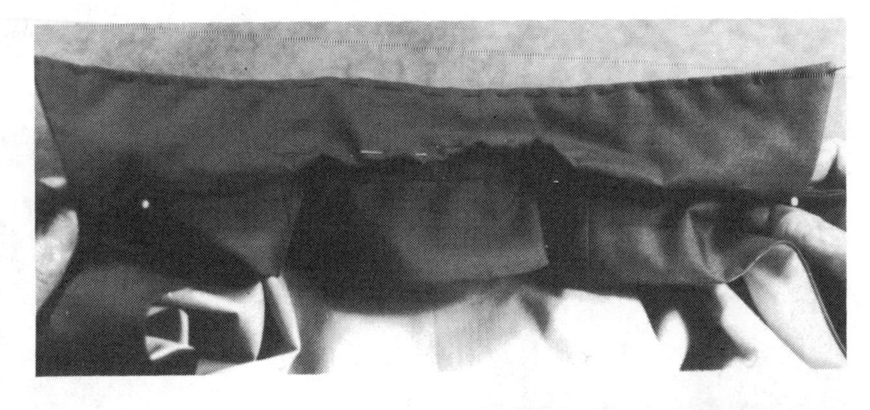

Pin or baste the upper edge of the collar to preserve the seam. It must stay slightly to the underside. With the center back of the collar over your fingers, roll the collar and pin the roll line. Try the garment on and check the roll of the collar. When the roll is satisfactory, pin close to the roll line to hold it.

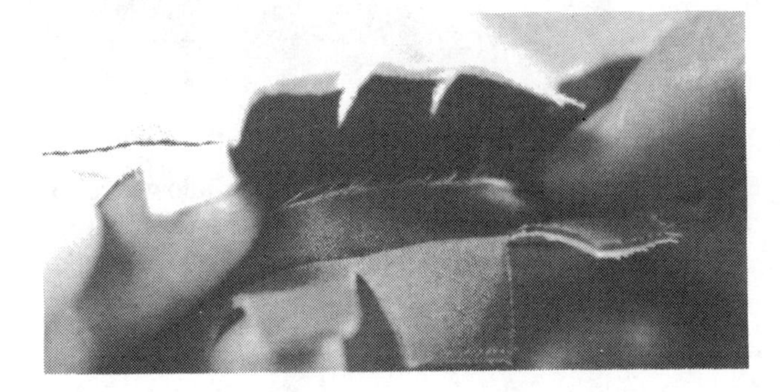

With the seams open lay the upper collar seam on the under collar seam.

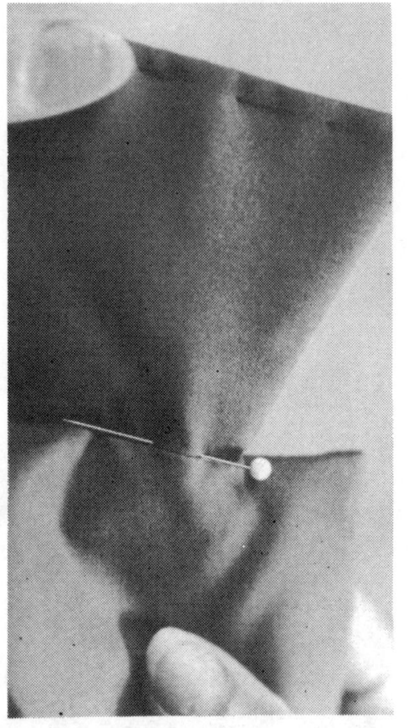

On the right side, hold the collar seam smooth from the front junction and pin in the seam line.

Finishing the collar with a back neck facing

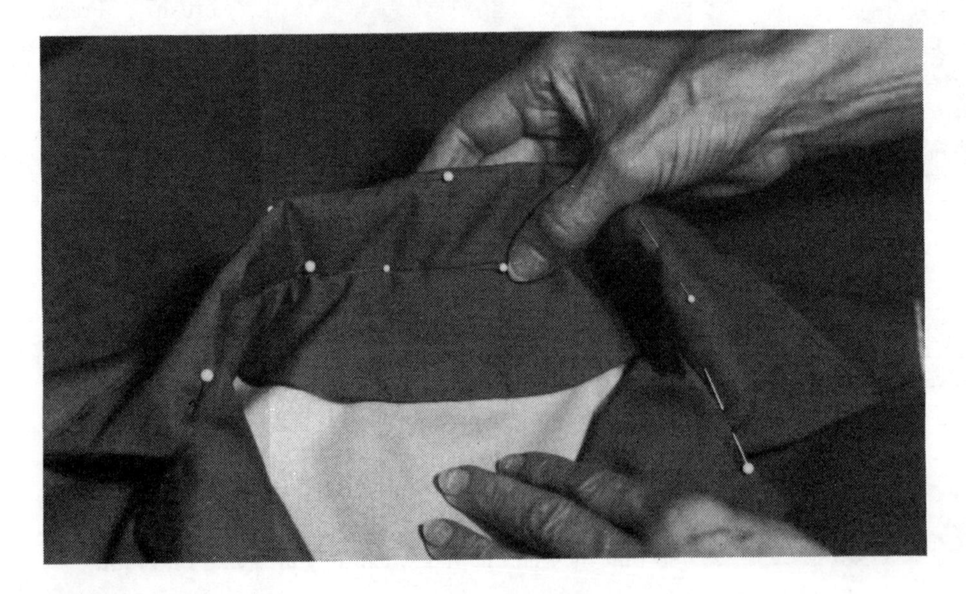

Fold the collar/lapel junction on the roll line and continue pinning along the under collar neck seam. The turn of cloth may prevent the under collar and upper collar seam from meeting exactly. Pin them as the collar dictates.

Lift the facing and hand backstitch the seams together. Hand stitch with a double thread (waxed) and a backstitch. Stitch the garment neck seam to the facing neck seam. Do not stitch below the seam line; it will show on the right side of the garment. Stitch close to the seam. The stitching stays in permanently.

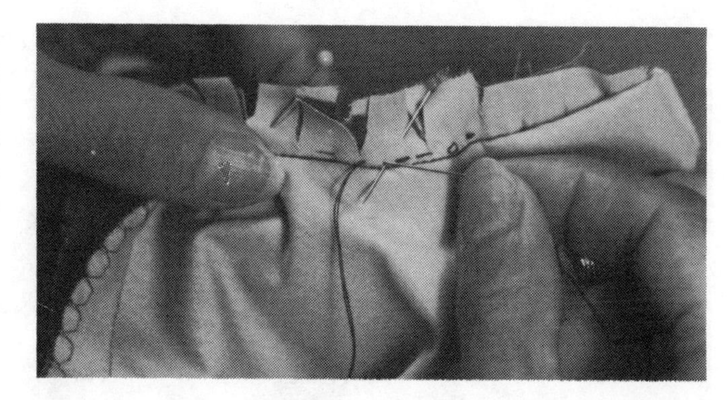

Finishing the collar without a back neck facing.

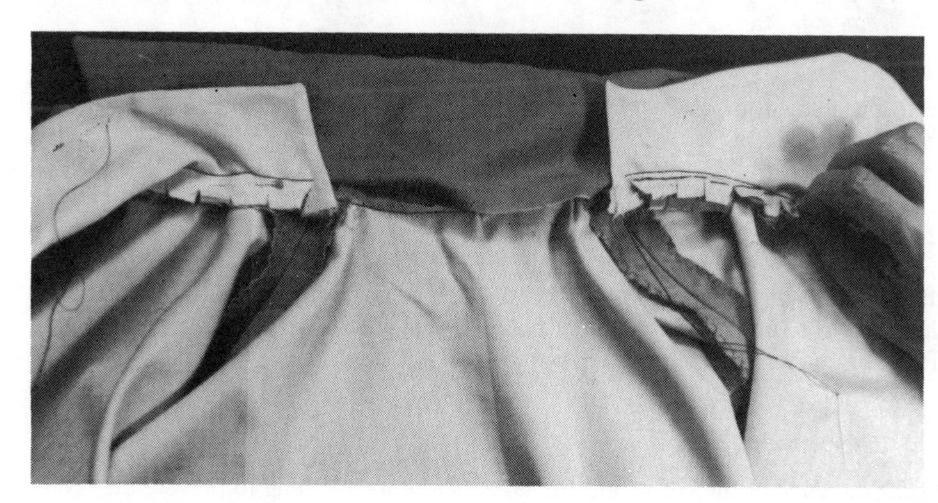

Hand stitch the garment neckline to the facing neckline from the shoulder seam to the end of the collar on both sides of the garment. Clip the back neck seam at the end of the stitching which is 1/4″ from the end of the front facing.

Trim the back neckline seam to 1/4″ from shoulder seam to shoulder seam. Press the seam up into the collar along the back neckline.

On the back neckline turn all seams in toward the collar. Always have the collar rolled as it will lie on you before pinning this seam. It's easiest to do this on a sleeve roll. Fasten the collar to the sleeve roll with the collar rolled as it will be on you.

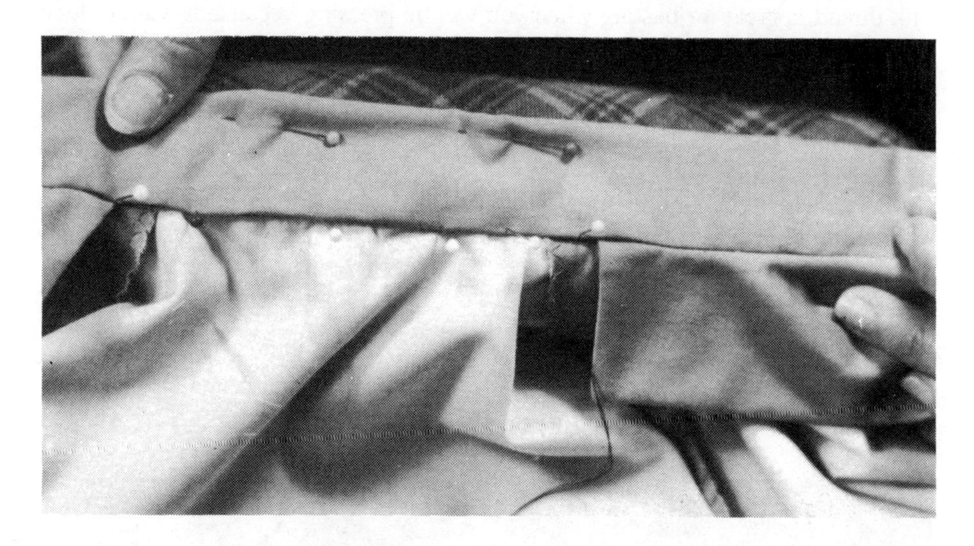

This allows enough fabric to let the collar roll as it should. Fold the upper collar seam allowance in so it just covers the neck seam. Stick pins into the sleeve roll all along the seam.

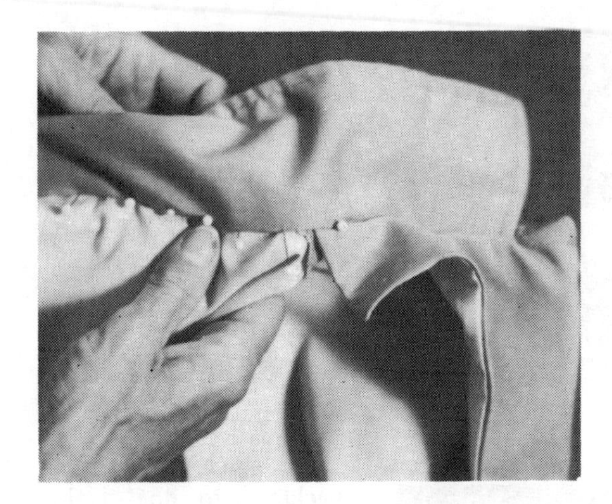

Then pull the collar off the roll and finish pinning. Hand baste before stitching.

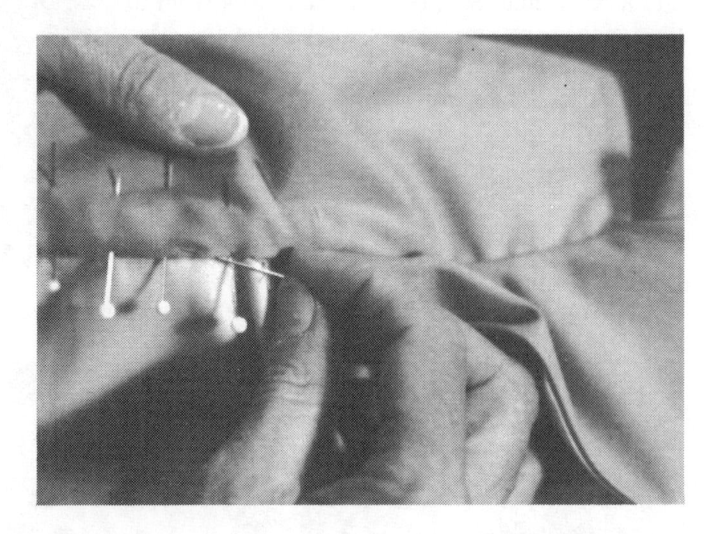

I usually machine stitch close to the fold on a garment that will be washed and hand stitch a finer garment using a hidden whip stitch.

Finishing the collar with lining instead of a back neck facing.

Hand stitch the garment neckline to the facing neckline from the end of the collar to the shoulder seam on both sides of the garment. Leave a long thread to finish stitching the neckline and to secure the stitches after the lining is in place. Refer to Couture Tailoring, pages 299 and 315-316.

Topstitching and pressing the collar and lapel

If you are topstitching, hand baste the edge of the collar and the lapel before topstitching to prevent the layers from slipping. If you are not topstitching, hand baste with silk thread to hold the seam correctly while you press. Silk thread is great for basting when you will be pressing because it will not leave an indent in the fabric. Refer to pages 72, 231, and 314.

Method Four

Garments which do not use a facing to finish the collar. If there is no collarband, attach the collar to the garment neckline in the same manner described below for the collar with a collarband.

Steps 1-6.

1. Interface, stitch, trim, turn, and press the collar.

Topstitch if the garment has topstitching. Refer to Collars, pages 161-164.

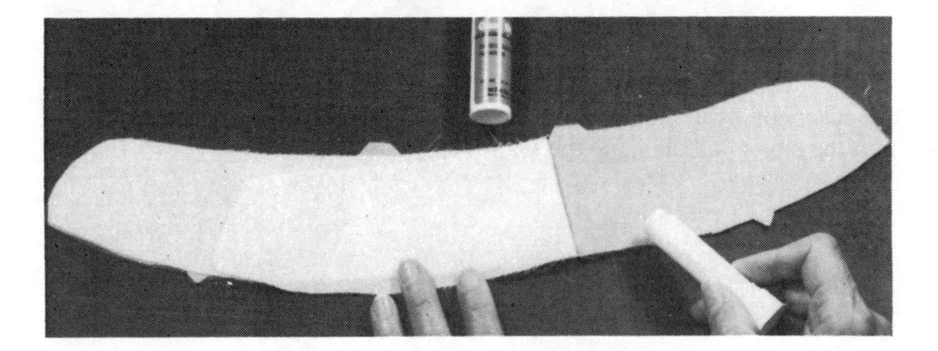

Also interface the under collar band.

2. Interface the garment opening.

Refer to Blouses and Dresses, pages 118-120. Stitch the shoulder seams of the garment. Refer to Sample Seams and Pressing Techniques, pages 58 and 65-67. Finish the shoulder seams. Refer to Seam Finishes, pages 68-71.

3. Attach the collar to the collarband.

With the right sides together, lay the collar on the collarband with the interfaced under collar next to the interfaced under collarband. Match the center fronts and the center back. Pin and baste in place.

Lay the upper collarband on the collar and pin in place through all thicknesses.

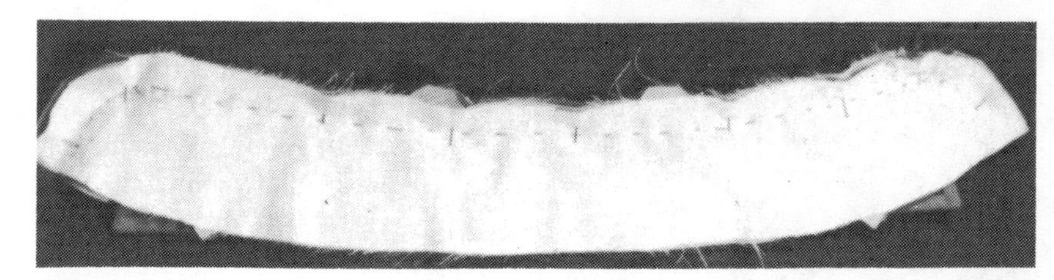

If your fabric is slippery and difficult to manage, hand baste the collar in place on the collarband. Be sure the center fronts and backs are matched on all the layers.

Stitch, being careful to match the curves on the ends of the collarband. It is so easy to have the curve a bit different on one end of the band. Refer to page 162.

Trim and grade the seam. Trim the collar seam to 1/4″. Trim the interfacings to the seam. Trim the collarband seam to 3/8″. Take notches out of the curved ends of the collar seam allowance.

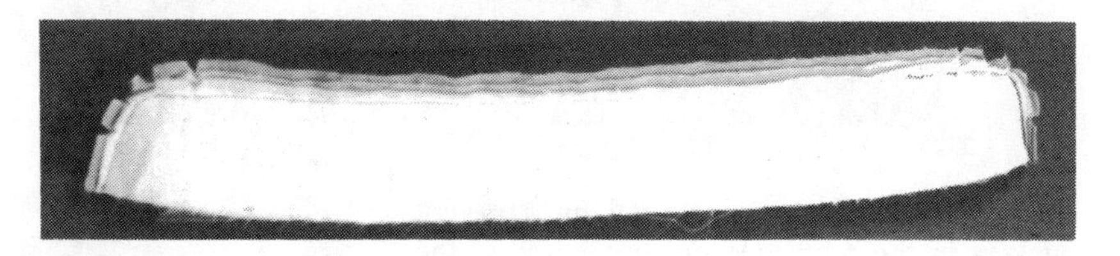

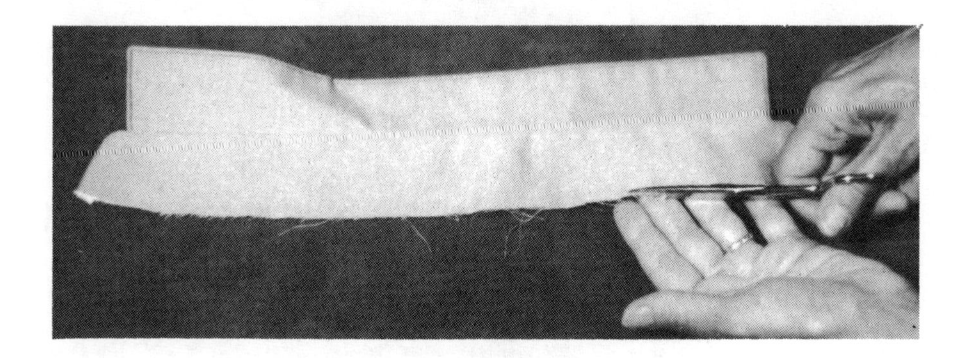

Press the band down in place. The neck edge of the collarbands must be even. Trim the neck edge of the collarbands if they are not even.

4. Attach the collarband to the garment.

With the right sides together, pin the under collarband to the neckline. Pin with the collar up, matching the center back of the collarband to the center back of the garment neckline. Pin the front edge of the garment neckline **exactly** on the seamline of the collarband. Keep the end seam of the collarband free. Refer to the picture on the upper left on page 172.

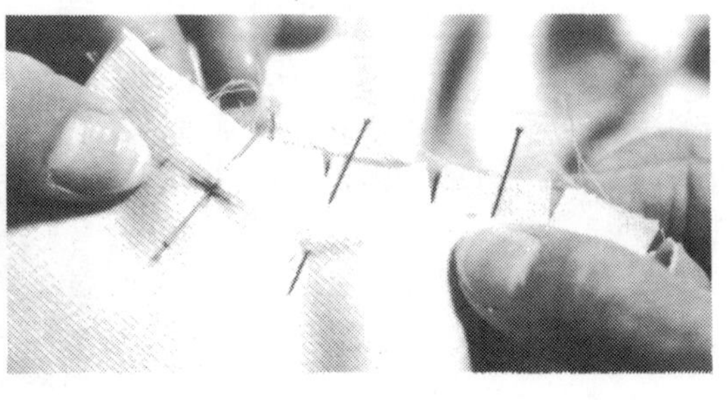

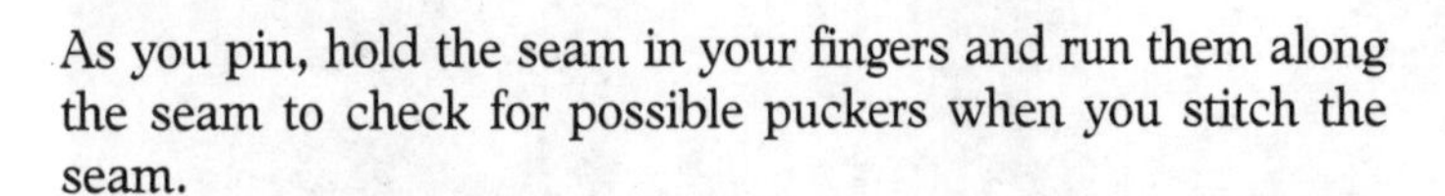

As you pin, hold the seam in your fingers and run them along the seam to check for possible puckers when you stitch the seam.

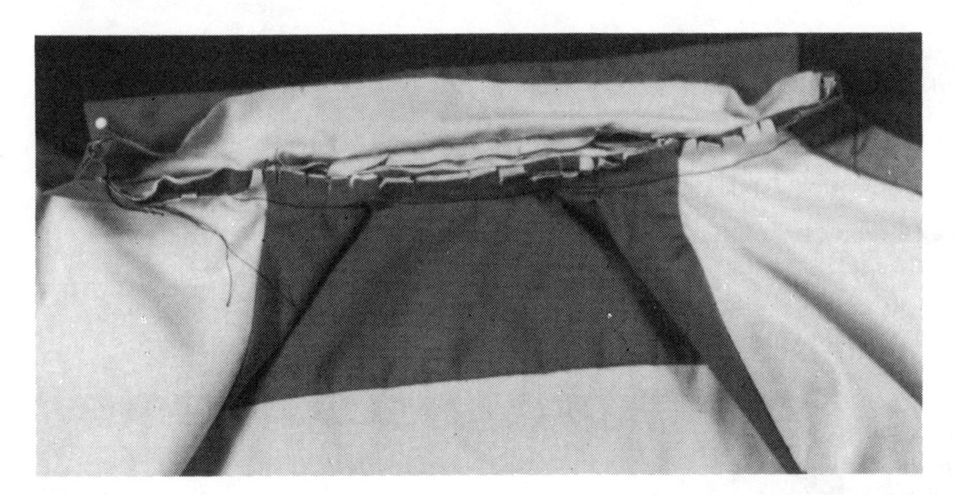

With the garment up, stitch the collarband to the garment. DO NOT catch the seam allowance of the collar in the stitching.

Gently pull the garment while stitching to prevent puckers in the seam. Do not backstitch at the center fronts. Leave long threads to tie later.

Check to make sure the collarbands are the same width, the collarband seams are free, and the garment center front is exactly on the collarband seam. If all is in order, tie the threads.

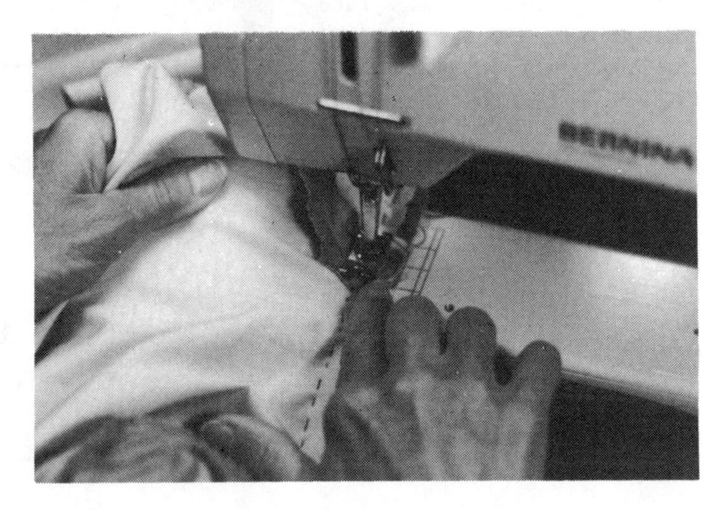

5. Machine stitch the collar front neck edge.

This can be done by hand but it looks more professional and wears better when done by machine.

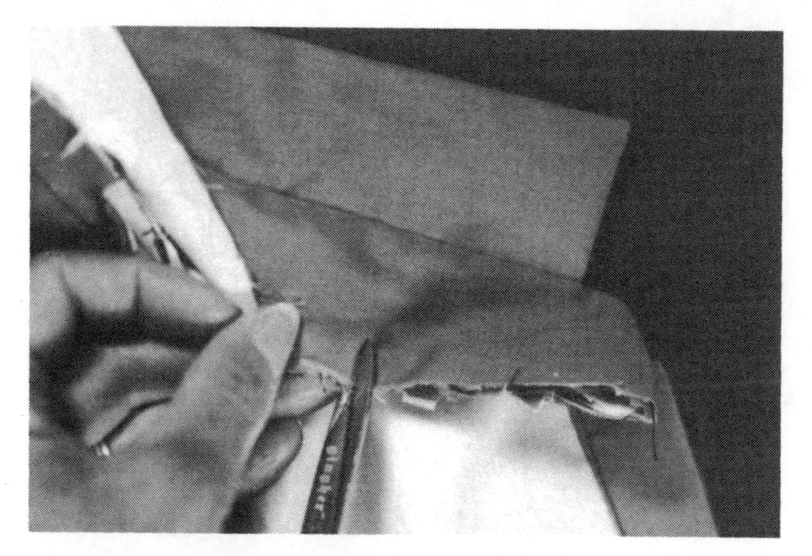

Lay the collarband seam edges together and clip once about 3-4″ from the front end of the band. The wider the collarband the farther back you can clip. The clip gives you a guide to keep you from stretching the upper collarband.

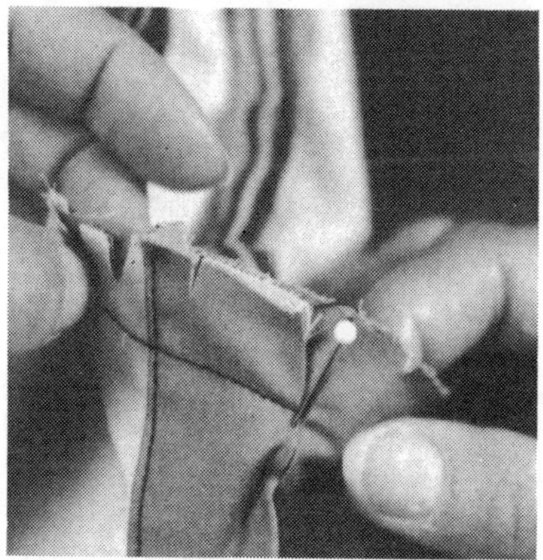

Put a pin, with the head of the pin toward the seam, very close to the collar end seam to hold the garment front in place.

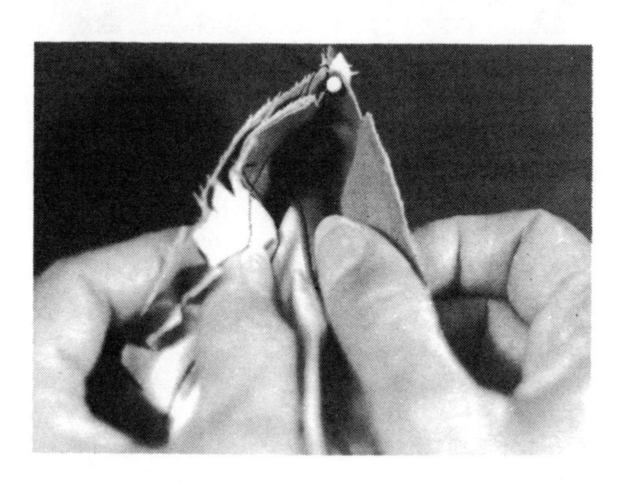

Turn the upper collarband back on itself so that the collarbands are right sides together, the edges even with the garment, and the collar in between like a sandwich. The width of the collarband determines how far you can stitch this seam. A wide band is much easier than a narrow band. If you can only do a small amount, it still allows you to trim the seam and have a very flat turn at the center front.

Pin to and match the clip you made in the band edges. **Be careful not to catch the garment or collar in the seam** when you are pinning. The collarbands are right sides together with the garment in between them like a sandwich. This is the same principal as the yoke, page 140, and the cuff, page 133.

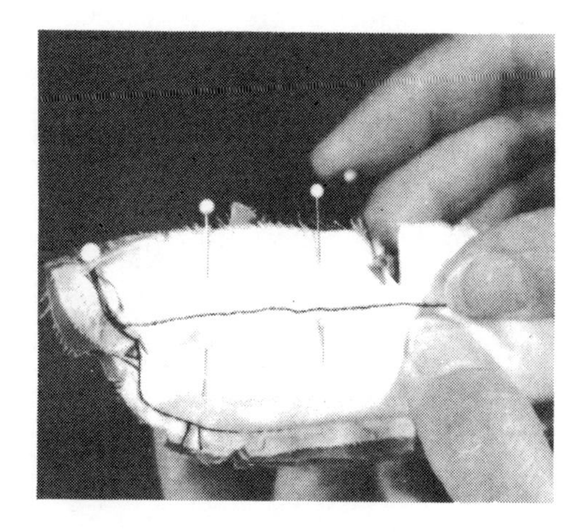

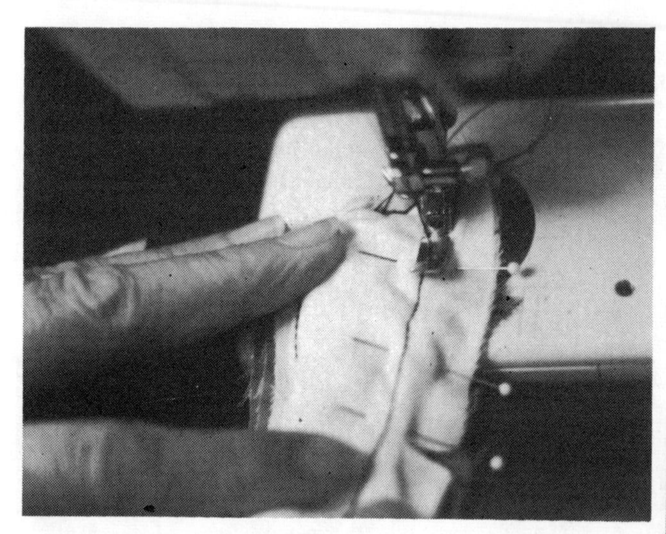

Stitch just inside the first row of stitching (toward the collar), using the stitching as a guide line. Use the zipper foot so you stitch on the previous line.

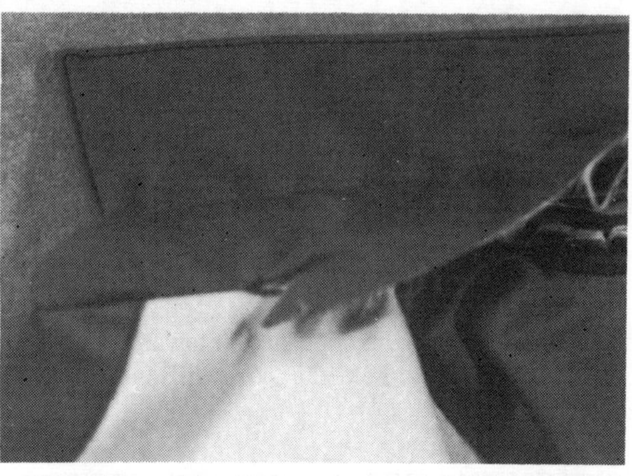

Turn and check the following points. Is the front edge even? Is the neck seam smooth? Is there any stitching showing? If the collar/garment junction looks good but you have some stitching showing, take out the stitches that show rather than ripping and restitching. You have stitched the seam twice so it is safe to take out the offending stitches.

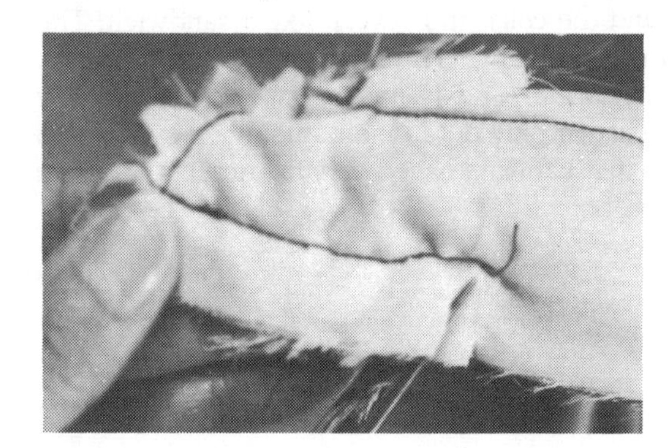

If it looks all right, turn it back as it was when you stitched and clip diagonally at the stopping point. This is a little difficult to turn back if the collar band is narrow. When you get proficient on this collar, you can skip checking your stitching.

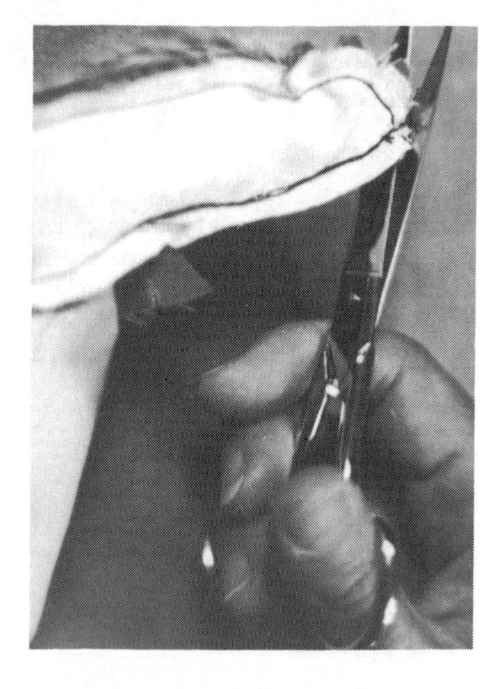

Trim the corner diagonally. Trim the seam to 1/4". Turn to the right side. Do both ends of the neckline.

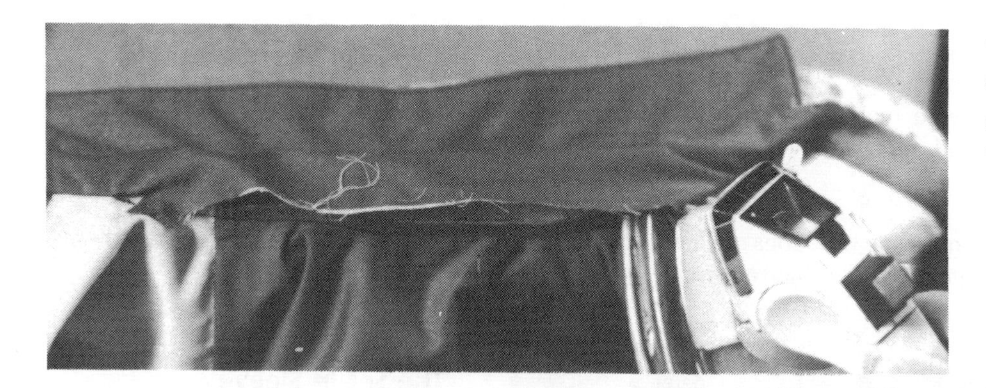

6. Finishing the collar

Trim the remaining neck seam to 1/4″ and press toward the collar band.

Fold the collar down as it will lie on the garment and press it in place. Fasten the garment to a sleeve roll and fold the upper band seam allowance in so that it just covers the neck seam. Stick pins down into the sleeve roll to hold the seam.

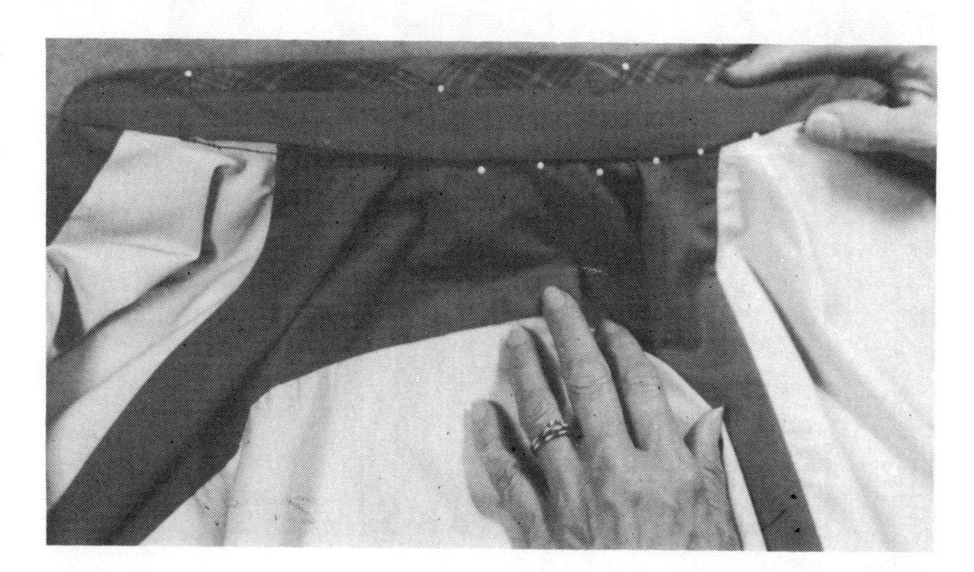

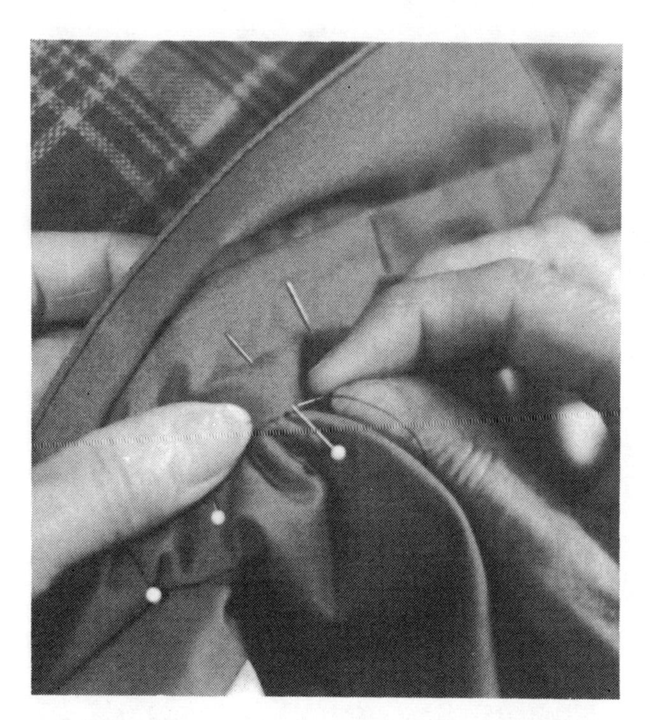

Gently pull the collar off the sleeve roll. Pull the collar free and finish pinning close to the folded edge. If you are hand stitching, you need not hand baste. If you are machine stitching close to the edge, hand baste before stitching. Then topstitch or edgestitch the collar band as directed on the pattern. Refer to pages 72, 231, and 314.

Proceed with the garment.

SLEEVES

Many seamtresses find sleeves a real challenge, especially the set-in sleeve. Sleeves must look right and be comfortable. This chapter covers which sleeves are the easiest and how to sew them and explains in detail how to tackle the hardest sleeve.

There are three sleeve styles and many variations of each style. Observe the different shapes of the sleeve patterns and the different look of the garment with the various sleeves styles.

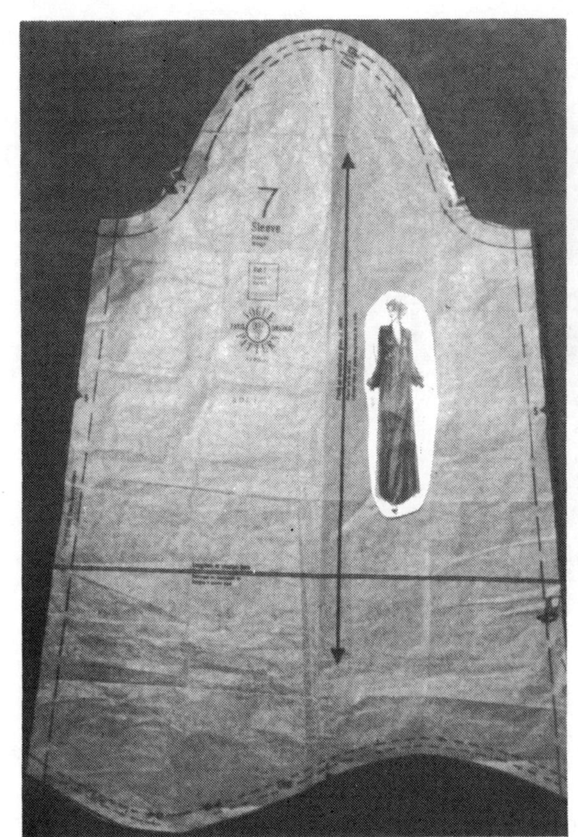

The Set-In Sleeve

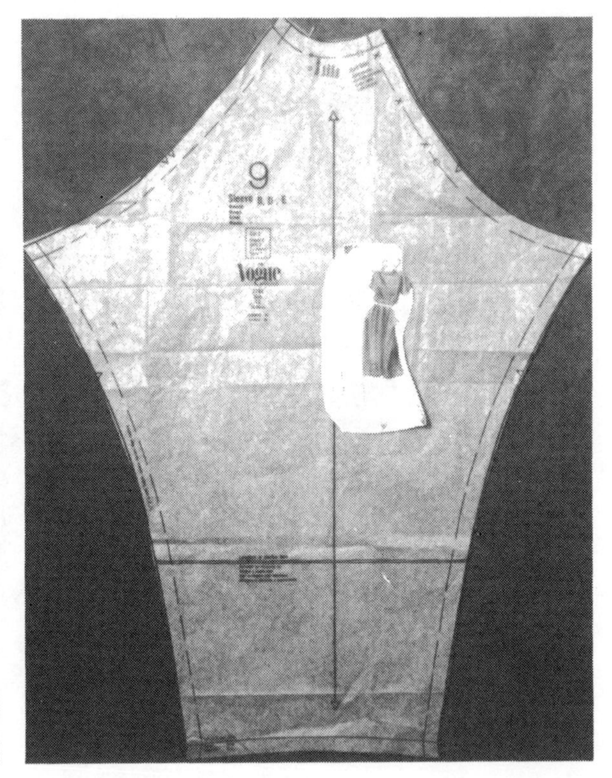

The Raglan Sleeve

The Kimono Sleeve

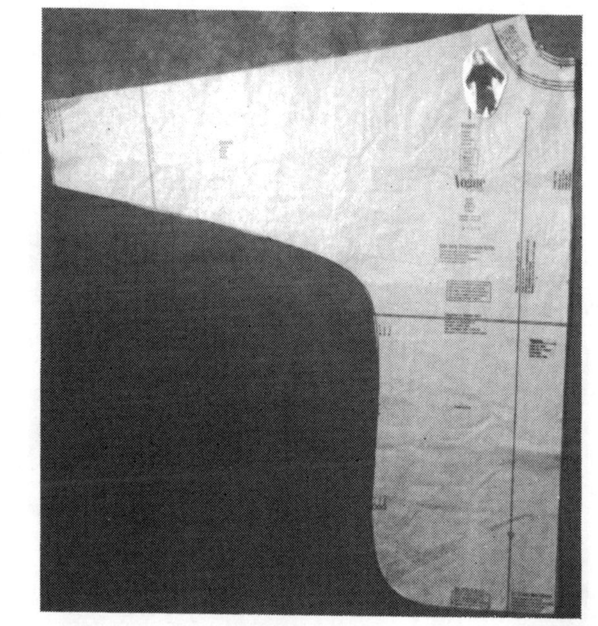

The raglan sleeve and the kimono (cut-on) sleeve are very easy to sew and the pattern directions are usually adequate.

My only advice would be in clipping the under arm area of the kimono (cut-on) sleeve.

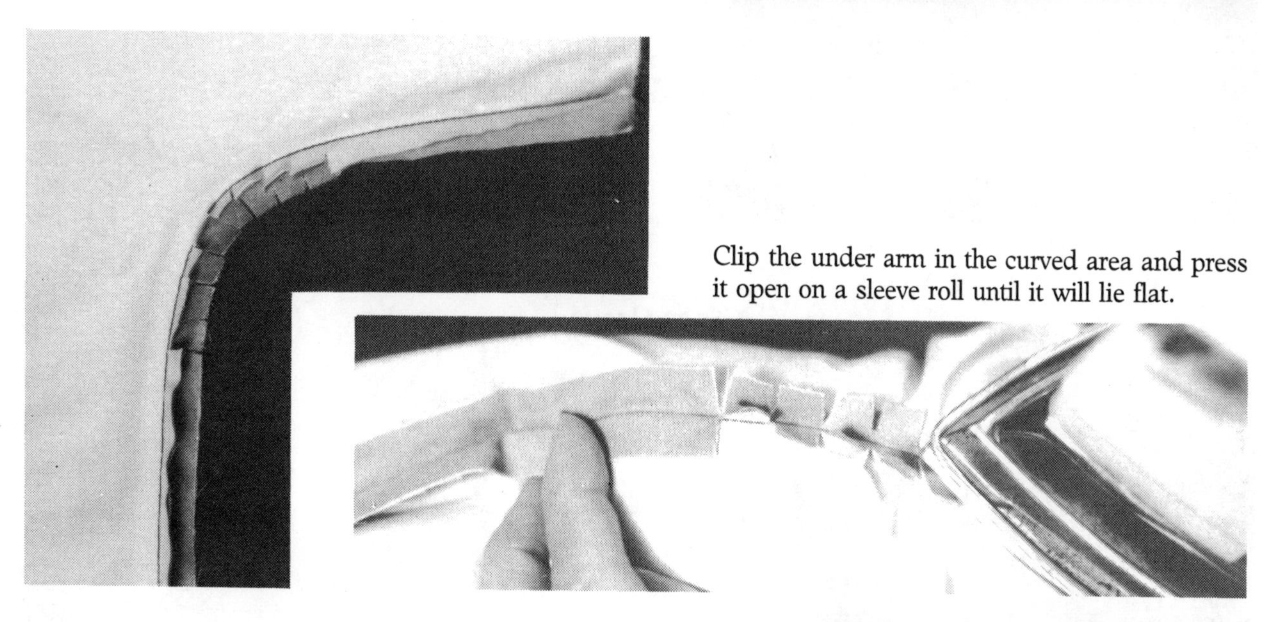

Clip the under arm in the curved area and press it open on a sleeve roll until it will lie flat.

Take a piece of rayon seam tape or straight piece of your fabric long enough to cover the clipped area and pin it to the open seam.

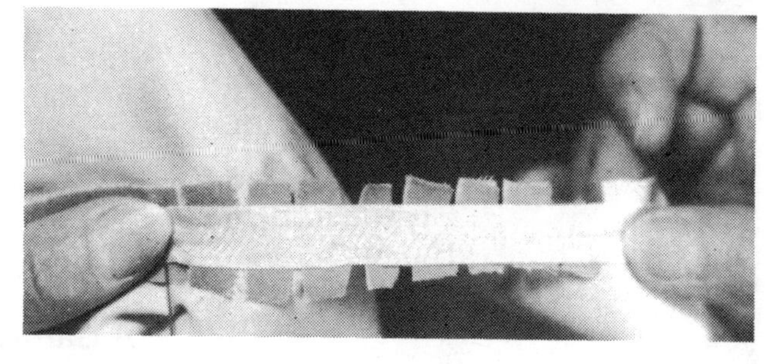

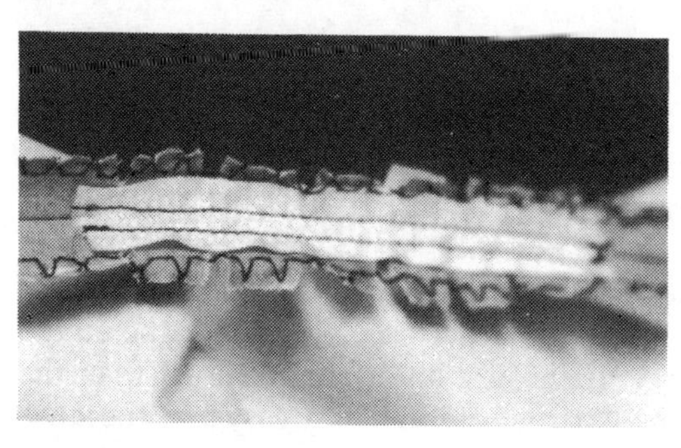

Stitch, with the seam up, about 1/4″ away from the seam. You are stitching through the seam tape and the clipped seam. Stitch both sides of the seam. This reinforces the clipped area and relieves all the pull on the seam.

The remainder of this chapter will deal with the set-in sleeve.

It is helpful to be able to recognize the different set-in sleeve styles and to recognize a well cut sleeve by the shape of the sleeve cap.

A very low cap on the sleeve pattern is either a dropped sleeve or a shirt sleeve. Either style is easy to construct. Often the pattern directions will show the **Open Method**, which is putting the sleeve on the garment before the side seams are stitched. Refer to pages 194-195.

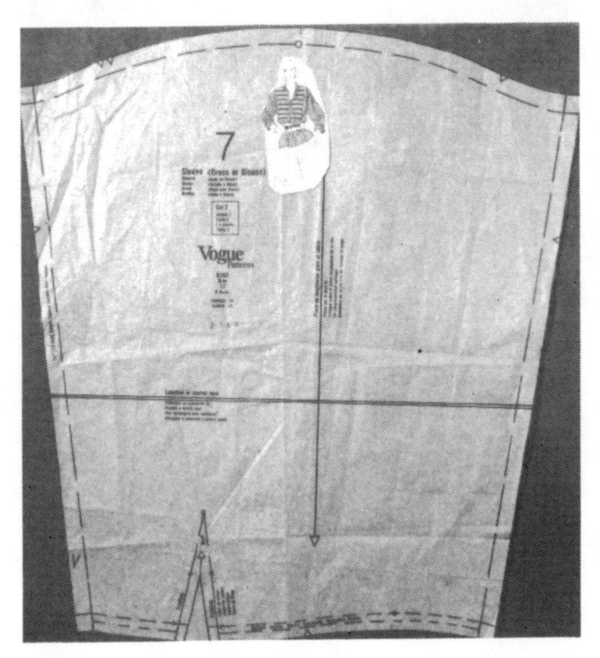

A Dropped Shoulder Sleeve

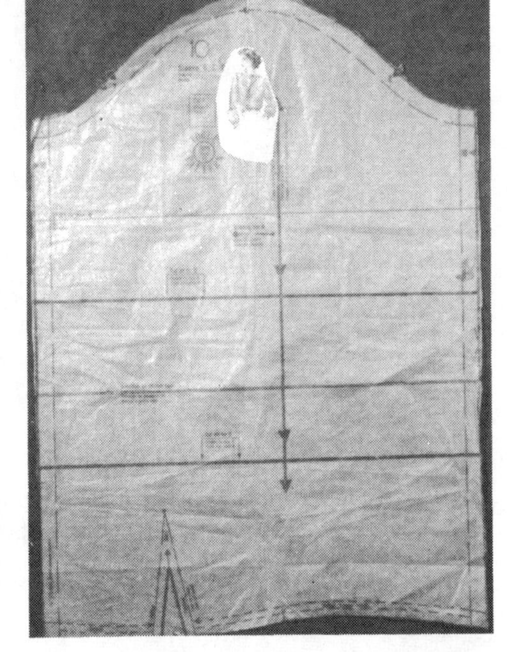

A Shirt Sleeve

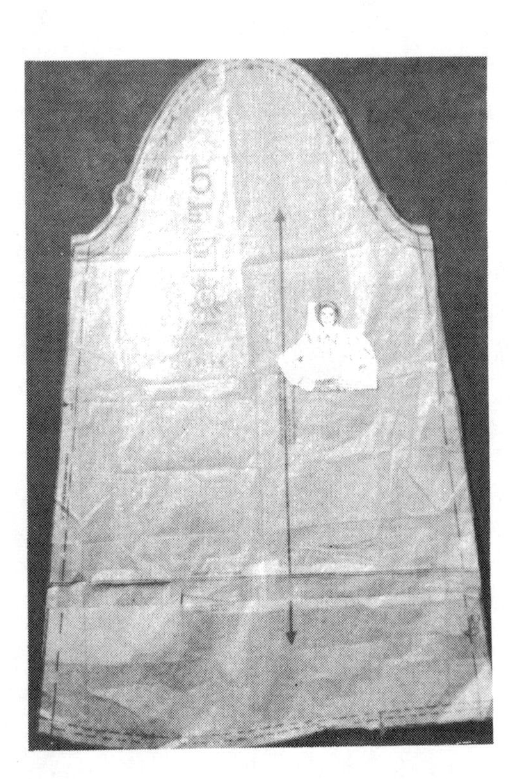

A Gathered Sleeve

The cap is quite wide and always will have gathering lines marked on the pattern. The wider the sleeve cap, the more gathered the cap will be. Gathered sleeves are harder to construct than the shirt or dropped sleeve, but they are still fairly easy to do because you don't have to work in the ease in the sleeve cap.

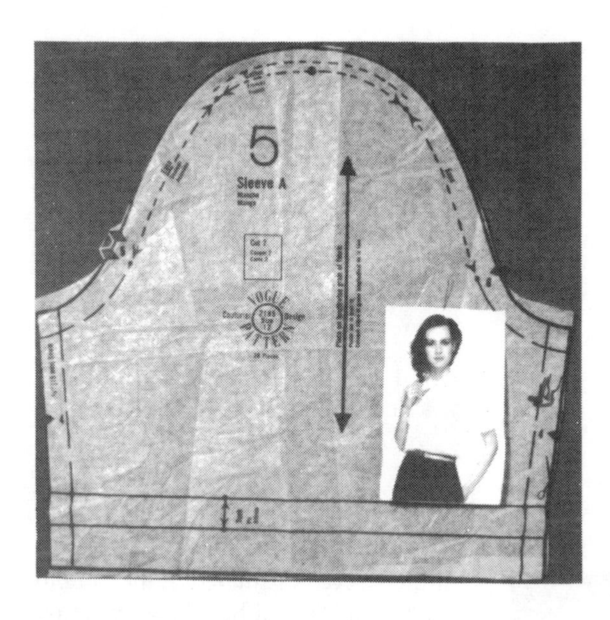

This gathered sleeve has a fairly high cap so it will have a larger puff. The arm hole was raised for a more comfortable fit in a fairly close fitting garment

This gathered sleeve has a lower cap and so a smaller puff, even though it is as wide as the sleeve above. The armhole was raised and the sleeve was lengthened.

A gathered or pleated sleeve often needs support for the gathers. For a puff support and/or shoulder pads, refer to Shoulder Pads, pages 333-335

A Fitted Sleeve

The fitted sleeve with no gathers is the most difficult sleeve. A well cut fitted sleeve in a fairly close-fitting garment will have a high cap. The back of the cap is wider than the front cap. If you have a wide back and need reach room, a bit more width can be added to the back of the sleeve as was done in the picture above of the gathered sleeve. Refer to Pattern Adjustments, pages 8-9.

You can see that the back is a bit wider when you fold the sleeve in half. The large dot marking the shoulder is usually exactly in the middle of the cap.

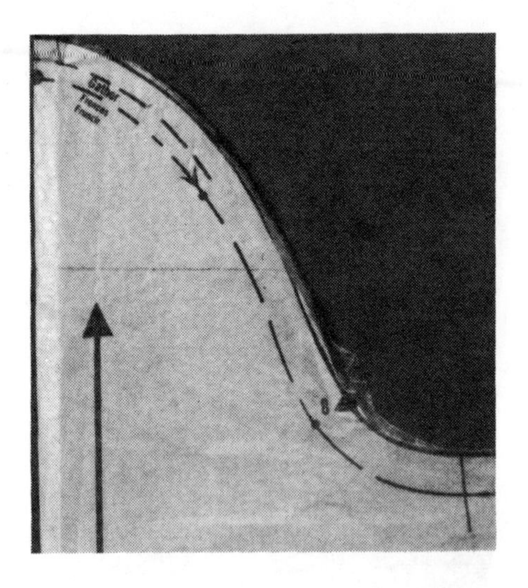

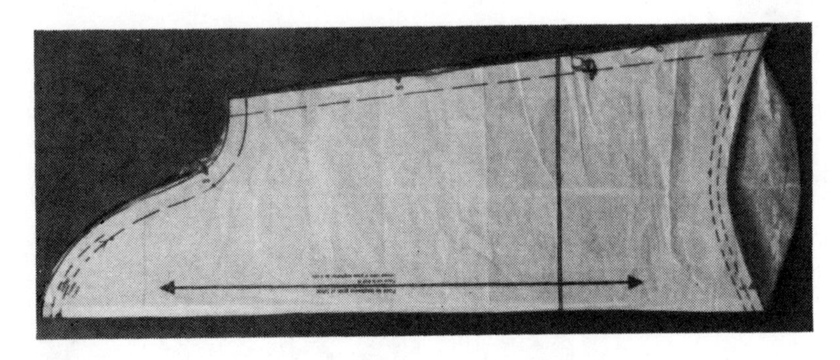

If the sleeve is gathered at the bottom with a cuff, it will be a little longer on the back of the sleeve to accommodate the elbow. The deeper the curve the more dramatic the drape at the bottom of the sleeve. If the sleeve is very full with a deep curve at the bottom, the cuff is usually wide. This helps keep the sleeve out of the soup.

Three Methods Of Setting In Sleeve

Open Method

Directions begin on page 194

Use the Open Method for the dropped shoulder sleeve and the shirt sleeve. Some designs must have this type construction because of the cut. Check your pattern instruction sheet. If it is directing you to use the Open Method, follow the instructions. The Open Method also works well for casual knit garments.

The Open Method of setting in a regular set-in sleeve never fits as well as the Modified Open Method or a regular Set-In Sleeve because the seam under the arm is not a continuous seam. It is broken by the side seam. The side seam is a continuous seam from the bottom of the blouse to the end of the sleeve.

Set-In Sleeve

Directions begin on page 196.

This method of setting in sleeves must be used on a two-piece sleeve and is the best way of setting in the sleeve if you have not used the pattern before. It gives you the opportunity of pin fitting the sleeve before it is permanently stitched.

Modified Open Method

Directions begin on page 203

The Modified Open Method finished is the same as the Set-In sleeve but it has the ease of putting the sleeve in flat.

A set-in sleeve fits better and is more comfortable because the sleeve seam is a circle. The Modified Open Method works well when the pattern has been fitted and you have previously checked and adjusted the hang and fit of the sleeve and the fit of the garment.

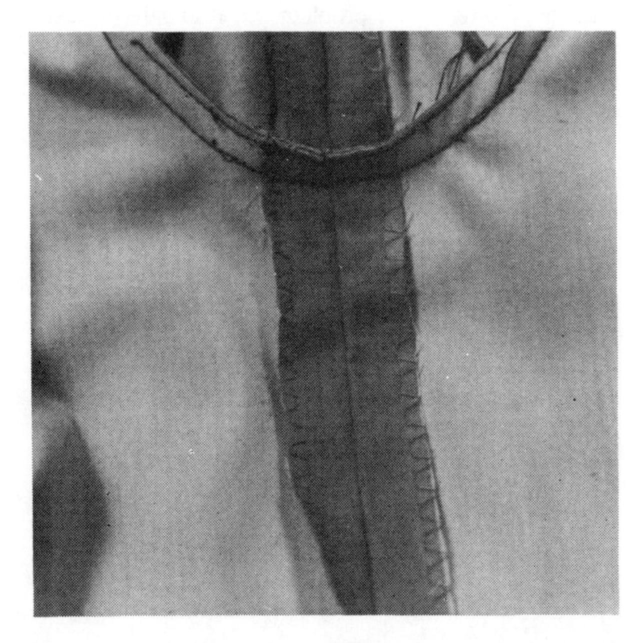

Essentials For Fitting The Set In Sleeve

Check before cutting by pinning the tissue together. The shoulder seam of the garment must fit you. The shoulder seam should be exactly at the top of the shoulder and divide the body about in half. Many people have a forward shoulder which makes it necessary to lengthen the back shoulder and sometimes to remove some length from the front shoulder. Refer to Fitting Your Garments-Pattern Adjustment, pages 8-9. A few people have square shoulders and it is necessary to have extra length on both the front and back of the pattern.

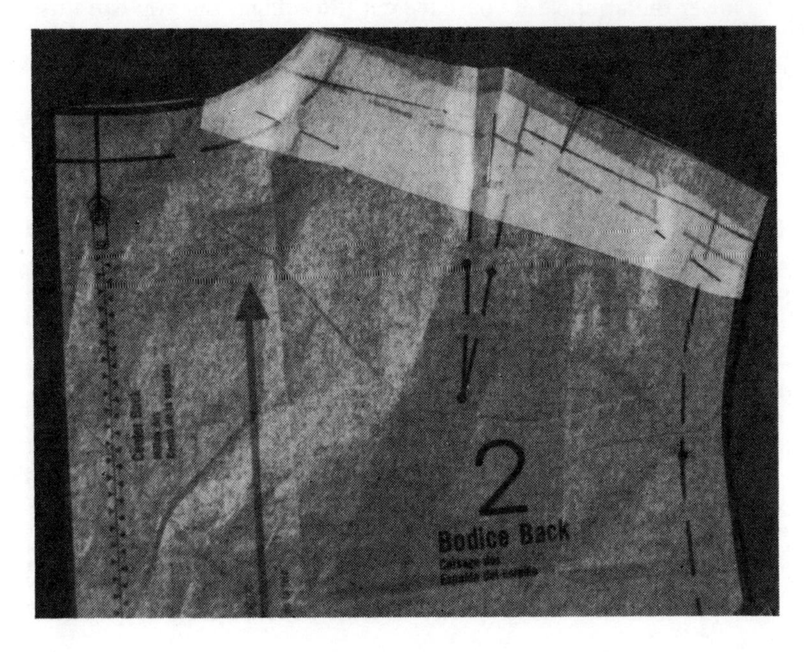

If you are in doubt add length to the back shoulder and, if needed, the front shoulder. Pin fit the shoulder seam during construction and trim any excess. Since garments hang from the shoulders use any changes you made when pin fitting on any pattern you use.

The sleeve must fit your arm. The minimum amount of ease for a fitted garment over the snug biceps measurement is 1½″. Check the measurement of the sleeve at the armhole.

If the sleeve is too small slash the pattern and spread the cap until it will fit your arm with the 1½″ ease. This method of adding width to the armhole does not make the armhole seam longer, it only makes the cap wider and shortens the cap. I usually do not find the shorter cap a problem but it is safe to add a bit to the cap length if widening shortened it significantly. Mark the pattern seamline of the cap on your fabric. Pin fit the sleeve. Trim the excess length if it is not needed.

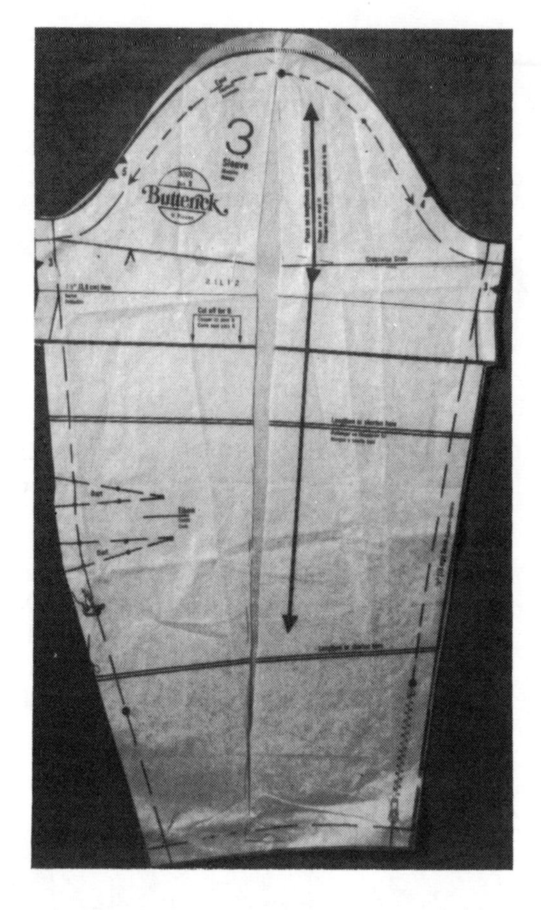

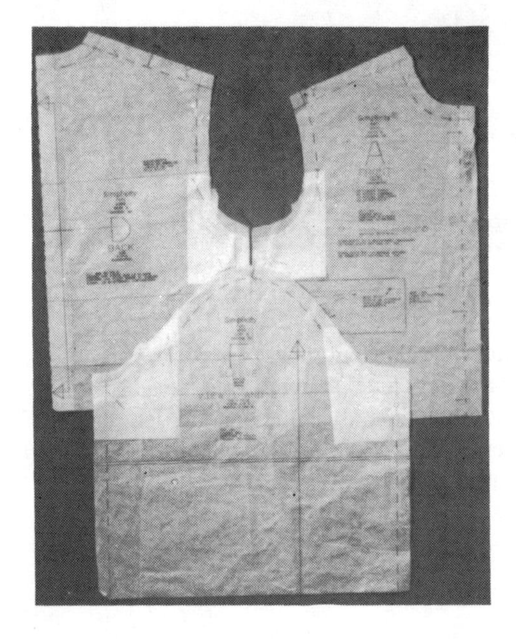

The looser the garment, the lower the armhole can be designed. The closer the fit of the garment, the higher up into the armhole the garment must be fit for you to move easily.

If your garment is a close fit, raise the armhole of the pattern about 1/2″ and the armhole of the sleeve the same amount. You can't ruin anything by cutting the armhole higher. You can always lower the armhole if you have cut it too high, but you can raise it only the amount of your seam allowance if it is cut too low. Some patterns have a narrow, deep armhole, and often a more shallow, wider armhole is more comfortable.

For a set in sleeve with a smooth cap—CHECK THE EASE BEFORE YOU CUT! Stand the tape measurement on edge on the seamline and measure the entire sleeve cap from seamline to seamline. Measure the armhole seam from underarm seam to underarm seam. Subtract the armhole measurement from the sleeve measurement to get the amount of ease the pattern has allowed.

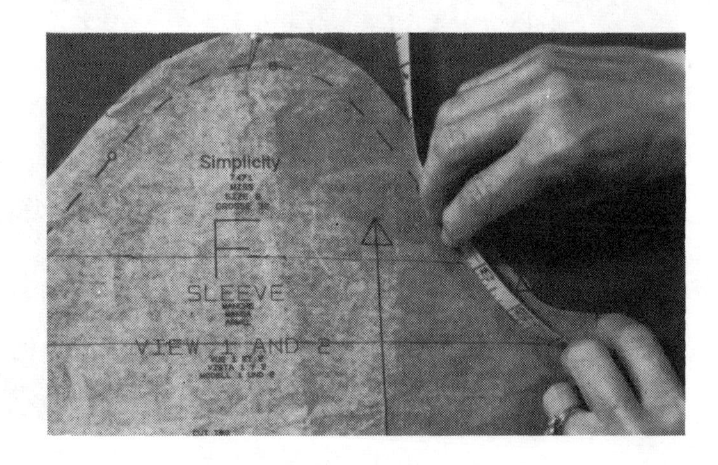

Most patterns allow 1″-1½″ of ease in the sleeve cap measurement over the armhole measurement. The sleeve will usually go in very nicely with that amount of ease allowed. If the ease is more than 1½″, the sleeve can be very difficult to get in without puckers. In that case take some ease out of the cap. If you are using a firm or crisp fabric that will not ease, you must take some room out of the cap without taking too much off the cap length.

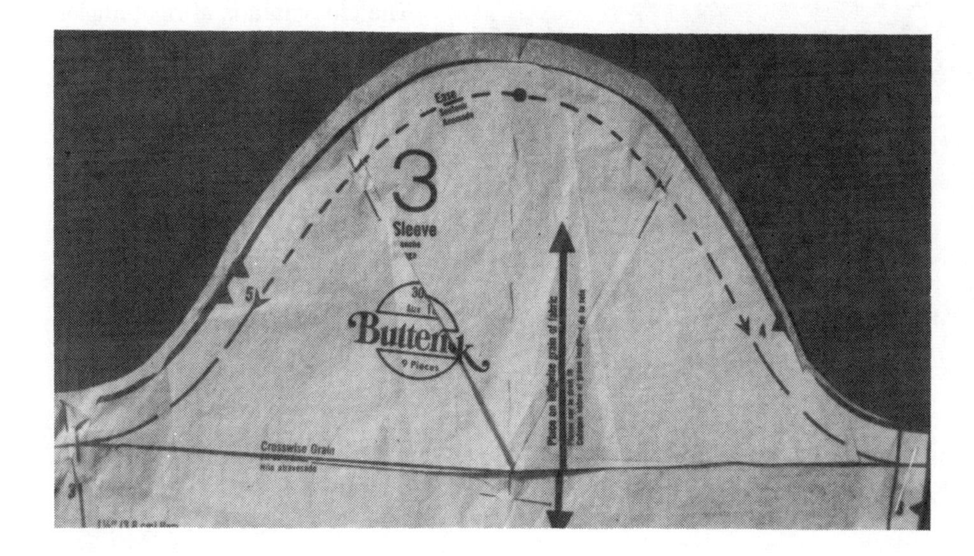

If your sleeve pattern has only one seam at the armhole, slash the pattern as shown and lap the slashes until you have reduced the ease to 3/4-1″. Mark the new pattern seam line and pin fit the sleeve. Trim any excess cap.

Ultrasuede will ease a maximum of 3/4″. A sleeve pattern that has two parts, an under and upper sleeve, is always my choice for Ultrasuede.

To remove the excess ease for Ultrasuede, take in the sleeve at the seamlines and taper to the normal seam 3″ from the armhole. This adjustment takes in the width of the cap but not the length. If you cannot take in the width enough to make the sleeve fit the armhole because of the measurement of the arm, take in the length a little also. I usually pin fit this so I don't take off too much. BE CAREFUL! It is very easy to make the cap too short.

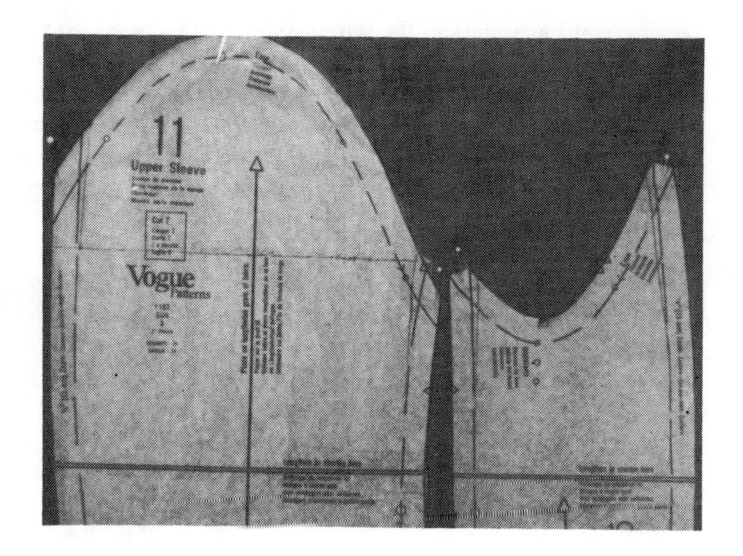

Always Mark On Your Sleeve

1. Mark the center of the sleeve on the cap. This is always marked on the pattern with a large dot.

2. Mark the underarm of the sleeve if the seam is not at the side seam, Mark the underarm of the garment if it is not at a side seam. This is usually marked with two small dots, one above the other.

3. Mark the back and front of your sleeve by cutting the notches out. The double notch is the back of the sleeve and the single notch is the front of the sleeve.

4. Mark the crossgrain line of the sleeve. If the pattern has been adjusted there is no need for the crossgrain line to be marked. However, if you are using the pattern for the first time and can not see the grain line of the fabric, it should be marked so you can check the hang of the sleeve.

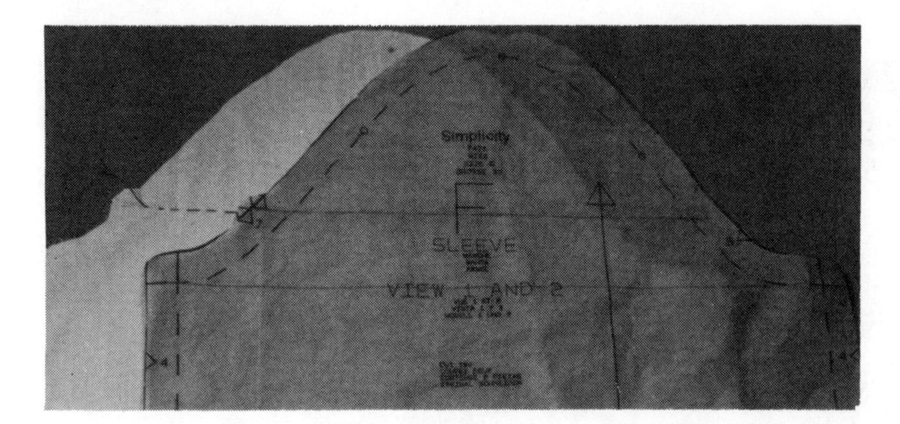

The crossgrain is at right angles to the straight of grain. To mark the crossgrain take a ruler and draw a line at right angles to the straight of grain on the pattern. Hand baste a line (thread trace) across the sleeve cap on the new crossgrain line.

5. Mark the notches and small dots on the bottom of the sleeve. If there is a cuff, mark the corresponding notches and small dots on the cuff interfacing so you can adjust the sleeve to the cuff as the pattern is marked.

Open Method

Prepare sleeves for the open method

Be sure you have marked the wrong side of the sleeves so you can identify a right and a left sleeve before you do the sleeve opening. Unless they are marked it is very easy to do both sleeves for the same arm. To prepare the sleeves for setting into the garment do the sleeve opening that is suitable for your fabric and the style of your garment. Refer to Blouses and Dresses, page 124-125. If you plan to use the No Slash Opening, put the sleeve on the garment before doing the sleeve opening. Check the pattern directions before easing the sleeve cap. If they do not tell you to do this step, it usually is not necessary.

Ease the sleeve cap using a machine baste on the 5/8″ seam line. If there is over 3/4″ ease in the sleeve cap or your fabric is crisp and does not ease well, put in a second row of stitching 1/4″ from the first row into the seam allowance.

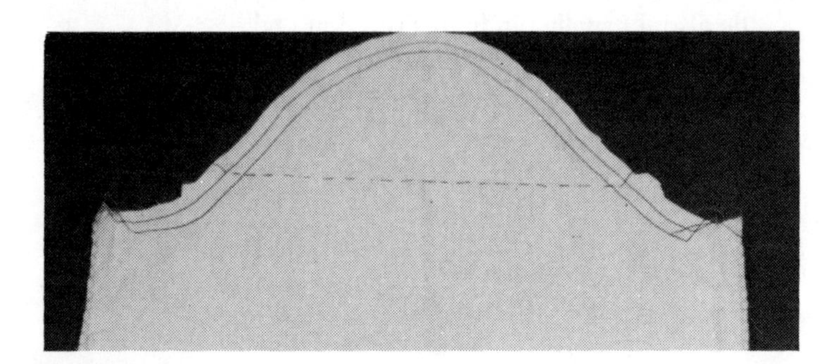

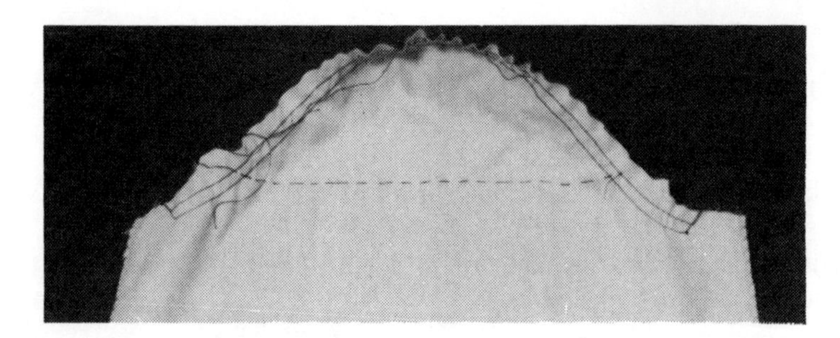

Pull the gathering thread up smaller than the sleeve opening. Then ease out the excess fullness so there are no gathers and the cap is shaped.

Open method of setting in a sleeve

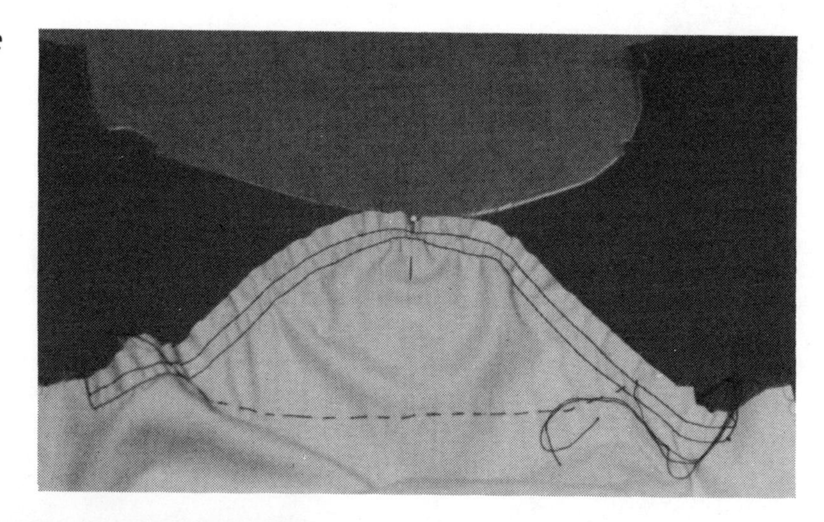

Lay the blouse out flat with the right side up. Lay the unstitched sleeve on the blouse with the right sides together. Match the center of the sleeve to the shoulder of the blouse.

Sometimes this will be a seam but if your pattern has a yoke or a forward shoulder seam, the shoulder will be marked with a large dot.

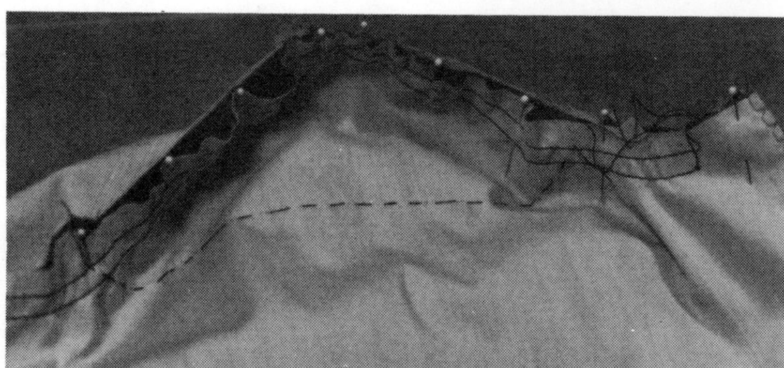

Match the edges of the sleeve to the armhole and ease the sleeve into the armhole of the blouse. With the blouse up, pin at close intervals.

Stitch the armhole seam. Check the seam to make sure it is smooth and nicely curved with no tucks stitched in. Stitch a second time 1/4" from the seam line. Use a seam finish for this stitch. Refer to Seam Finishes, pages 68-69.

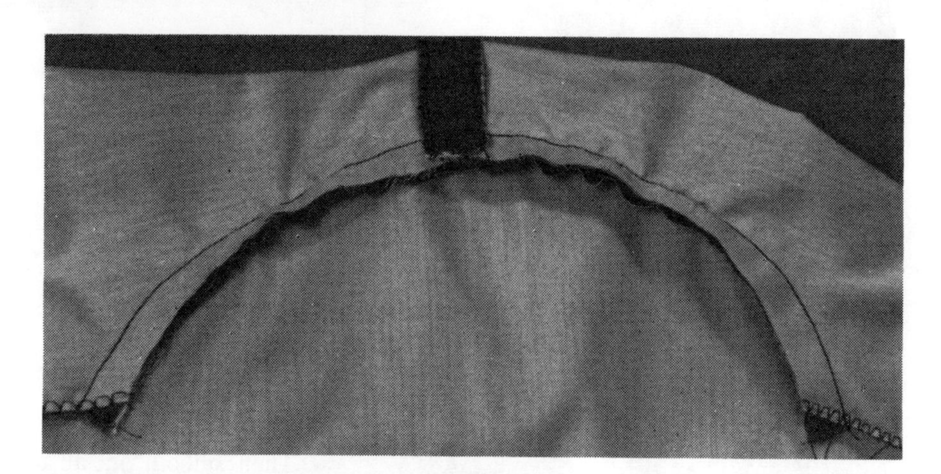

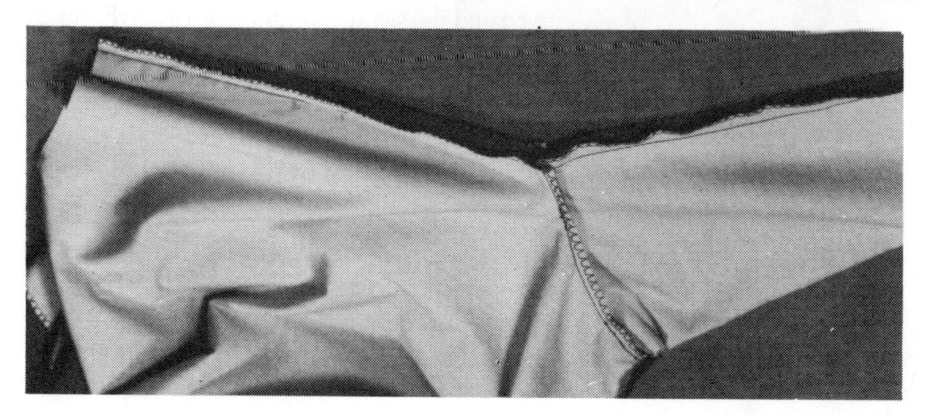

Lay the side seams and sleeve seams together matching the underarm seam and the bottom edges of the blouse and the sleeve. Refer to page 58. Stitch from the bottom of the blouse to the bottom of the sleeve. Finish the seam. Refer to Seam Finishes, pages 68-69.

Set-In Sleeve Method

Prepare sleeves for the Set-In mehod

To prepare the sleeves for setting into the garment do the sleeve opening that is suitable for your fabric and the style of your garment. Refer to Blouses and Dresses, pages 124-125. Be sure you have marked the wrong side of the sleeves so you can identify a right and a left sleeve before you do the sleeve opening. Unless they are marked it is very easy to do both sleeves for the same arm. Stitch the sleeve seam and finish the seam edges. Ease stitch or gather the cap and shrink the fullness out if necessary. Gather or tuck the bottom of the sleeve. If you are sure of the sleeve length, put the cuff on the sleeve before you put the sleeve on the garment. If it is the first time you have used the pattern, put the sleeve on the garment, then put the cuff on the sleeve. If you are using a shoulder pad, check the sleeve length with the shoulder pad in place. If the sleeve is too short — or too long — you can adjust the length. If the sleeve is too short, use a smaller seam allowance when stitching the cuff on the sleeve. If the sleeve is too long, shorten the sleeve before sewing the cuff in place.

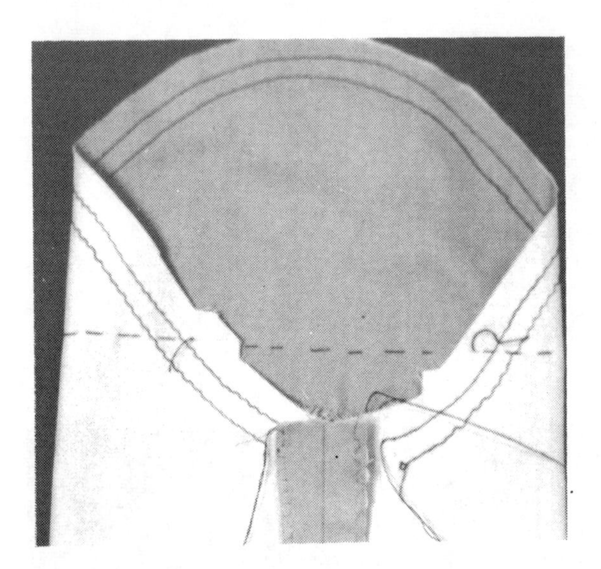

Put one row of gathering slightly inside the 5/8″ seam line around the entire sleeve and a second row of gathering stitches 1/4″ from the first row of basting into the seam allowance. Refer to Gathering. The second row makes it easier to control puckers.

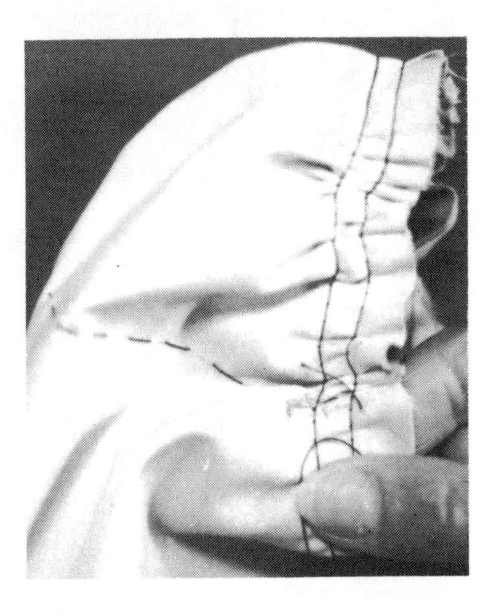

Working on the wrong side of the sleeve, pull up both threads together and gather the sleeve cap more tightly than is needed for the size of the armhole.

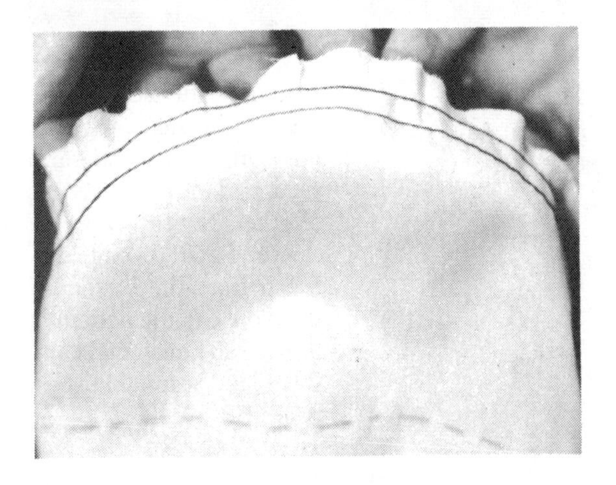

Then smooth out all the gathers until the sleeve cap is nicely curved and the seam allowance curves to the inside. You must have a little ease all around the sleeve, even at the center of the cap which is on the straight of the grain.

Measure the sleeve and the cap to assure you have taken in enough of the ease. This needn't be an exact measurement as you can easily adjust it. Wrap the gathering threads around a pin to hold that length.

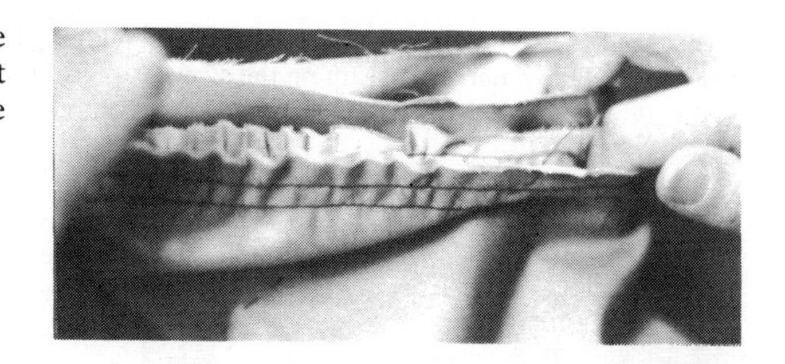

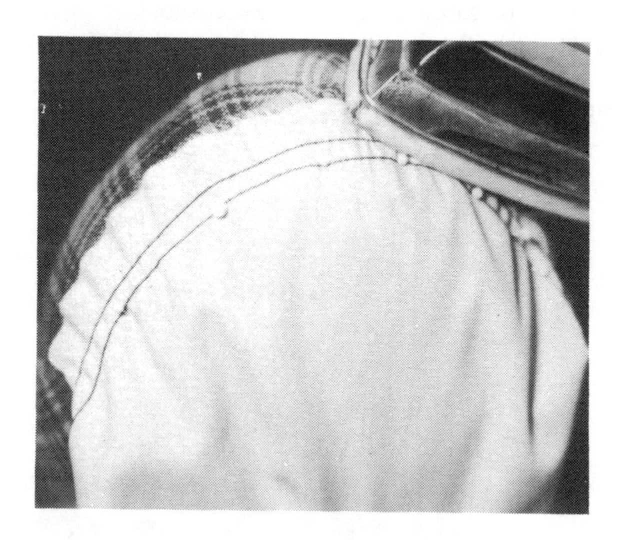

Place the sleeve cap on a ham and press the sleeve seam allowance to shrink in the ease. A ham holder makes this easier. Use plenty of steam when pressing. I don't always measure and steam the excess ease out of the sleeve cap, but if your fabric is difficult to ease it certainly helps. I do always take the time to measure and steam the ease when I am working with expensive fabric or tailoring a jacket or a coat.

Fitting The Sleeve in the Armhole

A set-in sleeve with a smooth cap is a challenge we all face in sewing. Each type of fabric handles differently, some ease nicely, some don't. A basic knowledge of sleeves can help us understand why we sometimes have problems setting sleeves into a garment.

Think of sleeves as two circles that must fit into each other. The armhole is one circle, and if you make the seam deeper than 5/8″ in the armhole that circle becomes larger. If you stitch the seam narrower than 5/8″ the circle becomes smaller.

The sleeve is another circle. If you take a deeper seam on the sleeve cap it becomes smaller. If you take a shallow seam on the sleeve cap it becomes larger.

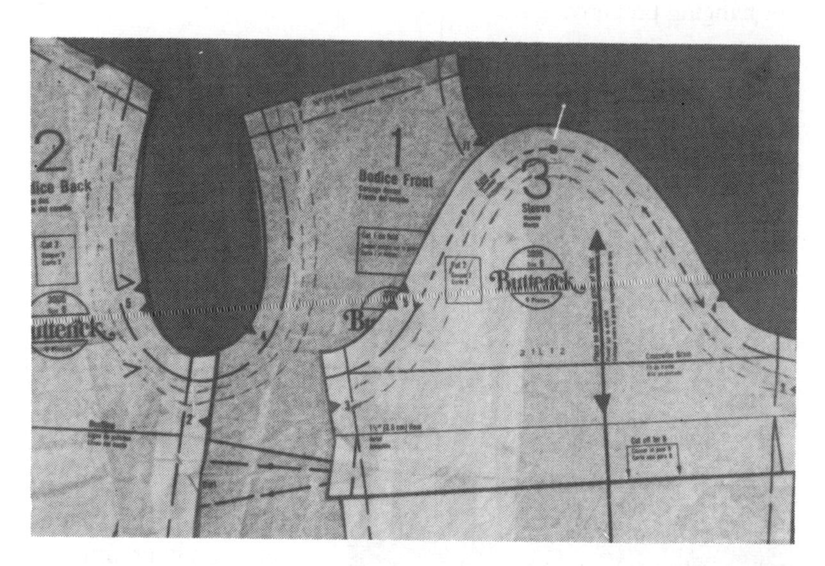

That is why it doesn't work if you just try to let the seam out or take it in a bit when stitching in a sleeve. When you stitch the seam deeper while the sleeve is getting smaller the armhole is getting bigger. If you take a shallow seam the armhole is getting smaller and the sleeve is getting larger.

If you need to set the sleeve in deeper at the shoulder, unless you have extra ease in the sleeve cap (over 1″) you need to take a narrower seam on the sleeve cap. Taking a deeper seam at the shoulder demands more sleeve so by taking a narrower seam on the cap you accommodate the larger armhole.

Put the garment on. If a shoulder pad is being used, slip the pad under the garment and position it to extend past the armhole seam 1/4″. Your shoulder determines where the center of the sleeve should be placed. The model has a shoulder that is forward, so the back shoulder was lengthened to make the shoulder seam fit her properly. Since the shoulder seam was altered the sleeve cap must be pivoted to correspond with the shoulder.

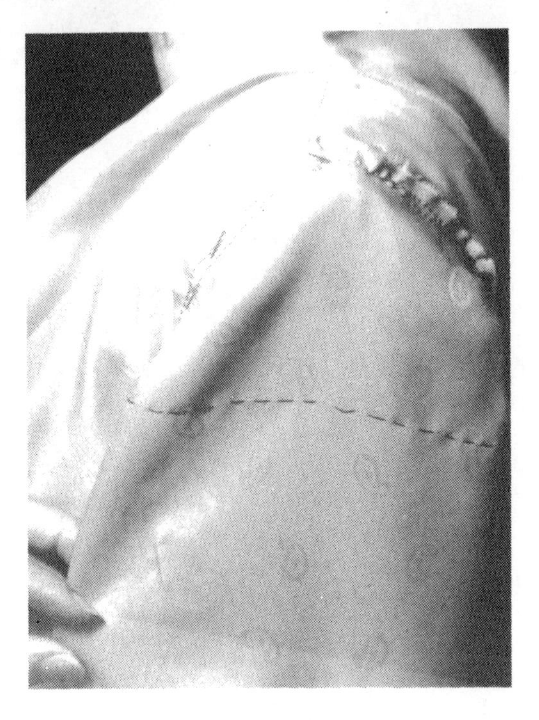

Put the sleeve on, matching the center of the sleeve to the shoulder dot. Pin a small area of the sleeve cap on both the front and the back of the sleeve. Is the sleeve hanging properly with the crosswise grain horizontal to the floor and the straight of the grain hanging plumb from the shoulder to the elbow? This sleeve is not hanging properly.

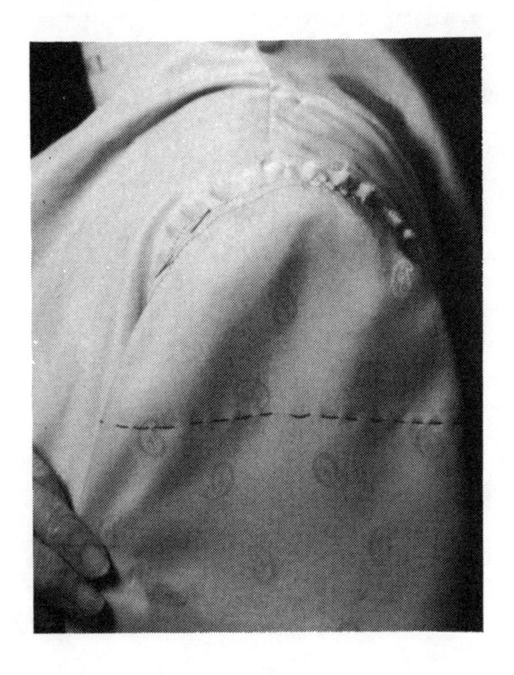

A sleeve is like a wall. It must be straight to look correct and feel comfortable. If you have a shoulder that is forward, you must pivot the sleeve cap forward to correspond with your shoulder. Check the hang of the sleeve. If the crossgrain line is not hanging parallel to the floor, move the center of the sleeve until the crossgrain line of the sleeve is horizontal to the floor and the straight of grain is hanging plumb from the shoulder to the elbow. Mark a new center on the sleeve cap to correspond with the shoulder seam marking. This sleeve is hanging properly. Take the garment off and mark both sleeves the same.

Pin fit the sleeve in the armhole

With both the sleeve and the garment right side out match the underarm of the sleeve to the underarm of the garment.

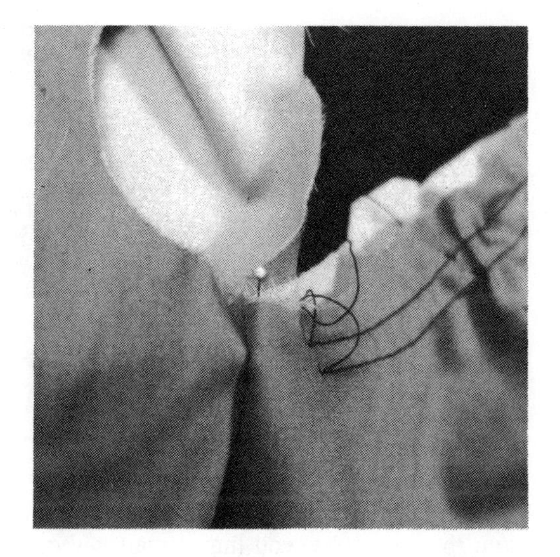

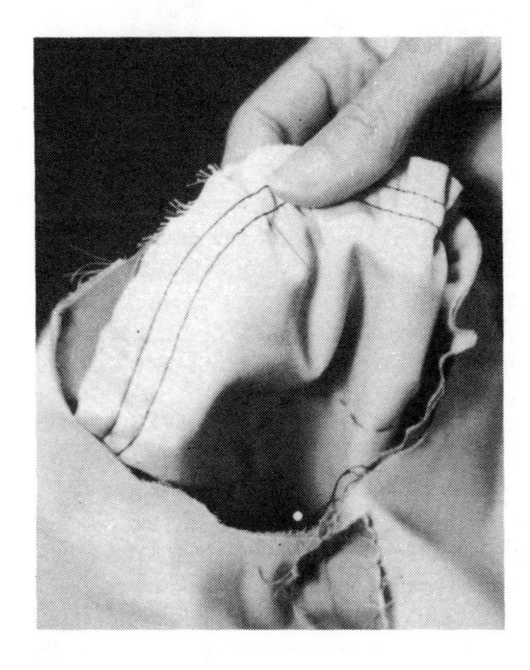

Match the center of the sleeve to the shoulder line. If you have pin fit and changed the center of the sleeve, use the new marking. Pin from the shoulder to the underarm on both the front and back shoulder. If the sleeve will not go in nicely with the notches matched, it is not necessary to match the notches on the sleeve to the notches on the garment. If needed, scoot some of the ease just where the arm separates from the body. That is where you get the most pull on a sleeve.

Adjust the ease by working first with the sleeve inside the armhole. As you are pinning hold the seam in your fingers and run them along the seam to check for puckers.

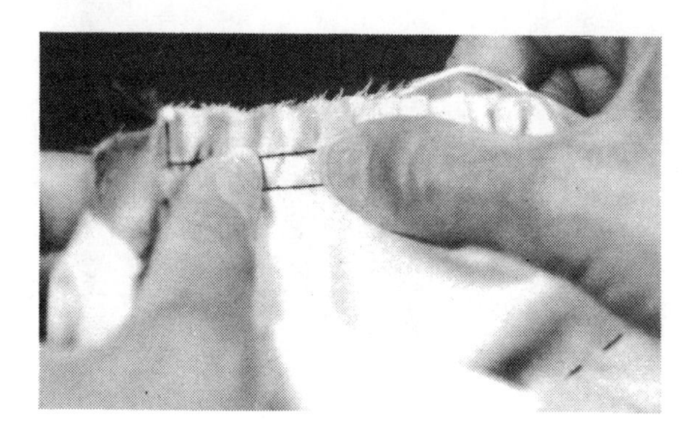

Then check the seam again with the seam over your fingers making sure the sleeve fits the armhole without puckers. Most of the time you can achieve this without disturbing the underarm seam. But, if you moved the center of the sleeve and the underarm seams are not matching but the sleeve looks and feels good, pin it as you have adjusted it.

Pin baste (pin along the seam line) or hand or machine baste. Check the fit before permanently stitching and trimming the armhole seam.

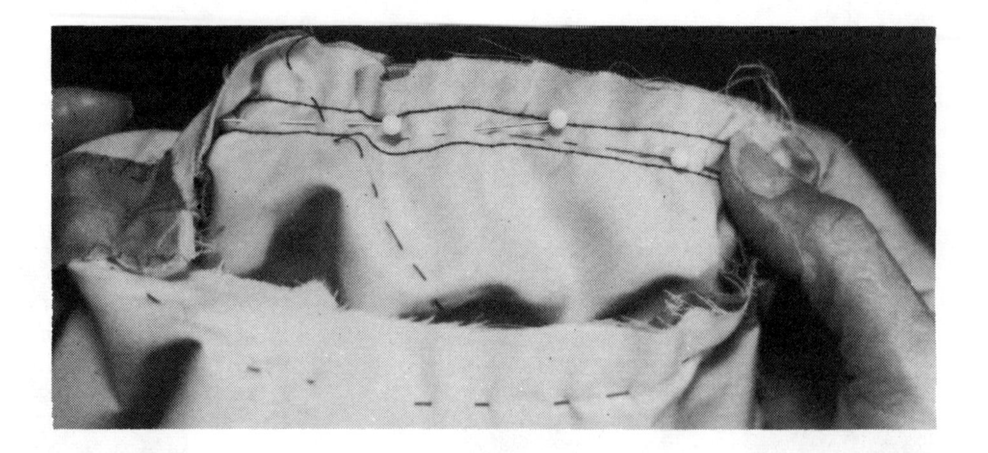

Slip the garment back on and check the hang again. Also check the comfort of the sleeve. Make sure you have room to move. Can you hug a man without too much pull across the back? If necessary, you can let out the seam on the back armhole to give yourself a little more room to reach. Can you square your shoulders without too much pull across the front? If it is too snug, let out the front armhole a bit. Does it cut you in the front armhole? If it cuts you in the front, stitch a little deeper curve in the armhole in that area. If the sleeve cap appears too wide in the front or back, it's always possible to pin the excess out, but be sure and check the comfort. You cannot remove all the ease in the armhole front and back and still have room to move in the garment without tearing the fabric.

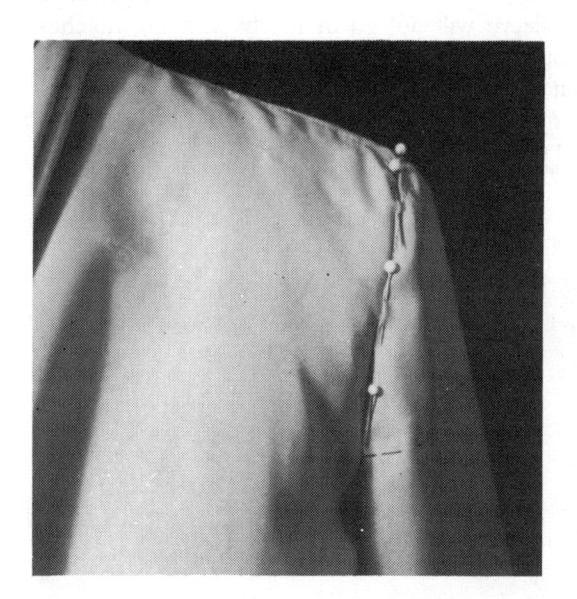

The sleeve in the picture was pin fit for comfort and moving ease but still has a problem. The sleeve needs more cap length. Notice the crossgrain line pulling up in the middle of the sleeve. To correct this problem all the seam allowance available in the cap area can be used to let the crossgrain drop at the center of the sleeve.

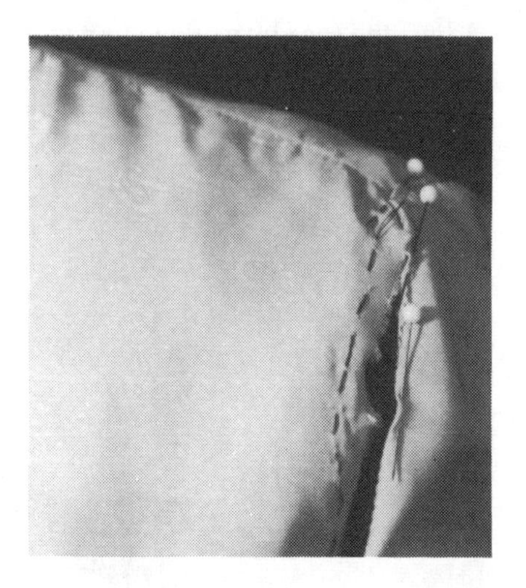

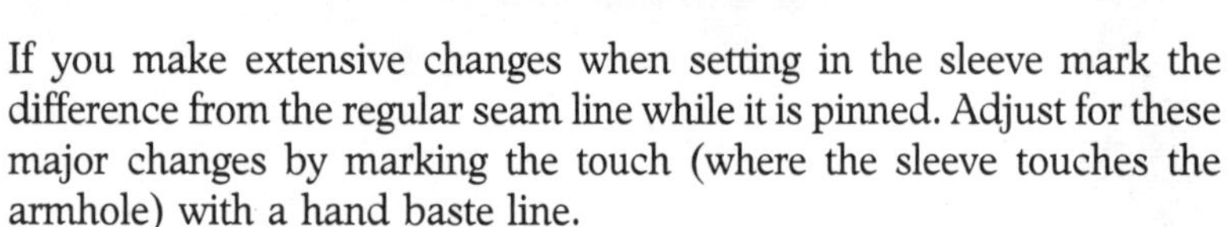

If you make extensive changes when setting in the sleeve mark the difference from the regular seam line while it is pinned. Adjust for these major changes by marking the touch (where the sleeve touches the armhole) with a hand baste line.

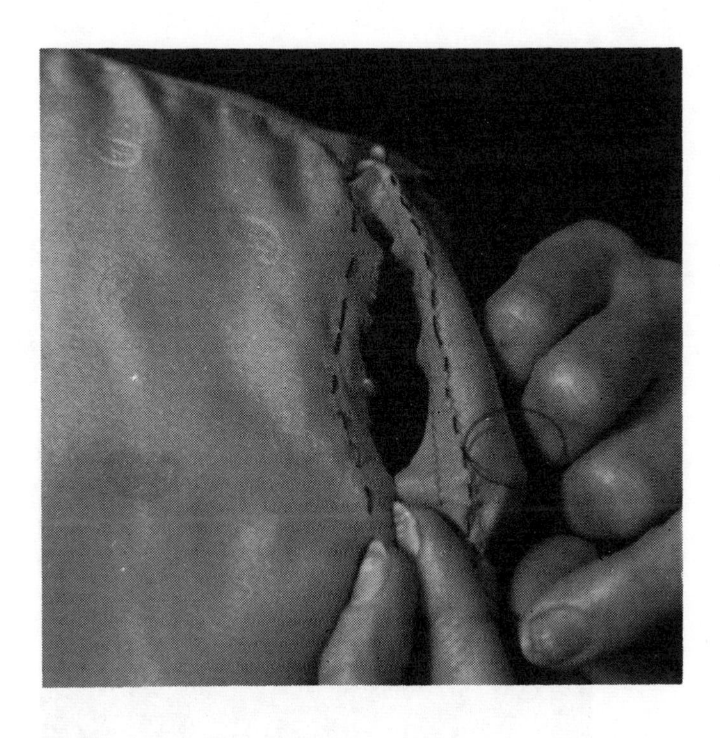

Also adjust for the changes by marking the turn (where the sleeve seam folds under) with a hand baste line.

Then put the opposite sleeve and armhole in the one that is marked and transfer the markings so both sleeves are set in the same way.

Exception: If you have enough differences in your shoulders sometimes both sleeves must be pin fit for them to fit properly and be comfortable. Be careful. Don't overfit and make them appear different. You can adjust for some differences with shoulder pads.

If you feel that you can't move without the whole garment coming up, it is not high enough in the armhole. Raise the armhole as much as the seam allowance will allow.

If the armhole is uncomfortably high lower the seam and trim the seam to the normal seam allowance.

If you change anything, rebaste and try on again to make sure you still have the necessary room to move.

Don't be afraid to adjust the sleeve until you are satisfied with the way it fits and looks. Then adjust your pattern as you have adjusted your garment so you can use it as a guide the next time you do a similar sleeve.

Stitch the set-in sleeve into the armhole

Before sewing the sleeve, pull the shoulder seam back a little. Often the shoulder seam will cause a strain on the armhole seam at the center of the sleeve.

Stitch the sleeve on the 5/8″ seam line or on the baste or pin line if you have altered the seam. Stitch the sleeve in a curve. Don't try to stitch a straight line.

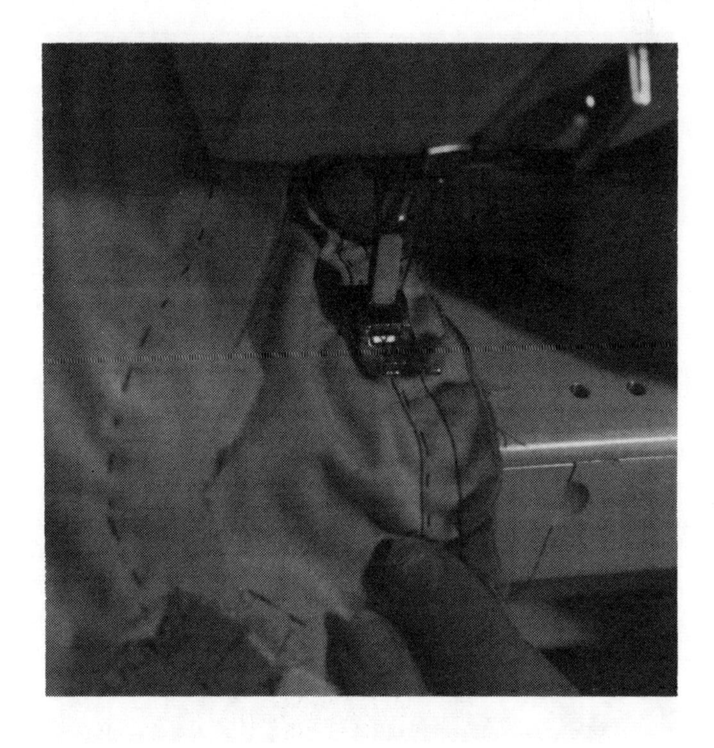

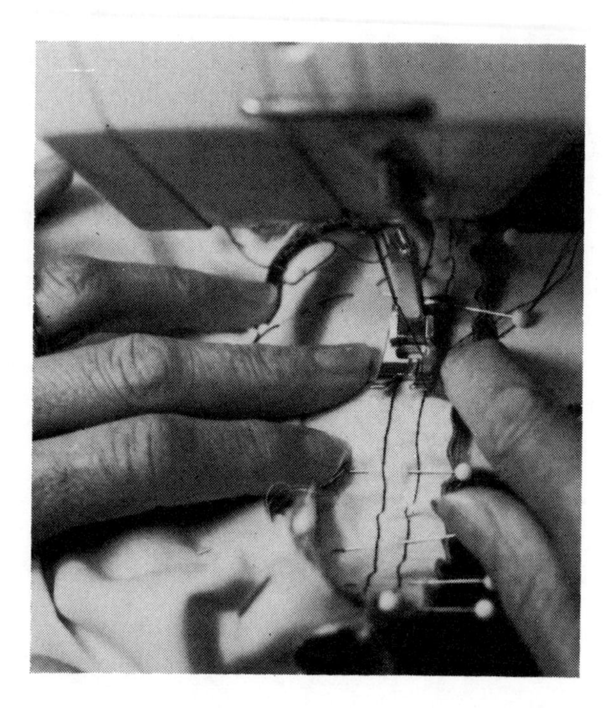

I always stitch with the sleeve up so I can work in the ease by holding the seam on both sides of the needle as I am stitching. Gently tug the garment underneath at a right angle to the needle to prevent puckers.

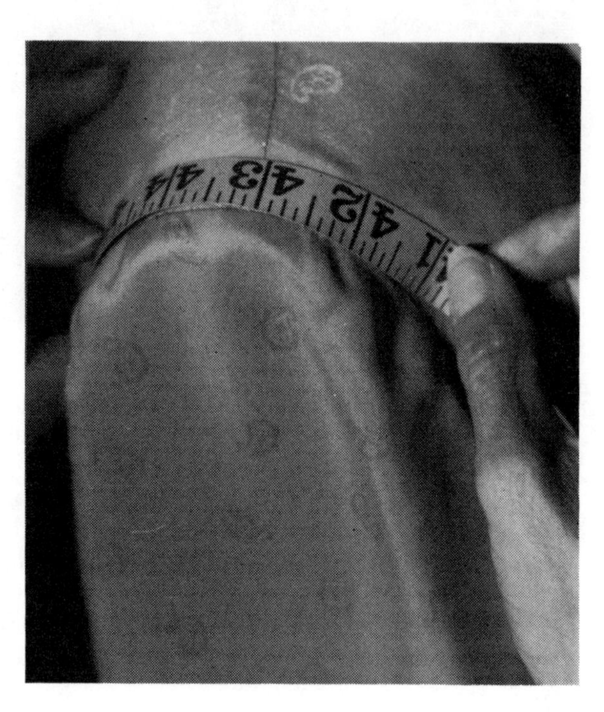

After stitching check the seam on the wrong side. The armhole seam should be smooth with no tucks or puckers.

Check the seam on the right side. Put the garment on a dress form or a ham. Check the seam on the garment side. The armhole seam should be smooth, no dips or funny curves. Lay a tape measure with the edge on the seam over the shoulder on the seamline to make sure you have a nice smooth seam line over the shoulder. This is especially important when you are using a shoulder pad.

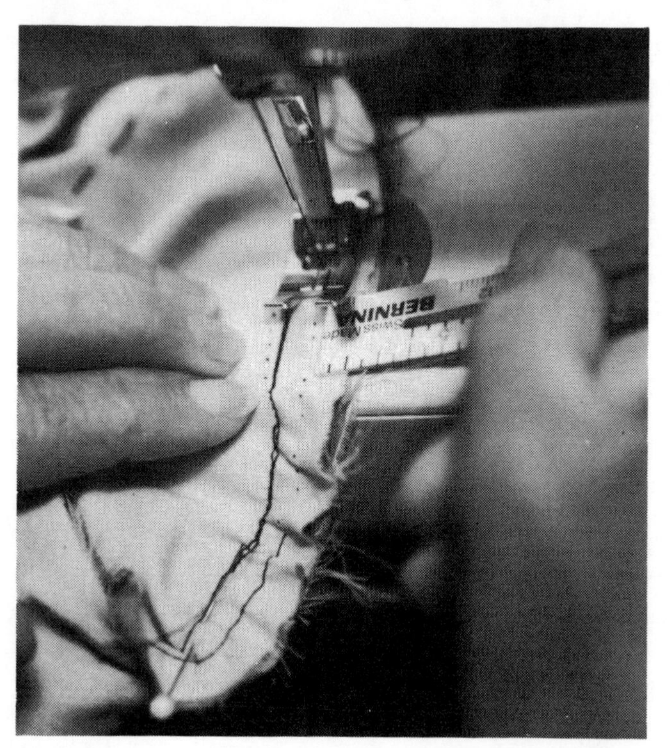

Remove all the bastings. Finish the seam in the same manner the rest of the seams of the garment are finished. If you have done French seams on the garment do a self-bound French seam on the armhole. Refer to Seam Finishes, page 70. For another seam finish stitch the sleeve 1/4″ into the seam allowance, either with a straight stitch, and overlock, or with the serger. I smooth the excess bubbles out of the seam with a sewing gauge (a small metal ruler) just ahead of the needle as I stitch. Trim the seam to the second row of stitching.

On the wrong side of the garment press the seam flat on a curved surface such as a ham. Then lightly press the seam toward the armhole. Some styles dictate pressing all or part of the seam toward the garment. Check the pattern directions and follow them.

If your set-in sleeve requires a shoulder pad or a puff support refer to Shouder Pads, pages 327 and 335.

If the cuff is not already on the sleeve, stitch the cuff on the sleeve, refer to Blouses and Dresses, pages 132-134. If there is no cuff, treat the bottom of the sleeve as your pattern directs.

Proceed with the garment. Follow the pattern directions and pertinent chapters of this book.

Modified Open Method

Prepare sleeves for the Modified Open Method

Be sure you have marked the wrong side of the sleeves so you can identify a right and a left sleeve before you do the sleeve opening. Unless they are marked it is very easy to do both sleeves for the same arm. To prepare the sleeves for setting into the garment do the sleeve opening that is suitable for your fabric and the style of your garment. Refer to Blouses and Dresses, pages 124-125. If you plan to use the No Slash Opening put the sleeve on the garment before doing the sleeve opening.

Ease stitch or gather the cap and shrink the fullness if necessary. Refer to Open Method, page 194, and to Set-In Method, page 196. Tuck the bottom of the sleeve but wait to gather the bottom of the sleeve until the sleeve seam is stitched and the edges finished.

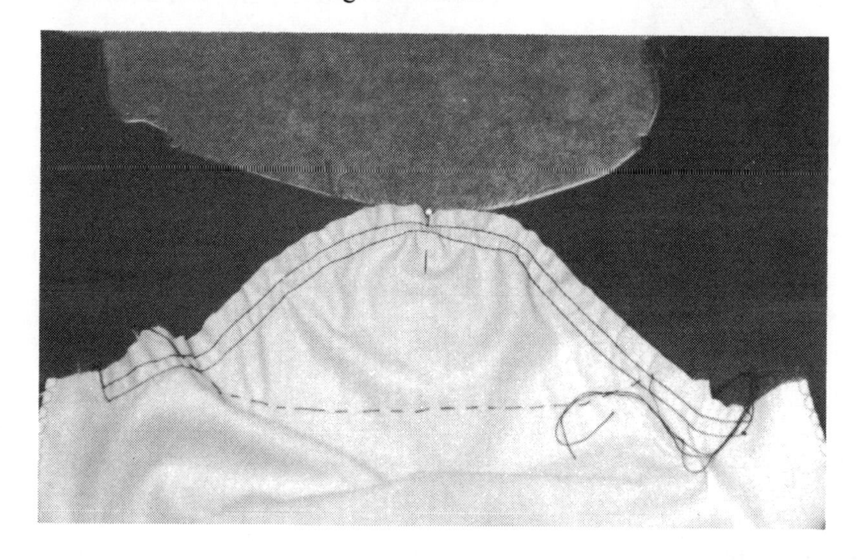

Lay the blouse out flat with the right side up. Lay the unstitched sleeve on the blouse with the right sides together. Match the center of the sleeve to the shoulder of the blouse.

Sometimes this will be a seam but if your pattern has a yoke or a forward seam, the shoulder will be marked with a large dot.

Modified Open Method of setting in a sleeve

Match the edges of the sleeve to the armhole and ease the sleeve into the armhole of the blouse. Pin at close intervals. Stitch, leaving about 1″ open on either end of the armhole at the side seam. Check the seam to make sure it is smooth and nicely curved with no tucks stitched in.

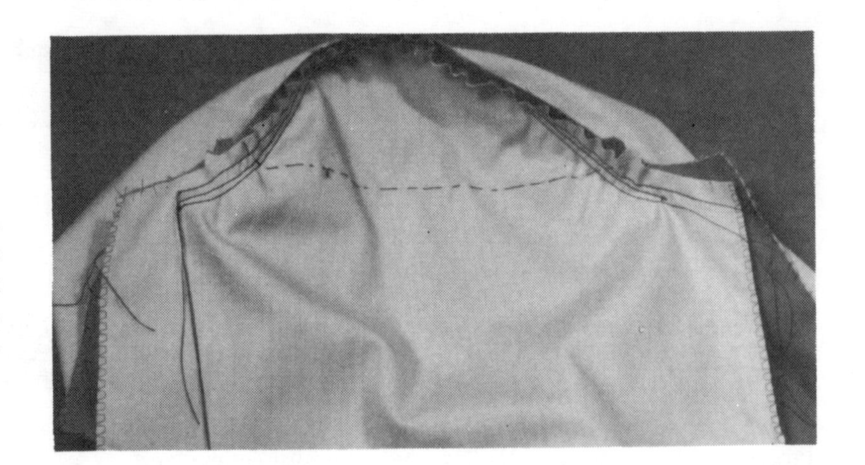

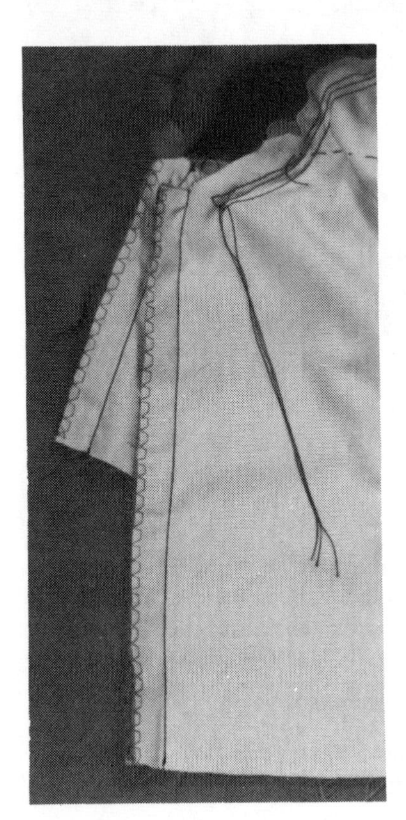

Stitch the side seams of the blouse and stitch the sleeve seams. Close them completely. Refer to Sample Seams and Pressing Techniques, pages 58 and 65-67.

Finish the seams. Often for a shirt blouse I will stitch the seams together with a serger or an overcast stitch. For a sheer fabric I would use a French seam. Let your fabric dictate the seam finish. Refer to Seam Finishes, pages 68-70.

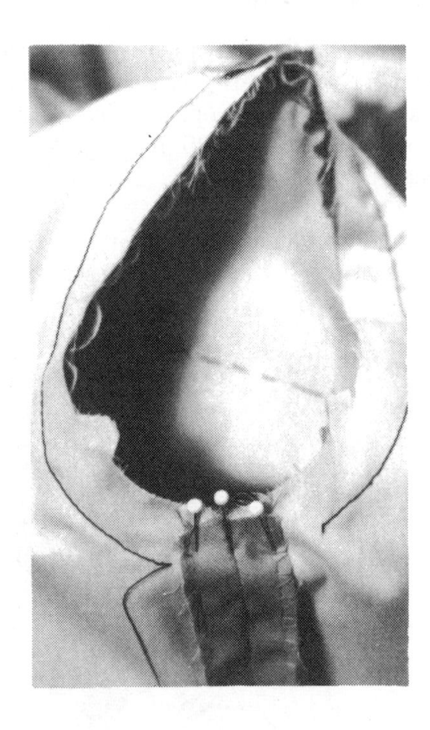

Pull the sleeve to the right side of the blouse. On the wrong side match the sleeve seam and the side seam at the armhole. Sew the small opening closed. Finish the armhole seam in the same manner as the other seams. If you used a French Seam on the straight seams, use the Self Bound French Seam for the curved armhole seam. Refer to Seam Finishes, page 70.

Stitch the cuff on the sleeve, refer to pages 132-134. If there is no cuff, treat the bottom of the sleeve as your pattern directs.

Proceed with the garment. Follow the pattern directions and pertinent chapter of this book.

Buttonholes ■ 6

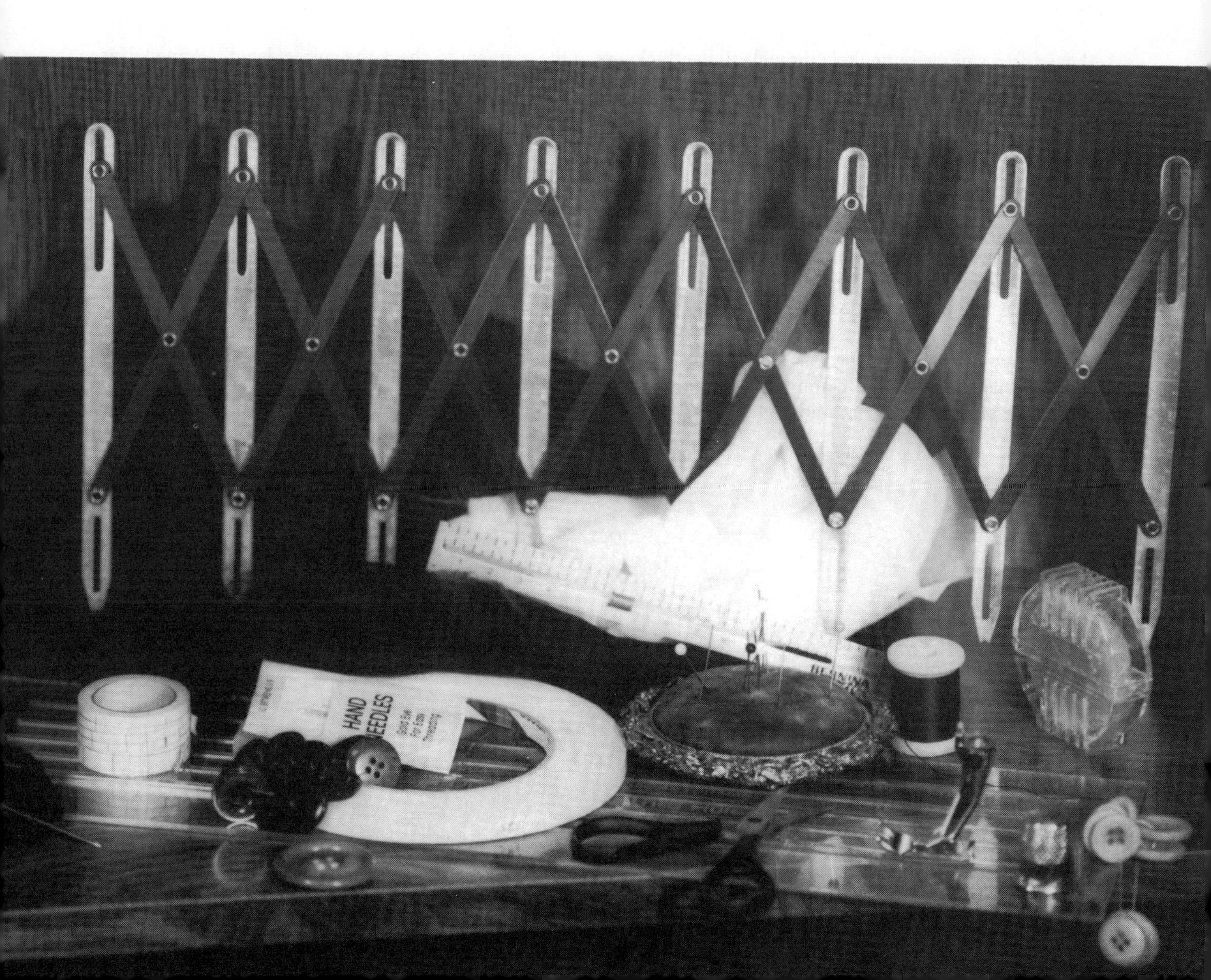

MACHINE BUTTONHOLES

Computer sewing machines make some of this chapter obsolete. However, sewers who are only dreaming of a computer machine and even those who have one still must mark the buttonhole location and must guide them straight on the garment.

Marking And Making Machine Buttonholes

Your garment is done except for the buttonholes. After investing so much time and work in a garment, a poor buttonhole is upsetting. If you do a bad buttonhole on the garment, it can be taken out and redone **before** it is cut. Work from the bobbin side and pull a bobbin thread to rip a buttonhole more easily. Practice making buttonholes with your machine until you are comfortable making them on the finest of fabrics.

I almost never use the pattern to determine the correct placement of the buttonholes.

Exception: A tailored garment with an open lapel. The lapel is drafted to that particular buttonhole placement.

Use the pattern as a guide for spaces between the buttonholes, distance from the front edge, and the direction of the buttonhole, either vertical or horizontal. Buttonholes are normally horizontal. Occasionally, some design feature dictates changing the direction. Buttonholes in garments with a front band are always vertical. The buttonholes in a collar band and on cuffs are always horizontal, even on a garment where all the other buttonholes are vertical.

Always do a sample buttonhole through all the thickness of the garment to check the correct length. Some fabrics are more difficult to do buttonholes through than others. A sample buttonhole is helpful in testing your fabric as well as the length of the buttonhole.

Placement of buttonholes

Try the garment on and pin it together at the bustline. Straighten your shoulders and check for pulls across the bustline. The blouse should not gape. The buttonhole can be a bit below the bust tip or even with the bust tip, whichever is best for that particular garment. Take the garment off, being careful to keep the marking pin in place. That is the buttonhole marking which determines the placement of the other buttonholes.

Pin or baste the facing, if there is a facing, to keep it flat while making the buttonholes. Space the buttonholes from the bustline using the pattern as a guide for the distances between buttonholes. Place a pin to mark each buttonhole at right angles to, and a little from, the front edge of the garment.

A Simflex Expanding Measure is helpful in spacing buttonholes, especially for an even number of buttonholes.

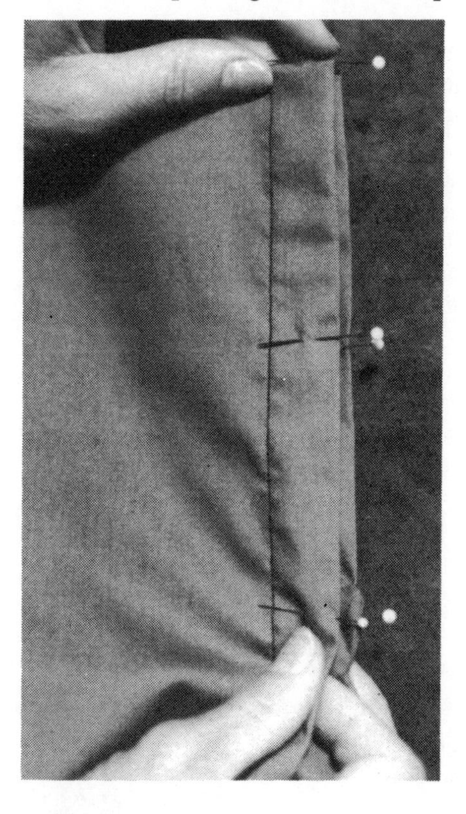

An uneven number of buttonholes can be spaced easily. Mark the first and last buttonhole, fold the garment in half, mark the fold with a pin to mark the middle buttonhole. Continue dividing the space until you have located each buttonhole.

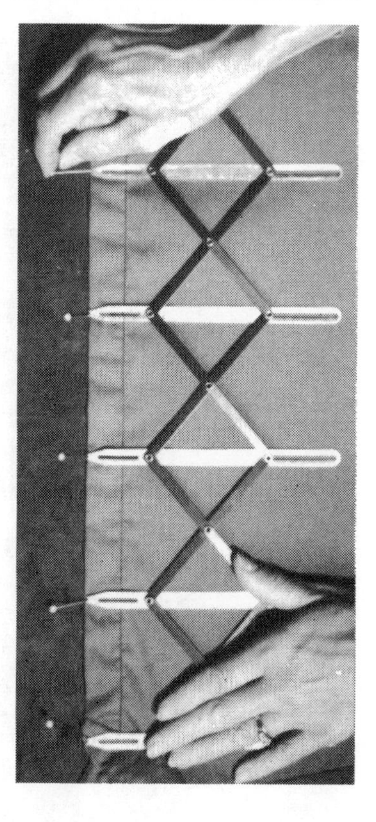

Marking buttonhole placement

Women's garments always lap to the left, men's lap to the right. I am referring to women's garments. Mark the buttonhole placement on the right front or the left back of the garment. I mark with tape, either Tape-Stitch, which pulls apart in narrow widths, or 1/4" wide masking tape. Always test the tape on your fabric. Tape damages some fabrics such as corduroy. Mark buttonholes on those fabrics with a thread trace or a disappearing marking pencil. I prefer tape; it is fast and accurate. **Never leave tape on the fabric overnight;** it can adhere and be very difficult to remove.

Measuring the length of buttonholes

Do a sample buttonhole through all the thicknesses on the garment to check the correct length.

Measure your button with the measuring tape. Measure the diameter of the button plus the depth of the button. This is usually the length of the buttonhole.

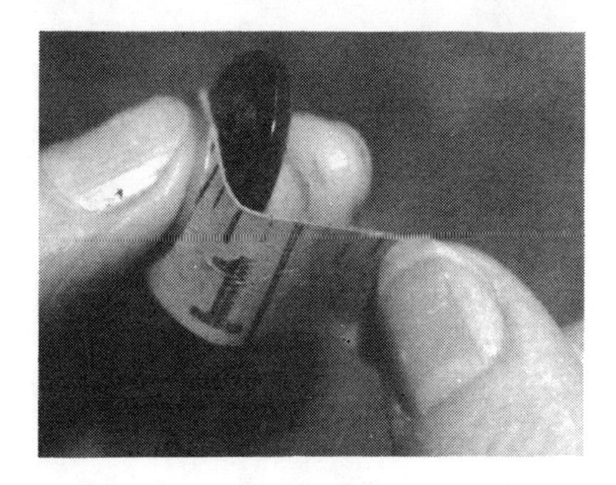

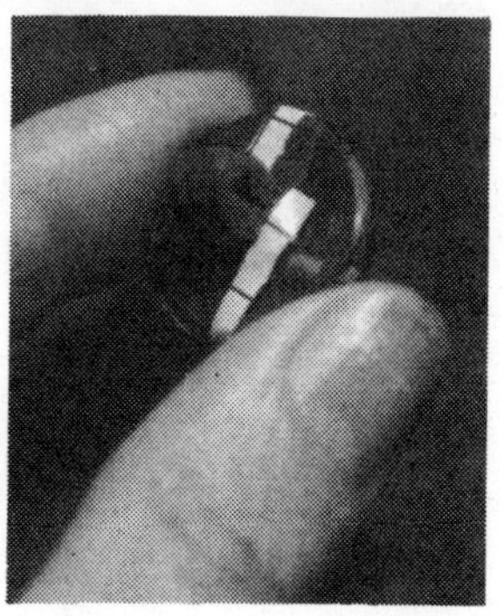

Measure a round ball button with a narrow piece of paper, going completely around the button. Divide the paper in half to determine the length of the buttonhole.

Marking Horizontal Buttonholes

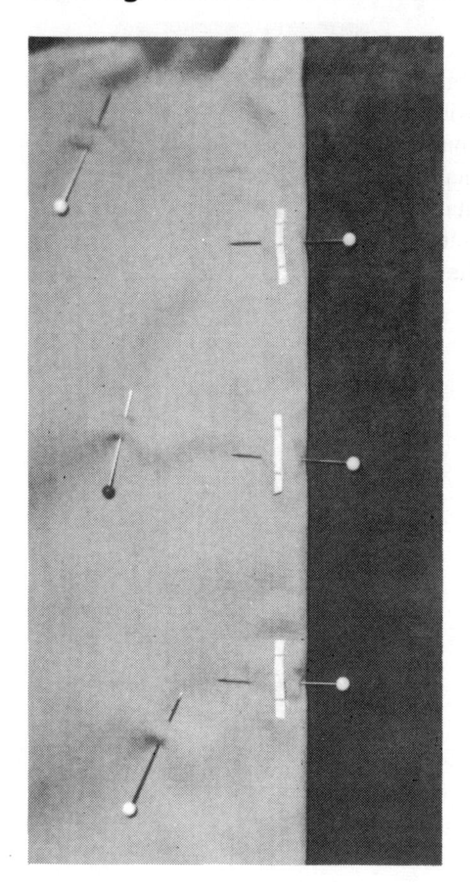

If you have a computerized sewing machine, mark the location and the distance from the front edge. Also, put the horizontal piece of tape on the fabric to keep the buttonhole at right angles to the front edge.

Mark horizontal buttonholes with a pin at right angles to the front edge. The buttonhole normally begins 1/8″ from the center front — usually 3/8″ to 5/8″ from the edge of the garment. The pattern is drafted for a certain width, check the distance from the edge on your pattern. Put a piece of tape (vertical) that distance from the edge of the garment at each buttonhole.

A common length for buttonholes is 5/8″. For easy measuring of that length when marking the buttonholes, use the tape measure, which is 5/8″ wide.

Put a second piece of tape to mark the length of the buttonhole.

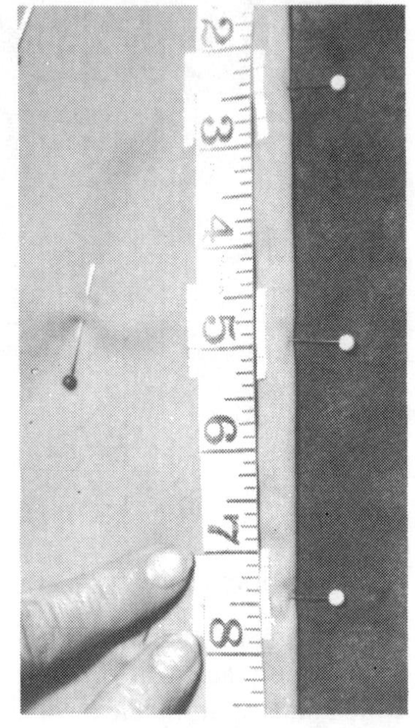

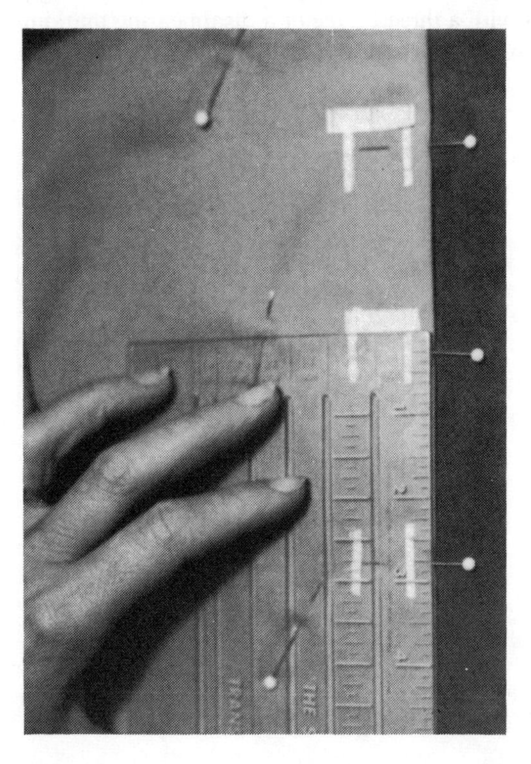

Use a third piece of tape at right angles (horizontal) to the center front, 1/4″ from the pin. The horizontal piece of tape keeps the buttonhole at a right angle to the front edge of the garment. A see-through ruler is a big help in placing the tape and checking to make sure the buttonholes are evenly spaced and in a straight line on the garment. The tape can be in one long piece (faster to put on) or short pieces.

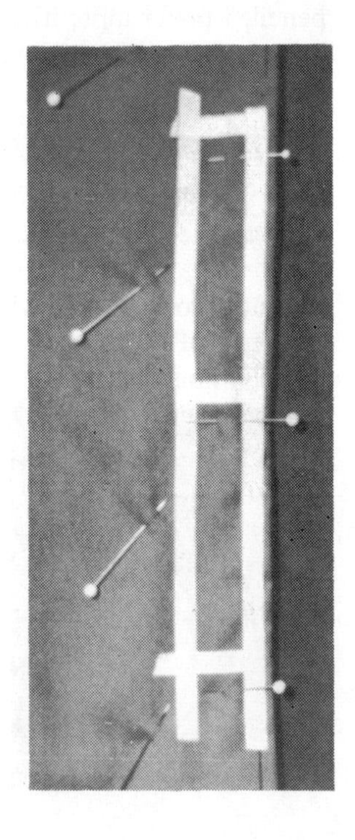

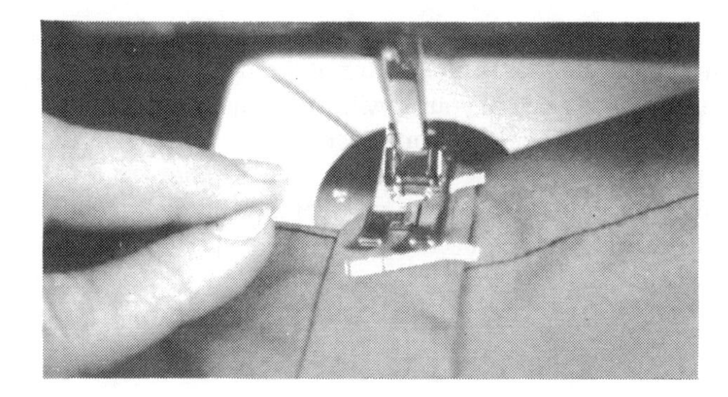

Collarband:

Mark the length of the buttonhole with tape. Place the presser foot in the center of the band and keep the edge of the foot straight with the collarband as you do the buttonhole.

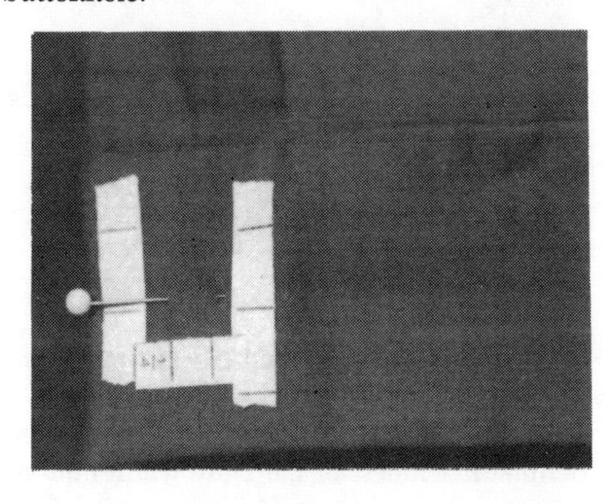

Cuffs:

If there is only one buttonhole on the cuff, it always goes in the center of the cuff.

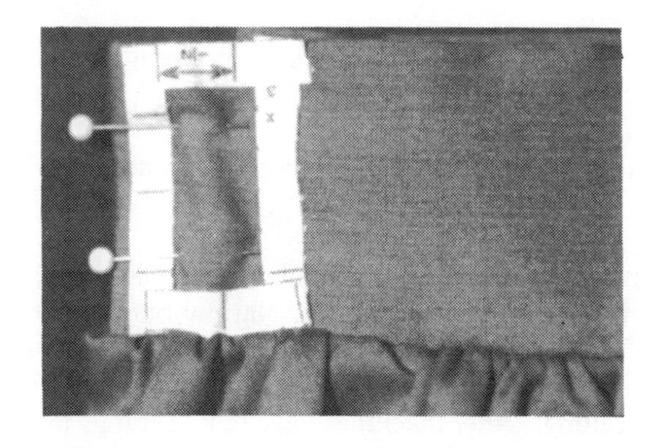

If there are two buttonholes on the cuff, they should be placed evenly apart and a minimum of 1/2" from the edges of the cuff. Two buttonholes hold a cuff closed better than one.

When all the tape is in place, remove the pins. If the tape does not adhere well to the fabric, put a pin across each piece of tape to hold it in place until you are ready — at the machine — to make that buttonhole.

Marking Vertical Buttonholes

If you have a computerized sewing machine, mark the beginning of each buttonhole. Mark the distance from the edge of the fabric with a piece of vertical tape on the bed of the sewing machine.

Mark vertical buttonholes with a pin at right angles to the front edge. Measure and mark with tape, about half the length of the buttonhole above the pin marking the location.

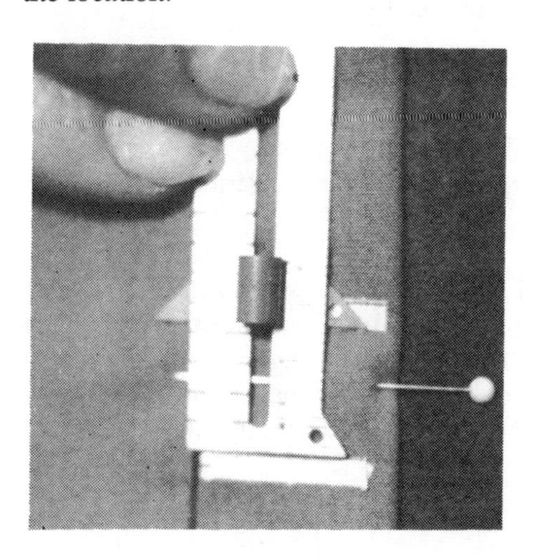

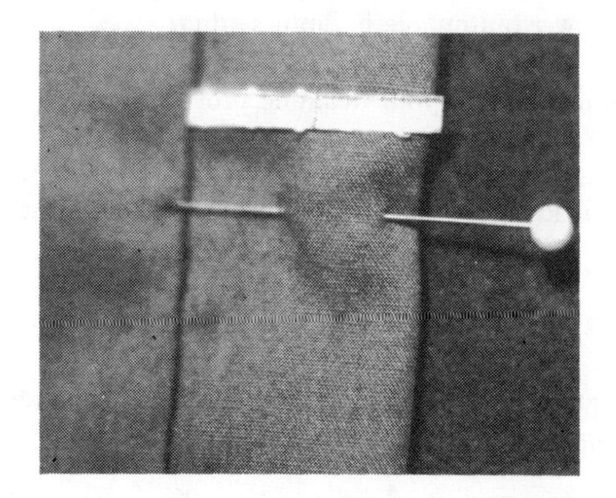

Measure and mark with tape, about half the length of the buttonhole below the pin marking the location.

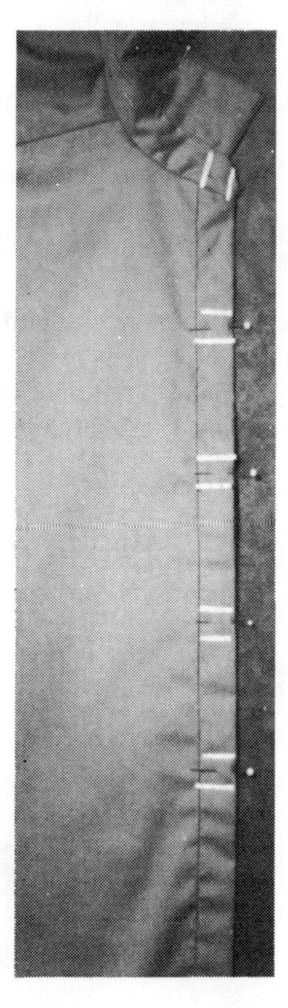

Blouse front marked with vertical buttonholes, and a horizontal buttonhole in the collarband.

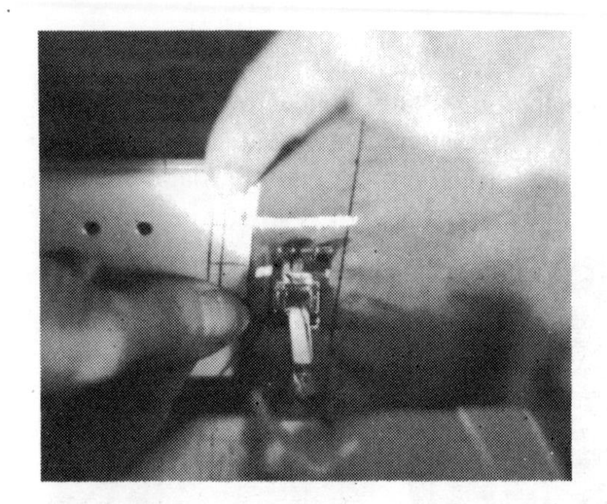

Vertical buttonholes are made in the middle of the front band. At the machine, place the foot in the center of the band. Put a piece of tape vertically on the bed of your sewing machine along the front edge of the garment. Keep the front edge of the garment on the tape as you do the buttonholes. Or check the distance from the front edge on your pattern and put a piece of tape on the machine the correct distance from the needle.

Setting The Machine For Buttonholes

Check your machine instruction book. In general, you must do the following. (I use the automatic setting on the Bernina machines for the 2mm width buttonholes.)

1. **Adjust the stitch length** to a close satin stitch. Set the machine for a wide zig-zag. Shorten the stitch length until you have a satin stitch — not heavy but close.

2. **Stitch width.** Follow your machine instruction manual. Normal width is 2mm for the buttonhole legs and 4mm for the bar-tack. This will make buttonholes in medium to heavy weight fabrics. Narrow buttonhole width is slightly over 1mm for the legs and 3mm for the bar-tack. This will make buttonholes in fine fabrics.

3. **Needle position.** Some machines have only a center needle setting. Other machines have more settings for the placement of the needle. Many machines have an automatic setting that changes the needle position automatically.

   Multiple needle positions are helpful when edge stitching, topstitching, and for making narrow buttonholes in fine fabrics such as crepe de chine and silky polyesters. The regular or automatic setting makes a wide, heavy appearing buttonhole in fine fabrics. The upper buttonhole is 1mm setting; the lower buttonhole is 2mm setting.

4. Change to the buttonhole foot if your machine provides one.

5. Tighten the bobbin tension to hold the stitches slightly to the under side of the fabric. (The Bernina machine has a little hole to thread through on the bobbin to give the extra tension needed.)

Cord Buttonholes in Knit Fabrics

On knit fabric be sure and cord the buttonholes or they will become larger as you wear the garment. The fabric has give and the zig-zag stitch has give, allowing them to grow.

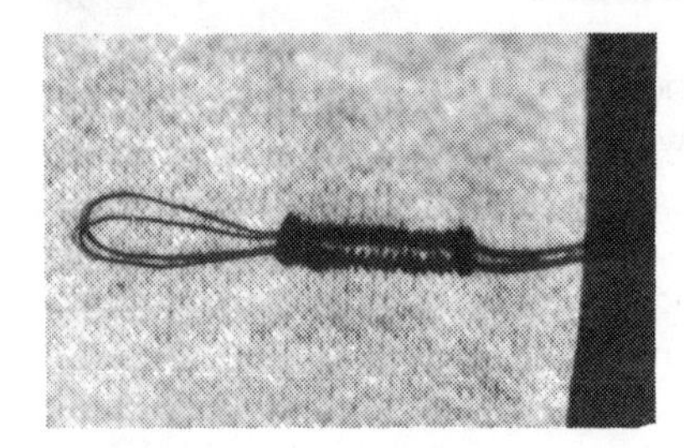

Cord the buttonhole by placing a strong thread or several strands of your sewing thread under the zig-zag stitch. (I prefer sewing thread.) Some machines have a buttonhole foot that makes cording easy to do. (Check your sewing machine instruction book.) Wait to tie the cording thread until the buttonhole has been cut and the button slipped through it. Then secure the cord ends.

Manual Directions For Regular (2mm) Buttonholes

The pictures show horizontal buttonholes.

Put the needle 2mm to the left of center. (Bernina machines as far left as possible.)

Set the zig-zag width to 2mm. (On Bernina machines this is between 1½ and 2.) Put the needle in the fabric just clearing the first piece of tape. If doing horizontal buttonholes, put the edge of the pressure foot along the horizontal piece of tape. If doing vertical buttonholes, put the edge of the fabric along the tape on the bed of the machine.

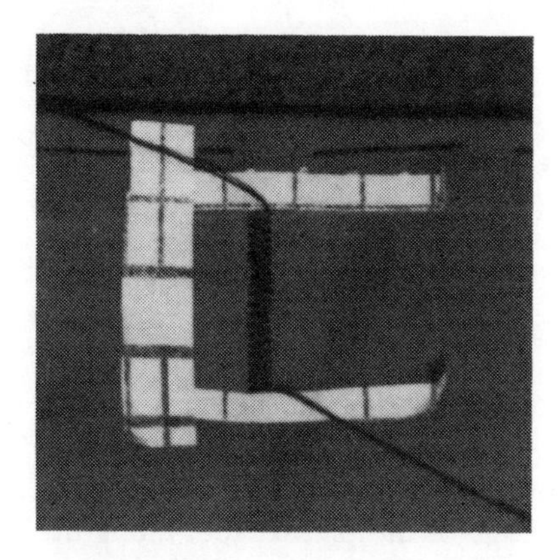

Stitch the first leg of the buttonhole. Stitch to the second piece of tape and stop with the needle to the right side.

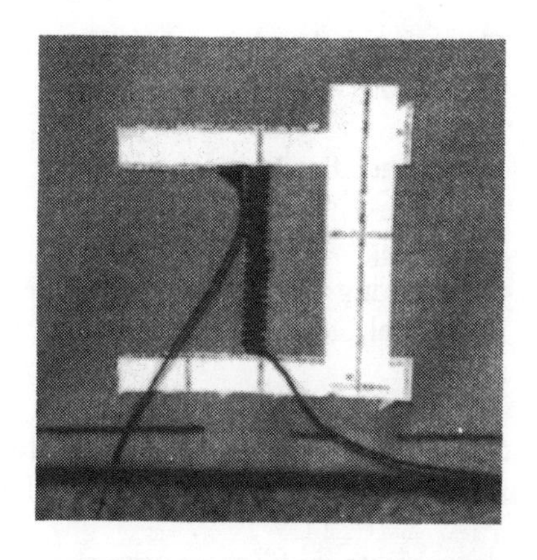

Leave the needle in the fabric, lift the presser foot, and pivot the fabric. Put the presser foot down, hold the fabric so it can't travel, or lower the feed dogs, and take one or two stitches to check the distance from the first leg. You must have a tiny space between the two rows of zig-zag stitching. Correct the spacing, if needed, by repositioning the presser foot.

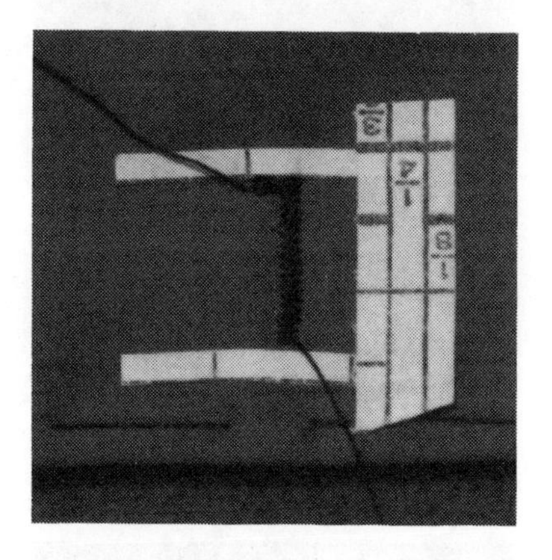

With the presser foot down, manually lift the needle. Set the zig-zag width to 4mm to bar-tack the end of the buttonhole. (On Bernina machines, the setting is 4.) Manually operate the machine to check the correct placement. The bar-tack must cover both legs of the buttonhole. Correct the spacing, if needed, by repositioning the presser foot. If the feed dogs are down, raise them. **Bar-tack: While slightly holding the fabric, do 4 or 5 complete stitches.**

Lift the needle up manually and change the zig-zag back to the narrow setting, 2mm. (On the Bernina, between 1 and 1½.) You must have a tiny space between the two rows of zig-zag stitching. Correct the spacing, if needed, by repositioning the presser foot.

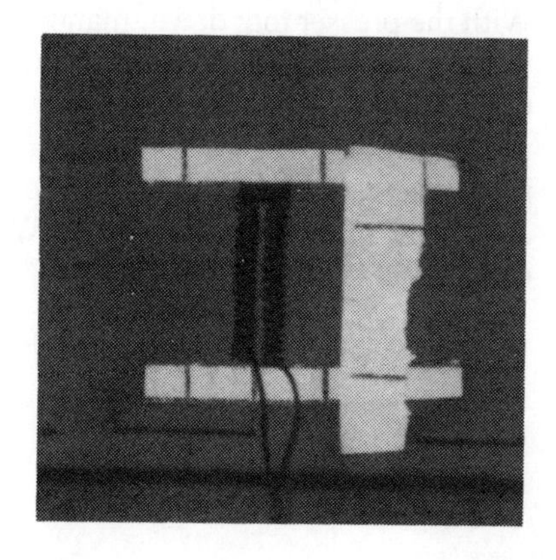

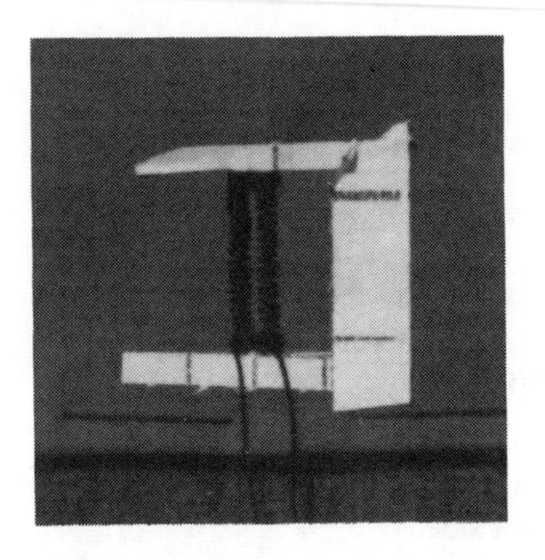

With the needle up, set the zig-zag width back to 4mm. (On the Bernina, 4.) **Backstitch 4 or 5 complete stitches for the final bar-tack** at the end of the buttonhole. The bar-tack must cover both legs of the buttonhole. Correct the spacing, if needed, by repositioning the presser foot.

Either pull the threads through to tie them or backstitch. To backstitch, set the zig-zag to 0 or straight stitch, leave the needle position to the left and backstitch to lock the stitches.

Manual Directions For Narrow (1mm) Buttonholes

The computerized Bernina does this narrow buttonhole using a half pattern width setting. The pictures show vertical buttonholes.

Put the needle 1mm left of center. (On the Bernina machines, the setting is one notch left of center.)

Set the zig-zag width slightly past 1mm. (On the Bernina machines, slightly over 1.) Put the needle in the fabric just clearing the first piece of tape. If doing horizontal buttonholes, put the edge of the presser foot along the horizontal piece of tape. If doing vertical buttonholes, put the edge of the fabric along the tape on the bed of the machine.

Stitch the first leg of the buttonhole. Stitch to the second piece of tape and stop with the needle to the right side.

Leave the needle in the fabric, lift the presser foot, and pivot the fabric. Put the presser foot down, hold the fabric so it can't travel, or lower the feed dogs and take one or two stitches to check the distance from the first leg. You must have a tiny space between the two rows of zig-zag stitching. Correct the spacing, if needed, by repositioning the presser foot.

With the presser foot down, manually lift the needle. Set the zig-zag width to 3mm to bar-tack the end of the buttonhole. (On Bernina machines, the setting is 3.) Manually operate the machine to check the correct placement. The bar-tack must cover both legs of the buttonhole. Correct the spacing, if needed, by repositioning the presser foot. If the feed dogs are down, raise them. **Bar-tack: While slightly holding the fabric, do 2 or 3 complete stitches.**

Lift the needle up manually and change the zig-zag back to the narrow setting, slightly over 1mm. (On the Bernina, slightly over 1.) **Stitch the second leg of the buttonhole.** You must have a tiny space between the two rows of zig-zag stitching. Correct the spacing, if needed, by repositioning the presser foot.

With the needle up, set the zig-zag width back to 3mm. (On the Bernina machine, 3.) **Backstitch 2 or 3 complete stitches for the final bar-tack** at the end of the buttonhole. The bar-tack must cover both legs of the buttonhole. Correct the spacing, if needed, by repositioning the presser foot.

Either pull the threads through to tie them or backstitch. To backstitch, set the zig-zag to 0 or straight stitch, leave the needle position to the left, and backstitch along the edge of the leg to lock the stitches.

Finishing The Buttonhole

If you did not backstitch, pull the threads to the inside or the wrong side of the garment and tie the threads. I prefer to pull them to the inside. Sometimes you must thread them through a needle to pull them to the inside. Beeswax the thread ends for ease in threading the needle.

Cut the buttonholes open carefully with a buttonhole cutter, a ripper, or fine scissors. If you use a ripper, begin by inserting the ripper close to a bar-tack. Cut to the center of the buttonhole. Insert the ripper at the opposite end and cut again to the middle. Be careful. It is easy to cut through the buttonhole if you start at one end and just cut to the other bar-tack. If you cut any threads as you open the buttonhole, go back over that segment with the narrow zig-zag setting.

BOUND BUTTONHOLES

Bound buttonholes should be done on only the finest garments. They are seen only on very expensive ready-to-wear clothing and fine couture garments. Many designers do not put them on their ready-to-wear collections because of the cost of labor. Even though most purchased garments no longer have bound buttonholes, I love the look of a well-made bound buttonhole. I still use them on my very best garments. For the most part, I reserve them for dressy coats, suits, and jackets.

Purchase the buttons for the garment before you make the bound buttonholes. Measure the diameter plus the thickness of the button to determine the length. Refer to Machine Buttonholes, page 207. Bound buttonholes are usually 1/4" wide. For lightweight fabric they should be a bit narrower, between 1/8" and 1/4". If the fabric is very heavy, they can be a bit wider but never more than 3/8".

Always make the bound buttonholes before you put any pieces of the garment together. It is much easier to make bound buttonholes while you have only one piece of fabric to handle.

Always make a sample buttonhole. Making a sample not only checks the length of the buttonhole but it also lets you see how your fabric handles. If the fabric ravels, fuse a lightweight fusible interfacing on the buttonhole area. Try a sample buttonhole through the fashion fabric and the interfacing. (The buttonholes are stronger when done through the interfacing.) If the two layers of fabric are thick and hard to turn, eliminate the interfacing in the buttonhole. If you are doing the buttonhole through the interfacing, put the interfacing on the garment before doing the buttonholes. If the interfacing is too heavy, do the buttonholes before applying the interfacing. Then cut a hole in the interfacing slightly larger than the buttonhole and pull the buttonhole through the interfacing. Refer to Couture Tailoring, pages 276-277.

Bound buttonholes are easy to make using this method. I also use this method for welt pockets. Refer to Welt Pockets, page 235. Bound buttonholes require accurate measuring, stitching, and **practice.** If you have not done bound buttonholes, practice making buttonholes until you are pleased with one before you attempt them on your garment. Do not try to make too many buttonholes at one time. Do three or four and take a break. If you are not pleased with a finished bound buttonhole, you can take the buttonhole edges off and put them on again. **Never remove the organdy rectangle.**

Preparation For Bound Buttonholes

For each buttonhole you will need a piece of lightweight fabric. Crisp organdy is the best. Refer to Inner Construction, page 21. If you are making several buttonholes, use a strip of organdy instead of a small piece for each buttonhole. It is much easier to keep the buttonholes in a straight line and in the proper location with the strip of organdy cut the same shape as the garment front.

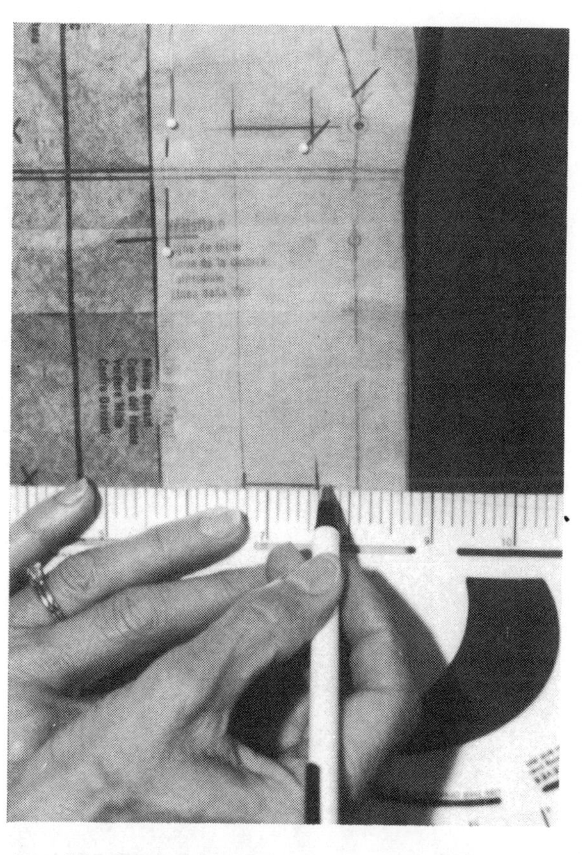

Put the organdy on the pattern, keeping the grain lines of the organdy straight. Mark the buttonhole placement lines on the organdy with a pencil. Also mark the center front if it is marked on the pattern.

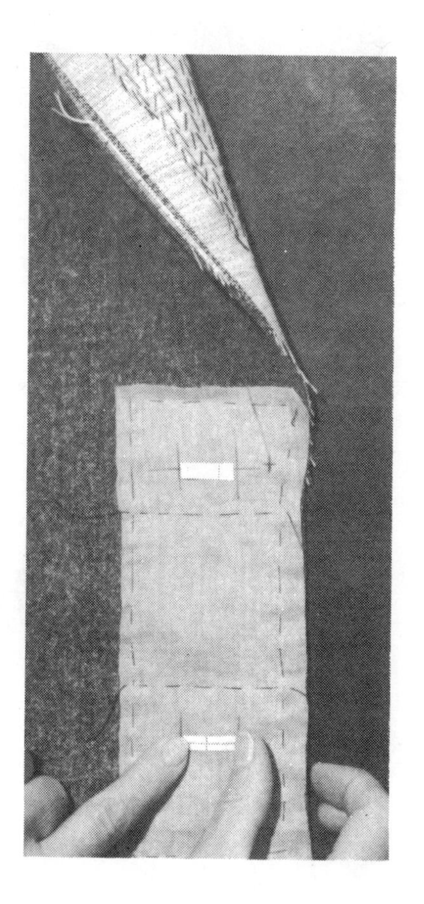

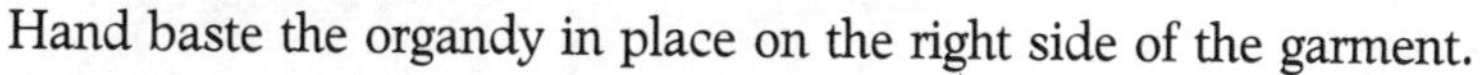

Hand baste the organdy in place on the right side of the garment.

Cut a piece of yellow sewing tape the length and just slightly narrower than the width needed for the finished buttonhole. Place it on the buttonhole placement line. If you are doing more than one buttonhole, put tape for each one and make sure the buttonholes are evenly placed and in a straight line 1/8″ over the center front toward the front edge of the garment. Place the pattern over the top of the organdy to check the placement of the buttonholes.

Stitch The Bound Button

Stitch around the tape using 15-20 stitches per inch. Overlap the stitches on one long side of the buttonhole. Do not start or end on a corner. It helps to use a thread just a bit off-color on the bobbin so you can see the stitching when you do the final stitching on the buttonhole. Remove the tape and save it for finishing the facing side of the buttonhole.

Clip through the center and diagonally into each corner. This makes a little pie on each end. Be careful not to clip the stitching but you must clip to it. Remove the basting holding the organdy in place.

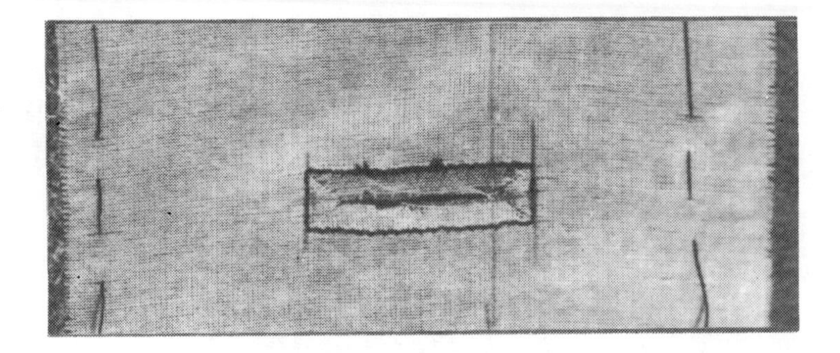

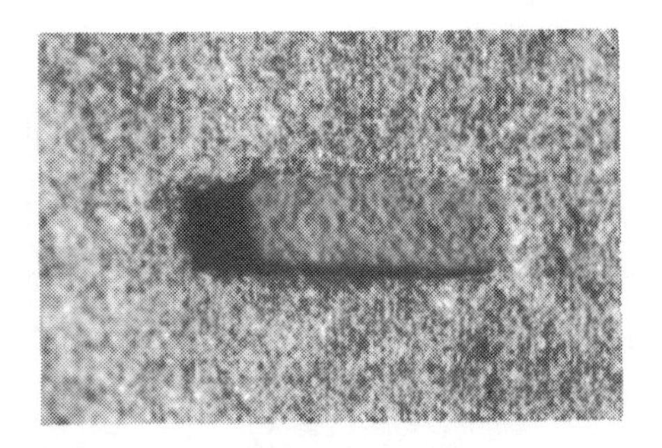

Pull the organdy through to the wrong side of the garment and press, making certain the organdy does not show on the right side of the garment. This makes a reinforced rectangular opening.

Make The Buttonhole Edges

Cut two pieces of your fabric 1¾″ wide and 1″ longer than the finished buttonhole. Place the right sides together and machine baste down the center of the strip.

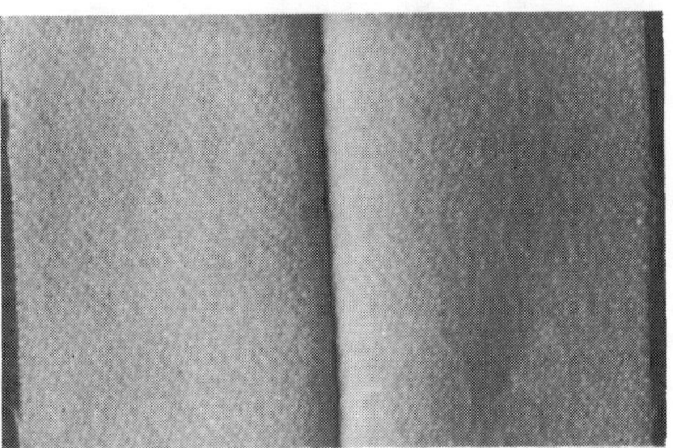

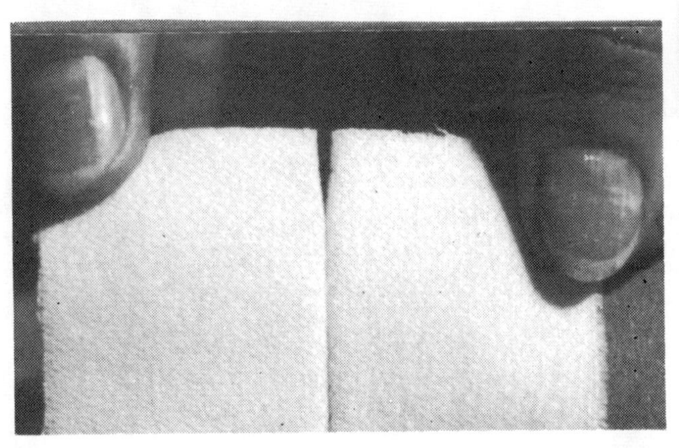

Bring the wrong sides together and press. This makes a strip with the baste holding the folds together.

Handstitch The Buttonhole Edges To The Buttonhole

Center the fold of the strip under the window in the fabric and pin it in place. The easiest, most accurate way to attach the strip to the garment is to baste with a hidden baste stitch with matching thread from the right side. You can see what you are doing and make sure the strip is held straight and even on both sides. After it is basted with matching thread, machine stitch it for strength. To baste use a beeswaxed thread with a knot. Start on the inside between the fashion fabric and the organdy. Take a small stitch in the strip. Take a small stitch in the fold of the garment and come up, just catching the fold in the strip. Baste the long edges and slip through the ends without stitching if you wish to cord the buttonhole. Cording raises the buttonholes slightly and strengthens the buttonhole.

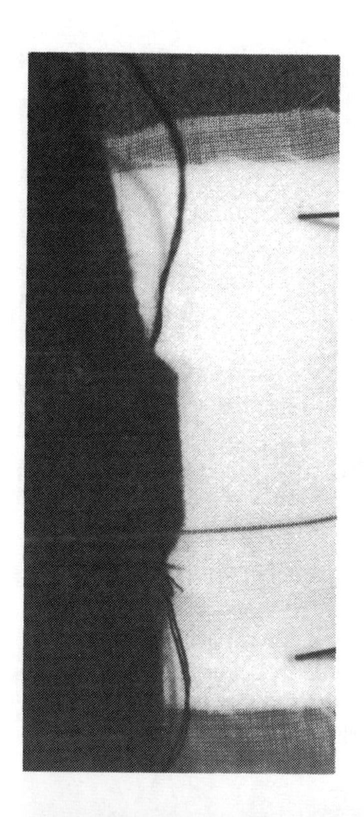

Machine Stitch The Buttonhole Edges

Fold the garment back to the inside exposing the long edges of the buttonhole and machine stitch the long edges just inside the first stitching line. Stitch both long sides of the buttonhole. Be sure and stitch to the corner. It is easier to pull out a stitch than it is to fill stitches in if you did not stitch far enough. Do not backstitch. Leave the threads long.

Check to make sure you have stitched to the corners and make sure the sides of the buttonholes are even. The stitching lines must be parallel and at equal distance from the center line of the buttonhole. Pull the threads to the inside and tie with a tailor's knot. Do not cut the threads.

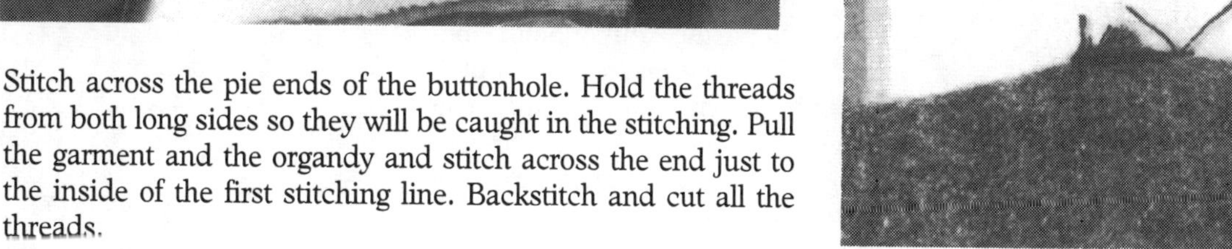

Cord the buttonhole

If you want to cord the buttonhole, do it now. I often cord the buttonhole. Cording raises the buttonholes slightly and strengthens the buttonhole. Slip the cording through the buttonhole edges with a large needle. Yarn works very well to cord the buttonhole.

Stitch across the pie ends of the buttonhole. Hold the threads from both long sides so they will be caught in the stitching. Pull the garment and the organdy and stitch across the end just to the inside of the first stitching line. Backstitch and cut all the threads.

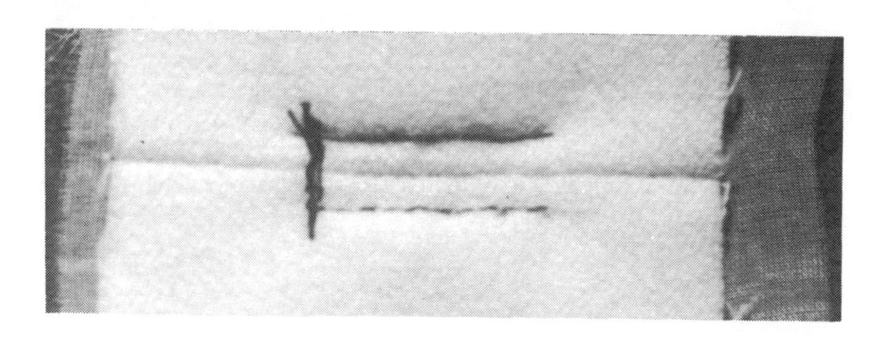

Picture of one end stitched. Stitch both ends.

Grade The Buttonhole

Trim the strip, and grade the seams to prevent bulk. Leave the layer closest to the garment the longest and trim all the other layers as shown. Leave the buttonhole closed until you have made the opening in the facing and the facing is stitched to the buttonhole.

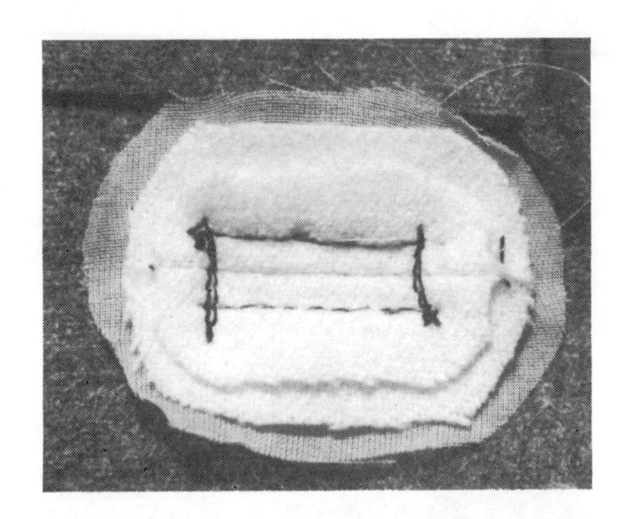

Make The Buttonhole Opening In The Facing

When your facing is in place, baste a piece of organdy or lining on the right side of the facing covering all the buttonholes so one edge of the organdy or lining is over the front edge of the fabric. Pin the facing securely to the garment.

On the right side of the garment, stick pins through the buttonhole corners.

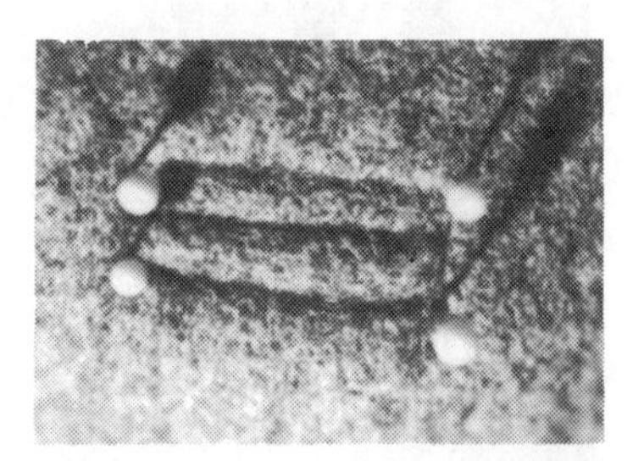

Position a piece of tape (hopefully the one you saved when you did the buttonhole) between the pins. Stitch around the tape. You are stitching through the organdy and the facing.

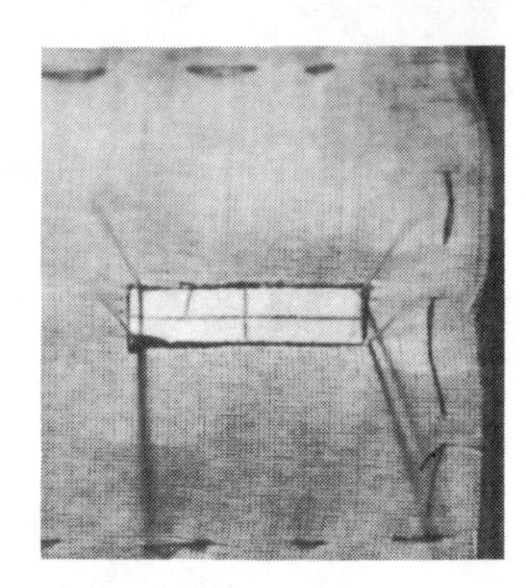

Since the facing has a tendency to move, check the position of the rectangle stitching in the facing before cutting. Insert a pin along the long stitching line through all the layers of the garment. (As shown in the picture above.)

The pin should be along the edge of the buttonhole on the right side of the garment. The ends of the rectangle and the buttonhole should line up. Correct the placement if necessary.

Cut through the center of the rectangle you have stitched and diagonally into the corners. Pull the organdy to the wrong side and press.

The picture shows the bound buttonholes trimmed and graded and the facing with the back of the buttonhole cut and pressed.

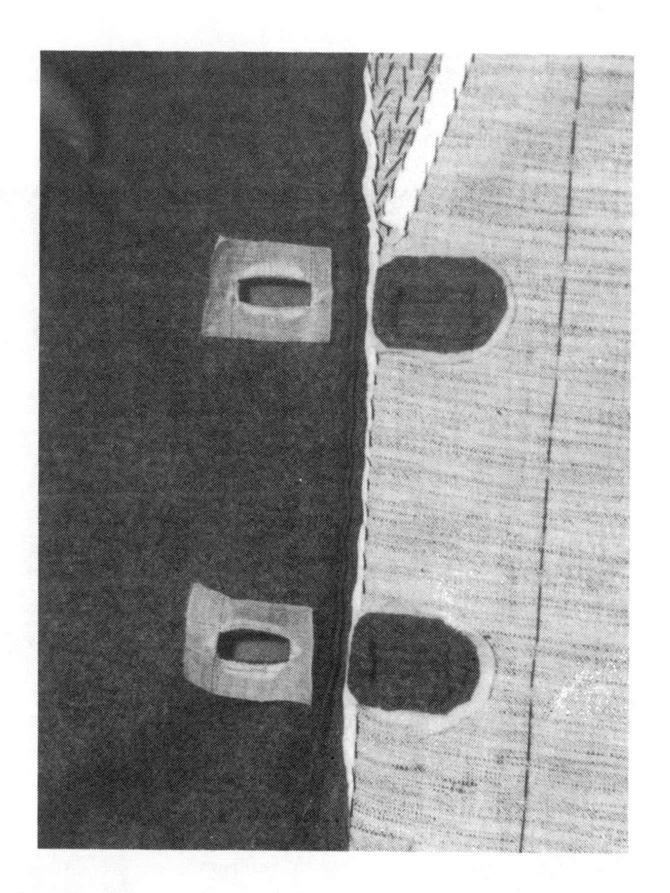

Handstitch, with a hidden slip stitch, the facing window to the back of the buttonhole. Open the buttonhole by carefully pulling the basting thread holding the lips together.

Proceed with the garment as the pattern directs or refer to pertinent chapters of this book.

SEWING ON BUTTONS

Button Placement

With the wrong sides together lay the front edges of the garment together with all edges even. Put a pin through each buttonhole.

Horizontal buttonholes. Put the pin 1/8″ from the bar-tack closest to the center front.

Vertical buttonholes. Put the pin through the middle of the hole.

Then put corresponding pins on the right side of the left front. Make sure all the pins are equal distance from the garment edge and that the overlap of the garment is the correct depth. Check the pattern for overlap width.

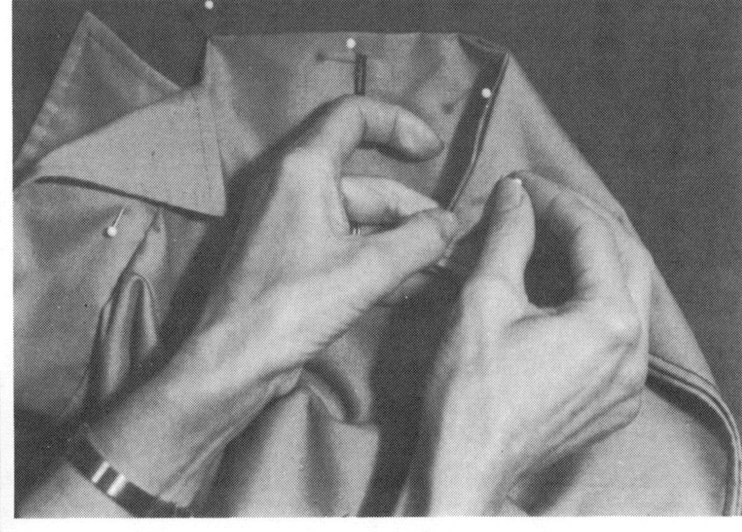

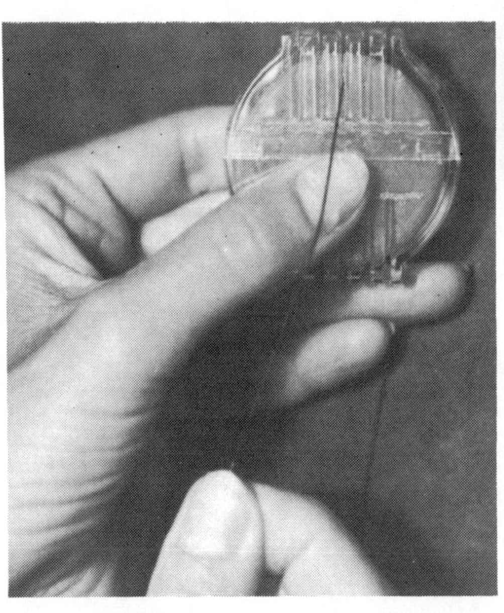

Sewing On Buttons

For ease in threading the needle and for ease in any handstitching, beeswax a long thread and press it lightly. This strengthens and stiffens the thread and keeps it from knotting. Thread a needle so the thread is double for sewing on buttons.

Take several small stitches on the button placement mark to secure the thread. Hold the button between the forefinger and thumb of your left hand and put the needle up through the first hole of the button. Put the needle down through the adjoining hole and into the fabric so you have a small stitch.

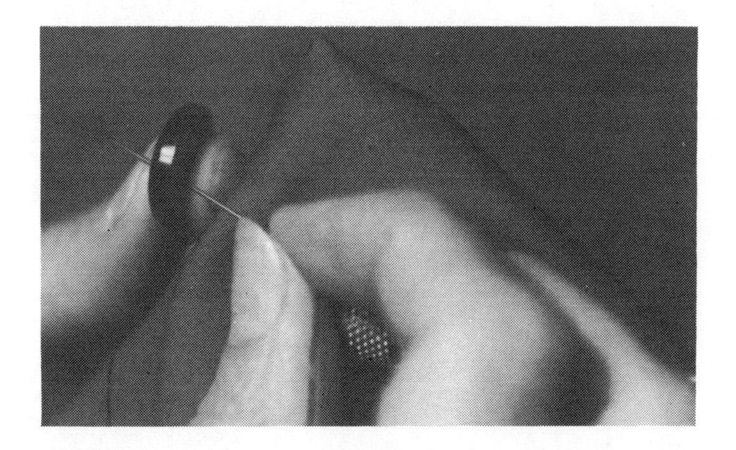

Don't pull the stitches too tight. All buttons need enough of a thread shank so there are no pulls on the garment when the garment is buttoned. The length of thread shank depends on the weight of the fabric. Allow a little more than you think is needed as it tends to shrink when you wrap the shank. Sometimes you need the full depth of your forefinger. Other shanks can be quite short.

Take the same number of stitches in each button. If one button becomes loose, restitch all the buttons.

Wrap the remaining thread snugly around the shank. Take several securing stitches in the fabric and shank and tie off the thread with a slip knot.

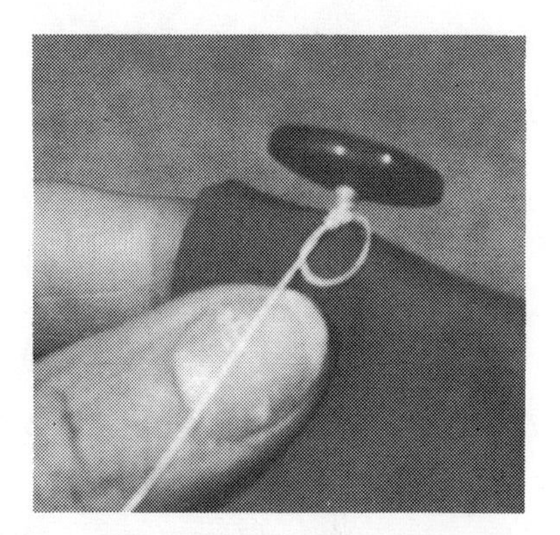

If your fabric is heavy or loosely woven, a backing button should be used. Be sure the backing button has the same number of holes as your fashion button.

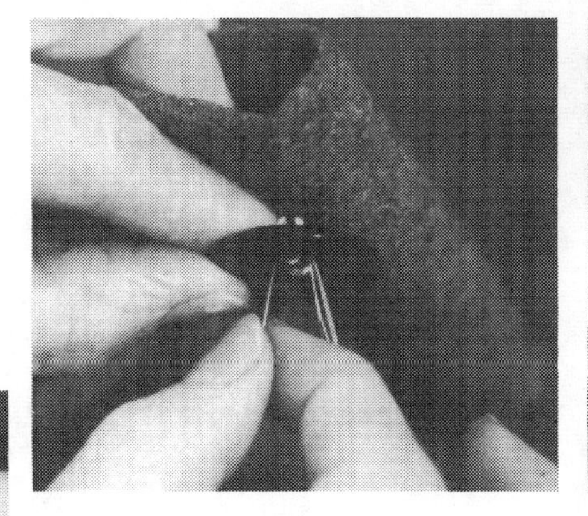

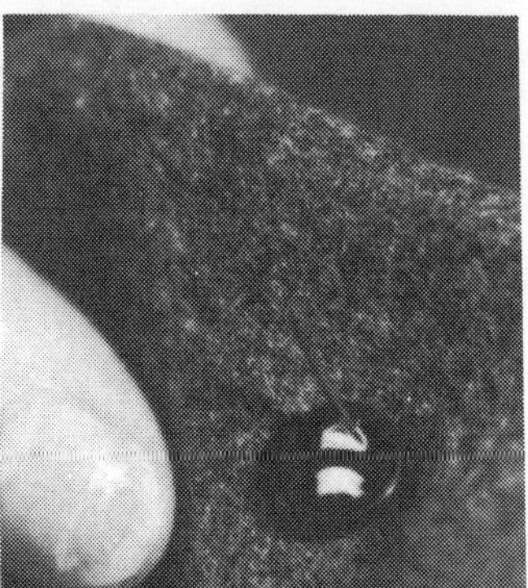

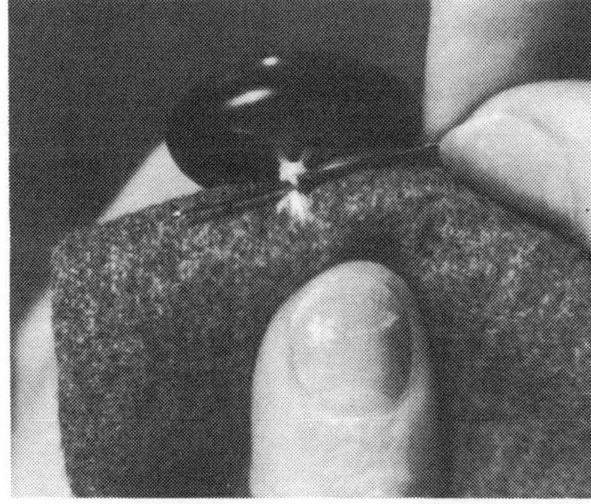

The same procedure is used with a backing button except that the stitches would go through the second button with the fabric in between the buttons. Wrap the shank and tie the threads between the fashion button and the right side of the fabric.

Pockets ■ 7

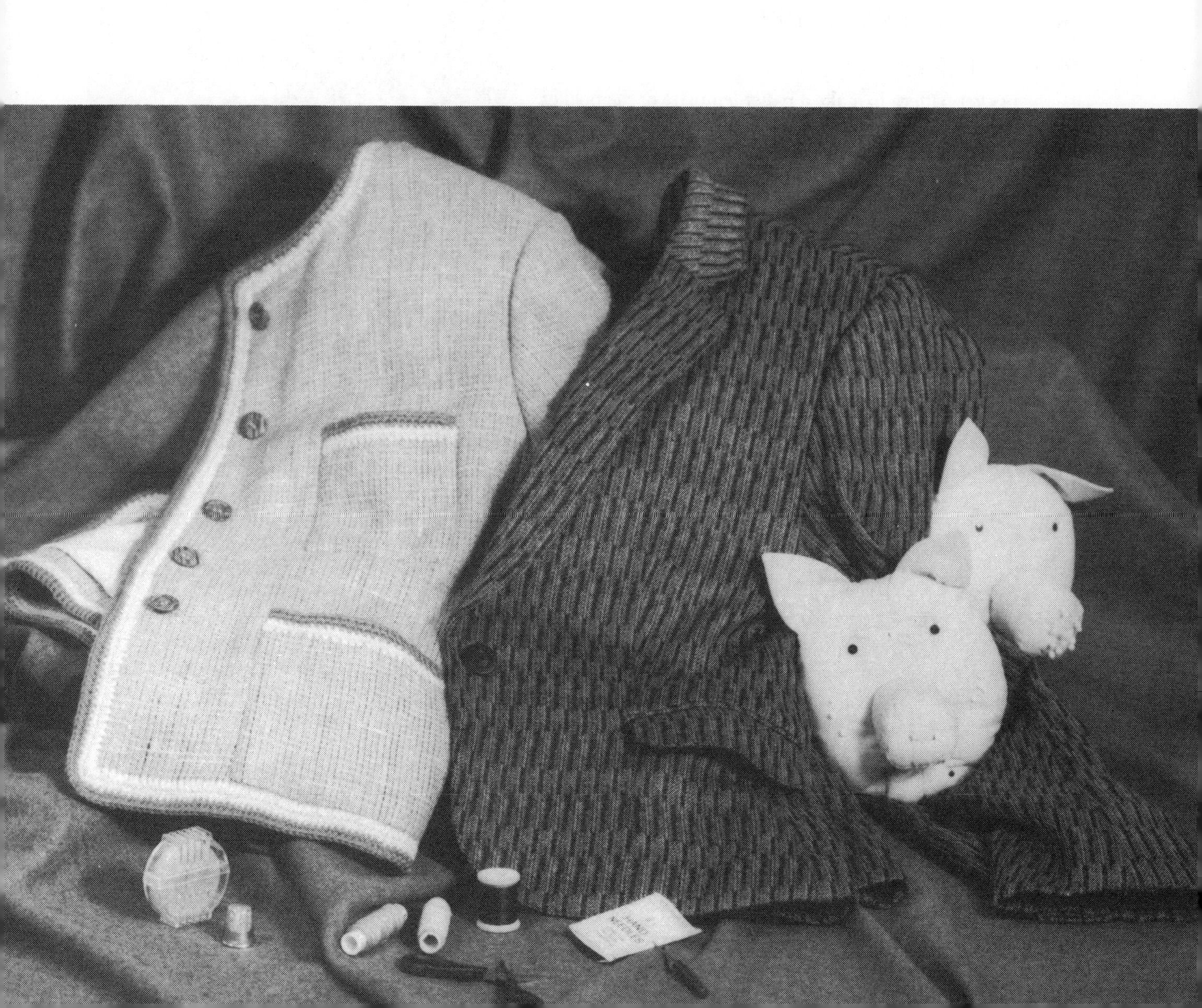

PATCH POCKETS

Patch pockets seem to be an easy thing to do. But it is difficult to get patch pockets with curved corners stitched evenly on both sides, and to get two patch pockets exactly the same size. There are two methods of doing patch pockets. The fast method and the couture method.

Fast Patch Pockets

Use this method when you need to line or face a pocket and you don't want to take the time to do it by hand. The pocket lining can be seen if you topstitch 1/4" from the edge. It works well when using fusible interfacing. I use this method if I am Fusible Tailoring a jacket or coat.

Couture Patch Pockets

Refer to page 227.

This is the best way of doing a patch pocket. The lining is finished inside the edge of the pocket. It never shows. This method works even if you are not interfacing or lining the pocket. For an uninterfaced and unlined pocket finish the edge of the pocket facing. With the right sides together stitch the ends, turn right side out and use the template to press the pocket.

FAST PATCH POCKETS

Pocket Preparation

Use the pocket pattern to make a paper template of the pocket with the seams removed. Use it as a guide when you stitch the pocket. This assures two pockets exactly the same size and shape.

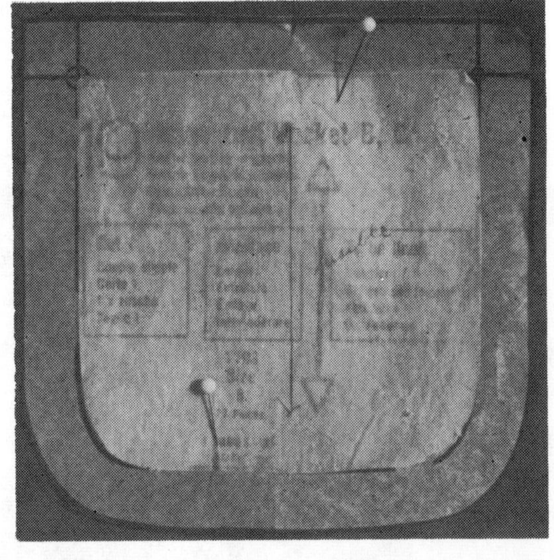

Mark the facing fold line of the pocket with a snip or with pins. Interface the pocket if needed. If you are topstitching, trim 5/8" off the fusible interfacing. Use the paper template as a pattern for cutting the interfacing. Trim 1/2" off the interfacing if the pocket will be attached to the garment by hand. If you are topstitching, the topstitching will hold the interfacing. If you are not topstitching, the interfacing must be caught in the seam.

Fuse the interfacing to the wrong side of the pocket with the top edge of the interfacing on the fold line of the pocket facing.

Stitch The Pocket

Sew the lining to the pocket facing, right sides together. Leave a small opening in the middle of the seam for turning the pocket.

Press the seam toward the lining.

Fold the pocket on the fold line with the wrong sides together and press.

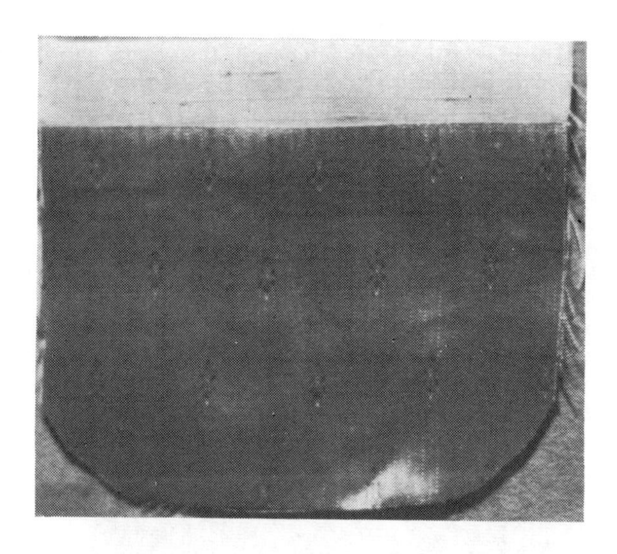

Trim the lining so that it exactly matches the pocket. If the lining is smaller than the pocket mark the difference so you can allow for a smaller seam when you stitch the pocket to the lining.

Fold the pocket on the fold line, right sides together. Scoot the lining out so that it extends past the pocket edge just a 1/16 of an inch. Pin firmly. There will be a little bubble in the pocket as it is pinned to be slightly larger than the lining. This will hold the lining to the inside so that it won't show on the right side of the garment.

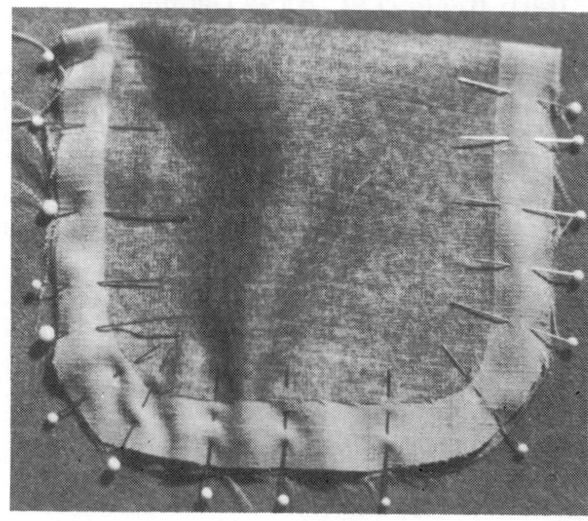

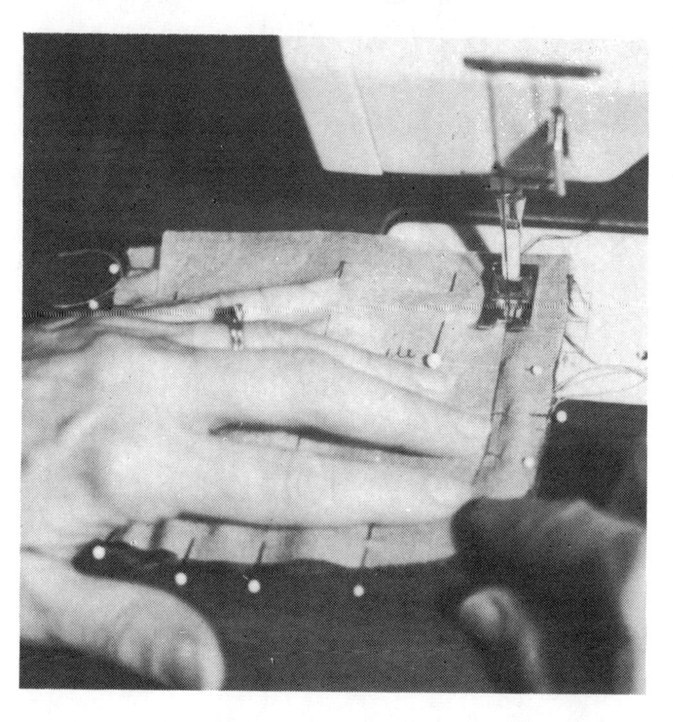

Pin the template on over the interfacing. Stitch, using the template as a guide. Stitch the corners slowly, picking up the presser foot and moving the fabric if needed. The knee lift on the Bernina machine is a wonderful help here as you lift the presser foot with your knee keeping both hands on the pockets as you are stitching the corners.

Trim the seam to 1/4″ and snip the excess fabric from the curves.

Turn the pocket through the opening and hand baste around the outer edge. Make sure the lining is lying to the underside of the pocket. Press. Slip stitch the small opening closed.

Attach The Pocket To The Garment

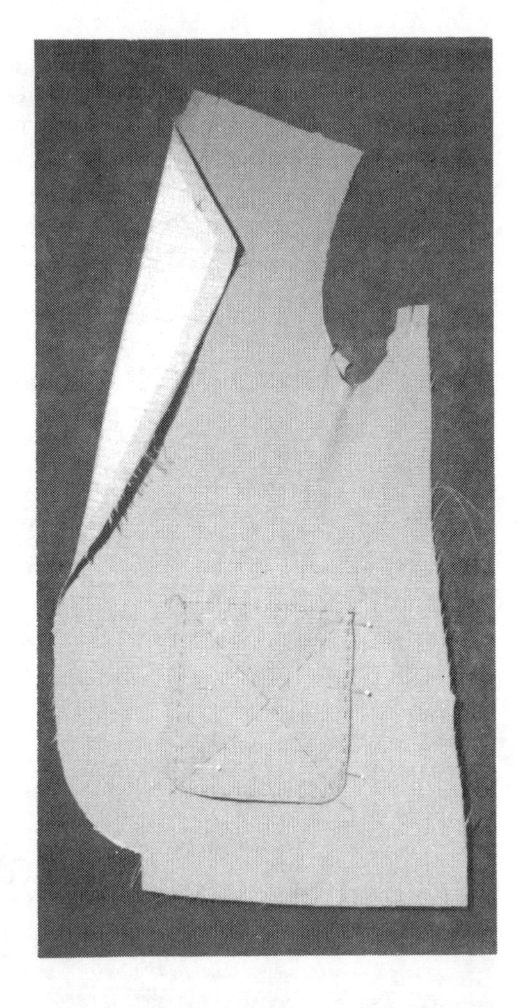

Baste the pockets on the garment with a big cross. Check the location. Refer to Couture Patch Pockets page 230. Patch pockets may be fastened to the jacket with narrow strips of fusible web or glue stick. This will keep the pocket from slipping while you are stitching them. Patch pockets are usually topstitched in place. If you wish to attach them by hand refer to Couture Patch Pockets page 231.

Refer to Topstitching and Edgestitching pages 72, 231, and 314.

COUTURE PATCH POCKETS

This is the best way of doing a patch pocket. This method works even if you are not interfacing or lining the pocket. For an uninterfaced and unlined pocket finish the edge of the pocket facing. With the right sides together stitch the ends, turn right side out and use the template to press the pocket. If you are interfacing and lining a pocket and want to eliminate the hand work use Fast Patch Pockets page 224.

Patch pockets seem like an easy thing to do, but it is difficult to get two patch pockets exactly the same size and shape. To insure two pockets the same size and shape make a lightweight cardboard template of the pocket.

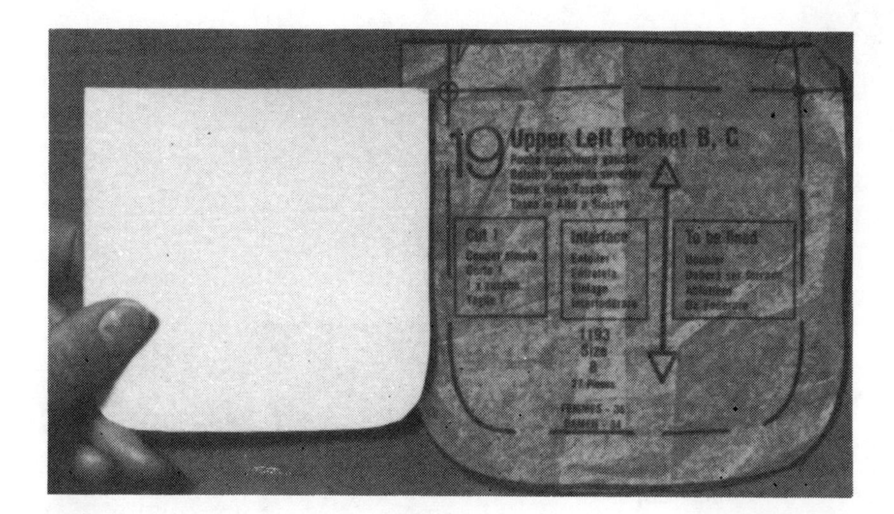

Pocket Preparation

Use the pocket pattern to make the template of the pocket. Place the pattern on the cardboard with a straight edge of the cardboard on the top fold line of the pocket Using a large pin poke holes exactly on the seam line. Mark the seam with a pencil following the pin holes. Trim off the pencil line as you cut the pocket out of the cardboard.

Lay the cardboard back on the pattern to check the curves and the size. It should be just slightly smaller than the seam line on the pattern.

Trim 5/8"-3/4" off the interfacing along the sides and bottom of the pocket. A heavier, bulky fabric would be trimmed the most to accommodate the turn of the cloth. A lightweight, flat fabric would be trimmed only 5/8".

Use a slightly lighter weight interfacing on the pockets than the interfacing you will be using on the garment front. Refer to Inner Construction, pages 21-22.

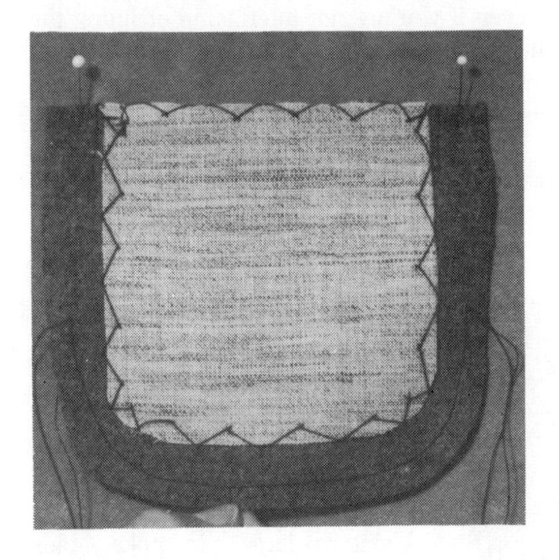

Fasten the interfacing to the wrong side of the pocket with a large catch stitch. The top edge of the interfacing must be on the fold line of the pocket.

Machine baste the lower section of the pocket around the curves 1/4″ from the cut edge. If the pocket is square miter the corners. Refer to Couture Tailoring, pages 301-302.

Stitch The Pocket

Stitch the lining to the pocket facing, right sides together.

Fold the pocket on the fold line, right sides together. Stitch the ends of the pocket to the seam line of the lining. Clip the fold and grade the seam. Turn the pocket right side out and gently push the corners out with a small screw driver or a point pusher.

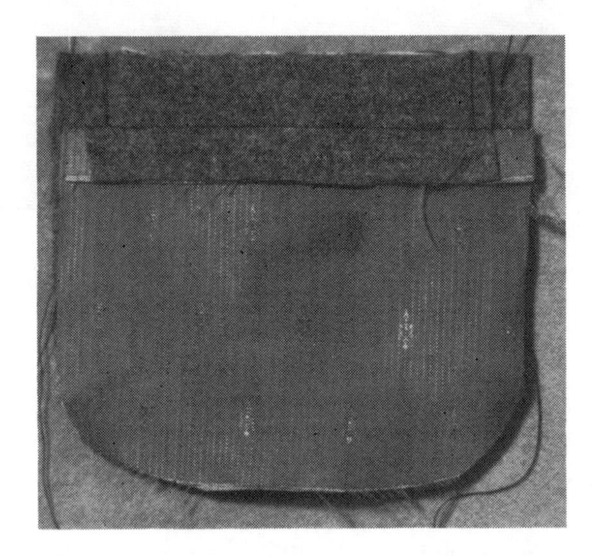

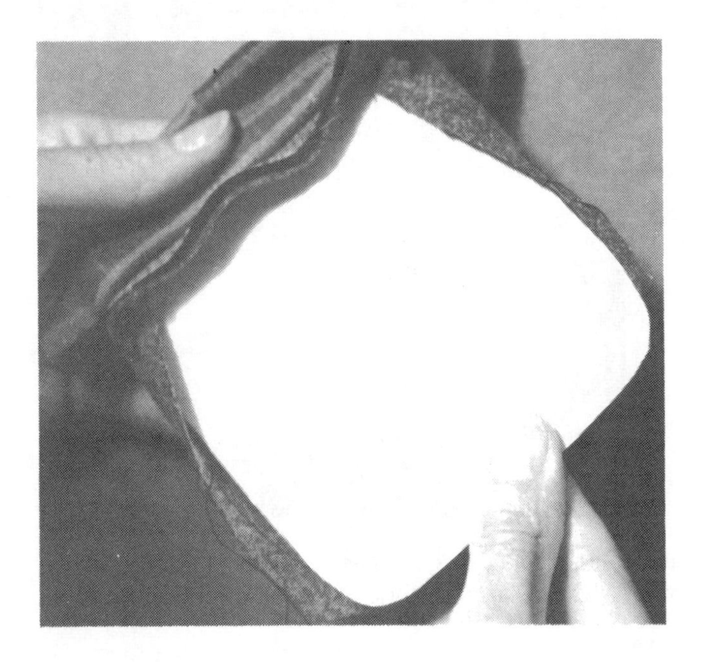

Slip the cardboard template into the top of the pocket. Make sure the cardboard is completely up to the fold and into the corners.

Pull the baste stitch around the curve so the seam folds to the inside snugly against the cardboard.

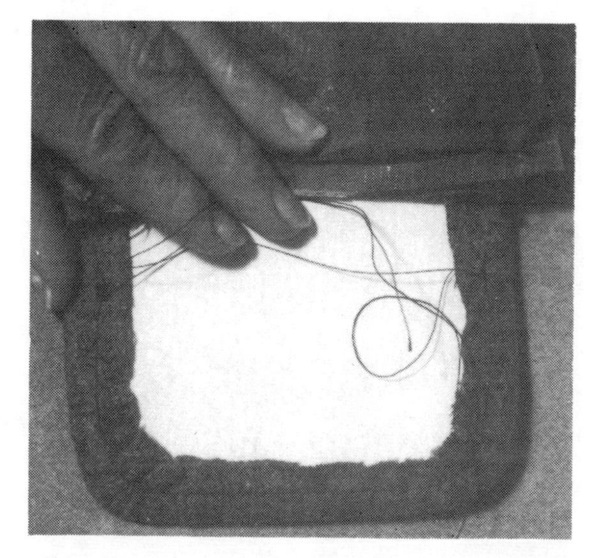

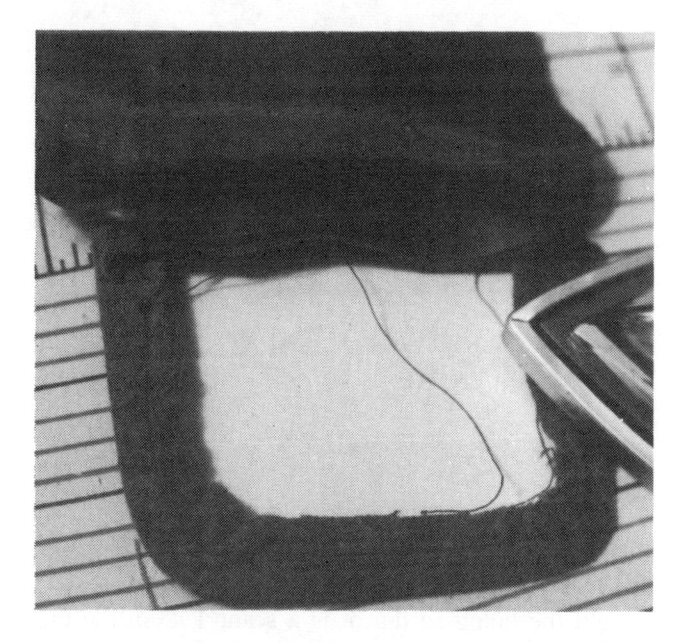

Press the pocket with the cardboard in the pocket. Hold the fabric snug against the cardboard while you press.

Clip excess fabric around the curves. Don't clip any closer than 1/4" from the seam. Slip the cardboard out of the pocket and hand baste, if needed, around the pocket to hold the crease.

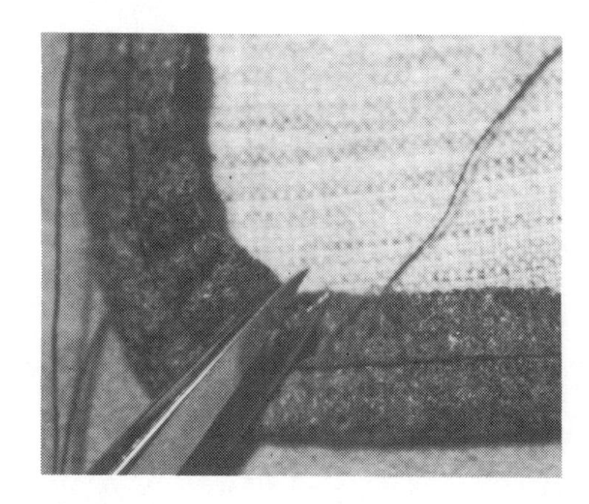

Clip the seam allowance of the pocket facing to remove the bulk where it is stitched to the lining.

Lay the lining down in place and pin the lining to the pocket. Trim the lining so that it is 1/8" larger than the pocket.

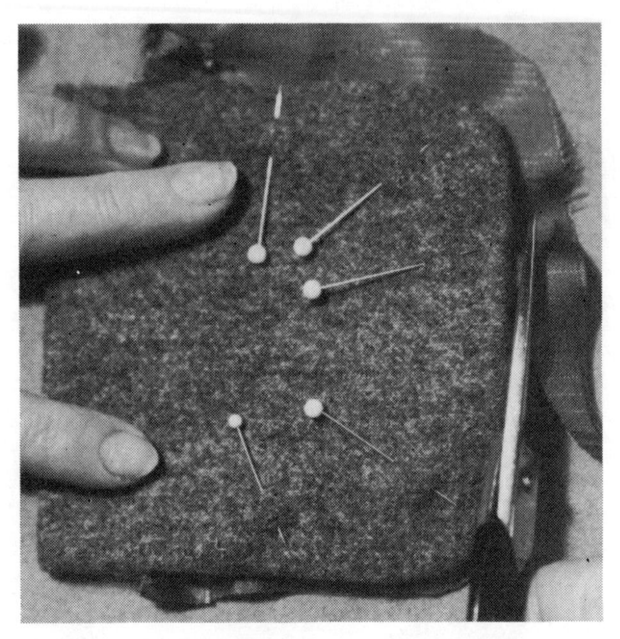

Fold the lining so that it is a scant 1/4" inside the edge of the pocket. Hand stitch the lining in place with a close hidden whip stitch.

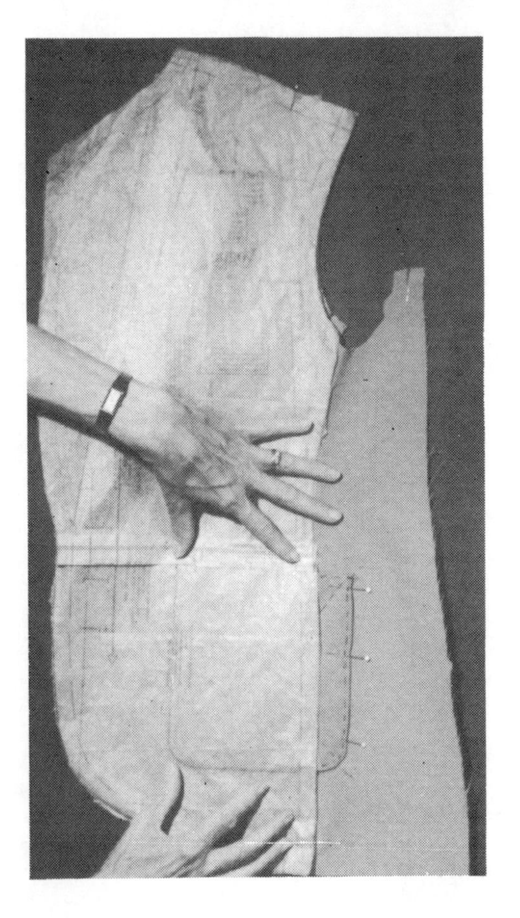

Press the pocket.

Attach the pockets to the garment

Place the pockets on the jacket and cross baste them to check the location. Cross basting keeps the pocket from slipping. Check the location by laying the tissue over the garment.

Be sure you allow enough room for the curve of the body. If you pin them flat on the table allow enough room for your hand to slip in. Check for the body curve when you check the pocket location.

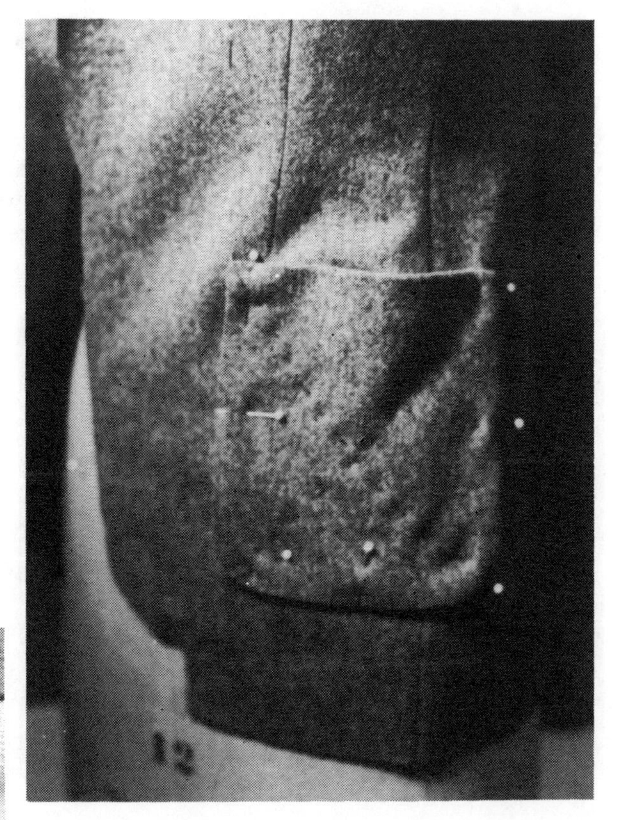

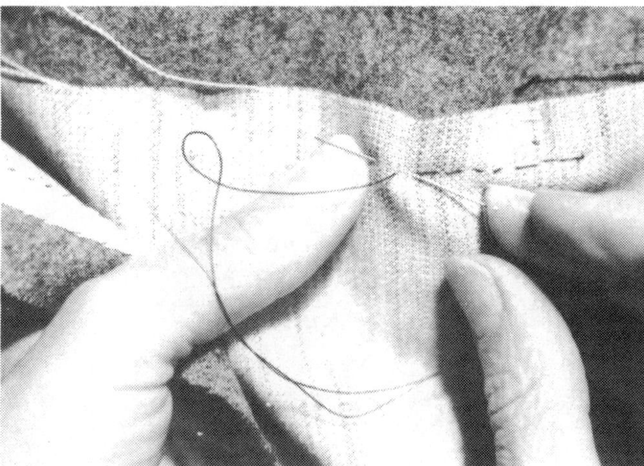

Either topstitch the pocket in place or hand stitch it on. If the pocket is to be hand stitched (no stitching will show on the right side of the garment) use a back stitch and stitch it from the wrong side of the garment. You can feel the edge of the pocket so you can stitch close to the edge of the pocket and it does not show on the right side of the garment.

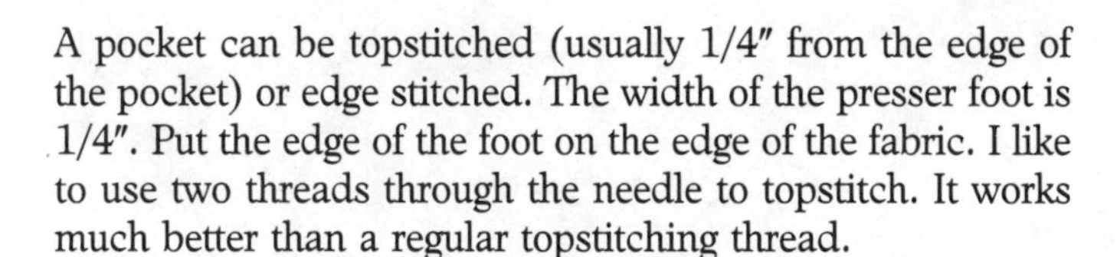

A pocket can be topstitched (usually 1/4″ from the edge of the pocket) or edge stitched. The width of the presser foot is 1/4″. Put the edge of the foot on the edge of the fabric. I like to use two threads through the needle to topstitch. It works much better than a regular topstitching thread.

If you are edge stitching try using the blind hem foot on your machine to keep the edge stitching straight and right on the edge. Your machine instruction book should tell you how to set the needle position for your machine. (Bernina machines have two settings. 1mm and 2mm to the left of the needle). Do a small sample with your blind hem foot to check the width of the edge stitch.

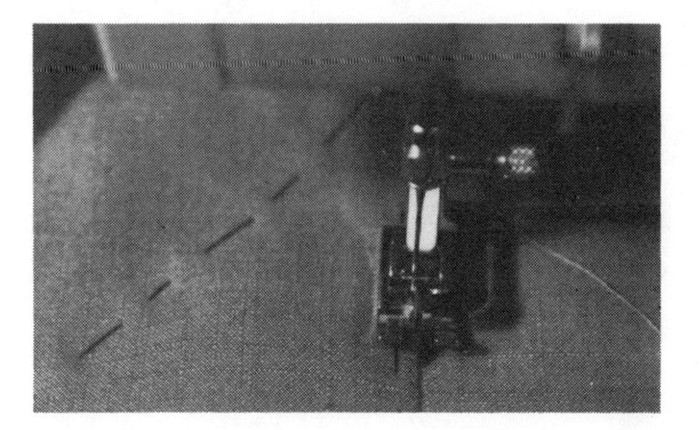

After pockets are done proceed with the garment.

WELT POCKETS

With this method welt pockets can be done on any fabric from a cotton knit to expensive cashmere coating. As with the bound buttonhole you are making a reinforced opening in the fabric and filling it. In a bound buttonhole you fill the opening with two strips of fabric that form the edges of the bound buttonhole. In welt pockets you can fill the opening in a variety of ways. An outside welt pocket, a single welt pocket, a single welt pocket with a flap, a double welt pocket, and a double welt pocket with a flap. They are pictured with a description.

An Outside Welt Pocket

An outside welt pocket is one in which the ends of the welt are stitched before it is attached to the opening. The outside welt stands up and covers the opening. Example: A breast pocket on a tailored jacket.

For detailed instructions for an outside welt pocket refer to page 237.

A Single Welt Pocket

A single welt pocket is one in which the ends and one long edge are stitched to the opening from the inside. The single welt pocket is combined with a flap on many blazers.

For detailed instruction for a single welt pocket refer to page 239.

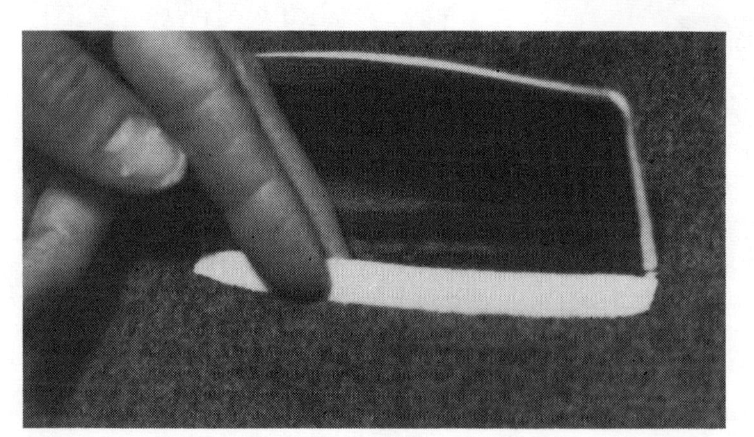

A Single Welt Pocket With A Flap

Refer to page 241 for detailed instructions.

A Double Welt Pocket

A double welt pocket is one which resembles a bound buttonhole and is done in the same manner. The double welt pocket is also combined with a pocket flap on many tailored garments.

For detailed instructions for a double welt pocket refer to page 244.

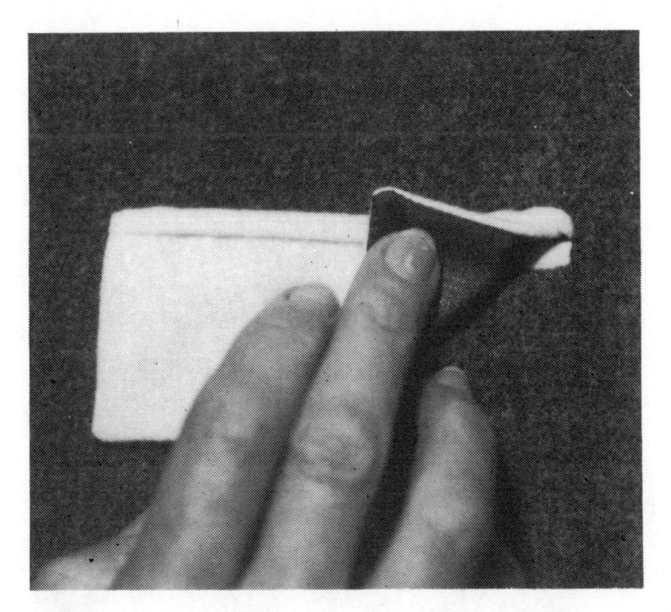

A Double Welt Pocket With A Flap

Refer to page 246 for detailed instructions.

Instructions For All Welt Pockets

Followed by detailed instructions for specific types of welt pockets:

All welt pockets must begin with a reinforced opening the length and width the pattern recommends. **Exception:** The opening for an outside welt pocket can be narrow, only 1/4″ deep. Outside welt pockets have a tendency to sag, hence a narrow opening is preferable to a deep (1/2″) opening.

Welt pockets are easy to make using this method. They do require accurate measuring, stitching, and **practice.** If you have never made a welt pocket practice making several before you do one on your garment. If you are not pleased with a finished welt pocket you can remove the welt and put it on again. **Never remove the organdy rectangle.**

Begin Every Welt Pocket With The Pocket Opening

You will need a piece of lightweight fabric for each welt pocket. Crisp organdy is the best, but regular organdy will work. Refer to Inner Construction page 21. Make the strip of organdy about 1″ larger on all edges over the size of the pocket opening. Keep the grainlines straight.

Do the following five steps for every welt pocket except the double welt without organdy on page 249.

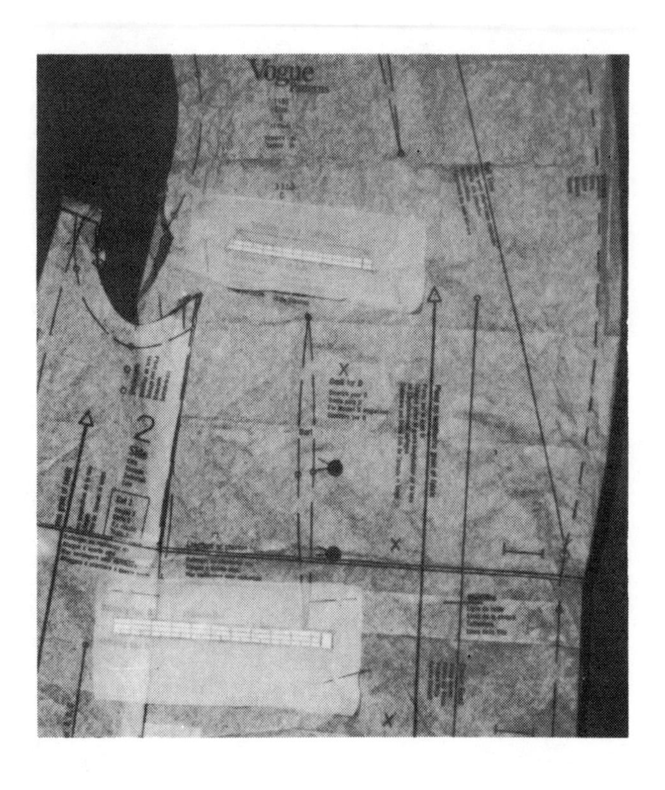

1. Working on a flat surface place the organdy on the pattern piece. Pin the organdy to the pattern keeping the grain lines straight.

   Put a piece of tape on the organdy the length, width, and shape of the pocket opening. Masking tape can be bought in 1/4″, 1/2″, and 3/4″ widths. Topstitching tape that pulls off in 1/8″ increments works well too.

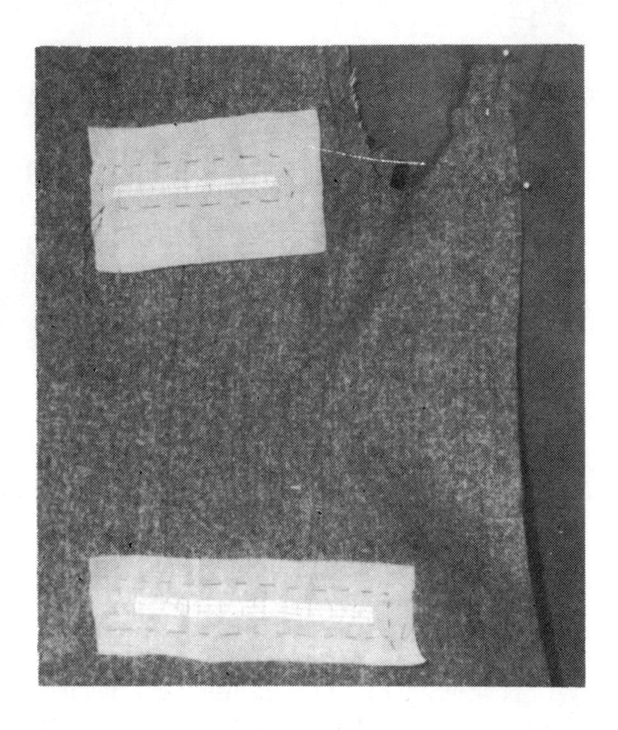

2. Remove the organdy from the pattern and put the organdy on the right side of the garment on the pocket location lines. Pin in place. Check one long edge of the tape with a ruler to make sure the pocket edges are straight. It is easy to pull the organdy a little and distort the line.

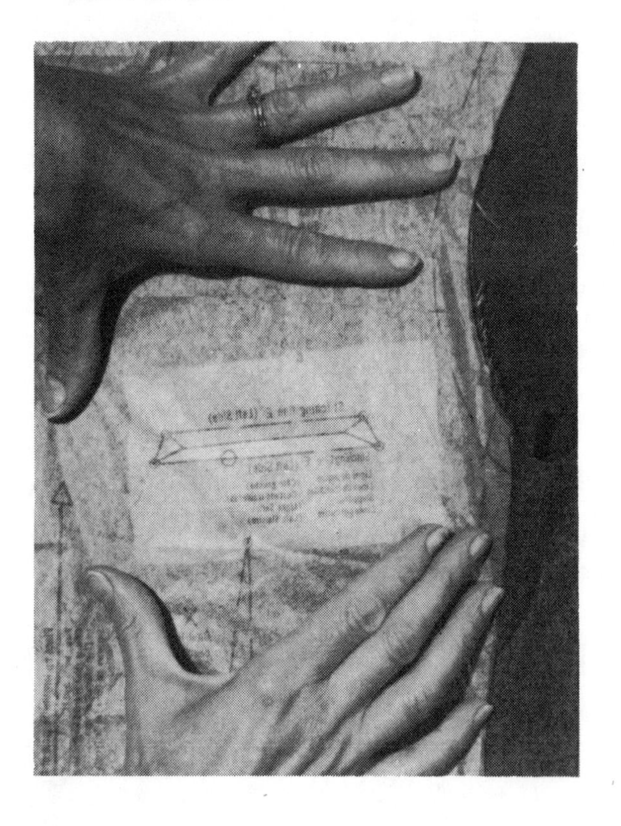

Check the pocket location by laying the pattern over the garment. If the organdy with the tape is exactly on the pocket location lines baste the outer edges of the organdy to hold it in place.

3. Stitch around the pocket opening, 15-20 stitches per inch, and overlap the stitches on a long side. It helps to use a color a few shades off for the bobbin thread so you can see the stitching when you attach the welts.

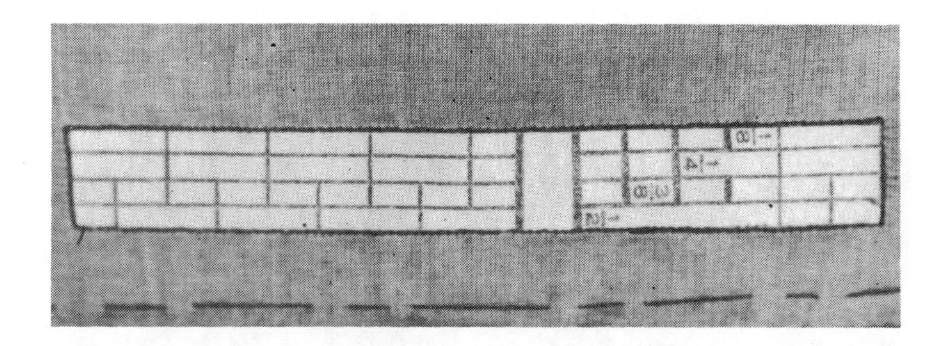

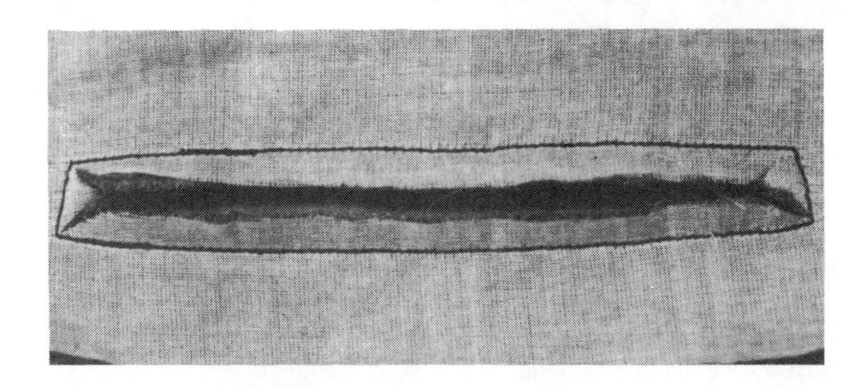

4. Remove the tape. Cut through the center of the pocket opening stopping about 1/2" short of the ends and clip diagonally into the corner. This makes a little pie on each end. Be careful not to clip the stitching, but you must clip to it. Remove the basting holding the organdy in place.

5. Pull the organdy to the wrong side of the garment and press. Press on a sleeve roll just enough to hold the fold. Make certain that no organdy shows on the right side of the garment.

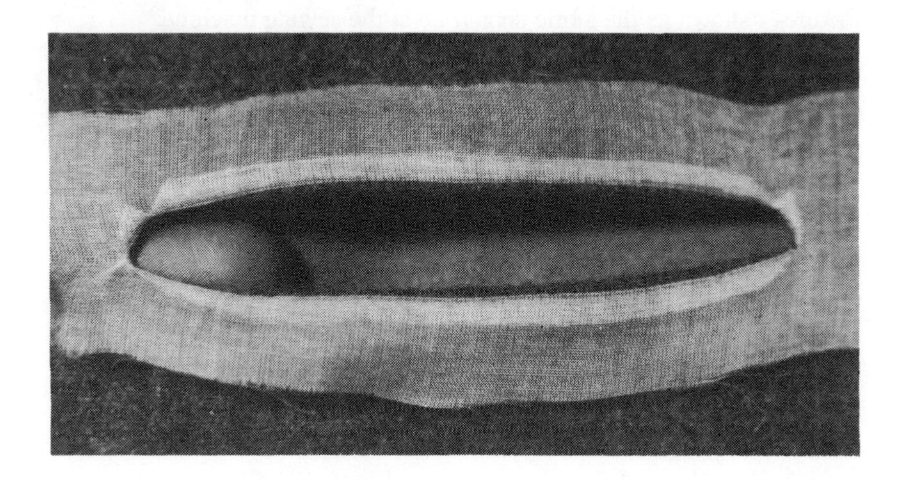

Attach The Welt And Flaps To The Pocket Opening

The easiest, most accurate way to attach double or single welts and the flaps to the garment is to hand baste them to the pocket opening with a permanent hidden baste stitch with matching thread from the right side. You can see what you are doing so you can make sure the welt or flap is held straight and is even on the entire pocket. After it is hand basted machine stitch it for strength.

Hand Baste The Welts And Flaps

To baste use a single bees waxed thread with a knotted end. Insert the needle at a corner between the fashion fabric and the organdy. Bring the needle to the right side in the corner.

Hand baste the welts and flaps continued:

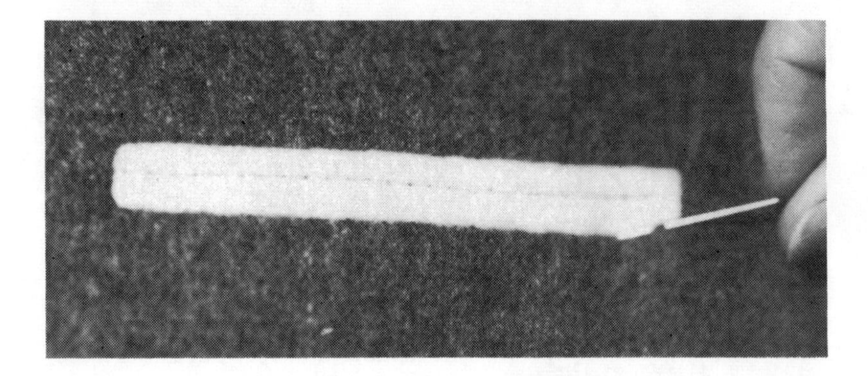

Take a small stitch completely through the welt or flap, and come up just catching the fold of the pocket opening. Slip the needle through the fold about 1/8" and take a second small stitch completely through the welt or flap. Come up again just catching the fold of the pocket opening. Continue the basting in this manner the length of the pocket opening.

Machine Stitch The Welts And Flaps

Fold the garment, right sides together, to expose the long edge of the pocket you have just hand basted and machine stitch the long edge on the hand baste line which will be just inside the first stitching line (the stitching with the off colored bobbin thread). Be sure and stitch to the corner. It is easier to pull out a stitch than it is to fill stitches in if you did not stitch far enough. Do not back stitch. Leave the threads long.

Picture is shown as the fabric should lie at the sewing machine.

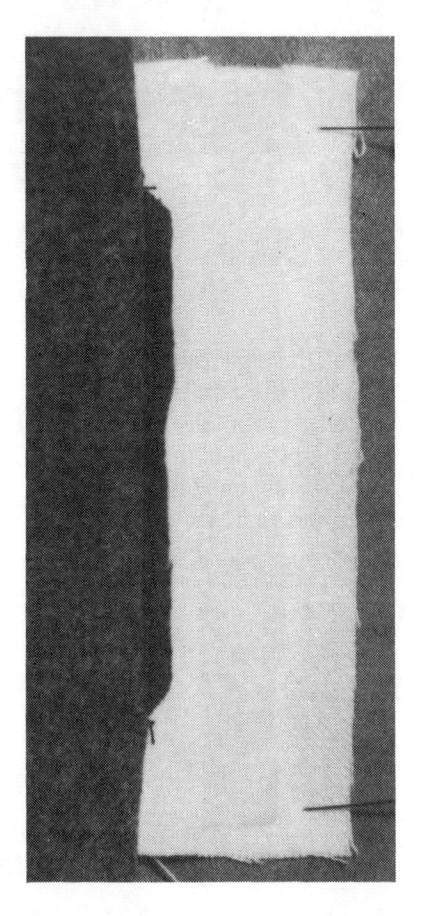

Check to make sure you have stitched to the corners, and make sure no organdy is showing on the right side of the garment. If you have organdy showing you did not stitch inside the first stitching line (toward the garment). Also make sure the sides of the pocket are even. If the pocket is stitched correctly pull the threads to the inside and tie with a tailors knot. Cut the threads a little way from the knot.

These steps must be done for every welt pocket except the double welt pocket without organdy.

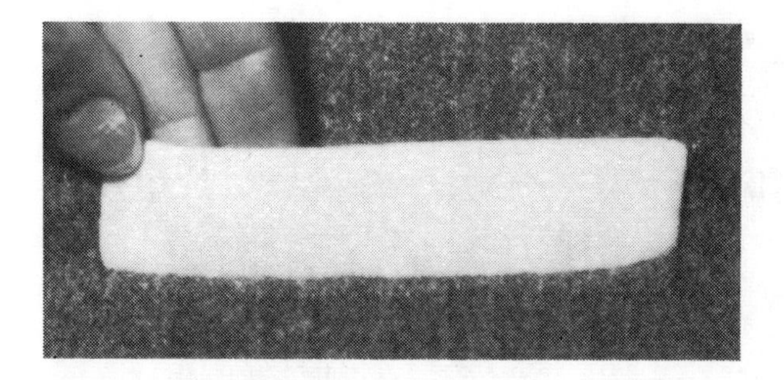

Outside Welt Pocket

The welt is wider than the pocket opening and covers the pocket opening. Make the pocket opening **before** you stitch the ends of the welt. The welt must be the **exact** size of the opening.

Pocket Preparation

Cut the pocket lining as the pattern directs. Then cut it on the slash line. This gives you two lining pieces for the pocket, one slightly smaller than the other.

Make the pocket opening by following steps 1-5 as described on pages 234-235.

Prepare the welt by interfacing and stitching the ends as the pattern directs. Wait to trim the ends. Turn the welt right side out and press. If the welt exactly fits the pocket opening trim and grade the end seams of the welt. If not adjust it as needed, then trim the edges. Top stitch if the pattern calls for it, or if you think the fabric needs top stitching.

Stitch The Pocket

Pin, hand baste, then stitch the large portion of the lining to the upper edge of the pocket opening. Center the lining so that you have equal amounts on each end of the pocket opening. Stitch on the seam line as the organdy was stitched.

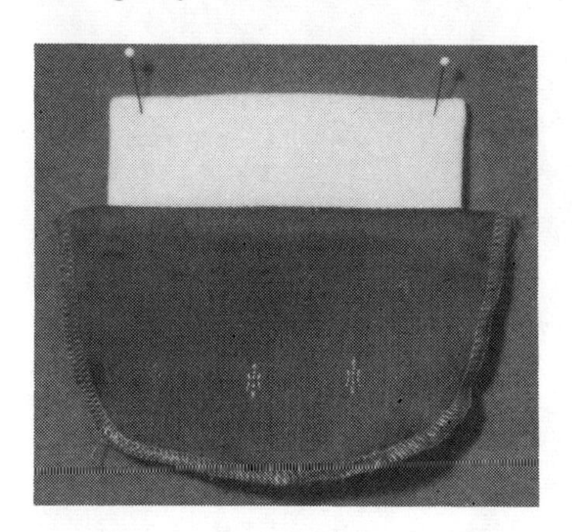

Pin the interfaced side of the welt to the right side of the small portion of the pocket lining. Center the welt on the lining as you pin. Stitch and press the seam toward the lining.

Slip the welt with the lining attached into the pocket opening with the seam allowance next to the organdy. Adjust the width of the welt to correspond with the pattern and pin to hold. Pin the upper lining out of the way. Hand baste the welt to the lower edge of the pocket opening. Refer to and follow hand basting and machine stitching the welts and flaps on pages 235-236.

Stitch across the pie ends of the pocket opening with a small hand backstitch. The bulk of the welt prevents doing the small pie ends on the machine. At the same time hand backstitch the ends of the welt to hold them in place. Begin stitching at the lower edge of the pie and continue up through the end of the welt. Even though you are stitching on the wrong side you can feel the edge of the welt. Backstitching on the wrong side of the garment is strong and does not show on the right side of the garment.

Stitch The Pocket Lining

Lay the pocket lining pieces as they will lie in the finished garment. If the pocket lining edges are not even when they are lying down in place trim them. Stitch the sides and the bottom of the pocket. Finish the edges with the serger or a machine finishing stitch.

Proceed with the garment.

Single Welt Pocket

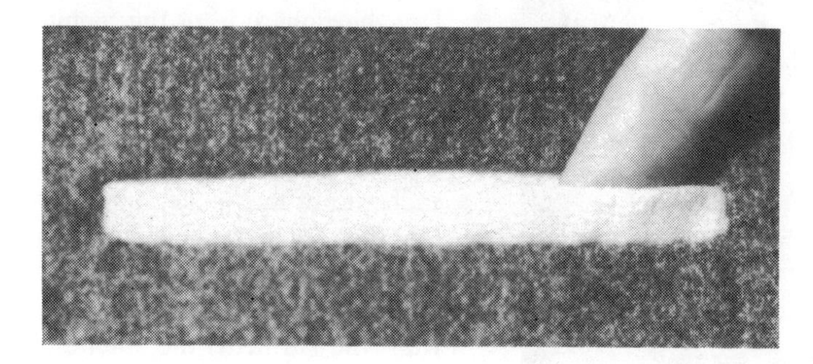

A single welt pocket is stitched on both ends and lower edge of the welt inside the garment. I have used this when I wanted a pocket and the pattern did not have a pocket. It is easy to put in at any angle because the organdy reinforces the opening. To prepare for a single welt pocket, do the following.

Pocket Preparation

Make the pocket opening following steps 1-5 as described on pages 234 and 235.

You can use the pattern welt pocket, lining, and facing pieces or you can make your own.

To make pocket lining pieces, cut the lining 1¼″ wider than the pocket opening and about 10-12″ in length. A one-piece pocket lining makes a pocket with a fold on the bottom edge. The pocket lining can be cut in two pieces with one piece about 4″ long and the second piece about 6″ long. If the pattern has a pocket lining that is not a rectangle, cut it in half at the slash cutting line marked on the pattern. You will now have two pieces, one slightly larger than the other, instead of one as your pattern directs. Cut the lining of lining fabric.

To make the welt pieces, cut the welt twice the width of the pocket opening plus two seam allowances and 1¼″ longer than the pocket opening. Fold the welt in half. Interface the welt to the fold line. Press the welt in half with the wrong sides together and baste the long unfinished edges together.

To make a pocket facing, cut the facing the same width as the lining and 2″ deep.

Stitch the facing to one end of the lining or, if the lining is in two pieces, to the small piece of lining. Press the seam toward the lining.

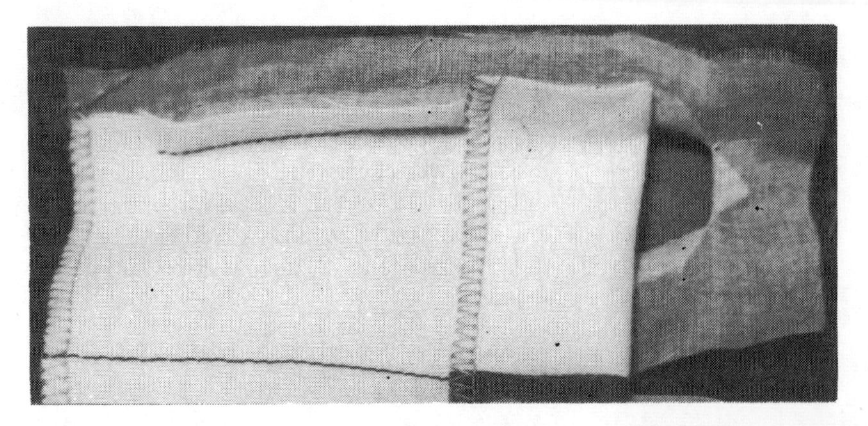

Stitch The Pocket

Lay the right side of the facing (with the pocket lining attached) on the organdy side of the pocket opening. Center the facing so that you have equal amounts on each end of the pocket opening. Pin, then stitch the pocket facing to the upper edge of the pocket opening. Stitch just inside (toward the garment) the stitching line holding the organdy.

Center the welt in the pocket opening. With the fold line along the upper edge of the pocket opening and the ends inside the garment, baste with a diagonal stitch as shown to hold the fold snugly against the long upper edge of the pocket. Make sure the fold of the welt is up into the corners of the opening.

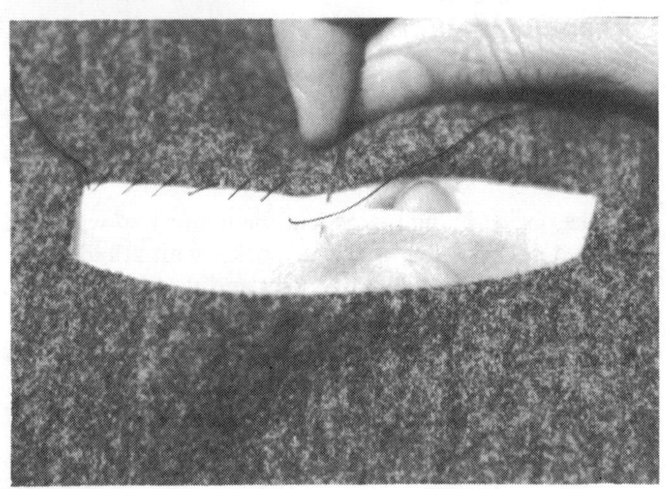

Keep the lining underneath free. Hand baste the welt to the lower edge of the pocket opening. Refer to and follow hand basting and machine stitching the welts on pages 235-236.

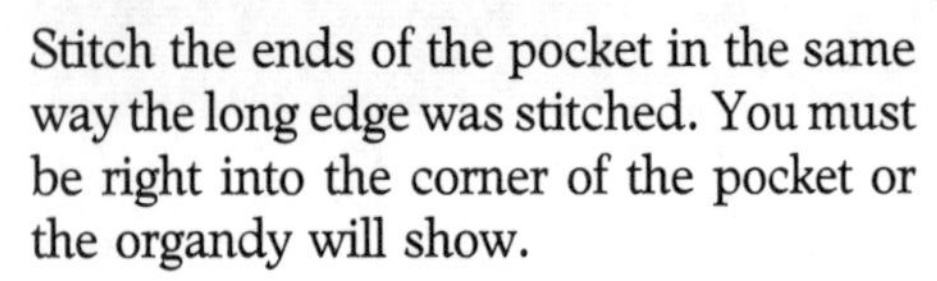

Stitch the ends of the pocket in the same way the long edge was stitched. You must be right into the corner of the pocket or the organdy will show.

Stitch The Pocket Lining

Grade the lower edge of the welt so you will be stitching lining to one layer of the welt. Stitch the remaining lining piece to the lower edge of the welt or if you had only one lining piece, attach the free edge to the lower edge of the welt. In that case, the bottom of the pocket would be a fabric fold as in the picture below.

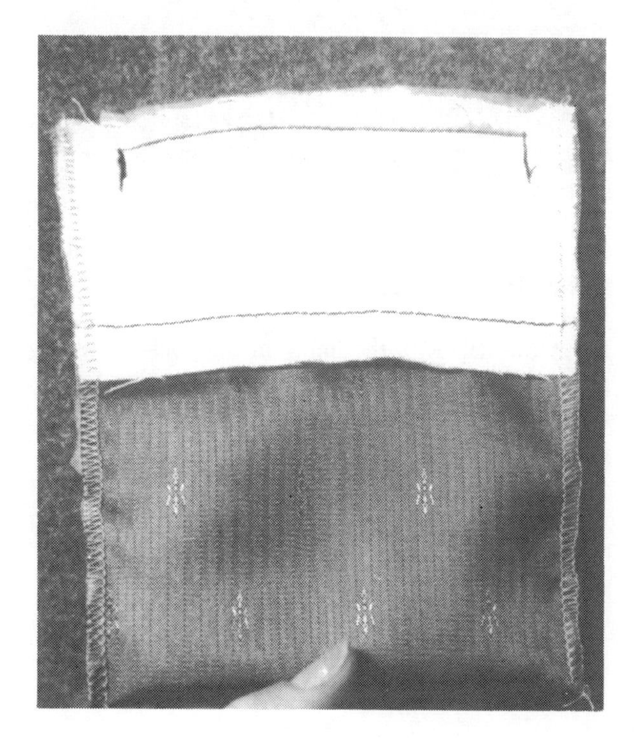

If the pocket lining edges of the two-piece lining are not even when they are lying down in place, trim them.

Finish the edges of the inside pocket. Either straight stitch and finish the edge with a zig-zag, do a French seam, or stitch the pocket edges with a serger.

Proceed with the garment. Wait to remove the basting holding the pocket edges until the garment is completed.

Single Welt Pocket With A Flap

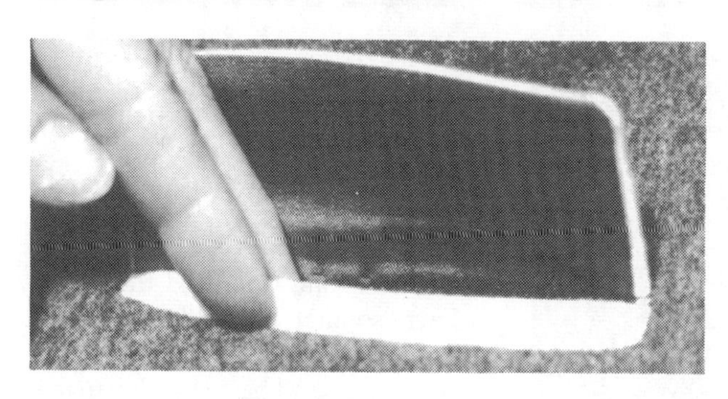

A single welt with a flap is done in the same manner as the single welt pocket except that the flap is stitched to the upper edge of the pocket opening in place of the facing.

Pocket Preparation

Make the pocket opening by following steps 1-5 described on pages 234-235.

Refer to Single Welt Pockets, page 239, for details in adapting pattern pieces or for making your own pattern pieces. You need a welt, a flap, and a lining for each pocket. You will not need a pocket facing.

Make the flap as the pattern directs. It must **exactly** fit the opening. Stitch the ends, press, and turn the flap. Check the size of the flap before you trim the end seams of the flap. If the flap exactly fits, trim and grade the end seams. Interface the welt to the fold and baste the cut edges together.

Center the flap on the lining with the right sides together. Pin, then machine stitch the flap to the lining. Press the seam toward the lining.

Stitch The Pocket

Insert the flap with the lining in the pocket opening and pin to the upper edge. Measure the flap for the correct width and pin in place.

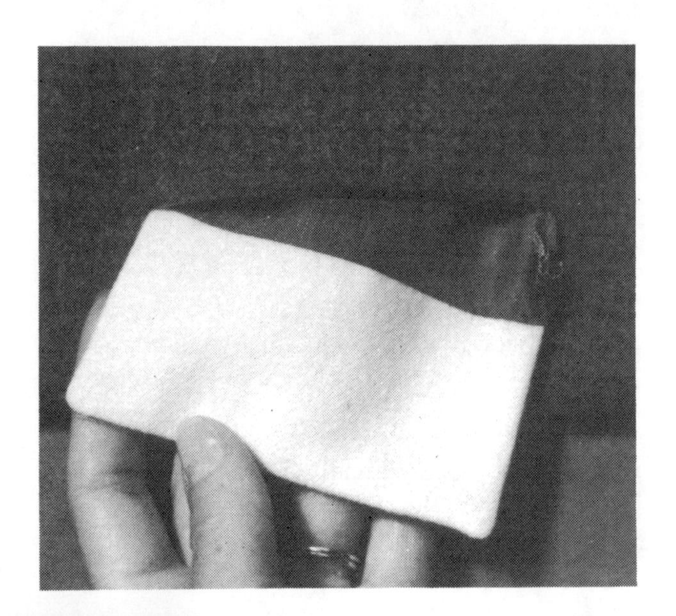

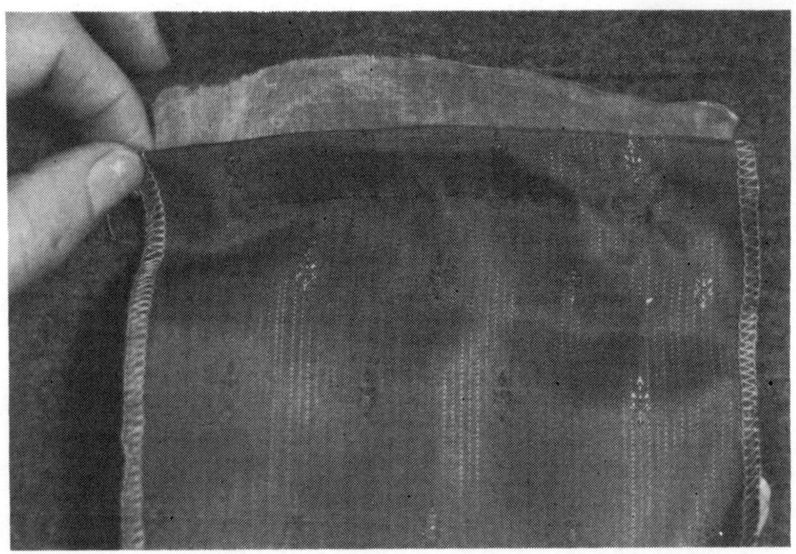

On the wrong side, fold the lining down so that the fold covers the upper welt edges and pin. On the right side, hand baste the flap to the upper edge of the pocket opening. You are hand basting and machine stitching through the lining, the flap, and the pocket opening. Refer to and follow hand basting and machine stitching the welts and flaps on pages 235-236.

Tuck the flap inside the pocket and center the welt on top of the flap with the fold snug against the upper edge of the opening. Diagonally baste the folded edge to hold it in place.

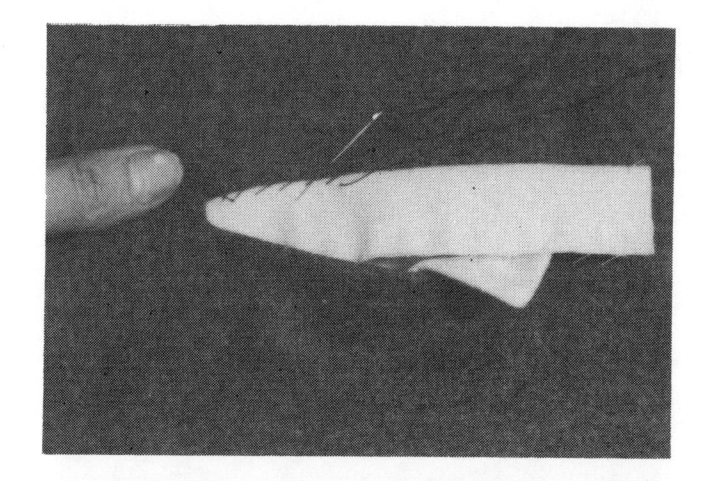

Hold the lining and the flap free. Hand baste the welt to the lower edge of the pocket opening. The Single Welt is pictured on the left on page 240. Refer to and follow hand basting and machine stitching the welts and flap on pages 235-236.

Trim the excess organdy. On the lower edge of the pocket opening, trim the layer of the welt closest to the garment so that it is slightly longer than the pocket opening seam allowance.

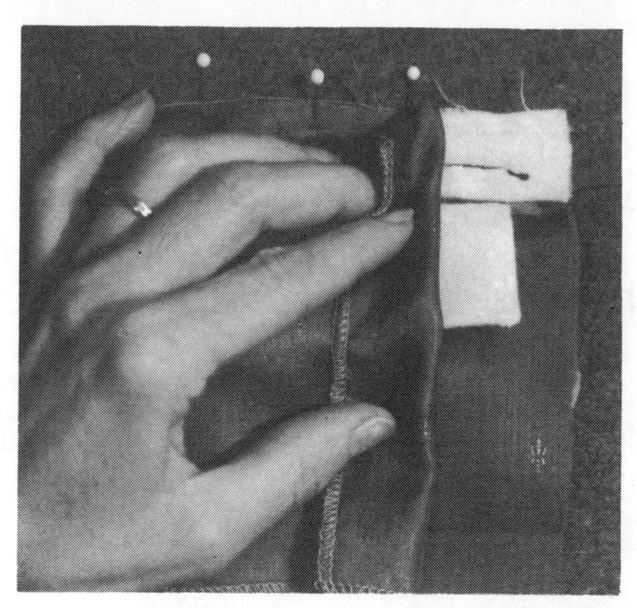

Stitch The Pocket Lining

Stitch the remaining lining piece to the lower edge of the welt or, if you had only one lining piece, attach the free edge to the lower edge of the welt. In that case the bottom of the pocket would be a fabric fold instead of a stitched seam. If the pocket lining edges of the two-piece lining are not even when they are lying down in place, trim them.

Remove the diagonal basting and bring the flap to the right side of the garment. Stitch the small pie ends of the welt in the same way as the long edges were stitched, catching the tied threads of the long edges. Check to make sure you stitched into the corner of the pocket or the organdy will show. If the small pie ends are stitched correctly, no puckers and no organdy showing, tie all the threads. Cut the threads a little way from the knot.

Finish the sides and the bottom (if it is not a fold) of the inside pocket. Either straight stitch and finish the edge with a finishing stitch, or do a French seam, or use the serger.

Proceed with the garment.

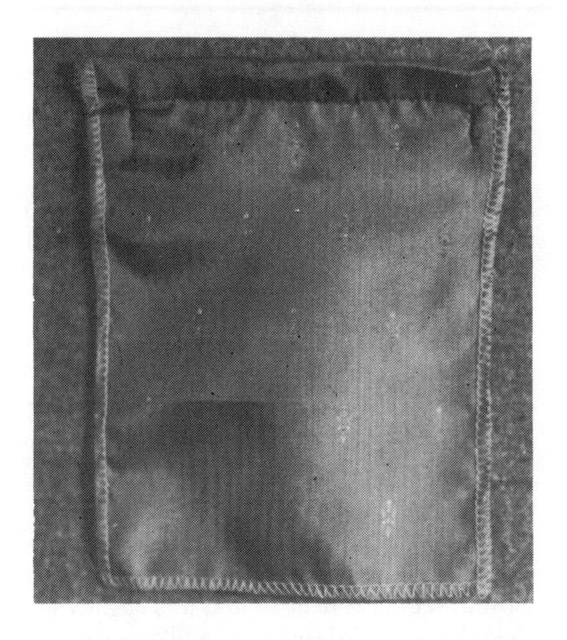

Double Welt Pockets

Double welt pockets without organdy

Pattern directions for double welt pockets use the fashion fabric instead of organdy when making the pocket opening. The pattern directions work for lightweight fabric in which a flap is not used. In heavier fabric, it is bulky and difficult to do well. It is an awkward method when you are using a flap. For detailed instructions a little easier than the pattern, refer to page 249.

Double welt pockets with organdy

This can be done in any weight fabric with or without a flap. No stitching shows on the right side of the garment.

Pocket Preparation

Make the pocket opening following steps 1-5 described on pages 234-235.

The pattern welt pocket and lining pieces are not correct for this method. Make your own welt pocket and lining pieces.

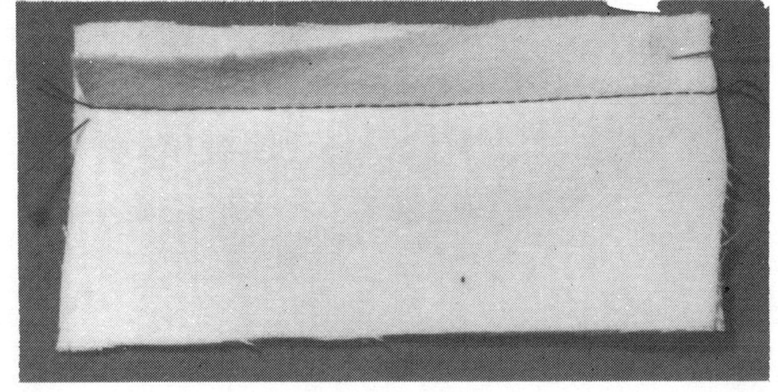

To make the welts, cut two pieces of your fabric 3″ wide and 1″ longer than the finished width of the pocket. Place the right sides together and machine baste 1″ from one edge the length of the strip. Bring the wrong sides together and press. This makes a strip with the baste holding the folds together.

To make a one-piece pocket lining, cut the lining $1\frac{1}{4}''$ wider than the pocket opening and about 10″ in length. A one-piece pocket lining makes a pocket with a fold on the bottom edge. The pocket lining can be cut in two pieces, each about 4″ in length. Cut the lining of lining fabric.

Stitch The Pocket

Place the strip with the narrow edge next to the organdy. Center the fold of the strip under the pocket opening and center the strip so that there are equal amounts on each end of the pocket opening. Pin it in place. Hand baste the upper and lower pocket openings. Refer to and follow hand basting and machine stitching the welts and flaps on pages 235-236. The Double Welt pocket is pictured on the left on page 236.

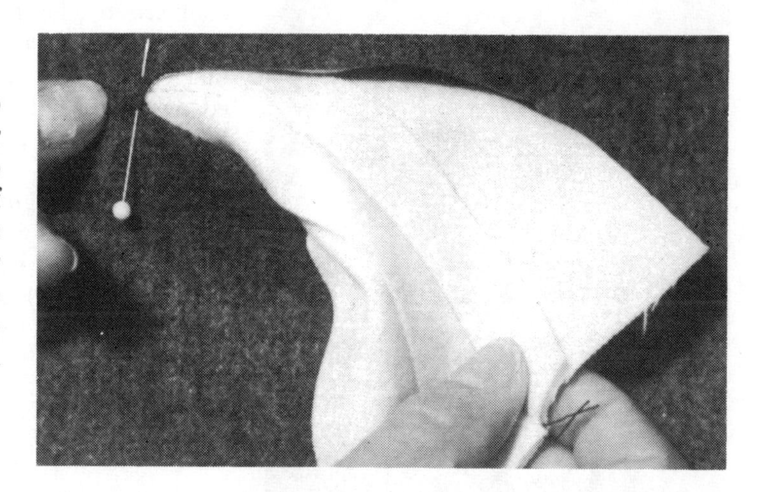

Cord The Pocket

If you want to cord the pocket, do it now. I sometimes cord a double welt pocket if it appears too flat. Cording raises the pocket edges and strengthens them. Slip the cording through the edges of the pocket with a large needle. Several layers of yarn work very well to cord the pocket. The picture of the step-sample has only one edge corded. Normally I would cord both edges.

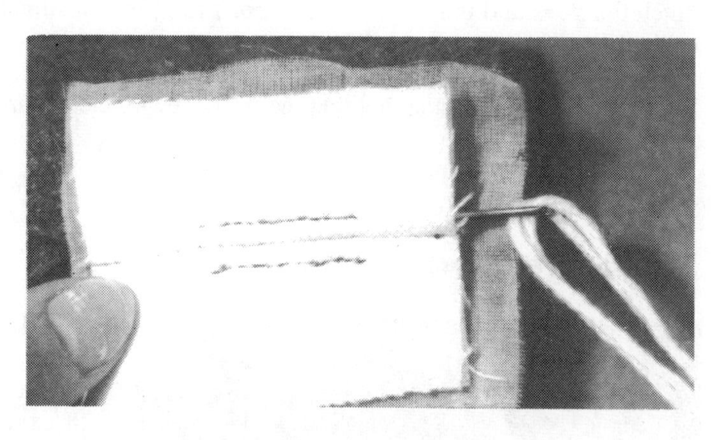

Stitch across the pie ends of the pocket. Hold the threads from both long sides so that they will be caught in the stitching. Tug the garment and the organdy and stitch across the end just to the inside of the first stitching line (toward the garment). Backstitch and cut all the threads.

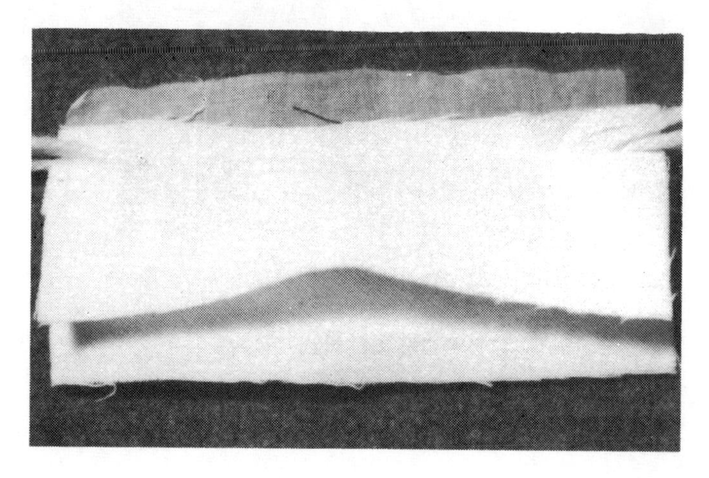

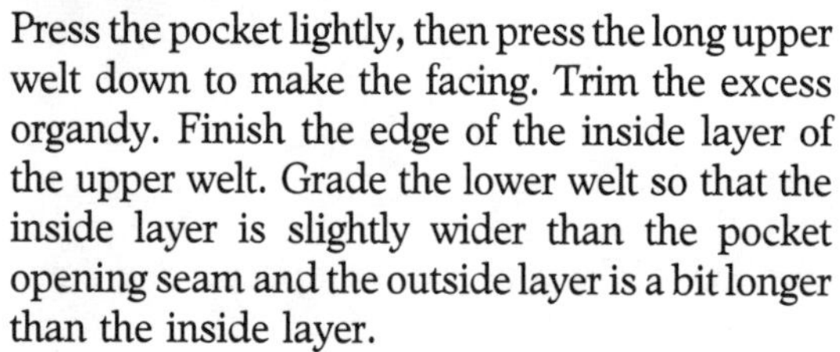

Press the pocket lightly, then press the long upper welt down to make the facing. Trim the excess organdy. Finish the edge of the inside layer of the upper welt. Grade the lower welt so that the inside layer is slightly wider than the pocket opening seam and the outside layer is a bit longer than the inside layer.

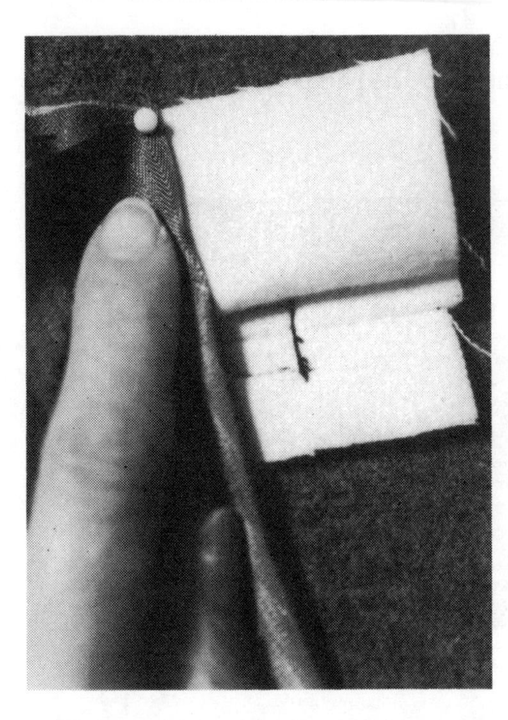

Stitch The Pocket Lining

Stitch the lining pieces or piece to the free edges of the welt — first the upper facing edge and second the lower edge of the welt.

If the pocket lining edges of the two-piece lining are not even when they are lying down in place, trim them.

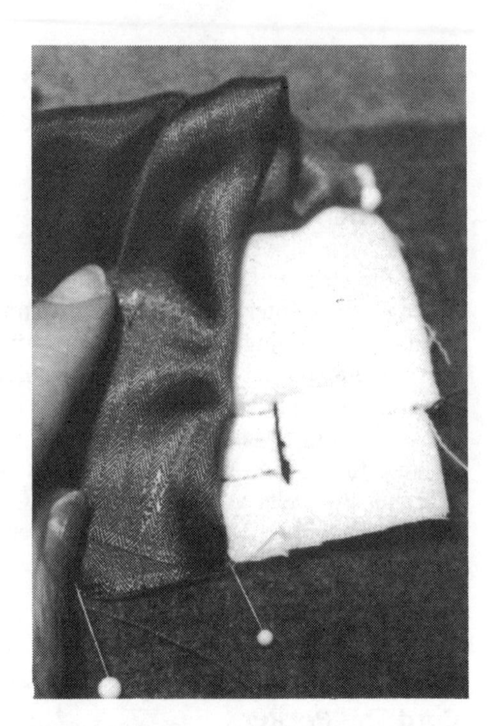

Stitch the sides and the bottom (if it is not a fold) with a straight stitch. Finish the edges with a finishing stitch, or do a French seam, or use the serger.

Wait to remove the basting holding the pocket edges closed until the garment is completed.

Proceed with your garment.

Double Welt Pocket With A Flap

The double welt pocket with a flap is made in much the same manner as the double welt pocket. Do not make the welt until the pocket edges are done. The flap must fit exactly and often is too large if it is done before the pocket edges are finished.

Pocket Preparation

Make the pocket opening by following steps 1-5 described on pages 234-235.

The pattern welt pocket and lining pieces are not correct for this method. Make your own welt pocket and lining pieces.

To make the welt pieces, cut two pieces of your fabric 2″ wide and 1″ longer than the finished width of the pocket. Place the right sides together and machine baste down the middle the length of the strip.

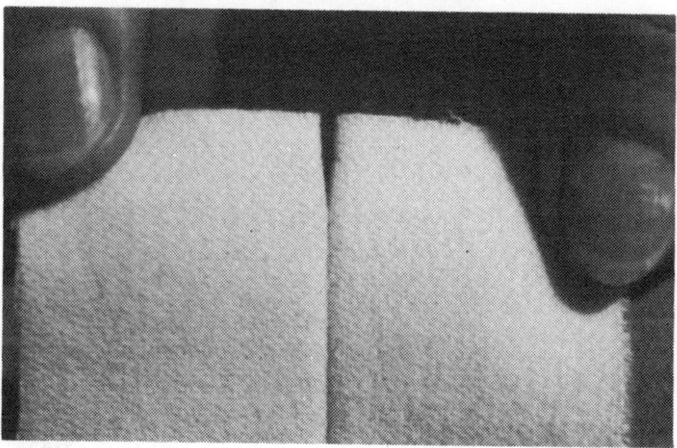

Bring the wrong sides together and press. This makes a strip with the baste holding the folds together for the welt edges of the pocket.

To make the pocket a one-piece lining, cut the lining 1¼″ wider than the pocket opening and about 10″ in length. A one-piece pocket lining makes a pocket with a fold on the bottom edge. The pocket lining can be cut in two pieces, one about 4″ and the other about 7″ in length. Cut the lining of lining fabric.

Stitch The Pocket

Place the welt strip next to the organdy. Center the fold of the welt strip under the pocket opening and center the strip so that you have equal amounts on each end of the pocket opening. Pin it in place. Hand baste the long upper and lower edges of the pocket opening. Refer to and follow hand basting and machine stitching the welt and flaps on pages 235-236. The Double Welt pocket is pictured on the left on page 236.

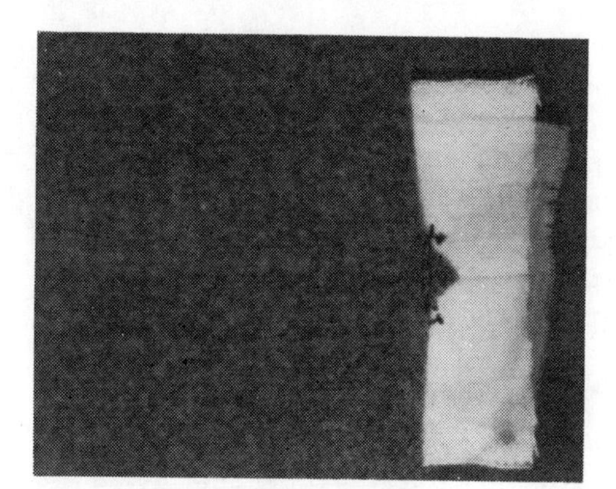

Fold the garment, right sides together, to expose the end of the pocket. Stitch across the pie end of the pocket. Stitch both ends. Hold the threads from both long sides so they will be caught in the stitching. Tug the garment and the organdy and stitch across the end just to the inside of the first stitching line (toward the garment). Backstitch and cut all the threads.

Prepare The Flap

Prepare the flap as the pattern directs but wait to trim the end seams until the welts are in the pocket. Turn the flap right side out and press. If the flap exactly fits the pocket opening, trim and grade the end seams of the flap. If not, adjust it as needed, then trim the edges. Topstitch, if the pattern calls for it or if the fabric needs topstitching.

Center the right side of the flap on the wrong side of the long piece of pocket lining with either a one- or two-piece lining. Pin and then stitch the flap to the lining. press the seam toward the lining.

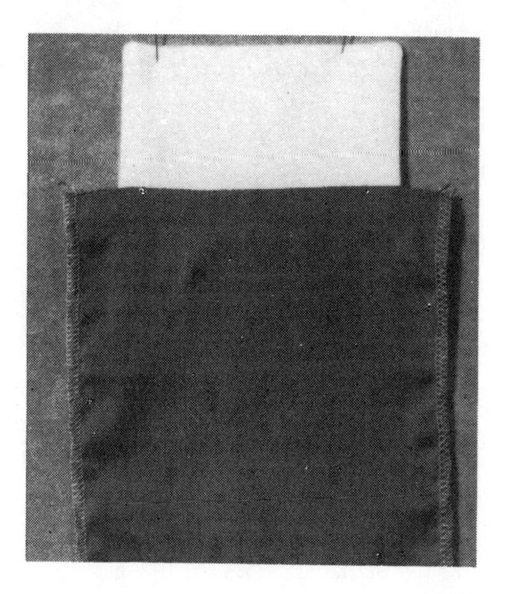

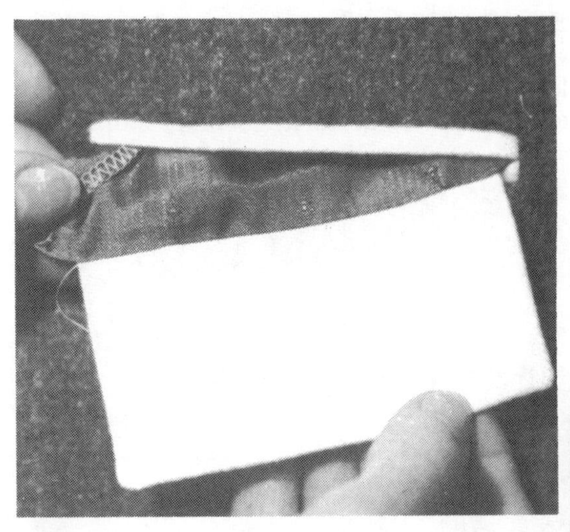

Insert the flap with the lining into the pocket opening. Measure the flap for the correct width and pin in place. Grade the edges of the upper welt.

Fold the lining down so that the fold of the lining is above the upper pocket opening seam allowance and pin. On the right side, hand baste along the upper pocket edge in the well of that seam. You are basting through the lining, the flap, and the pocket opening. Refer to and follow hand basting and machine stitching the welts and flaps on pages 235-236.

Trim any excess organdy. Trim the layer of the lower welt closest to the garment. Cut any tied threads.

Stitch The Pocket Lining

Stitch the free end of the pocket lining, or if you cut two pieces, stitch the small piece of lining to the right side of the free long edge of the lower welt. If the pocket lining edges of the two-piece lining are not even when they are lying down in place, trim them.

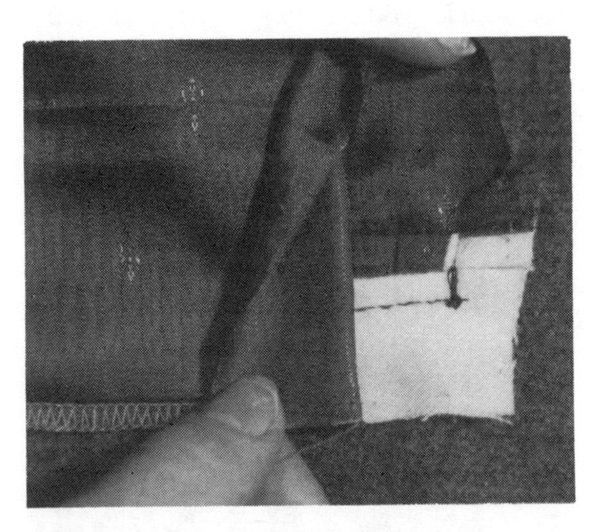

Stitch the sides and the bottom (if it is not a fold) of the pocket lining with a straight stitch and finish the edge with a finishing stitch, or do a French seam, or use the serger.

Proceed with the garment.

Double Welt Pockets Without Organdy

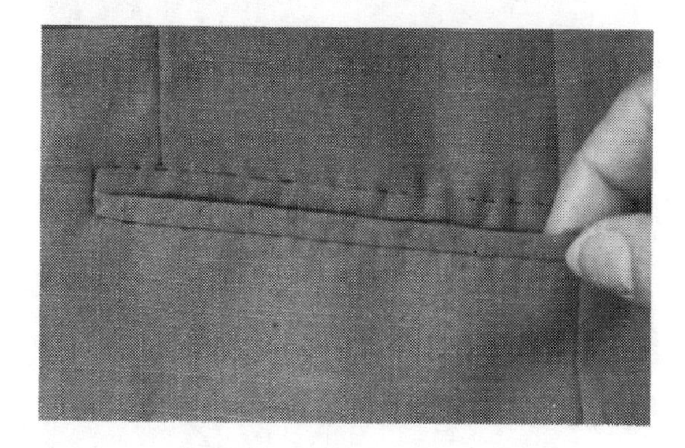

This method works for lightweight fabric when a flap is not used. In heavier fabric it is bulky and difficult to do well. It is an awkward method when you are using a flap. The stitching, either hand or machine done in the well of the seam, does show on the right side of the garment.

Pocket Preparation

Stitch the pocket pieces together as the pattern directs.

Using tape is the easiest way to mark and stitch the pocket location lines. Masking tape can be purchased in 1/4", 1/2", and 3/4" widths. Topstitching tape that pulls off in 1/8" increments works well too.

Put a piece of tape on the wrong side of the welt pocket fabric on the pocket location lines the length, width, and shape of the pocket opening.

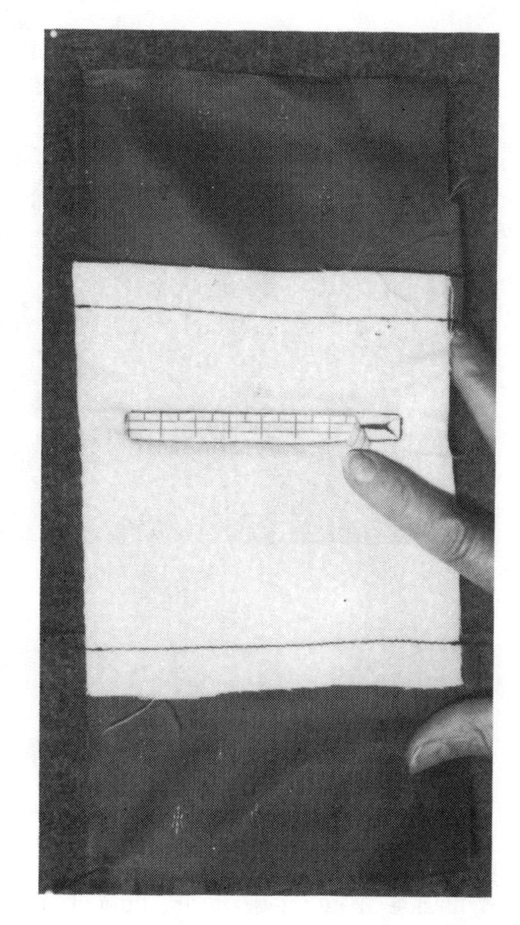

Stitch The Pocket

Stitch around the pocket opening, 15-20 stitches per inch, and overlap the stitches on a long side.

Remove the tape and cut exactly through the center of the pocket opening, stopping about 1/2" short of the ends. Clip diagonally into the corners. Clipping diagonally into the corners makes a little pie on each end. Be careful not to clip the stitching, but you must clip to it.

Since the pocket is pulled over the seam allowance to form the welt edges, it is important that you cut exactly through the center.

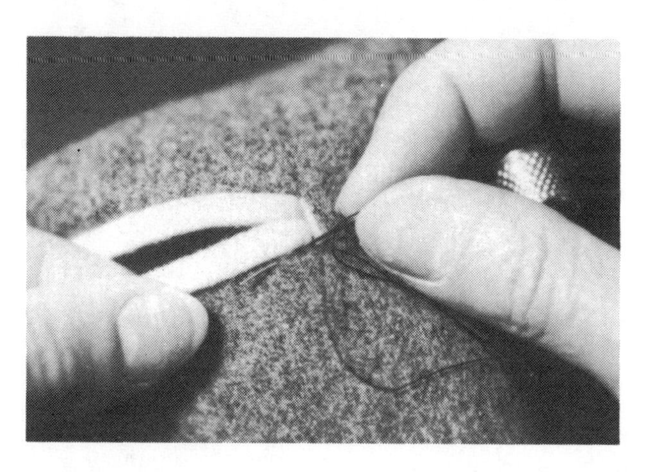

Press the opening to flatten the seam. Turn the pocket to the inside. Fold the fabric snugly over the seam allowance encasing the raw edges to form the welts. Hand stitch the entire length of the pocket opening in the crease of the seam. I don't like to stitch these long edges by machine because the machine stitch shows more than hand stitching on the right side of the garment.

Baste the edges of the pocket together with a diagonal baste stitch, as shown, to hold them in position until the pocket is completed.

Fold the pocket lining down in place and pin to hold it. Fold the garment right sides together, to expose the end of the pocket. Stitch the pie end of the pocket. Refer to page 245 for a picture of the pie end in the stitching position. Be sure you stitch inside the first stitching line (toward the garment).

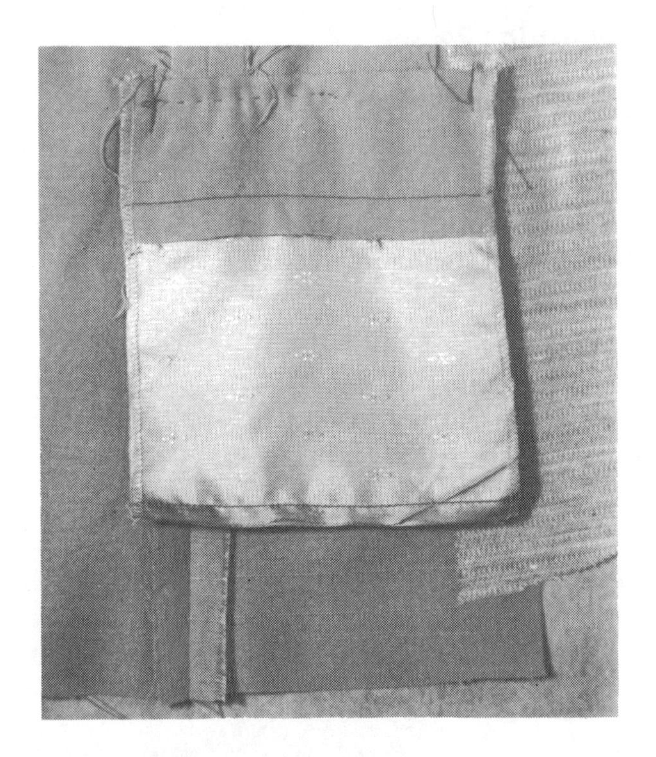

Stitch The Pocket Lining

Then stitch the bottom edges of the pocket together. Press the pocket. If the pocket seems a little insecure at the upper edge, do a second row of stitching on the right side along the seam line through all the layers. The picture shows a hand baste partially done along the upper edge to hold it more firmly.

Proceed with the garment.

Wait to remove the diagonal basting holding the pocket edges until the garment is completed.

Tailoring ■ 8

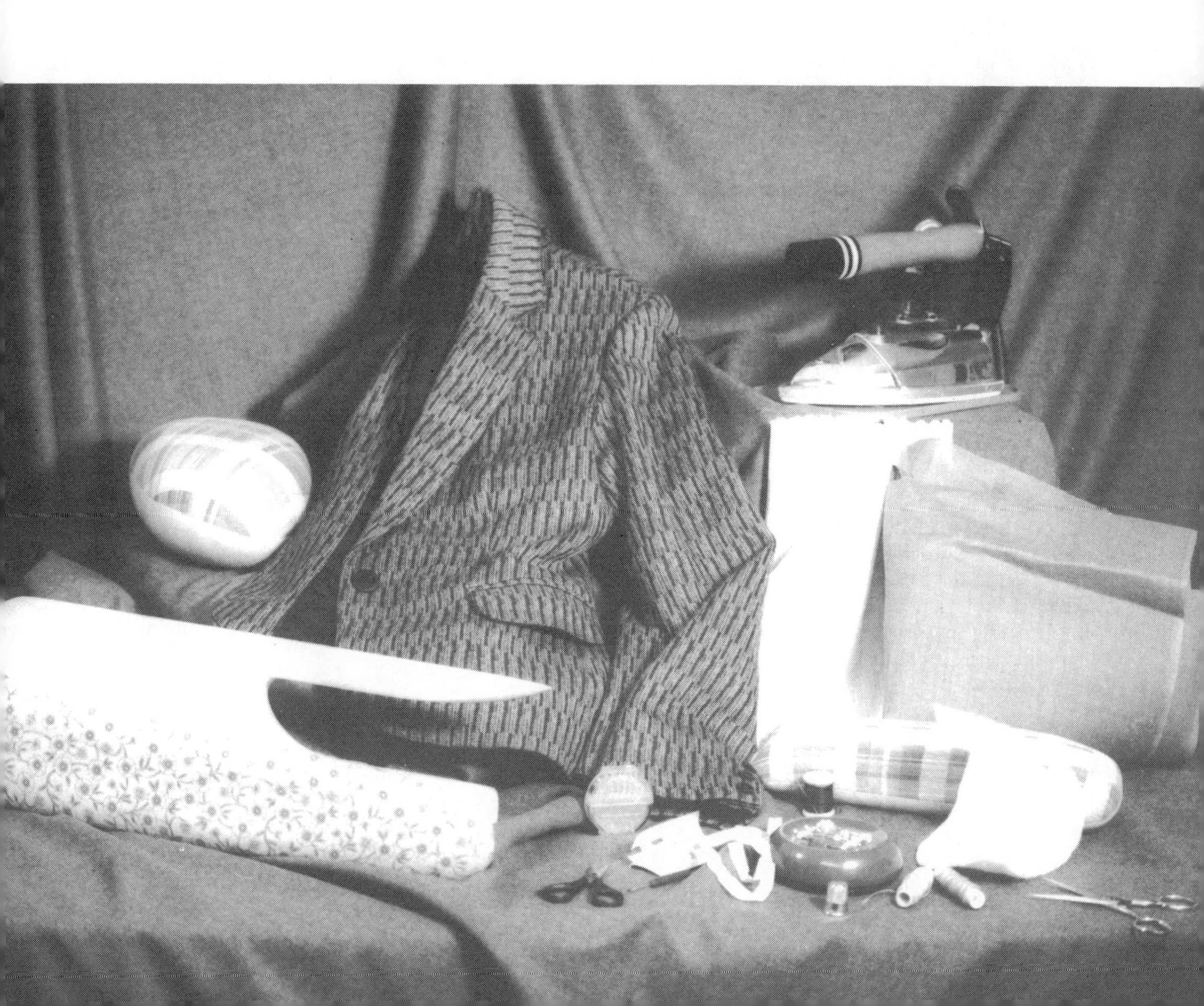

FUSIBLE TAILORING

I recommend this method for inexpensive fabrics and for garments you may want to launder. If you wish to launder the garment, be sure all the fabric and notions are washable. Fusible tailoring uses fusible interfacing which eliminates a lot of hand work. Do patch pockets and machine buttonholes to save time. Use fusible tailoring if the style is trendy and you do not expect to have the garment in your wardrobe very long. I always prefer the couture method if I am working with expensive fabric or expect to have the garment in my wardrobe for several years. If you simply do not have the time to do the couture tailoring, use fusible tailoring.

Supplies Needed For Fusible Tailoring

Pattern, fabric, interfacing, lining, shoulder pads, sleeve rolls, and buttons.

Fashion fabric:

Denim, corduroy, or often a blend of wool/polyester, linen/polyester, silk/polyester, etc.

Linings:

Any lining suitable for the fashion fabric. Refer to Inner Construction, pages 25-27.

Fusible interfacing:

A tailored garment should have interfacing in the armhole seam and needs a back interfacing to cushion the shouder pad and help strengthen the armhole. The garment and sleeve hem shoud be interfaced. Always do a sample of the fusible interfacing with the fashion fabric. It should not feel like a board. I prefer to use a double layer of fusible interfacing on the lapel and the undercollar rather than use a heavy fusible for the entire interfacing. If possible, use a bit stiffer interfacing for the undercollar and the collar stand than was used for the garment. A lightweight fusible or muslin should be used for the back interfacing. Example: Armo weft for the front interfacing, lapel piece, and hems. Fusible Acro for the undercollar and collar stand. Whisper weft for the back interfacing and for the pocket. If you have favorite fusible interfacings, test them with your fabric to make sure they would be suitable for fusible tailoring.

Shoulder pads and sleeve rolls:

Shoulder pads and sleeve rolls can be made or purchased. The shoulder pads pictured in this chapter are purchased. If you prefer to make the shoulder pads, refer to Shouder Pads, page 328. Make the sleeve rolls out of lightweight pellon fleece.

Check the Fit Of The Pattern

Cut the tissue apart and press it. Do any changes you normally do to your pattern. Since the design ease of outer garment patterns varies greatly be sure to check the amount of design ease allowed. I often make a muslin to check the fit, the hang, and the design ease. If you do not choose to make a muslin, check the amount of ease against a basic pattern or a favorite garment of a similar style. Lay the garment or pattern out flat and measure it. Check that measurement against the new pattern. At the very least, pin the tissue together and try it on. Refer to Fitting Your Garments - Pattern Adjustment, pages 6-9.

Adjust The Pattern Tissue

Do any further adjustments to the tissue that are necessary after checking the fit. Also check and change the following pattern pieces.

Undercollar pattern piece

The undercollar pattern piece should be on the bias with a center back seam. The bias helps to mold the collar. A seam at the center back insures the same grain on the ends of the collar. Change the pattern if needed.

Interfacing pattern pieces

The front interfacing pattern pieces for tailoring should include the shoulder and the front armhole.

The back interfacing pattern piece should include the shoulder and the back armhole. If the interfacing pieces (front and back) do not include the entire armhole, add to the pattern pieces. If there is no back interfacing pattern piece, make one. Refer to Couture Tailoring, page 268.

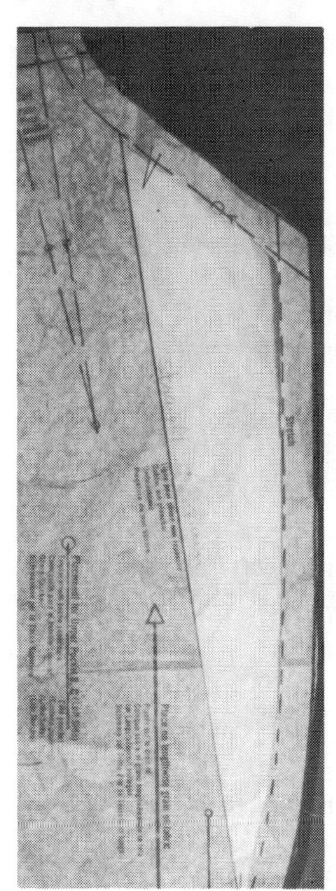

Make a trace of the **lapel**, 3/4″ smaller on the outer edges, and right on the roll line. Use the roll line as the straight of grain on this piece. This is especially important since you will not tape the roll line.

Make a trace of the **under collar** stand 3/4″ smaller on the outer edges and right on the roll line of the collar. Mark a bias straight of grain on the new pattern piece.

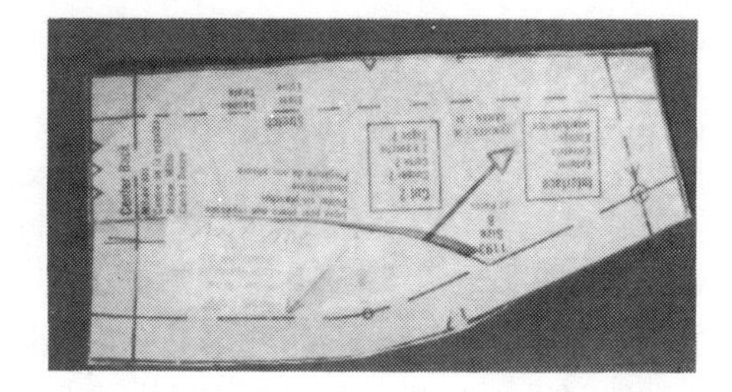

Adjust the lining tissue

If you do any pattern adjustments on the garment be sure that you do the same adjustments on the lining pattern pieces. Don't wait to adjust the lining pattern. It is easier and faster to adjust the lining when you are adjusting the garment.

Check the length of the lining pattern pieces. The lining must be at a minimum of 1/2″ longer than the finished garment.

Sometimes a pattern will be unlined and you want to line the garment. Refer to Couture Tailoring, pages 269-270, for directions to make lining pattern pieces for an unlined pattern.

Preparation For Cutting All The Fabrics

Straighten the fabric. Refer to Grain In Fabric, pages 16-17.

Preshrink the fabric and interfacing. Preshrink interfacing by soaking in warm water for about 10 minutes, drip the water out, lay on towel to dry. Refer to Preshrinking Fabric, page 18.

Cut All The Fabrics

Cut the garment

Refer to Cutting. If your fabric is heavier than those suggested on the pattern envelope, reserve a little extra fabric for the upper collar and the front facings. Check to make sure the pattern is large enough for the turn of cloth before cutting them. Refer to Sample Seams And Pressing Techniques, page 65.

Cut the interfacing

Cut the **front interfacing**. Cut the extra piece for the lapel.

Cut the **under collar interfacing** on the bias. Cut the extra piece for the collar stand also on the bias. Trim the center back seams of the undercollar interfacing. If possible, use a bit stiffer interfacing for the under collar and stand than was used for the rest of the garment.

Cut a **back interfacing** of muslin or lightweight fusible. If the back interfacing is of muslin the center back should be on a fold. If the back interfacing is a fusible and there is a center back seam cut the interfacing with a seam and fuse it to the backs before stitching the center back seam.

Cut **bias strips** 1/2″ wider than the hems of the garment. If you like a soft hem, make them 1″ wider than the hem.

Cut the **pocket interfacing** of lightweight fusible 5/8″ smaller than the pocket around the outer edges and right on the fold line at the top of the pocket. Refer to Fast Patch Pockets, page 224.

Cut the lining

Don't wait to cut the lining. If is easier and faster to do it while you are cutting the garment. If the garment has a back vent, do not cut the excess off the upper side of the vent until the lining is in the garment.

Mark All The Pieces Of The Garment

Garment and lining

Do all the marking called for by the pattern on your fabric, or if the marking would be covered by the interfacing, mark the interfacing.

Front interfacing

Mark the roll line, the center front line below the roll line of the lapel, the big dot at the end of the collar, and the dart if you have one, with a pencil. Refer to Couture Tailoring, page 272. Remove the corners of the interfacing at the neckline. Cut the dart out of the interfacing along the dart lines.

Fuse All The Interfacing Pieces On The Fashion Fabric

Protect your ironing surface with a press cloth. Put another press cloth over the area you are fusing to protect your iron. Be sure your interfacing is placed on the wrong side of the fashion fabric with the fusible side down.

Work at the ironing board. Lay the lapel piece on the lapel of the garment.

Lay your pattern back on the garment to check the placement before fusing.

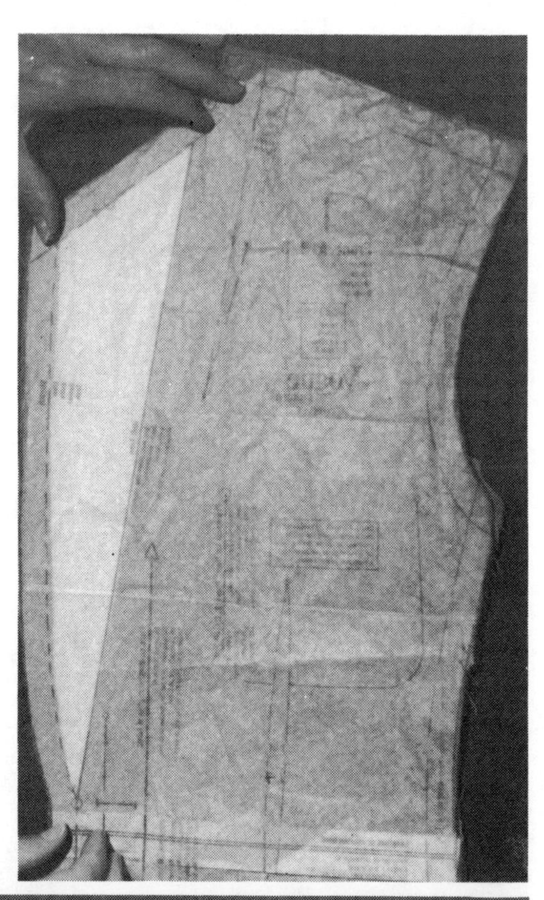

Fuse the front interfacing except the lapel area. Leave it free. Be sure to line up the edges of the shoulder, armhole, and lapel. Lining up everything carefully keeps the dart in the correct location.

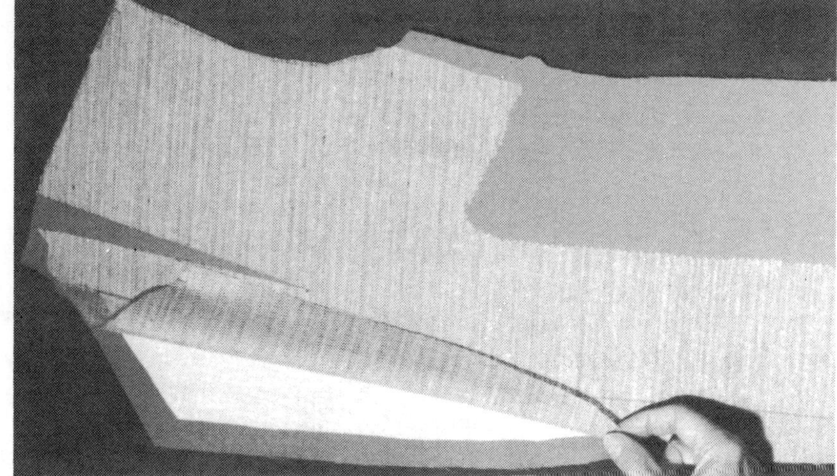

Turn the garment so that the right side is up and lay a folded towel along the roll line. Bring the lapel interfacing up over the lapel and the front and fuse it. Let it cool before moving it. This shaping takes the place of the pad stitching in couture tailoring.

If you are using fusible interfacing for the back, fuse it to each back piece. The picture shows the interfacing fused and the seam stitched and pressed.

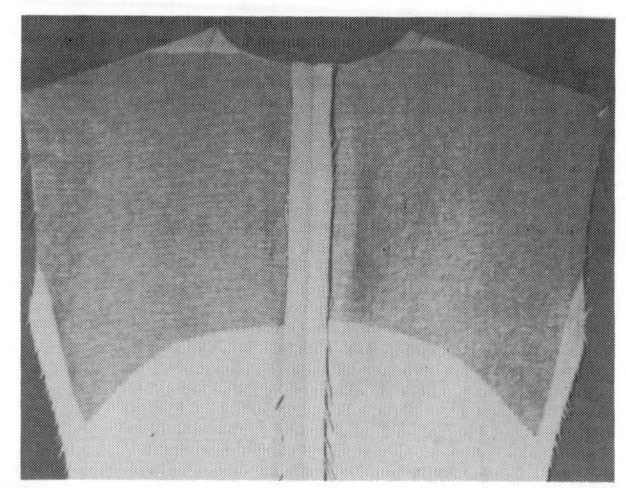

With the under collar in two pieces, fuse the collar stand on the under collar making sure the roll line is exactly on the roll line of the under collar. Check the position by laying the pattern on the under collar as was done on the lapel.

Fuse the complete under collar interfacing over the stand interfacing.

Fuse the interfacing on the pocket pieces. Refer to Fast Patch Pockets, page 224.

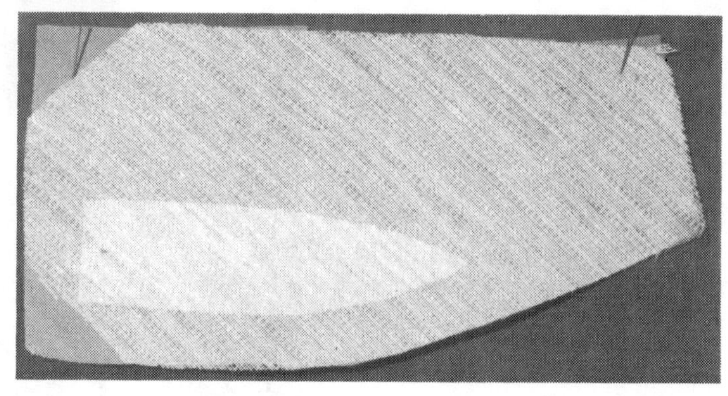

Stitch The Garment

Check the pattern directions. For speed of sewing stitch all the following areas at the same time. Refer to page 273.

- Stitch all the darts on the garment. Use tape along the dart stitching line to get a tapered dart and a nice smooth point. Refer to Couture Tailoring, page 273. Match the dart legs where you have interfaced.

Most darts in tailoring especially those that come from the neckline are cut open until the width of the dart is about 1/4″. The upper part of the dart is trimmed to about 1/2″ and pressed open to reduce bulk. Follow the pattern directions for trimming darts in this manner. **Never clip and trim a waistline dart or seam that will influence the fit of the garment until you have checked the fit.**

- Stitch the center front piece to the side front piece if you have a pattern that has no side seam.
- Stitch the back pieces together (center back seam).
- Stitch the back neck facing to the front facings at the shoulder.
- Stitch the center back seam of the under collar. Match the roll lines. After the seam is pressed open, stitch along the roll line.
- Stitch one seam on the sleeve if you have a two piece sleeve. Do not stitch the vent seam. If there is only one seam, wait to stitch it.

Pockets

If patch pockets are being used, make the patch pockets. Refer to Fast Patch Pockets, page 225-226.

Stitch The Lining

Refer to Couture Tailoring, page 275. If you have a serger, the seams could be serged. Check the fit of the garment first. **Exception:** Set the sleeve in the lining for Fusible Tailoring. At the underarm stitch the armhole seam only 1/4″ deep. Taper from a 5/8″ seam at the notch to a 1/4″ seam at the underarm. This allows enough room for the lining to go up and over the garment sleeve seam without any pulls.

Press All The Seams Of The Garment And Lining Open

If you have shaped seams that need clipping, **do not clip** any seam that will influence the fit of the garment until you have checked the fit.

Shape The Under collar

The fusible interfacing must be shaped before the upper and under collars are stitched together.

Press the collar flat first.

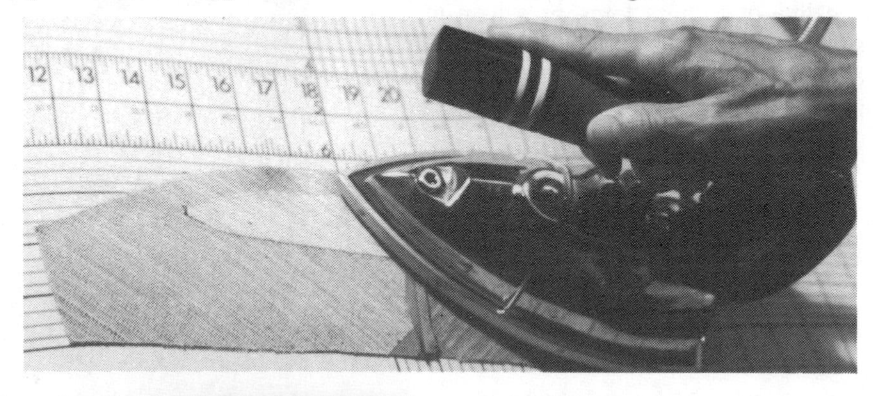

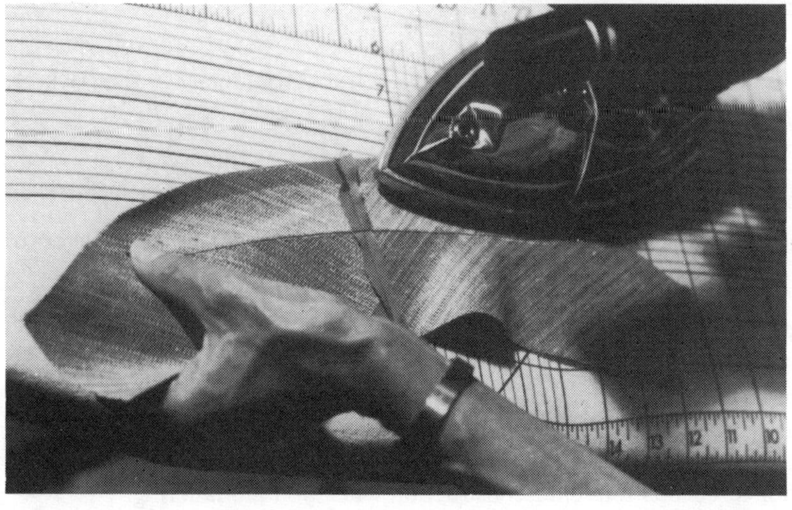

Then stretch the stand (not the roll line) with steam.

Fold the collar on the roll line and press gently stretching the stand.

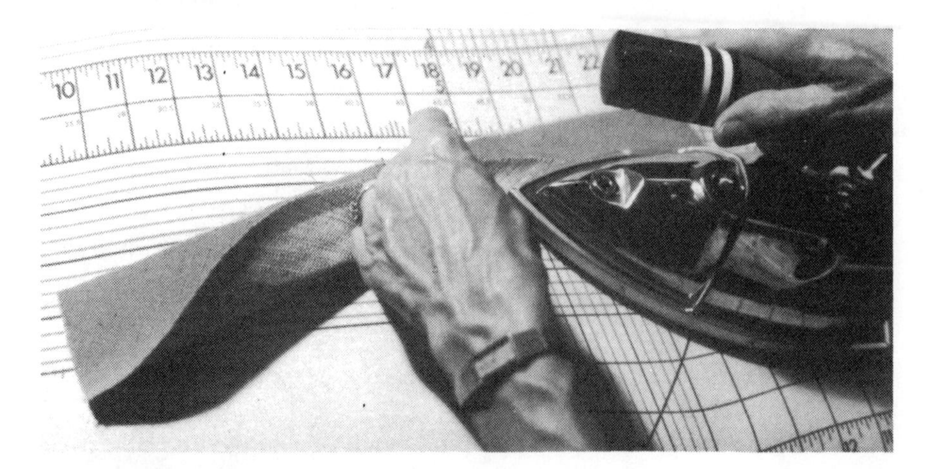

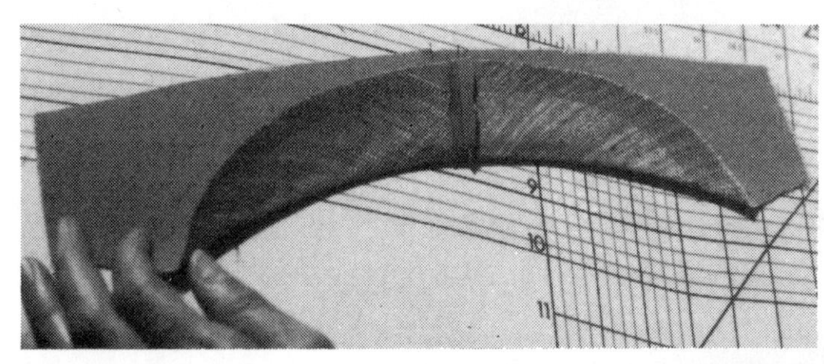

Press until the stand of the collar is shaped and lying flat against the fall of the collar.

While the collar still has steam from the iron in it put the collar around your neck, or the neckline of a dress form, or a ham to let it shape until it cools. Never lay it out flat again. Store the collar rolled until you are ready to use it.

Muslin Back Interfacing

If you are using a muslin for the back interfacing instead of a fusible, staystitch it directionally to the back of the jacket. Refer to Couture Tailoring, page 277.

Pockets

If patch pockets are being used, baste them in place and check the location before the final stitching. Refer to page 230.

Collar Construction In Fusible Tailoring

I like to stitch the collar together, press and turn it before it is attached to the garment. It is much easier to get a well turned collar and to attach it to the garment properly if you have the collar stitched and pressed before attaching it to the garment. Refer to Collars, pages 161-164 for general information on collar construction. Then refer to Couture tailoring, page 283-287 for directions for collar construction when you are tailoring.

Stitch The Garment

Stitch the garment shoulder and side seams. Refer to page 273. **Check the fit.** Try on the garment with the shoulder pads in place. Check the size and shape of the shoulder pads while you have the jacket on to check the fit. If you have a helper, have her mark the pads while the garment is on you. If not, put the garment on a dress form or put a ham in the armhole.

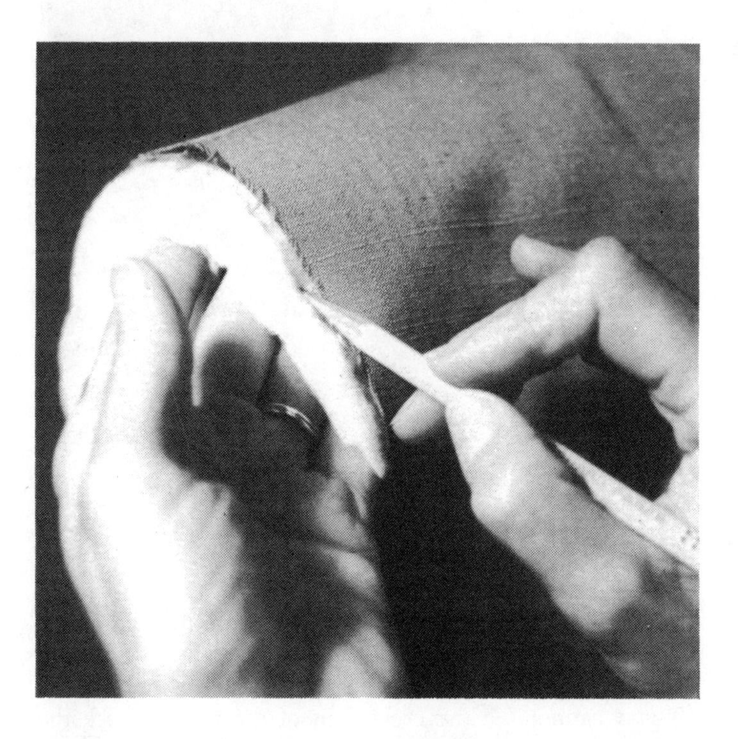

Slip the pad into the armhole so that all the edges of the pad are even with the armhole. Some edges may be extending. Mark the parts of the pad that are extending with a pencil line. Mark the location of the shoulder seam of the garment on the pad with a pencil line deep enough so that it is not lost if you need to trim excess from the pad. Label the pads for the left and right armhole. Remove the pad and trim the excess that was marked. The pad must be curved to fit the shoulder. If needed, pad stitch the pad to hold it in the correct curve. For padding instructions, refer to Shoulder Pads, page 329.

If you are not sure of the sleeve length, pin or baste the remaining sleeve seam. Pin the sleeve to the armhole with the shoulder pad in place and determine the hem turn of the sleeve.

Finish The Sleeves

Fuse the interfacing to the sleeve in the hem area

Measure and lightly crease the sleeve along the hem line.

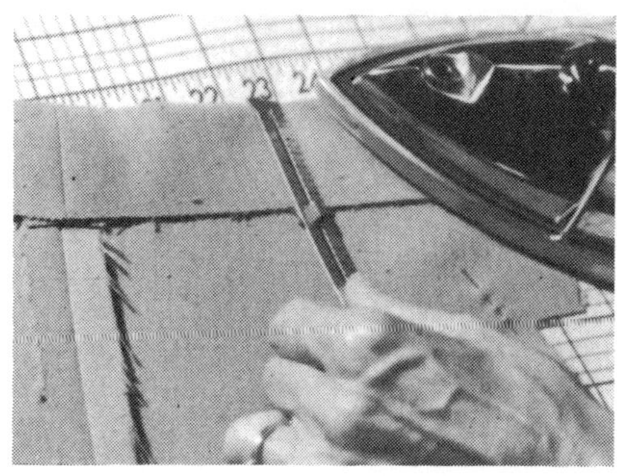

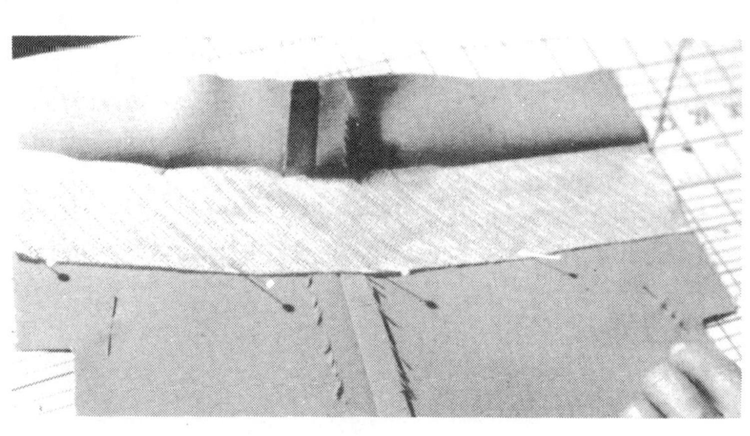

Lay the interfacing on the hemline extending up onto the sleeve body with the fusing side up. If you cut the interfacing wider for a soft hem, extend the interfacing 1/2" into the hem turn.

Shape the bias by holding it with pins.

Lay the hem up over the interfacing and fuse the hem to the interfacing. The fusible interfacing should extend about a 1/2″ beyond the edge of the hem. Any excess fullness of the hem should shrink and be held by the interfacing.

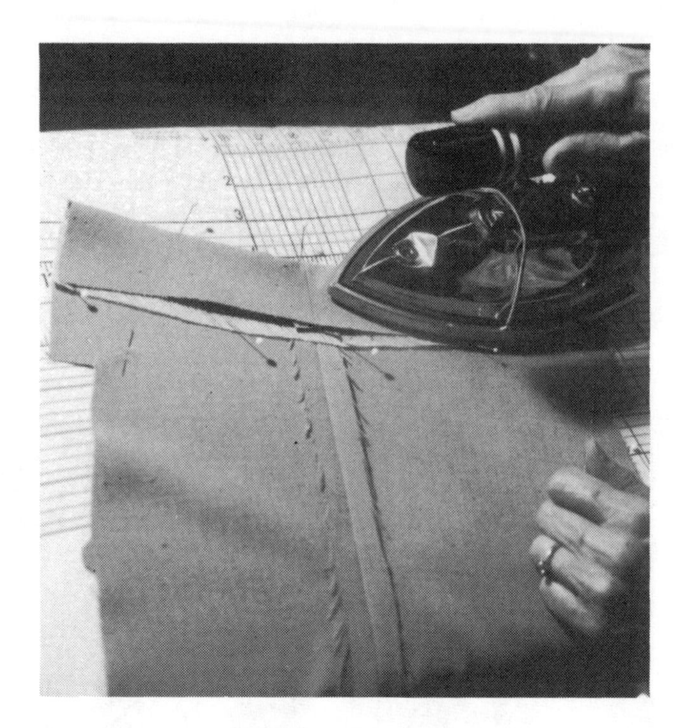

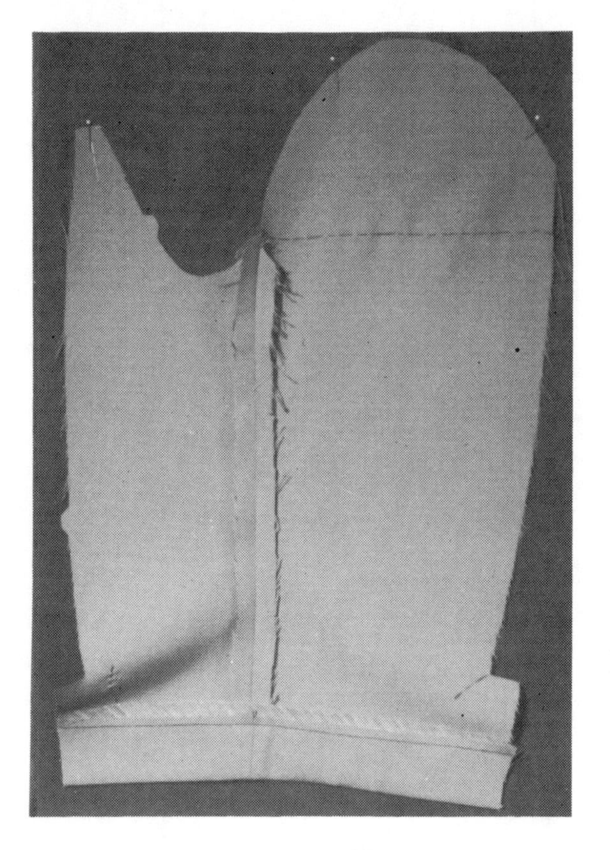

Stitch the hem to the interfacing 1/4″ from the hem edge. You are stitching through the hem edge and the interfacing.

If you cannot see the crossgrain of the fabric, mark the crossgrain line on the sleeve cap with a thread baste line. Refer to Sleeves, page 194.

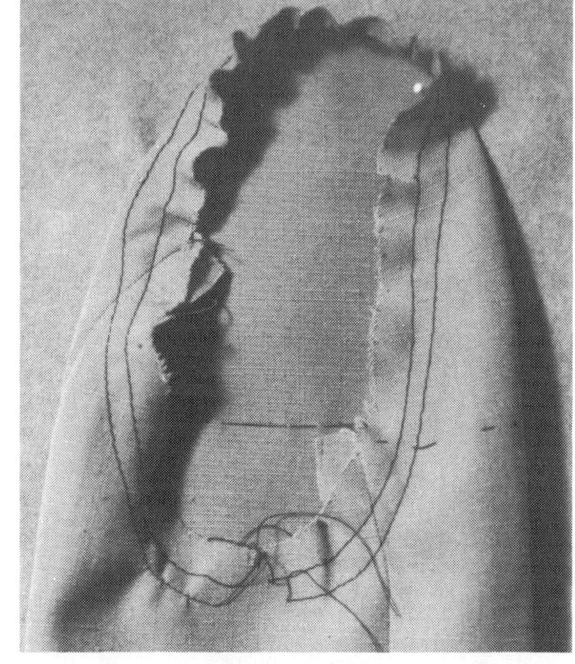

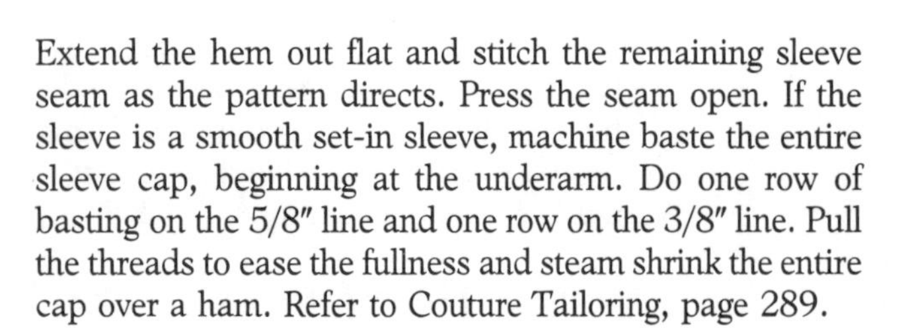

Extend the hem out flat and stitch the remaining sleeve seam as the pattern directs. Press the seam open. If the sleeve is a smooth set-in sleeve, machine baste the entire sleeve cap, beginning at the underarm. Do one row of basting on the 5/8″ line and one row on the 3/8″ line. Pull the threads to ease the fullness and steam shrink the entire cap over a ham. Refer to Couture Tailoring, page 289.

Hem The Sleeve

If you are sure of the length, hem the sleeve. If the pattern calls for mitering, refer to Couture Tailoring, pages 289-290.

Finish the ends of the sleeve hem by marking the hem turn with a pin.

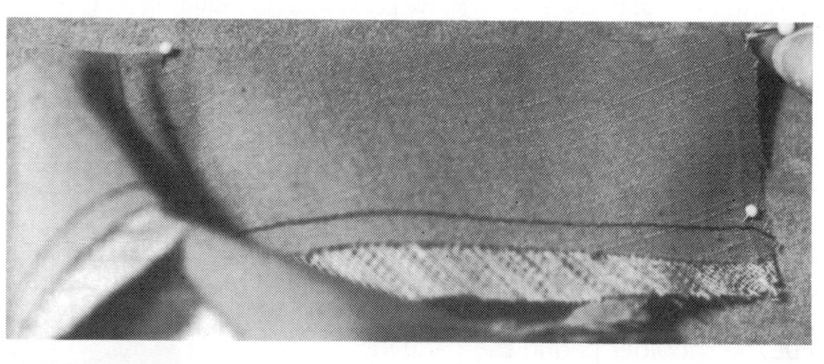

Fold the hem back on itself so the right sides are together and stitch a narrow seam.

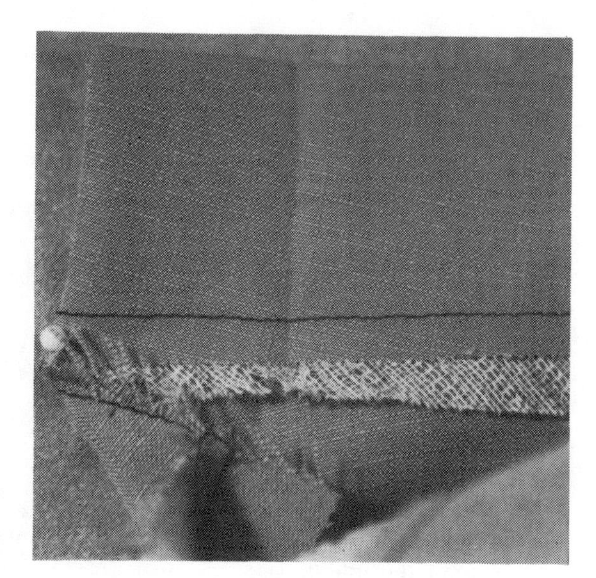

Turn right side out. Push the corners out and press making, sure the seam is to the under.

Hem the sleeve. Refer to Hems, pages 100-101.

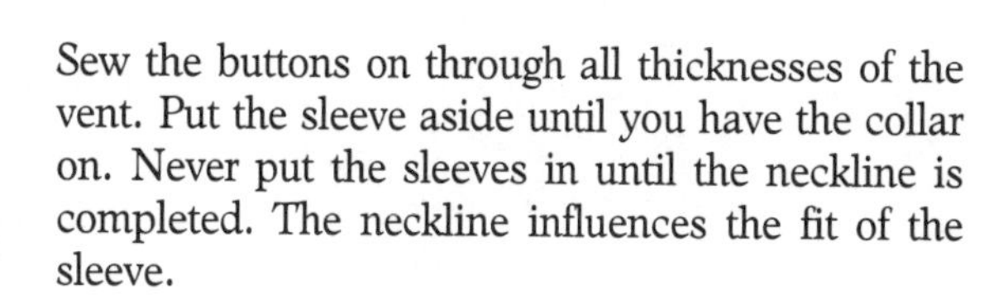

Sew the buttons on through all thicknesses of the vent. Put the sleeve aside until you have the collar on. Never put the sleeves in until the neckline is completed. The neckline influences the fit of the sleeve.

Stitch The Collar And The Facing To The Garment

Method Three:

Refer to Collars, pages 171-179, for general information on attaching the collar to the garment. Then follow the directions for attaching the collar when tailoring in the Couture Tailoring Chapter on pages 291-299.

Prepare To Set In Sleeves

Refer to Couture Tailoring, page 306.

Set In The Sleeves

Refer to Couture Tailoring, page 307.

Put the shoulder pad in the garment

Refer to Couture Tailoring, pages 308-309.

Put the sleeve roll in the garment

Refer to Couture Tailoring, page 310.

The Following Must Be Done Before Lining The Garment

Patch pockets

Patch pockets should be permanently stitched. Refer to Topstitching And Edgestitching, pages 72, 231 and 314.

Hem the garment

Apply the fusible interfacing to the garment hem, measure and lightly crease the garment along the hem line.

Lay the interfacing on the hemline extending up onto the garment body with the fusing side up. If you cut the interfacing wider for a soft hem, extend the interfacing 1/2" into the hem turn. Shape the bias by holding it with pins.

Lay the hem up over the interfacing and fuse the hem to the interfacing. The fusible interfacing should extend about 1/2" beyond the edge of the hem. Any excess fullness of the hem should shrink and be held by the interfacing.

Stitch the hem to the interfacing 1/4″ from the hem edge. You are stitching through the hem edge and the interfacing. Refer to Couture Tailoring, pages 312, for instructions on finishing the front edges of the garment. Refer to Hems, pages 100-101, for a description of the hemming stitch.

Topstitch and edge stitching

Refer to Topstitching and Edgestitching, page 72, Couture Tailoring, pages 305, 314, and Patch Pockets, page 231.

Buttonholes

Do machine buttonholes on the right front of the jacket. Refer to Machine Buttonholes. Or, if you prefer, take it to a tailor when it is finished and have keyhole buttonholes done on it.

Lining The Garment

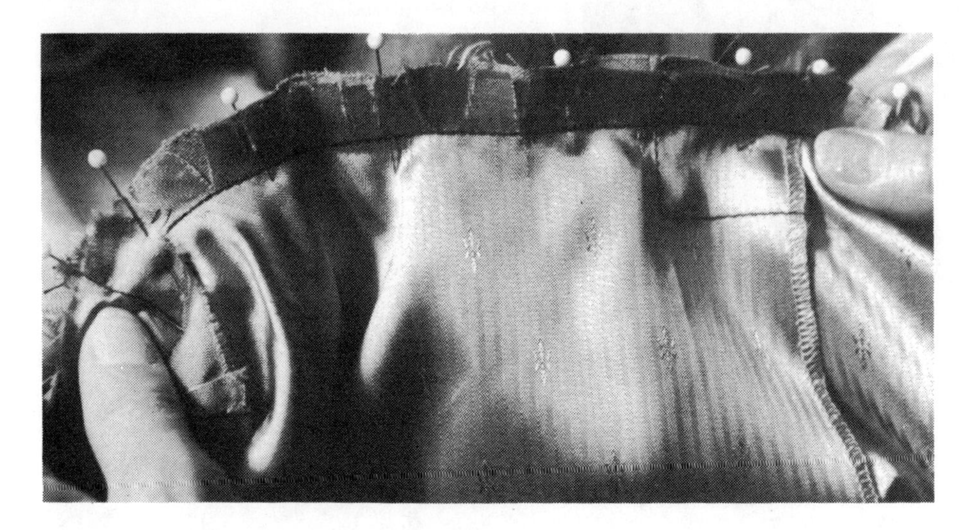

Pin the back lining to the garment's back neck facing. Match the center backs and the shoulder seams. Clip the lining to the stay stitching line until the seams fit. Stitch from the shoulder seam to the shoulder seam.

Lining without a back neck facing

Refer to Couture Tailoring, pages 315-316.

Finishing the collar without a back neck facing

Refer to Couture Tailoring, page 316.

Lay the lining into the garment, slip the sleeve lining into the jacket sleeve. Line up the side seams together, match the notches if you have them, if not, slip the lining up 3/8″ (it was lengthened that amount). Pin the seams together through the lining and the jacket.

Pin up the lining so it is even with the hem turn of the garment at the side seam. Turn up the lining the same amount at the front edge of the lining. Pin the front edges of the lining to the front facing, turn the lining in 5/8″. Keep the crossgrain lines of the lining lying straight so it isn't pulled up or down. Pin the front from the hem to about the armhole.

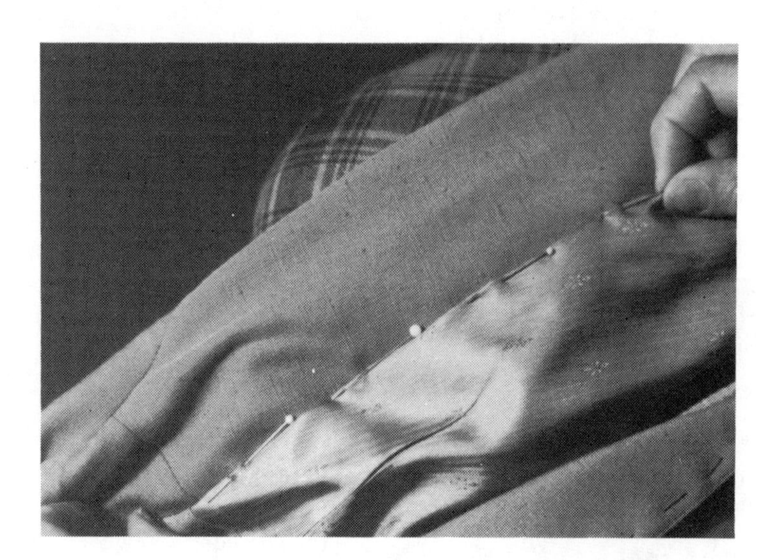

Then place the garment over a ham and continue pinning the lining up to the shoulder seam. Pinning over the ham helps to ease the lining onto the facing in the curved upper area. Check the outside of the garment to see if it is lying okay. (No pulls on the outside of the garment.)

Remove the pins along the side seam. Then pin the lining to the facing from the inside. Slip the first pins out and repin on the wrong side. Repinning in this manner keeps the lining in the correct position.

Machine stitch with the lining up. Leave about 2″ of the lining unstitched at the bottom to finish the hem.

Pin the other front. It is not necessary to pin and check the position of the second front. Measure and match the turn up of the lining (at the bottom front edge) to the first side. Pin the lining to the facing. Pin it flat to the armhole and then over the ham. Check it on the right side to make sure there are no pulls. Repin on the inside and stitch the second front.

Fasten The Lining To The Garment At The Armhole

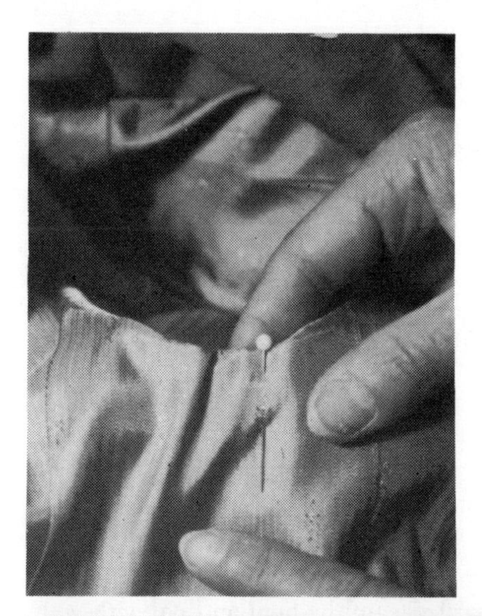

On the inside, lay the lining armhole so that the seam is at the same height as the edge of the seam allowance of the garment. (The lining seam was stitched on the 1/4″ to allow room for it to go up and over the garment seam.)

Tack the lining to the garment on the wrong side of the lining in the seam allowance.

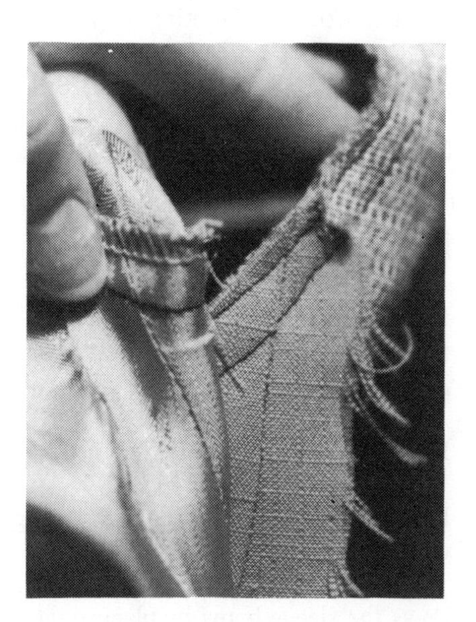

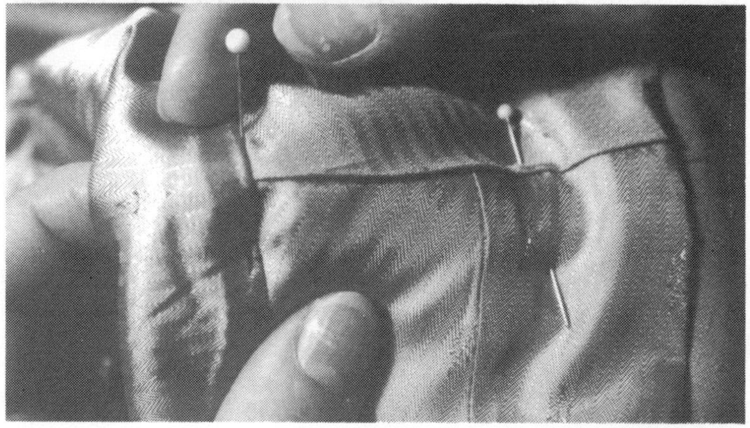

On the inside of the garment and on the right side of the lining line up the lining shoulder seam with the garment shoulder seam. Pin to hold the seams in together.

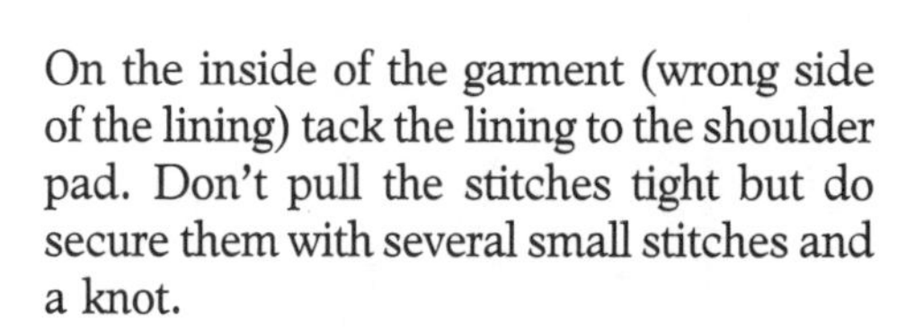

On the inside of the garment (wrong side of the lining) tack the lining to the shoulder pad. Don't pull the stitches tight but do secure them with several small stitches and a knot.

Hem The Lining

Refer to Couture Tailoring, pages 323-325. If there is a back vent in the garment, refer to Couture Tailoring, page 322.

Hem the sleeve

Refer to Couture Tailoring, pages 325-326.

Sew the buttons on

Sew the buttons on the front of the garment with a double thread. Refer to Sewing On Buttons, pages 220-221.

Press The Garment

Do not over press the garment. Press the roll line of the lapel over a towel as you did when you shaped the interfacing. Pressing over a towel keeps it a soft roll as it should always be on a lapel. Refer to Couture Tailoring, page 326.

Press the lining gently to flatten the seam connecting it to the jacket front facing.

Press the lining hem. I almost never press a sharp crease in a hem. Just steam the lining hem and pat the hem with your hand to flatten it.

Press the sleeve hems by placing the sleeve on a sleeve roll or a sleeve board. Steam the hem and pat with your hand to flatten it.

If you feel that you cannot do a professional job with the equipment you have, take the garment to the dry cleaners and have it professionally pressed.

COUTURE TAILORING

Many women who sew do not feel that they can attempt tailoring, especially couture tailoring. The word couture has come to mean fine sewing with special finishing touches usually done by hand. Couture is a custom made-to-fit garment. A ready-to-wear garment, even though expensive, is not couture.

The difference between Fusible Tailoring and Couture Tailoring is hand work. In Fusible Tailoring, the interfacings are fused, the front edges are not taped, and machine keyhole buttonholes and patch pockets are usually done. The lining is stitched together completely and put in the garment by machine. Many purchased garments are constructed in this manner to save labor costs.

In Couture Tailoring, the front interfacings and often the collars are pad stitched and the lapel is taped to shape and retain that shape. Bound buttonholes, welt pockets, and hand work in lining the garment are other touches that make a couture garment very comfortable and long wearing. Couture tailoring is not difficult but it does take time. It is worth the extra effort because you are making a superior garment that will wear for many years. A purchased garment done in this way costs many hundreds of dollars. Some garments do not require all the tailoring techniques included. Combine techniques from Fusible and Couture Tailoring to fit your needs.

Supplies Needed For Tailoring

Pattern, fabric, interfacing (the front interfacing, the sleeve, and the garment hem, are of hair canvas), collar linen or prepadded under collar (for the under collar), muslin (for the back interfacing), lining, and buttons. Other supplies you will need are edge tape, shoulder pads, and sleeve rolls. I make my own shoulder pads. They fit the armhole best. Pellon fleece works well for shoulder pads and sleeve rolls. Lambs wool works well for lightweight sleeve rolls.

Most fabric stores do not carry all the tailoring supplies I have listed. Usually you must purchase edge tape and collar linen from a tailor supply.

Heavy fabrics:

Use the channel method of interfacing in place of the taping. Taping works well for most fabrics but will not hold well in heavy fabrics such as bulky coatings. The muslin channel eliminates the bulk of the hair canvas from the seam line and holds the interfacing secure and makes possible a sharp, fine edge at the front edge of the garment.

To make a channel, you will need muslin the same length as the interfacing pattern piece.

Check The Fit Of The Pattern

Cut the tissue apart and press it. Do any changes you normally do to your pattern. Refer to Fitting Your Garments - Pattern Adjustment, pages 5-8.

Tailoring is an investment of time and often the fabric is expensive, so I take the time to make a muslin of the pattern to check the fit, the amount of ease, and hang of the pattern. To make a muslin, cut the muslin with both sleeves, the under collar, and the length of the pattern. You need not use the facings, hems, or upper collar. Try the muslin on with shoulder pads to check the fit. The ease of outer garments varies greatly. Be sure to check the amount of design ease. If you do not choose to make a muslin, check the amount of ease against a basic pattern or a favorite garment of similar style. Lay the garment or pattern out flat and measure it. Check that measurement against the new pattern. At the very least, pin the tissue together and try it on.

Adjust The Pattern Tissue

Do any further adjustments to the tissue that are necessary after checking the fit. Refer to Fitting Your Garments - Pattern Adjustment, pages 8-9.

Check and change the following pattern pieces, as needed.

Under collar pattern piece

The under collar pattern piece should be on the bias with a center back seam. Change the pattern if needed. The bias helps to mold the collar. A seam at center back insures the same grain on the ends of the collar.

Interfacing pattern pieces

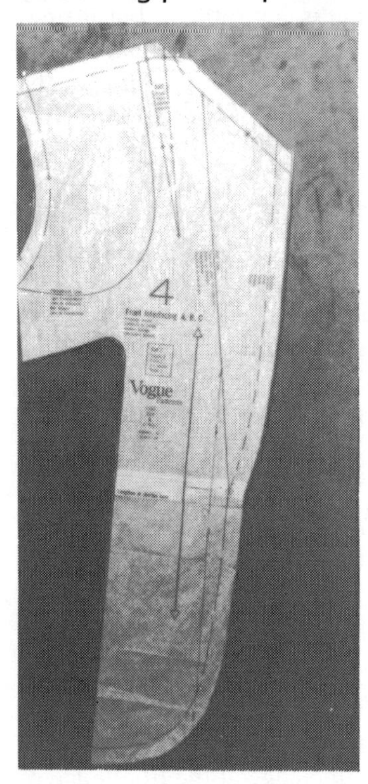

The front interfacing pattern pieces for tailoring should include the shoulder, and the entire armhole shown on the front pattern piece. If your pattern has 5/8" removed around the lapel edge, add it. Often when you are pad stitching you need the extra hair canvas on the lapel to allow for the roll. Trace the center front line and the buttonhole locations from the front pattern to the interfacing pattern.

The **back interfacing pattern** piece for tailoring should be on a fold at the center back. It should include the shoulder and the entire back armhole. If there is no back interfacing pattern piece, make one by tracing the back pattern in the same areas as shown here for a back interfacing. The interfacing should be from 4-7" long at the center back and 2½" deep at the armhole.

If the interfacing pieces, front and back, do not include the entire armhole, add it to the pattern pieces. If there is no side seam, add to the back pattern piece as shown in the picture. Lay the interfacing on the corresponding pattern, add tracing paper, and extend the interfacing to the front armhole. Make the interfacing about 2½" wide at the underarm.

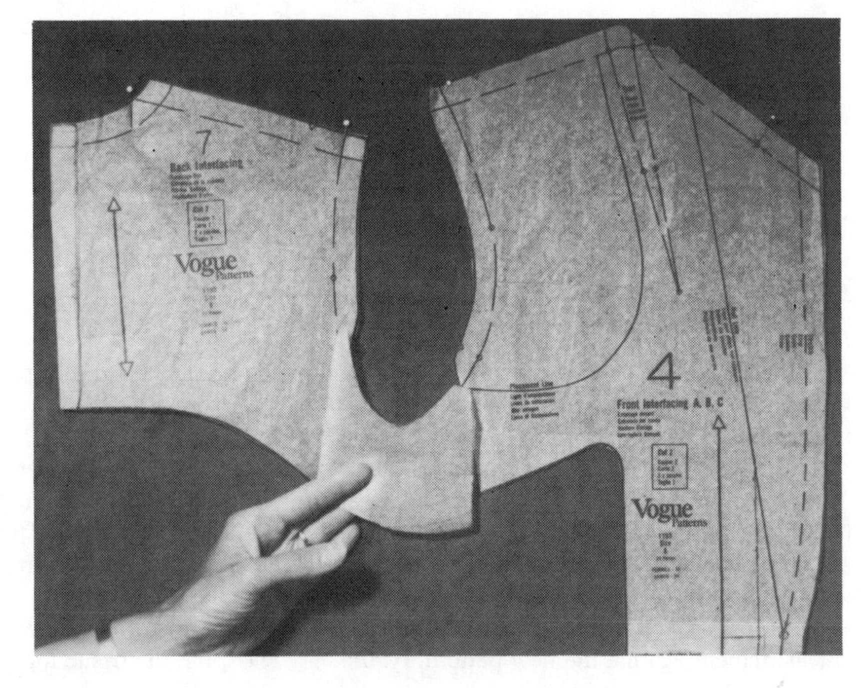

If you neglect adding interfacing to the entire armhole, it can be strengthened by adding a narrow tape to the armhole area that is not interfaced after the sleeve is stitched in. It will not wear as well as a garment that has an interfaced armhole.

Adjust the lining tissue

If you do any pattern adjustments on the garment, be sure that you do the same adjustments on the lining pattern pieces. Don't wait to adjust the lining pattern. It is easier and faster to do the lining now.

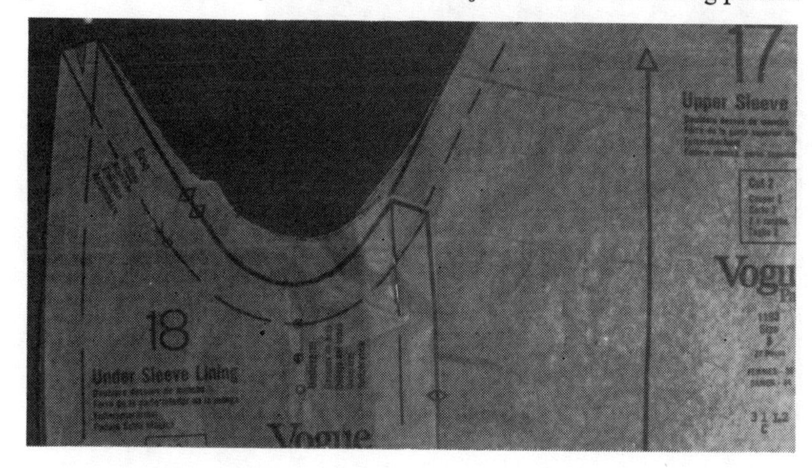

Also raise the sleeve lining 3/4" higher at the underarm only. The lining must go up and over the sleeve underarm seam so it needs the extra length.

Check the length of the lining pattern pieces. The lining must be a minimum of 1/2" longer than the finished garment.

Making Lining Pattern Pieces For An Unlined Pattern

Sometimes a pattern will be unlined and you want to line the garment. To make lining pattern pieces, copy the tissue as follows.

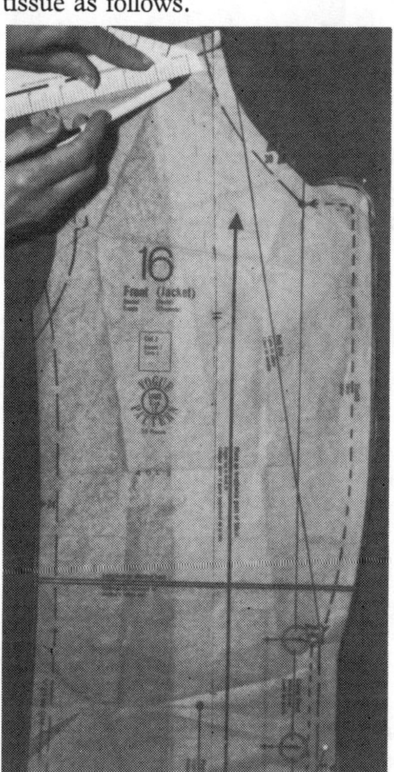

Front pattern

Lay the front facing under the garment front. Fasten the pieces to a flat surface to keep them from slipping.

Mark a cutting line for the lining $1\frac{1}{4}$" (two seam allowances) from the edge of the facing toward the front edge of the pattern in a straight line from the hem to about the bustline. Allow a 3/4" tuck (for ease in the bust area) at the shoulder. Join the marking at the shoulder (close to the neckline) to the cutting line you drew from the bust to the hem.

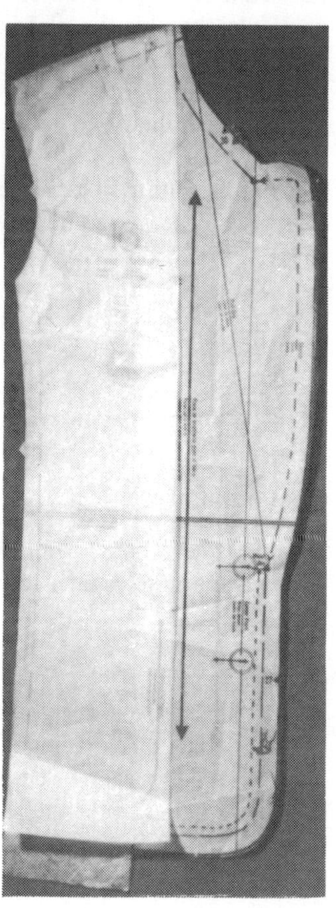

Lay tissue or tracing paper over the front pattern piece. Trace the straight of grain line and the cutting line for the lining from the pattern piece on the tracing paper copy. Mark the 3/4" tuck in the center of the front shoulder.

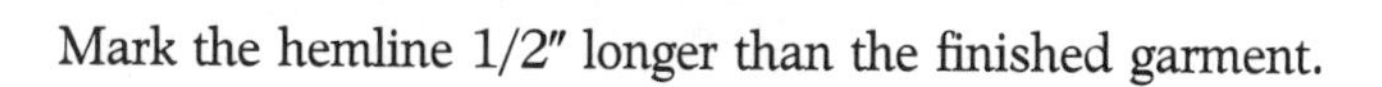

Mark the hemline 1/2" longer than the finished garment.

Cut out the lining pattern piece following the lines you have marked and the pattern edges where you have not marked. This is your front lining pattern piece.

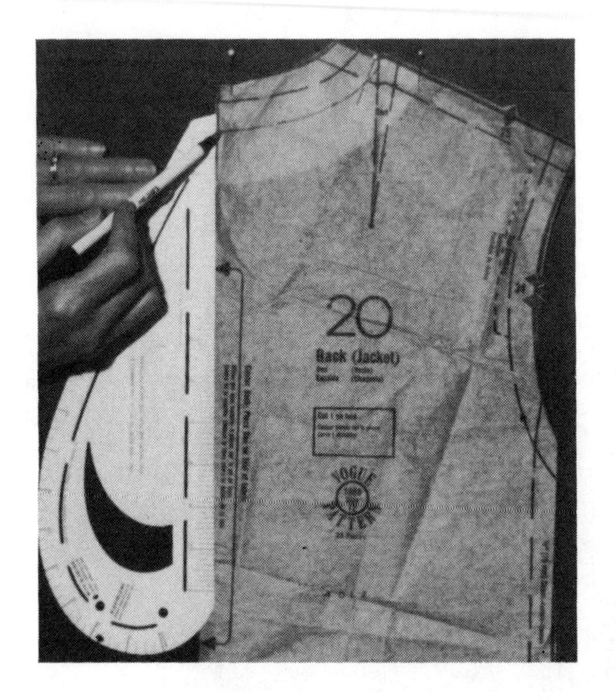

Back pattern

Lay the back neck facing under the back pattern piece. Mark a cutting line 1¼″ from the facing edge toward the neckline and shoulder. This is a curved line.

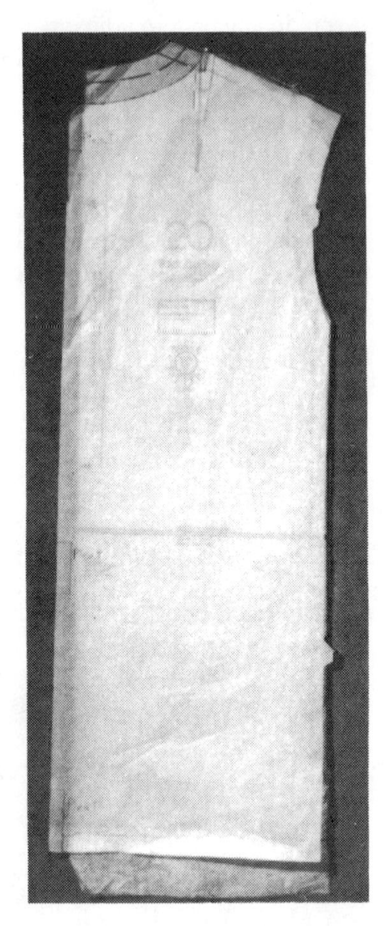

Lay tissue or tracing paper over the back pattern piece. Allow extra room at the center back to add a back pleat at the center back seam. Add a 1/2″ pleat for jackets, 1″ for coats, to the center back. Make the center back a fold unless the seam is very curved or you have a back vent. In that event you would need a seam plus the pleat. If you have shoulder darts, trace them on your copy. If the center back is not on a fold, trace the straight of grain line. Trace the cutting line for the lining from the pattern piece on the tracing paper copy. Mark the hemline 1/2″ longer than the finished garment.

Cut out the lining pattern piece following the lines you have marked and the pattern edges where you have not marked. This is your back lining pattern piece.

Side pattern pieces

Use the side pattern pieces as the pattern piece for the lining but shorten it so it is 1/2″ longer than the finished length of the garment.

Sleeve pattern

Use the sleeve pattern but shorten the pattern so it is 1/2″ longer than the finished length of the sleeve. Raise the sleeve armhole, refer to page 269.

Raglan Coats

Always use a back neck facing. If the pattern does not use one, adapt the pattern so that it has a back neck facing. A back neck facing is the same width as the front neck facing and always is on a fold at the center back. Lay the raglan pattern pieces together and make a trace of the top portion. Remove that amount from the top of the lining pattern plus the seam. Mark a cutting line for the lining. Refer to lining pattern pieces for an unlined garment, page 269.

Preparation For Cutting All The Fabrics

Straighten all the fabric. I have had poor results when attempting to straighten hair canvas. If the crossgrain of the hair canvas is crooked, leave it alone. Refer to Grain In Fabric, pages 15-17.

Preshrink all the fabrics. Preshrink the hair canvas by soaking in warm water for 10 minutes, and spinning the water out in the washing machine or by letting it drip dry. Do not dry hair canvas interfacing in the dryer. Preshrink the lining by pressing with a steam iron. Refer to Preshrinking Fabric, page 18.

Cut All The Fabrics

Cut The Garment

I do cut the notches outward when tailoring on both the garment and the lining. In construction you use the notches to match the lining to the garment.

If you are underlining, cut the underlining. Refer to Inner Construction, page 20.

If your fabric is heavier than the fabrics suggested on the pattern envelope, reserve a little extra fabric for the upper collar and the front facings. You will want to check and make sure the pattern is large enough for the turn of cloth before you cut them. Refer to page 65.

Upper collar

The upper collar is usually cut on the fold of the fabric. For a special fit or in unyielding fabric, it can be cut on the bias. I usually prefer to cut it on the crossgrain. Sometimes, if the fabric is soft, a bias upper collar will show ripples. The upper collar has to be cut larger than the under collar. The amount varies with the thickness of the fabric and the shape of the collar.

Cut The Interfacing

Cut the **front interfacing** pieces of hair canvas. Remove the corners of the interfacing at the shoulder/neckline junction.

Heavy fabrics

Use the channel method of interfacing in place of the taping. Cut the front interfacing of hair canvas. Remove the corners of the interfacing at the shoulder/neckline junction. Cut the channel of muslin 1½″ wide, the same grain as the front interfacing. Refer to page 274. Go 1″ beyond the big dot that marks the collar junction.

Cut the **back interfacing** of muslin or lightweight interfacing, **not** hair canvas. Remove the corners at the neckline/shoulder junction. Do not cut a back interfacing if you are underlining.

Cut **bias strips** 1/2″ wider than the hem for the sleeve and garment hem or use the pattern pieces if they are provided. If you like a soft hem, make the strips 1″ wider than the hem.

Cut enough **edge tape** to reach from the big dot at the neckline to the hem line of the garment and from the dot marking the bottom of the lapel roll line to the shoulder line plus a little extra. Measure the edge tape along the front seam line. Preshrink in hot water and let the edge tape dry.

Cut the **under collar** on the bias of collar linen instead of hair canvas. Trim the center back corners of the linen, removing it 1/8″ inside the sewing lines. Refer top page 272. This prevents it from turning back with the seam and making a lump. If using prepadded felt/collar linen, cut the under collar on the bias. A center back seam can be used but often the under collar is on the fold.

Cut The Lining

Don't wait to cut the lining. It is easier and faster to do it now. Cut notches in the lining as they were cut on the garment. The notches make it easy to match the seams of the lining to the seams of the garment which helps to get the lining set in the garment without any pulls.

If the garment has a back vent, do not cut the excess off the upper side of the vent until the lining is in the garment.

Mark All the Pieces Of The Garment

Garment and lining

Do all the marking called for by the pattern on your fabric. Refer to Marking, pages 39-45. If you are setting in the sleeve without any help, mark the crossgrain line with a hand baste line. This will help you get the sleeve to hang properly. Refer to Sleeves, pages 193-194.

Any marking that will be covered by the interfacing pieces should be marked with pencil on the interfacing instead of the fashion fabric.

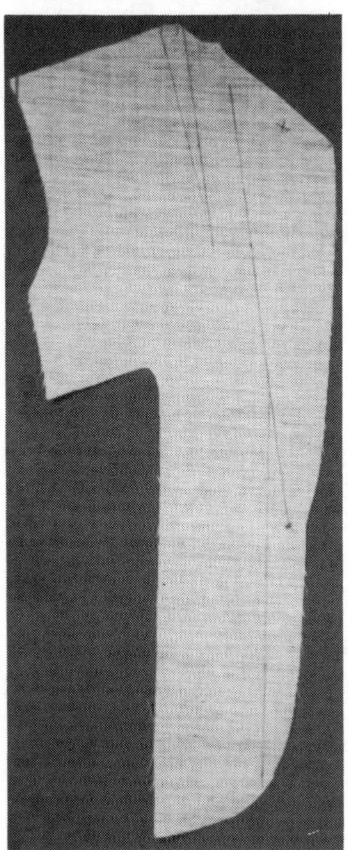

Front interfacing

Mark the roll line, the center front line, the big dot marking the collar junction, and the darts. Mark the darts on the interfacing by drawing the dart leg lines.

Back interfacing

Mark the darts by drawing the dart leg lines.

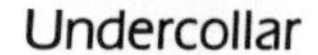

Undercollar

On the linen, mark the roll line as indicated on the pattern. Mark the 5/8" stitching lines on all edges. If you are machine padding, mark the padding design as shown. Stop them 1/8" from the seam allowance.

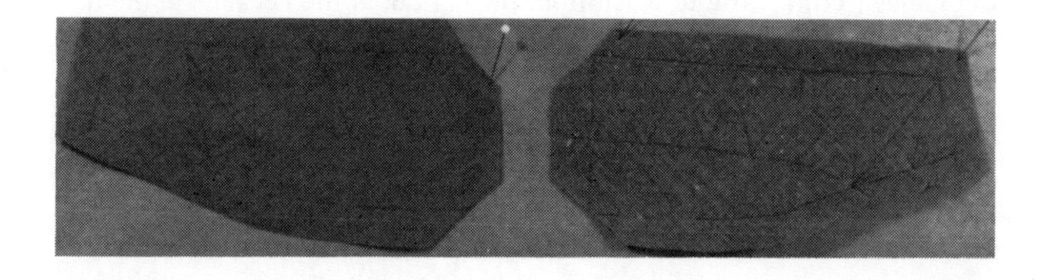

Bound Buttonholes And Welt Pockets

If you are doing bound buttonholes or welt pockets, do a sample buttonhole or pocket through the fabric and the interfacing. If the sample is too heavy to turn nicely, do a sample without the interfacing. Buttonholes and welt pockets are stronger with the interfacing included, but it is better to do them without the interfacing if it is too heavy to turn nicely. If the buttonhole or welt pocket sample looks better without the interfacing, do them on the appropriate jacket fronts before the interfacing is applied. If the buttonhole and the welt pockets are fine with the interfacing, wait to do them until the interfacing pieces are on the jacket. Refer to Bound Buttonholes, page 214, and Welt Pockets, page 232.

Stitch The Garment

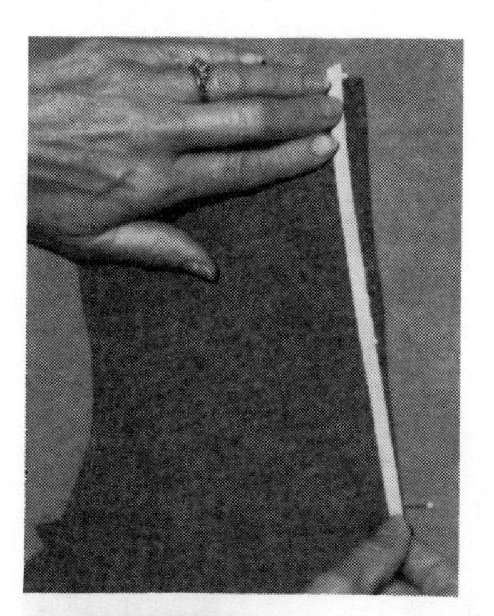

- Stitch all the darts on the garment.

  Use tape along the dart stitching line to get a tapered dart and a nice smooth point. Stitch the dart and remove the tape.

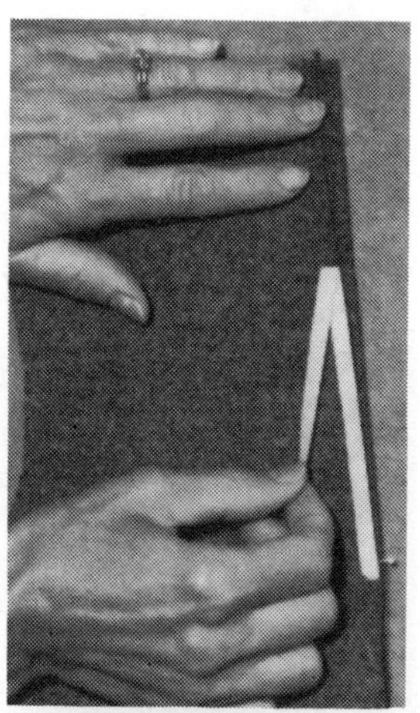

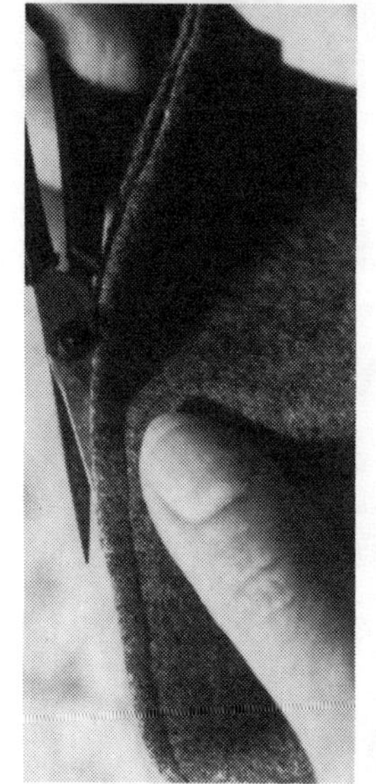

Most darts in tailoring, especially those that come from the neckline, are cut open until the width of the dart is about 1/4". The upper part of the dart is trimmed to about 1/2" and pressed open to reduce bulk. Follow the pattern directions for treating darts in this manner.

Never clip and trim a waistline dart or seam that will influence the fit of the garment until you have checked the fit.

Pin baste before stitching seams

I rarely baste a seam unless I am unsure of the fit. I do pin baste all seams before basting or stitching. I often pin baste to try on the garment by placing the pins on the seam line vertically.

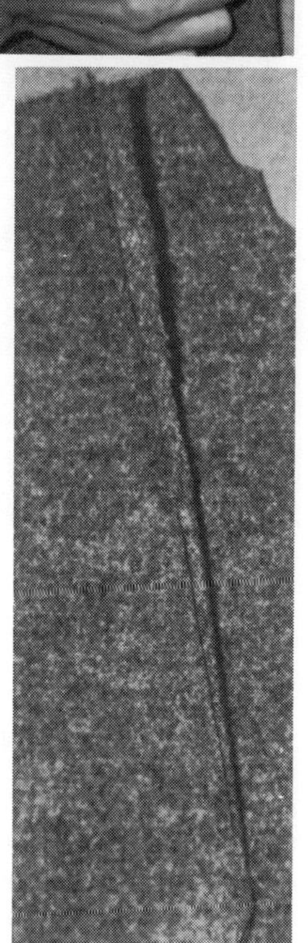

Lay both layers of fabric together on a flat surface, preferably one to which you can fasten the fabric. Example: Padded table, cutting board or an ironing board. Match the top and bottom edge of the seam with the two seam allowances lying even. If the seams are angled, match the seam junctions instead of the edges. Pin the layers to your working surface so they are taut. Pin from one end to the middle of the piece. Pin the opposite end to the middle. Insert the pins into the seam allowance with the head of the pin toward the seam. Having the pin head toward the seam facilitates removing the pins quickly as you sew. On straight seams, pin about every 6". On curved seams, pin more closely.

- Stitch the center front piece to the side front piece if you have a pattern that has no side seam.
- Stitch the back pieces together (center back seam). Do not stitch the fronts to the back.
- Stitch the back neck facing to the front facings at the shoulder.
- Stitch one seam on the sleeve if you have a two-piece sleeve. Do not stitch the vent seam. If there are is one seam, don't stitch it until the interfacing is applied to the hem area of the sleeve.

Press All The Seams Open

If you have shaped seams that need clipping, do not clip any seam that will influence the fit of the garment until you have checked the fit of the garment. Refer to Pressing Techniques, pages 66-67.

Pockets

If patch pockets are being used, make the patch pockets. Baste them in place and check the location before the final stitching. Refer to Couture Patch Pockets, page 227.

Stitch The Interfacing Pieces

Slash all the darts in the interfacings down the center. Overlap until the dart legs match and stitch with a step zigzag stitch. Reinforce the point of the dart with a small piece of muslin. Glue stick the muslin in place, then stitch. Trim the excess fabric from along the zigzag stitching line.

Heavy fabrics

Use the channel method of interfacing in place of the taping. Staystitch (one layer of fabric) the muslin strip on the 1/2" and the 5/8" line from the lapel edge. Press. Then lay it onto the hair canvas interfacing with the outer edges even and stitch on the 7/8" and 1" line from the outer edge through both thicknesses. Press. Trim the hair canvas out of the seam line. **Do NOT trim the muslin.**

Stitch bias hem pieces together if needed by lapping them on the straight of grain and stitching through the two layers with a step zigzag. Refer to page 311. Trim any excess fabric to the stitching line.

Stitch The Lining

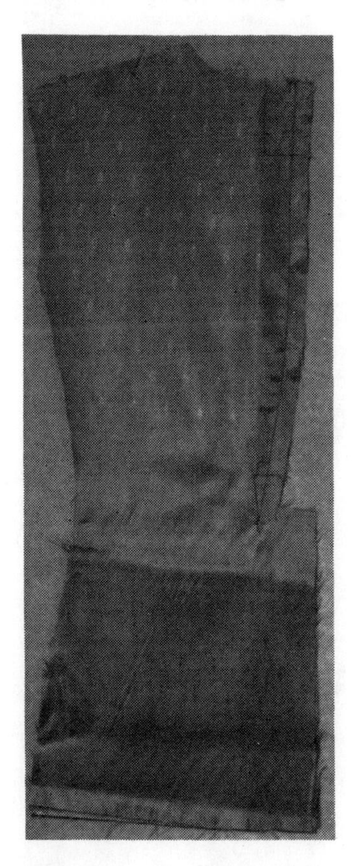

Secure the pleats at the center back by stitching tucks on the wrong side of the lining at the neckline, the waistline, and the hem line. Omit the waist tuck in very loose garments. Press the back pleat to the left.

Secure the pleats in the bust area in the same manner. Press the front pleats toward the center.

Stitch all seams in the lining. **Do not** set the sleeve into the lining.

If no back facing is being used, leave two inches of lining shoulder seams open toward the neckline.

Staystitch the back neckline a fat 1/2″ from the cut edge.

Press the shoulder seams toward the back. Press all other seams open.

Put the lining aside until you are ready for it.

Raglan coat linings

Follow the directions above except set the sleeve into the lining. Machine stitch the sleeve, once on the 5/8″ line and again on the 3/8″ line. Trim to the last stitching.

Do The Bound Buttonholes And Welt Pockets

If the buttonhole or welt pocket sample looked best without the interfacing, do them on the appropriate jacket fronts now before the interfacing is applied. Refer to Bound Buttonholes, page 214, and Welt Pockets, page 232.

The pictures show bound buttonholes on both the right and wrong side of the fabric.

Interfacing In Tailoring

Apply the interfacing to the garment.

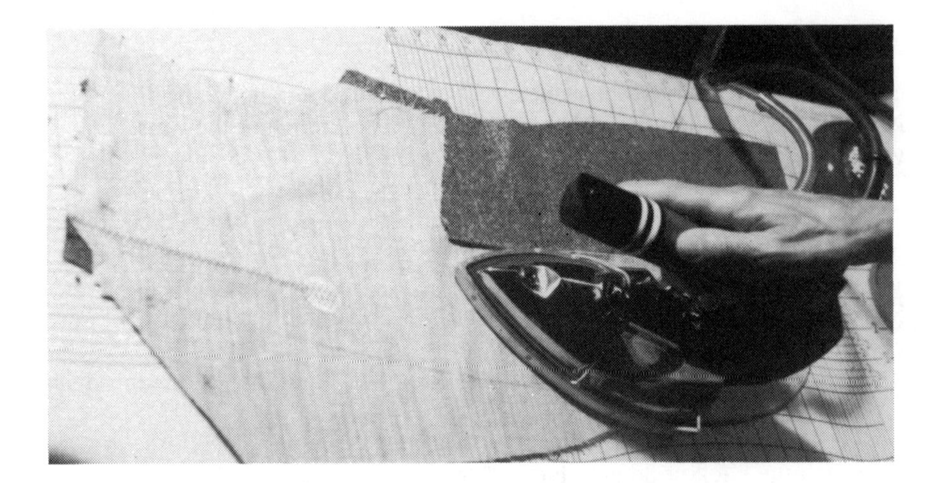

Front interfacing

Press the jacket front and the interfacing together. Be sure to line up the front edges, the shoulder, and the armhole edges carefully; otherwise, you will destroy the bust curve.

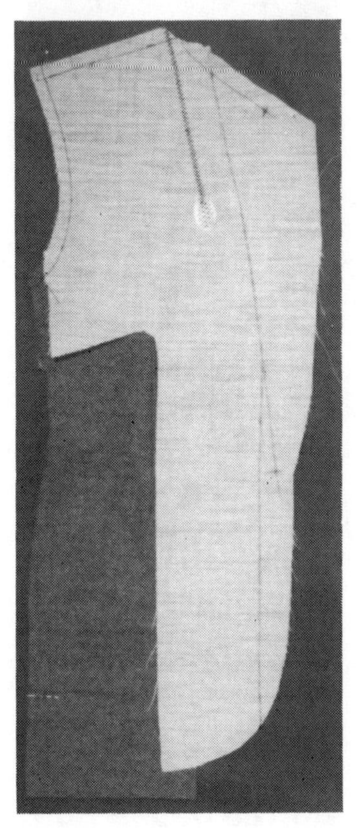

With the fabric flat on the table, hand baste through both thicknesses on the roll line and center front below the roll line. Pin baste the interfacing to the garment on the front neckline, the shoulder, the armhole, and down the sides as needed.

Staystitch the interfacing to the fabric. Staystitch directionally 1/2″ from the edge of the fabric on the shoulder and armholes and down the side as needed. Stitching directionally means to stitch with the grain of the fabric. Determine how the threads are lying on the cut edges. Stitch in the same direction the threads lie. Staystitch the neckline exactly on the 5/8″ line. **Stop at the big dot** leaving the lapel area loose.

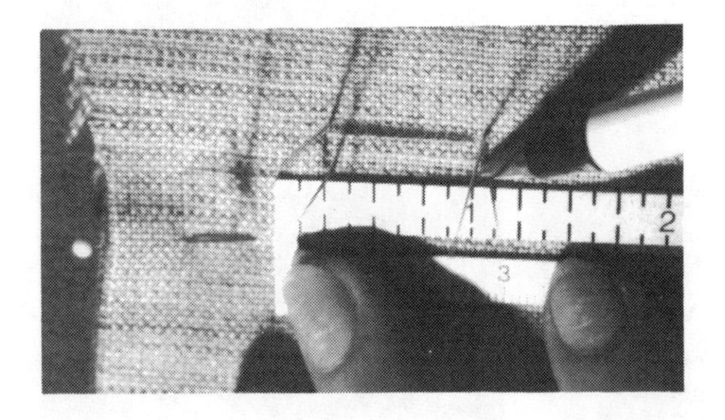

If the buttonholes were done in the fashion fabric and not through the interfacing, wait to baste the center front. Mark the buttonhole locations on the interfacing. On the right side of the garment stick pins through the four corners of the buttonholes. Draw a square on the interfacing and cut it out.

Pull the buttonhole edges through the holes. Be sure they are just large enough so that you do not have bubbles between the buttonholes in the interfacing.

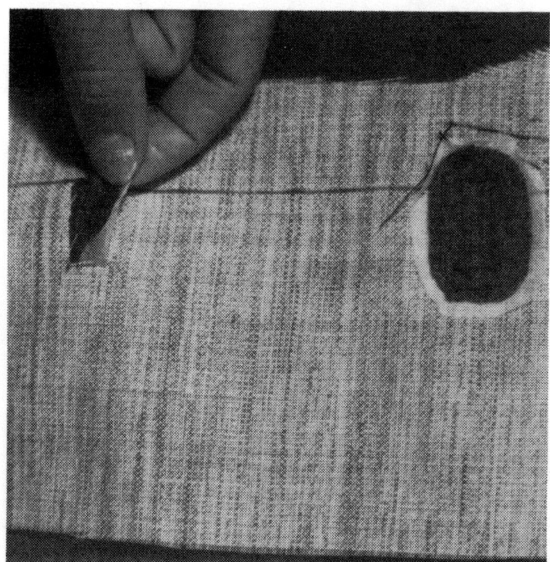

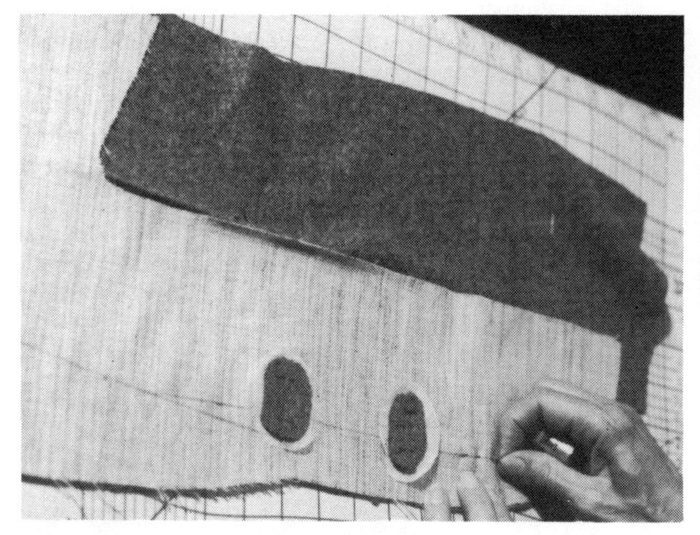

Then, with the fabric flat on the table, baste the center front through both the interfacing and the fashion fabric, skipping over the buttonholes.

Channel method for heavy fabrics

Attach the interfacing with the channel in the same manner as on page 276.

Exception: The roll line area is left free until the pad stitching is finished, then that area of the lapel is staystitched.

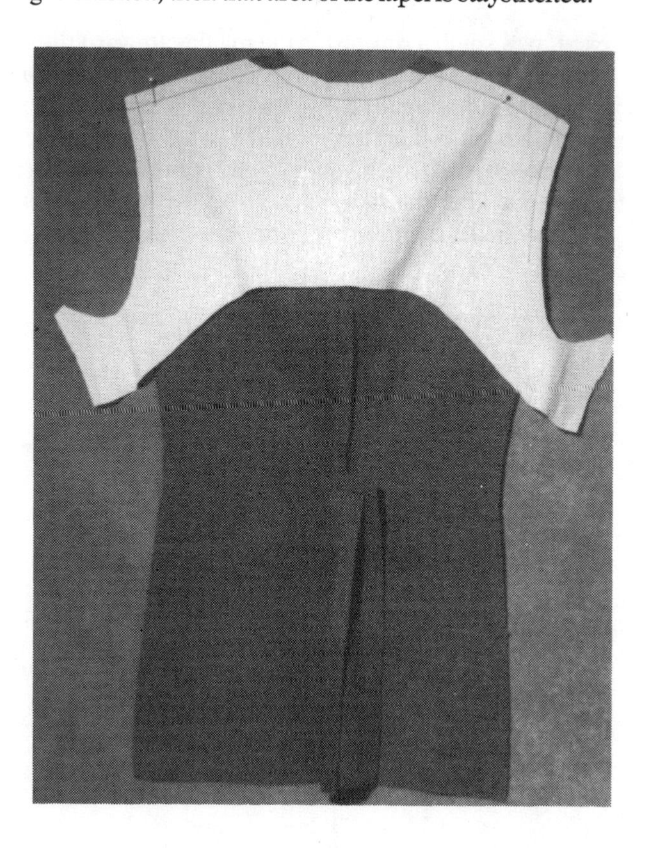

Back interfacing

Press the jacket back and the interfacing together. Line up the shoulders, the neckline, and the armhole edges. Pin baste the interfacing to the garment on the back neckline, the shoulder, the armhole, and down the sides as needed. If there is no side seam, leave the muslin free a few inches above the seam line.

Directionally staystitch the interfacing to the fabric. Stitching directionally means to stitch with the grain of the fabric. Determine how the threads are lying on the cut edges. Stitch in the same direction the threads lie. Staystitch the shoulder, the armhole, and the side seams 1/2″ from the edge of the fabric. Staystitch the neckline exactly on the 5/8″ line.

Pad Stitch The Lapel

Pad stitches are taken at right angles to the roll line. Stitches are 3/8″ to 1/2″ apart, rows 1/4″ to 3/8″ apart. The stitches go through the interfacing and just catch the fashion fabric. The stitch should barely show on the right side of the fabric. The left hand is under the work and guides the needle depth. Just touch the left hand with the needle.

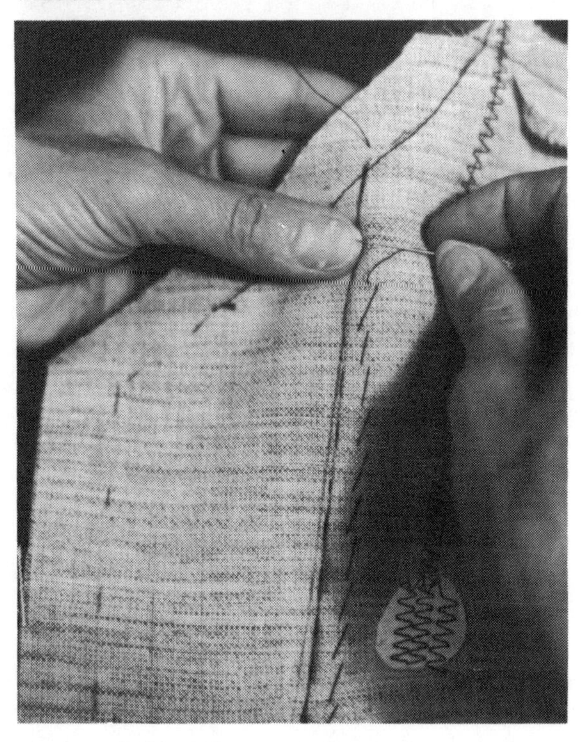

Mark a line 3/4″ from the edge of the lapel and leave that area unpadded. Thread a short needle (No. 9 or 10 betweens or quilting) with beeswaxed thread. Beeswax enough thread to pad the lapel, about 4 pieces. Refer to page 220. Sit in a comfortable place so you can hold the work firmly against a table or your lap. On the right front, begin the padding at the bottom of the roll line and stitch to the neckline. On the left front begin the padding at the top of the roll line and stitch to the bottom of the roll line. Begin by pad stitching one row outside the roll line (toward the armhole) with the fabric flat. Then pad stitch back and forth without turning the fabric.

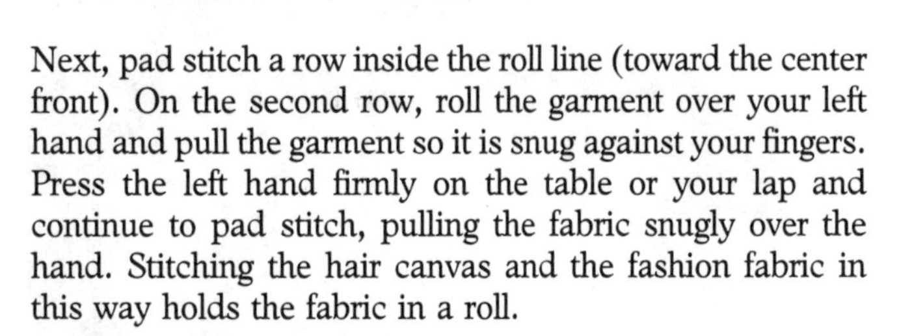

Next, pad stitch a row inside the roll line (toward the center front). On the second row, roll the garment over your left hand and pull the garment so it is snug against your fingers. Press the left hand firmly on the table or your lap and continue to pad stitch, pulling the fabric snugly over the hand. Stitching the hair canvas and the fashion fabric in this way holds the fabric in a roll.

As you pad stitch, roll the fabric over your fingers and pull it snug on each successive row so you can just see the previous row of pad stitching. Go up and down with lines parallel to the roll line. Do not turn the fabric. Pad the entire area from the roll line to within 3/4″ of the lapel edge.

When the lapel is completely padded, it should look like the picture to the right.

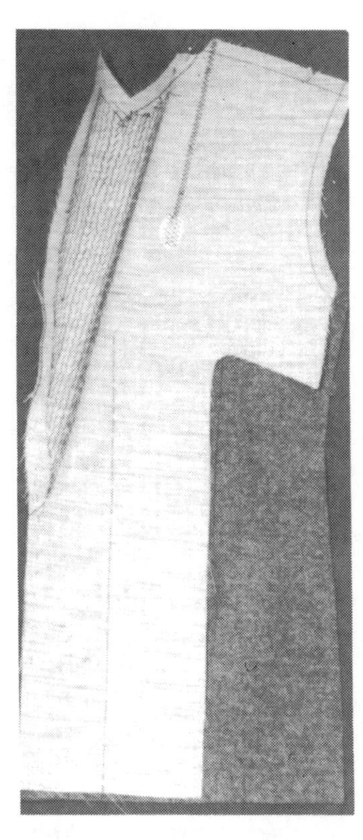

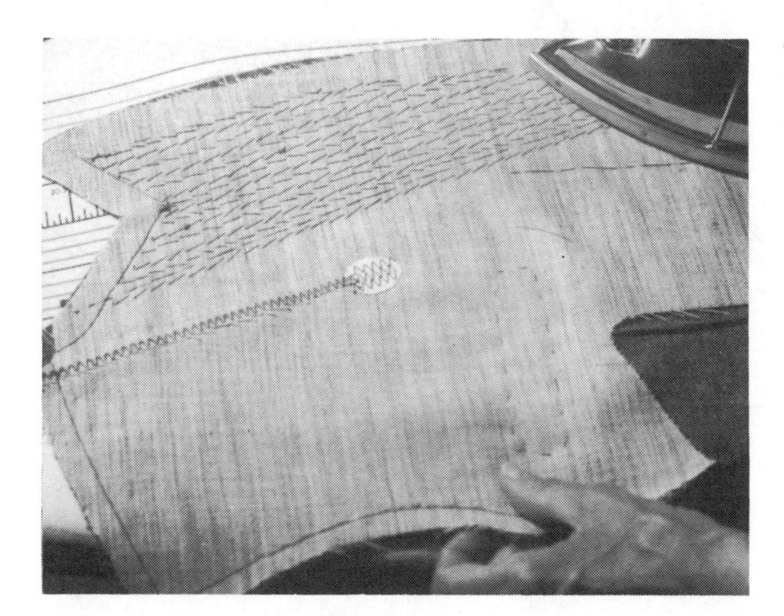

Then press the lapel area flat.

Do The Bound Buttonholes And Welt Pockets

If the buttonholes and the welt pockets were best done through the interfacing, do them on the right jacket front now before the taping is done. Refer to Bound Buttonholes, page 214, and Welt Pockets, page 232.

Tape The Lapel Edges

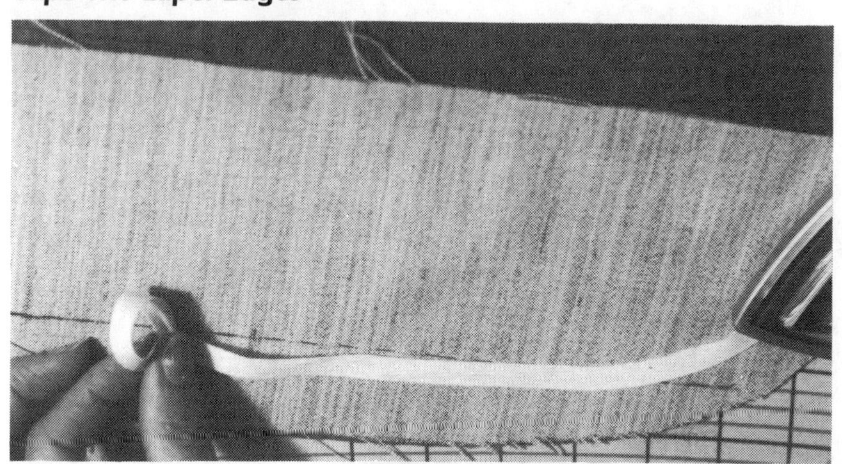

Work at the ironing board. Start at the bottom of the garment and work up to the lapel area. Shape the edge tape by pressing with steam so that the tape corresponds to any curves on the front of the garment.

Lay the tape so the outside edge of the tape is exactly on the 5/8″ line. If the bottom of the garment is straight, begin the taping at the hemline. Pin the tape to the interfacing and garment until you reach the dot marking the lapel.

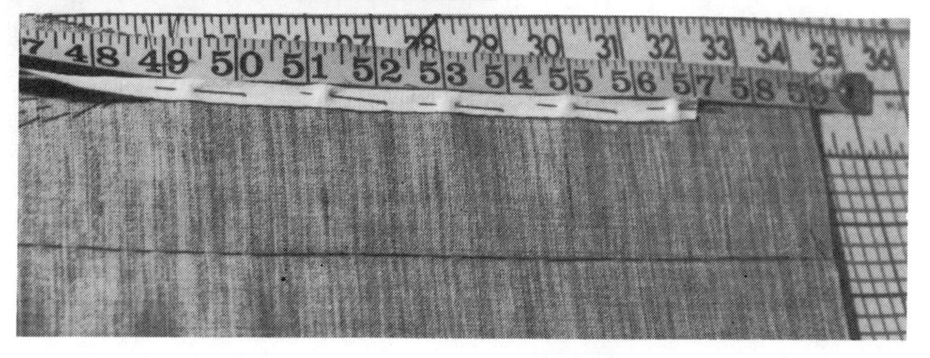

If the bottom of the garment is curved, begin the tape on the hem line at the edge of the interfacing. The tape measure is 5/8″ wide and helps get a straight line on the edge tape. The outer edge of the edge tape is the stitching line of the lapel. It must be a nice straight line or an even curve.

At the dot marking the beginning of the lapel, put a securing pin through all the thickness of the fabric into the ironing board. Shorten the tape 1/8″ on a short lapel, 1/4″ on a long lapel (almost to the waistline) by pinning a small tuck in the lapel. Then lay the edge tape over the tuck and secure it through the ironing board at the top edge of the lapel.

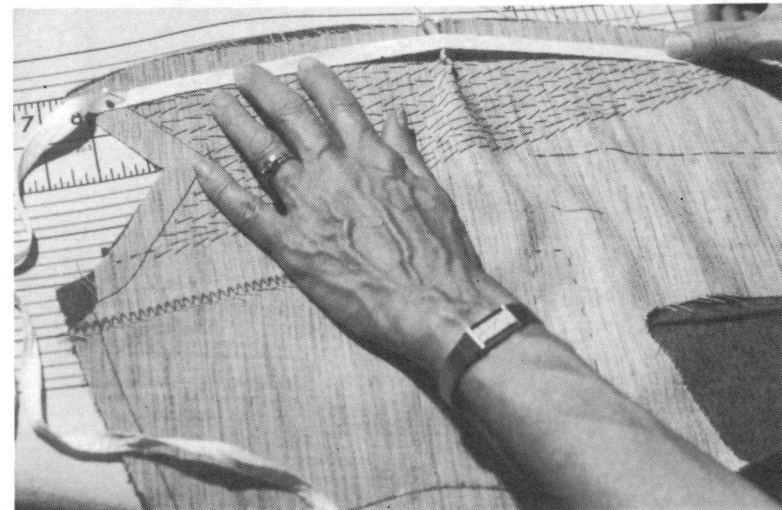

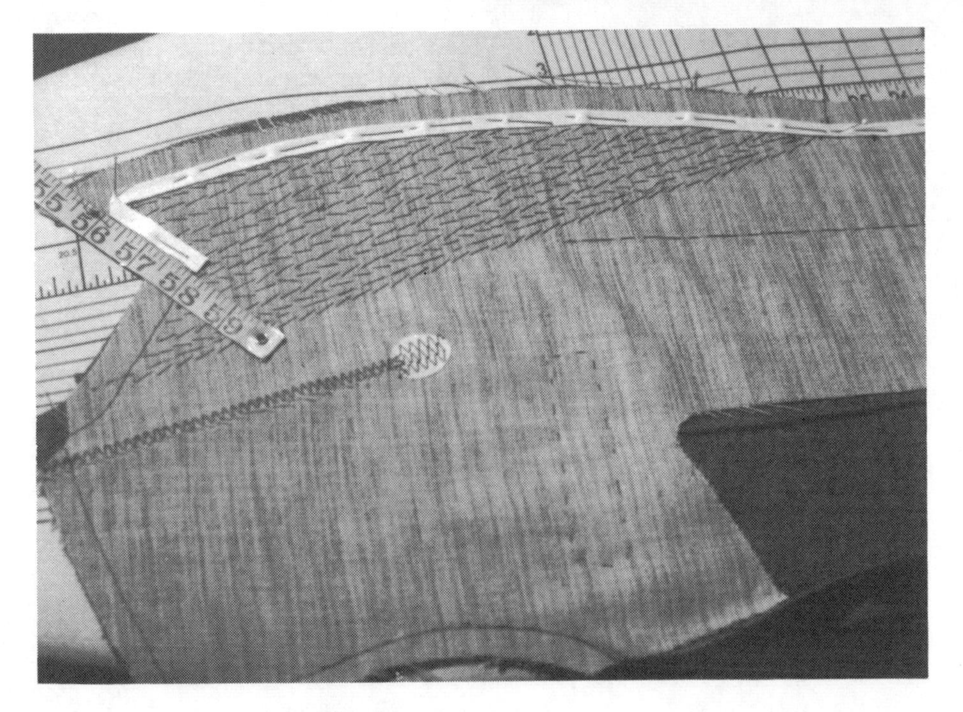

Release the tuck and steam the area to shrink the excess fabric. Stretch the tape to fit the lapel. Continue pinning the tape around the lapel point, folding the tape at the point. Stop the tape exactly at the big dot marking the collar junction. With the garment lying flat on the table, pin or hand baste through the center of the tape, catching all thickness of the fabric.

Taping The Roll Line

Tailors call this Bridal Tape. The roll line is a bias area and is taped to prevent stretching. If the lapel is short (above the bustline), it is not as necessary to tape the roll line. For long lapels (below the bustline), it is important to tape the roll line. Shorten the tape 1/4″ for a small bustline, 3/8″ for a medium bustline and 1/2″ for a full bustline.

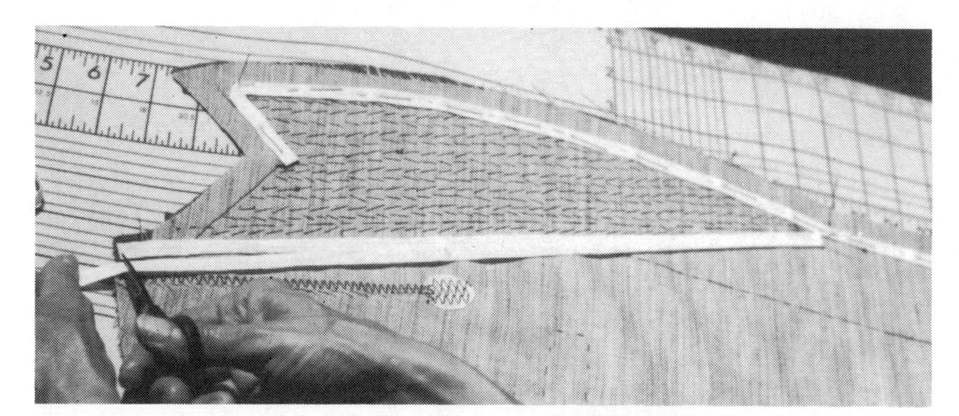

Place the tape on the armhole side of the roll line from the bottom of the roll line to the edge of the shoulder at the neckline. Cut it at the shoulder and cut a second piece the same length for the other front.

Fasten the tape through the garment to a firm surface at the beginning of the roll line. Pull the tape to shorten the needed amount for the size of the bust cup.

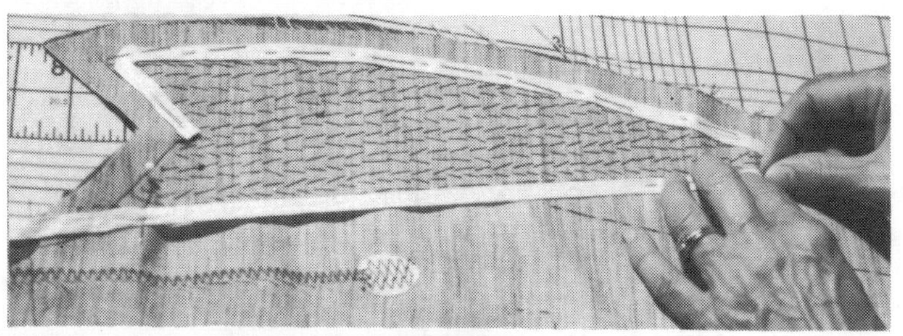

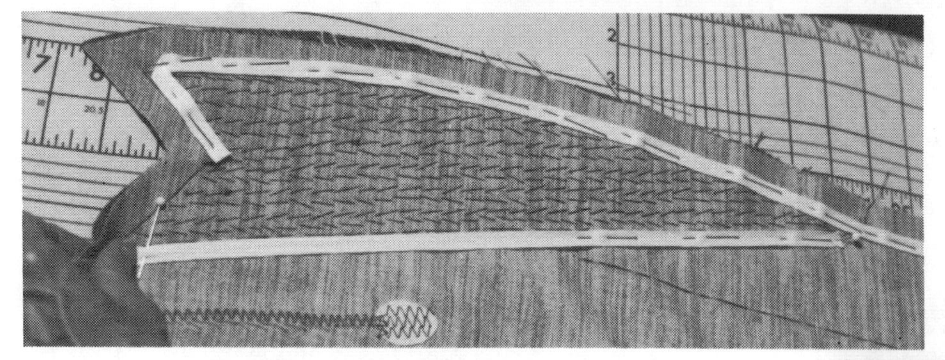

Pin the tape to the firm surface. Then while you are stretching the tape, pin through all thicknesses of fabric, the length of the tape. Stop 5/8″ below the neck seamline.

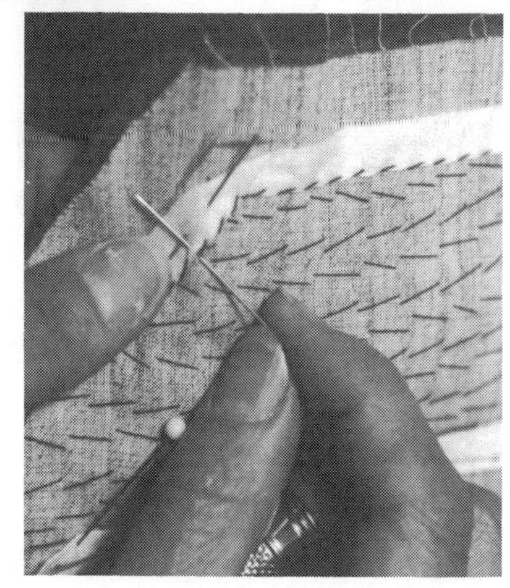

When both fronts are taped, lay them together to compare the front length. They must be the same length. Adjust the tape if necessary.

Stitch the inner edge of the tape to the hair canvas from the bottom of the garment to the notch with a small whip stitch.

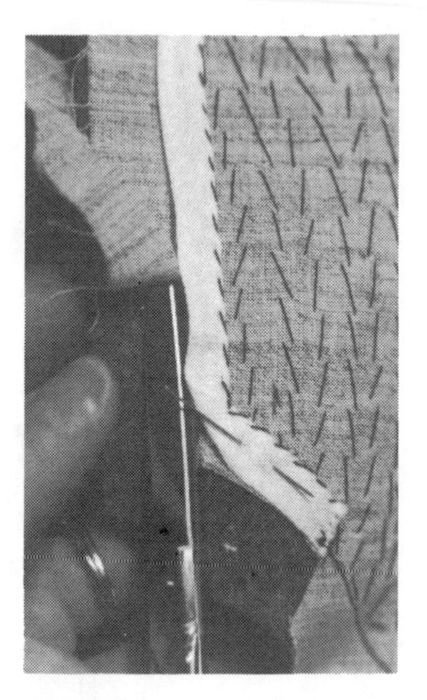

Trim the hair canvas from the seam line so that the edge of the canvas is just slightly under the tape. Trim the entire lapel area.

Hand stitch, with a small whip stitch, the outer edge of the seam tape to the fashion fabric from the bottom of the garment up to the collar junction.

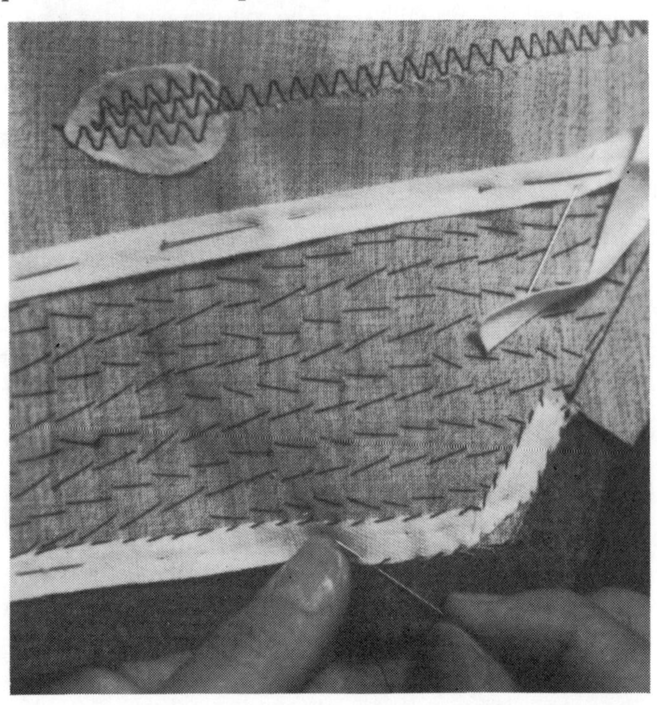

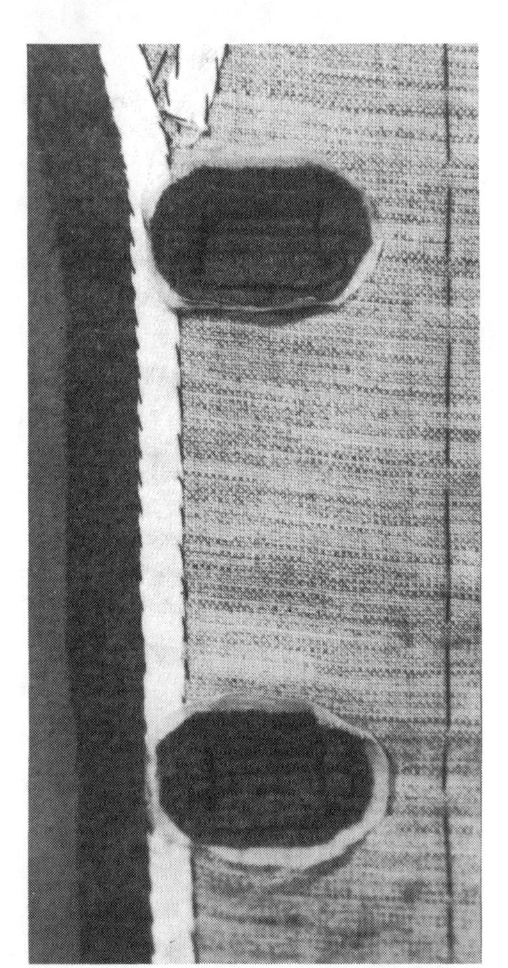

Keep the bound buttonholes free of the edge tape. They will extend over the inner edge. Just don't catch them when you are hand stitching the tape.

Hand stitch with a small whip stitch both edges of the edge tape (bridal tape) through all the layers of fabric. The loose end of the tape will be attached to the under collar roll line after the collar is stitched on.

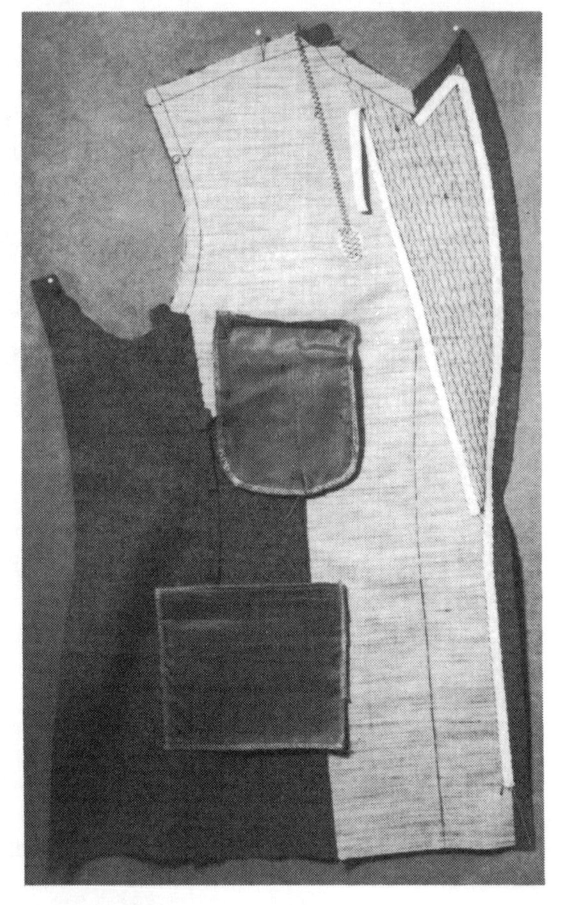

Complete both fronts with pad stitching, taping, bound buttonholes, and welt pockets. Patch pockets should be basted in place until after the first fitting. Then they can be stitched on the garment. Refer to pages 72, 231, and 314.

Collars In Tailoring

The best interfacing for the collar is collar linen. Tailors call collar linen tailor's elastic because it shapes and holds that shape. There are three options for attaching the interfacing to the collar. **Hand padding, machine padding, and pre-padded collar linen.** Refer to pages 299-305 for detailed instructions for the pre-padded collar. The pre-padded collar is used extensively in men's tailoring. Use it when the collar will not be worn up or if you are a bit short of fabric for the under collar. Pre-padded collar linen can be found at a tailor supply.

I like to stitch the collar together, press and turn it before it is attached to the garment. It is much easier to get a well-turned collar and to attach it to the garment properly if you have the collar stitched and pressed before attaching it to the garment. **Exception:** If you are using a pre-padded felt under collar which must be attached by hand, do not stitch and turn the collar before attaching it to the garment.

Interfacing The Under Collar When Hand Padding Or Machine Padding The Under Collar

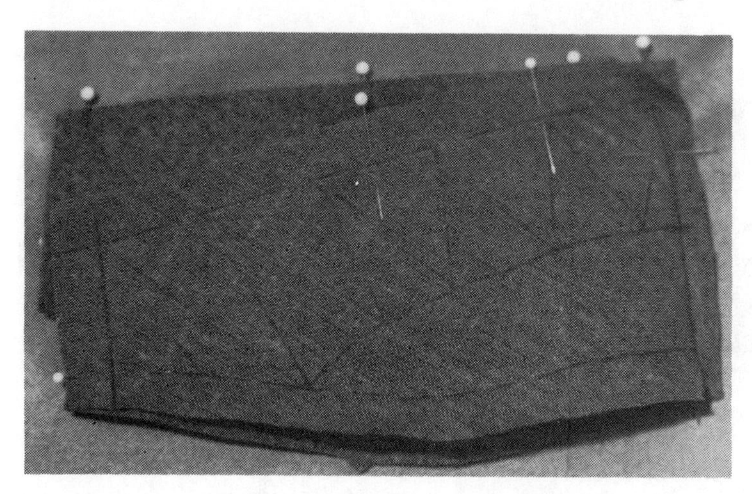

Pin the collar linen to the wrong side of the under collar with the marking on the outside. The linen in the picture has been marked for machine padding. If you are hand padding, mark the roll line and the 5/8" seam lines. Pin the under collars together at the center back, matching the roll lines. Stitch through all four thicknesses on the center back seam. Press the seam open. On the seam allowance trim the linen to 1/4". Trim the collar to 3/8".

Hand Pad Stitching The Under Collar

If the collar will be flipped up in wearing so the under collar would show, pad stitch the under collar by hand as you did on the lapel area.

Roll the collar on the roll line when you are pad stitching the stand. Otherwise pad it flat with the pad design shown in the picture. The pad stitching is done in the same manner as the lapel was done only the rows are a bit closer together on the stand of the collar.

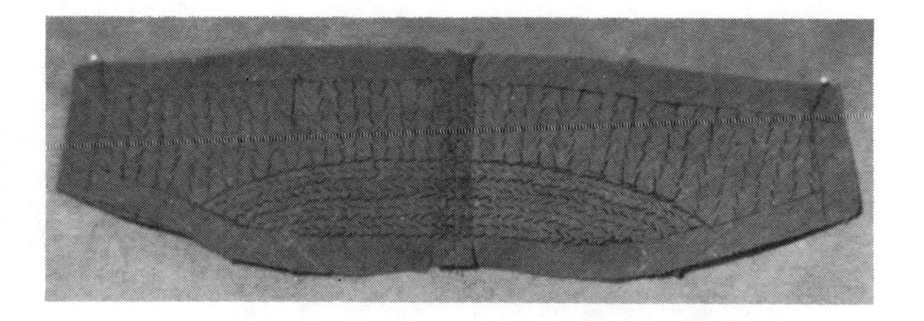

Machine pad stitching the under collar

If the collar will always lie down, pad stitch the collar by machine.

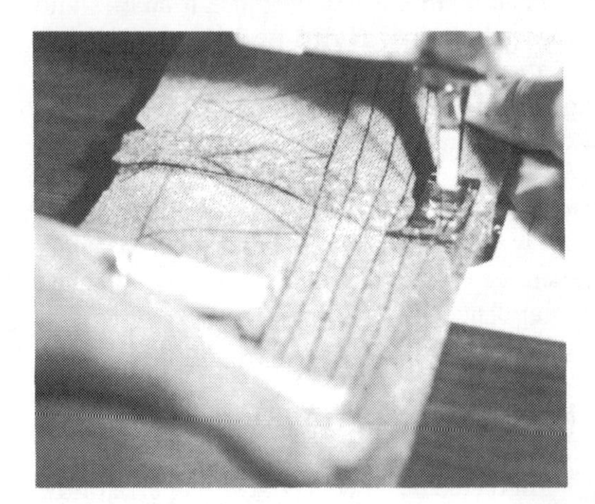

With all the edges even stitch slong the roll line. Don't go into the seam allowances. Then, stretching the collar and linen, machine stitch pad rows on the collar stand until the last row is 1/4″ from the seam. Staystitch the lower edge of the collar on the 5/8″ seamline stretching only the stand area.

The picture shows the stand machine pad stitched and the neck edge of the collar staystitched on the 5/8″ seamline.

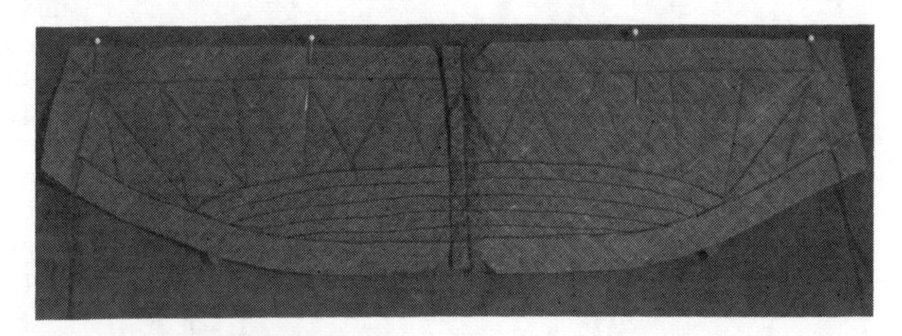

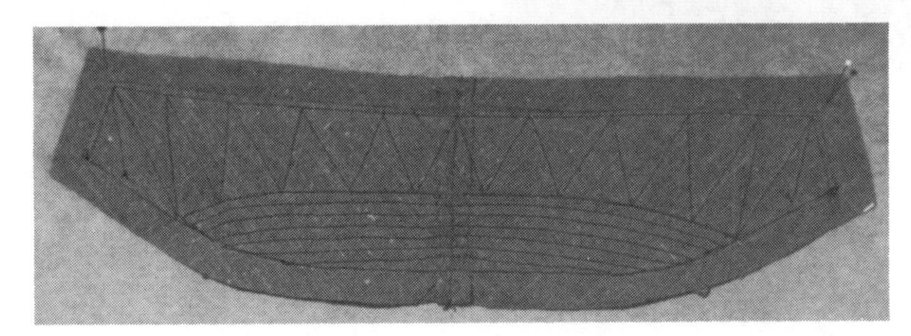

With the collar flat stitch along the padding lines on the main part of the collar, staying 3/4″ from the edge of the collar.

Staystitch the ends and top of the collar on the 3/4″ line, pivoting at the corners.

Shape The Under Collar

Press the collar flat first.

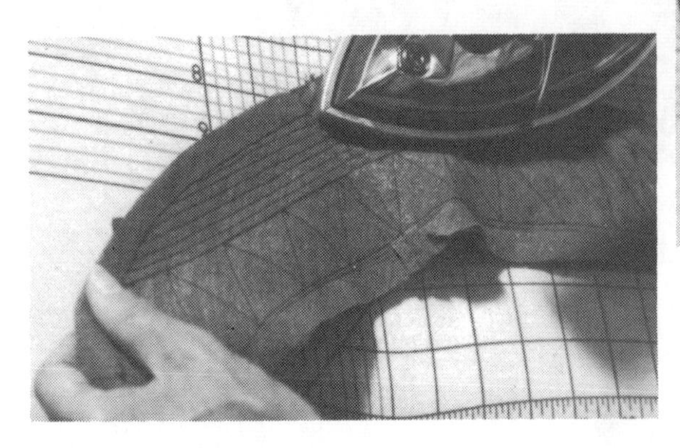

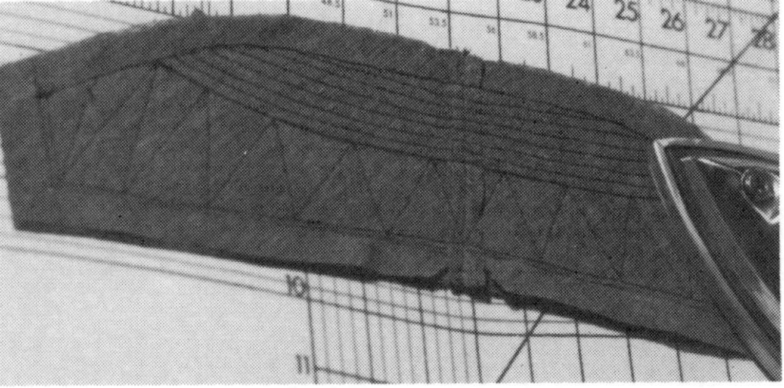

Then stretch the stand (not the roll line) with steam.

Fold the collar on the roll line and press gently, stretching the stand.

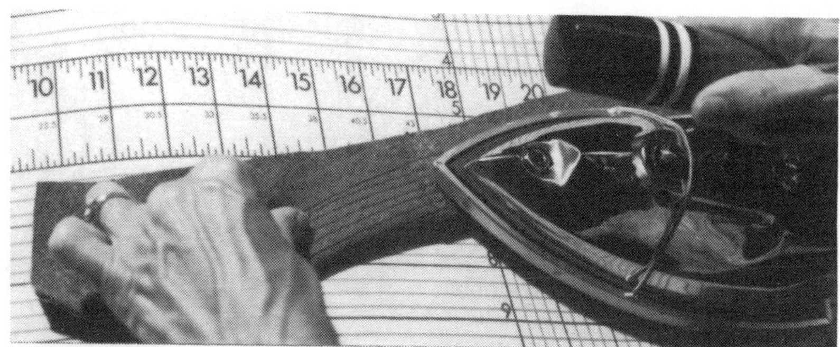

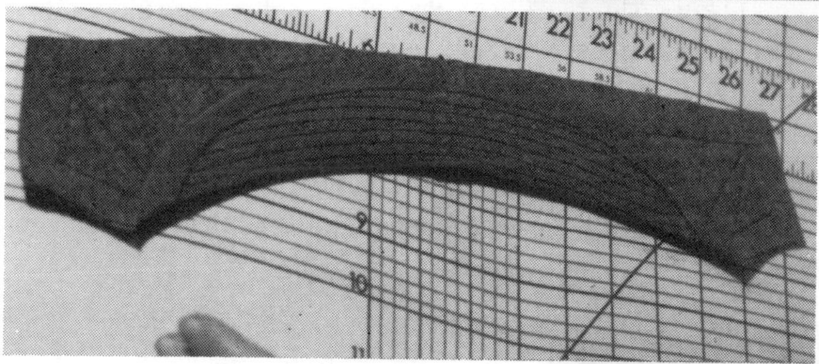

Press until the stand of the collar is shaped and lying flat against the fall of the collar.

While the collar still has steam from the iron in it, put the collar around your neck or the neckline of a dress form or a ham to let it shape until it cools. Never lay it out flat again. Store the collar rolled until you are ready to use it.

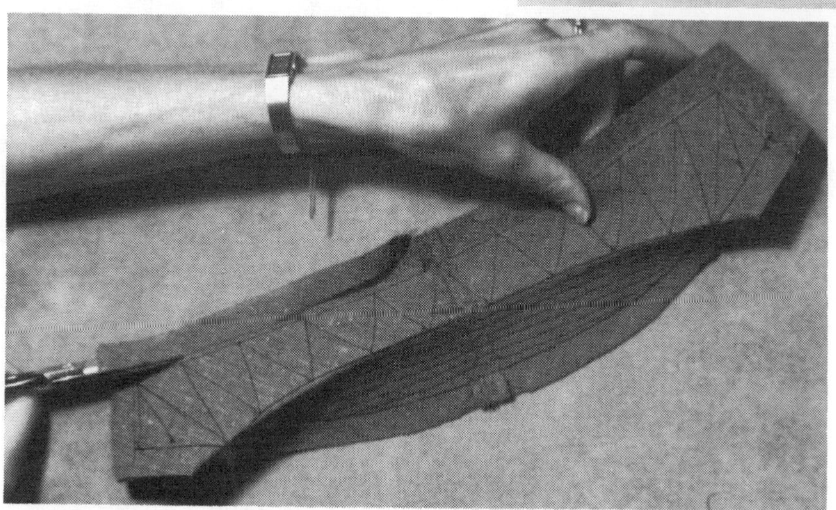

Trim only the collar **linen** along the 5/8″ line on the end and top of the collar only. (Where the staystitching was 3/4″). **The cut edge of the collar linen is the stitching line. It must be straight.** DO NOT trim the linen along the neck edge.

Collar Construction

Refer to Collars, pages 161-164, for general information on collar construction. Then use the following directions for collars when you are tailoring.

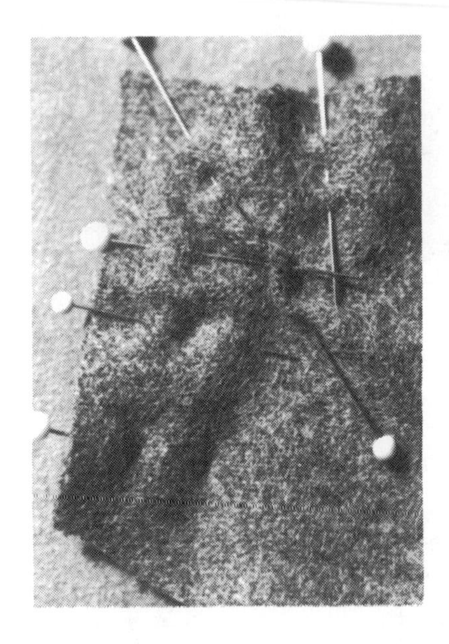

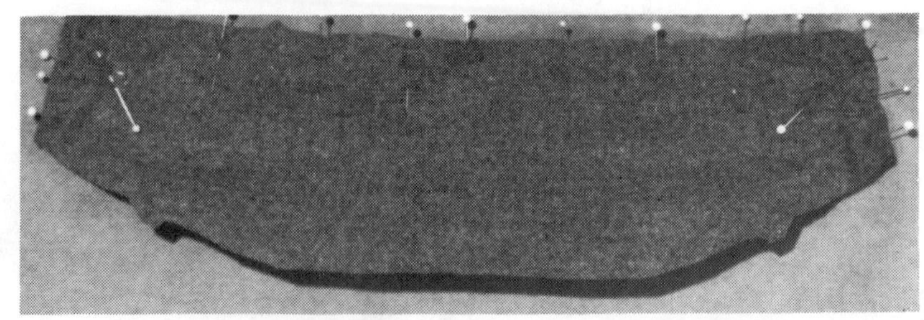

Pin the upper and under collar together. First pin the front edge of the collar at the big dot. This keeps the collars flat together along the neckline. Second pin the center back. Continue to pin the collar from the center back to each end. The result is a bubble at the corner of the collar.

Pin in a tailor's blister. A tailor's blister is a small tuck pinned in the fabric to hold the ease needed for turn of cloth at the corner. Hold the blister back from the 5/8″ seam allowance. (If the fabric is very thin and flat, don't use a blister.)

Stitch the under collar to the upper collar on the outer edges and the ends. Sew the end of the collar a little bow-legged so it won't dip in. Do this also on the end of the lapel.

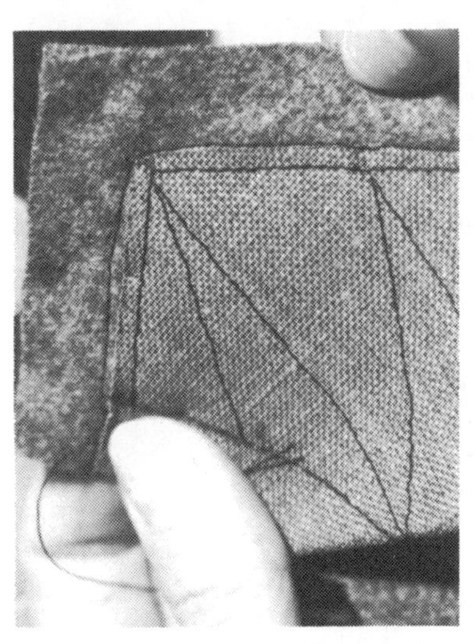

Start and stop at the big dot marking the collar/lapel junction and leave long threads for tying. Stitch with the interfacing up, just missing the linen. The linen is not included in the seam. Stitch the corner by pivoting on the needle unless the fabric is heavy, then stitch the corner with one stitch on the diagonal. Check the corners before trimming to be sure they are the same.

Trim the seams to 1/4″ on the under collar, 3/8″ on the upper collar. Trim the corner to 1/4″. Tie the long threads. Do not cut them.

Press the seams on the point presser. Check the corner and trim more if needed. Refer to Collars, pages 162-164. Turn and press the collar edge ONLY. Press with the under collar up. Use plenty of steam. Be careful. Don't let the extra fabric at the corner squeeze out at the seam edge. Finish pressing with the upper collar up. Use a press cloth. Do not press the roll line.

With the collar rolled on the roll line, trim the under collar and the top collar even at the neck edge. Keep the collar rolled, not flat, until you are ready to put it on the garment.

Shoulder Pads

Make the shoulder pads. If you prefer, purchase the pads. Purchased pads must be fitted to the armhole. Refer to Fusible Tailoring, page 259. If they are flat, they must be pad stitched to shape them. Refer to Shoulder Pads, page 329.

Stitch The Garment Seams

Stitch the garment shoulder and side seams; refer to pages 39 and 273. Check the fit. Try the jacket on with the shoulder pads in place. Do any adjustments needed to the shoulder seams and the side seams of the garment.

If you are not sure of the sleeve length, pin or baste the remaining sleeve seam. Pin the sleeve into the armhole with the pad in place and determine the hem turn of the sleeve.

Then press the shoulder and side seams and catch stitch the side seams to the interfacing. Only clip fitting seams when necessary after making sure the garment fits. Clip any seams that need clipping to allow them to lie flat.

Finish The Sleeves

Apply the interfacing to the sleeve

Measure and lightly crease the sleeve along the hemline.

If you cut the interfacing wider for a soft hem, press a fold 1/2" wide the length of the interfacing. Lay the fold on the hem line as directed.

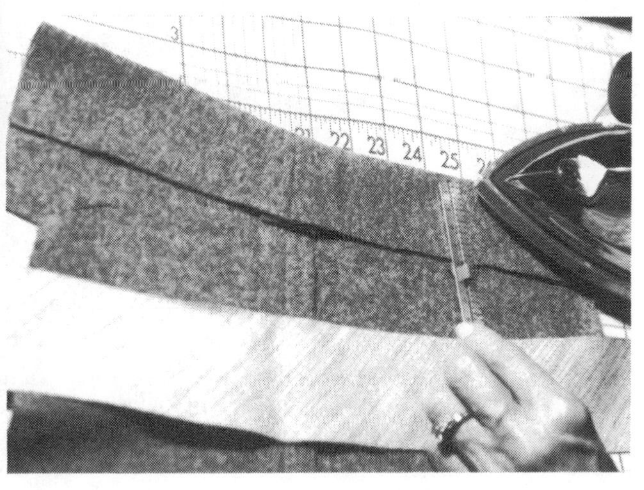

Lay the interfacing on the hemline extending up onto the sleeve body. Steam shape the interfacing to the sleeve.

Lay the hem up over the interfacing. The interfacing should extend about 1/2″ beyond the edge of the hem. Steam any excess fullness of the hem to shrink it.

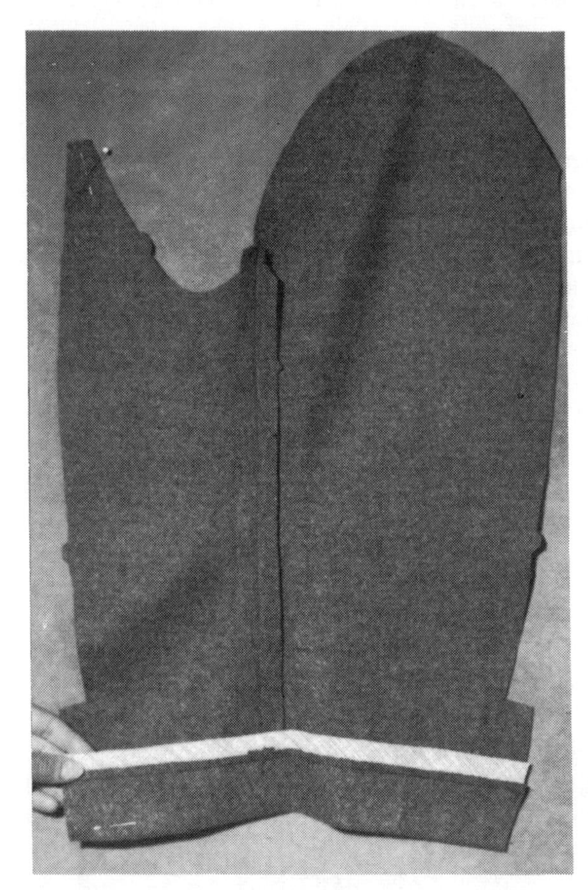

Pin the hem to the interfacing, then stitch 1/4″ from the hem edge. You are stitching the hem edge to the interfacing.

Stitch And Finish The Sleeve

If you cannot see the crossgrain of the fabric, mark the cross grain with a thread baste line. Refer to Sleeves, page 194. Extend the hem out flat and stitch the remaining sleeve seam as the pattern directs.

Machine baste two rows as shown and ease the cap of the sleeve if it is a smooth set-in sleeve. Follow the pattern directions for any other type of sleeve.

Pull up the threads and steam shrink the entire cap over a ham. The ham is resting in a ham holder to hold it steady while the sleeve cap is being shrunk.

Preparation For Hemming The Sleeves

If you are sure of the length, hem the sleeve. If the pattern calls for mitering, only miter the upper corner (the largest part of a two-piece sleeve). It is very difficult to get a sleeve hem even when you miter both corners. Mitering does reduce the bulk but the sleeve hem cannot be let down after it is mitered.

Miter the upper sleeve vent opening

To miter, fold the hem as it will lie. Mark with a pin the bottom corner, the upper edge of the hem where it touches the sleeve vent, and the sleeve vent where it touches the hem, as shown in the picture.

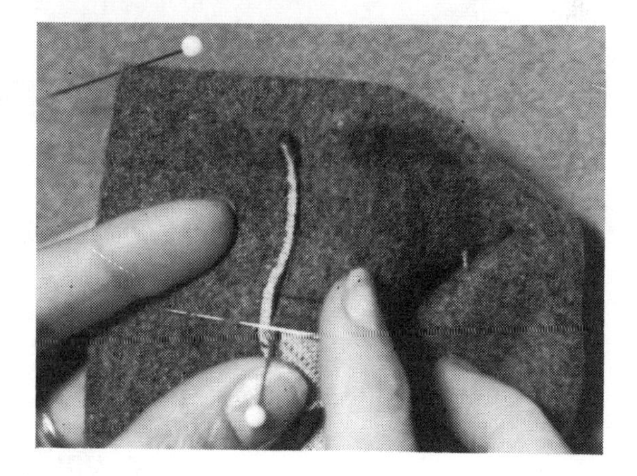

Lay the sleeve hem and the vent right sides together and match the pins at the hem line and the vent. The pin marking the hem turn on the corner should be on the angle. Put a piece of tape from the top edge of the hem to the hem turn. Stitch along the tape.

Turn and press the miter.

Remove the tape and trim the seam and the hem interfacing as shown in the picture.

Finish the lower sleeve vent opening

Check the length of the under sleeve with the vent as it will lie and correct the hem turn if needed.

On the under sleeve finish the end of the sleeve hem by marking the hem turn with a pin.

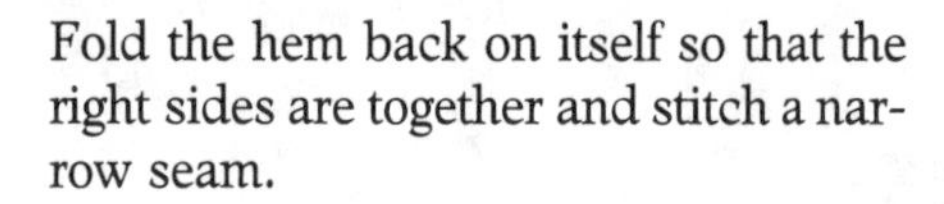

Fold the hem back on itself so that the right sides are together and stitch a narrow seam.

Turn right side out. Push the corner out and press, making sure the seam is to the under.

Hem The Sleeves

Refer to Hems, pages 100-101.

Stitch the buttons on through all thickness of the vent. Put the sleeves aside until you have the collar on.

Never put set-in sleeves in until the neckline is completed. The neckline influences the fit of the sleeve.

Stitch The Collar To The Garment

Method Three

Stitch the collar and the facings to the jacket in the following sequence. Refer to Collars, pages 171-179, for information on attaching the collar to the garment. Then follow the directions for attaching the collar when tailoring.

Stitch The Under Collar To The Neckline

Pin the **under collar** to the jacket neckline on the 5/8″ seam line with the collar up. Match the center backs and work from the center back to either end of the collar.

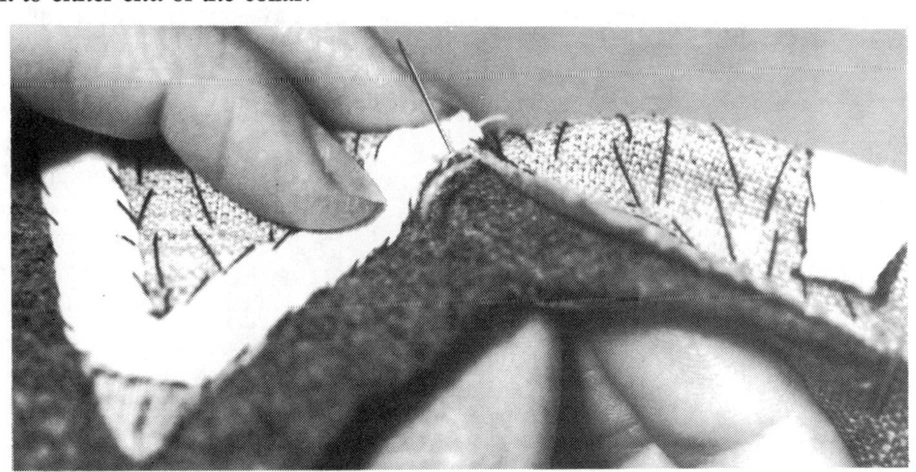

Carefully match the big dot marking the collar junction. Pin so that the collar end seam is free.

Carefully match the roll of the collar to the roll line of the lapel. The under collar was stretched when it was shaped for the roll. Gently push it into the neckline. Stretch the neckline in the shoulder area to fit the collar and, if necessary, clip the neckline. Be careful. Don't clip deeper than 3/8″.

As you pin, hold the seam in your fingers. Run them along the seam to check for possible puckers when you stitch the seam. If the seam feels smooth, you can usually stitch it without any puckers. Hand baste the seam for more control. When everything looks and feels good, stitch the under collar to the garment with the garment up. Gently tug the garment as you stitch to help prevent puckers in the seam. When stitching the under collar to the neckline, keep the collar end seam free and the upper collar pulled out of the way. Don't backstitch. Leave long threads. (You will be tying them later.)

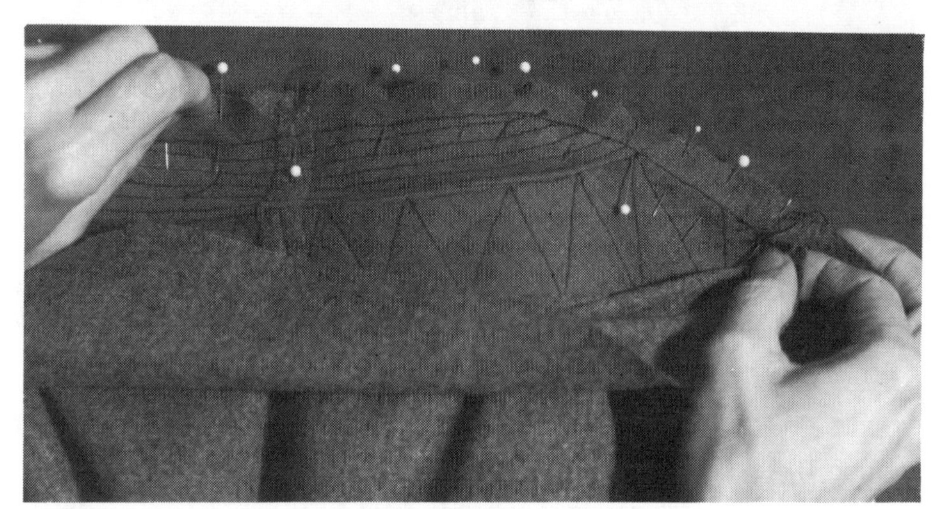

Stitch The Upper Collar To The Facings Or Facing If You Have Only A Front Facing

Pin the **upper collar** to the facing. Pin with the collar up, matching the center backs, notches, and the big dot marking the collar junction. Work from the center back to either end of the collar.

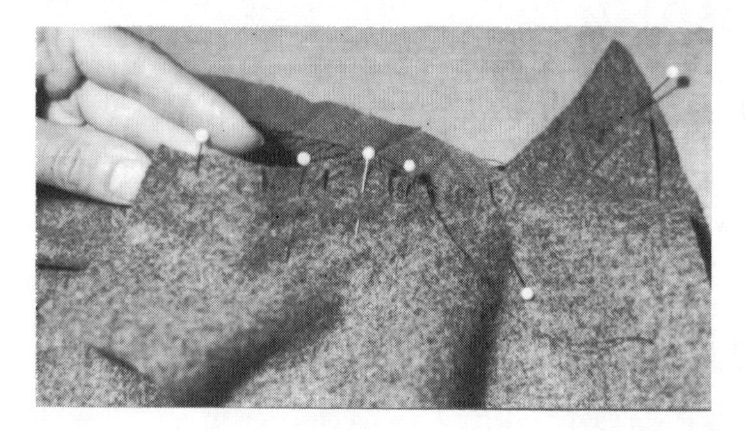

If there is no back neck facing, be sure the front facings end at the shoulder seam marking on the collar. The shoulder seam is marked by two small dots on the collar pattern. If you neglected to mark it, lay the upper collar on the neckline and put a pin through the collar at the shoulder seam. The 5/8″ seam line of the facing should come to that mark on the collar.

Stretch the facing neckline in the shoulder area to fit the collar. If necessary, clip the neckline. Be careful. Don't clip deeper than 3/8″. As you are pinning, hold the seam in your fingers and run them along the seam to check for possible puckers when you stitch. Hand baste the seam before stitching for more control.

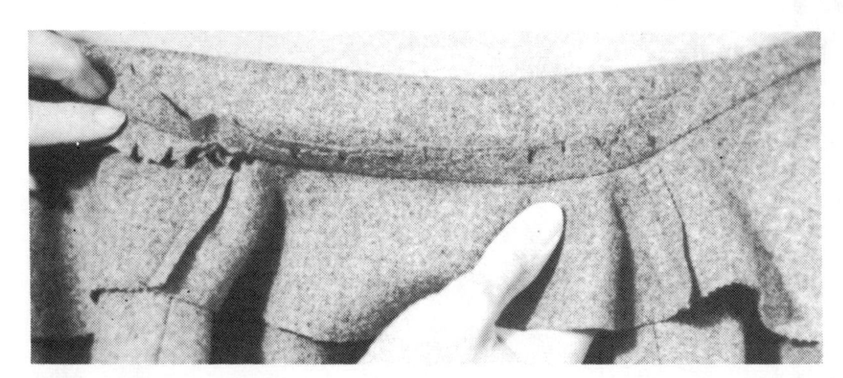

Stitch the upper collar to the facing or facings if you are using a back neck facing. Stitch with the facings up and as you stitch gently tug the garment on both sides of the needle to prevent puckers in the seam. Keep the collar end seam free. Don't back-stitch. Leave long threads. (You will be tying them later.)

Stitch The Lapel

First check the lie of the lapel. With the collar and lapel right side out, arrange the seam as it must be when it is stitched. The end seam of the collar must not show. It must lie to the under side of the collar. For detailed information on pinning the lapel, refer to Collars, pages 174-175.

Pin the collar/lapel junction correctly as shown in the Collar chapter. Pin a tailor's blister on the corner of the lapel in the same way you did on the corners of the collar, page 286. (The tailor's blister preserves enough fabric for the turn of cloth at the corner. If the fabric is very thin and flat, don't use the blister.)

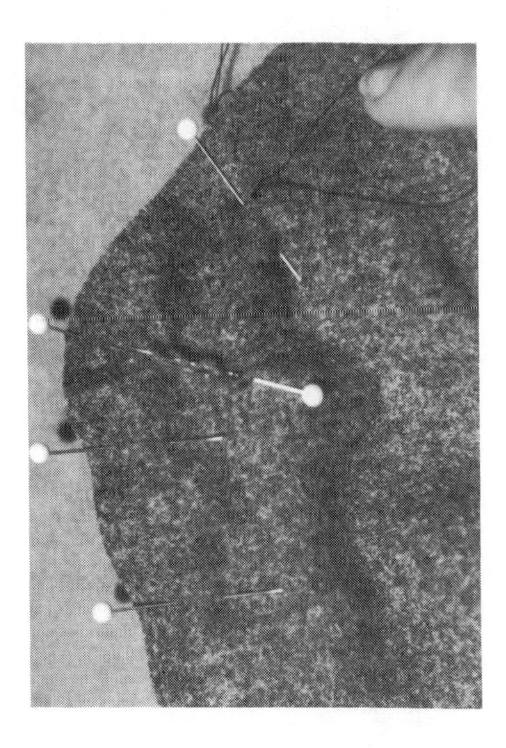

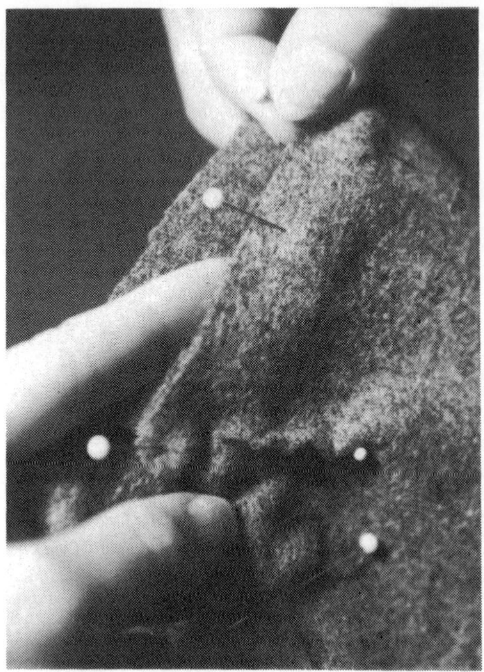

Pin the entire facing from the collar junction to the bottom of the lapel. Pin with the facing up and the lapel seam over your hand to allow the right ease. Ease the facing onto the garment from the corner of the lapel to the bottom of the roll line.

From the bottom of the roll line to the bottom of the garment the facing must lie flat (no ease).

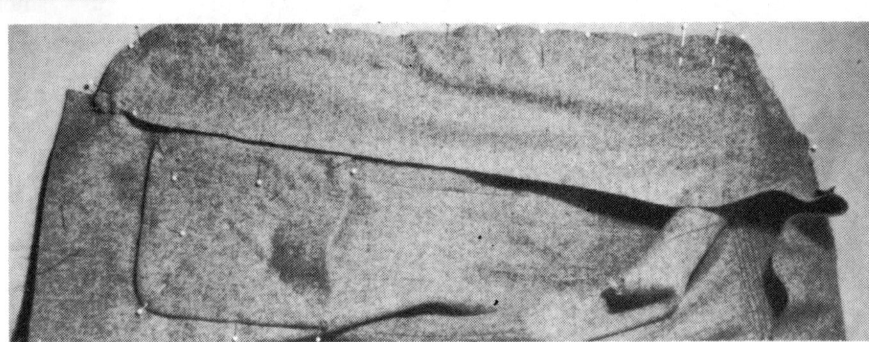

At the hem of a curved front, turn the facing back 1/8″ to hide the raw edge.

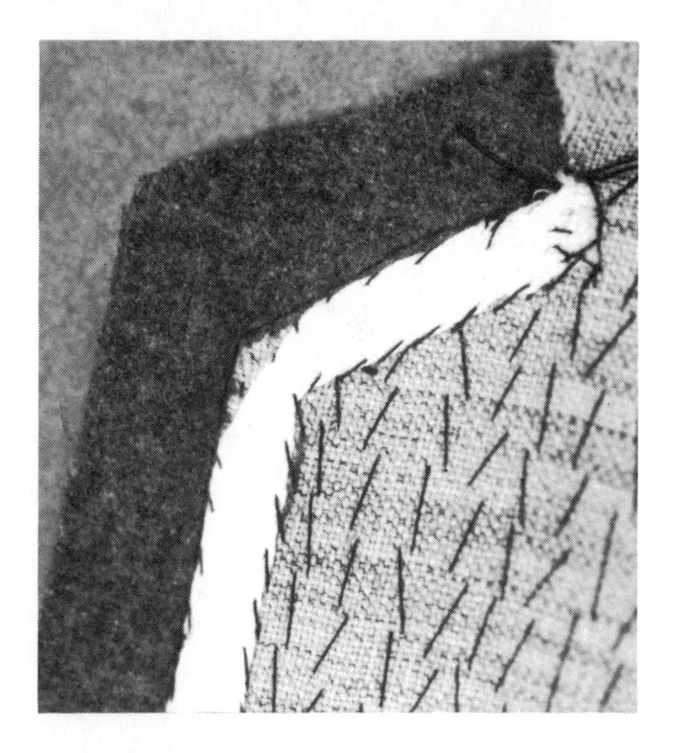

Then stitch with the interfacing up from the collar junction to the bottom edge of the garment. Stitch close to but not on the edge tape. The lapel seam must be the same depth (5/8″) as the collar seam. Stitch the end of the lapel a little bowlegged. A slightly curved line instead of exactly along the edge tape. Do not backstitch; leave long threads for tying later.

On a curved hem, stitch across the edge of the facing which was pinned back 1/8″ to hold the turn of the fabric. Backstitch.

Check These Points

- Be sure the front extensions at the end of the collar are of equal length on both sides of the garment.
- Be sure the collar points are of equal size and shape at the center front.
- The seams on the end of the collar must lie to the under side as it was pressed.
- The lapel seam must lie to the under side so that it does not show when the lapel is folded back against the garment.
- The lapel ends must lie flat. If they want to curl out, you have not allowed enough fabric for the turn of cloth on the corner of the lapel.

When everything looks satisfactory, pull all the threads of the four seams to one side of the fabric and tie the threads. The four seams are the collar end seam, the under collar seam, the upper collar seam, and the lapel seam. The picture of the inside of the collar shows all the seams except the lapel seam.

If you have trouble pulling the threads to one side of the fabric, thread them on a needle to get them on one side of the fabric for tying. If you have stopped short of the large dot, put a hand needle on the long thread and close the hole with small hand stitches. When all the seams are correct and the collar looks good turned to the right side, tie all the threads securely, and clip the thread, leaving about 1/4″ beyond the knot.

Clipping, Trimming, and Pressing Seams

Trim the hair canvas, muslin, and collar linen to 1/8″ from the seam line. At all seam junctions, trim the seam allowance out of the seam allowance to eliminate bulk. Refer to Collars, page 171.

Clip the neck seam of the garment and the neck seam of the facing until they lie flat when they are on grain as they will lie in the garment. **DO NOT trim these seams. Just clip.**

Trim the under collar to 1/4″. You needn't trim the upper collar.

Trim the lapel seam to eliminate all unnecessary bulk at the collar/lapel junction.

Trim the end of the collar seam allowance and neckline seam allowance to lie in a miter. In this way, trim both the upper and under collar seams where they lie up into the collar.

Trim the lapel and the front of the garment by grading as was done on the collar. Trim to 1/4″ first on what will lie on the underside. Measure the 1/4″ until you can judge the distance. Trim the sections that lie next to the outside of the garment to 3/8″. The grading reverses at the roll line of the lapel. Trim the point of the lapel as you did the point of the collar. Refer to Collars, pages 162-164.

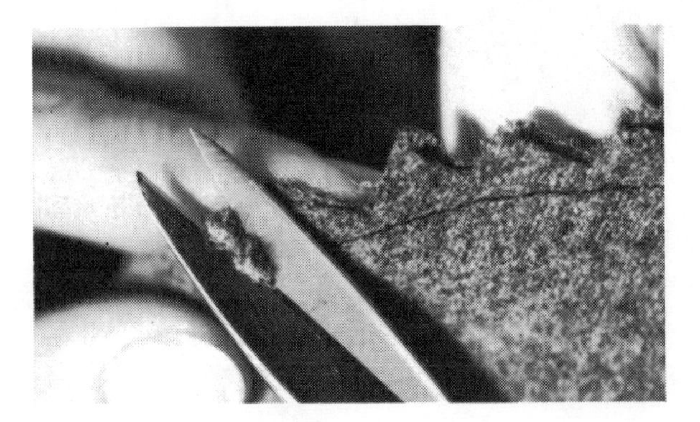

If the bottom of the garment is curved, take bits out of the curve.

Paint the seams with a paint brush, then press. This keeps the moisture just where you need it.

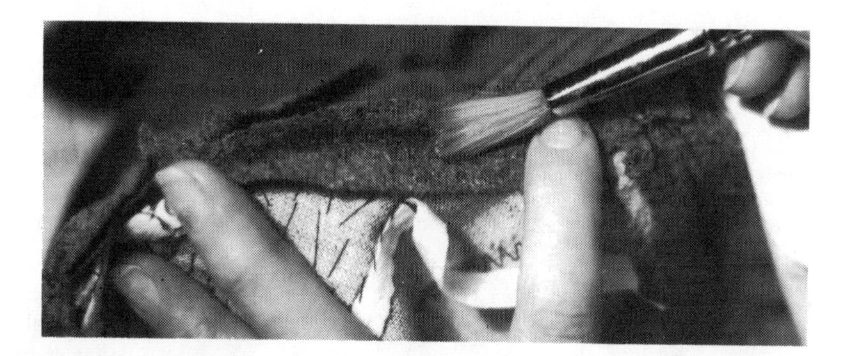

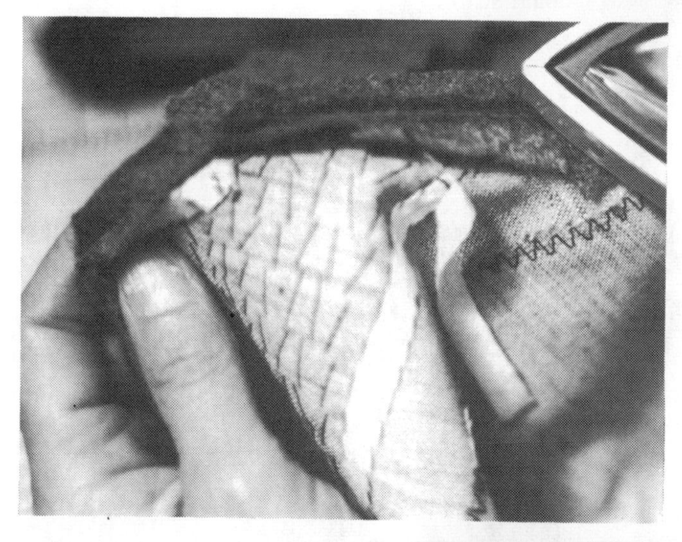

Press the seams open on a point presser. Press the under collar seam, the upper collar seam, and the lapel seam. As you press make sure you have clipped the neckline seams so that they lie flat when they are lying on grain.

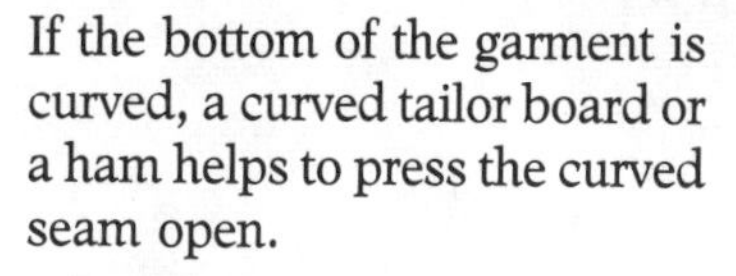

If the bottom of the garment is curved, a curved tailor board or a ham helps to press the curved seam open.

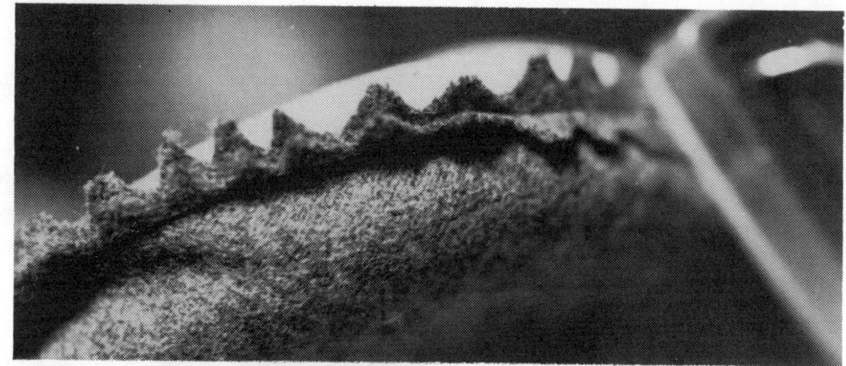

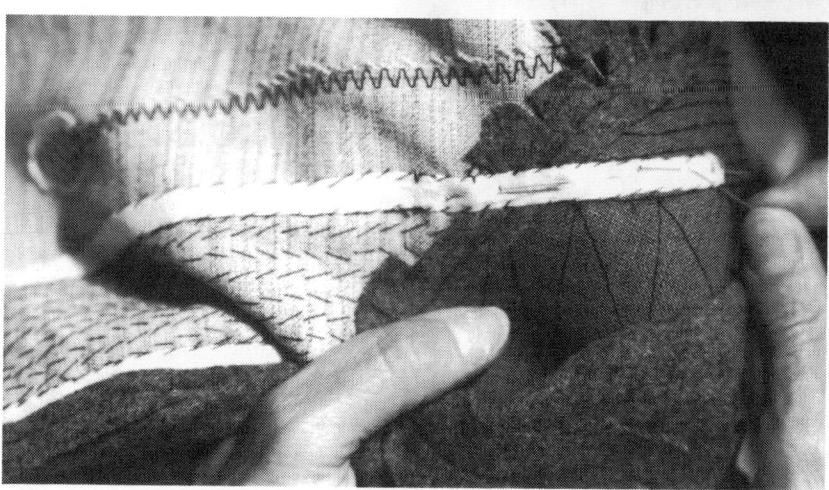

Bring the edge tape from the lapel over the under collar seam and lay it along the collar roll line. Make sure the roll line is smooth from the garment to the collar. If it is not, change the tape on the roll line until it is a smooth line. Hold the tape taut and pin in place. Hand stitch both edges of the tape to the under collar.

Finishing The Collar

Directions are given for garments with a back neck facing and with a lining in place of a back neck facing.

Finishing the collar with a back neck facing

Hand baste the upper edge of the collar to preserve the seam. It must stay slightly to the under side.

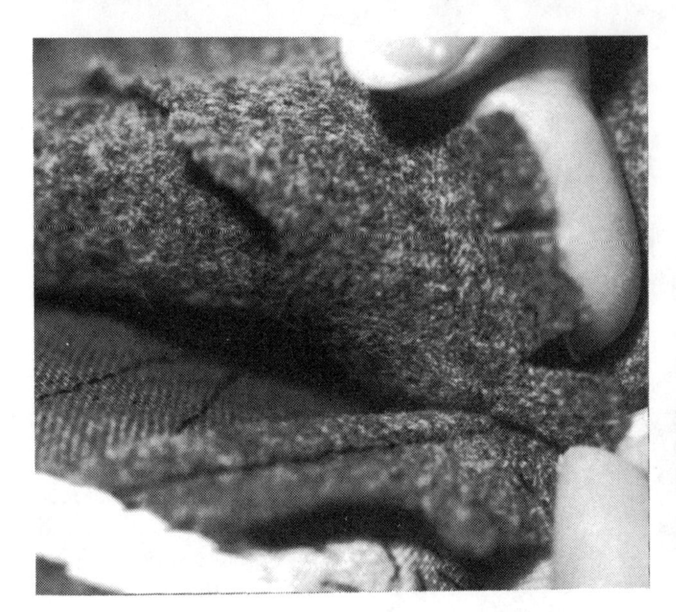

With the seams open, lay the upper collar seam on the under collar seam.

On the right side of the garment, hold the collar seam smooth from the collar junction and pin the open seam lines together.

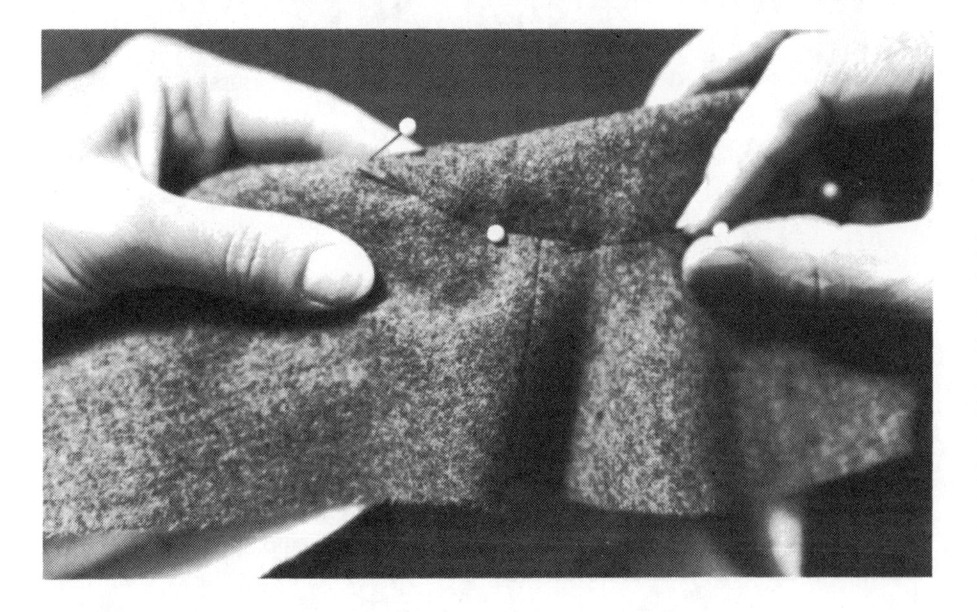

Fold the lapel/collar junction on the roll line of the collar and continue pinning the collar seams together. The seam lines may not match exactly because of the turn of cloth and the roll of the collar. Pin the entire collar seam in this manner with the collar folded on the roll line.

Lift the facing and hand stitch the seams together as closely to the garment seam line as possible. Stitch from one end of the collar to the other with a beeswaxed double thread and a large back stitch.

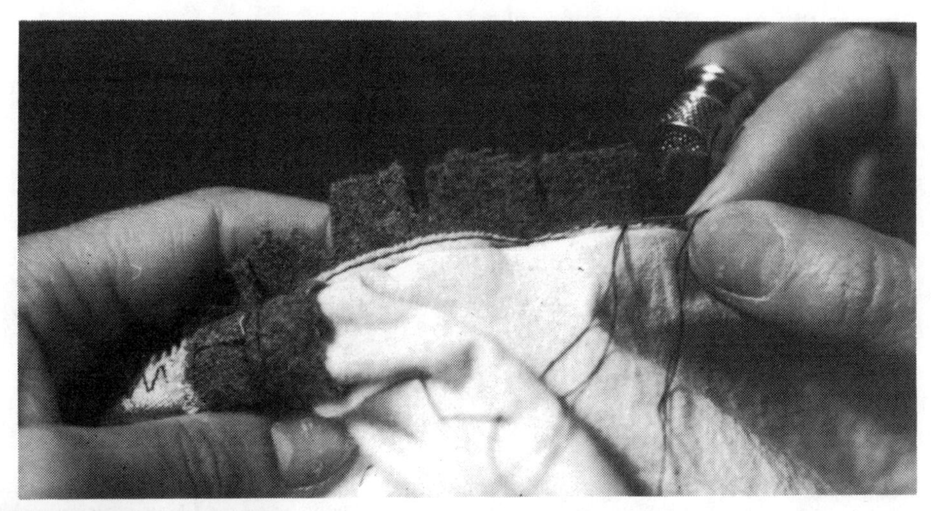

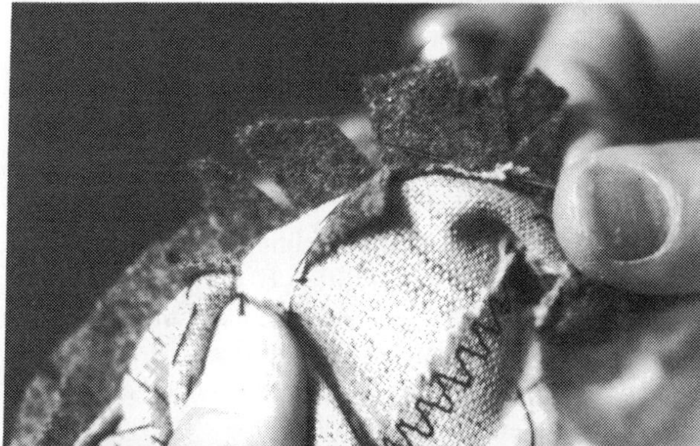

At the roll line where the edge tape crosses the seam, fasten the facing seam to the tape.

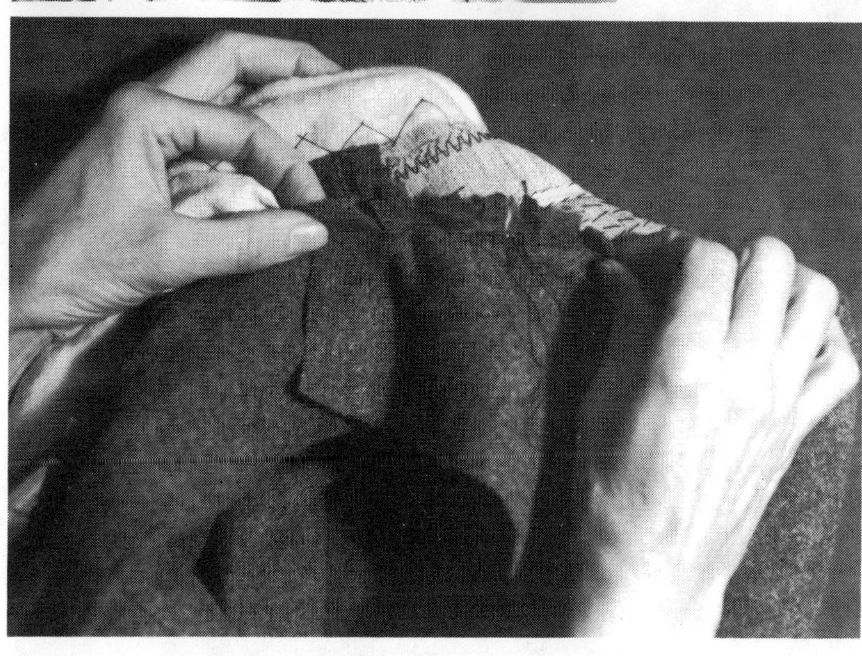

Finishing the collar with lining instead of a back neck facing

When lining is being used in place of the back neck facing the collar cannot be completely finished until the lining is attached. The procedure is the same as for a collar with a back neck facing except the neckline seam is only partially stitched.

Hand stitch the garment neckline to the facing neckline from the end of the collar to the shoulder seam on both sides of the garment. Leave a long thread to finish stitching the neckline and to secure the stitches after the lining is in place.

Directions continue on page 305.

Pre-Padded Under Collar

Cut the under collar of the bias pre-padded collar linen using the pattern tissue. Use the center back seam if you can. Eliminate the center back seam and cut the under collar on a fold if you are short of material. The grain lines on the ends of the collar are a bit different but since there is no grain line in felt it doesn't seem to affect the collar.

Prepare the pre-padded under collar

Mark a 5/8″ seam line on all the collar edges. Mark the roll line.

Seam shape the under collar.

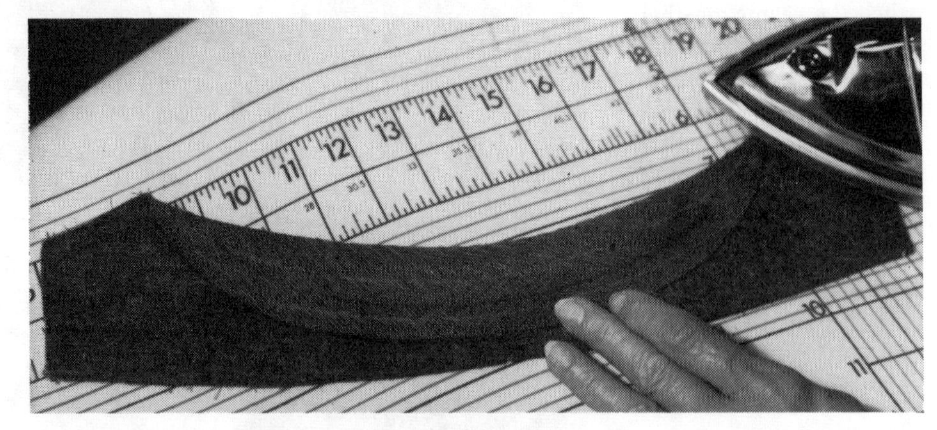

Trim 5/8″ from the neck edge only of the under collar. You are cutting both the linen and felt. Then trim 1/16″ of only the collar linen to expose the felt. Trim 5/8″ from only the linen on the end of the collar. Wait to trim the felt on the end of the collar.

Attach The Pre-Padded Under Collar

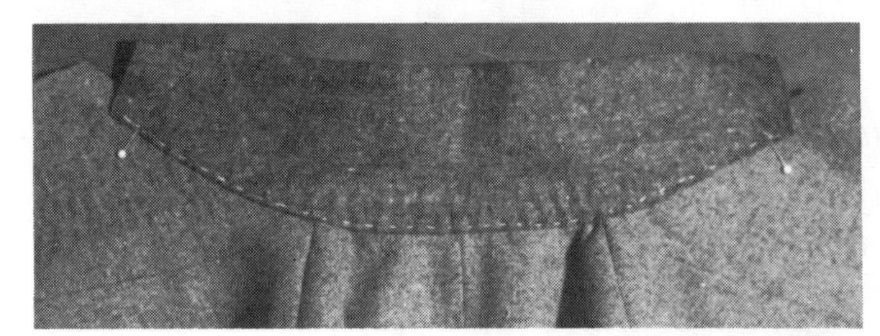

Pin, then hand baste the under collar to the garment neckline, laying the cut edge of the felt on the 5/8″ staystitched line of the neckline. At the collar junction set the collar slighlty deeper than 5/8″. Check to make sure both lapel length and collar ends are the width.

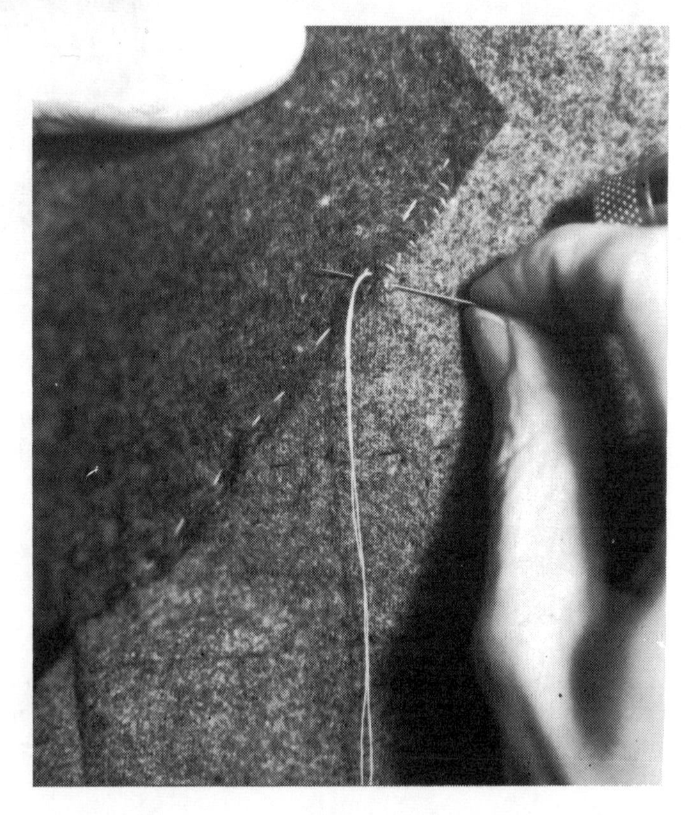

Fell stitch the collar all along the neckline. To fell stitch, beeswax the thread and knot one end. Start by bringing the needle up from underneath slightly inside the edge of the felt. The stitches should be about 1/10″ apart and about 1/10″ deep. Bring the thread straight down and insert the needle into the neckline. Bring the needle up at a slight angle through the felt. Continue this stitch on the entire neckline.

Begin stitching at the collar junction. The end of the collar has not been trimmed so the 5/8″ seam allowance is extending beyond the starting point.

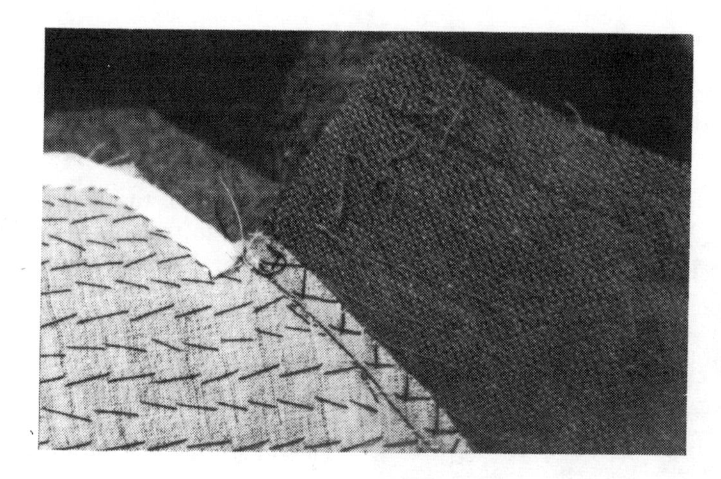

On the wrong side trim the front neckline seam, along the collar only, to 1/4". Do not trim the back neckline seam. Catch-stitch the seam allowance of both the front and back neckline to the collar linen.

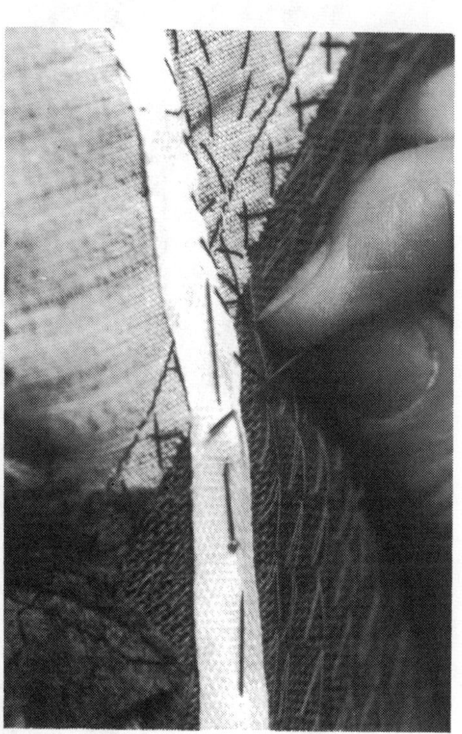

Hold the edge tape taut and stitch the edge tape to the roll line of the collar. Refer to page 297.

Prepare the upper collar

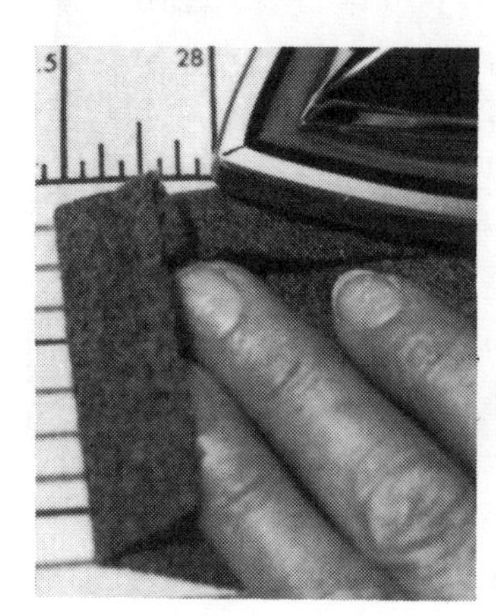

Miter the upper corners of the collar. To miter press the seam allowances of the upper collar edges to the wrong side of the collar.

Mark where the seam allowance edges touch with pins. Mark the corner with pins.

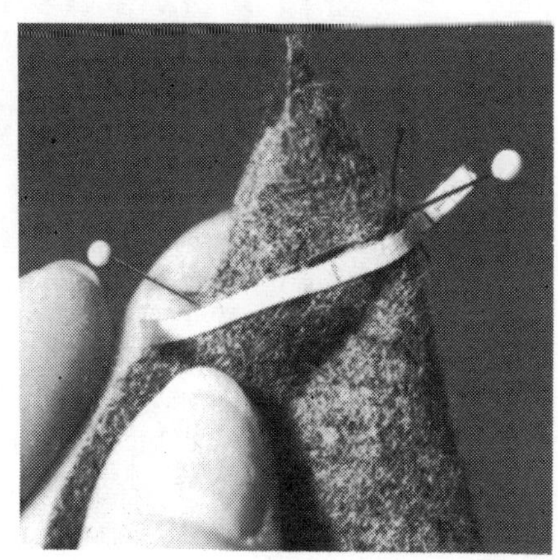

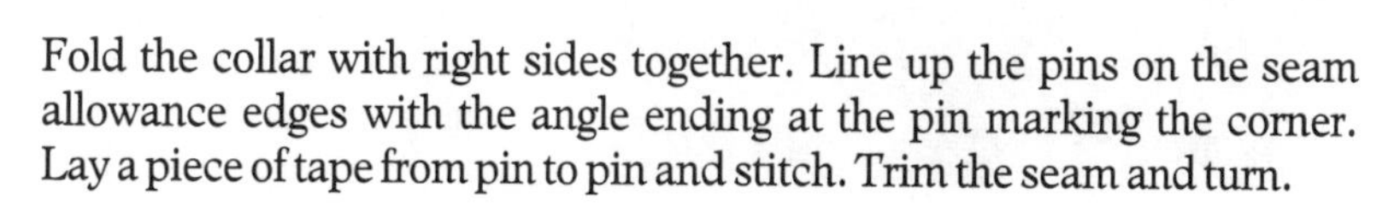

Fold the collar with right sides together. Line up the pins on the seam allowance edges with the angle ending at the pin marking the corner. Lay a piece of tape from pin to pin and stitch. Trim the seam and turn.

Stitch the upper collar to the facings or facing if there is only a front facing

Pin then stitch the upper collar to the front facing or facings if the pattern has a back neck facing. If there is no back neck facing, be sure the facing ends at the shoulder seam on the collar. The shoulder seam is marked on the collar pattern by two small dots.

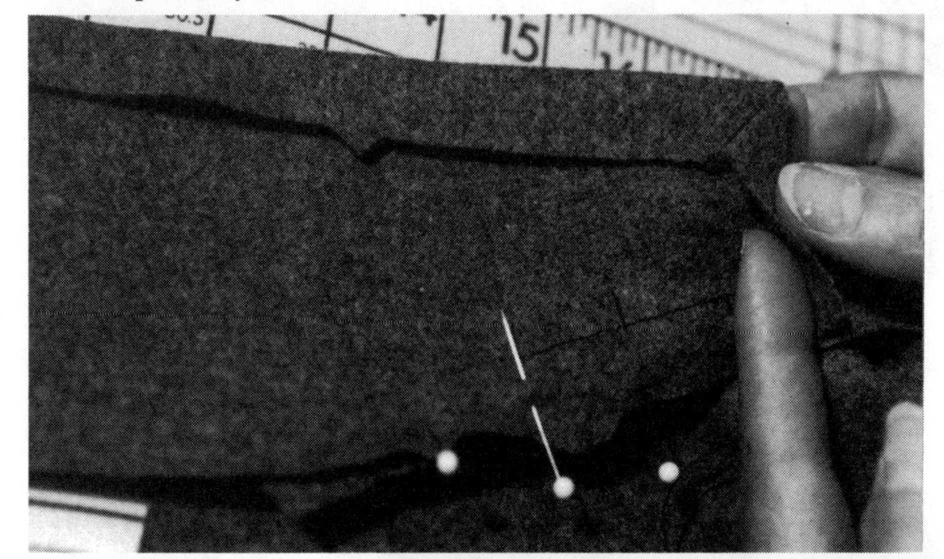

The 5/8″ line of the facing must come to that marking on the collar. Keep the seam allowance of the collar free. The 5/8″ seam allowance of the collar end seam must be exactly on the collar junction marking on the front facing. Leave long threads at the end of the collar and tie them. Wait to cut the threads until you are fell stitching the collar.

Press the seams open and clip the facing seam to allow it to lie flat when it is lying on grain as it will in the garment.

Trim the collar to 1/4″ and the facing seam to 3/8″.

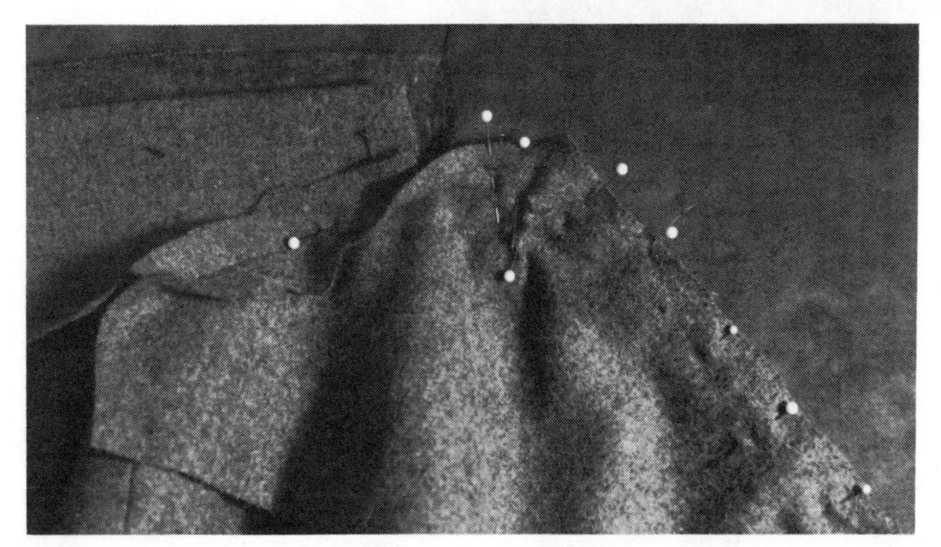

Stitch The Lapel

Pin then stitch the facing to the lapel from the collar junction to the hem. Refer to page 294. The collar is not stitched at this time. The upper collar must just cover the collar linen on the end of the collar. The lapel is easier to control with the pre-padded collar because the ends and top of the collar are fell-stitched in place. Refer to Collars, pages 174-175.

Trim, grade, and press the lapel seam only

Refer to pages 296-297.

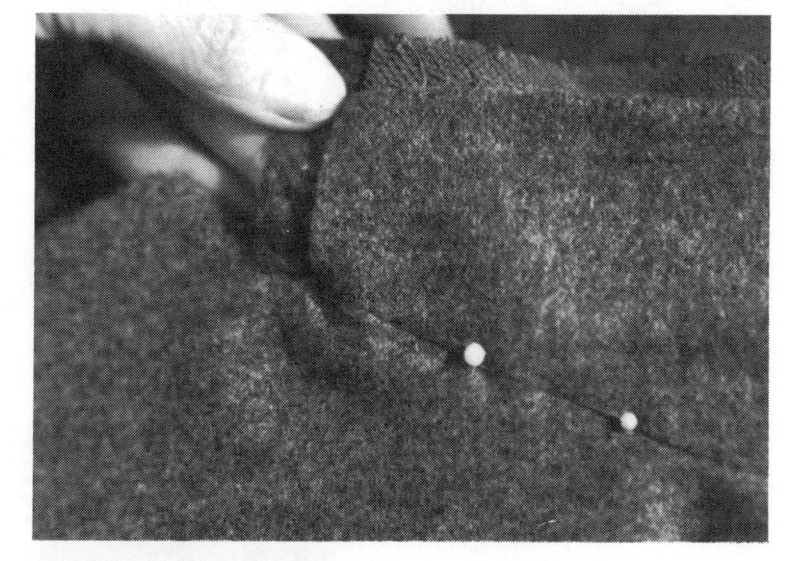

Attach The Upper Collar

On the right side of the garment hold the collar seam smooth from the collar junction to the roll line. Pin through the seam.

Lift the facing and on the inside catch stitch the collar seam allowance to the hair canvas from the collar junction to the roll line.

Baste the end and the upper edge of the upper collar to the felt at the 5/8″ line marked on the collar linen. Baste about 1/4″ from the edge.

Fold the lapel/collar junction on the roll line of the collar and continue pinning the collar seams together. The seam lines may not match exactly because of the turn of cloth and the roll of the collar. Pin the entire collar seam in this manner with the collar folded on the roll line.

Lift the facing and on the inside catch stitch the facing seam allowance to the hair canvas and muslin from roll line to roll line along the back neckline. If lining is used in place of the back neck facing, wait to fasten the neckline until the lining is stitched in place.

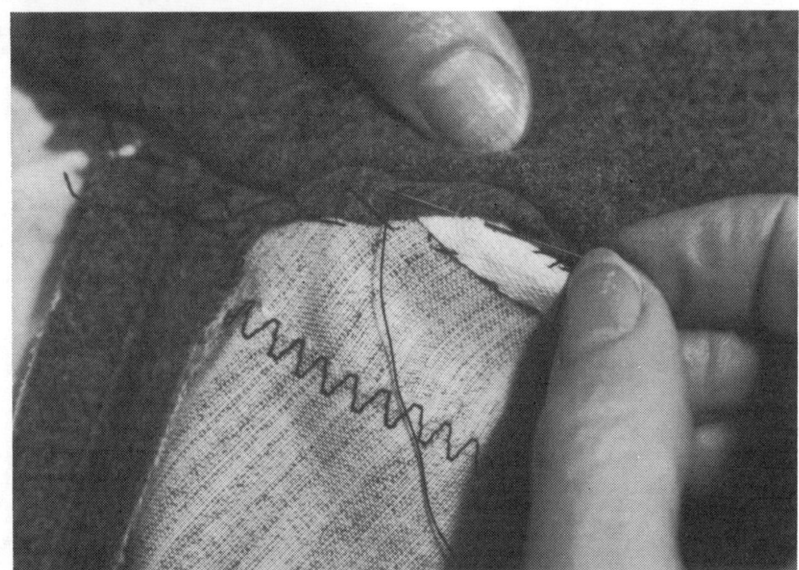

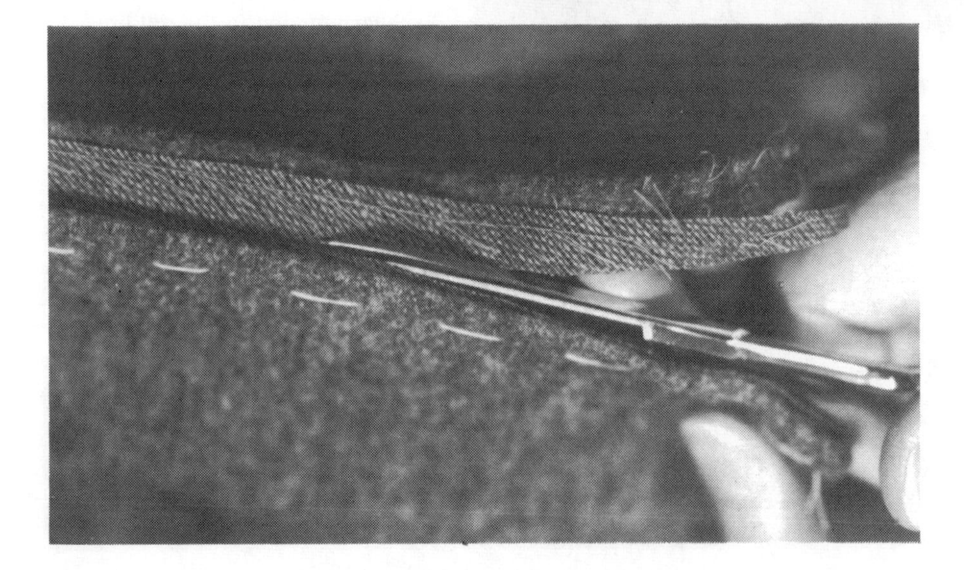

Trim the under collar felt so that it is slightly smaller than the upper collar. Trim the linen 1/16″ more.

Fell-stitch the under collar to the upper collar on the ends and upper edge of the collar. Press the edges of the collar. Press the collar on the roll over a ham to shape the upper collar to the roll line.

Hand baste the edge of the collar and lapel edge so that the seam favors the under.

Remember to reverse at the roll line on the lapel. The seam should lie toward the wrong side of the garment below the roll line and toward the right side of the garment above the roll line.

Silk thread is great for basting when you will be pressing with the basting threads in. It is easier to get the seam to lie correctly if you baste before pressing. Press the edge. Be careful to keep everything lying on grain as you press.

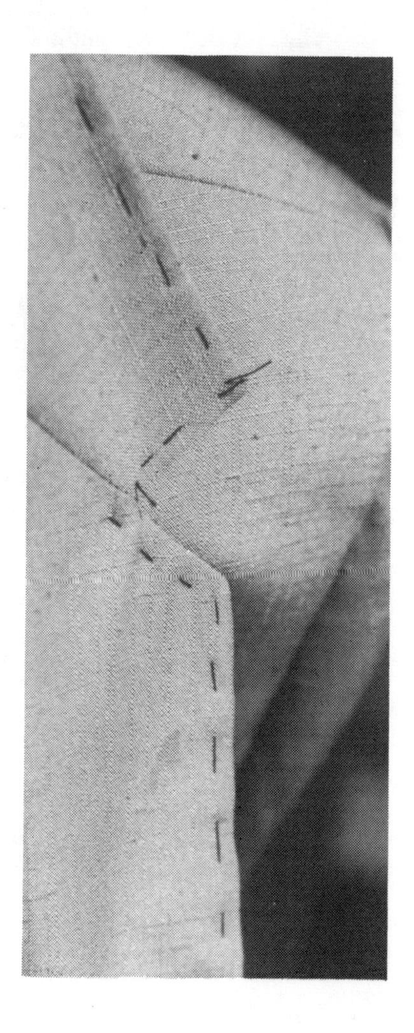

Prepare To Set In The Sleeves

The shoulder pads were made when you checked the sleeve length. If you purchased shoulder pads, fit them to the armhole. Refer to Fusible Tailoring, page 259. Fitting and shaping the pad is already done if you made the shoulder pads.

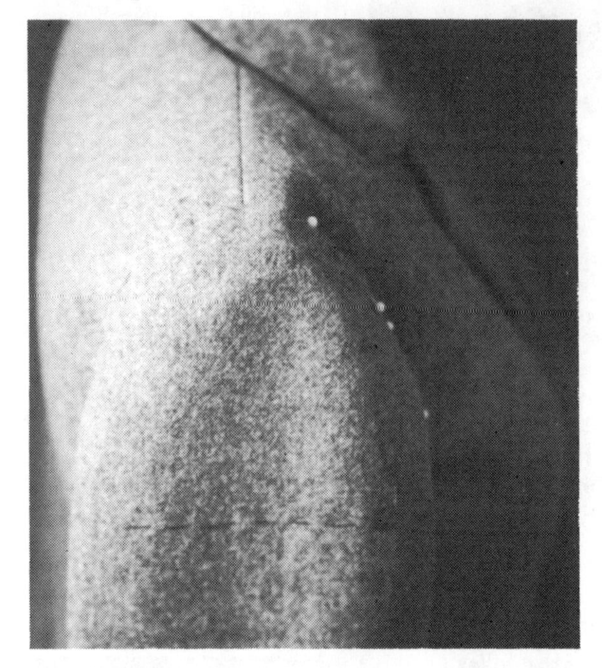

Check the fit and the hang of the sleeve with a pad slipped in place. The crossgrain line must be horizontal to the floor. Pin the sleeve at the shoulder so that the hang is correct. Then pin or hand baste the sleeves into the jacket and check the comfort and the hang before you stitch them in permanently. Refer to Sleeves, pages 197-201.

If the sleeve needs changes in the sleeve cap or the armhole seamlines, mark any difference from the regular seam line.

Do this by marking the touch (where the sleeve touches the armhole) with a hand baste line.

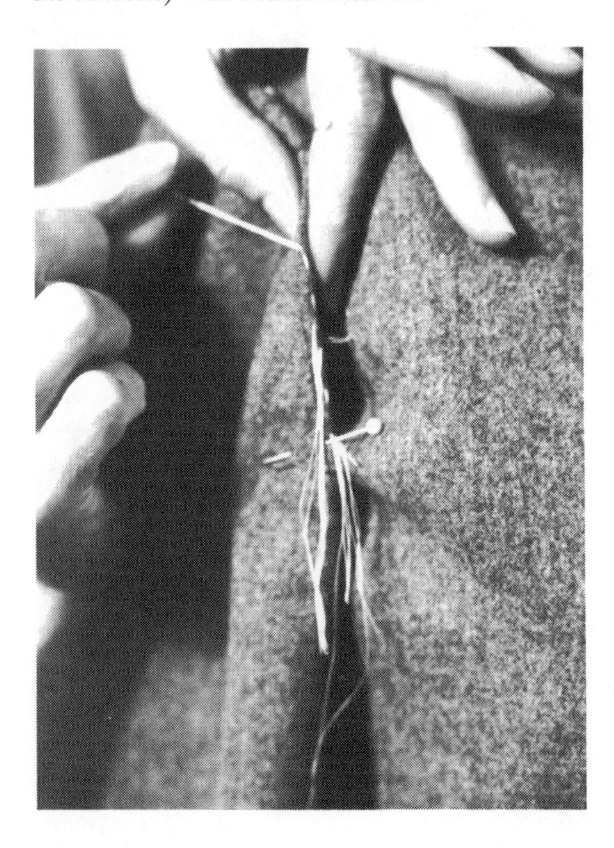

Also mark the turn (where the sleeve seam folds under) with a hand baste line.

Then lay the opposite sleeve and armhole in the one that is marked and transfer the markings so that both sleeves are set in the same manner. Hand baste or pin the sleeve in and stitch. **Exception:** If one shoulder is very different from the other shoulder and the sleeve will not hang properly if they are done the same, you must pin fit each sleeve.

Set In The Sleeves

Stitch both sleeves in after the fit has been checked. For general information on setting in sleeves, refer to Sleeves, pages 201-203.

Stitch the sleeve on the 5/8″ line. After stitching, check for puckers on the sleeve and armhole. Put the garment on a dress form or ham. Check the seam on the garment side. Lay a tape measure with the edge on the seam over the shoulder to make sure you have a nice smooth seam line on the shoulder. This is especially important when you are using shoulder pads.

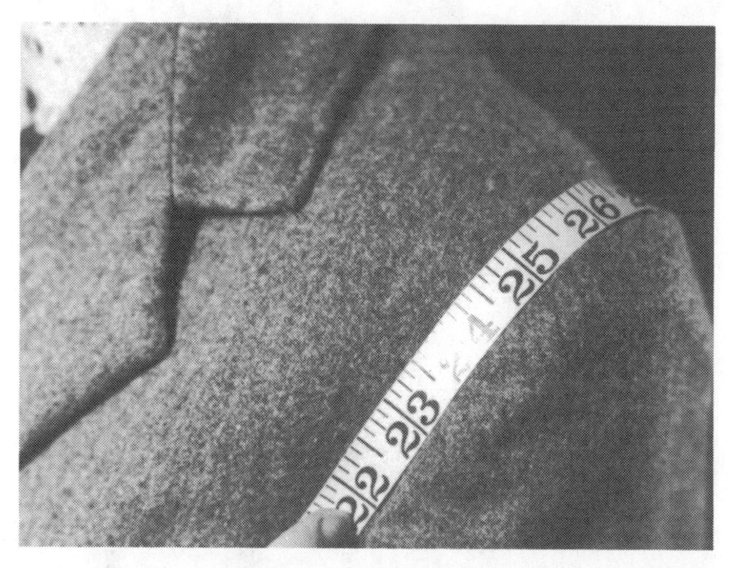

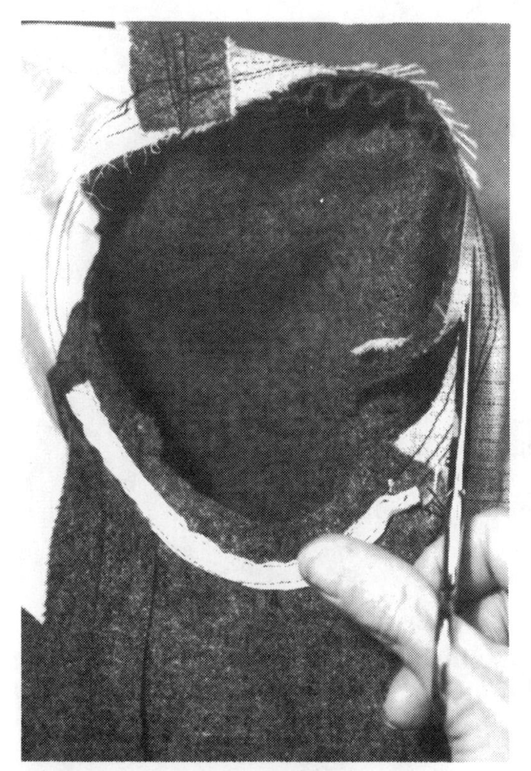

Remove the bastings. Stitch again 1/4″ from the first stitching line, easing in the fullness.

Tape the sleeve in the bias area if the entire armhole was not interfaced. If the fabric is very heavy or loosely woven, tape over the interfacing. To tape, hold the tape taut in the curve of the armhole and hold the sleeve in its curve as you stitch. The tape can be caught in both the 5/8″ and the 3/8″ stitching lines.

Trim the sleeve seam to the 3/8″ stitching line in the underarm area. If you like a crisp look in the shoulder area, trim the entire armhole to the 3/8″ stitching line. If you prefer a soft shoulder line, trim only the underarm area and leave the remaining sleeve seam a full 5/8″.

Press the sleeve seam on the inside of the garment over the ham. Extend the tip of the iron slightly over the seam. Press completely around the armhole. Press the seam on the outside after the shoulder pads and sleeve rolls are in.

Put The Shoulder Pads In The Garment

Always pin the pad on the right side of the garment with the garment over your hand.

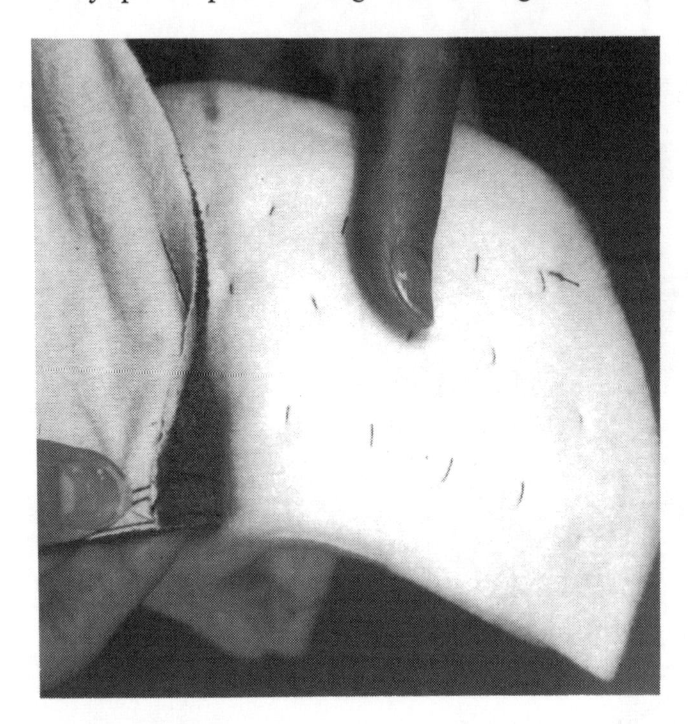

On the inside, put the shoulder line marking on the pad at the shoulder seam. Place the edge of the pad 1/4″-3/8″ beyond the armhole stitching line. Pin to hold at the shoulder seam. Also pin the edge of the pad to the edge of the front armhole seam just enough to insure that it will stay in place.

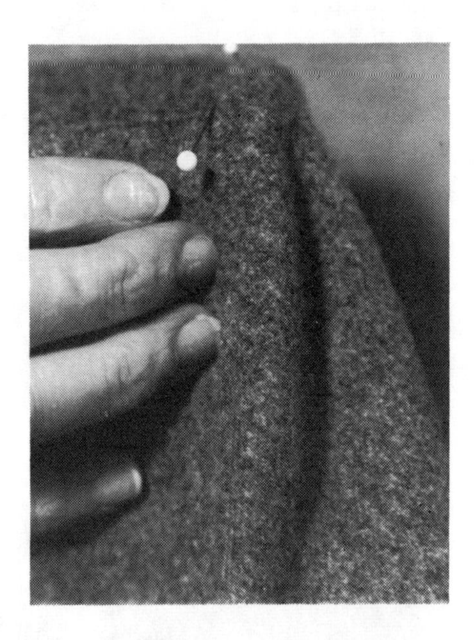

On the outside, push your fingers against the armhole seam, smoothing the garment against the pad. Pin in the well of the seam, catching the pad. **On the inside,** check to make sure that the edge of the pad is extending past the armhole seam. **On the outside,** unpin one side of the armhole (to free the pad for stitching to the shoulder seam).

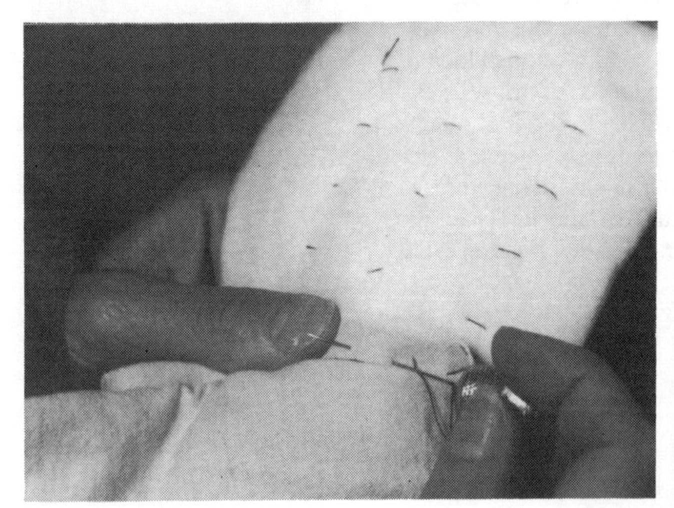

On the inside, flip the loose area of the pad up and permanently hand baste the shoulder pad to the shoulder seam. Use long loose stitches through the top layers of the pad. Secure the beginning and end with close stitches and a knot.

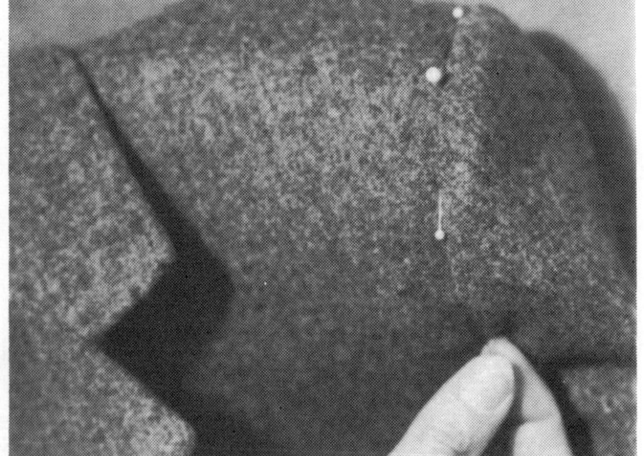

On the outside, repin the loose side of the pad along the well of the seam.

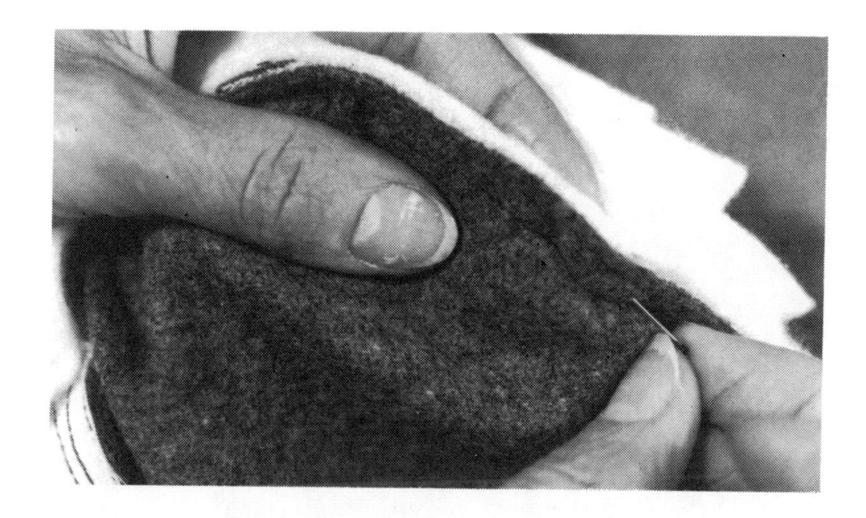

On the inside, permanently hand baste the layer of the pad closest to the garment to the armhole seam allowance. Make sure the baste stitch does not pull the seam or cause any pulls on the right side of the garment. Secure the beginning and end with several close stitches and knot.

Catch stitch the shoulder pad edges to the interfacings

With the garment over your hand pin **on the outside** of the garment, catching the shoulder pad edges underneath.

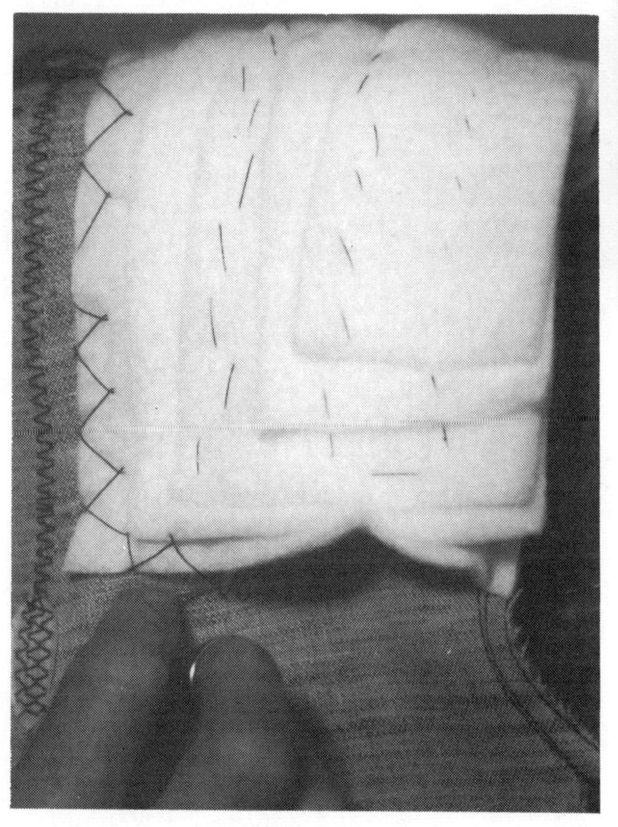

On the inside, catch stitch with a large stitch the outer layer of the shoulder pad to the interfacing. Do not catch the fashion fabric.

Put The Sleeve Roll In The Garment

The sleeve roll or sleeve head buffers the sleeve seam and gives a nice roll to a well done sleeve.

Use a 1½" wide piece of lambs wool cut on the bias or pellon fleece 1½" wide cut on the crossgrain about the length of the shoulder pad. Pellon fleece makes a better roll for heavy weight fabric and lambs wool works best for lightweight fabric.

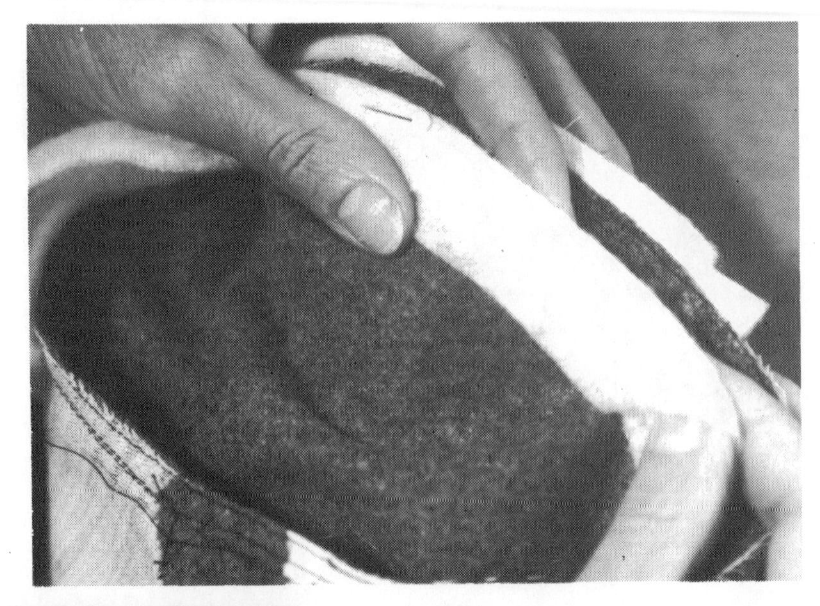

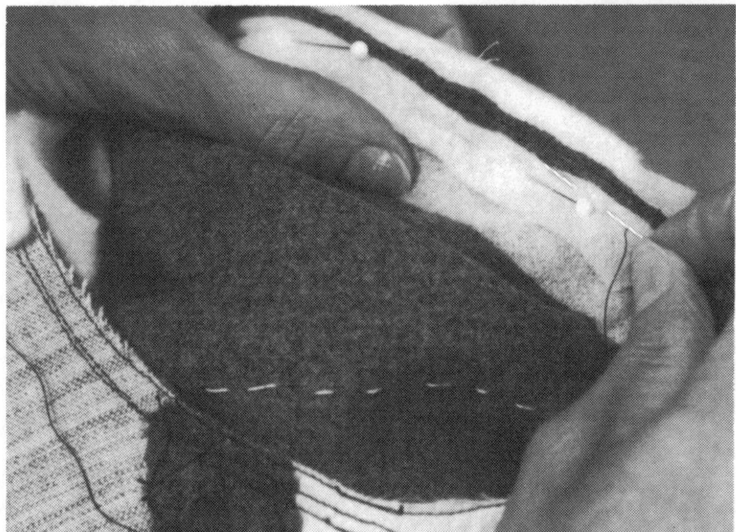

Fold the sleeve roll in half so that it is graded with the longest edge next to the sleeve. Stretch it slightly to fit without bubbles on the longest edge next to the garment. Pin it to the armhole seam.

Permanently baste the folded edge of the sleeve roll to the seam allowance of the armhole. The sleeve roll should lie smoothly against the sleeve when it is finished.

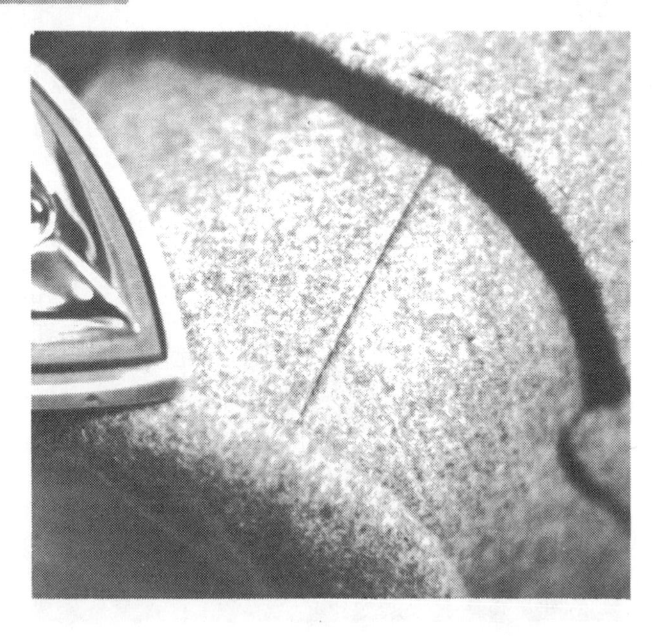

Press the sleeve. You can ruin the sleeve by over pressing. Put your hand in the sleeve with your fingers against the pad and press the sleeve seam with lots of steam. When it gets too hot for your fingers it's enough for the sleeve. While the steam is still in the fabric press the seam with your hand. That is enough.

The Following Must Be Done Before Lining The Garment

Finish the bound buttonholes

Finish the bound buttonholes on the facing side. Wait to attach the back of the buttonhole until the hem is done. Refer to the Bound Buttonholes, pages 218-219.

Finish the pockets

Outside welt pockets should have the ends hand stitched from the wrong side of the garment with a backstitch. Refer to page 238. Patch pockets should be permanently stitched. If you are hand stitching the patch pockets in place, stitch them from the wrong side of the garment with a backstitch. Refer to page 231.

Preparation For Hemming The Garment

Interface the garment hem

Lightly crease the garment along the hemline. If the garment is a coat, the hem should be marked and trimmed so that it is a standard depth. Refer to Hems, pages 97-98 and 101. If the garment is a jacket, after the hem is lightly creased, pin it up and try it on to check the length. For a soft hem, refer to page 288.

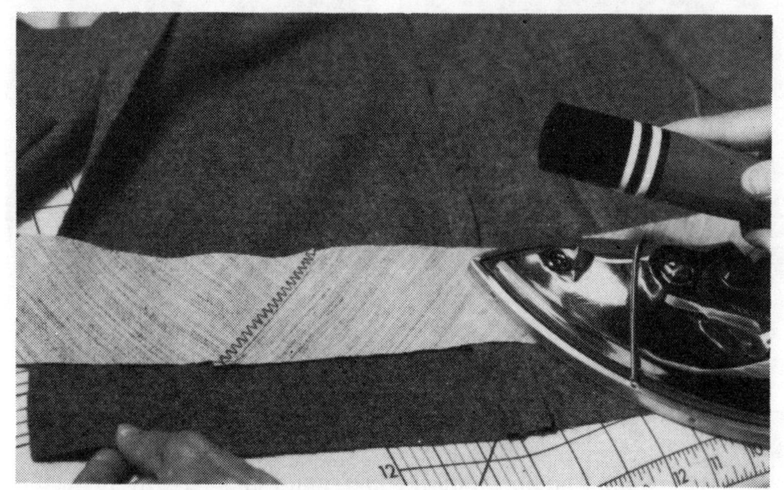

Lay the interfacing on the hemline, extending up into the garment. Steam shape the interfacing to the garment. Cut the interfacing so it overlaps the front interfacing about 1/2". At a back vent, it should come to the fold line of the vent.

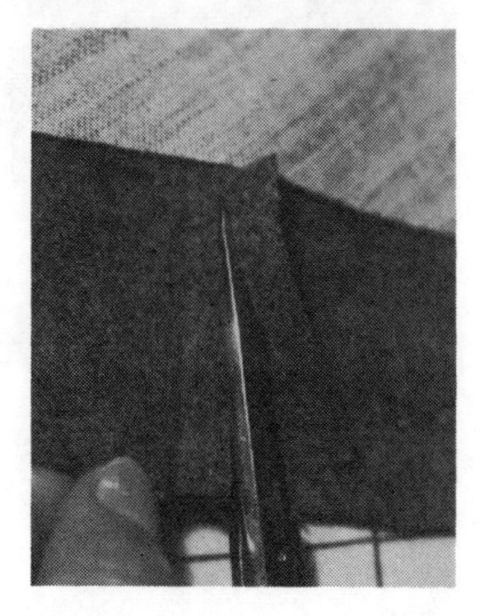

Trim the garment seam allowance in the hem to 3/8" to grade them. Only trim the seam allowance if you are sure that you will never need to let out the seams. It is better not to remove the small amount of bulk in the hem if you might need to alter the garment at some later date.

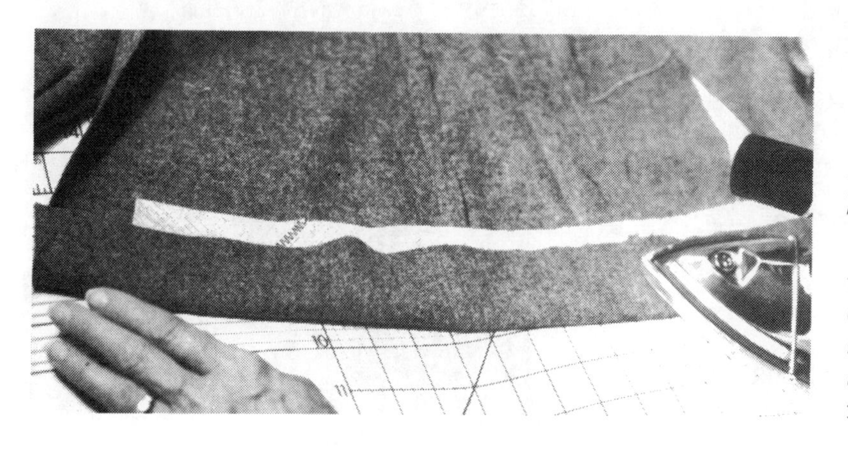

Lay the hem up over the interfacing. The interfacing should extend about 1/2" beyond the edge of the hem. Pin the hem to the interfacing. Steam any excess fullness from the hem, then stitch 1/4" from the hem edge. You are stitching the hem edge to the interfacing.

On a garment with a straight bottom, the hem should continue to the end of the facing. If the garment needed to be lengthened and you have trimmed the facing hem, you cannot lengthen the garment. The hem interfacing will extend 1/4″ beyond the edge of the front interfacing.

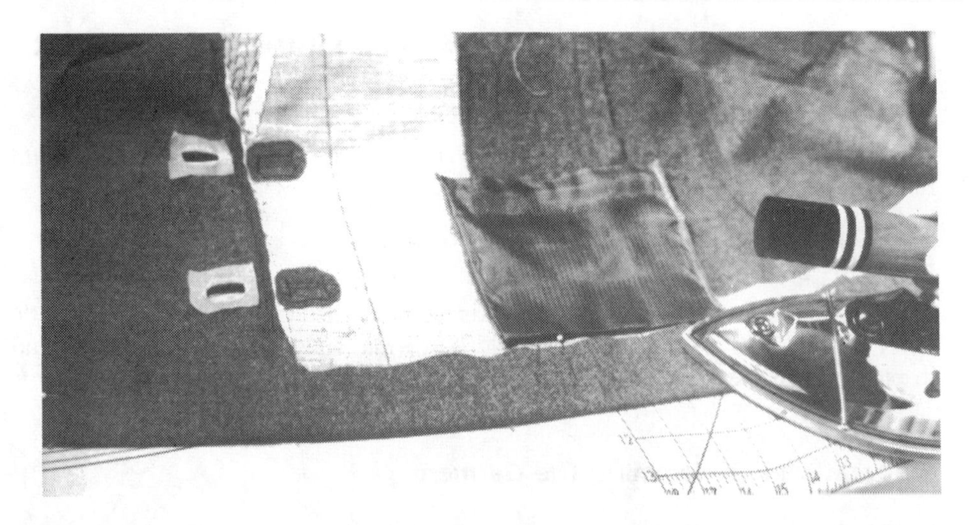

On the garment/facing seam line, hand baste the hem to the garment in the hem turn at the front edge of the garment. This holds those seams tightly together while they are pressed and usually topstitched and gives a nice crisp turn at the bottom corner of the garment.

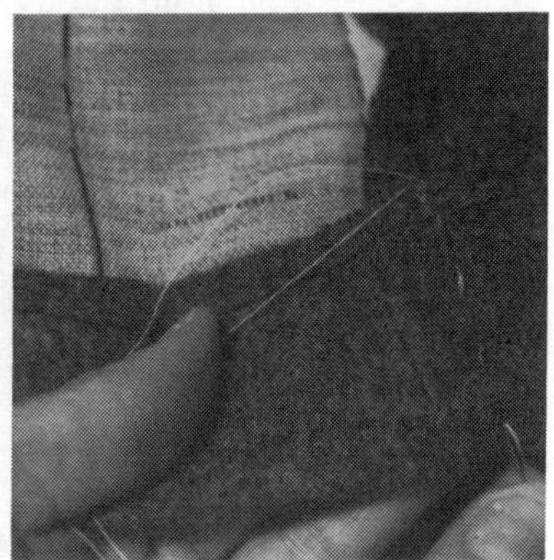

On a garment with a curved bottom, the hem ends at the front facing. The front facing edge should be folded back a small amount and should be hand stitched to the hem.

Back Vent

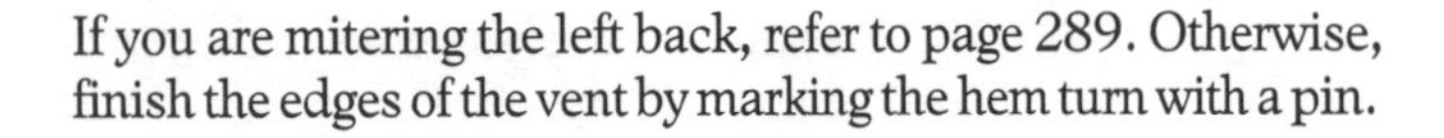

If you are mitering the left back, refer to page 289. Otherwise, finish the edges of the vent by marking the hem turn with a pin.

Fold the hem toward the garment with the right sides together. On the upper layer of the vent (left back with no interfacing in the hem turn of the vent), stitch the end with only a scant 1/4″ seam. On the under layer of the vent (the right back), stitch the end with a 5/8″ seam. The picture is of the under layer of the vent. Trim the interfacing as shown so the lining will cover the interfacing.

Turn the vent ends to the right side and press.

Hem The Garment

Fold the interfacing edge back and hem the interfacing to the garment. Refer to Hems, page 101.

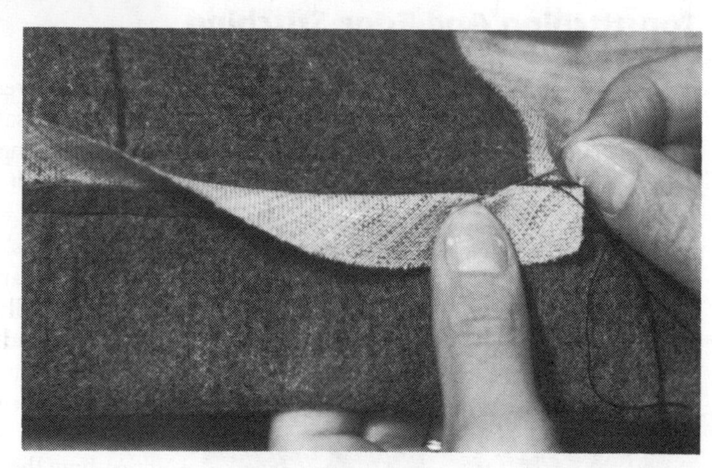

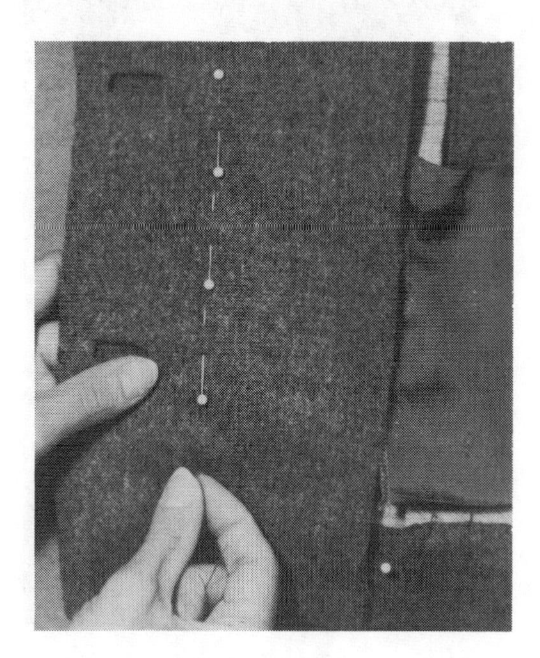

Tailor Baste The Facing To The Interfacing

On loosely woven or bulky fabric, tailor baste the facing to the interfacing on both fronts.

On the right front, tailor baste from the buttonholes to the edge of the facing and tailor baste below the buttonholes.

Tailor baste the entire left front.

Put a row of pins about 1″ from the front edge through the facing and garment. Baste at 1″ intervals until you are about 1″ from the edge of the facing.

Fold the facing back and take a large stitch at right angles to the facing, catching the interfacing to the facing. The stitch in the facing should be very small. The stitch in the interfacing can be larger. The stitches must be loose enough so they do not pull the facing. When one row is done, put another row of pins about 1″ from the first row until you are basted to within 1″ of the facing edge.

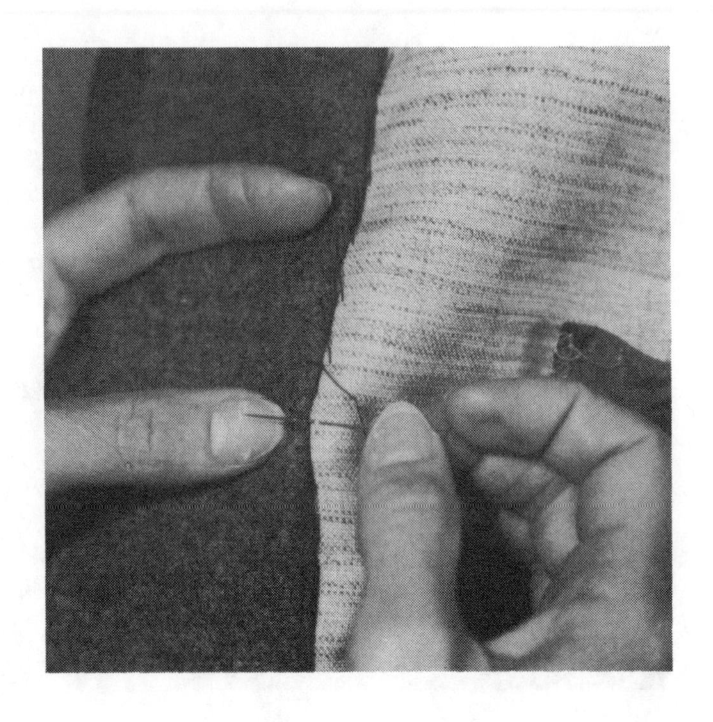

Topstitching And Edge Stitching

It is always your choice to topstitch, edgestitch, or only to press. Sometimes the fabric or the style will decide for you. If you are unsure of which would look best, do a sample. Then choose what looks the best to you. Always hand baste before you topstitch or edgestitch. Basting holds all the layers together and helps you to achieve a professional job. Refer to page 305. Also refer to Topstitching and Edgestitching, pages 72 and 164.

Topstitching is usually 1/4″ from the edge of the lapel, collar, welt pocket flap, or the edge of patch pockets. Sometimes the pattern will call for other areas to be topstitched. I often topstitch with two strands of thread through the needle as in the picture to the left. Notice how the collar is stitched.

Edgestitching is 1/16″ from the edge of the fabric and is used to hold the edge flat. It is not meant to be a trimming. Use the blind hem foot of your machine to help you edgestitch straight. Refer to Patch Pockets, page 231.

Lining The Garment

The lining can be put in entirely by hand as the pattern suggests. Or the neckline and facing area can be stitched by machine and the remainder done by hand. I use the machine method.

Clip the lining to the staystitching around the back neckline. **Pin** the lining to the back facing, matching the centers and the shoulder seams. The closeup picture shows the lining pinned. **Machine stitch** from shoulder seam to shoulder seam.

Lining without a back neck facing

Do steps 1-3 in sequence.

1. Stitch about 3″ of the front lining to the garment facing at the top of the facing to complete the front shoulder area.

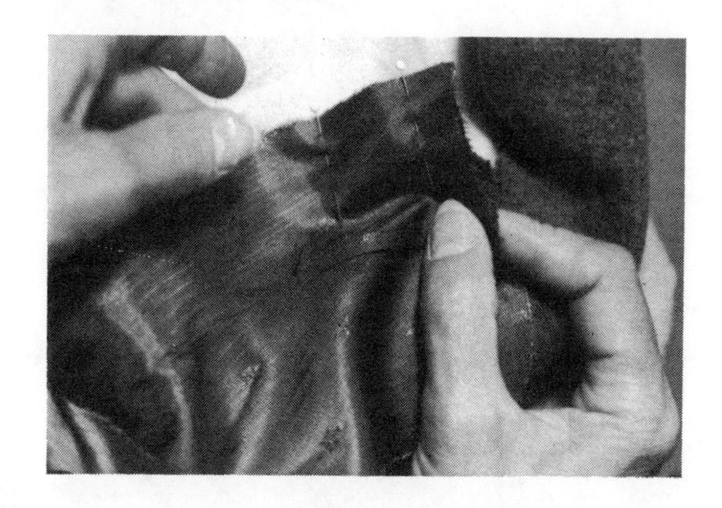

2. Stitch the shoulder seam of the back lining to the shoulder seam of the front facing/lining.

3. Stitch the back neckline of the lining to the upper collar. Press the seam open clipping the lining until it lies flat.

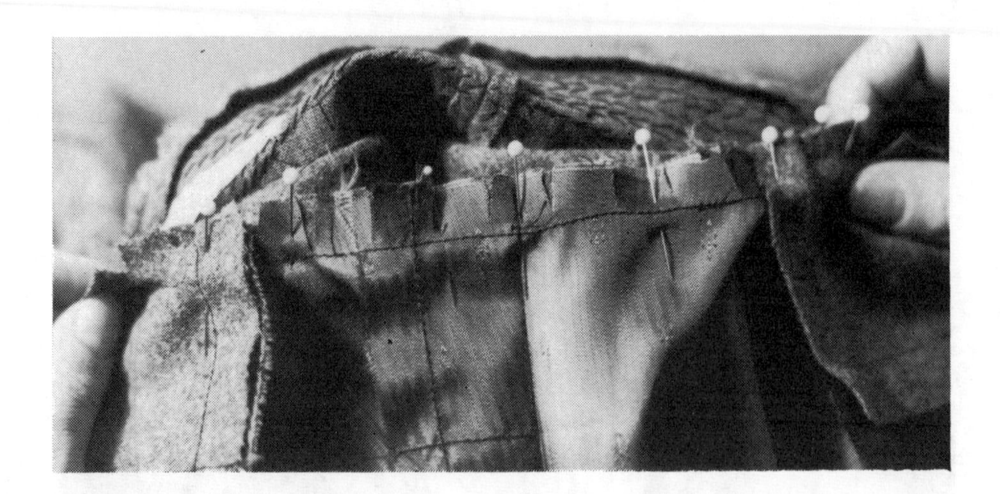

Finish the collar without a back neck facing

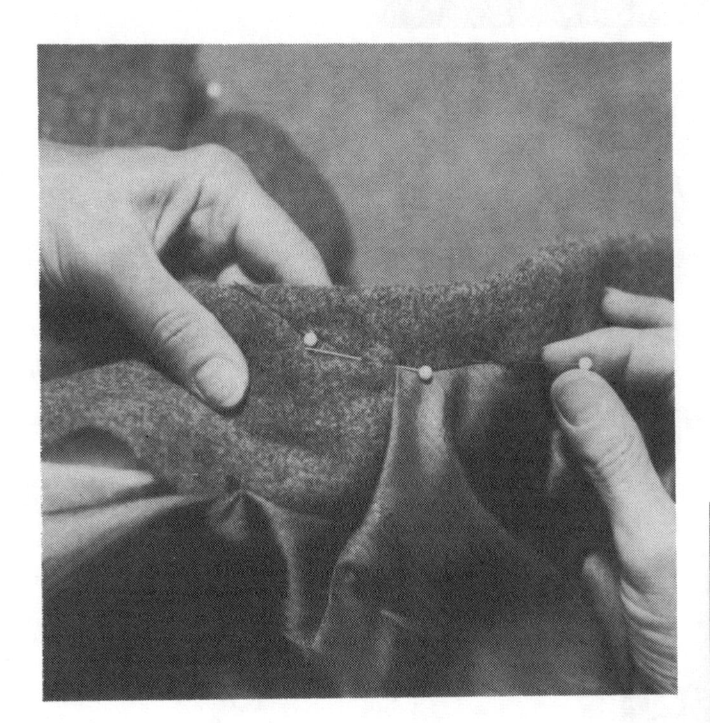

Fold the collar on the roll line and pin the collar seams together. The seam lines may not match exactly because of the turn of cloth and the roll of the collar.

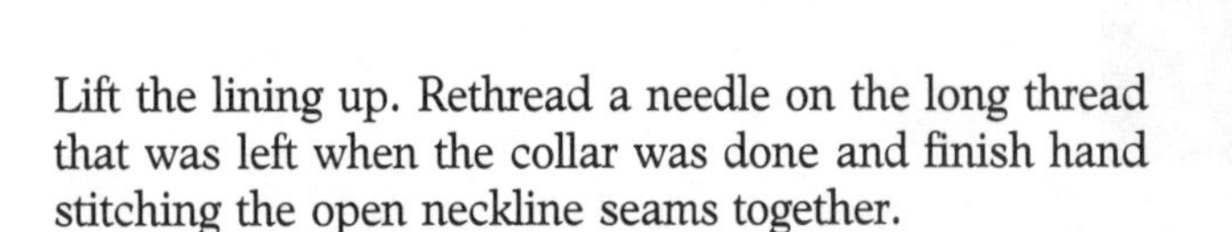

Lift the lining up. Rethread a needle on the long thread that was left when the collar was done and finish hand stitching the open neckline seams together.

Preparation for stitching the lining to the front facing

Pin the lining to the back and front armhole. Work down from the shoulder and really stretch the lining to make it fit. Match the seams of the lining to the seams of the garment.

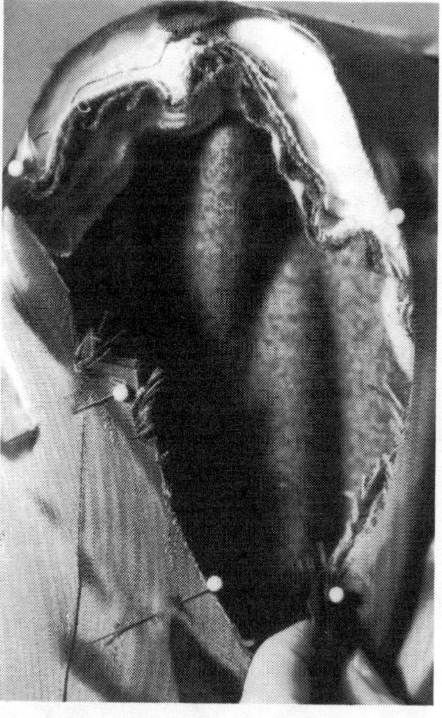

The shoulder pad makes the lining a tight fit when it is turned to the wrong side. The garment armhole has been trimmed. The lining armhole has not been trimmed. Allow the lining to extend past the seam line of the garment. Check the right side of the garment to be sure there are no pulls showing on the right side of the garment.

On the seam closest to the front of the garment match the side seams of the lining to the side seams of the garment. Match the notches of lining side seams to the notches of the garment. Pin the seams together.

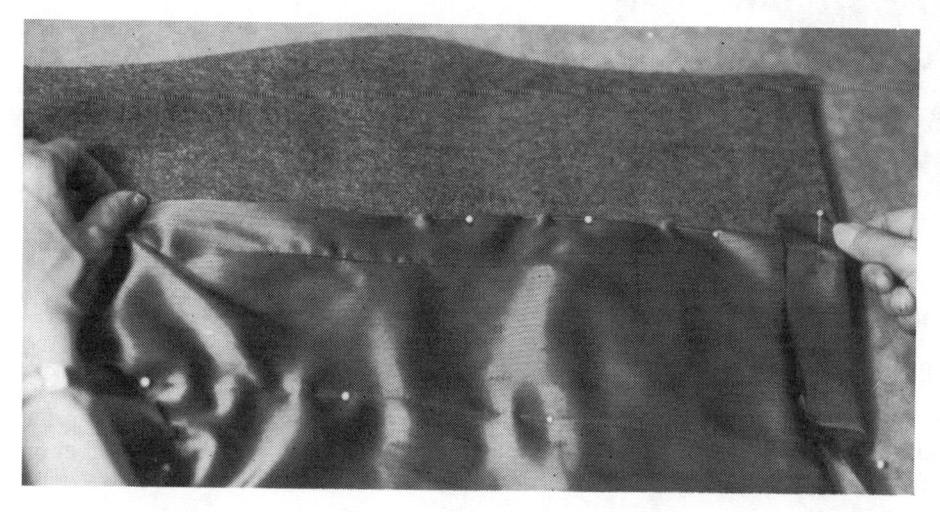

Pin up the hem at the side seam so it is even with the bottom edge of the garment. Turn up the hem the same amount at the front of the lining.

Pin the front edge of the lining to the front facing. Turn under the seam allowances. The grain line of the lining must be horizontal to the hem with no pull up or down. Pin the lining to the facing until you reach about the level of the armhole.

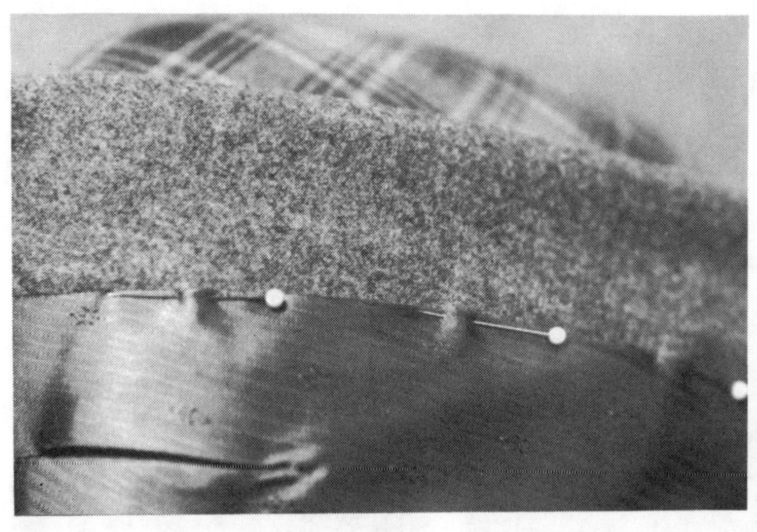

Then place the garment over a ham and continue pinning the lining to the facing up to the shoulder seam. Pinning over the ham curve helps ease the lining onto the facing. It is very easy to pull the lining in this area and cause pulls on the outside of the garment.

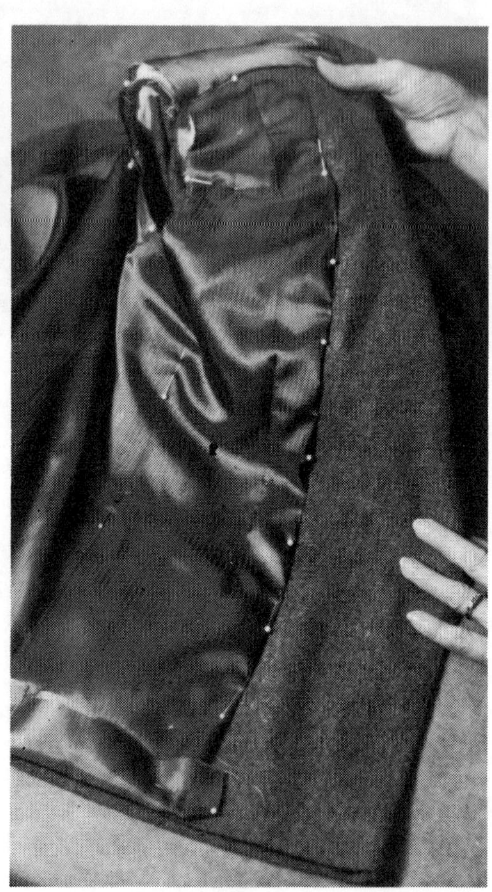

The lining can be stitched by hand. I prefer to stitch it by machine. I have found that it looks better and is stronger. Also it is faster to stitch it by machine.

After the lining is pinned to the facing remove the pins around the armhole and along the side seams.

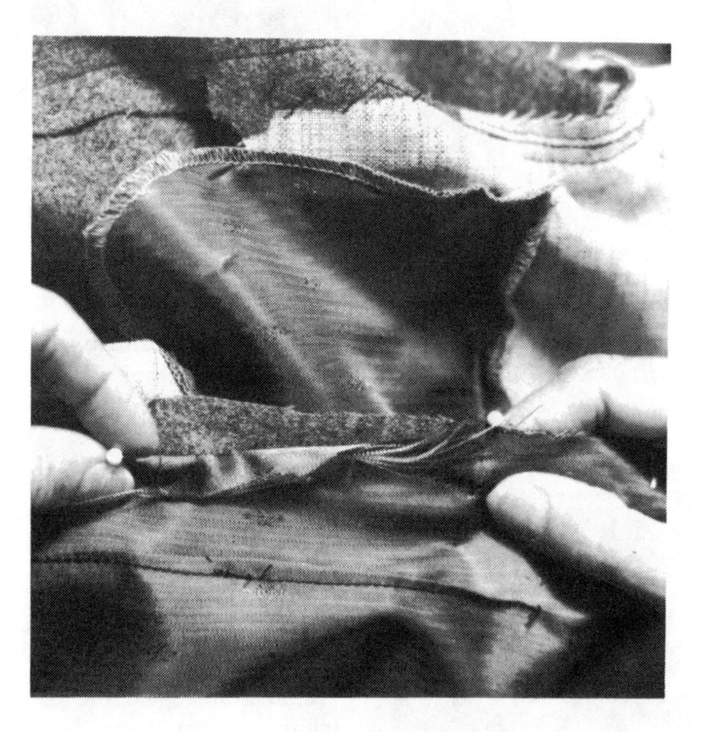

Repin the lining to the facing from the inside

Hold the two layers of fabric and slip the pins from the right side to the inside to repin the seam. Repinning in this manner keeps the lining in the correct position.

Stitch the lining to the front facing

Machine stitch with the lining up. Leave about two inches unstitched at the bottom to finish the hem.

Pin the other front. It is not necessary to check the position of the second front. Measure the turn up on the lining at the bottom and pin the lining to the facing. Pin it flat to the armhole and then over the ham. Repin on the inside and stitch the second front.

Stitch the lining to the armhole

Repin around the armhole. Stretch the lining to make it fit. Match the seams of the lining to the seams of the garment. The garment armhole has been trimmed. The lining armhole has not been trimmed. Allow the lining to extend past the seam line of the garment. Check the right side of the garment to be sure there are no pulls showing on the right side of the garment.

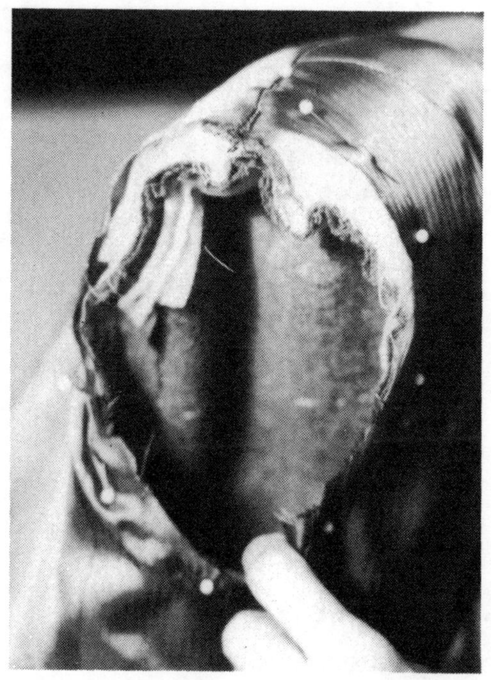

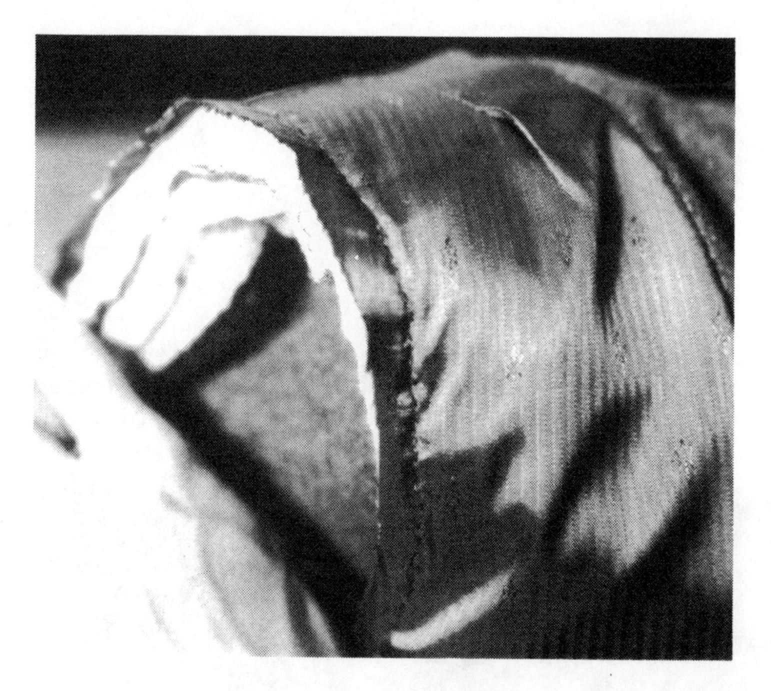

Fasten the lining to the garment seam allowance around the armhole with a double thread and a short backstitch. Work close to the seam line. In the shoulder pad area lengthen the stitch and stitch into the pad. Don't pull too tight. The shoulder pad must not be distorted. Stitch the underarm area on the sleeve side so you can see the seam and the shoulder pad area on the garment side. Trim the excess lining.

Traveling thread

Attach all the seams of the lining to the garment seams except the center back seam. Lay the open seams of the lining on the open seams of the garment. Match the notches and pin the seams together. Allow a slight ease on the lining.

Begin with the seam closest to the front of the garment.

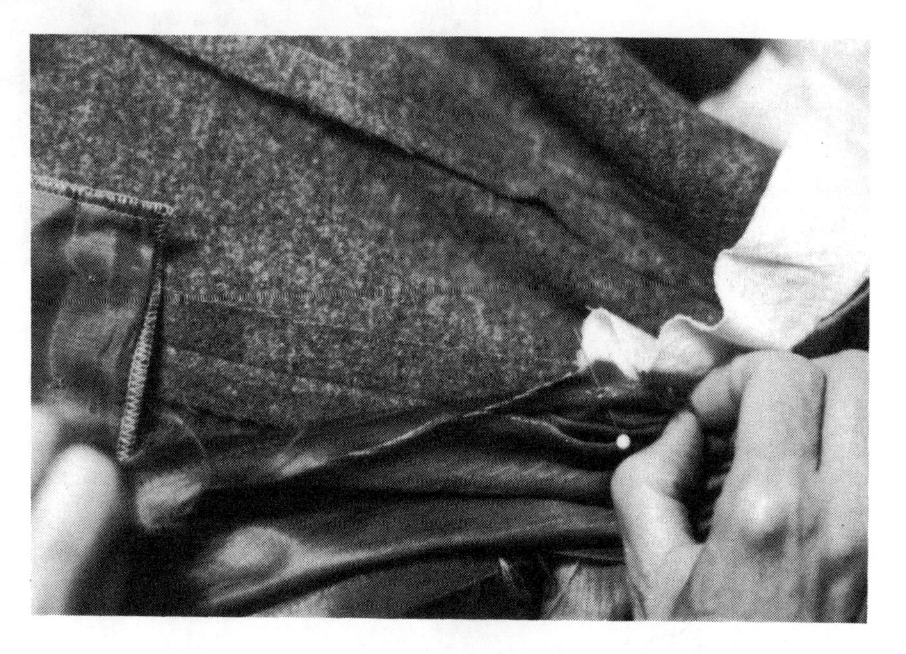

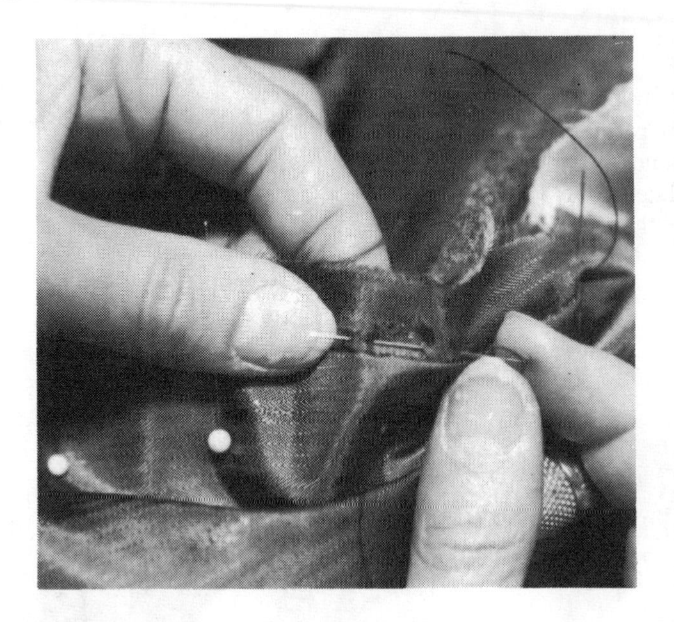

Permanently hand baste close to one side of the seamline, using a continuous beeswaxed thread or a quilting thread (already waxed). Leave a 2″ end with a knot on the thread on both ends. This allows for the thread to move (called a traveling thread) and eliminates pulls on the garment while holding the lining firmly in place.

Notice in the picture below how the thread is held. It can move so you don't get any pulls on the garment.

Leave about 2″ of the seam unfastened at the top and bottom of each seam.

Do all the seams in this manner except the center back seam.

Lining The Sleeve

With the sleeve lining wrong side out, slip it into the correct garment sleeve. Turn the garment sleeve wrong side out and lay the matching seams together and pin. Match the notches of the lining to the corresponding notches of the sleeve. If there are no notches to guide you, make sure you have enough lining at the armhole to go over the seam and turn under 1/4″. (This is the area where you raised the armhole 3/4″ when you cut the sleeve lining.) If you didn't cut it higher, scoot the lining up so that you have enough room to go over the seam and turn under 1/4″.

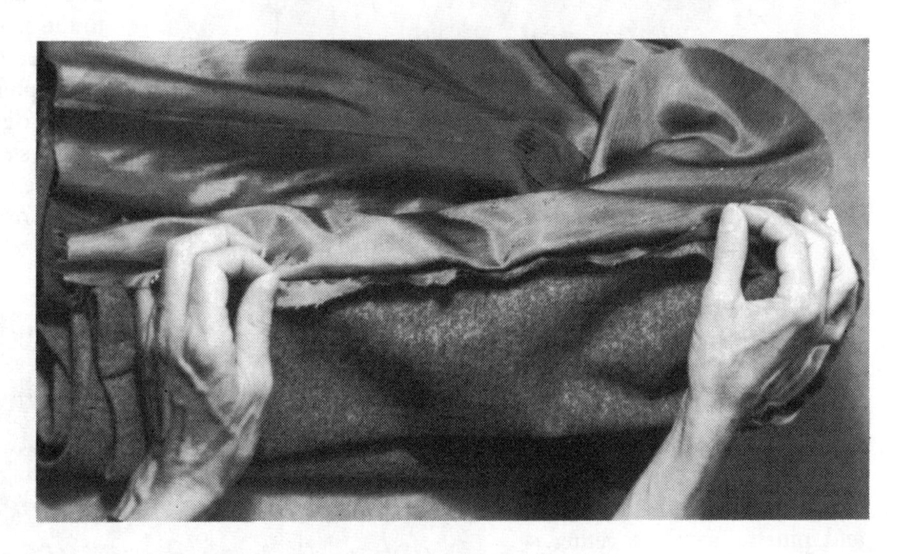

Hand baste the lining seams to the sleeve seams in the same manner as you did the garment. Turn the sleeve right side out.

Starting at the underarm, pin the sleeve lining to the garment lining. Pin a small area on either side of the underarm. Turn under only 1/4″. Do not clip.

Go to the center of the cap and turn in a normal 5/8″ seam allowance. Work from the center on both the front and the back. Turn in the 5/8″ seam allowance everywhere except the small area of the underarm where it is only turned under 1/4″.

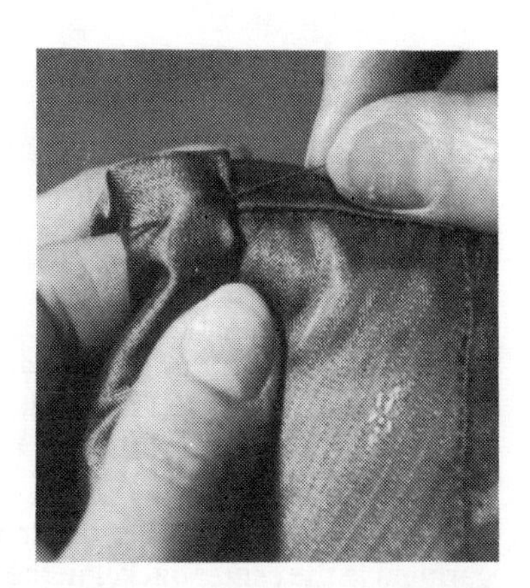

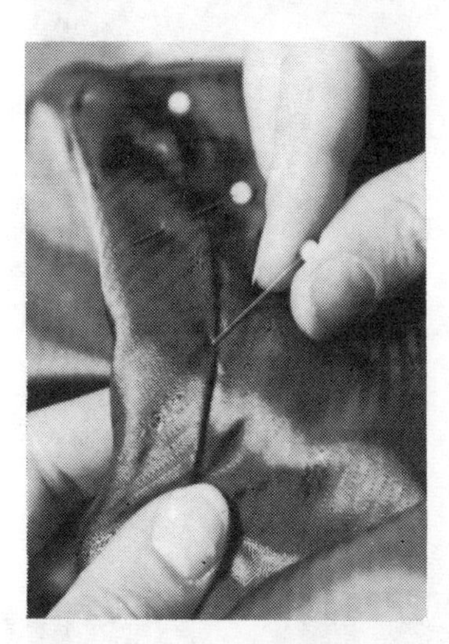

Move any excess fullness on the cap toward the underarm. You need the ease where the sleeve strains when you move. If it is too tight there, it will pull out with wear. Pin around the whole armhole, distributing the ease evenly around the sleeve.

After it is all pinned, stitch the sleeve lining to the garment lining. Stitch around the armhole with a double thread using a small stitch. Ease a little with each stitch. Go under the garment lining and come up in the fold of the sleeve lining. Begin stitching at the underarm and hand stitch the entire armhole just inside the stitching line holding the garment lining to the armhole.

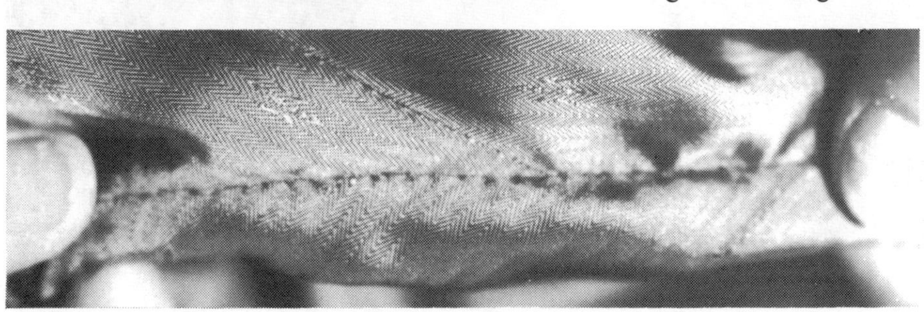

Hemming The Lining

This method of hemming the lining is commonly called a jump hem. The hem fold is loose so there is never a pull on the garment.

A back vent in a lining

If there is a back vent, do it before proceeding with the hem. Mark the cutting and fold lines but never cut the left side out before you attach it to the garment as the pattern directs. It is so easy to cut the wrong side before it is stitched into the garment.

Hold the garment by the collar and with it hanging pin the lining to the garment at the center back. Pin the vent to the garment at the top of the vent.

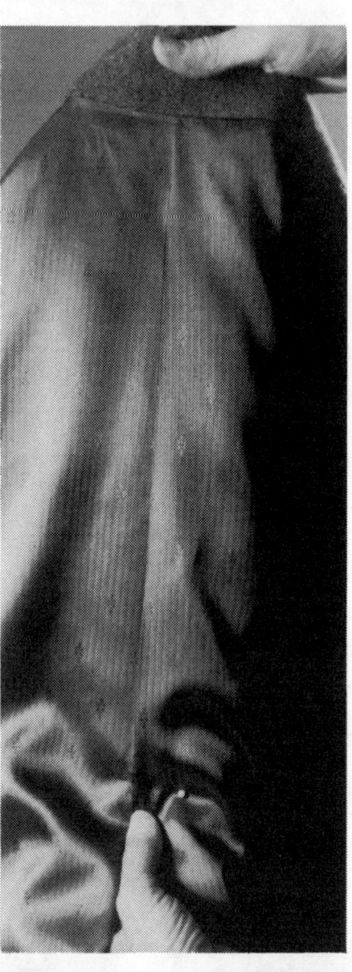

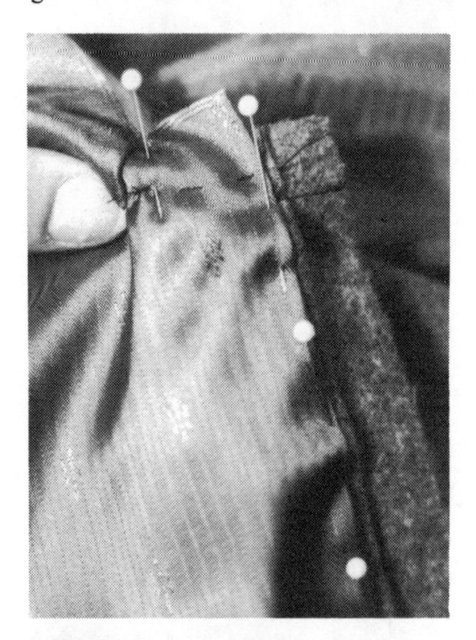

On the under side of the vent baste the top edges to hold the lining in place. Fold the seam allowance under so that it exposes a little of the fashion fabric and pin it along the edge. Stop about an inch from the top of the hem.

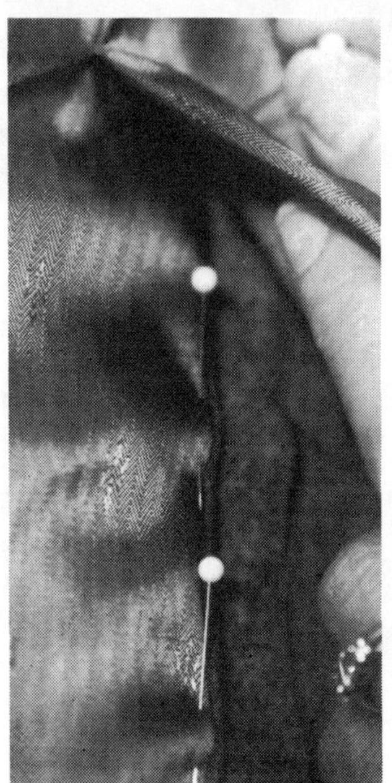

On the top side of the vent put a pin in from the right side of the lining to mark where the lining will clear the pleat underneath.

Reinforce that pin by stitching a small V. Clip to the point of the V. Be careful. Check as you are clipping to make sure you are just to the edge of the under pleat. Trim the excess lining on the marked lines.

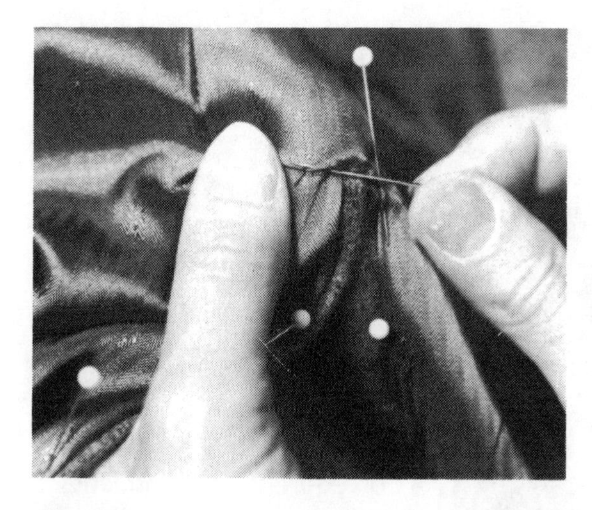

Fold in the upper part of the pleat. Turn the corner neatly.

On the upper part of the pleat pin the lining to the garment seam line of the pleat. The pins are almost hidden by the under side of the vent.

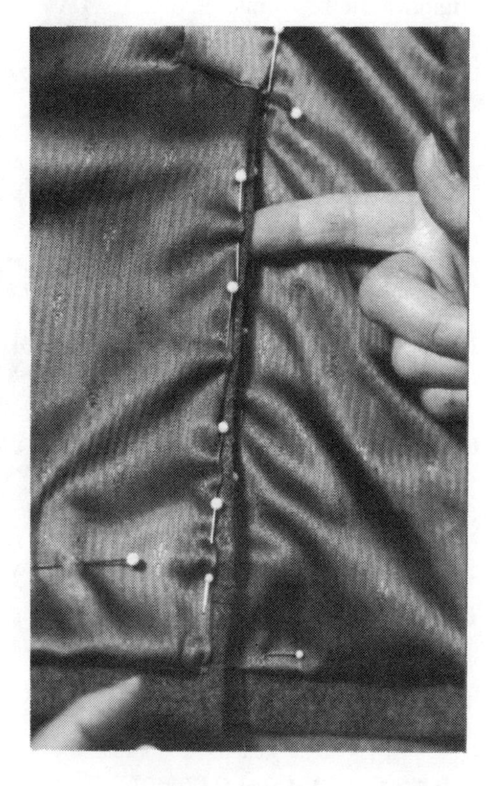

The upper part of the pleat (closest to the right of the garment) is lying underneath in the picture. Turn up the hem of the lining as described below. After everything is pinned check to make sure there are no pulls on the right side of the garment. Then invisibly stitch the edges.

Do the jump hem on the garment lining

Hold the garment by the collar and with it hanging pin the lining to the garment at the center back. Refer to the upper right picture on the previous page.

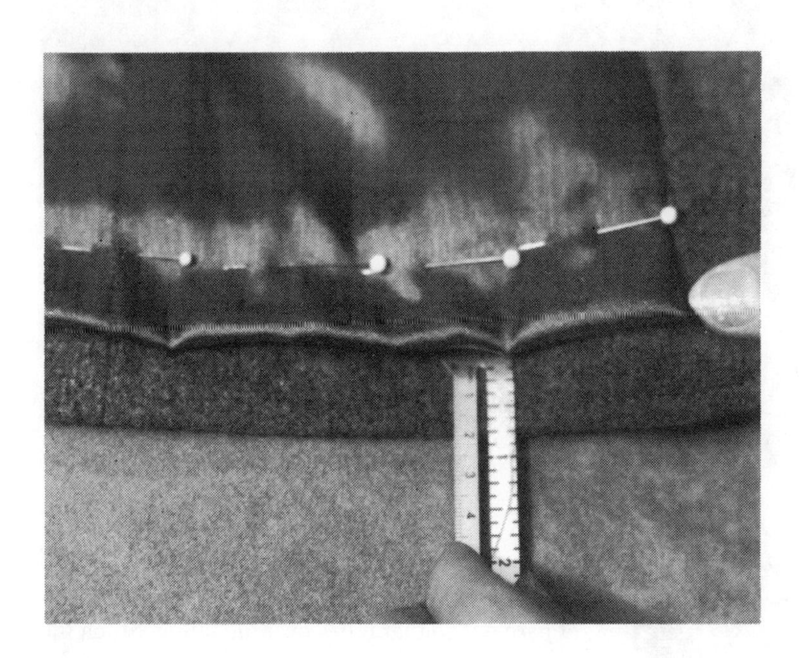

Lay the garment on a table and turn the lining hem in so that it clears the garment hem by 1/2- 3/4″. Pin through the lining (two thicknesses of the lining) and the garment along the hemline of the garment. (You can feel the hemline.) Match the seams of the lining to the garment seams with a slight ease in the lining. Adjust the lining seams if they don't fit. If there is a lot of excess length, trim the lining so it is 1/2″ longer than the hem turn of the garment.

Fold the lining up and pin again, this time catching a single thickness of lining. Remove the first pins.

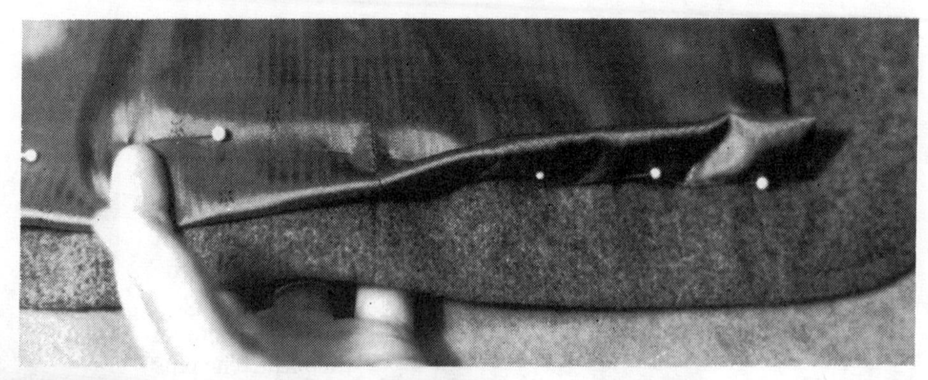

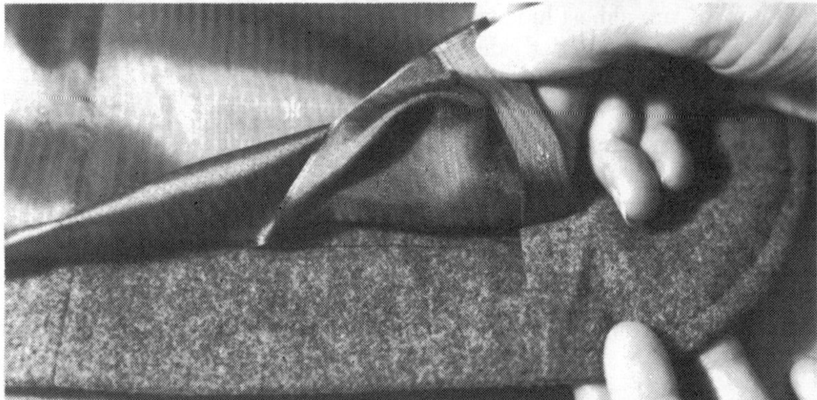

Curved front on a garment

On a garment with a curved front keep the seam allowance of the lining at the bottom of the facing folded under when you turn up the hem. That turns the corner neatly on the front edge of the lining.

Straight front on a garment

On a garment with a straight front treat the lining at the corner as follows. Mark the hem turn of the garment with a pin. Turn the lining up so that it clears the garment hem by 1/2 - 3/4″. Pin through the lining (two thicknesses of the lining) and the garment along the facing seamline.

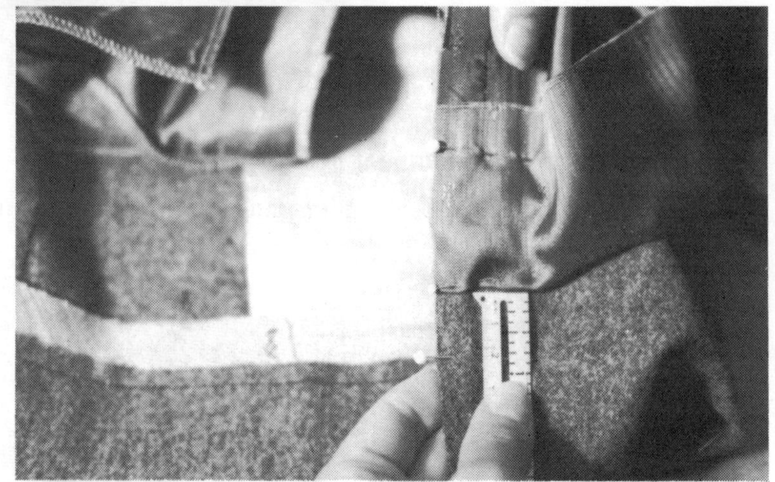

Fold the hem up, right side of hem to right side of garment so that it lies over the lining. Stitch the facing seam from the hem turn and overlap the previous stitching line.

Turn the hem right side out. The facing is hemmed exactly the same length as the garment. I never cut the facing hem. If the garment needed to be lengthened and you have trimmed the facing hem, you cannot lengthen the garment.

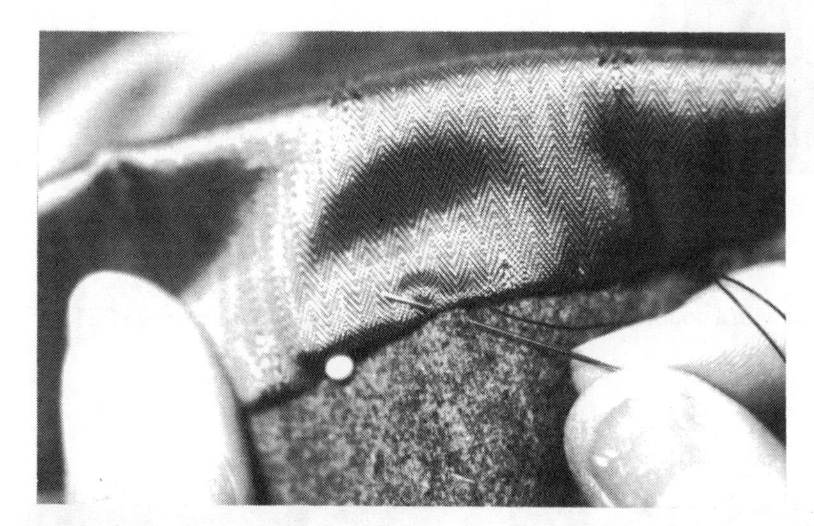

Slipstitch the lining to the garment hem. Stitch, just covering the stitching line holding the interfacing to the hem. Use a single thread and hem with the stitches about 3/8″ apart.

Hem The Sleeves

If the sleeves are not hemmed, refer to pages 289-291. If the buttons are not already on the sleeve, sew them on now. Sometimes they are only trim. Usually they hold the vent closed. They are rarely intended to button and would serve no function buttoned. The buttons must be sewn on before the sleeve lining is hemmed. They do not get sewn through the lining. Refer to the pattern for the location and the number of buttons. Sew the buttons through all thicknesses of the vent. No shank is needed on the sleeve buttons. Refer to Sewing on Buttons, page 220.

Hem the sleeve lining

Trim off any excess lining to within 1/4″ of the bottom edge of the sleeve hem. Turn the edge of the lining under and pin it along the stitching line holding the interfacing to the hem.

Slipstitch the lining to the garment hem. Stitch just covering the stitching line holding the interfacing to the hem. Use a single thread and hem with the stitches 3/8″ apart.

Be careful to hem from the inside. Do not turn the sleeve wrong side out to do the hem. The sleeve is such a small circle that the eases are wrong when you turn it wrong side out to hem.

Sew The Buttons On

Sew the buttons on the left front of the garment with a double waxed thread. Refer to Sewing on Buttons, page 221.

Press The Garment

Do not over-press the garment.

Press the roll line of the lapel over a towel to shape the roll and keep it soft as it should be. There should never be a hard crease on a lapel.

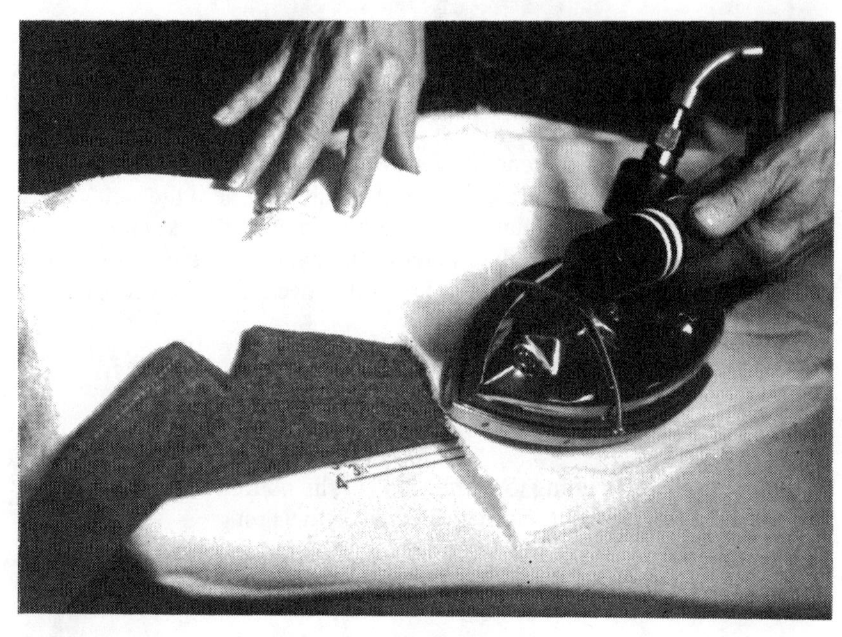

Press the lining gently to flatten the seam connecting it to the jacket front facing.

Press the lining hem. I almost never press a sharp crease in a hem. Just steam the lining hem and pat with your hand to flatten it.

If you feel that you cannot do a professional job with the equipment you have, take the garment to the dry cleaners and have it professionally pressed.

SHOULDER PADS

Shoulder pads go in and out of style. It is nice when pads are in style. They are slimming because they balance the hip line. They are a big help if the shoulders are sloped or uneven. Adjustments can be made in the pads to correct figure faults. Some support is needed in outer garments even when pads are out of style. When pads are in style they are found in most blouses and dresses as well as outer wear.

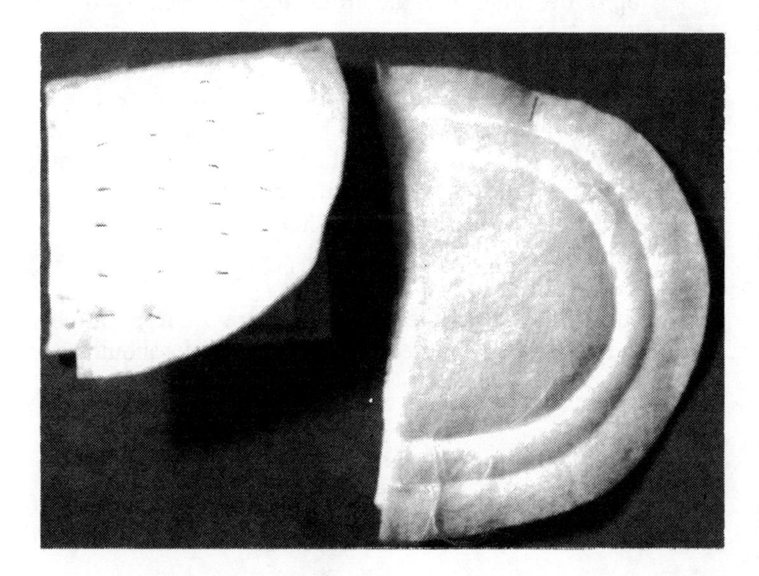

Purchased pads often have to be shaped to fit the armhole and curved to fit the shoulder. If you are purchasing pads, check to see if they are washable or drycleanable. Many purchased pads are made of foam or cotton batting and tend to wad up or mash when they are laundered. Pads made of pellon fleece are washable.

The pad on the right is a purchased pad just as it came from the package. The pad on the left is a handmade pad.

A square pad is specifically for a set-in sleeve. It also looks good in some kimono and dropped shoulder sleeves. A curved pad is for a raglan, kimono, or dropped shoulder sleeve. Always use the curved pad in a curved or raglan sleeve. Try the square pads in other style sleeves. Use the shape and size pad that gives you the look you want. Most pads have a front and back. The back is curved and the front is squared to fill out the hollow between the bust and the shoulder. Patterns that call for pads have the pad thickness added to the shoulder and the sleeve cap. If you do not want that much pad, you must adjust the pattern for a smaller pad, taking in the shoulder seam and the sleeve cap.

Supplies Needed For Making A Shoulder Pad

1/4 to 3/8 yard of pellon fleece. Pellon fleece made by Pellon is thinner than Thermolan Plus made by Stacy. Keep both weights of fleece on hand and mix the weights of pellon fleece to get the pad thickness that looks the best in your garment.

Shoulder pads in a lined garment do not need to be covered. Shoulder pads in unlined garments should be covered or make a shoulder pad pocket for the pad. You will need about 1/4 to 3/8 yards of lining fabric or light weight cotton/polyester such as batiste to cover a pad or to make a shoulder pad pocket. The size of the pad will determine the amount of fabric. If your garment is lightweight, the fashion fabric scraps can usually be used to cover the shoulder pad or make the shoulder pad pocket.

Shoulder Pad Patterns

I have included some of my favorite pad patterns at the end of this chapter. Make a trace of the pattern and make the smaller layers as you would to make any shoulder pad pattern.

Square Shoulder Pads

To make a square shoulder pad pattern to fit a specific armhole, follow steps 1-5.

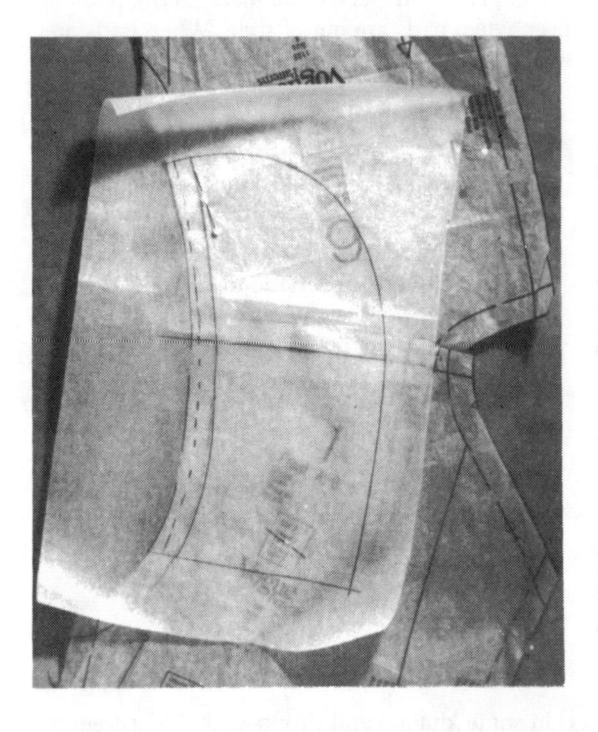

1. Lay the front and back pattern together at the shoulder line. Be sure you have the shoulder seam lines one on top of the other with the armhole edges even.

2. Lay tracing paper on top of the pattern and trace the shoulder line. Trace the armhole seamline. Mark a line 3/8″ beyond the seam line. The back of the pad should extend about 3½″-4″ down the back armhole. The front is a little longer, 4″-5″ down the front armhole. The edge closest to the neckline should be about 1″ from the neckline.

   Curve the back of the pad and square the front of the pad to fill the hollow between the bust and the shoulder.

3. Fold enough tissue or tracing paper so that you can cut out the number of layers needed to make the tissue pattern of the pad. The thickness of the pellon determines the number of layers. Two layers make a 1/8″ thick pad, 4 layers make about a 3/8″ thick pad, 5 layers make about a 1/2″ thick pad and 8-9 layers make about a 1″ thick pad.

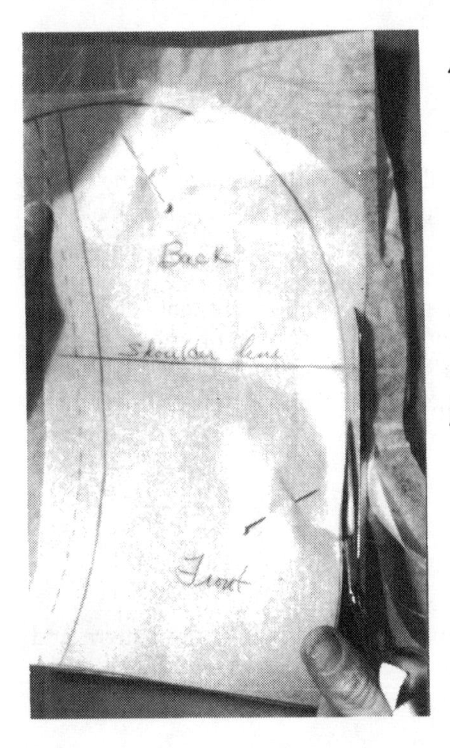

4. Lay the tissue trace of the shoulder pad on enough layers of tissue to make the size pad you want and cut all the tissues to match your pattern. Remove the pattern but keep all the layers pinned together.

5. Trim 1/2″ off the outer edge of all the layers, leaving the armhole edge untrimmed. Remove one tissue and trim 1/2″ off the outer edges of the remaining pieces. Keep doing this until you have graded each pattern to be 1/2″ smaller than the one before it.

Cutting the shoulder pad

Cut two of each pattern piece of pellon fleece. Pellon fleece has no grain so it can be cut in any direction.

Mark the shoulder line on the outside of the largest layer. Take the pattern off the pellon and lay the largest layer so you have a right and left pad. Lay the other layers on in succession, keeping the armhole edges even.

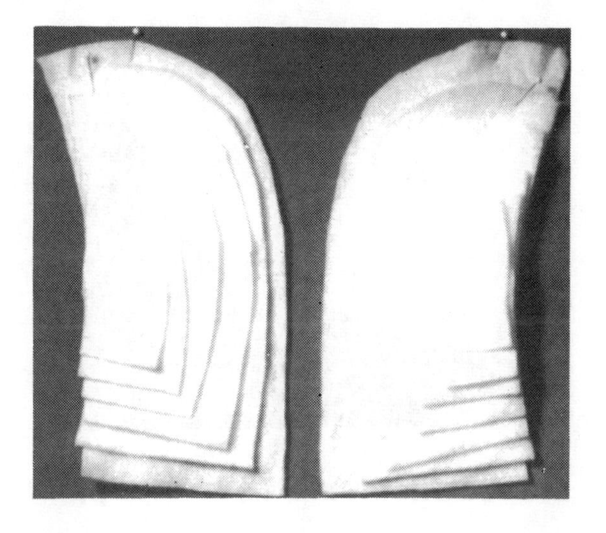

Padding the shoulder pad

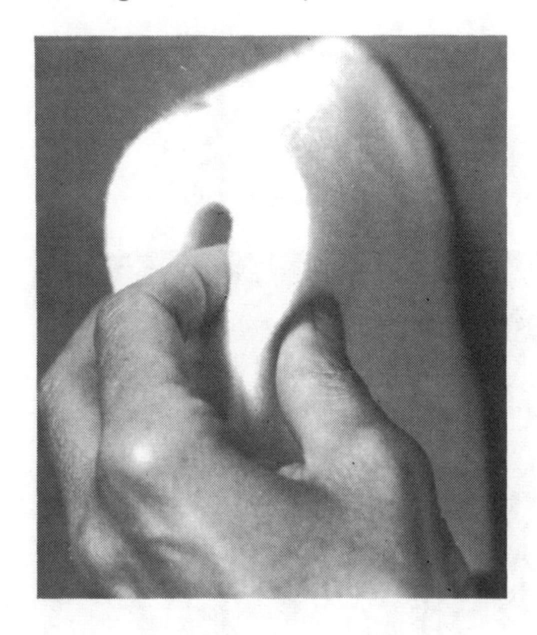

Thread a long needle and knot the thread. Hold all the layers with the largest one on top. Fold them over your fingers and pin them to hold the rounded shape. Pad stitch with the pad rolled over the fingers. If in padding the layers shift and are not graded, trim the edges until they are graded.

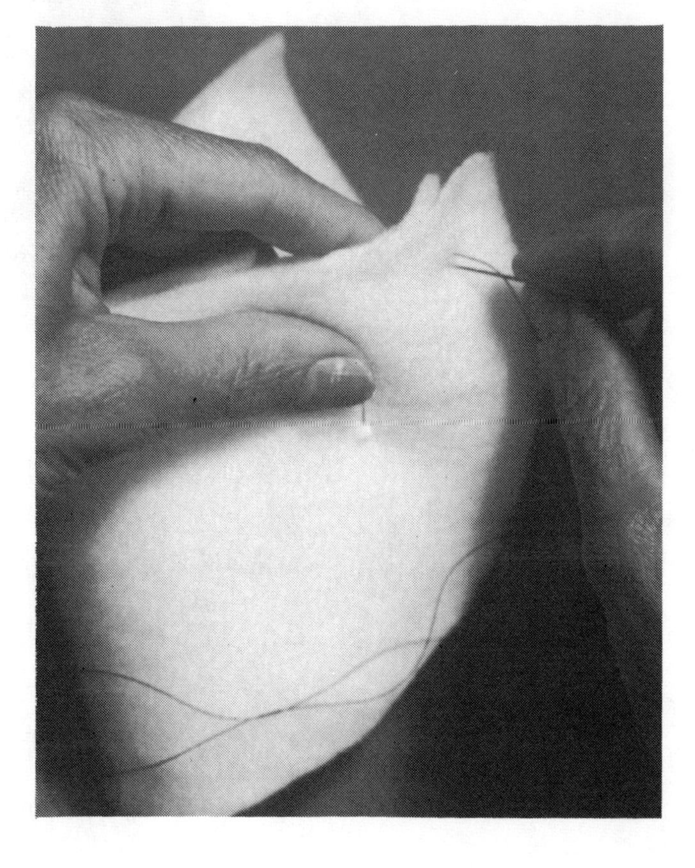

Begin padding on the underside close to one end and close to the armhole edge. Put the needle through the pad and bring it to the top side of the pad. Insert the needle about 1/4″ from the thread and take a long stitch on the underside of the pad. Pull the long stitch taut and continue pad stitching along the armhole with short stitches on the top side of the pad and long stitches on the underside. The pad must curve enough to fit nicely over the shoulder. Pad back and forth until all the layers of the pad are held together. Three or four rows of padding will do. Keep the thread taut but don't pull it tight enough to dimple the pad.

The completed shoulder pad should be curved to fit the shoulder as in the picture. Store the pads in a roll until they are needed.

Curved Shoulder Pad For Dropped, Kimono, Or Raglan Sleeves

Extend the shoulder line about 1¾″ and curve to the armhole at the front and back. Cut 2 of the shaped layers with one layer 1/2″ smaller than the largest one. Use the regular shape of the pad for the remaining layers. Refer to page 328.

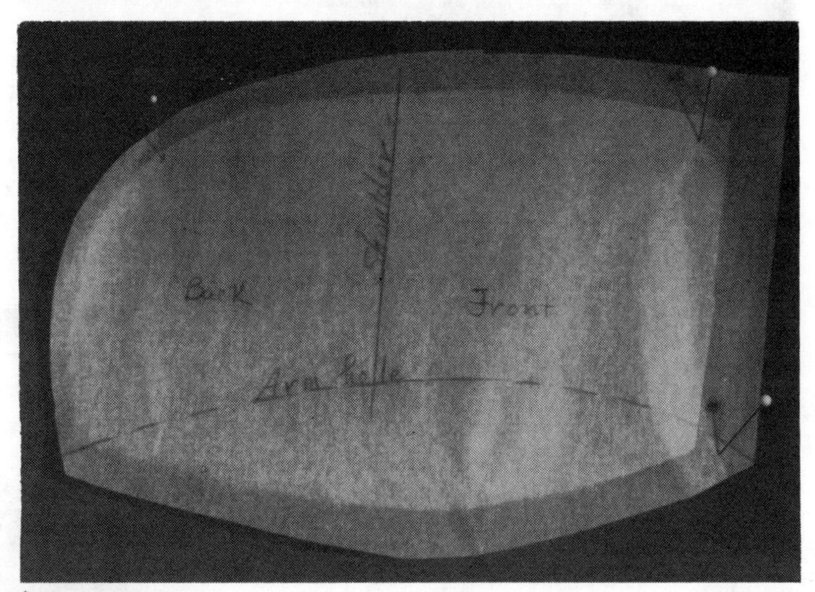

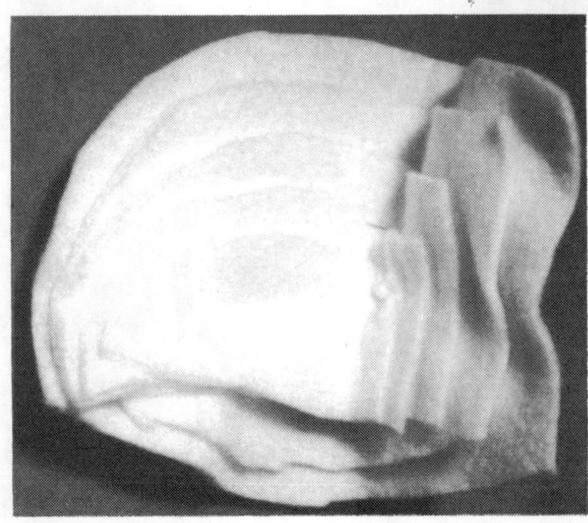

Mark the shoulder line on the outside of the largest layer. Take the pattern off the pellon and lay the largest layer so you have a right and left pad. Lay the other layers on in succession keeping the armhole edges even.

Pad all the layers of the pad with the extended layers on the outside of the pad. After the pad is padded take darts as needed out of the overhang to shape the pad to the shoulder. Several smaller darts are better than one large one. Don't get the dart too deep. Press the pad on a ham to soften the shoulder line.

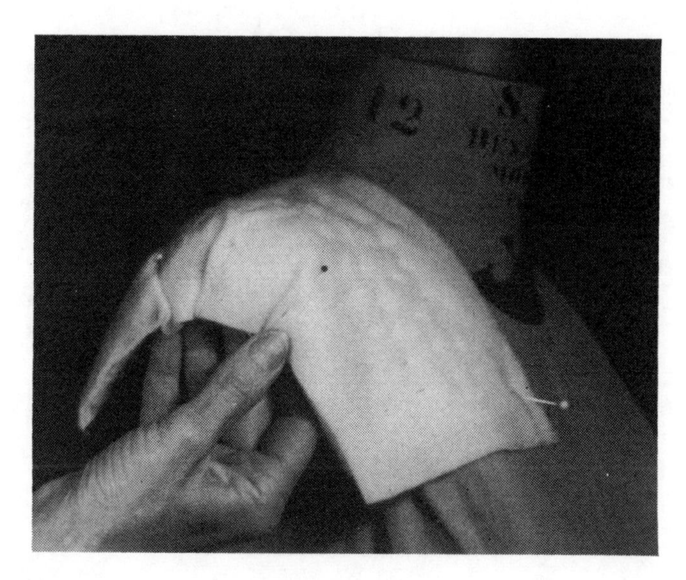

Covering Shoulder Pads And Making Pad Pockets

Shoulder pads in a lined garment do not need to be covered. If the garment is unlined the pads should by covered or a shoulder pad pocket should be made. A shoulder pad pocket is much like a pad cover except the shoulder edge is open and you can slip the pad into it. The pad pocket has the advantage of using the same pads for several garments and also you can very the thickness of the pad. That is especially nice for a blouse when you might want a thicker pad when you wear the blouse alone and a thinner pad when you wear the blouse with a suit. Fasten the pad to the shoulder pad pocket with pins or velcro.

Depending on the pad size, you will need 1/4 to 3/8 yards of lining fabric or lightweight cotton/polyester such as batiste. If your garment is lightweight the fashion fabric scraps can usually be used to cover the shoulder pad or make a pad pocket.

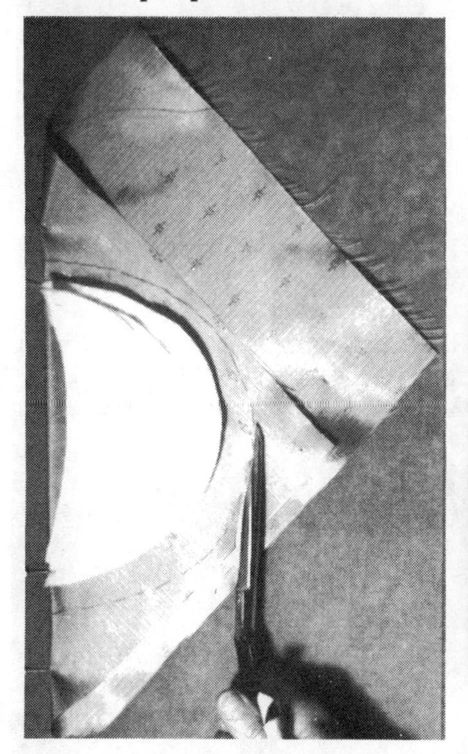

To cover the pad or to make a pad pocket, fold a large enough piece of lining on the bias to accommodate the pad plus 5/8″ seam allowance. Lay the armhole side of the pad on the bias fold so the ends of the pad are touching the fold line. Cut around the pad leaving a seam allowance.

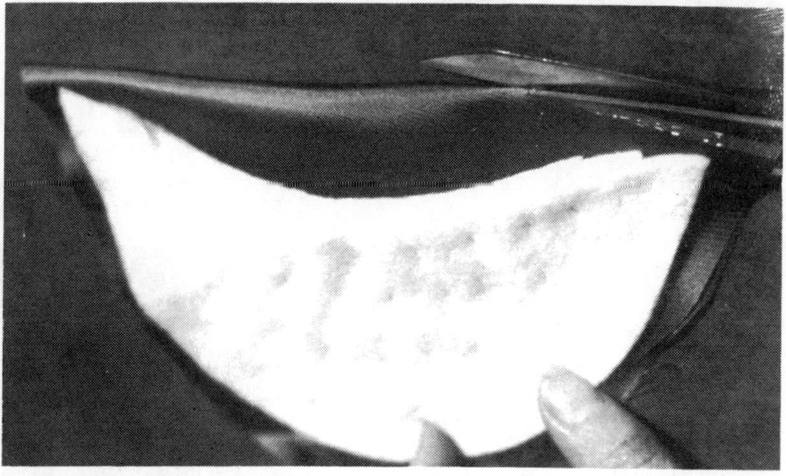

To make a pad pocket, also cut the lining along the fold. Do not cut the fold if you are covering the pad.

Covering The Pads

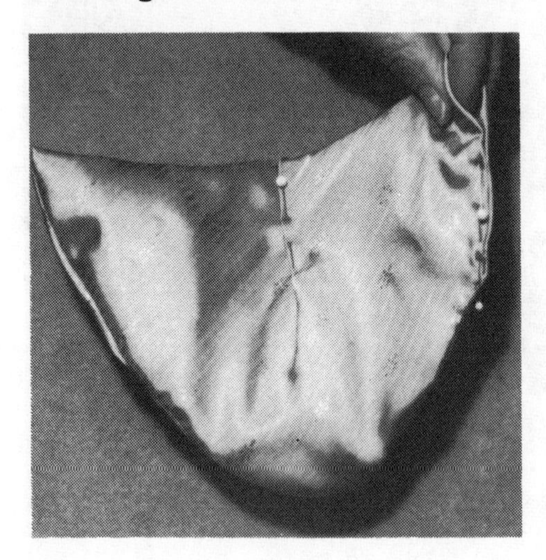

Stitched and turned

The pad cover can be stitched with wrong sides together leaving a small opening to turn it right side out and to put the pad into the covering. Slip the pad in and slipstitch the opening closed.

Pin a tuck in the underside of the cover to hold the pad in its curve and to tack the pad to the cover.

Serged, or overlocked

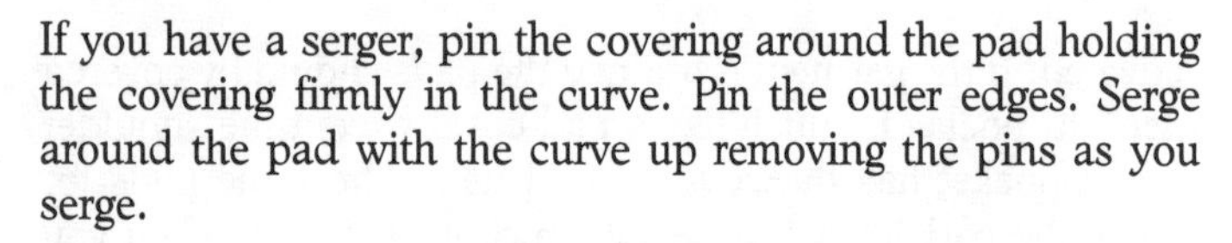

If you have a serger, pin the covering around the pad holding the covering firmly in the curve. Pin the outer edges. Serge around the pad with the curve up removing the pins as you serge.

On the underside, tack the pad cover to the pad. If a small dart in the covering is needed to hold the pad curve, put one in when you tack the pad to the covering.

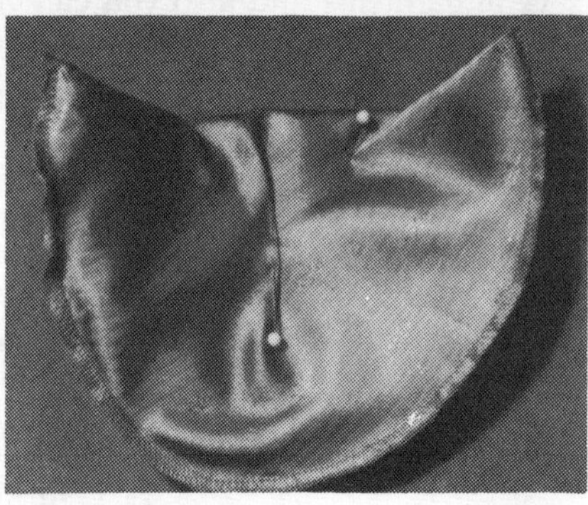

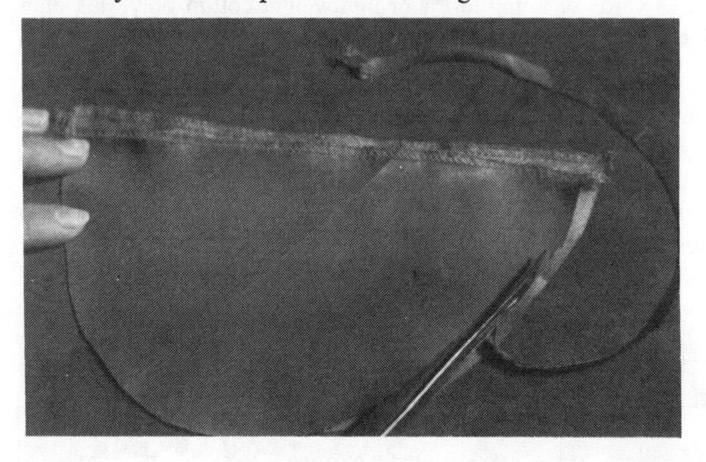

Pad pockets

Trim 1/4" off around the curved area of one layer of the pocket.

Stitch the bias area one layer at a time to finish the edge of the fabric.

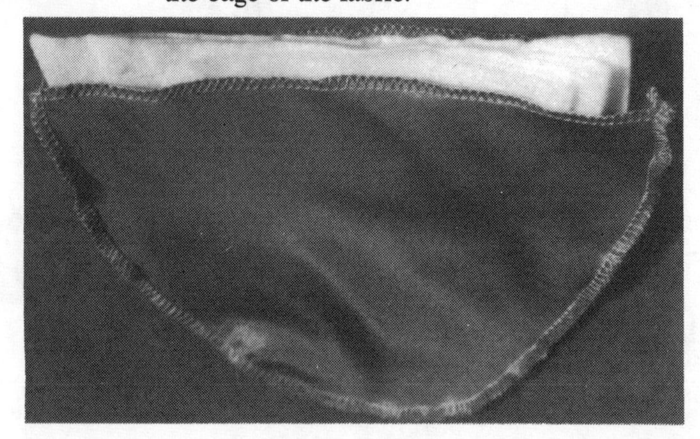

Lay the curved areas together with the wrong sides of the fabric together and stretch the small layer to fit the larger one. Stitch the curved area together to form a pocket.

Putting Pads In Garments

Blouses and dresses are done in the same manner as a jacket except that sometimes you do not have shoulder seams or armhole seams to fasten the pad to.

Pad pockets are done in the same way as a pad. Position the pocket with the pad inside in the correct place on the garment. Attach the largest layer of the pad pocket to the garment.

Put the garment on and position the pad. A square pad should be put out to the edge of your shoulder. The pad can be extended beyond that a bit but your shoulder must support the pad. Keep a rounded pad cupped around the shoulder. A raglan pad cannot extend past the shoulder or it will pull the front of the garment off the shoulders.

The square pad should extend 1/4" - 3/8" into the armhole on the entire length of the pad. If it does not, shape the pad to fit the armhole. This is easiest to do before the sleeve is set in. Refer to Fusible Tailoring, page 259.

Always pin the pad to the garment from the outside with the garment over your hand, on the body, a dress form, or a ham. Then stitch from the inside. All stitches holding the pad to the garment must be secure but done with a light hand. Don't nail them down. Check for pulls on the outside after each step. Refer to Couture Tailoring, pages 308-309.

Sleeve Rolls

A light sleeve roll can be used on any set-in sleeve to cushion the armhole seam. The sleeve roll can be bias of self fabric, outing flannel, lambs wool, or pellon fleece. Pellon fleece would be the heaviest and can be cut on the crossgrain.

Refer to Couture Tailoring, page 310, for directions for attaching the sleeve roll.

Attaching A Shoulder Pad To Raglan, Kimono, or Dropped Sleeve

Position the pad in the same manner as a set-in sleeve. Pin it to the shoulder seam or any seam you can to hold it in place. Hand baste from the inside to the seam or seams. Pads that are just tacked at the corners are bound to come out. Baste the outer layer of the entire pad to the shoulder seam allowances.

Gathered Sleeve Pad And/Or Puff Support

Some sleeves use both the puff support and a shoulder pad. Follow the pattern directions for the type of sleeve support needed.

To make a puff support cut a piece of bias on the fold in the shape of a crescent of organdy, taffeta or self fabric. Net works well too, but it does scratch. Make the puff support twice as long as the area on the armhole that has gathers.

Put two rows of gathering stitches on the curved edge of the pad support.

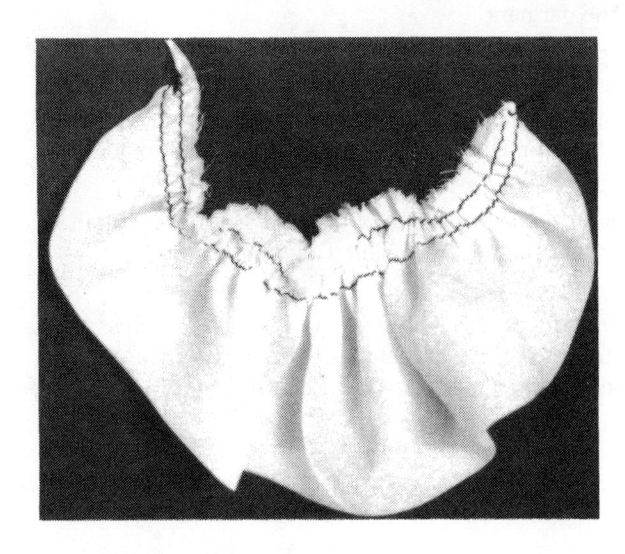

Gather the curved edge and pull up the gathering threads to form a support for the puff sleeve.

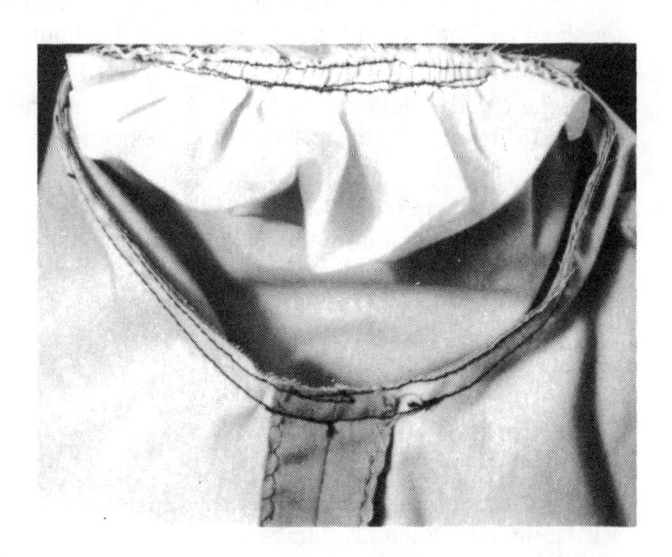

Tie off the gathering thread and sew the gathered edge into the top of the sleeve.

If the sleeve needs both a pad and a puff support, the puff support is put in first then the pad is added. If the sleeve is to have only a pad, it is positioned out into the sleeve cap and the sleeve seam in the pad area is pressed and held into the garment. Both these applications are pictured. Notice what a difference it makes when the sleeve seam is pressed toward the garment.

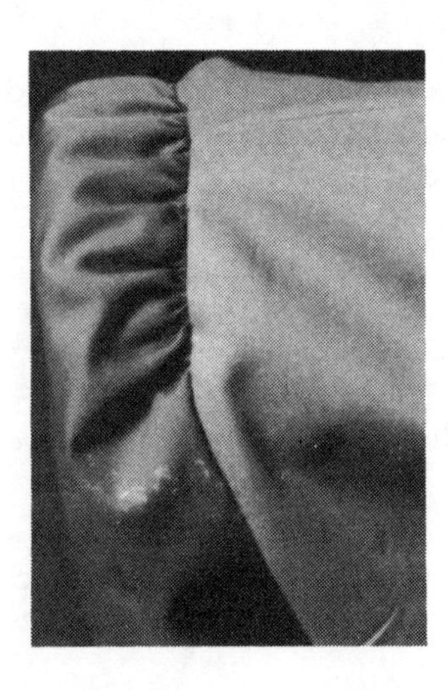

If the puff is to be flat, clip the seam slightly below the puff and press the puffed area of the armhole seam toward the garment. In this case only a shoulder pad is used and it extends into the cap of the sleeve to support it. Most patterns will set any puffed sleeve deeper on the shoulder to help support the puff. Pin-fit a gathered sleeve for the best results.

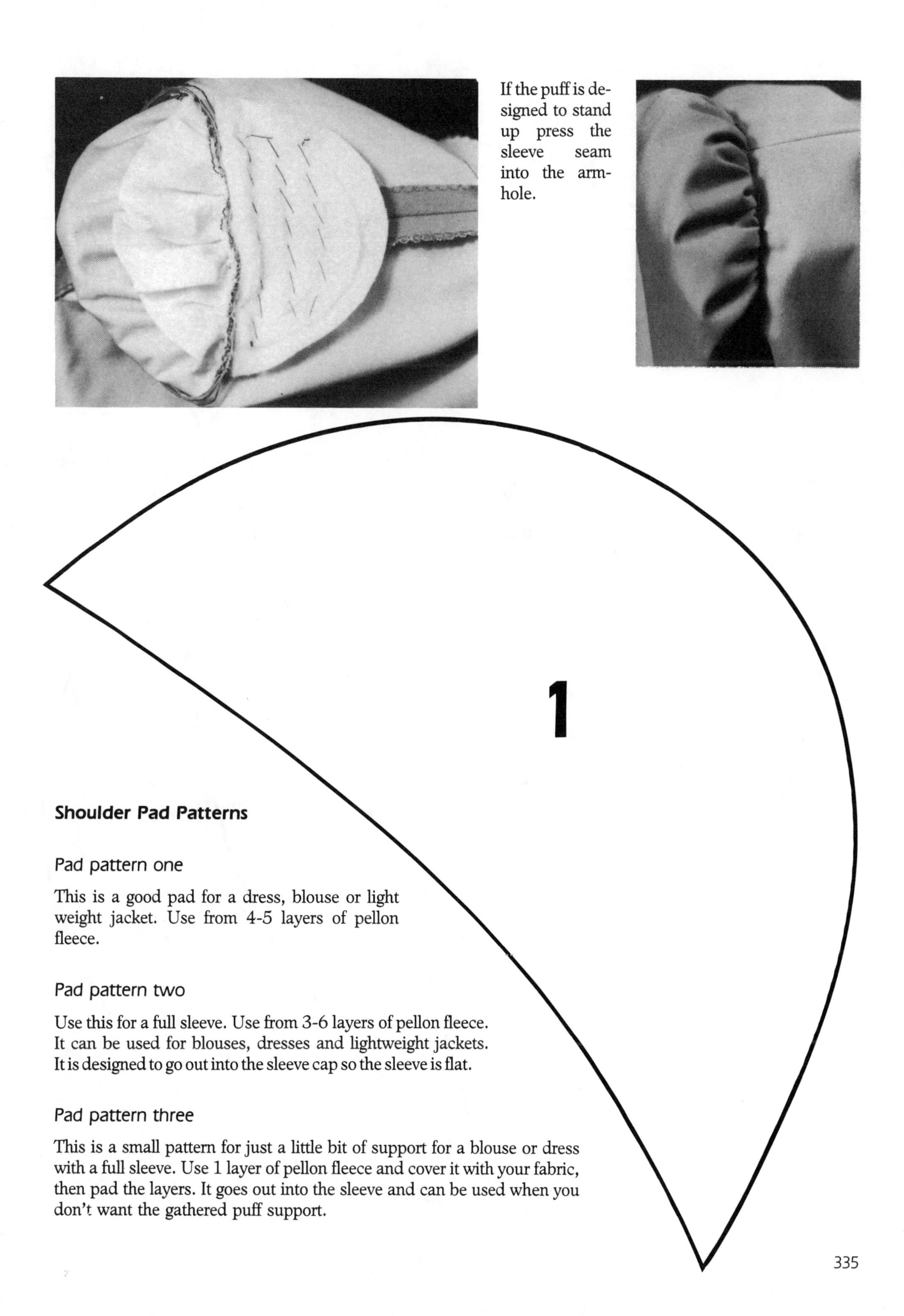

If the puff is designed to stand up press the sleeve seam into the armhole.

Shoulder Pad Patterns

Pad pattern one

This is a good pad for a dress, blouse or light weight jacket. Use from 4-5 layers of pellon fleece.

Pad pattern two

Use this for a full sleeve. Use from 3-6 layers of pellon fleece. It can be used for blouses, dresses and lightweight jackets. It is designed to go out into the sleeve cap so the sleeve is flat.

Pad pattern three

This is a small pattern for just a little bit of support for a blouse or dress with a full sleeve. Use 1 layer of pellon fleece and cover it with your fabric, then pad the layers. It goes out into the sleeve and can be used when you don't want the gathered puff support.

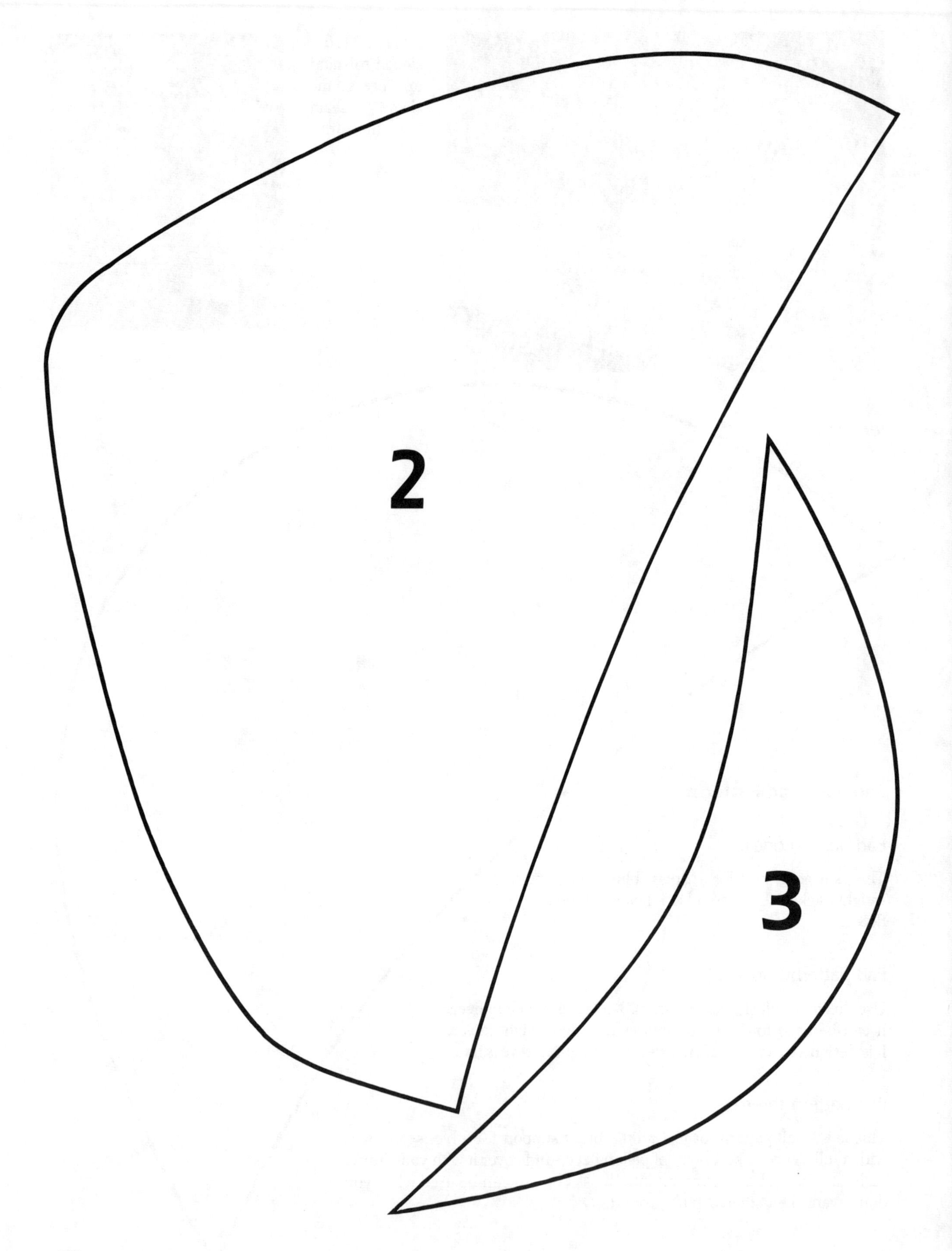
2
3

Index

D

E

F

G

H

I

K